JavaScript
The Definitive Guide

JavaScript
The Definitive Guide

Second Edition

David Flanagan

O'REILLY™

Cambridge · Köln · Paris · Sebastopol · Tokyo

JavaScript: The Definitive Guide, Second Edition
by David Flanagan

Published by O'Reilly & Associates, Inc., 101 Morris Street, Sebastopol, CA 95472.

Editor: Frank Willison

Production Editor: David Futato

Printing History:

August 1996:	Beta Edition.
January 1997:	Second Edition.

This book is printed on acid-free paper with 85% recycled content, 15% post-consumer waste.
O'Reilly & Associates is committed to using paper with the highest recycled content available
consistent with high quality.

ISBN: 1-56592-234-4

Table of Contents

Preface

In recent months, the pace of technical innovation has shot through the roof. It's been said that the Internet has turned "man-months" into "web-weeks." It's hard to keep up!

When Netscape released a final version of Navigator 2.0, I imagined that JavaScript would finally be stable, and that the time was ripe for a book documenting it. Soon after I started writing, a beta release of Netscape 3.0 was announced. It seems like I've been playing catch-up ever since. In order to keep up with this rapidly evolving language, we printed a "beta edition" of this book which documented the final beta release of Navigator 3.0.

With the beta edition released, I was able to catch my breath and really document JavaScript the way it needed to be documented. This edition is far superior to the last. It is over one hundred pages longer and contains several new chapters, many practical new examples, far fewer errors, and dramatically improved coverage of cookies, the Image object, LiveConnect, and other topics.

Fortunately (for my sanity), this edition of the book goes to print *before* the first beta version of Navigator 4.0, a.k.a. Communicator, is released. The word is that there will be a lot of powerful and interesting new JavaScript features in Navigator 4.0, and you can be sure that we'll update this book to cover them when the final version of 4.0 comes out. In the meantime, I hope you'll agree that this book is truly *the* definitive guide to JavaScript.

Conventions Used in This Book

I use the following formatting conventions in this book:

- **Bold** is used for headings in the text, and occasionally to refer to particular keys on a computer keyboard or to portions of user interfaces, such as the **Back** button or the **Options** menu.

- *Italics* are used for emphasis, and to signify the first use of a term. Italics are also used for email addresses, web sites, FTP sites, file and directory names, and newsgroups. Furthermore, italics are in this book for the names of Java classes, to help keep Java class names distinct from JavaScript names.

- `Letter Gothic` is used in all JavaScript code and HTML text listings, and generally for anything that you would type literally when programming.

- `Letter Gothic Oblique` is used for the name of function arguments, and generally as a placeholder to indicate an item that would be replaced with some actual value in your programs.

Request for Comments

Please help us at O'Reilly to improve future editions by reporting any errors, inaccuracies, bugs, misleading or confusing statements, and plain old typos that you find anywhere in the book. Email your bug reports and comments to us at: *bookquestions@ora.com*.

Please also let us know what we can do to make the book more useful to you. We take your comments seriously, and will try to incorporate reasonable suggestions into future editions of the book.

You can reach us at:

O'Reilly & Associates, Inc.
101 Morris Street
Sebastopol, CA 95472
1-800-998-9938 (in the US or Canada)
1-707-829-0515 (international/local)
1-707-829-0104 (FAX)

Finding Examples Online

The examples used in this book are available via anonymous FTP on O'Reilly's FTP server. They may be found at:

ftp://ftp.ora.com/pub/examples/nutshell/javascript

Acknowledgments

Writing this book would not have been nearly as exciting if Brendan Eich and his team at Netscape had not kept adding new features as I wrote! I, and many JavaScript developers, owe Brendan a tremendous debt of gratitude for developing JavaScript, and for taking the time out of his crazy schedule to answer our questions and even solicit our input. Besides patiently answering my many questions, Brendan also read and provided helpful comments on the beta edition of this book.

Nick Thompson and Richard Yaker at Netscape were also very helpful during the development of the book. Nick answered many of my questions about LiveConnect, and took the time to review and comment on a draft of Chapter 19, *LiveConnect: JavaScript and Java*. Richard found answers for me to many miscellaneous questions, and also provided me with the list of known bugs that are described in Appendix B, *Known Bugs*. Lynn Rollins, a partner at R&B Communications, and a contractor for Netscape, pointed out errors in the Beta edition of the book and also shared with me some of the less publicized features of JavaScript in Navigator 3.0.

Much of my information about Internet Explorer comes from Shon Katzenberger Ph.D., Larry Sullivan, and Dave C. Mitchell, three of the primary developers of Microsoft's version of JavaScript. Shon and Larry are the Software Design Engineers who developed Microsoft's version of the JavaScript interpreter and Microsoft's version of the JavaScript client-side object model, respectively. Dave was the Test Lead for the project. All three reviewed the Beta edition of the book and provided me a wealth of information about Internet Explorer that was simply lacking before. Dave was particularly helpful in answering my last minute questions about IE's capabilities.

Neil Berkman, a software engineer at Bay Networks in Billerica, MA, as well as Andrew Schulman and Terry Allen at O'Reilly were technical reviewers for the Beta edition. Their comments made that edition (and therefore this one) stronger and more accurate. Andrew was also the editor for the Beta edition of this book, and Frank Willison is editor of the current edition. I am grateful to them both.

David Futato was the production manager for this edition of the book and the last. He coordinated the whole process of production, and for the Beta edition, it was he who worked weekends and nights in order to give me time to squeeze the last few new Beta 6 features in. Chris Reilley produced the figures for the book. Edie

Freedman designed the cover, and Nancy Priest and Mary Jane Walsh designed the internal format, which was implemented by Lenny Muellner, with help from Erik Ray. Seth Maislin indexed this book.

Finally, my thanks, as always and for so many reasons, to Christie.

David Flanagan
November 1996

Introduction to JavaScript

JavaScript is a lightweight interpreted programming language with rudimentary object-oriented capabilities. The general-purpose core of the language has been embedded in Netscape Navigator and other web browsers and embellished for web programming with the addition of objects that represent the web browser window and its contents. This "client-side" version of JavaScript allows "executable content" to be included in web pages—it means that a web page need no longer be static HTML, but can include dynamic programs that interact with the user, control the browser, and dynamically create HTML content.

Syntactically, the core JavaScript language resembles C, C++ and Java, with programming constructs such as the `if` statement, the `while` loop, and the `&&` operator. The similarity ends with this syntactic resemblance, however. JavaScript is an untyped language, which means that variables do not have to have a type specified. Objects in JavaScript are more like Perl's associative array than they are like structures in C or objects in C++ or Java. Also, as mentioned, JavaScript is a purely interpreted language, unlike C and C++, which are compiled, and unlike Java, which is compiled to byte-code before being interpreted.

This chapter is a quick overview of JavaScript; it explains what JavaScript can do and also what it can't, and exposes some myths about the language. The chapter demonstrates web programming with some real-world JavaScript examples, explains the many versions of JavaScript, and also addresses security concerns.

1.1 Executable Content: JavaScript in a Web Page

When a web browser is augmented with a JavaScript interpreter, it allows "executable content" to be distributed over the Internet in the form of JavaScript "scripts."[*] Example 1-1 shows a simple JavaScript program, or script, embedded in a web page. When loaded into a JavaScript-enabled browser, it produces the output shown in Figure 1-1.

Example 1-1: A Simple JavaScript Program

```
<HTML>
<BODY>
<SCRIPT LANGUAGE="JavaScript">
document.write("<h2>Table of Factorials</h2>");
for(i = 1, fact = 1; i < 10; i++, fact *= i) {
    document.write(i + "! = " + fact);
    document.write("<br>");
}
</SCRIPT>
</BODY>
</HTML>
```

As you can see in this example, the <SCRIPT> and </SCRIPT> tags are used to embed JavaScript code within an HTML file. We'll learn more about the <SCRIPT> tag in Chapter 10, *Client-Side Program Structure*. The main feature of JavaScript demonstrated by this example is the use of the document.write() method.[†] This method is used to dynamically output HTML text that will be parsed and displayed by the web browser; we'll encounter it many more times in this book.

Besides allowing programmatic control over the content of web pages, as shown in Figure 1-1, JavaScript allows programmatic control over the browser, and also over the content of HTML forms that appear in a web page. We'll learn about these and other capabilities of JavaScript in more detail later in this chapter, and in much more detail later in this book.

Not only can JavaScript control the content of HTML forms, it can also control the behavior of those forms! That is, a JavaScript program might respond in some way when you enter a value in an input field or click on a checkbox in a form. JavaScript can do this by defining "event handlers" for the form—pieces of JavaScript code that are executed when a particular event occurs, such as when

---

[*] Currently the only JavaScript-enabled browsers are Netscape Navigator versions 2.0 and 3.0, and Microsoft Internet Explorer version 3.0.

[†] "Method" is the object-oriented term for function or procedure; you'll see it used throughout this book.

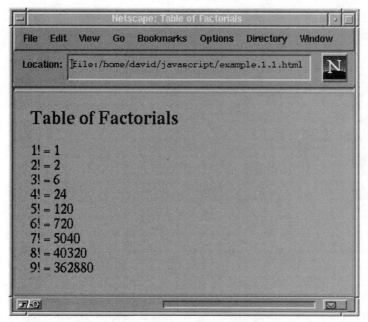

Figure 1–1: A web page generated with JavaScript

the user clicks on a button. Example 1-2 shows the definition of a very simple HTML form that includes an event handler that is executed in response to a button click. Figure 1-2 illustrates the result of clicking the button.

Example 1–2: An HTML Form with a JavaScript Event Handler Defined

```
<FORM>
<INPUT TYPE="button"
      VALUE="Click here"
      onClick="alert('You clicked the button')">
</FORM>
```

The onClick attribute shown in Example 1-2 is an HTML extension added by Netscape specifically for client-side JavaScript. All JavaScript event handlers are defined with HTML attributes like this one. The value of the onClick attribute is a string of JavaScript code to be executed when the user clicks the button. In this case, the onClick event handler calls the alert() function. As you can see in Figure 1-2, this function pops up a dialog box to display the specified message.

The examples above highlight only the simplest features of client-side JavaScript. The real power of JavaScript on the client side is that scripts have access to a hierarchy of objects that are based on the content of the web page. If you treat JavaScript as simply a new programming language, you're missing the whole point. What's exciting about JavaScript is the context that this language is

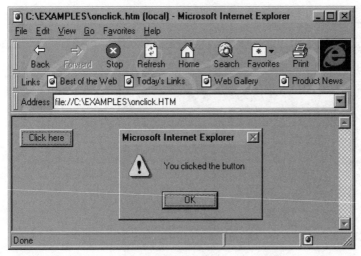

Figure 1–2: The JavaScript response to an event

embedded in. The interactions between JavaScript code and the web browser and the browser's contents are what matter most. A script can access an array of all hypertext links in a page, for example, and it can also read and write data from and to each of the elements in each of the forms in a page. In Netscape Navigator 3.0, JavaScript can also manipulate the images in a web page, and communicate with the Java applets and plug-ins on the page. Mastering the use of these client-side "document objects" is the real key to using JavaScript effectively in web pages.

1.2 JavaScript Myths

JavaScript is a new technology that is rapidly changing. It is not yet well understood and is the subject of a fair bit of misinformation and confusion. Before we proceed any further with our exploration of JavaScript, it is important to debunk some common myths about the language.

1.2.1 JavaScript Is Not Java Simplified

One of the most common misconceptions about JavaScript is that it is a "simplified version" of Java, the programming language from Sun Microsystems. Other than an incomplete syntactic resemblance and the fact that both Java and JavaScript can deliver "executable content" over networks, the two languages are entirely unrelated. The similarity of names is purely a marketing ploy (the language was originally called LiveScript, and its name was changed to JavaScript at the last minute).

JavaScript and Java do, however, make a good team. The two languages have disjoint sets of capabilities. JavaScript can control browser behavior and content but cannot draw graphics or perform networking. Java has no control over the browser as a whole, but can do graphics, networking, and multithreading. In Navigator version 3.0, JavaScript can communicate with the Java interpreter built into the browser and can work with and control any Java applets in a web page. This means that in this version of Navigator, JavaScript really can "script" Java. This new feature is called LiveConnect, and it also allows Java code to invoke JavaScript commands. Chapter 19, *LiveConnect: JavaScript and Java* describes LiveConnect in detail.

1.2.2 JavaScript Is Not Simple

JavaScript is touted as a "scripting language" instead of a "programming language," the implication being that scripting languages are simpler, that they are programming languages for nonprogrammers. Indeed, JavaScript appears at first glance to be a fairly simple language, perhaps of the same complexity as BASIC. Further experience with JavaScript, however, reveals complexities that are not readily apparent. For example, the use of objects as arguments to functions requires a careful understanding of the difference between passing arguments "by value" and passing arguments "by reference." There are also a number of tricky details to understand about converting data values from one type to another in JavaScript. Even the seemingly simple document.write() method that we saw in Example 1-1 has nonintuitive aspects.

This is not to say that JavaScript is beyond the reach of nonprogrammers. It *will* be useful to nonprogrammers, but only for limited, cookbook-style tasks. For better or worse, complete mastery of JavaScript requires sophisticated programming skills.[*]

1.3 What JavaScript Can Do

JavaScript is a relatively general-purpose programming language, and, as such, you can write programs in it to perform arbitrary computations. You can write simple scripts, for example, that compute Fibonacci numbers, or search for primes. In the context of the Web and web browsers, however, these aren't particularly interesting applications of the language. As mentioned earlier, the real power of JavaScript lies in the browser and document-based objects that the language supports. To give you an idea of JavaScript's potential, the following subsections list and explain the important capabilities of JavaScript and of the objects it supports.

---

[*] And a good programmer's guide and reference, like the one you are reading!

1.3.1 Control Document Appearance and Content

The JavaScript Document object, through its `write()` method that we have already seen, allows you to write arbitrary HTML into a document as the document is being parsed by the browser. For example, this allows you to always include today's date in a document, or to display different text on different platforms, or even perhaps extra text to appear only on those browsers that support JavaScript.

You can also use the Document object to generate documents entirely from scratch. Furthermore, properties of the Document object allow you to specify colors for the document background, the text, and for the hypertext links within it. What this amounts to is the ability to generate dynamic and conditional HTML documents, a technique that works particularly well in multiframe documents. Indeed, in some cases, dynamic generation of frame contents allows a JavaScript program to entirely replace the use of a traditional CGI script.

1.3.2 Control the Browser

Several JavaScript objects allow control over the behavior of the browser. The Window object supports methods to pop up dialog boxes to display simple messages to the user and to get simple input from the user. This object also defines a method to create and open (and close) entirely new browser windows, which can have any specified size and can have any combination of user controls. This allows you, for example, to open up multiple windows to give the user multiple views of your web site. New browser windows are also useful for temporary display of generated HTML, and, when created without the menu bar and other user controls, can serve as dialog boxes for more complex messages or user input.

JavaScript does not define methods that allow you to directly create and manipulate frames within a browser window. However, the ability to dynamically generate HTML allows you to programmatically write the HTML tags that will create any desired frame layout.

JavaScript also allows control over which web pages are displayed in the browser. The Location object allows you to download and display the contents of any URL in any window or frame of the browser. The History object allows you to move forward and back within the user's browsing history, simulating the action of the browser's **Forward** and **Back** buttons.

Finally, yet another method of the Window object allows JavaScript to display arbitrary messages to the user in the status line of any browser window.

1.3.3 Interact with Document Content

The JavaScript Document object, and the objects it contains, allow programs to read, and sometimes interact with, portions of the document. It is not possible to read the actual text itself (although this will probably be possible in a future release of JavaScript) but, for example, it is possible to obtain a list of all hypertext links in a document.[*] In Navigator 3.0, it is even possible to use JavaScript to obtain an array of all images and Java applets embedded in a document.

By far the most important capability for interacting with document contents is provided by the Form object, and by the Form element objects it can contain: the Button, Checkbox, Hidden, Password, Radio, Reset, Select, Submit, Text and Textarea elements. These element objects allow you to read and write the values of any input element in any form in the document. For example, the Internal Revenue Service could create a web page that contains a U.S. 1040EZ income tax return. When the user enters his filing status and gross income, JavaScript code could read the input, compute the appropriate personal exemption and standard deduction, subtract these values from the income, and fill in the result in the appropriate data field of the form. This technique is frequently seen in JavaScript calculator programs, which are common on the Web, and in fact, we'll see a tax calculator example, much like the one described above, a little later on in this chapter.

While HTML forms have traditionally be used only with CGI scripts, JavaScript is much more practical in some circumstances. Calculator programs like those described above are easy to implement with JavaScript, but would be impractical with CGI, because the server would have to be contacted to perform a computation every time the user entered a value or clicked on a button.

Another common use for the ability to read user input from form elements is for verification of a form before it is submitted. If client-side JavaScript is able to perform all necessary error checking of a user's input, then the required CGI script on the server side becomes much simpler, and no round trip to the server is necessary to detect and inform the user of the errors. Client-side JavaScript can also perform preprocessing of input data, which can reduce the amount of data that must be transmitted to the server. In some cases, client-side JavaScript can eliminate the need for CGI scripts on the server altogether! (On the other hand, JavaScript and CGI do work well together. For example, a CGI program can dynamically create JavaScript code "on the fly," just as it dynamically creates HTML.)

---

[*] For important security reasons in Navigator 2.0 and 3.0, this is only true when the script reading the list of links (or other information) was loaded from the same web server as the page containing the links. Because of this security restriction, you currently cannot download an arbitrary page off the Web, and have JavaScript return you an array of the hypertext links on that page—i.e., you cannot write a web crawler in JavaScript. See Chapter 20, *JavaScript Security*, for a full discussion of this restriction and its resolution in a future version of JavaScript.

1.3.4 Interact with the User

An important feature of JavaScript is the ability to define "event handlers"—arbitrary pieces of code to be executed when a particular event occurs. Usually, these events are initiated by the user, when (for example) she moves the mouse over a hypertext link or enters a value in a form or clicks the **Submit** button in a form. This event-handling capability is a crucial one, because programming with graphical interfaces, such as HTML forms, inherently requires an event-driven model. JavaScript can trigger any kind of action in response to user events. Typical examples might be to display a special message in the status line when the user positions the mouse over a hypertext link, or to pop up a confirmation dialog box when the user submits an important form.

1.3.5 Read and Write Client State with Cookies

"Cookies" are Netscape's term for small amounts of state data stored permanently or temporarily by the client. They are transmitted back and forth to and from the server and allow a web page or web site to "remember" things about the client—for example, that the user has previously visited the site, or that they have already registered and obtained a password, or that they've expressed preferences about colors or layouts of web pages. Cookies help you provide the state information that is missing from the stateless HTTP protocol of the Web. The "My Yahoo!" site at *http://my.yahoo.com/* is an excellent example of the use of cookies to remember a user's preferences.

When cookies were invented, they were intended for use exclusively by CGI scripts, and although stored on the client, they could only be read or written by the server. Their purpose was to allow CGI scripts to generate and send different HTML to the client depending on the value of the cookies. JavaScript changes this. JavaScript programs can read and write cookie values, and as we've noted above, they can dynamically generate HTML based on the value of cookies. The implications of this are subtle. CGI programming will still be an important technique in many cases that use cookies. In some cases, however, JavaScript can entirely replace the need for CGI.

1.3.6 Interact with Applets

In Navigator 3.0, JavaScript can interact with Java applets that are running in the browser. This important feature is part of Netscape's "LiveConnect", a communication layer that allows Java applets, Netscape plug-ins, and JavaScript code talk with and control one another. Using LiveConnect, JavaScript code can read and write properties of, and invoke methods of, Java applets and plug-ins. This capability is tremendously powerful, and truly allows JavaScript to "script" Java.

1.3.7 Manipulate Embedded Images

In Navigator 3.0, JavaScript can change the images displayed by an <IMG> tag. This allows sophisticated effects, such as having an image change when the mouse passes over it or when the user clicks on a button elsewhere in the browser. When Navigator 3.0 was released recently, this capability spawned a burst of creativity on web sites designed for the new browser.

1.3.8 Still More Features

In addition to all of the above, there are quite a few other JavaScript capabilities:

- As mentioned at the start of this section, JavaScript can perform arbitrary computation. JavaScript has a floating-point data type, arithmetic operators that work with it, and a full complement of the standard floating-point mathematical functions.

- The JavaScript Date object simplifies the process of computing and working with dates and times.

- The Document object supports a property that specifies the "last modified" date for the current document. You can use it to automatically display a time-stamp on any document.

- JavaScript has a window.setTimeout() method that allows a block of arbitrary JavaScript code to be executed some number of milliseconds in the future. This is useful for building delays or repetitive actions into a JavaScript program.

- The Navigator object (named after the web browser, of course) has variables that specify the name and version of the browser that is running, and also has variables that identify the platform it is running on. These variables allow scripts to customize their behavior based on browser or platform in order, for example, to take advantage of extra capabilities supported by some versions or to work around bugs that exist on some platforms.

- In Navigator 3.0, JavaScript uses the navigator.plugins[] array to specify which "plug-ins" are installed in the browser; JavaScript uses the navigator.mimeTypes[] array to specify which MIME data formats are recognized by the browser.

- In Navigator 3.0, the scroll() method of the Window object allows JavaScript programs to scroll windows in the X and Y dimensions.

1.4 What JavaScript Can't Do

JavaScript has an impressive list of capabilities. Note, however, that they are confined to browser-related and HTML-related tasks. Since JavaScript is used in a limited context, it does not have features that would be required for standalone languages:

- JavaScript does not have any graphics capabilities, except for the ability to format and display HTML (which, however, does include images, tables, frames, forms, fonts, and other user-interface elements).

- For security reasons, client-side JavaScript does not allow the reading or writing of files. Obviously, you wouldn't want to allow an untrusted program from any random web site to run on your computer and rearrange your files!

- JavaScript does not support networking of any kind, except—an important exception!—that it can cause a web browser to download the contents of arbitrary URLs.

- Finally, JavaScript doesn't have any multithreading capabilities, except whatever comes implicitly from the web browser's internal use of threads.

1.5 An Example: Calculating Your Taxes with JavaScript

Example 1-3 is a listing of a complete, non-trivial JavaScript program. The program calculates the estimated U.S. federal income tax you will have to pay for 1996.[*] The program is displayed in Figure 1-3. As you can see, it consists of an HTML form displayed within an HTML table. To use it, you enter your filing status, adjusted gross income, and a couple of other pieces of data. Every time you enter data into the form, JavaScript recomputes all the fields and displays your estimated tax at the bottom.

This example is a fairly complex one, but is worth taking the time to look over. You shouldn't expect to understand all the JavaScript code at this point, but studying the program will give you a good idea of what JavaScript programs look like, how event handlers work, and how JavaScript code can be integrated with HTML forms.

The beginning of the program defines "constructor functions" for two data types we'll use in the tax calculation. These new datatypes are `TaxBracket` and `TaxSchedule`. The next portion of the program creates and initializes an array of

---

[*] If you are not a U.S. resident, you won't have to pay, but you should study this example anyway!

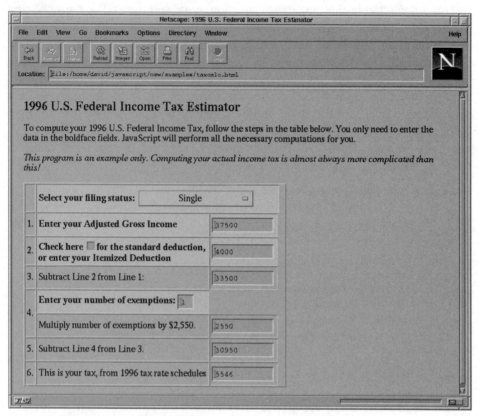

Figure 1–3: A JavaScript tax estimator

four TaxSchedule objects, each of which contains five TaxBracket objects. This is the data that the program will use to compute income tax.

Next comes the definition of a function named compute(). This is the function that computes the estimated tax you'll have to pay. It doesn't just perform the computation, however. It also reads the user's input from the form, and stores the result of the tax computation, along with intermediate results in the computation back into the form. The variable f in this function refers to the HTML form, and the various elements of the form are accessed by name. Thus, you'll see expressions like f.income.value to refer to the string that the user entered in the income field. The names for these fields will be assigned when the form is itself defined. Note that this compute() function both reads and writes the value of expressions like f.income.value and f.standard.checked—querying and setting the values displayed in the form. If you follow the comments, and refer occasionally to the reference section (Part III of this book), you may be able to follow the logic behind the tax computation.

After the definition of the `compute()` function, we reach the end of the JavaScript `<SCRIPT>`. The rest of the file consists of HTML, but this does not mean that JavaScript is not involved. After some brief instructions to the user, the HTML begins to define the form displayed by the program. The form is contained within an HTML table which makes things somewhat harder to figure out. Note, though, that every input element defined in the form has a `NAME` attribute, so that JavaScript can refer to it by name. And note that every input element has an event handler defined. These event handlers all call the `compute()` function defined earlier in the program. This means that whenever the user enters a value, all values in the form will be recomputed and redisplayed.

Example 1–3: Estimating Your Taxes with JavaScript

```
<HEAD>
<TITLE>1996 U.S. Federal Income Tax Estimator</TITLE>
<SCRIPT>
// These functions define the data structures we'll use to store
// tax bracket and tax schedule data for computing taxes.
function TaxBracket(cutoff, percentage, base)
{
    this.cutoff = cutoff;          // how much money to be in this bracket
    this.percentage = percentage;  // what the tax is in this bracket
    this.base = base;              // combined tax from all lower brackets
}
function TaxSchedule(b0, b1, b2, b3, b4)
{   // A tax schedule is just 5 brackets
    this[0] = b0; this[1] = b1; this[2] = b2; this[3] = b3; this[4] = b4;
}


// Taxes are computed using a tax schedule that depends on your filing status,
// so we create an array and store four different schedules in it.
var Schedules = new Object();  // create the array.


// Schedule X: Single
Schedules[0] =  new TaxSchedule(new TaxBracket(263750, .396, 84020.5),
    new TaxBracket(121300, .36, 32738.5), new TaxBracket(58150, .31, 13162),
    new TaxBracket(24000, .28, 3600), new TaxBracket(0, .15, 0));


// Schedule Z: Head of Household
Schedules[1] = new TaxSchedule(new TaxBracket(263750, .396, 81554),
    new TaxBracket(134500, .36, 35024), new TaxBracket(83050, .31, 19074.5),
    new TaxBracket(32150, .28, 4822.5), new TaxBracket(0, .15, 0));


// Schedule Y1: Married, Filing Jointly
Schedules[2] = new TaxSchedule(new TaxBracket(263750, .396, 79445),
    new TaxBracket(147700, .36, 37667), new TaxBracket(96900, .31, 21919),
    new TaxBracket(40100, .28, 6015), new TaxBracket(0, .15, 0));
```

Example 1–3: Estimating Your Taxes with JavaScript (continued)

```
// Schedule Y2: Married, Filing Separately
Schedules[3] = new TaxSchedule(new TaxBracket(131875, .396, 39722.5),
    new TaxBracket(73850, .36, 18833.5), new TaxBracket(48450, .31, 10959.5),
    new TaxBracket(20050, .28, 3007.5),  new TaxBracket(0, .15, 0));

// The standard deduction allowed by tax law depends on filing status,
// so we've got to store this data in an array as well.
var StandardDeductions = new Object();
StandardDeductions[0] = 4000; StandardDeductions[1] = 5900;
StandardDeductions[2] = 6700; StandardDeductions[3] = 3350;

// This function computes the tax and updates all the elements in the form.
// It is triggered whenever anything changes, and makes sure that
// all elements of the form contain legal values and are consistent.
function compute()
{
    var f = document.taxcalc;  // This is the form we'll we working with.

    // get the filing status
    var status = f.status.selectedIndex;

    // line 1, adjusted gross income
    var income = parseFloat(f.income.value);
    if (isNaN(income)) { income = 0; f.income.value = "0"; }
    f.income.value = Math.round(income);

    // line 2, the standard or itemized deduction
    var deduction;
    if (f.standard.checked)
        deduction = StandardDeductions[status];
    else {
        deduction = parseFloat(f.deduction.value);
        if (isNaN(deduction)) deduction = 0;
        if (deduction < StandardDeductions[status]) {
            deduction = StandardDeductions[status];
            f.standard.checked = true;
        }
    }
    f.deduction.value = Math.round(deduction);

    // Line 3: Subtract line 2 from line 1
    var line3 = income - deduction;
    if (line3 < 0) line3 = 0;
    f.line3.value = line3;

    // Line 4: exemptions
    var num_exemptions = parseInt(f.num_exemptions.value);
    if (isNaN(num_exemptions)) num_exemptions = 1;
```

Example 1–3: Estimating Your Taxes with JavaScript (continued)

```
      f.num_exemptions.value = num_exemptions;
      var exemption = num_exemptions * 2550;
      f.exemption.value = exemption;

      // Line 5: subtract Line 4 from Line 3.
      var line5 = line3 - exemption;
      if (line5 < 0) line5 = 0;
      f.line5.value = line5;

      // Line 6: tax from schedules.
      // determine which tax schedule to use, based on filing status
      var schedule = Schedules[status];
      // determine which tax bracket to use within that schedule
      for(var i = 0; i < 5; i++) if (line5 >= schedule[i].cutoff) break;
      var bracket = schedule[i];
      // then compute the tax based on that bracket
      var tax = (line5 - bracket.cutoff) * bracket.percentage + bracket.base;
      f.tax.value = Math.round(tax);
}
</SCRIPT>
</HEAD>
<BODY>
<H1>1996 U.S. Federal Income Tax Estimator</H1>
To compute your 1996 U.S. Federal Income Tax, follow the steps in the
table below. You only need to enter the data in the boldface fields.
JavaScript will perform all the necessary computations for you.
<P>
<I>This program is an example only. Computing your actual income tax is
almost always more complicated than this!</I>

<!--
   -- The code below is an HTML table inside of an HTML form. It gets tricky!
   -- Notice the event handlers on all the form input elements.
   -->
<FORM NAME="taxcalc">
  <TABLE BORDER CELLPADDING=3>
    <TR>                                        <!-- Filing status -->
      <TD> </TD>
      <TD COLSPAN=3 BGCOLOR="d0d0d0">
        <B>Select your filing status:</B>
        <SELECT NAME="status" onChange="compute()">
          <OPTION VALUE=0 SELECTED>Single
          <OPTION VALUE=1>Head of Household
          <OPTION VALUE=2>Married, Filing Jointly
          <OPTION VALUE=3>Married, Filing Separately
        </SELECT>
      <TD></TR>
```

Example 1-3: Estimating Your Taxes with JavaScript (continued)

```
    <TR>                                        <!-- Line 1: Income -->
      <TD>1.</TD>
      <TD BGCOLOR="d0d0d0"><B>Enter your Adjusted Gross Income</B></TD>
      <TD BGCOLOR="d0d0d0">
        <INPUT TYPE=text NAME="income" SIZE=12 onChange="compute()">
      </TD></TR>
    <TR>                                        <!-- Line 2: Deduction -->
      <TD>2.</TD>
      <TD BGCOLOR="d0d0d0">
        <B>Check here
        <INPUT TYPE=checkbox NAME="standard" CHECKED onClick="compute()">
        for the standard deduction,<BR>or enter your Itemized Deduction</B>
      </TD>
      <TD BGCOLOR="d0d0d0">
        <INPUT TYPE=text NAME="deduction" SIZE=12
               onChange="this.form.standard.checked = false; compute()">
      </TD></TR>
    <TR>                                        <!-- Line 3: subtraction -->
      <TD>3.</TD>
      <TD>Subtract Line 2 from Line 1:</TD>
      <TD><INPUT TYPE=text NAME="line3" SIZE=12 onChange="compute()"></TD></TR>
    <TR>                                        <!-- Line 4: Exemption -->
      <TD ROWSPAN=2>4.</TD>
      <TD BGCOLOR="d0d0d0">
        <B>Enter your number of exemptions: </B>
        <INPUT TYPE=text NAME="num_exemptions" SIZE=2 onChange="compute()">
      </TD><TD></TD></TR>
    <TR>                                        <!-- Line 4, continued -->
      <TD>Multiply number of exemptions by $2,550.</TD>
      <TD><INPUT TYPE=text NAME="exemption" SIZE=12 onChange="compute()"></TD>
    </TR>
    <TR>                                        <!-- Line 5: subtraction -->
      <TD>5.</TD>
      <TD>Subtract Line 4 from Line 3.</TD>
      <TD><INPUT TYPE=text NAME="line5" SIZE=12 onChange="compute()"></TD></TR>
    <TR>                                        <!-- Line 6: Tax -->
      <TD>6.</TD>
      <TD>This is your tax, from 1996 tax rate schedules</TD>
      <TD><INPUT TYPE=text NAME="tax" SIZE=12 onChange="compute()"></TD></TR>
  </TABLE>
<FORM>
</BODY>
```

1.6 Flavors and Versions of JavaScript

So far, we've been discussing JavaScript as if there were only one language to consider. In fact, there are several different varieties or flavors of JavaScript, and within these, there are different language versions. The subsections below sort it all out.

1.6.1 Standalone JavaScript

JavaScript was designed as a lightweight, general purpose scripting language, suitable for use in many different contexts. As such, there is a core JavaScript language, which is embellished with the necessary objects when it is embedded in a particular context. This book discusses the core language plus all the extensions it uses when embedded in a web browser. As we'll see below, JavaScript has also been embedded in web servers. In Example 1-3, all of the JavaScript code that queries and sets the fields of an HTML form is web-browser–specific, and is not part of the standalone core language. On the other hand, the code that defines data structures and performs computations is part of the core.

The core JavaScript language was, and continues to be, developed by Netscape (despite the word "Java" in its name, JavaScript is not a product of Sun Microsystems nor of JavaSoft). Netscape's press release announcing JavaScript[*] lists 28 companies that "have endorsed JavaScript as an open standard object scripting language and intend to provide it in future products." According to this press release, JavaScript is "an open, freely licensed proposed standard available to the entire Internet community." Netscape has released a reference implementation of the core JavaScript language in the form of a standalone version known as "JSRef". The JSRef distribution contains complete C source code for the JavaScript interpreter, so that it can be embedded into other products. Both JSRef and the language specification that accompanies it are currently available only to licensees of Netscape's Open Network Environment (ONE). (Obtaining an ONE license is free.)

Because JSRef was not available in time from Netscape, Microsoft was forced to develop their own version of the JavaScript interpreter. They have named their standalone version of the language "JScript" and have made it available for licensing as well. Microsoft intends to keep JScript compatible with JavaScript.

---

[*] You can find it at: *http://home.netscape.com/newsref/pr/newsrelease67.html*

1.6.2 JavaScript 1.0 and 1.1

There are currently two versions of the core JavaScript language. The version that was included in Navigator 2.0 is JavaScript 1.0. The version that is in the current JSRef and in Navigator 3.0 is 1.1. When Navigator 4.0 is released, it will contain JavaScript 1.2.

There are some significant differences between these various versions of the language. For example, JavaScript 1.1 provides much better support for arrays than JavaScript 1.0 does. Similarly, JavaScript 1.1 supports something known as a "prototype object" that makes it much easier to define complex data types. JavaScript 1.2 will also add new features to the language: current expectations are that this new version will include support for string matching with regular expressions and also for a C-style `switch/case` statement.

When JavaScript is embedded in a web browser, the differences between versions go beyond the core language features described above, of course. For example, Navigator 3.0 defines new objects, not available in Navigator 2.0, that allow JavaScript to manipulate images and applets. It is difficult to say whether these new features are enhancements of JavaScript 1.1 over JavaScript 1.0, or whether they are simply new features of Navigator 3.0 that are not available in Navigator 2.0. Note that in this book, Navigator 3.0 is sometimes used as a synonym for JavaScript 1.1 and Navigator 2.0 as a synonym for JavaScript 1.0, although this usage is not strictly accurate.

Finally, note that the version of JavaScript implemented in Internet Explorer is not JavaScript 1.1, but does support some JavaScript 1.1 features. The differences between the Microsoft and Netscape versions of JavaScript will be noted throughout this book.

1.6.3 Client-Side JavaScript

When a JavaScript interpreter is embedded in a web browser, the result is client-side JavaScript. This is by far the most common "flavor" of JavaScript; when most people refer to JavaScript, they usually mean client-side JavaScript. This book documents client-side JavaScript, along with the core JavaScript language that client-side JavaScript incorporates.

As of this writing, there are only two browsers, Netscape Navigator (versions 2.0 and 3.0) and Internet Explorer (version 3.0), that support client-side JavaScript. With Netscape's release of JSRef, we may see other browsers adopt the language as well. Unfortunately for those of us who want to write portable code, there are quite a few differences between JavaScript as implemented in Netscape's Navigator and JavaScript as implemented in Microsoft's Internet Explorer. While this book attempts to document both browsers, you'll notice that it documents Navigator by default, and Internet Explorer as a special case where it differs from Navigator.

There are a couple of reasons for this bias towards Navigator. First, Netscape created JavaScript, and so their implementation must be considered the definitive one. Second, Navigator was simply there first, and most JavaScript programmers have more experience with Navigator than they do with Internet Explorer. Third, Navigator has a more fully developed implementation of JavaScript. In Internet Explorer 3.0, JavaScript is implemented basically at the JavaScript 1.0 level. In future releases, we can expect to see Navigator and Internet Explorer come much closer to each other in terms of the features they implement.

1.6.4 VBScript

Besides supporting JavaScript, Internet Explorer 3.0 also support another scripting language, VBScript, which is short for "Visual Basic, Scripting Edition". VBScript is *not* another version of JavaScript, obviously, but is worth mentioning here anyway. As we've noted, standalone JavaScript becomes client-side JavaScript when the JavaScript interpreter is integrated into a web browser and when the web browser provides objects representing browser windows, documents, forms, and so on, that JavaScript can manipulate.

The engineers at Microsoft took this idea a small step further and kept the language interpreter and browser object model separate. By doing so, they allow arbitrary scripting languages (such as JavaScript and VBScript) to be integrated with the browser and given the ability to work with browser objects. Navigator does not support, and probably never will support, VBScript, but if you are a developer already familiar with Visual Basic, and you know that your pages will only be viewed through Internet Explorer, you may choose to use VBScript instead of JavaScript.

This book does not document VBScript. It does document all the client-side objects, what Microsoft calls the "object model" that JavaScript and VBScript use, however. Thus while the chapters on the core JavaScript language won't be of interest to VBScript programmers, the rest of this book will.

1.6.5 Server-Side JavaScript

We've seen how the core JavaScript language has been extended for use in web browsers. Netscape has also taken the core language and extended it in an entirely different way for use in web servers. Netscape calls their server-side JavaScript product "LiveWire," not to be confused with LiveConnect, documented in Chapter 19, or with LiveScript, which was the original name for JavaScript. As this book goes to press, the current versions of LiveWire are based on JavaScript 1.0.

There are not currently any server-side JavaScript products from other vendors. Other vendors may choose to embed JavaScript in their servers, or, because compatibility on the server side is not nearly as important as it is on the client side, other vendors may prefer to use proprietary scripting languages in their server products.

Server-side JavaScript provides an alternative to CGI scripts. It goes beyond the CGI model, in fact, because server-side JavaScript is embedded directly within HTML pages and allows executable server-side scripts to be directly intermixed with web content. Whenever a document containing server-side JavaScript code is requested by the client, the server executes the script or scripts contained in the document and sends the resulting document (which may be partially static and partially dynamically generated) to the requester. Because execution speed is a very important issue on production web servers, HTML files that contain server-side JavaScript are precompiled to a binary form that may be more efficiently interpreted and sent to the requesting client.

An obvious capability of server-side JavaScript is to dynamically generate HTML to be displayed by the client. Its most powerful features, however, come from the server-side objects it has access to. The File object, for example, allows a server-side script to read and write files on the server. And the Database object allows scripts to perform SQL database queries and updates.

Besides the File and Database objects, server-side JavaScript also provides other powerful objects, including the Request and Client objects. The Request object encapsulates information about the current HTTP request that the server is processing. This object contains any query string or form values that were submitted with the request, for example. The Client object has a longer lifetime than the Request object and allows a server-side script to save state across multiple HTTP requests from the same client. Because this object provides such an easy way to save state between requests, writing programs with server-side JavaScript feels much different from writing simple CGI scripts. In fact, it makes it feasible to go beyond writing scripts and to easily create what Netscape's documentation calls "web applications."

Because LiveWire is, at least at this point, a proprietary vendor-specific server-side technology, rather than an open client-side technology, it is not documented in this book. Nevertheless, the chapters of this book that discuss the core JavaScript language will still be valuable to LiveWire programmers.

1.7 JavaScript Security

Early versions of client-side JavaScript were plagued with security problems. In Navigator 2.0, for example, it was possible to write JavaScript code that would automatically steal the email address of any visitor to the page containing the code. More worrisome was the related capability to send email in the visitor's name, without the visitor's knowledge or approval. This was done by defining an HTML form, with a `mailto:` URL as its `ACTION` attribute and using `POST` as the submission method. With this form defined, JavaScript code could then call the form object's `submit()` method when the page containing the form was first loaded. This would automatically generate mail in the visitor's name to any desired address. The mail would contain the visitor's email address, which could be stolen for use in Internet marketing, for example. Furthermore, by setting appropriate values within the form, this malicious JavaScript code could send a message in the user's name to any email address.

Fortunately, practically all known security issues in JavaScript have been resolved in Navigator 3.0. Furthermore, Navigator 4.0 will implement a completely new security model that promises to make client-side JavaScript even more secure. Chapter 20 contains a complete discussion of security in client-side JavaScript.

1.8 Using the Rest of This Book

The rest of this book is in four parts. Part I, immediately following this chapter, documents the standalone JavaScript language. This is the core language common to both client-side and server-side implementations of JavaScript. Chapters 2 through 5 begin this section with some bland but necessary reading—these chapters cover the topics necessary when learning any new programming language.

- Chapter 2, *Lexical Structure*, explains the basic lexical structure of the language.

- Chapter 3, *Variables and Data Types*, documents the data types supported by JavaScript and also covers the related topics of literals and identifiers.

- Chapter 4, *Expressions and Operators*, explains expressions in JavaScript, and documents each of the operators supported by JavaScript. Experienced C, C++, or Java programmers will be able to skim much of this chapter.

- Chapter 5, *Statements*, describes the syntax and usage of each of the JavaScript statements. Again, experienced C, C++, and Java programmers will be able to skim some, but not all, of this chapter.

The next four chapters of this first section become more interesting. They still cover the core of the JavaScript language, but document parts of the language that will not already be familiar to you, even if you already know C or Java. These chapters must be studied carefully if you want to really understand JavaScript:

- Chapter 6, *Functions*, documents how functions are defined, invoked, and manipulated in JavaScript.

- Chapter 7, *Objects*, explains objects, the most important JavaScript data type. This chapter includes a discussion of creating objects and defining object methods, among other important topics.

- Chapter 8, *Arrays*, describes the creation and use of arrays in JavaScript.

- Chapter 9, *Further Topics in JavaScript*, covers advanced topics that were not covered elsewhere. You can skip this chapter the first time through the book, but the material it contains is important to understand if you are ever to become a JavaScript expert.

Part II of the book documents client-side JavaScript. The chapters in this part document the web browser objects that are at the heart of client-side JavaScript, and provide detailed examples of their use. Any interesting JavaScript program running in a web browser will rely heavily on features specific to the client-side. You should read chapters 10, 11, and 12 first. After that, you can read chapters 13 through 20 in any order you choose, although you'll probably get the most out of this part if you read them in the order they are presented.

- Chapter 10, *Client-Side Program Structure*, explains the various ways in which JavaScript is integrated into web pages for execution on the client side. It also discusses the order of execution of JavaScript programs and the event-driven programming model.

- Chapter 11, *Windows and the JavaScript Name Space*, documents the most central and important object of client-side JavaScript, the Window object. It also covers issues related to this Window object, such as the name space, variable lifetime, and garbage collection.

- Chapter 12, *Programming with Windows*, discusses and illustrates specific programming techniques using the Window object.

- Chapter 13, *The Navigator, Location, and History Objects*, documents the Navigator, Location, and History objects and shows examples of using them.

- Chapter 14, *Documents and Their Contents*, explains the Document object, which is perhaps the second most important object in client-side programming. It also illustrates programming techniques that use this object.

- Chapter 15, *Saving State with Cookies*, illustrates the use of "cookies" to save state in web programming.

- Chapter 16, *Special Effects with Images*, explains the Image object and demonstrates some special graphical effects you can produce with JavaScript.

- Chapter 17, *Forms and Form Elements*, documents the Form object, another very crucial object in client-side JavaScript. It also documents the various form element objects that appear within HTML forms, and shows examples of JavaScript programming using forms.

- Chapter 18, *Compatibility Techniques*, discusses the important issue of compatibility in JavaScript programming. It discusses compatibility between Navigator and Internet Explorer, between different versions of Navigator, and between JavaScript-enabled browsers and browsers that do not support the language.

- Chapter 19, *LiveConnect: JavaScript and Java*, explains how you can use JavaScript to interact with Java classes and objects, and even communicate with and control Java applets. It also explains how you can do the reverse—invoke JavaScript code from Java applets.

- Chapter 20, *JavaScript Security*, provides an overview of security issues in JavaScript. It explains the steps taken to plug security holes in Navigator 2.0, and the new "tainting" security model that is forthcoming in Navigator 4.0.

Part III is the reference section that makes up the second half of this book. It contains complete documentation for all JavaScript objects, methods, properties, functions, and event handlers, both for core and client-side JavaScript.

Finally, Part IV is a section of appendices that you may find useful. They include lists of commonly encountered bugs, a list of differences between JavaScript in Navigator and Internet Explorer, and other helpful information.

1.9 Exploring JavaScript

The way to really learn a new programming language is to write programs with it. As you read through this book, I encourage you to try out JavaScript features as you learn about them. There are a number of ways you can do this, and a number of techniques that make it easy to experiment with JavaScript.

The most obvious way to explore JavaScript is to write simple scripts. JavaScript has powerful enough features that even simple programs, only a few lines long, can produce complex results. We saw an example that computed factorials at the beginning of this chapter. Suppose you wanted to modify it as follows to display Fibonacci numbers instead:

```
<SCRIPT>
document.write("<h2>Table of Fibonacci Numbers</h2>");
for(i=0,j=1,k=0,fib=1; i<50; i++,fib=j+k,k=j,j=fib) {
```

```
        document.write("Fibonacci(" + i + ") = " + fib);
        document.write("<br>");
    }
    </SCRIPT>
```

This code may be convoluted (and don't worry if you don't yet understand it) but the point is that when you want to experiment with short programs like this, you can simply type them up and try them out in your web browser using a local `file:` URL. For simple JavaScript experiments like this, you can usually omit the `<HTML>`, `<HEAD>`, and `<BODY>` tags in your HTML file, and you can even omit the `LANGUAGE="JavaScript"` attribute that you would include in the `<SCRIPT>` tag of any production code you wrote.

For even simpler experiments with JavaScript, you can sometimes use the `javascript:` URL pseudo-protocol to evaluate a JavaScript expression and return the result. A JavaScript URL consists of the `javascript:` protocol specifier followed by arbitrary JavaScript code (with statements separated from one another by semicolons). When the browser "loads" such a URL, it executes the JavaScript code. The value of the last expression in such a URL is converted to a string, and this string becomes the "document" specified by the URL. For example, you might type the following JavaScript URLs into the **Location** field of your web browser to test your understanding of some of JavaScript's operators and statements:

```
javascript:5%2
javascript:x = 3; (x < 5)? "x is less": "x is greater"
javascript:d = new Date(); typeof d;
javascript:for(i=0,j=1,k=0,fib=1; i<10; i++,fib=j+k,k=j,j=fib) alert(fib);
```

While you can type these URLs directly into the **Location** field of Navigator, you cannot do the same in Internet Explorer 3.0. These URLs will work correctly in IE 3.0 in hypertext links and the like, but they cannot be entered directly.

In Navigator 2.0 and 3.0 (but not Internet Explorer 3.0), if you specify the URL `javascript:` by itself, Navigator will display a JavaScript interpreter screen, and JavaScript code entered into the input field in the lower frame will be evaluated and the results displayed in the upper frame. Figure 1-4 shows this special interpreter screen, with some example code evaluated. In this case, the JavaScript code shown pops up a dialog box that displays the name and value of each of the properties of the browser window.

Figure 1-4 also shows some other useful techniques for experimenting with JavaScript. First, it shows the use of the `alert()` function to display text. This function pops up a dialog box and displays plain text (i.e., not HTML formatted) within it. It also demonstrates the `for/in` loop, which loops through all the properties of an object. This is quite useful when trying to discover which objects have what properties. The `for/in` loop is documented in Chapter 5, *Statements*.

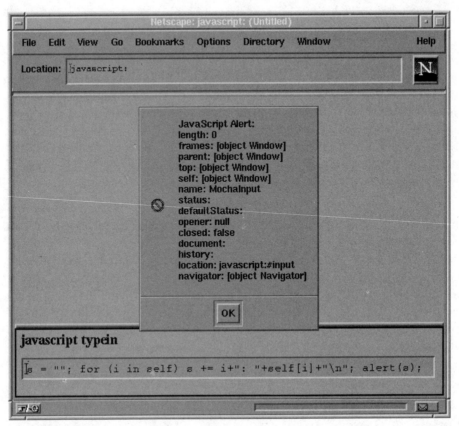

Figure 1-4: The javascript: interpreter screen

While exploring JavaScript, you will probably write code that doesn't work as you expect it to, and will want to debug it. The basic debugging technique for JavaScript is like that in many other languages—insert statements into your code to print out the value of relevant variables so that you can try to figure out what is actually happening. As we've seen, you can sometimes use the `document.write()` method to do this. This method doesn't work from within event handlers, however, and has some other shortcomings as well, so it's often easier to use the `alert()` method to display debugging messages in a separate dialog box.

The `for/in` loop mentioned above is also very useful when debugging. You can use it, along with the `alert()` method to write a function that displays a list of the names and values of all properties of an object, for example. This kind of function can be quite handy when exploring the language or trying to debug code.

Good luck with JavaScript, and have fun exploring!

I

Core JavaScript

This part of the book, Chapters 2 through 9, documents the core JavaScript language, as it is used in web browsers, web servers, and even in standalone JavaScript implementations. This part is a JavaScript language reference, and after you read through it once to learn the language, you may find yourself referring to it to refresh your memory about some of the trickier points.

2

Lexical Structure

The lexical structure of a programming language is the set of elementary rules that specify how you write programs in the language. It is the lowest-level syntax of a language, and specifies such things as what variable names look like, what characters are used for comments, and how one program statement is separated from the next. This short chapter explains the lexical structure of JavaScript: it covers the above topics and others.

2.1 Case Sensitivity

JavaScript is a case-sensitive language. This means that language keywords, variables, function names, and any other identifiers must always be typed with a consistent capitalization of letters. The `while` keyword, for example, must be typed "while", and not "While" or "WHILE". Similarly, `online`, `Online`, `OnLine`, and `ONLINE` are four distinct variable names.

Note that HTML is not case-sensitive, which, because of its close association with JavaScript, can be confusing. In particular, names of event handlers[*] are often typed in mixed-case in HTML (`onClick` or `OnClick`, for example) but must be all lowercase when referenced from JavaScript (`onclick`).

2.1.1 Case Sensitivity in Internet Explorer

In Internet Explorer 3.0, the core JavaScript language is case-sensitive, as it is in Navigator. Unfortunately, all of the objects, and their methods and properties, added to this core language by client-side JavaScript are case-insensitive in IE. The Date and Math objects are a built-in part of core JavaScript, so they are case-

---

[*] Event handlers are pieces of JavaScript code used as the value of HTML attributes.

sensitive in IE; to compute a sine, you must invoke `Math.sin()`, exactly as shown here. On the other hand, the Document object is part of client-side JavaScript, so it is not case-sensitive. This means that where you would type `document.write()` in Navigator, you could use `Document.Write()`, `DOCUMENT.WRITE()`, or even `DoCuMeNt.WrItE()` in Internet Explorer.

All user-defined variables, functions, and objects are case-sensitive in IE; it is just the client-side objects and their predefined methods and properties that are not. This does mean, however that you need to be careful how you name your variables and properties. For example, the Window object has a property named `parent`. In Navigator, it would be perfectly safe to create a new property of a Window object and name it `Parent`. This would not be okay in IE, however, and would either cause an error or overwrite the value of the `parent` property.

The reason that client-side objects are not case-sensitive in IE is that IE allows the same client-side objects to be used by the VBScript scripting language. VBScript, like Visual Basic, is not case-sensitive, so Microsoft felt that their client-side objects must not be either. Because of Microsoft's requirement for VBScript, it is not likely that the client-side objects will become case-sensitive in a future version of IE; this is an incompatibility that we will have to live with.

This incompatibility presents a worst-of-both-worlds situation. Because Navigator is case-sensitive, you must be sure to type all your object, method, and property names in exactly the correct case. But because IE is not case-sensitive, you can't take advantage of Navigator's case sensitivity to create different variables with the same spelling and different capitalizations.

2.2 Whitespace and Line Breaks

JavaScript ignores spaces, tabs, and newlines that appear between "tokens" in programs, except those that are part of string constants. A "token" is a keyword, variable name, number, function name, or some other place where you would obviously not want to insert a space or a line break. If you place a space or tab or newline within a token, you obviously break it up into two tokens—123 is a single numeric token and 12 3 contains two separate tokens (and constitutes a syntax error, incidentally).

Because you can use spaces, tabs, and newlines freely in your program (except in strings and tokens) you are free to format and indent your programs in a neat and consistent way that makes the code easy to read and understand.

2.3 Optional Semicolons

Simple statements in JavaScript are generally followed by a semicolon character, just as they are in C, C++, and Java. This serves to separate them from the following statement. In JavaScript, however, you are allowed to omit this semicolon if your statements are each placed on a separate line. For example, the following code could be written without semicolons:

```
a = 3;
b = 4;
```

But when formatted as follows, the semicolons are required:

```
a = 3; b = 4;
```

Omitting semicolons is not a good programming practice; you should get in the habit of using them.

2.4 Comments

JavaScript supports both C-style and C++–style comments. Any text between a // and the end of a line is treated as a comment and is ignored by JavaScript. Also, any text (which may cover multiple lines) between the characters /* and */ is treated as a comment.

In addition, JavaScript recognizes the HTML comment opening sequence <!--. JavaScript treats this as a single-line comment, just as it does the // comment, and does not recognize the HTML comment closing sequence -->. There is a special purpose for recognizing the HTML comment but treating it differently from HTML. In a JavaScript program, if the first line begins <!--, and the last line ends //-->, then the entire program is contained within an HTML comment and will be ignored (instead of formatted and displayed) by browsers that do not support JavaScript. Since the first line begins with <!-- and the last line begins with //, JavaScript ignores both, but does not ignore the lines in between. In this way, it is possible to hide code from web browsers that can't understand it, without hiding it from those that can. Because of the special purpose of the <!-- comment, you should use it only in the first line of your scripts; other uses would be confusing.

2.5 Literals

A literal in JavaScript is a data value that appears directly in a program. These are numbers, strings (in single or double quotes), the Boolean values true and false, and the special value null. The specific syntax of each type of literal is described in the following subsections.

2.5.1 Integer Literals

Base-10 integers may be represented simply as an optional minus sign followed by a sequence of digits that does not begin with the digit zero.

```
[-](1-9)(0-9)*
```

For example:

```
3
-12
10000000
```

Since JavaScript represents all numbers as floating-point values, you can specify extremely large integer values, but you may lose precision in the trailing digits.

2.5.2 Octal and Hexadecimal Literals

You may also specify integers as octal (base-8) and hexadecimal (base-16) values. An octal value begins with an optional minus sign, followed by the digit zero, followed by a sequence of digits, each between 0 and 7:

```
[-]0(0-7)*
```

As in C and C++, a hexadecimal literal begins with an optional minus sign followed by "0x" or "0X", followed by a string of hexadecimal digits. A hexadecimal digit is one of the digits 0 through 9, or the letters a (or A) through f (or F), which are used to represent values ten through fifteen.

```
[-]0(x|X)(0-9|a-f|A-F)*
```

Examples:

```
-0123
0377
0xff
-0xCAFE911
```

2.5.3 Floating-Point Literals

Floating-point literals can have a decimal point; they use the traditional syntax for scientific notation exponents. A floating-point value is represented as:

- An optional plus or minus sign, followed by

- The integral part of the number, followed by

- A decimal point and the fractional part of the number.

Exponential notation may be represented with additional syntax:

- The letter e or E, followed by

- An optional plus or minus sign, followed by

- A one, two, or three digit integer exponent. The preceding integral and fractional parts of the number are multiplied by ten to the power of this exponent.

More succinctly, the syntax is:

```
[(+|-)][digits][.digits][(E|e)[(+|-)]digits]
```

Examples:

```
3.14
-1.414
.333333333333333333
6.02e+23
1.4738223E-32
```

Note that JavaScript does not specify the maximum and minimum representable sizes of numbers. It is probably safe to assume that every implementation uses IEEE double-precision format, which has a maximum value of approximately $\pm1.79E+308$ and a minimum value of approximately $\pm4.94E-324$.

2.5.4 String Literals

Strings are any sequence of zero or more characters enclosed within single or double quotes (' or "). Double-quote characters may be contained within strings delimited by single-quote characters, and single-quote characters may be contained within strings delimited by double quotes. Examples of string literals are:

```
'testing'
"3.14"
'name="myform"'
"Wouldn't you prefer O'Reilly's book?"
```

HTML uses double-quoted strings.[*] Since JavaScript code often contains embedded HTML strings, and is often embedded within HTML strings (for event handler specifications), it is a good idea to use single quotes around your JavaScript strings. In the example below, the string "Thank you" is single-quoted within a JavaScript expression, which is double-quoted within an HTML event-handler attribute:

```
<A HREF="" onClick="alert('Thank you')">Click Me</A>
```

---

[*] The original versions of HTML required double-quoted strings, though most popular web browsers now allow single-quoted strings as HTML attribute values as well.

On the other hand, when you use single quotes to delimit your strings, you must be careful with English contractions and possessives like "can't" and "O'Reilly's". Since the apostrophe is the same as the single-quote character, you must use the backslash character (\) to escape any apostrophes that appear in single-quoted strings. This use of the backslash is explained in the section that follows.

2.5.5 Escape Sequences in String Literals

The backslash character (\) has a special purpose in JavaScript strings. Combined with the character that follows it, it represents a character that is not otherwise representable within the string, just like in C or C++. For example, the characters \n are an escape sequence that represents a newline character. When we type the string literal, we type two individual characters, the backslash and the n, but the string itself contains only a single newline character at that location.[*]

Another example, mentioned above, is the \' escape which represents the single quote (or apostrophe) character. This escape sequence is useful when you need to include an apostrophe in a string literal which is contained within single quotes. You can see why we call these "escape sequences"—the backslash allows us to "escape" from the usual interpretation of the single-quote character; instead of using it to mark the end of the string, we use it as an apostrophe. Table 2-1 lists the JavaScript escape sequences and the characters they represent.

There is one escape sequence that deserves special comment. *xxx* represents the character with the Latin-1 (ISO8859-1) encoding specified by the three octal digits *xxx*. You can use this escape sequence to embed accented characters and special symbols into your JavaScript code, even though those characters cannot be typed from a standard keyboard. For example, the sequence \251 represents the copyright symbol.

Table 2-1: JavaScript Escape Sequences

Sequence	Character Represented
\b	Backspace
\f	Form feed
\n	Newline
\r	Carriage return
\t	Tab

---

[*] Bear in mind that HTML ignores newlines, so a \n escape sequence in HTML will not produce a newline in the browser display: for that you need to output <BR> or <P>. Thus, the \n escape might be useful in a string you pass to alert(), but not in a string you pass to document.write().

Table 2-1: JavaScript Escape Sequences (continued)

Sequence	Character Represented
\ '	Apostrophe or single quote
\ "	Double quote
\xxx	The character with the encoding specified by the three octal digits *xxx*.

2.5.6 Boolean Literals

The *Boolean* data type in JavaScript represents a "truth value"—i.e., whether something is true or false. Any kind of comparison operation in JavaScript yields a Boolean value that specifies whether the comparison succeeded or failed. Since there are two possible truth values, there are two Boolean literals: the keywords true or false. These literals are commonly used in JavaScript code like the following:

```
while(done != true) {
    ...
    if ((a == true) || (b == false) || (i > 10)) done = true;
}
```

2.5.7 The null Literal

There is one final literal used in JavaScript: the null keyword. All other literals represent a value of a particular data type. null is different—it represents a lack of value. In a sense, null is like zero, but for data types other than numbers. We'll see more about null in Chapter 3, *Variables and Data Types*.

2.6 Identifiers

An *identifier* in JavaScript is a name used to refer to something else. That is, it is a variable or function name. The rules for legal identifier names are the same in JavaScript as they are in most languages. The first character must be a letter (lowercase or uppercase) or an underscore (_). Subsequent characters may be any letter or digit or an underscore. (Numbers are not allowed as the first character so that JavaScript can easily distinguish identifiers from numbers.) These are legal identifiers:

```
i
my_variable_name
v13
_dummy
```

In Navigator 3.0, the $ character is also legal in JavaScript identifiers, in any position including the first. This change was made for compatibility with Java identifiers. Therefore, in Navigator 3.0 scripts, the variable names in the following assignments are also legal:

```
A$ = "I'm a BASIC programmer";
$VMS = true;
```

Internet Explorer 3.0 does not support $ in identifier names, but a future version of the language will.

2.7 Reserved Words

There are a number of "reserved words" in JavaScript. These are words that you cannot (or should not) use as identifiers (such as variable names) in your JavaScript programs. Table 2-2 lists the keywords in JavaScript. These words have special meaning to JavaScript—they are part of the language syntax itself. This means that they should not be used as identifiers. Table 2-3 lists keywords from Java. Although JavaScript does not currently use any of these keywords, it might in future versions; you should avoid using them in your programs. Finally, Table 2-4 lists other identifiers to avoid. While these identifiers are not strictly reserved, they are the names of datatypes, functions, and variables that are predefined by client-side JavaScript; using them may cause unexpected behavior in your programs. Note that since Internet Explorer is not case-sensitive, you should avoid all variations of these identifiers in Table 2-4, whether in lower- or uppercase.

Table 2-2: Reserved JavaScript Keywords

break	false	in	this	void
continue	for	new	true	while
delete	function	null	typeof	with
else	if	return	var	

Table 2-3: Java Keywords Reserved by JavaScript

abstract	default	implements	private	throw
boolean	do	import	protected	throws
byte	double	instanceof	public	transient
case	extends	int	short	try
catch	final	interface	static	
char	finally	long	super	
class	float	native	switch	
const	goto	package	synchronized	

Table 2-4: Other Identifiers to Avoid

alert	escape	JavaPackage	onunload	setTimeout
Anchor	eval	length	open	status
Area	FileUpload	Link	opener	String
Array	focus	Location	Option	Submit
assign	Form	location	Packages	sun
blur	Frame	Math	parent	taint
Boolean	frames	MimeType	parseFloat	Text
Button	Function	name	parseInt	Textarea
Checkbox	getClass	navigate	Password	top
clearTimeout	Hidden	Navigator	Plugin	toString
close	History	navigator	prompt	unescape
closed	history	netscape	prototype	untaint
confirm	Image	Number	Radio	valueOf
Date	isNaN	Object	ref	Window
defaultStatus	java	onblur	Reset	window
Document	JavaArray	onerror	scroll	
document	JavaClass	onfocus	Select	
Element	JavaObject	onload	self	

3

Variables and Data Types

This chapter introduces two of the most important concepts of programming languages: variables and data types. A variable is a name associated with a data value; we say that the variable "stores" or "contains" the value. Variables allow us to store and manipulate data in our programs.

Just as fundamental as variables are data types. These, as the name suggests, are the types of data that our programs can manipulate. In Chapter 2, *Lexical Structure*, we saw that we can include numeric, string, and Boolean literals directly in our programs. This chapter provides more detail about these data types, and also introduces three new ones: functions, objects, and arrays.[*] Later chapters of the book will provide much more detail about functions, objects, and arrays.

3.1 Variables

In Chapter 2, we considered JavaScript literals: constant values embedded directly (or literally) into a JavaScript program. A program that operated only on constant, literal values would not be a very interesting one, and so JavaScript (and all programming languages) use *variables*. Variables are names that have values assigned to them. They provide a way to manipulate values by name. The value associated with a name need not be constant; new values may be assigned to existing names. Since the value associated with a name may vary, the names are called variables. For example, the following line of JavaScript assigns the value 2 to a variable named i.

---

[*] Technically, objects and arrays are actually two distinct uses of a single data type. Because they are used in such distinct ways, we will usually consider them as separate types in this book.

```
i = 2;
```

And the following line adds 3 to i and assigns the result to a new variable sum:

```
sum = i + 3;
```

3.1.1 Variable Declaration

Although it is often unnecessary, it is good programming style to *declare* variables before using them. You do this with the var keyword, like this:

```
var i;
var sum;
```

You can also declare multiple variables with the same var keyword:

```
var i, sum;
```

And you can combine variable declaration with initial assignment to the variable:

```
var i = 2;
```

As mentioned above, however, variable declaration is not usually required. The first time you use a variable that is not already declared, it will automatically be declared. The only time you actually need to declare a variable with var is when declaring a local variable inside a function definition (we haven't introduced functions yet) and that variable name is also in use as a "global" variable outside of the function. If you simply used the variable in the function without declaring it, then JavaScript would assume you meant the global variable declared outside the function, and would not automatically declare a local one within the function.

3.1.2 Untyped Variables

An important difference between JavaScript and languages like Java and C is that JavaScript is *untyped*. This means, in part, that variables can hold values of any data type, unlike Java and C variables which can only hold one type of data. For example, it is perfectly legal in JavaScript to assign a number to a variable and later assign a string to it:

```
i = 10;
i = "ten";
```

In C, C++, or Java, these lines of code would be illegal.

A related implication of the fact that JavaScript is an untyped language is that variable declarations do not have to specify a data type for the variable as they do in C, C++, and Java. In those languages, you declare a variable by specifying the name of the data type it will hold and following that by the variable:

```
int i;  // a declaration of an integer variable in C, C++, or Java
```

As we've seen, we just use the `var` keyword to declare variable in JavaScript, with no need to specify a type:

```
var i;  // a declaration of an untyped JavaScript variable.
```

In fact, although it is good programming style to declare variables in JavaScript, it is usually unnecessary, precisely because JavaScript is untyped.

Another feature of JavaScript's lack of typing is that values are conveniently and automatically converted from one type to another. If you attempt to append a number to a string, for example, JavaScript will automatically convert the number to the corresponding string so that it can be appended. We'll see more about data type conversion in Chapter 9, *Further Topics in JavaScript*.

JavaScript is obviously a simpler language for being untyped. The advantage of typed languages, like C++ and Java, is that they enforce rigorous programming, and therefore make it easier to write, maintain, and reuse long, complex programs. Since most JavaScript programs are shorter "scripts," this rigor is not necessary, and we benefit from the simpler syntax.

3.2 Numbers

Numbers are the most basic data type there is, and require very little explanation. As we saw in Chapter 2, numeric literals can be integer or floating-point, and integers can be expressed in decimal, octal, or hexadecimal notation. JavaScript differs from programming languages like C and Java in that it does not make a distinction between integer value and floating point values. All numbers in JavaScript are represented as floating-point values. JavaScript represents numbers using the standard 8-byte IEEE floating-point numeric format, which means that it can represent numbers as large as $\pm1.7976931348623157\times10^{308}$, and numbers as small as $\pm2.2250738585072014\times10^{-308}$.[*]

3.2.1 Arithmetic and Mathematical Functions

JavaScript programs work with numbers using the arithmetic operators that the language provides. These include + for addition, - for subtraction, * for multiplication, and / for division. Full details on these and other arithmetic operators are in Chapter 4, *Expressions and Operators*.

In addition to these basic arithmetic operations, JavaScript supports more complex mathematical operations through a large number of mathematical functions that

---

* This format will be familiar to Java programmers as the format of the `double` type. It is also the `double` format used in almost all modern implementations of C and C++.

are a core part of the language. For convenience, these functions are all stored as properties of a single object named `Math`, and so we use always use the literal name `Math` to access them. For example, to compute the sine of the numeric value x, we would write code like this:

```
sine_of_x = Math.sin(x);
```

And to compute the square-root of a numeric expression, we might use code like this (note the use of the * operator for multiplication):

```
hypot = Math.sqrt(x*x + y*y);
```

See the Math object and subsequent listings in the reference section of this book for full details on all the mathematical functions supported by JavaScript.

3.2.2 Special Numeric Values

There are several special numeric values used by JavaScript. When a floating-point value becomes larger than the largest representable type, the result is a special infinity value, which JavaScript prints as `Infinity`. Similarly, when a negative value becomes more negative than the most negative representable number, the result is negative infinity, printed as `-Infinity`. (Internet Explorer 3.0 prints these special infinity values in a less intuitive fashion; this will be fixed.)

Another special JavaScript numeric value is returned when a mathematical operation (such as division by zero) yields an undefined result or an error. In this case, the result is the special Not-a-Number value, printed as `NaN`. The special Not-a-Number value has special behavior: it does not compare equal to any number, including itself! For this reason, a special function `isNaN()` is required to test for this value. In Navigator 2.0, the `NaN` value and the `isNaN()` do not work correctly on Windows and other platforms. On 2.0 Windows platforms, 0 is returned instead of `NaN` when a numeric value is undefined. Similarly, `NaN` does not work in Internet Explorer 3.0, although it will in future versions. In IE 3.0, `isNaN()` always returns `false`, and functions return 0 instead of `NaN`.

In Navigator 3.0 (but not IE 3.0), there are constants defined for each of these special numeric values. These constants are listed in Table 3-1.

Table 3-1: Special Numeric Constants

Constant	Meaning
`Number.MAX_VALUE`	Largest representable number
`Number.MIN_VALUE`	Most negative representable number
`Number.NaN`	Special not-a-number value

Table 3–1: Special Numeric Constants (continued)

Constant	Meaning
Number.POSITIVE_INFINITY	Special value to represent infinity
Number.NEGATIVE_INFINITY	Special value to represent negative infinity

3.3 Strings

A string is a string of letters, digits, punctuation characters, and so on—it is the JavaScript data type for representing text. As we saw in Chapter 2, string literals may be included in your programs by enclosing them in matching pairs of single or double quotes.

One of the built-in features of JavaScript is the ability to concatenate strings. If you use the + operator with numbers, it adds them. But if you use this operator on strings, it joins them by appending the second to the first. For example:

```
msg = "Hello, " + "world";   // produces the string "Hello, world"
greeting = "Welcome to my home page," + " " + name;
```

To determine the length of a string—the number of characters it contains—you use the length property of the string. If the variable s contains a string, you access its length like this:

```
s.length
```

There are a number of methods that you can use to operate on strings. For example, to find out what the last character of a string s is, you could use:

```
last_char = s.charAt(s.length - 1)
```

To extract the second, third, and fourth characters from a string s, you would write:

```
sub = s.substring(1,4);
```

To find the position of the first letter 'a' in a string s, you could use:

```
i = s.indexOf('a');
```

There are quite a few other methods you can use to manipulate strings. You'll find full documentation of these methods in the reference section of this book, under the headings "String", "String.charAt", and so on.

When we introduce the object data type below, you'll see that object properties and methods are used in the same way that string properties and methods are used in the examples above. This does not mean that strings are a type of object. In fact, strings are a distinct JavaScript data type. They use object syntax for accessing properties and methods, but they are not themselves objects. We'll see just why this is at the end of this chapter.

Note that JavaScript does not have a `char` or character data type, like C, C++, and Java do. To represent a single character, you simply use a string that has a length of 1.

3.4 *Boolean Values*

The number and string data types have an infinite number of possible values. The Boolean data type, on the other hand, has only two. As we saw in Chapter 2, the two legal Boolean values are the keywords `true` and `false`. A Boolean value represents a "truth value"—it says whether something is true or not.

Boolean values are generally the result of comparisons we make in our JavaScript programs. For example, when we write:

```
a == 4
```

we are testing to see if the value of the variable a is equal to the number 4. If it is, then the result of this comparison is the Boolean value `true`. If a is not equal to 4, then the result of the comparison is `false`. If Boolean values are usually generated by comparisons, they are generally used in JavaScript control structures. For example, the `if/else` statement in JavaScript will perform one action if a Boolean value is `true` and another action if the value is `false`. Generally, we will combine a comparison that creates a Boolean value directly with a statement that uses it. The result looks like this:

```
if (a == 4)
  b = b + 1;
else
  a = a + 1;
```

This code checks if a equals 4. If so, it adds 1 to b; otherwise, it adds 1 to a.

Instead of thinking of the two possible Boolean values as `true` and `false`, it is sometimes convenient to think of them as "on" (`true`) and "off" (`false`) or "yes" (`true`) and "no" (`false`). Sometimes it is even useful to consider them equivalent to 1 (`true`) and 0 (`false`). (In fact, JavaScript does just this and converts `true` and `false` to 1 and 0 when necessary.)

C and C++ programmers should note that JavaScript has a distinct Boolean data type, unlike C and C++ which simply use integer values to simulate Boolean values. Java programmers should note that although JavaScript has a Boolean type, it is not nearly as "pure" as the Java Boolean data type—JavaScript Boolean values are easily converted to and from other data types, and so in practice, the use of Boolean values is much more like their use in C and C++ than in Java.

3.5 Functions

A function is a piece of JavaScript code that is defined once in a program and can be executed, or *invoked*, many times by the program. JavaScript functions can be passed *arguments* or *parameters* that specify the value or values that the function is to operate upon, and can return values. Functions are defined in JavaScript with code like the following:

```
function square(x)
{
    return x*x;
}
```

Once a function is defined, you can invoke it by following the function's name with a comma-separated list of arguments within parentheses. The following lines are function invocations:

```
y = square(x);
compute_distance(x1, y1, z1, x2, y2, z2)
click()
y = sin(x);
```

An unusual feature of JavaScript is that functions are actual data types. In many languages, including Java, functions are a syntactic feature of the language, and can be defined and invoked, but they are not data types. The fact that functions are true data types in JavaScript gives a lot of flexibility to the language. It means that functions can be stored in variables, arrays, and objects, and it means that functions can be passed as arguments to other functions. This can quite often be useful. We'll learn more about defining and invoking functions, and also about using them as data values, in Chapter 6, *Functions*.

Since functions are data types just like numbers, and strings, they can be assigned to object properties just like other values can. When a function is assigned to a property of an object (described below), it is often referred to as a *method* of that object. Some special methods of certain objects are automatically invoked by the web browser when the user interacts with the browser (by clicking the mouse, for example). These special methods are called *event handlers*. We'll see more about methods in Chapter 7, *Objects*, and about event handlers in Chapter 10, *Client-Side Program Structure*.

3.6 Objects

An object is a collection of named pieces of data. These named pieces of data are usually referred to as *properties* of the object. (Sometimes they are called "fields" of the object, but this usage can be confusing.) To refer to a property of an object, we refer to the object, and follow this reference with a period, and follow the period with the name of the property. For example, if an object named `image` has properties named `width` and `height`, we can refer to those properties like this:

```
image.width
image.height
```

Properties of objects are, in many ways, just like JavaScript variables and can contain any type of data, including arrays, functions, and other objects. Thus, you might see JavaScript code like this:

```
document.myform.button
```

which refers to the `button` property of an object which is itself stored in the `myform` property of an object named `document`.

As mentioned above, when a function value is stored in a property of an object, that function is often called a *method*, and the property name becomes the method name. To invoke a method of an object, use the `.` syntax to extract the function value from the object, and then use the `()` syntax to invoke that function. To invoke the `write()` method of the `document` object, we use code like this:

```
document.write("this is a test");
```

Objects in JavaScript have the ability to serve as associative arrays—that is, they can associate arbitrary data values with arbitrary strings. When objects are used in this way, a different syntax is generally required to access the object's properties: a string containing the name of the desired property is enclosed within square brackets. Using this syntax we could access the properties of the `image` object mentioned above with code like this:

```
image["width"]
image["height"]
```

Associative arrays are a powerful data type, and are useful for a number of programming techniques. We'll learn more about objects in their traditional and associative array usages in Chapter 7.

3.7 Arrays

An array is a collection of data values, just as an object is. While each data value contained in an object has a name, each data value in an array has a number, or *index*. In JavaScript, arrays are indexed (i.e., individual numbered values are retrieved from the array) by enclosing the index within square brackets after the array name. For example, if an array is named a, and i is an integer, then a[i] is an element of the array. Array indexes begin with zero. Thus a[2] refers to the *third* element of the array a.

Arrays may contain any type of JavaScript data, including references to other arrays or to objects or functions. So, for example, the JavaScript code:

```
document.images[1].width
```

refers to the width property of an object stored in the second element of an array stored in the images property of the document object.

Note that the arrays described here differ from the associative arrays described in the previous section. The "regular" arrays we are discussing are indexed by integers. Associative arrays are indexed by strings. Also note that JavaScript does not support multidimensional arrays, except as arrays of arrays. Finally, because JavaScript is an untyped language, the elements of an array do not all need to be of the same type, as they do in typed languages like Java. We'll learn more about arrays in Chapter 8, *Arrays*.

3.8 Null

The JavaScript keyword null is a special value that indicates "no value." Technically speaking, null is a value of object type, so when a variable holds the value null, you know that it does not contain a valid object or array. For that matter, you also know that it does not contain a valid number, string, Boolean or function.

C and C++ programmers should note that null in JavaScript is not the same as 0 as it is in those languages. In certain circumstances, null will be converted to a 0, but the two are not equivalent.

3.9 Undefined

There is another special value occasionally used by JavaScript. This is the "undefined" value returned when you use a variable that doesn't exist, or a variable that has been declared, but never had a value assigned to it, or an object property that doesn't exist.

Unlike the `null` value, there is no `undefined` keyword for the undefined value. This can make it hard to write JavaScript code that detects this undefined value. The undefined value is not the same as `null`, but for most practical purposes, you can treat it as if it is. This is because the undefined value compares equal to `null`. That is, if we write:

```
my.prop == null
```

the comparison will be true both if the `my.prop` property doesn't exist, or if it does exist but contains the value `null`.

In Navigator 3.0 and later, you can distinguish between `null` and the undefined value with the `typeof` operator (which is discussed in detail in Chapter 4). This operator returns a string that indicates the data type of any value. We said above that `null` is actually a object value, and when we use `typeof` on `null`, it indicates this by returning the string "object":

```
type = typeof null;                    // returns "object"
```

However, when we apply `typeof` to a variable that has had no value assigned (or to an undefined variable or property), it returns the string "undefined":

```
var new_undefined_variable;
type = typeof new_undefined_variable  // returns "undefined"
```

The implication of this "undefined" result is interesting. It means that the undefined value is a completely different data type than any other value in JavaScript.

3.10 The Date Object

The sections above have described all of the fundamental data types supported by JavaScript. Dates and times are not one of these fundamental types. But JavaScript does provide a type (or *class*) of object that represents dates and times, and can be used to manipulate this type of data. A Date object in JavaScript is created with the `new` operator and the `Date()` constructor:

```
now = new Date();   // create an object representing the current date and time
xmas = new Date(96, 11, 25);  // Create a Date object representing Christmas
```

Methods of the Date object allow you to get and set the various date and time values, and to convert the Date to a string, using either local time or GMT time. For example:

```
xmas.setYear(xmas.getYear() + 1);   // Change the date to next Christmas
document.write("Today is: " + now.toLocaleString());
```

In addition, the Date object also defines functions (not methods; they are not invoked through a Date object) to convert a date specified in string or numeric form to an internal millisecond representation that is useful for some kinds of date arithmetic.

You can find full documentation on the Date object and its methods in the reference section of this book. Unfortunately, the Date object is plagued with various bugs in Navigator 2.0. Appendix B, *Known Bugs*, contains details.

3.11 Data Type Wrapper Objects

When we introduced strings earlier in this chapter, we pointed out a strange feature of that data type: to operate on strings, we use object notation. For example, a typical operation involving strings might be the following:

```
s = "These are the times that try people's souls.";
last_word = s.substring(s.lastIndexOf(" ")+1, s.length);
```

If we didn't know better, it would appear that s was an object, and that we were invoking methods and reading property values of that object.

In Chapter 6, we'll see something similar: functions also have properties that we can access using object notation. What's going on? Are strings and functions objects, or are they distinct data types? In Navigator 3.0, the typeof operator assures us that strings have a data type "string" and that functions are of type "function" and that neither is of type "object". Why then, do they use object notation?

The truth is that each primitive data type (i.e., the data types that are not objects or arrays) has a corresponding object type defined for it. That is, besides supporting the number, string, Boolean and function data types, JavaScript also supports Number, String, Boolean, and Function object types. These object types are "wrappers" around the primitive data types—they contain the same primitive data value, but also define the properties and methods that we use to manipulate that data (or to manipulate strings and functions, at least; the Number and Boolean objects are not as useful as the String and Function objects.)

As an untyped language, JavaScript can very flexibly convert values from one type to another. When we use a string in an "object context", (i.e., when we try to access a property or method of the string) JavaScript internally creates a String wrapper object for the string value. This String object is used in place of the primitive string value; the object has properties and methods defined, and so the use of the primitive value in an object context succeeds. The same is true, of course, for the other primitive types and their corresponding object wrappers; we just don't use the other types in an object context nearly as often as we use strings in that context.

When we use a string in an object context, note that the String object that is created is a transient one—it is used to allow us to access a property or method, and then it is no longer needed and is reclaimed by the system. Suppose s is a string, and we determine the length of the string with a line like this:

```
len = s.length;
```

In this case, s remains a string; the original string value is not itself changed. A new transient String object is created, which allows us to access the length property, and the transient object is discarded, with no change to the original value s. If you think that this scheme sounds elegant and bizarrely complex at the same time, you are right. Don't worry, however, the conversion to a transient object is done quite efficiently within JavaScript.

If for some reason we want to use a String object explicitly in our program, we will have to create a non-transient one that will not be automatically discarded by the system. We create String objects just as we create other objects, with the new operator. (The new operator will be introduced in Chapter 4, and we'll learn more about object creation in Chapter 7.) For example:

```
s = "hello world";              // a primitive string value
S = new String("Hello World");  // a String object
```

Once we have created a String object S, what can we do with it? Nothing that we can't do with the corresponding primitive string value. If we use the typeof operator, it will tell us that S is indeed an object, and not a string value, but except for that case, we'll find that we can't distinguish between the a primitive string and the String object. This is for two reasons. First, as we've seen, strings are automatically converted to String objects whenever necessary. But it turns out that the reverse is also true. Whenever we use a String object where a primitive string value is expected, JavaScript will automatically convert the String to a string. So if we use our String object with the + operator, a transient primitive string value will be created so that the string concatenation operation can be performed:

```
msg = S + '!';
```

Bear in mind that everything we've said in this section about string values and String objects applies also to the other primitive types and their corresponding Number, Boolean, and Function objects. You can learn more about these object types from their respective entries in the reference section of this book. In Chapter 9 we'll see more about this primitive type/object duality, and about automatic data conversion in JavaScript.

4

Expressions and Operators

Expressions and operators are fundamental to most programming languages. This chapter explains how they work in JavaScript. If you are familiar with C, C++, or Java, you'll notice that expressions and operators in JavaScript are very similar, and you'll be able to skim this chapter quickly. If you are not a C, C++, or Java programmer, this chapter will teach you what you need to know about expressions and operators in JavaScript.

4.1 Expressions

An *expression* is a "phrase" of JavaScript that a JavaScript interpreter can *evaluate* to produce a value. Simple expressions are constants (e.g., string or numeric literals) or variable names, like these:

```
1.7                            // a numeric literal
"Oh no!  We're out of coffee!" // a string literal
true                           // a Boolean literal
null                           // the literal null value
i                              // the variable i
sum                            // the variable sum
```

The value of a constant expression is simply the constant itself. The value of a variable expression is the value that the variable refers to.

These expressions are not particularly interesting. More complex (and interesting) expressions can be created by combining simple expressions. For example, we saw that 1.7 is an expression and i is an expression, so the following is also an expression:

```
i + 1.7
```

The value of this expression is determined by adding the values of the two simpler expressions. The plus sign in this example is an *operator* that is used to combine two expressions into a more complex expression. Another operator is - which is used to combine expressions by subtraction. For example:

```
(i + 1.7) - sum
```

This expression uses the - operator to subtract the value of the sum variable from the value of our previous expression i + 1.7. JavaScript supports a number of other operators, besides + and -, which we'll learn about in the next section.

4.2 Operator Overview

If you are a C, C++, or Java programmer, then the JavaScript operators will almost all be already familiar to you. Table 4-1 summarizes the operators, and you can refer to this table for reference. In the table, the column labeled **P** gives the operator precedence, and the column labeled **A** gives the operator associativity, which can be L (left-to-right) or R (right-to-left).

If you do not already know C, C++, or Java, the sections that follow the table explain how to interpret the table and explain what each of the operators does.

Table 4-1: JavaScript Operators

P	A	Operator	Operand Type(s)	Operation Performed
0	L	.	object, property	property access
	L	[ ]	array, integer	array index
	L	( )	function, args	function call
1	R	++	number	pre-or-post increment (unary)
	R	--	number	pre-or-post decrement (unary)
	R	-	number	unary minus (negation)
	R	~	integer	bitwise complement (unary)
	R	!	Boolean	logical complement (unary)
	R	typeof	any	return data type (unary)
	R	new	constructor call	create new object (unary)
	R	void	any	return undefined value (unary)
2	L	*, /, %	numbers	multiplication, division, remainder

Table 4-1: JavaScript Operators (continued)

P	A	Operator	Operand Type(s)	Operation Performed
3	L	+, -	numbers	addition, subtraction
	L	+	strings	string concatenation
4	L	<<	integers	left shift
	L	>>	integers	right shift with sign-extension
	L	>>>	integers	right shift with zero extension
5	L	<, <=	numbers or strings	less than, less than or equal
	L	>, >=	numbers or strings	greater than, greater than or equal
6	L	==	primitive types	equal (have identical values)
	L	!=	primitive types	not equal (have different values)
	L	==	reference types	equal (refer to same object)
	L	!=	reference types	not equal (refer to different objects)
7	L	&	integers	bitwise AND
8	L	^	integers	bitwise XOR
9	L	|	integers	bitwise OR
10	L	&&	Booleans	logical AND
11	L	||	Booleans	logical OR
12	R	? :	Boolean, any, any	conditional (ternary) operator
13	R	=	variable, any	assignment
	R	*=, /=, %=, +=, -=, <<=, >>=, >>>=, &=, ^=, |=	variable, any	assignment with operation
14	L	,	any	multiple evaluation

4.2.1 Number of Operands

In general, there are three types of operators. Most JavaScript operators, like the + operator that we saw in the previous section, are *binary operators* that combine two expressions into a single, more complex expression. That is, they operate on two operands. JavaScript also supports a number of *unary operators*, which convert a single expression into a single more complex expression. The - operator in the expression -3 is a unary operator which performs the operation of negation on the operand 3. Finally, JavaScript supports one *ternary operator*, ? :, which combines the value of three expressions into a single expression.

4.2.2 Type of Operands

When constructing JavaScript expressions, you must pay attention to the data types that are being passed to operators, and to the data types that are returned. Different operators expect their operands' expressions to evaluate to values of a certain data type. For example, it is not possible to multiply strings, so the expression "a" * "b" is not legal in JavaScript. Note, however, that JavaScript tries to convert expressions to the appropriate type whenever possible, so the expression "3" * "5" is legal. Its value is the number 15, not the string "15".

Furthermore, some operators behave differently depending on the type of the operands. Most notably, the + operator adds numeric operands but concatenates string operands. And if passed one string and one number, it converts the number to a string and concatenates the two resulting strings. For example, '1' + 0 yields the string '10'.

Finally, note that operators do not always return the same type as their operands. The comparison operators (less than, equal to, greater than, etc.) take operands of various types, but when comparison expressions are evaluated, they always return a Boolean result that indicates whether the comparison is true or not. For example, the expression a < 3 returns true if the value of variable a is in fact less than 3. As we'll see, the Boolean values returned by comparison operators are used in if statements, while loops, and for loops—JavaScript statements that control the execution of a program based on the results of evaluating expressions that contain comparison operators.

4.2.3 Operator Precedence

In Table 4-1 the column labeled **P** specifies the *precedence* of each operator. Operator precedence controls the order in which operations are performed. Operators with a lower number in the **P** column are performed before those with a higher number. Somewhat confusingly, we say that operators that are performed first (with a lower **P** number) have *higher* precedence.

Consider the following expression:

```
w = x + y*z;
```

The multiplication operator * has a higher precedence than the addition operator +, so the multiplication is performed before the addition. Furthermore, the assignment operator = has the lowest precedence, and so the the assignment operator = has the lowest assignment is performed after all the operations on the right-hand side are completed. Operator precedence can be overridden with the explicit use of parentheses. To force the addition to be performed first in the above example, we would write:

```
w = (x + y)*z;
```

In practice, if you are at all unsure about the precedence of your operators, the simplest thing is to use parentheses to make the evaluation order explicit. The only rules that are important to know are that multiplication and division are performed before addition and subtraction, and that assignment has very low precedence and is always performed last.

4.2.4 Operator Associativity

In Table 4-1 the column labeled **A** specifies the associativity of the operator. A value of L specifies left-to-right associativity, and a value of R specifies right-to-left associativity. The associativity of an operator specifies the order in which operations of the same precedence are performed. Left-to-right associativity means that operations are performed from left to right. For example:

```
w = x + y + z;
```

is the same as:

```
w = ((x + y) + z);
```

because the addition operator has left-to-right associativity. On the other hand, the following (almost nonsensical) expressions:

```
x = ~-~y;
w = x = y = z;
q = a?b:c?d:e?f:g;
```

are equivalent to:

```
x = ~(-(~y));
w = (x = (y = z));
q = a?b:(c?d:(e?f:g));
```

because the unary, assignment, and ternary conditional operators have right-to-left associativity.

4.3 Arithmetic Operators

Having explained operator precedence, associativity, and other background material, we can start to describe the operators themselves. This section details the arithmetic operators.

4.3.1 Addition (+)

The + operator adds its two numeric operands. If both operands are strings, then it returns a string that is the result of concatenating the second operand onto the first. If either operand is a string, then the other is converted to a string, and the two strings are concatenated. Furthermore, if either operand is an object, then both operands are converted to strings and concatenated.

4.3.2 Subtraction (−)

The − operator subtracts its second operand from its first. Both operands must be numbers. Used as a unary operator, − negates its operand.

4.3.3 Multiplication (*)

The * operator multiplies its two operands, which must both be numbers.

4.3.4 Division (/)

The / operator divides its first operand by its second. Both operands must be numbers. If you are a C programmer, you might expect to get an integer result when you divide one integer by another. In JavaScript, however, all numbers are floating-point, so all divisions have floating-point results: 5 / 2 evaluates to 2.5, not 2.

4.3.5 Modulo (%)

The % operator computes the first operand modulo the second operand. That is, it returns the remainder when the first operand is divided by the second operand an integer number of times. Both operands must be numbers. For example, 5 % 2 evaluates to 1.

While the modulo operator is typically used with integer operands, it also works for floating-point values. For example, 4.2 % 2.1 == 0.

4.3.6 Unary Negation (−)

When − is used as a unary operator, before a single operand, it performs unary negation, i.e., it converts a positive value to an equivalently negative value, and vice versa.

4.3.7 Increment (++)

The ++ operator increments (i.e., adds 1 to) its single operand, which must be a variable, an element of an array, or a property of an object that refers to a numeric value. The precise behavior of this operator depends on its position relative to the operand. When used before the operand, where it is known as the pre-increment operator, it increments the operand and evaluates to the incremented value of that operand. When used after the operand, where it is known as the post-increment operator, it increments its operand, but evaluates to the *unincremented* value of that operand.

For example, the following code sets both i and j to 2:

```
i = 1;
j = ++i;
```

But these lines set i to 2 and j to 1:

```
i = 1;
j = i++;
```

This operator, in both its forms, is most commonly used to increment a counter that controls a loop.

4.3.8 Decrement (−−)

The −− operator decrements (i.e., subtracts 1 from) its single numeric operand, which must be a variable, an element of an array, or a property of an object. Like the ++ operator, the precise behavior of −− depends on its position relative to the operand. When used before the operand, it decrements and returns the decremented value. When used after the operand, it decrements, but returns the *undecremented* value.

4.4 Comparison Operators

This section describes the JavaScript comparison operators. These are operators that compare values of various types and return a Boolean value (true or false) depending on the result of the comparison. As we'll see in Chapter 5, *Statements*, they are most commonly used in things like if statements and while loops to control the flow of program execution.

4.4.1 Equality (= =)

The == operator returns true if its two operands are equal, and returns false if they are not equal. The operands may be of any type, and the definition of "equal" depends on the type.

In JavaScript, numbers, strings, and Boolean values are compared *by value*. This means that two variables are equal only if they contain the same value. For example, two strings are equal only if they each contain exactly the same characters. In this case, there are two separate values involved, and the == operator checks that these two values are identical.

On the other hand, objects and arrays are compared *by reference*. This means that two variables are equal only if they refer to the same object. Two separate arrays will never be equal, by the definition of the == operator, even if they contain identical elements. For two variables that contain references to objects, arrays, or functions, they are equal only if they refer to the same object, array, or function. If you want to test that two separate objects contain the same properties or that two separate arrays contain the same elements, you'll have to check the properties and elements yourself. (And, if any of the properties or elements are themselves objects or arrays, you'll have to decide which kind of equality you want to test for.)

In Navigator 3.0, functions are compared by reference, just as objects and arrays are. Prior to 3.0, functions may not be used with the == operator.

Usually, if two values have different types, then they are not equal. Because JavaScript automatically converts data types when needed, though, this is not always the case. For example, the expression "1" == 1 evaluates to true in JavaScript. Similarly, and not surprisingly to C or C++ programmers, true == 1 and false == 0 are also both true expressions. In Navigator 2.0, null is equal to 0, but this was a bug was fixed in 3.0. Be careful when comparing values of different types: if you compare a string to a number, and the string cannot be converted to a number, then Navigator 2.0 and 3.0 will produce an error message. Internet Explorer takes the simpler, and probably correct, course and returns false in this case.

Note that the equality operator == is very different from the assignment operator =, although in English, we often read both as "equals". It is important to keep the two operators distinct and to use the correct one in the correct situation. To keep them straight, it may help to read the assignment operator = as "is assigned" or as "gets".

4.4.2 Inequality (!=)

The != operator tests for the exact opposite of the == operator. If two variables are equal to each other, then comparing them with the != operator will return false. On the other hand, comparing two objects that are not equal to each other with != will return `true`. As we'll see, the ! operator computes the Boolean NOT operation. This makes it easy to remember that != stands for "not equal to."[*] See the discussion of the == operator for details on how equality is defined for different data types.

4.4.3 Less Than (<)

The < operator evaluates to `true` if its first operand is less than its second operand; otherwise it evaluates to `false`. The operands must be numbers or strings. Strings are ordered alphabetically, by character encoding.

4.4.4 Greater Than (>)

The > operator evaluates to `true` if its first operand is greater than its second operand; otherwise it evaluates to `false`. The operands must be numbers or strings. Strings are ordered alphabetically, by character encoding.

4.4.5 Less Than or Equal (<=)

The <= operator evaluates to `true` if its first operand is less than or equal to its second operand; otherwise it evaluates to `false`. The operands must be numbers or strings. Strings are ordered alphabetically, by character encoding.

4.4.6 Greater Than or Equal (>=)

The >= operator evaluates to `true` if its first operand is greater than or equal to its second operand; otherwise it evaluates to `false`. The operands must be numbers or strings. Strings are ordered alphabetically, by character encoding.

4.5 String Operators

As we've noted in the previous sections, there are several operators that have special effects when their operands are strings.

The + operator concatenates two string operands. That is, it creates a new string that consists of the first string followed by the second. Thus, for example, the following expression evaluates to the string "hello there":

```
"hello" + " " + "there"
```

---

[*] There is one case in which the != operator is not the exact opposite of ==, when a != b is not identical to !(a == b). This occurs with the NaN value (Not-a-Number), which is never equal or inequal to itself. That is, if either operand is NaN, both == and != return `false`.

And the following lines produce the string "22":

```
a = "2"; b = "2";
c = a + b;
```

The <, <=, >, and >= operators compare two strings to determine what order they fall in. The comparison uses alphabetical order. Note, however, that this "alphabetical order" is based on the ASCII or Latin-1 (ISO8859-1) character encoding used by JavaScript. In this encoding, all capital letters come before (are "less than") all lowercase letters, which can cause unexpected results. It means, for example, that the following expression evaluates to true:

```
"Zoo" < "aardvark"
```

The == and != operators work on strings, but, as we've seen, these operators work for all data types, and they do not have any special behavior when used with strings.

The + operator is a special one—it gives priority to string operands over numeric operands. As noted earlier, if either operand to + is a string (or an object) the the other operand (or both operands) will be converted to strings and concatenated, rather than added. On the other hand, the comparison operators only perform string comparison if *both* operands are strings. If only one operand is a string, JavaScript attempts to convert it to a number. The following lines illustrate:

```
1 + 2          // Addition. Result is 3.
"1" + "2"      // Concatenation. Result is "12".
"1" + 2        // Concatenation; 2 is converted to "2". Result is 12.
11 < 3         // Numeric comparison. Result is false.
"11" < "3"     // String comparison. Result is true.
"11" < 3       // Numeric comparison; "11" converted to 11. Result is false.
"eleven" < 3   // Causes error because "eleven" can't be converted to a number.
```

Finally, it is important to note that when the + operator is used with strings and numbers, it may not be associative. That is, the result may depend on the order in which operations are performed. This can be seen with examples like this:

```
s = 1 + 2 + "blind mice";       // yields "3 blind mice"
t = "# of blind mice: " + 1 + 2; // yields "# of blind mice: 12"
```

The reason for this surprising difference in behavior is that the + operator works from left to right, unless parentheses change this order. Thus the two lines above are equivalent to these:

```
s = (1 + 2) + "blind mice";       // 1st + yields number; 2nd yields string
t = ("# of blind mice: " + 1) + 2; // both operations yield strings
```

4.6 Logical Operators

The logical operators expect their operands to be Boolean values, and they perform "Boolean algebra" on them. In programming, they are usually used with the comparison operators to express complex comparisons that involve more than one variable.

4.6.1 Logical And (&&)

The && operator evaluates to true if and only if its first operand *and* its second operand are both true. If the first operand evaluates to false, then the result will be false, and && operator doesn't even bother to evaluate the second operand. This means that if the second operand has any side effects (such as those produced by the ++ operator) they might not occur. In general, it is best to avoid expressions like the following that combine side effects with the && operator:

```
(a == b) && (c++ < 10)   // increment may or may not happen
```

4.6.2 Logical Or (| |)

The | | operator evaluates to true if its first operand *or* its second operand (or both) are true. Like the && operator, the | | operator doesn't evaluate its second operand when the result is determined by the first operand (i.e., if the first operand evaluates to true, then the result will be true regardless of the second operand, and so the second operand is not evaluated). This means that you should generally not use any expression with side effects as the second operand to this operator.

4.6.3 Logical Not (!)

The ! operator is a unary operator; it is placed before a single operand. Its purpose is to invert the Boolean value of its operand. For example, if the variable a has the value true, then !a has the value false. And if p && q evaluates to false, then !(p && q) evaluates to true.

4.7 Bitwise Operators

Despite the fact that all numbers in JavaScript are floating-point, the bitwise operators require numeric operands that have integral values. They operate on these integer operands using a 32-bit integer representation instead of the equivalent floating-point representation. These operators may return NaN if used with operands which are not integers or which are too large to fit in a 32-bit integer representation. Four of these operators perform Boolean algebra on the individual bits of the operands, behaving as if each bit in each operand was a Boolean value and performing similar operands to the logical operators we saw earlier. The other three bitwise operators are used to shift bits left and right.

If you are not familiar with binary numbers and the binary representation of decimal integers, you can skip the operators described in this section. The purpose of these operators is not described here; they are used for low-level manipulation of binary numbers and are not commonly used in JavaScript programming.

4.7.1 Bitwise And (&)

The & operator performs a Boolean AND operation on each bit of its integer arguments. A bit is set in the result only if the corresponding bit is set in both operands.

4.7.2 Bitwise Or (|)

The | operator performs a Boolean OR operation on each bit of its integer arguments. A bit is set in the result if the corresponding bit is set in one or both of the operands.

4.7.3 Bitwise Xor (^)

The ^ operator performs a Boolean "exclusive OR" operation on each bit of its integer argument. Exclusive OR means either operand one is true or operand two is true, but not both. A bit is set in the result of this operation if a corresponding bit is set in one (but not both) of the two operands.

4.7.4 Bitwise Not (~)

The ~ operator is a unary operator that appears before its single integer argument. It operates by reversing all bits in the operand. Because of how signed integers are represented in JavaScript, applying the ~ operator to a value is equivalent to changing its sign and subtracting 1.

4.7.5 Shift Left (<<)

The << operator moves all bits in its first operand to the left by the number of places specified in the second operand, which should be an integer between 1 and 31. For example, in the operation a << 1, the first bit (the ones bit) of a becomes the second bit (the twos bit), the second bit of a becomes the third, etc.

A zero is used for the new first bit, and the value of the 32nd bit is lost. Shifting a value left by one position is equivalent to multiplying by 2. Shifting two positions is equivalent to multiplying by 4, and so on.

4.7.6 Shift Right with Sign (>>)

The >> operator moves all bits in its first operand to the right by the number of places specified in the second operand (an integer between 1 and 31). Bits that are shifted off the right are lost. The bits filled in on the left are the same as the sign bit of the original operand to preserve the sign of the result: If the first operand is positive, the result will have zeros filled in the high bits; if the first operand is negative, the result will have ones filled in the high bits. Shifting a value right one place is equivalent to dividing by two (discarding the remainder), shifting right two places is equivalent to integer division by four, and so on.

4.7.7 Shift Right Zero Fill (>>>)

The >>> operator is just like the >> operator, except that the bits shifted in on the left are always zero, regardless of the sign of the first operand.

4.8 Assignment Operators

As we saw in the discussion of variables in Chapter 3, *Variables and Data Types*, = is used in JavaScript to assign a value to a variable. For example:

```
i = 0
```

While you might not normally think of such a line of JavaScript as an expression that has a value and can be evaluated, it is in fact an expression, and technically speaking, = is an operator.

The = operator expects its left-hand operand to be a variable, or the element of an array or a property of an object, and expects its right-hand operand to be an arbitrary value of any type. The value of an assignment expression is the value of the right-hand operand. As a side effect, the = operator assigns the value on the right to the variable, element, or property on the left so that future uses of the variable, element, or property refer to the value.

Because = is defined as an operator, you can include it in more complex expressions. For example, you can assign and test a value in the same expression with code like this:

```
(a = b) == 0
```

If you do this, be sure you are clear on the difference between the = and == operators!

The assignment operator has right-to-left associativity, which means that when multiple assignment operators appear in an expression, they are evaluated from right to left. This means that you can write code like the following to assign a single value to multiple variables:

```
i = j = k = 0;
```

Remember that each assignment expression has a value that is the value of the right-hand side. So in the above code, the value of the first assignment (the right-most one) becomes the right-hand side for the second assignment (the middle one) and this value becomes the right-hand side for the last (leftmost) assignment.

As we'll see in Chapter 7, *Objects*, you can use the `Object.assign()` method in Navigator 3.0 to override the behavior of the assignment operator.

N3

4.8.1 *Assignment with Operation*

Besides the normal = assignment operator, JavaScript also supports a number of other assignment operators that provide a shortcut by combining assignment with some other operation. For example, the += operator performs addition and assignment. The following expression:

```
total += sales_tax
```

is equivalent to this one:

```
total = total + sales_tax
```

As you might expect, the += operator works for numbers or strings. For numeric operands, it performs addition and assignment, and for string operands, it performs concatenation and assignment.

Similar operators include −=, *=, &=, and so on. Table 4-2 lists them all. In general, the expression:

```
a op= b
```

where *op* is an operator, is equivalent to:

```
a = a op b
```

Table 4-2: Assignment Operators

Operator	Example	Equivalent
+=	a += b	a = a + b
−=	a −= b	a = a − b
*=	a *= b	a = a * b

Table 4-2: Assignment Operators (continued)

Operator	Example	Equivalent
/=	a /= b	a = a / b
%=	a %= b	a = a % b
<<=	a <<= b	a = a << b
>>=	a >>= b	a = a >> b
>>>=	a >>>= b	a = a >>> b
&=	a &= b	a = a & b
|=	a |= b	a = a | b
^=	a ^= b	a = a ^ b

bitwise operators

4.9 Miscellaneous Operators

JavaScript supports a number of other miscellaneous operators, described in the sections below.

4.9.1 The Conditional Operator (?:)

The conditional operator is the only ternary operator (three operands) in JavaScript and is sometimes actually called the ternary operator. This operator is sometimes written ?:, although it does not appear quite that way in code. Because this operator has three operands, the first goes before the ?, the second goes between the ? and the :, and the third goes after the :. It is used like this:

```
x > 0 ? x*y : -x*y
```

→ 1,0

The first operand of the conditional operator must have a Boolean value—usually this is the result of a comparison expression. The second and third operands may have any value. The value returned by the conditional operator depends on the Boolean value of the first operand. If that operand is true, then the value of the conditional expression is the value of the second operand. If the first operand is false, then the value is the value of the third operand.

While you can achieve similar results using the if statement, the ?: operator is a very handy shortcut in many cases. Here is a typical usage, which checks to be sure that a variable is defined, uses it if so, and provides a default value if not.

```
greeting = "hello " + ((name != null) ? name : "there");
```

This is equivalent to, but more compact than, the following if statement:

```
greeting = "hello ";
if (name != null)
    greeting += name;
else
    greeting += "there";
```

4.9.2 The typeof Operator

The typeof operator is available in Navigator 3.0 and Internet Explorer 3.0. typeof is an unusual operator because it is not represented by punctuation characters but instead by the typeof keyword. It is a unary operator that is placed before its single operand, which can be of any type. The value of the typeof operator is a string indicating the data type of the operand.[*]

Possible values are "number", "string", "boolean", "object", "function", and "undefined" for undefined values. Both arrays and objects return the "object" value. typeof may be used as follows:

```
typeof i
(typeof value == "string") ? "'" + value + "'" : value
```

Note that you can place parentheses around the operand to typeof, which will make typeof look like the name of a function rather than an operator keyword:

```
typeof(i)
```

4.9.3 Object Creation Operator (new)

As we saw earlier, numbers, strings, and Boolean values are represented through textual literals in JavaScript. That is, you just type their string representation into your program, and then your program can manipulate that value. As we'll see later, you can use the function keyword to define functions that your program can work with. But JavaScript supports two other data types as well—objects and arrays. Object and array values cannot simply be typed into your JavaScript programs; they must be created. The new operator is used to do this.

The new operator is one, like typeof, that is represented by a keyword rather than by special punctuation characters. This is a unary operator that appears before its operand. It has the following syntax:

```
new constructor
```

---

[*] This means that typeof typeof x, where x is any value, will always yield the value "string".

constructor must be a function-call expression (i.e., it must include an expression that refers to a function, and this function should be followed by an optional argument list in parentheses). As a special case, for this new operator only, JavaScript simplifies the grammar by allowing the parentheses to be omitted if there are no arguments in the function call. Example uses of the new operator are:

```
o = new Object;      // optional parentheses omitted here
d = new Date();
c = new rectangle(3.0, 4.0, 1.5, 2.75);
obj[i] = new constructors[i]();
```

The new operator works as follows: first, it creates a new object with no properties defined. Next, it invokes the specified constructor function, passing the specified arguments, and passing the newly created object as the value of the this keyword. The constructor function can then use the this keyword to initialize the new object in any way desired. We'll learn more about the this keyword and about constructor functions in Chapter 7.

In Navigator 3.0, you create a JavaScript array with the new Array() syntax. In Navigator 2.0, there is not an Array() constructor function defined. In this version of JavaScript, you can create an array with the Object() constructor instead. Some programs will define their own custom Array() constructor.

We'll see more about creating and working with objects and arrays in Chapter 7 and Chapter 8, *Arrays*.

4.9.4 The delete Operator

If you are a C++ programmer, then you probably expect JavaScript to have a delete operator that destroys objects created with the new operator. JavaScript does have such an operator, but it does not behave in the same way the C++ delete. In Navigator 2.0 and 3.0, delete simply sets its operand (a variable, object property, or array element) to null. You could obviously do this with an assignment statement just as easily, and in fact, delete is depricated in Navigator 2.0 and 3.0; you should not use it at all. This mostly-useless version of the operator was created in a beta version of Navigator 2.0, and never quite got removed from the language. In Navigator 4.0, however, we can expect to see a new, non-depricated, delete operator which is more functional—it will actually delete, or undefine a variable or object property.

Note that even this new Navigator 4.0 delete operator will not be the same as the C++ delete—it simply undefines a variable or property, and does not actually delete or destroy or free up the memory associated with an object created with new. The reason that a C++-style `delete` is not necessary is that JavaScript provides automatic "garbage collection"—when objects and other values are no longer being used, the memory associated with them is automatically reclaimed by the system. You don't have to worry about deleting objects or freeing or releasing memory that is no longer in use. Garbage collection in JavaScript is discussed in more detail in Chapter 11, *Windows and the JavaScript Name Space.*

4.9.5 *The void Operator*

The `void` operator is supported in Navigator 3.0, but not in Internet Explorer 3.0. IE will support it in a future version.

`void` is a unary operator that appears before an expression with any value. The purpose of this operator is an unusual one: it always discards its operand value and simply returns an undefined value. The only occasion on which you are likely to want to do this is in a `javascript:` URL, in which you want to evaluate an expression for its side effects, but do not want the browser to display the value of the evaluated expression. Thus, you might use the `void` operator in HTML like the following:

```
<A HREF="javascript:void document.form1.submit();">Submit Form</A>
```

4.9.6 *The Comma Operator (,)*

The comma operator is a simple one. It evaluates its left argument, evaluates its right argument, and then returns the value of its right argument. Thus, this line:

```
i=0, j=1, k=2;
```

is equivalent to:

```
i = 0;
j = 1;
k = 2;
```

This strange operator is useful only in a few limited circumstances in which you need to evaluate several independent expressions with side effects in a situation where only a single expression is allowed. In practice, the comma operator is only frequently used in conjunction with the `for` loop statement, which we'll see later in Chapter 5.

4.9.7 *Array and Object Access Operators*

As noted briefly in Chapter 3, you can access elements of an array using square brackets `[ ]`, and you can access elements of an object using a dot (`.`); both of these are treated as operators in JavaScript.

The . operator expects an object as its left operand, and the name of an object property or method as the right operand. This right operand should not be a string or a variable that contains a string, but should be the literal name of the property, without quotes of any kind. Here are some examples:

```
document.lastModified
navigator.appName
frames[0].length
document.write("hello world")
```

object. property

object. method

If the specified property does not exist in the object, JavaScript does not issue an error, but instead simply returns the special undefined value as the value of the expression.

Most operators allow arbitrary expressions for either operand, as long as the type of the operand is suitable. The . operator is an exception: the right-hand operand must be a literal property name. Nothing else is allowed.

The [ ] operator allows access to array elements and also to object properties, and it does so without the restrictions that the . operator places on the right-hand operand. If the first operand (which goes before the left bracket) refers to an array, then the second operand (which goes between the brackets) can be an arbitrary expression that evaluates to an integer. For example:

```
frames[1]
document.forms[i + j]
document.forms[i].elements[j++]
```

If the first operand to the [ ] operator is a reference to an object, on the other hand, then the second operand may be an arbitrary expression that evaluates to a string that names a property of the object. Note that in this case, the second operand is a string, not a literal name. It should be a constant in quotes, or a variable or expression that refers to a string. This works like associative arrays in the Perl and awk programming languages. For example:

```
document["lastModified"]
frames[0]['length']
data["val" + i]
```

The [ ] operator is usually used to access the elements of an array. It is less convenient than the . operator for accessing properties of an object because of the need to quote the name of the property. When an object is used as an associative array, however, and the property names are dynamically generated, then the . operator cannot be used, and only the [ ] operator will do. This is commonly the case when you use the for/in loop, which will be introduced in Chapter 5. For example, the following JavaScript code uses a `for/in` loop and the `[ ]` operator to print out the name and value of all properties f in an object o:

```
for (f in o) {
    document.write('o.' + f + ' = ' + o[f]);
    document.write('<BR>');
}
```

4.9.8 Function Call Operator

The `( )` operator is used to invoke functions in JavaScript. This is an unusual operator in that it does not have a fixed number of operands. The first operand is always the name of a function or an expression that refers to a function. This is followed by the left parenthesis and any number of additional operands, which may be arbitrary expressions, each separated from the next with a comma. The right parenthesis follows the final operand. The `( )` operator evaluates each of its operands, and invokes the function specified by the first, with the value of the remaining operands passed as arguments. Examples:

```
document.close()
Math.sin(x)
alert("Welcome " + name)
Date.UTC(99, 11, 31, 23, 59, 59)
funcs[i].f(funcs[i].args[0], funcs[i].args[1])
```

5

Statements

As we saw in the last chapter, *expressions* are JavaScript "phrases" that can be evaluated to yield a value. Operators within an expression may have "side effects," but in general, expressions don't "do" anything. To make something happen, you use a JavaScript *statement*, which is akin to a complete sentence or command.

A JavaScript program is simply a collection of statements. Statements usually end with a semicolon. In fact, if you place each statement on a line by itself, you may omit the semicolon. There are circumstances in which you are required to use the semicolon, however, so it is a good idea to get in the habit of using it everywhere.

The following sections describe the various statements in JavaScript and explain their syntax.

5.1 Expression Statements

The simplest kind of statements in JavaScript are expressions that have side effects. We've seen this sort of statement in the section on operators in Chapter 4, *Expressions and Operators*. One major category of these are assignment statements. For example:

```
s = "Hello " + name;
i *= 3;
```

Related to assignment statements are the increment and decrement operators, ++ and −−. These have the side effect of changing a variable value, just as if an assignment had been performed:

```
counter++;
```

Function calls are another major category of expression statements. For example:

```
alert("Welcome, " + name);
window.close();
```

These functions calls are expressions, but also produce an effect on the web browser, and so they are also statements. If a function does not have any side effects, then there is no sense in calling it, unless it is part of an assignment statement. So, for example, you wouldn't just compute a cosine and discard the result:

```
Math.cos(x);
```

Instead, you'd compute the value and assign it to a variable for future use:

```
cx = Math.cos(x);
```

5.2 Compound Statements

Earlier, we saw that the comma operator can be used to combine a number of expressions into a single expression. JavaScript also has a way to combine a number of statements into a single statement, or *statement block*. This is done simply by enclosing any number of statements within curly braces. Thus, the following lines act as a single statement and can be used anywhere that JavaScript expects a single statement.

```
{
    x = Math.PI;
    cx = Math.cos(x);
    alert("cos(" + x + ") = " + cx);
}
```

Note that although this statement block acts as a single statement, it does *not* end with a semicolon. The primitive statements within the block end in semicolons, but the block itself does not.

Combining expressions with the comma operator is an infrequently used technique in JavaScript. On the other hand, combining statements into larger statement blocks is extremely common. As we'll see in the following sections, a number of JavaScript statements themselves contain statements (just as expressions can contain other expressions); these statements are *compound statements*. Formal

JavaScript syntax specifies that these compound statements contain a single sub-statement. Using statement blocks, you can place any number of statements within this single allowed substatement.

5.3 *if*

The if statement is the fundamental "control statement" that allows JavaScript to "make decisions," or to execute statements conditionally. This statement has two forms. The first is:

```
if (expression)
    statement
```

In this form, the *expression* is evaluated. If it is true, then *statement* is executed. If the *expression* is false, then *statement* is not executed. For example:

```
if (name == null)
    name = "John Doe";
```

Note that the parentheses around the expression are a required part of the syntax for the if statement. Although they look extraneous, they are actually a required part of the complete statement.

As mentioned above, we can always replace a single statement with a statement block. So the if statement might also look like this:

```
if ((address == null) || (address == "")) {
    address = "undefined";
    alert("Please specify a mailing address.");
}
```

Note that the indentation used in these examples is not mandatory. Extra spaces and tabs are ignored in JavaScript and since we used semicolons after all the primitive statements, these examples could be written all on one line if we wanted to. Using line breaks and indentation as shown here, however, makes the code easier to read and understand.

The second form of the if statement introduces an else clause that is executed when the *expression* is false. Its syntax is:

```
if (expression)
    statement1
else
    statement2
```

In this form of the statement, the *expression* is evaluated, and if it is `true`, then *statement1* is executed; otherwise *statement2* is executed. For example:

```javascript
if (name != null)
    alert("Hello " + name + "\nWelcome to my home page.");
else {
    name = prompt("Welcome!\n What is your name?");
    alert("Hello " + name);
}
```

When you have nested `if` statements with `else` clauses, some caution is required to ensure that the `else` clause goes with the appropriate `if` statement. Consider the following lines:

```javascript
i = j = 1;
k = 2;
if (i == j)
    if (j == k)
        document.write("i equals k");
else
    document.write("i doesn't equal j");    // WRONG!!
```

In this example, the inner `if` statement forms the single statement allowed by the syntax of the outer `if` statement. Unfortunately, it is not clear (except from the hint given by the indentation) which `if` the `else` goes with. And in this example, the indenting "hint" is wrong, because a JavaScript interpreter will actually interpret the above as:

```javascript
if (i == j)
{
    if (j == k)
        document.write("i equals k");
    else
        document.write("i doesn't equal j");    // OOPS!
}
```

The rule in JavaScript (as in most programming languages) is that an `else` clause is part of the nearest `if` statement. To make this example less ambiguous and easier to read, understand, maintain, and debug, you should use curly braces:

```javascript
if (i == j)
{
    if (j == k) {
        document.write("i equals k");
    }
}
else { // what a difference the location of a curly brace makes!
    document.write("i doesn't equal j");
}
```

5.4 *while*

Just as the `if` statement is the basic control statement that allows JavaScript to "make decisions," the `while` statement is the basic statement that allows JavaScript to perform repetitive actions. It has the following syntax:

```
while (expression)
    statement
```

The `while` statement works like this: first, the *expression* is evaluated. If it is `false`, JavaScript moves on to the next statement in the program. If it is `true`, then *statement* is executed, and *expression* is evaluated again. Again, if the value of *expression* is `false`, then JavaScript moves on to the next statement in the program; otherwise it executes the *statement* that forms the "body" of the loop. This cycle continues until the *expression* evaluates to `false`, at which point the `while` statement ends and JavaScript moves on. Note that you can create an infinite loop with the syntax `while(true)`.

You usually do not want JavaScript to perform exactly the same operation over and over again, so in almost all loops, there are one or more variables that change with each *iteration* of the loop. Since the variables change, the actions performed by executing *statement* may differ each time through the loop. Furthermore, if the changing variable or variables are involved in the *expression*, then the value of the expression may be different each time through the loop. This is important, or an expression that starts off `true` would never change, and the loop would never end! Here is an example `while` loop:

```
count = 0;
while (count < 10) {
    document.write(count + "<br>");
    count++;
}
```

As you can see, the variable `count` starts off at 0 in this example, and is incremented each time the body of the loop runs. Once the loop has executed ten times, the expression becomes false (i.e., the variable `count` is no longer less than 10), the `while` statement finishes, and JavaScript can move on to the next statement in the program. Most loops will have a counter variable like `count`. The variable names `i`, `j`, and `k` are commonly used as a loop counters, though you should use more descriptive names if it makes your code easier to understand.

5.5 *for*

The `for` statement is a loop that is often more convenient than the `while` statement. The `for` statement takes advantage of a pattern common to most loops (including the `while` loop example above). Most loops have a counter variable of some kind. This variable is initialized before the loop starts. Then it is tested as part of the *expression* evaluated before each iteration of the loop. Finally, the counter variable is incremented or otherwise updated at the end of the loop body just before the expression is evaluated again.

The initialization, the test, and the update are the three crucial manipulations of a loop variable, and the `for` statement combines these three and makes them an explicit part of the loop syntax. This makes it especially easy to understand what a `for` loop is doing, and prevents mistakes such as forgetting to initialize or increment the loop variable. The syntax of the `for` statement is:

```
for(initialize ; test ; increment)
    statement
```

The simplest way to explain what this `for` loop does is to show the equivalent `while` loop:*

```
initialize;
while(test) {
    statement
    increment;
}
```

That is, the *initialize* expression is evaluated once, before the loop begins. To be useful, this is an expression with side effects, usually an assignment. The *test* expression is performed before each iteration and controls whether the body of the loop is executed. If the *test* expression is `true`, then the *statement* that is the body of the loop is executed. Finally, the *increment* expression is evaluated. Again, this must be an expression with side effects in order to be useful. Generally it will be an assignment expression or will use the `++` or `--` operators.

The example `while` loop of the previous section can be rewritten as the following `for` loop, which counts from 0 to 9:

```
for(count = 0 ; count < 10 ; count++)
    document.write(count + "<br>");
```

Notice how this syntax places all the important information about the loop variable on a single line, which makes it very clear how the loop will execute. Also

---

* As we'll see when we consider the `continue` statement, this `while` loop is not an exact equivalent to the `for` loop.

note that placing the increment expression in the `for` statement itself simplifies the body of the loop to a single statement, and we don't even need to use curly braces to produce a statement block.

Loops can become a lot more complex than these simple examples, of course, and sometimes there will be more than one variable changing with each iteration of the loop. This is the only place that the comma operator is commonly used in JavaScript—it provides a way to combine multiple initialization and increment expressions into a single expression suitable for use in a `for` loop. For example:

```
for(i = 0, j = 10 ; i < 10 ; i++, j--)
    sum += i * j;
```

5.6 *for...in*

The `for` keyword is used in two ways in JavaScript. We've just seen how it is used in the `for` loop. It is also used in the `for/in` statement. This statement is a somewhat different kind of loop with the following syntax:

```
for (variable in object)
    statement
```

The `variable` should be the name of a variable, or should be an element of an array or a property of an object; it should be something suitable as the left-hand side of an assignment expression. `object` is the name of an object, or an expression that evaluates to an object. As usual, the `statement` is a primitive statement or statement block that forms the body of the loop.

You can loop through the elements of an array by simply incrementing an index variable each time through a `while` or `for` loop. The `for/in` statement provides a way to loop through the properties of an object. The body of the `for/in` loop is executed once for each property of `object`. Before the body of the loop is executed, the name of one of the object's properties is assigned to `variable`, as a string. Within the body of the loop, you can use this variable to look up the value of the object's property with the `[ ]` operator. For example, the following `for/in` loop prints out the name and value of each property of an object:

```
for (prop in my_object) {
    document.write("name: " + prop  "; value: " + my_object[prop], "<br>");
}
```

The `for/in` loop does not specify in what order the properties of an object will be assigned to the variable. There is no way to tell in advance, and the behavior may differ between implementations or versions of JavaScript.

The `for/in` loop does not actually loop through all possible properties of all objects. The rules below specify exactly which properties the statement does list and which it does not in Navigator 3.0. Internet Explorer may use somewhat different rules:

- It lists any user-defined properties or methods explicitly set in a user-defined or system object.

- In general, it lists the properties, but not the methods, of built-in and HTML objects. Certain properties, such as the `constructor` property are never listed, and some built-in objects may have object-specific listing behavior. This object-specific behavior may differ between Navigator and Internet Explorer.

- It lists all defined indexes of user-defined arrays, but does not list the `length` property of those arrays.

- It lists the `length` property and indices of built-in and HTML arrays.

- It does not list properties of functions, methods, or constructors.

- It does not list the constants defined by the `Math` and `Number` objects, such as `Math.PI`. (Since `Math` and `Number` are constructor functions, this follows from the above point.)

- It does not list object properties or methods implicitly defined in an object with the `var` or `function` keywords. (In client-side JavaScript, defining a variable with `var` is the same as defining a property of the same name in the current Window object, except for the different treatment of these two cases by the `for/in` loop.) Properties implicitly defined by the `var` keyword at any time will never again be listed, even if the property is afterwards directly and explicitly set in the object. This last is not true for the `function` keyword.

5.7 *break*

The `break` statement has a very simple syntax:

```
break;
```

This statement is valid only within the body of a `while`, `for`, or `for/in` loop. Using it outside of a loop is a syntax error. When executed, the `break` statement exits the currently running loop. This statement is usually used to exit a loop prematurely when, for whatever reason (perhaps when an error condition arises), there is no longer any need to complete the loop. The following example searches the elements of an array for a particular value. If the value is found, a `break` statement terminates the loop:

```
for(i = 0; i < a.length; i++) {
    if (a[i] == target)
        break;
}
```

5.8 *continue*

The `continue` statement is related to the `break` statement and has a syntax that is just as simple:

```
continue;
```

Like the `break` statement, `continue` can be used only within the body of a `while`, `for`, or `for/in` loop. Using it anywhere else will cause a syntax error.

When the `continue` statement is executed, the current iteration of the enclosing loop is terminated, and the next iteration begins. In a `while` loop, the specified *expression* is tested again, and if `true`, the loop body is executed. In a `for` loop, the *increment* expression is evaluated, then the *test* expression is tested again to determine if another iteration should be done. In a `for/in` loop, the loop starts over with the next property name being assigned to the specified variable.

The following example shows the `continue` statement being used to abort the current iteration of a loop when an error occurs:

```
for(i = 0; i < data.length; i++) {
    if (data[i] == null)
        continue;  // can't proceed with undefined data
    total += data[i];
}
```

Note the difference in behavior of the `continue` statement for the `while` and `for` loops—a `while` loop returns directly to its condition, but a `for` loop first evaluates it increment expression, and then returns to its condition. Above, in the discussion of the `for` loop, we explained the behavior this loop in terms of an "equivalent" `while` loop. But because the `continue` statement behaves differently for these two loops it is never possible to perfectly simulate a `for` loop with a `while` loop.

5.9 *with*

JavaScript interfaces with the web browser through an "object hierarchy" that contains quite a few arrays nested within objects and objects nested within arrays. In order to refer to the components that make up a web page, you may find yourself referring to objects with cumbersome expressions like the following:

```
frames[1].document.forms[0].address_field.value
```

The with statement provides a way to simplify expressions like this one, and reduce your typing. It has the following syntax:

```
with (object)
    statement
```

object is an expression that evaluates to an object. This specified object becomes the default object for all expressions in *statement*, which is a primitive statement or statement block. Any time an identifier appears within *statement*, that identifier is looked up as a property of *object* first. If the identifier is defined as a property of *object*, then this is the definition used. If the identifier is not defined there, then JavaScript looks up its value as it normally would.

For example, you might use the with statement to simplify the following code:

```
x = Math.sin(i * Math.PI / 20);
y = Math.cos(i * Math.PI / 30);
```

Using with, you might write:

```
with(Math) {
    x = sin(i * PI / 20);
    y = cos(i * PI / 30);
}
```

Similarly, instead of calling document.write() over and over again in a JavaScript program, you could use a with(document) statement, and then invoke write() over and over again instead.

You can nest with statements arbitrarily. Note that the *object* expression in a nested with statement may itself be interpreted depending on the *object* in a containing with statement.

If the *object* in a with statement contains properties that have the same name as top-level variables, the with statement effectively hides the top-level variable—when you use the name of that variable you now refer to the object's property instead. If you need to explicitly refer to a hidden top-level variable *var*, you can usually use this syntax:

```
top.var
```

We'll see why this works when we study the Window object in Chapter 11, *Windows and the JavaScript Name Space*. Note that this technique will not work if top is the name of a property of the *object* in any enclosing with statement.

It is important to understand that the with statement only works with properties that already exist in the specified *object*. If you assign a value to a variable that does not exist as a property of the specified *object*, then that property is not created in the *object*. Instead, JavaScript searches the containing with statements, if any, for a property with that name, and then searches for a top-level variable with that name. If no such property or variable is found, then a new top-level variable is created. The rule to remember is that new properties cannot be added to an object if you refer to the object implicitly through a with statement. To create a new property in the object, you must refer to it explicitly.

To really understand how the with statement works, we need to briefly consider how variables are looked up in JavaScript. We'll return to this topic in detail in Chapter 11. Suppose JavaScript needs to look up the value of the name n. It proceeds as follows:

- If n is referred to within a with statement, then it first checks to see if n is a property of the *object* of that statement. If so, it uses the value of this property.

- If the first enclosing with statement does not provide a definition for n, then JavaScript checks any other enclosing with statements in order (remember that they can be nested to any depth). If any of objects specified in these statements define a property n, then that definition is used.

- If the reference to n occurs within a function, and no enclosing with statements yield a definition for it, then JavaScript checks to see if the function has any local variables or arguments named n. If so, it uses this value.

- Finally, if no definition for n has been found then JavaScript checks to see if there is a top-level variable named n, and uses it if so.

- If n is not defined in any of these places, then an error occurs.

5.10 var

We saw the var statement in Chapter 3, *Variables and Data Types*; it provides a way to explicitly declare a variable or variables. The syntax of this statement is:

```
var name_1 [ = value_1] [ ..., name_n [= value_n]]
```

That is: the var keyword is followed by a variable name and an optional initial value, or it is followed by a comma-separated list of variable names, each of which can have an initial value specified. The initial values are specified with the = operator and an arbitrary expression. For example:

```
var i;
var j = 0;
var x = 2.34, y = 4.12, r, theta;
```

If no initial value is specified for a variable with the `var` statement, then the variable will be defined, but its initial value will be the special JavaScript undefined value.

The `var` statement should always be used when declaring local variables within functions. Otherwise, you run the risk of overwriting a top-level variable of the same name. For top-level variables, the `var` statement is not required. Nevertheless, it is a good programming practice to use the `var` statement whenever you create a new variable. It is also a good practice to group your variable declarations together at the top of the program or at the top of a function.

Note that the `var` statement can also legally appear as part of the `for` and `for/in` loops, in order to declare the loop variable as part of the loop itself. For example:

```
for(var i = 0; i < 10; i++) document.write(i, "<BR>");
for(var i = 0, j=10; i < 10; i++,j--) document.write(i*j, "<BR>");
for(var i in o) document.write(i, "<BR>");
```

This syntax behaves just as it does in C++ and Java—the variable declared with this syntax is not local to the loop; its scope is the same as it would be if it had been declared outside of the loop.

5.11 *function*

Earlier, we saw that the `( )` operator is used to invoke a function. Before a function can be invoked, however, it must be defined (except for those that are predefined by JavaScript); the `function` statement is used to define a new function. It has the following syntax:

```
function funcname([arg1 [,arg2 [..., argn]]]) {
    statements
}
```

funcname is the name of the function that is being defined. This must be a literal name, not a string or an expression. *arg1*, *arg2*, and so on to *argn* are a comma-separated list of any number (including zero) of argument names for the function. These are also literal names, not strings or expressions. These names can be used as variables within the body of the function; when the function is executed, they will be assigned the values specified in the function call expression.

The `function` statement differs from statements like the `while` and `for` loops. In those loops, the body of the loop is a single statement, which can be a single primitive statement or a block of statements enclosed in curly braces. For the `function` statement, however, curly braces are a required part of the syntax, and any number of JavaScript statements may be contained within. Even if the body of a function consists of only a single statement, the curly braces must still be used. Here are some example function definitions:

```
function welcome() { alert("Welcome to my home page!"); }

function print(msg) {
    document.write(msg, "<br>");
}

function hypotenuse(x, y) {
    return Math.sqrt(x*x + y*y);     // return is documented below
}

function factorial(n) {              // a recursive function
    if (n <= 1) return 1;
    else return n * factorial(n - 1);
}
```

The most important way that the `function` statement differs from other statements is that the statements that form the body of the function are *not* executed. Instead, they are stored as the definition of a new function named *funcname*, and may be executed at any later time with the ( ) function call operator.

We'll learn more about functions in Chapter 6, *Functions*.

5.12 *return*

As you'll recall, function invocation with the ( ) operator is an expression. All expressions have values, and the `return` statement is used to specify the value "returned by" a function. This value is the value of the function invocation expression. The syntax of the `return` statement is:

```
return [ expression ];
```

When the `return` statement is executed, the *expression* is evaluated, and returned as the value of the function. Execution of the function stops when the return statement is executed, even if there are other statements still remaining in the function body. The `return` statement can be used to return a value like this:

```
function square(x) { return x*x; }
```

The `return` statement may also be used without an *expression* to simply terminate execution of the function without returning a value. For example:

```
function display_object(obj) {
    // first make sure our argument is valid
    // and skip rest of function if it is not.
    if (obj == null) return;
```

```
    // rest of the function goes here...
  }
```

If a function executes a return statement with no *expression*, or if it never executes a return statement (i.e., it simply executes all the statements in the body and implicitly returns) then the value of the function call expression will be undefined (i.e., the special JavaScript undefined value).

It is a syntax error to use the return statement anywhere except in a function body.

5.13 The Empty Statement

One final legal statement in JavaScript is the empty statement. It looks like this:

```
  ;
```

Executing the empty statement obviously has no effect and performs no action. You might think that there would be little reason to ever use such a statement, but it turns out that the empty statement is occasionally useful when you want to create a loop that has an empty body. For example:

```
// initialize an array a
for(i=0; i < a.length; a[i++] = 0) ;
```

To make your code clear, it can be useful to comment your empty statements as such:

```
for(i=0; i < a.length; a[i++] = 0) /* empty */ ;
```

5.14 Summary of JavaScript Statements

This chapter has introduced each of the statements of the JavaScript language. Table 5-1 summarizes these statements, their syntax, and their purpose.

Table 5–1: JavaScript Statement Syntax

Statement	Syntax	Purpose
break	`break;`	Exit from the innermost loop.
continue	`continue;`	Jump to top of containing loop.
empty	`;`	Do nothing.
for	`for (initialize ; test ; increment)` `statement`	Easy-to-use loop.
for/in	`for (variable in object)` `statement`	Loop through properties of object.

function	`function funcname([arg1 [..., argn]]) {`
	    `statements`
	`}`
		Declare a function.

if/else	`if (expression)`
	    `statement1`
	`[ else`
	    `statement2 ]`
		Conditionally execute code.

return	`return expression;`	Return a value from a function.
var	`var name_1 [ = value_1 ]` `[ ..., name_n [ = value_n]] ;`	Declare and initialize variables.
while	`while (expression)` `statement`	Basic loop construct.
with	`with (object)` `statement`	Specify the current name space.

6

Functions

Functions are an important and complex part of the JavaScript language. This chapter examines functions from several points of view. First, functions are introduced from the syntactic standpoint, explaining how functions are defined and invoked. Second, it is shown that functions are data types in JavaScript, with examples of the useful programming techniques that are possible by treating functions as data. Finally, the Function object and its properties are discussed, which support a number of advanced techniques for manipulating functions and their arguments.

Functions in JavaScript are closely integrated with JavaScript objects, and there are features of functions that are not documented in this chapter. Chapter 7, *Objects*, explains the specialized uses of functions as methods, constructors, and event-handlers.

6.1 Defining and Invoking Functions

As we saw in Chapter 5, *Statements*, functions are defined with the `function` keyword, followed by:

- the name of the function

- a comma-separated list of argument names in parentheses

- the JavaScript statements that comprise the body of the function, contained within curly braces

Example 6-1 shows the definition of several functions. Although these functions are short and very simple, they all contain each of the elements listed above. Note that functions may be defined to expect varying numbers of arguments, and that they may or may not contain a `return` statement. The `return` statement was introduced in Chapter 5; it causes the function to stop executing and return the value of its expression (if any) to the caller. If a function does not contain a `return` statement, then it simply executes each statement in the function body and returns no value to the caller.

Example 6-1: Defining JavaScript Functions

```
// A short-cut function, sometimes useful instead of document.write()
// This function has no return statement, so it returns no value.
function print(msg)
{
    document.write(msg, "<BR>");
}


// A function that computes and returns the distance between two points.
function distance(x1, y1, x2, y2)
{
    var dx = (x2 - x1);
    var dy = (y2 - y1);
    return Math.sqrt(dx*dx + dy*dy);
}


// A recursive function (one that calls itself) that computes factorials.
// Recall that x! is the product of x and all positive integers less than it.
function factorial(x)
{
    if (x <= 1)
        return 1;
    else
        return x * factorial(x-1);
}
```

Once a function has been defined, it may be invoked with the ( ) operator, introduced in Chapter 4, *Expressions and Operators*. Recall that the parentheses appear after the name of the function, and that a comma-separated list of argument values (or expressions) appear within the parentheses. The functions defined in Example 6-1 could be invoked with code like the following:

```
print("Hello, " + name);
print("Welcome to my home page!");
total_dist = distance(0,0,2,1) + distance(2,1,3,5);
print("The probability of that is: " + factorial(13)/factorial(52));
```

When you invoke a function, each of the expressions you specify between the parentheses is evaluated, and the resulting value is used as an *argument* or *parameter* of the function. These values are assigned to the variables named (within parentheses) when the function was defined, and the function operates on its parameters by referring to them by name. Note that these parameter variables are only defined while the function is being executed; they do not persist once the function returns.

Since JavaScript is an untyped language, you are not expected to specify a data type for function arguments, and JavaScript does not check that you have passed the type of data that the function expects. If the data type of an argument is important, you can test it yourself with the `typeof` operator. JavaScript does not check that you have passed the correct number of arguments, either. If you pass more arguments than the function expects, the extra values will simply be ignored. If you pass fewer than expected, then some of the parameters will be given the undefined value—which will, in many circumstances, cause your function to behave incorrectly. Later in this chapter we'll see a technique you can use to test that the correct number of arguments have been passed to a function.

Note that because our `print()` function does not contain a `return` statement and does not return a value, it cannot be used as part of a larger expression. The `distance()` and `factorial()` functions, on the other hand, can be used as parts of larger expressions, as shown in the examples above.

6.2 *Functions as Data Types*

The most important features of functions is that they can be defined and invoked, as shown in the previous section. Function definition and invocation are syntactic features of JavaScript, and of most other programming languages. In JavaScript, however, functions are not only syntax, but also data. In some languages, like Java, functions are part of a program, but cannot be manipulated by the program—you cannot, for example, pass one function as an argument to another function in Java. Other languages, like C and C++, are more flexible—while a function defined in C is not actually a data type, "function pointers" can be manipulated by the program, and it is possible to pass these function pointers to other functions and to assign them to variables.

JavaScript goes even further than C. Functions in JavaScript are data, and thus can be treated like any other data value—assigned to variables, stored in the properties of objects or the elements of arrays, passed to functions, and so on. Because JavaScript is an interpreted language, and because it treats functions as a distinct data type, the language (in Navigator 3.0) even allows functions to be defined dynamically, at run-time! We'll see how this is done when we consider the Function object later in this chapter.

We've seen that the `function` keyword is the syntax used to define a function in a JavaScript program. To understand how functions are JavaScript data as well as JavaScript syntax, we've got to understand what the `function` keyword really does. `function` creates a function, as we've seen, but it also defines a variable. In this way, the `function` keyword is like the `var` keyword. Consider the following function definition:

```
function square(x) { return x*x; }
```

This code does the following:

- Defines a new variable named `square`.

- Creates a new data value, of type function. This function value expects a single argument named `x`, and has a body that consists of a single statement: "`return x*x;`".

- Assigns the newly created function value to the newly defined variable.

When we consider function definition in this light, it becomes clear that the name of a function is really immaterial—it is simply the name of a variable that holds the function. The function can be assigned to another variable, and will still work the same:

```
function square(x) { return x*x; }
a = square(4);    // a contains the number 16
b = square;       // now b refers to the same function as square does.
c = b(5);         // c contains the number 25
```

Functions can also be assigned to object properties:

```
o = new Object;
o.sq = square;
y = o.sq(16);     // y equals 256
```

Functions don't even require names, as when we assign them to array elements:

```
a = new Array(10);
a[0] = square;
a[1] = 20;
a[2] = a[0](a[1]);  // a[2] contains 400
```

Note that the function invocation syntax in this last example looks strange, but is still a legal use of the JavaScript ( ) operator!

Example 6-2 is a detailed example of the things that can be done when functions are used as data. It demonstrates how functions can be passed as arguments to other functions, and also how they can be stored in associative arrays (which were introduced in Chapter 3, *Variables and Data Types*, and are explained in detail in Chapter 7.) This example may be a little tricky, but the comments explain what is going on; it is worth studying carefully.

Example 6-2: Using Functions as Data

```
// We define some simple functions here
function add(x,y) { return x + y; }
function subtract(x,y) { return x - y; }
function multiply(x,y) { return x * y; }
function divide(x,y) { return x / y; }

// Here's a function that takes one of the above functions
// as an argument and invokes it on two operands
function operate(operator, operand1, operand2)
{
    return operator(operand1, operand2);
}

// We could invoke this function like this to compute
// the value (2+3) + (4*5):
var i = operate(add, operate(add, 2, 3), operate(multiply, 4, 5));

// Now we store the functions defined above in an associative array
var operators = new Object();
operators["add"] = add;
operators["subtract"] = subtract;
operators["multiply"] = multiply;
operators["divide"] = divide;
operators["pow"] = Math.pow;   // works for predefined functions too.

// This function takes the name of an operator, looks up
// that operator in the array, and then invokes it on the
// supplied operands. Note the syntax used to invoke the
// operator function.
function operate2(op_name, operand1, operand2)
{
    if (operators[op_name] == null) return "unknown operator";
    else return operators[op_name](operand1, operand2);
}

// We could invoke this function as follows to compute
// the value ("hello" + " " + "world"):
var j = operate2("add", "hello", operate2("add", " ", "world"))

// Using the predefined Math.pow() function
var k = operate2("pow", 10, 2)
```

If the preceding example does not convince you of the utility of being able to pass functions as arguments to other functions, and otherwise treat functions as data values, consider the `Array.sort()` method. This function sorts the elements of an array, but because there are many possible orders to sort things into (numerical order, alphabetical order, date order, ascending, descending, and so on) it takes a function as an argument to tell it how to perform the sort. This function has a very simple job—it is passed two elements of the array, which it compares, and then returns a value specifying which element is larger and which is smaller. This function argument makes the `Array.sort()` method perfectly general and infinitely flexible—it can sort any type of data into any conceivable order!

6.3 *The Function Object*

In Chapter 3 we saw that each of the primitive (i.e., non-object) JavaScript data types has a corresponding "wrapper" object type that is used to provide properties and methods for the data type. Recall that JavaScript automatically converts primitive values to the corresponding object type, when those values are used in an "object context"—i.e., when you try to access their properties or methods. Because the conversion is so transparent to the programmer, it can seem as if primitive types, like strings, have properties and methods.

Since, as we've seen, functions are not just a syntactic feature of JavaScript, but also a data type, JavaScript provides the Function object type as a wrapper. The Function object has two properties: `arguments`, which contains an array of arguments passed to the function, and `caller` which refers to the function that called the current function. Additionally, in Navigator 3.0, the Function object has a constructor function that can be used (with the `new` keyword) to define new functions dynamically, at run-time. The subsections below explain exactly how these two properties and the constructor function work.

Before we consider the properties of the Function object, there are a couple of important points we must note about their use. The first point is that the `arguments` and `caller` properties of the Function object are only defined while the function is being executed. If you try to access these properties from outside the function, their value will be `null`.

The second point to note is that in order to refer to these Function properties from inside a function, the function must refer to itself. It would seem logical that JavaScript would define a special keyword that refers to "the currently running function" to support this self-reference. There are two likely candidates, but unfortunately, neither of them do what we want: the `this` keyword, when used in a function refers to the object through which the function was invoked (we'll see more about this when we consider methods in Chapter 7), and the `self` keyword (really a property name, not a keyword, as we'll see in Chapter 11, *Windows and the JavaScript Name Space*) refers to the current browser window, not the current function. The current version of JavaScript simply does not have a keyword to refer to the current function, although this may be added in a future version of the language.

So, a function can refer to itself simply by using its name. As we saw in the previous section, this name is nothing more that a variable name or an object property, or even a numbered element of an array. Remember that a function is just a data value—if you can refer to this value in order to invoke the function, then you can generally refer to it in the same way from inside the function body. A function f might refer to elements of its arguments[] array like this:

```
function f() { return f.arguments[0] * f.arguments[1]; }
```

When we introduce the constructor function of the Function object, we'll actually show a way to create unnamed functions, and you may encounter occasional circumstances in which the body of a function does not know how to refer to itself. If you encounter one of these rare cases in Navigator 3.0, you can refer to the current function by passing the string "this" to the eval() method (a method of the Function object, as it is of all objects). For example, you could refer to the caller property of the current function, without explicitly naming it, like this:

```
eval("this").caller
```

With these notes about the use of the Function object's properties in mind, we can finally go ahead and consider the properties themselves.

6.3.1 The arguments[] Array

The arguments[] property of a Function object refers to an array that contains the complete set of argument values passed to the function for the current invocation. JavaScript allows any number of argument values to be passed to any function, regardless of the number of argument names that appear in the function definition. If you define a function named f with a single argument named x, then within the function, the value of the argument x is the same as f.arguments[0]. If you invoke this function and pass it two arguments instead of just one, then the second argument won't have a name within the function but will be available as f.arguments[1]. Like most arrays, the arguments[] array has a length property that specifies the number of elements. Thus, for a function f, f.arguments.length specifies the number of argument values that were passed for the current invocation.

The arguments[] array is useful in a number of ways. As Example 6-3 shows, you can use it to check that a function is invoked with the correct number of arguments, since JavaScript doesn't do this for you.

Example 6-3: Checking for the Correct Number of Arguments

```
function f(x, y, z)
{
    // first, check that the right # of arguments were passed.
    if (f.arguments.length != 3) {
        alert("function f called with " + f.arguments.length +
            "arguments, but it expects 3 arguments.");
        return null;
    }
    // now do the actual function...
}
```

The arguments[ ] array also opens up an important possibility for JavaScript functions: they can be written so that they work with any number of arguments. Example 6-4 shows how you can write a max() function that accepts any number of arguments and returns the value of the largest argument it is passed.

Example 6-4: A Multi-Argument max() Function

```
function max()
{
    var m = -Number.MAX_VALUE; // Navigator 3.0 only. In 2.0 use -1.79E+308

    // loop through all the arguments, looking for, and
    // remembering, the biggest.
    for(var i = 0; i < max.arguments.length; i++)
        if (max.arguments[i] > m) m = max.arguments[i];
    // return the biggest.
    return m;
}

var largest = max(1, 10, 100, 2, 3, 1000, 4, 5, 10000, 6);
```

You can also write functions that have some named arguments, followed by some unnamed arguments. Example 6-5 shows such a function; it is a constructor function that creates an array, initializes a size property as specified by a named argument len, and then initializes an arbitrary number of elements, starting with element 1, of the array to the values of any additional arguments. (JavaScript programs in Navigator 2.0 often use a function like this, as seen in Chapter 8, *Arrays*.)

Example 6-5: Creating and Initializing an Array

```
function InitializedArray(len)
{
    this.size = len;  // In 2.0, this sets array element 0.
    for (var i = 1; i < InitializedArray.arguments.length; i++)
        this[i] = InitializedArray.arguments[i];
}
```

A final note about the `arguments[ ]` array: the `arguments` property of a Function object actually holds a copy of the Function object itself. In other words, if f is a function, and F is the corresponding Function object, then each of the following lines of code refers to the same thing:

```
f.arguments
F.arguments
F
F.arguments.arguments.arguments
```

It is a strange implementation, but what it means is that it is the Function object itself that maintains the array of arguments (as we'll see in Chapter 8, arrays and objects are the same thing in JavaScript, and an object can have both properties and array elements.) So, instead of writing `f.arguments[i]`, you can just write `f[i]`, and instead of `f.arguments.length`, you can write `f.length`. This feature is not guaranteed to continue to work in future versions of JavaScript; using the `arguments` property is the officially supported way to access function arguments.

6.3.2 *The caller Property*

The other property of the Function object is `caller`. This property is a reference to the function (the function value itself, not the Function object wrapper) that invoked the current one. If the function was invoked from the top level of the script, rather than from a function, then this property will be `null`. Because `caller` is a reference to a function value, you can do anything with it that you can do with any other function reference. You can call it, or pass it to other functions, causing a kind of recursion.

Unfortunately, since the `caller` property refers to a function that is not the currently executing function, you cannot inspect the `arguments` or `caller` property of the function referred to by the `caller` property. That is, the following JavaScript expressions evaluate to `null`:

```
f.caller.caller        // doesn't work
f.caller.arguments[1]  // doesn't work
```

It is a shame that these kinds of expressions do not return meaningful values, because it would allow us to write functions that produce stack traces, for example, or a function that could be invoked for the purpose of checking that its caller was invoked with the correct number and type of arguments.

6.3.3 *The Function() Constructor*

We said in Chapter 4 that the `new` operator is used to create new objects; this object is used with a special "constructor function" that specifies the type of object to be created. Many JavaScript object types define constructor functions that can

be used to create objects of that type. The Function object type is no exception—
it provides the Function() constructor which allows us to create new Function
objects. This constructor works in Navigator 3.0, but not in Internet Explorer 3.0. It
will be implemented in a future version of IE.

The Function() constructor provides a technique for defining functions without
using the function keyword. You can create a new Function object with the
Function() constructor like this:

```
var f = new Function("x", "y", "return x*y;");
```

This line of code creates a new function (wrapped within a new Function object)
that is equivalent (almost) to a function defined with the syntax we're already
familiar with:

```
function f(x, y) { return x*y; }
```

The Function() constructor expects any number of string arguments. The last
argument in the list becomes the body of the function—it can contain arbitrary
JavaScript statements, separated from each other with semicolons. All other arguments to the Function() constructor are strings that specify the names of the
arguments to the function being defined. If you are defining a function that takes
no arguments, then you simply pass a single string—the function body—to the
constructor.

There are a couple of reasons you might want to use the Function() constructor.
Recall that the function keyword defines a variable, just like the var does. So the
first reason to use the Function() constructor is to avoid having to give your
function a temporary variable name when you are just going to immediately assign
it to an object property (making a method of that object, as we'll see in Chapter
7). For example, consider the following two lines of code:

```
function tmp_area() { return Math.PI * this.radius * this.radius; }
Circle.area = tmp_area
```

The Function() constructor allows us to do this in a single step without creating
the temporary tmp_area variable:

```
Circle.area = new Function("return Math.PI * this.radius * this.radius;");
```

Another reason you might want to use the Function() constructor is to define
temporary or "anonymous" functions that are never given a name. Recall the
Array.sort() method mentioned earlier in this chapter: it takes a function as an
argument, and that function defines how the elements of the array are sorted.
Strings and numbers already have a well-defined sort order, but suppose we were
trying to sort an array of objects each of which represented a complex number. To
do this, we might use the magnitude of the number, or its overall "distance" from

the origin as the value which we would compare to do the sort. It is simple enough to right an appropriate function to perform this comparison, but if we only plan to sort this array of complex number objects once, we might not want to bother defining the function with the `function` keyword and giving it a permanent name. Instead, we might simply use code like the following to dynamically create a Function object and pass it to the `sort()` method without ever giving it a name. (Recall that just as JavaScript automatically converts primitive types to their corresponding wrapper objects, so to does it convert in the other direction. So the Function object created in the example will be automatically converted to a function value appropriate for the `sort()` method.

```
complex_nums.sort(
        new Function("a", "b",
                "Math.sqrt(a.x*a.x+a.y*a.y)-Math.sqrt(b.x*b.x+b.y*b.y);"));
```

The only difference between functions defined with the `function` keyword and those defined with the `Function()` constructor has to do with how they are printed. (Try it! Use `document.write()` or `alert()`.) When a function is printed (or otherwise converted to a string) the function name, arguments, and body are displayed, along with the `function` keyword. The result of converting a function to a string is a string that contains a legal JavaScript function definition. When a function is defined with `function`, it is given a name as part of the function definition syntax, and this name appears when the function is printed. Functions defined with `Function()`, however, do not have a name, and so are printed with the name "anonymous". For this reason, functions defined in this way are sometimes referred to as "anonymous functions".

6.3.4 Function Properties

There are several interesting facts about functions that you should be aware of. You can combine these facts into a useful programming technique.

6.3.4.1 Functions are objects

One of the interesting features of JavaScript functions is that you can assign properties to them. For example:

```
function f() { alert('hello world!'); }
f.i = 3;
```

This code creates a function f, and then assigns a property i to it. Later, we can use this property just like any other:

```
var i = f.i + 2;
```

What is unusual about this is that we are assigning a property to a primitive function value. JavaScript does actually allow us to assign properties to other primitive types, but those properties don't persist. Consider this code:

```
n = 1;      // A number
n.i = 2;    // Convert it to a Number object and give that object a property
typeof n.i  // This tells us n.i is undefined; the property is transient.
```

When properties are assigned to primitive numbers, Booleans, and strings, JavaScript converts those primitive types to temporary Number, Boolean, and String objects, and assigns the property to those objects. The objects only persist while the expression is being evaluated, and, once discarded, the property no longer exists.

The reason this doesn't happen with functions is that all JavaScript functions are objects. The Function object is obviously an object type, but even primitive function types are objects that can have properties assigned to them. Because functions are such an important and integral part of the language, however, they are usually treated as a special primitive type.

6.3.4.2 *Function arguments and variables are properties*

In all versions of JavaScript, global variables are actually properties of some top-level object. In client-side JavaScript, as we'll see, this top-level object is the browser window or frame that contains the JavaScript code. This raises the obvious question: if global variables are properties of an object, what are local function variables? It would make sense that they, too, are properties of some object. The only obvious object is the function (or Function) itself. The following code demonstrates:

```
function f(x)
{
    var y = 3;       // a local variable
    return f.x + f.y; // refer to the argument and variable as properties
}
```

If we invoke the function, we see that function arguments and local variables really can be accessed as properties of the function itself:

```
result = f(2);       // returns 5
```

However, if we try to read these properties ourselves, we will be unable to:

```
typeof f.x   // yields "undefined"
typeof f.y   // yields "undefined"
```

What this means is that, like the `arguments[]` array and the `caller` property, the local variable and argument properties are only accessible while the function is running. When the function returns, JavaScript deletes these properties.

6.3.4.3 Function properties simulate static variables

Knowing that local variables are implemented as transient properties of a function is not particularly useful in itself, but it does lead us to a useful programming technique. In C and C++, a `static` variable in a function is one that is local to the function, but which has a value that persists across invocations of the function—that is, its value is not reset every time the function is called, and you can use it to save state so that a function could keep track of how many times it had been invoked, for example. A static variable in a function is a global variable, because it retains its value. And it is also like a local variable because it is invisible outside the function, which means that you do not have to give it a unique name or worry about collisions with other global variables or about cluttering up the name space. This is often a very useful combination of features.

JavaScript does not support static variables directly, but it turns out that we can simulate them with function properties. We've seen that function properties for local variables and arguments are created when a function is invoked and are deleted when the function returns. You can create other properties of a function, however, that will not be deleted like this. Because local variables are looked up as properties of the function, any properties you add will appear to be local variables. They differ from local variables, however, in that they are not deleted and reset every time the function is called, so they can retain their value. At the same time, though, they are properties of a function instead of global variables, so they do not clutter the name space. These are exactly the features we desire in a static variable.

Example 6-6 shows a function that uses a "static variable" to keep track of how many times it has been called. You'll probably find many more realistic uses for static variables in your own programming. As a rule of thumb, never use a global variable where a static variable would work as well.

Example 6-6: Using Static Variables

```
function count()
{
    // counter is a static variable, defined below.
    // Note that we use it just like a local variable.
    alert("You've called me " + counter + " time(s).");
    // Increment the static variable. This incremented value
    // will be retained and will be used the next time we are called.
    counter++;
}
```

Example 6–6: Using Static Variables (continued)

```
// To define the static variable, just set it as a property of the function:
// Note that the only shortcoming of this technique is that static
// variables can only be defined after they are used in the function.
count.counter = 1;
```

6.4 Built-in Functions

This chapter has focused on the use of functions that you define yourself. Bear in mind that JavaScript also provides a number of built-in functions that are part of the language. For example, the `parseInt()` function converts a string to an integer, and the `Math.sin()` function computes the sine of a number. For the most part, built-in functions behave just like user-defined functions: you can assign them to new variables, object properties, and array elements, and you can invoke them through these new variable names, properties or array elements. Practically the only discernible difference between a built-in function and a user-defined one becomes apparent when you try to print the value of a built-in function: the body of the function is replaced with the string "[native code]", indicating that the function is not itself implemented in JavaScript.

6.5 Event Handlers

An event handler is a special-purpose function, one that is used only in client-side JavaScript. Event-handler functions are defined unusually—instead of using the `function` keyword (or the `Function()` constructor) and being defined as part of a JavaScript program, they are defined as fragments of JavaScript within the HTML tags of certain elements on a web page.

Event-handler functions are also unusual in how they are used. They are not usually invoked by your JavaScript program; instead, they are invoked by the web browser itself, whenever certain "events" occur within the element with which they are associated. For example, you can associate an event handler with a button in an HTML form. When the user clicks on the button, the JavaScript code in the event handler will be automatically invoked by the browser. The following piece of HTML code creates a button with the words "Click me!"; clicking the button runs an piece of JavaScript code that adds together two numbers and displays the result in a dialog box:

```
<FORM>
<INPUT TYPE="submit" VALUE="Click me!"
        onClick="var sum=1+2; alert(sum);">
</FORM>
```

This piece of JavaScript code is actually a function. That is, defining an event handler in an HTML tag does create a JavaScript function object, just as other function definitions do, and this object can be used as other function objects are. The main difference is that the function will be invoked automatically by the browser in response to appropriate user actions.

Event handlers are part of client-side JavaScript, not part of the core language. Therefore, their definition and use will be described in greater detail in Chapter 10, *Client-Side Program Structure*.

7

Objects

Chapter 3, *Variables and Data Types,* explained that objects are one of the fundamental data types in JavaScript. They are also one of the most important. This chapter describes JavaScript objects in detail. Basic usage of objects, described in the first section below, is straightforward, but as we'll see in later sections, objects have more complex uses and behaviors.

7.1 Object Properties

An *object* is a data type that contains named pieces of data. Each named datum is called a *property*. Each property has a name, and the object associates a value with each property name. A property value may be of any type. In effect, the properties of an object are variables within the "name space" created by the object.

7.1.1 Reading and Writing Object Properties

You normally use the . operator to access the value of an object's properties. The value on the left of the . should be a reference to an object (usually just the name of the variable that contains the object reference). The value on the right of the . should be the name of the property. This must be an identifier, not a string or an expression. For example, you refer to the property p in object o with o.p. Or, you refer to the property document in the object parent with parent.document. The . operator is used for both reading and writing object properties. For example:

```
// Read a property value:
w = image.width;

// Set a property value:
window.location = "http://my.isp.com/my_home_page/index.html";
```

```
// Read one property and set it in another property
image.src = parent.frames[1].location
```

7.1.2 Defining New Object Properties

You can add a new property to an object simply by setting its value. Thus, you might add a property to the object win with code like the following:

```
win.creator = self;
```

This line assigns the value of self to the creator property of the object win. If the creator property does not already exist, then it will be created so that the value can be assigned to it.

7.1.3 Undefined Object Properties

If you attempt to read the value of a property that does not exist—i.e., has never had a value assigned to it—you will retrieve the special JavaScript undefined value (which was introduced in Chapter 3).

Once a property has been defined in an object, however, there is no way to undefine it. You may set the value of a property to the special undefined value, by assigning the value of an undefined property, but this just changes the value of the property without actually undefining it. You can demonstrate that the property still exists by using a for/in loop to print out the name of all defined properties:

```
for (prop in obj)
    property_list += prop + "\n";
alert(property_list);
```

7.2 Creating New Objects with Constructors

As we saw briefly in Chapter 4, *Expressions and Operators*, the new operator creates a new object. For example:

```
o = new Object();
```

This syntax creates an "empty" object, one that has no properties defined. There are certain occasions in which you might want to start with an empty object of this sort, but in "object-oriented" programming, it is more common to work with objects that have a predefined set of properties. For example, you might want to define one or more objects that represent rectangles. In this case, each rectangle object should have a width property and a height property.

To create objects with properties such as `width` and `height` already defined, we need to write a *constructor* to create and initialize these properties in a new object. A constructor is a JavaScript function with three special features:

- It is invoked through the `new` operator.

- It is passed a reference to a newly created, "empty" object as the value of the special `this` keyword, and it is responsible for performing appropriate initialization for that new object.

- It should not return a value; if it uses the `return` statement, it should do so without a value to be returned.

Example 7-1 shows how the constructor function for a rectangle object might be defined and invoked.

Example 7–1: A Rectangle Object Constructor Function

```
// define the constructor.
// Note how it initializes the object referred to by "this"
function Rectangle(w, h)
{
    this.width = w;
    this.height = h;
}

// invoke the constructor to create two rectangle objects
// Notice that we pass the width and height to the constructor, so it
// can initialize each new object appropriately.
rect1 = new Rectangle(2, 4);
rect2 = new Rectangle(8.5, 11);
```

Notice how the constructor performs its initialization on the object referred to by the `this` keyword. A constructor will generally perform initialization based on the argument values that are passed to it. Some constructors may also initialize other properties of a new object (setting them to constant values, for example). Keep in mind that a constructor function simply initializes the specified object; it does not have to return that object.

Also notice how we define a "class" of objects simply by defining an appropriate constructor function—all objects created with that constructor will have the same properties. It is stylistically important to give constructor functions a name that indicates the class of objects they will "construct." For example, creating a rectangle with `new construct_rect(1,2)` is a lot less intuitive than `new Rectangle(1,2)`.

7.2.1 The constructor Property

In Navigator 3.0, but not in Internet Explorer 3.0, all objects have a `constructor` property that refers to the constructor function that was used to create the object. Since the constructor function determines the "class" of an object, the `constructor` property in a sense specifies the "type" of any given object. For example, you might use code like the following to determine the type of an unknown object:

```
if ((typeof n == "object") && (n.constructor == Number))
    // then do something with the Number object...
```

7.3 Methods

A *method* is nothing more than a JavaScript function that is invoked through an object. Recall that functions are data values, and that there is nothing special about the name they are defined with—a function can be assigned to any variable, or even to any property of an object. If we have a function f, and an object o, then we can define a method named m with the following line:

```
o.m = f;
```

Having defined the method m( ) of the object o, we invoke it like this:

```
o.m();
```

Or, if m( ) expects two arguments, we might invoke it like this:

```
o.m(x, x+2);
```

Invoking o.m( ) this way is the same as calling f( ), except for one point: when the function is invoked as a method, through the object o, the this keyword will refer to that object within the body of the method. When the same function object is invoked directly as f( ), the this keyword will not contain a meaningful value.[*]

This discussion of the this keyword should begin to make it clear why we use methods at all. Any function that is used as a method is effectively passed a third argument—the object through which it is invoked. Typically, a method performs some sort of operation on that object, and the method invocation syntax is a par-

---

[*] As you may have discovered by now, variables in client-side JavaScript are all implicitly properties of the current Window object, so invoking f( ) is equivalent to invoking window.f( ): the this keyword in both these cases refers to the current window. (See Chapter 11, *Windows and the JavaScript Name Space*, for an extended discussion of this somewhat odd aspect of JavaScript.)

ticularly elegant way to express the fact that a function is operating on an object. Compare the following two lines of code:

```
o.m(x,y);
f(o,x,y);
```

The hypothetical method m() and function f() may perform exactly the same operation on the object o, but the method invocation syntax more clearly indicates the idea that it is the object o that is the primary focus or target of the operation.

The typical usage of methods is more clearly illustrated through an example. Example 7-2 returns to the Rectangle objects of Example 7-1 and how a method that operates on Rectangle objects can be defined and invoked.

Example 7-2: Defining and Invoking a Method

```
// This is a function. It uses the this keyword, so
// it doesn't make sense to invoke this function by itself; it
// needs instead be made a method of some object, some object that has
// "width" and "height" properties defined.
function compute_area()
{
    return this.width * this.height;
}


// Create a new Rectangle object, using the constructor defined earlier
var rect = new Rectangle(8.5, 11);

// Define a method by assigning the function to a property of the object
rect.area = compute_area;

// Invoke the new method like this:
a = rect.area();    // a = 8.5*11 = 93.5
```

There is a shortcoming that is evident in Example 7-2: before you can invoke the area() method for the rect object, you must assign that method to a property of the object. While we can invoke the area() method on the particular object named rect, we can't invoke it on any other Rectangle objects without first assigning the method to them. This quickly becomes tedious. Example 7-3 defines some additional Rectangle methods and shows how they can automatically be assigned to all Rectangle objects with a constructor function.

Example 7-3: Defining Methods in a Constructor

```
// First, define some functions that will be used as methods
function Rectangle_area() { return this.width * this.height; }
function Rectangle_perimeter() { return 2*this.width + 2*this.height; }
function Rectangle_set_size(w,h) { this.width = w; this.height = h; }
function Rectangle_enlarge() { this.width *= 2; this.height *= 2; }
```

Example 7-3: Defining Methods in a Constructor (continued)

```
function Rectangle_shrink() { this.width /= 2; this.height /= 2; }

// Then define a constructor method for our Rectangle objects.
// The constructor initializes properties, and also assigns methods.
function Rectangle(w, h)
{
    // initialize object properties
    this.width = w;
    this.height = h;

    // define methods for the object
    this.area = Rectangle_area;
    this.perimeter = Rectangle_perimeter;
    this.set_size = Rectangle_set_size;
    this.enlarge = Rectangle_enlarge;
    this.shrink = Rectangle_shrink;
}

// Now, when we create a rectangle, we can immediately invoke methods on it:
r = new Rectangle(2,2);
a = r.area();
r.enlarge();
p = r.perimeter();
```

7.4 Object Prototypes

We've seen that a constructor function defines a "class" of objects in JavaScript—all objects created with a given constructor will be initialized in the same way and will therefore have the same set of properties. These properties may include methods, for (as we've also seen) you can use a constructor function to assign a set of methods to each object that is a member of the class.

In Navigator 3.0 and Internet Explorer 3.0, there is another way to specify the methods, constants, and other properties that all objects in a class will support. The technique is to define the methods and other properties in a *prototype object* for the class. A prototype object is a special object, associated with the constructor function for a class, that has a very important feature: any properties defined by the prototype object of a class will appear as properties of every object of that class. This is true of properties that are added to the prototype both before and after the objects are defined. The properties of the prototype object of a class are shared by all objects of that class (i.e., objects do not get their own unique copy of the prototype properties, so memory usage is minimal).

The properties of the prototype object for a class can be read through all objects of the class, and, although they appear to be, they are not actually properties of those objects. There is a single copy of each prototype property, and this copy is shared by all objects in the class. When you read one of these properties of an object, you are reading that shared value from the prototype object. When you set the value of one of these properties for a particular object, on the other hand, you are actually creating a new property for that one object. From that point on, for that one particular object, the newly created property "shadows," or hides, the shared property in the prototype object. Figure 7-1 illustrates how a private, non-shared property can shadow a shared prototype property.

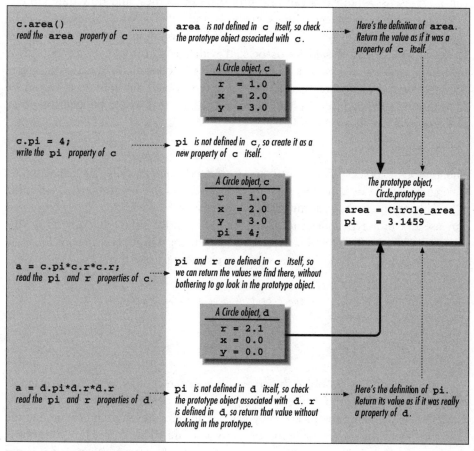

Figure 7-1: Objects and prototypes

Because prototype properties are shared by all objects of a class, it only generally makes sense to use them to define properties that will be the same for all objects within the class. This makes them ideal for defining methods. Other properties with constant values (such as mathematical constants) are also suitable for definition with prototype properties. If your class defines a property with a very commonly used default value, you might define this property, and the default value in a prototype object. Then the few objects that want to deviate from the default value can create their own private, unshared, copy of the property, defining their own nondefault property value.

After all this discussion of how prototype objects and their properties work, we can now discuss where you can find prototype properties, and how they are created. The prototype object defines methods and other constant properties for a class of objects; classes of objects are defined by a common constructor; therefore, the prototype object should be associated with the constructor function. This is indeed the case. If we were to define a `Circle()` constructor function to create objects that represent circles, then the prototype object for this class would be `Circle.prototype`, and we could define a constant that would be available to all Circle objects like this:

```
Circle.prototype.pi = 3.14159;
```

The prototype object of a constructor is created automatically by JavaScript. In Navigator, it is created the first time the constructor is used with the `new` operator. What this means is that you must create at least one object of a class before you can use the prototype object to assign methods and constants to objects of that class. So, if we have defined a `Circle()` constructor, but not yet used it to create any Circle objects, we'd define the constant property `pi` like this:

```
// First create and discard a dummy Circle object.
// All this does is force the prototype object to be created.
new Circle();

// Now we can set properties in the prototype
Circle.prototype.pi = 3.14159;
```

This requirement that an object be created before the prototype object is available is an unfortunate blemish in the JavaScript language design. If you forget to create an object before using the prototype you'll get an error message indicating that the prototype object does not have the property you are trying to set (i.e., the object does not exist). It is an annoyance, but a minor one. In Internet Explorer, it is not necessary to create a dummy object to force the prototype object to be created; IE provides a prototype object for all JavaScript functions, whether they are used as constructors or not.

Prototype objects and their properties can be quite confusing. Figure 7-1 illustrates several of the important prototype concepts; you should study it carefully. In addition to the figure, Example 7-4 is a concrete example of how you can use prototypes to help you define a class of objects. In this example, we've switched from our Rectangle class to a new Circle class. The code defines a `Circle` class of objects, by first defining a `Circle()` constructor method to initialize each individual object, and then by setting properties on `Circle.prototype` to define methods, constants, and defaults shared by all instances of the class.

Example 7-4: Defining a Class with a Prototype Object

```
// Define a constructor method for our class.
// Use it to initialize properties that will be different for
// each individual circle object.
function Circle(x, y, r)
{
    this.x = x;  // the X coordinate of the center of the  circle
    this.y = y;  // the Y coordinate of the center of the circle
    this.r = r;  // the radius of the circle
}


// Create and discard an initial Circle object.
// Doing this forces the prototype object to be created
new Circle(0,0,0);


// Now define a constant; a property that will be shared by
// all circle objects. Actually, we could just use Math.PI,
// but we do it this way for the sake of example.
Circle.prototype.pi = 3.14159;


// Now define some functions that perform computations on circles
// Note the use of the constant defined above
function Circle_circumference() { return 2 * this.pi * this.r; }
function Circle_area() { return this.pi * this.r * this.r; }

// Make these functions into methods of all Circle objects by
// setting them as properties of the prototype object.
Circle.prototype.circumference = Circle_circumference;
Circle.prototype.area = Circle_area;

// Now define a default property. Most Circle objects will share this
// default value, but some may override it by setting creating their
// own unshared copy of the property.
Circle.prototype.url = "images/default_circle.gif";

// Now, create a circle object, and use the methods defined
// by the prototype object
c = new Circle(0.0, 0.0, 1.0);
```

Example 7-4: Defining a Class with a Prototype Object (continued)

```
a = c.area();
p = c.circumference();
```

An important point to note about prototypes is that in Navigator 3.0, you can use them with built-in object types, not just those that you define yourself. For example, if you wrote a function that operated on a string object, you could assign it as a method to `String.prototype`, and make it accessible as a method of all JavaScript strings. This technique does not work in Internet Explorer 3.0. IE 3.0 does not support the prototypes for Boolean and Number objects, and the properties of `String.prototype` are only available to actual String objects, not primitive string values, as they are in Navigator. These shortcomings will be fixed in a future version of IE.

Finally, a couple of points to remember about prototypes are that they are not available in Navigator 2.0, and that prototype properties are shared by all objects of a given class, regardless of whether the prototype property is defined before or after any given object is created.

7.5 Classes in JavaScript

Although JavaScript supports a data type we call an "object", the language's lack of strong typing and a formal inheritance mechanism mean that it is not a truly object-oriented language. Still, JavaScript does a good job of simulating the features of object-oriented languages like Java and C++. For example, we've been using the term "class" in the last few sections of this chapter, despite the fact that JavaScript does not officially define or support classes. This section will explore some of the parallels between JavaScript and the true object-oriented features of Java and C++.

We start by defining some basic terminology. An object, as we've already seen, is a data structure that "contains" various pieces of named data, and may also contain various methods to operate on those pieces of data. An object groups related data values and methods into a single convenient package, which generally makes programming easier, by increasing the modularity and reusability of code. Objects in JavaScript may have any number of properties, and properties may be added to an object dynamically. This is not the case in strictly typed languages like Java and C++—in those languages, each object has a predefined set of properties, (or fields, as they are often called) and each property contains a value of a predefined type. So when we are using JavaScript objects to simulate object-oriented programming techniques, we will generally define in advance the set of properties that each object will have, and the type of data that each property will hold.

In Java and C++, a *class* is thing that defines the structure of an object. It is the class that specifies exactly what fields an object contains, and what types of data each holds. It is also the class that defines the methods that operate on an object. JavaScript does not have a formal notion of a class, but, as we've seen, it approximates classes with its constructors. A constructor function can create a standard set of properties for each object it initializes. Similarly, in Navigator 3.0, the prototype object associated with the constructor can define the methods and constants that will be shared by each object initialized by the constructor.

In both JavaScript and true object-oriented languages, there may be multiple objects of the same class. We often say that an object is an *instance* of its class. Thus, there may be many instances of any class. Sometimes we use the term *instantiate* to describe the process of creating an object (an instance of a class).

In Java, it is a common programming convention to name classes with an initial capital letter, and to name objects with lower case letters. This helps to keep classes and objects distinct from each other in our code, and this is a useful convention to follow in JavaScript programming as well. In previous sections, for example, we've defined the `Circle` and `Rectangle` "classes," for example, and have created instances of those classes named `c` and `rect`.

The fields defined by a Java class may be of four basic types: "instance" variables, "instance" methods, "static" or "class" variables, and "static" or "class" methods. The paragraphs below explain the differences between these types of fields, and show how they are simulated in JavaScript.

An "instance variable" is a variable of an instance, or object. It is a variable contained in an object. Each object has its own separate copy of this variable; if there are ten objects of a given class, then there are ten copies of this variable. In our Circle class, for example, every circle object has a `r` property that specifies the radius of the circle. In this case `r` is an instance variable. Since each object has its own copy of instance variables, these variables are accessed through individual objects. If `c` is an object that is an instance of the Circle class, for example, then we refer to its radius as:

```
c.r
```

By default, any object property in JavaScript is an instance variable, but to truly simulate object-oriented programming, we will say that instance variables in JavaScript are those properties that are created and/or initialize in an object by the constructor function.

An "instance method" is much like an "instance variable" except that it is a method rather than a data value. (In Java, functions and methods are not data types, as they are in JavaScript, so this distinction is more clear). Instance methods are invoked on a particular "instance" or object. The `area()` method of our Circle class is an instance method. It is invoked on a Circle object c like this:

```
a = c.area();
```

Instance methods use the `this` keyword to refer to the object or instance they are operating on. An instance method can be invoked for any instance of a class, but this does not mean that each object contains its own private copy of the method, as it does its instance variables. Instead, each instance method is shared by all instances of a class. In JavaScript, we define an instance method for a class by setting a property in the constructor's prototype object to a function value. This way, all objects created by that constructor share a reference to the function, and can invoke it using the method invocation syntax shown above. (Prior to Navigator 3.0, instance methods can be defined in a constructor function, as instance variables are; this is less efficient, though.)

A "class" or "static" variable in Java is a variable that is associated with a class itself, rather than with each instance of a class. No matter how many instances of the class are created, there is only one copy of each class variable. Just as instance variables are accessed through an instance of a class, class variables are accessed through the class itself. `Number.MAX_VALUE` is an example of a class variable in JavaScript—the `MAX_VALUE` property is accessed through the `Number` class. Because there is only one copy of each class variable, class variables are essentially global variables. What is nice about them, however, is that by being associated with a class, they have a logical niche, a position in the JavaScript name space, where they are not likely to be overwritten by other variables with the same name. As is probably clear, we simulate a class variable in JavaScript simply by defining a property of the constructor function itself. For example, to create a class variable `Circle.PI` to store the mathematical constant, often used with circles, we could do the following:

```
Circle.PI = 3.14;
```

Finally, we come to class methods. A "class" or "static" method is a method associated with a class rather than with an instance of a class. Class methods are invoked through the class, rather than through a particular instance of the class. `Math.sqrt()`, `Math.sin()`, and other methods of the `Math` object are class methods. Because class methods are not invoked through a particular object, they cannot use the `this` keyword—`this` refers to the object that an *instance* method is invoked for. Like class variables, class methods are "global." Because they do not operate on a particular object, static methods can often more easily be thought of as functions that happen to be invoked through a class. Again, associating these functions with a class gives them a convenient niche in the JavaScript name space, and prevents "name space collisions" from occurring in case some other class happens to define a function with the same name. To define a class method in JavaScript, we simply set the appropriate function as a property of the constructor.

Example 7-5 is a re-implementation of our Circle class that contains examples of each of these four basic types of fields.

Example 7-5: Defining Instance/Class Variables and Methods

```
function Circle(radius) {   // the constructor defines the class itself
    // r is an instance variable; defined and initialized in the constructor
    this.r = radius;
}

// Circle.PI is a class variable--it is a property of the constructor function
Circle.PI = 3.14159;

// Here is a function that computes a circle area.
function Circle_area() { return Circle.PI * this.r * this.r; }

// Here we make the function into an instance method by assigning it
// to the prototype object of the constructor. Remember that we have to
// create and discard one object before the prototype object exists
new Circle(0);
Circle.prototype.area = Circle_area;

// Here's another function. It takes two circle objects are arguments and
// returns the one that is larger (has the larger radius).
function Circle_max(a,b) {
    if (a.r > b.r) return a;
    else return b;
}

// Since this function compares two circle objects, it doesn't make sense as
// an instance method operating on a single circle object. But we don't want
// it to be a standalone function either, so we make it into a class method
// by assigning it to the constructor function:
Circle.max = Circle_max;

// Here is some code that uses each of these fields:
c = new Circle(1.0);      // create an instance of the Circle class
c.r = 2.2;                // set the r instance variable
a = c.area();             // invoke the area() instance method
x = Math.exp(Circle.PI);  // use the PI class variable in our own computation.
d = new Circle(1.2);      // create another Circle instance
bigger = Circle.max(c,d); // use the max() class method.
```

7.6 Objects as Associative Arrays

We've seen the . operator used to access the properties of an object. It is also possible to use the [ ] operator, more commonly used with arrays, to access these properties. Thus, the following two JavaScript expressions have the same value:

```
object.property
object["property"]
```

The important difference to note between these two syntaxes is that in the first, the property name is an identifier, and in the second, the property name is a string. We'll see why this is so important below.

In C, C++, Java, and similar strongly typed languages an object can have only a fixed number of properties (or "fields," as they're often called), and the names of these properties must be defined in advance. Since JavaScript is a loosely typed language, this rule does not apply—a program can create any number of properties in any object. When you use the . operator to access a property of an object, however, the name of the property is expressed as an identifier, and identifiers must be "hardcoded" into your JavaScript program. That is, identifiers are not a JavaScript data type; they must be typed literally into a JavaScript program, and cannot be manipulated by the program.

On the other hand, when you access a property of an object with the [ ] array notation, the name of the property is expressed as a string. Strings are JavaScript data types, and they can be manipulated and created while a program is running. So, for example, you could write the following code in JavaScript:

```
var addr = "";
for(i = 0; i < 4; i++) {
    addr += customer["address" + i]
}
```

This code fragment reads and concatenates the properties address0, address1, address2, and address3 of the customer object.

The code fragment above demonstrates the flexibility of using array notation to access properties of an object with string expressions. We could have actually written that example using the . notation, but there are cases for which only the array notation will do. Suppose, for example, that you are writing a program that uses network resources to compute the current value of the user's stock market investments. The program allows the user to type in the name of each stock they own, and also the number of shares of each stock. You might use an object named portfolio to hold this information. The object would have one property for each stock; the name of the property would be the name of the stock, and the property value would be the number of shares of that stock. So, for example, if a user held 50 shares of stock in Netscape Communications Corp., then the `portfolio.nscp` property would have the value 50.

One part of this program would be a loop that prompts the user to enter the name of a stock they own, and then asks them to enter the number of shares they own of that stock. Inside the loop, you'd have code something like the following:

```
stock_name = get_stock_name_from_user();
shares = get_number_of_shares();
portfolio[stock_name] = shares;
```

Since the user enters stock names at run-time, there is no way that you can know the property names ahead of time. Since you can't know the property names when you write the program, there is no way you can use the . operator to access the properties of the `portfolio` object. You can use the `[]` operator, however, because it uses a string value (which is dynamic and can change at run-time), rather than an identifier (which static and must be hard-coded in the program), to name the property.

When an object is used this fashion, it is often called an *associative array*—a data structure that allows you to dynamically associate arbitrary data values with arbitrary strings. JavaScript objects are actually implemented internally as associative arrays. The . notation for accessing properties makes them seem like the static objects of C++ and Java, and they work perfectly well in that capacity. But they also have the very powerful ability to associate values with arbitrary strings. In this respect, JavaScript objects are much more like Perl arrays than like C++ or Java objects.

Chapter 5, *Statements*, introduced the `for/in` loop. The real power of this JavaScript statement becomes clear when we consider its use with an associative array. To return to the stock portfolio example, we might use code that looked like the following after the user had entered her portfolio and we were computing its current total value:

```
value = 0;
for (stock_name in portfolio) {  // for each stock in the portfolio
    // get the per share value and multiply it by the number of shares
    value += get_share_value(stock_name) * portfolio[stock_name];
}
```

We couldn't write this code without the `for/in` loop, because the names of the stocks aren't known in advance, and this is the only way to extract those property names from the associative array (i.e., JavaScript object) named `portfolio`.

7.7 Special Object Methods

For any object in JavaScript, there are three special methods that control the way the object is manipulated. Each of these methods is automatically invoked by JavaScript to manipulate the object in some way. By providing a custom definition of the method, you can control the way an object is manipulated. The methods are toString(), which is invoked to convert the object to a string, valueOf(), which is invoked to convert the object to a number or other nonobject type, and assign(), which is invoked to assign a value to the object. These three methods are detailed in the sections below.

7.7.1 The toString() Method

The toString() method takes no arguments and returns a string, which should somehow represent the type and/or value of the object referred to by this. JavaScript invokes this method whenever it needs to convert an object to a string. This occurs, for example, when you use the + operator to concatenate a string with an object, or when you pass an object to a method like document.write(). The default toString() method for user-defined objects is not very informative. For example, the following lines of code simply cause the browser to display the string "[object Object]":

```
c = new Circle(1, 0, 0);
document.write(c);
```

You can define your own toString() method so that your objects can be converted to more meaningful strings that contain more information about the object being converted. This is very useful when debugging programs, and if the string conversions are chosen carefully, it can also be useful in the programs themselves.

The toString() method is an excellent candidate, of course, for inclusion in a prototype object when defining a class of JavaScript objects. We might write and register a toString() method for our Circle class as follows:

```
function Circle_toString()
{
    return "[Circle of radius " + this.r + ", centered at ("
            + this.x + ", " + this.y + ").]";
}

Circle.prototype.toString = Circle_toString();
```

With this toString() method defined, a typical Circle object might be converted to "[Circle of radius 1, centered at (0,0).]".

7.7.2 The valueOf() Method

The `valueOf()` method is much like the `toString()` method, but is called when JavaScript needs to convert an object to some type other than an object or a string, typically a number. It takes no arguments, and should return a number, Boolean, or function that somehow represents the "value" of the object referred to by the `this` keyword.

Most objects are more complicated than number or Boolean values, and so the `valueOf()` method is not often used. In fact, its main purpose is for use with the Number, Boolean, and Function objects, for which it returns the corresponding number, Boolean, or function value. For most objects, the default `valueOf()` method simply returns the object itself; this is a way of indicating that the object could not be converted to any nonobject type. You may occasionally find circumstances in which you can meaningfully convert an object to a primitive type, and in these cases, you may want to provide a custom definition of the `valueOf()` method.

Suppose, for example, that you define a class of Complex objects that represent complex numbers. This class will define methods for arithmetic on complex numbers, but you'd still like to be able to use your Complex objects with the regular arithmetic operators, as if they were real numbers. You might do so with code like that shown in Example 7-6.

Example 7-6: Defining and Using the valueOf() Method

```
function Complex(x,y) {
    this.x = x;   // real part of complex number
    this.y = y;   // imaginary part of complex number
}

// force the prototype object to be created
new Complex(0,0);

// define some methods
Complex.prototype.valueOf = new Function("return this.x");
Complex.prototype.toString = new Function("return '{'+this.x+','+this.y+'}'");

// create new complex number object
c = new Complex(4,1);

// Now rely on the valueOf() operator to treat it like a real number.
// Note that this wouldn't work with the + operator--that would convert
// the object to a string and do string concatenation.
x = c * 2;        // x = 8
x = Math.sqrt(c);   // x = 2
```

7.7.3 The assign() Method

The assign() method is a new feature of Navigator 3.0, and supports a kind of C++–style "operator overloading" for the = operator. The assign() method of an object is invoked when that object appears on the left-hand side of an assignment operator. It is passed one argument, which is the value on the right-hand side of the operator. The purpose of the method is in some fashion to assign the value passed as an argument to the object referred to by the this keyword. The default version of this method simply performs an assignment, replacing the object on the left-hand side of the operator with the new value from the right-hand side. You would define a custom assign() method when you want the assignment to behave differently.

One use of the assign() method is to implement an assignment with side effects. Client-side JavaScript does this with the Location object stored in the Window.location property. When a string containing a URL is assigned to this Location object, two things happen. First, the URL is parsed, and its various components are assigned to the properties of the Location object. And second, and more importantly, the web browser reads the contents of the new URL and displays them. This all occurs as the side effect of an assignment, and is implemented with a custom assign() method.

Another use of the assign() method is to make objects read-only. If you define an assign method that does nothing, then no one will be able to change the value of the variable that holds your object. For example:

```
// give an object an empty assign() method
function no_op() { /* do nothing */ }
o = new Object();
o.assign = no_op;

// Now, no one can overwrite o. It will always contain the object we created.
o = 3;          // has no effect
o = new Date(); // has no effect

// Note, though that we can assign properties to o:
o.x = 3;        // this works fine
```

This technique can be extended to print issue a warning if any attempt is made to overwrite the object. You might do it with an assign() method defined like this:

```
function warn_on_assign(value) {
    alert('Attempt to set a read-only variable to:\n' + value);
}
ReadOnlyClass.prototype.assign = warn_on_assign;
```

Finally, the assign() method can be used to change the very way that assignment is done. Objects are usually assigned "by reference". That is, when one object is assigned to another, the contents of the object are not copied; instead, a reference to the new object merely overwrites a reference to the old. (The concept of assignment "by reference" is explained in detail in Chapter 9, *Further Topics in JavaScript.*) If you want the *contents* of an object to be copied when you assign one to another, you can do so with an assign() method like the following:

```
function assign_properties(value)
{
    // if the value is an object, copy it property by property
    // otherwise, do nothing and leave the variable unchanged.
    if (typeof value == "object")
        for (prop in value) this[prop] = value[prop];
}
MyClass.prototype.assign = assign_properties;
```

The assign() method is one of the most obscure and least elegant features of JavaScript. The JavaScript developers at Microsoft did not support it in Internet Explorer 3.0, and don't plan to support it in future versions of the language either. Even the JavaScript designers at Netscape aren't happy with assign(); they are thinking about providing similar functionality through a cleaner, more general mechanism in a future version of JavaScript. For these reasons, the assign() method may be one of the least portable features of JavaScript, and you should think twice before writing code that relies upon it.

8

Arrays

The last chapter documented the JavaScript object type—a data structure that contain named pieces of data. This chapter documents the array type—a data structure that contains numbered pieces of data. Note that the arrays we'll be discussing in this chapter are not the same thing as the "associative arrays" described the previous chapter, although, as we'll see, there is not as much difference among associative arrays, the "regular" arrays described here, and objects as it might first appear.

8.1 Array Elements

An array is a data type that contains or stores numbered pieces of data. Each numbered datum is called an *element* of the array, and the number assigned to an element is called its *index*. Because JavaScript is an untyped language, an element of an array may be of any type, and different elements of the same array may be of different types. Array elements may even contain other arrays, which allows you to create data structures that are arrays of arrays.

8.1.1 Reading and Writing Array Elements

You access an element of an array using the [ ] operator. A reference to the array should appear to the left of the brackets. Inside the brackets should appear an arbitrary expression that has a non-negative integer value. You can use this syntax to both read and write the value of an element of an array. Thus, the following are all legal JavaScript:

```
value = a[0];
a[1] = 3.14;
i = 2;
a[i] = 3;
a[i + 1] = "hello";
a[a[i]] = a[0];
```

In some languages, the first element of an array is at index 1. In JavaScript, as well as C, C++, and Java, however, the first element of an array is at index 0.*

8.1.2 Adding New Elements to an Array

In languages like C and Java, arrays have a fixed number of elements that must be specified when you create the array. This is not the case in JavaScript—arrays can have any number of elements, and you can change the number of elements at any time.

To add a new element to an array, simply assign a value to it:

```
a[10] = 10;
```

Arrays in JavaScript are *sparse*. This means that array indexes need not fall into a contiguous range of numbers, and that memory is allocated only for those array elements that are actually stored in the array. Thus, when you execute the following lines of code, JavaScript allocates memory only for array indexes 0 and 10,000, not for the 9,999 indexes between.

```
a[0] = 1;
a[10000] = "this is element 10,000";
```

8.1.3 Removing Elements from an Array

Once an element of an array has been defined, you can set its value to `null` or anything else, but there is no way to actually undefine that element, short of actually truncating the array, which (as we'll see later in the chapter) is possible in Navigator 3.0.

The `Select.options[]` array is an exception to this rule. It represents HTML elements in client-side JavaScript and has special behavior in Navigator 3.0, including the ability to delete individual elements. See the entry in the reference section of this book for more.

---

* Although, as we'll see later, index 0 is often not used in the Navigator 2.0 version of JavaScript.

8.2 *Multidimensional Arrays*

JavaScript does not support true multidimensional arrays, but it does allow you to approximate them quite nicely with arrays of arrays. To access a data element in an array of arrays, simply use the [ ] operator twice. For example, suppose the variable matrix is an array of arrays of numbers. Every element matrix[x] is an array of numbers. To access a particular number within this array you would write matrix[x][y].

Instead of using arrays of arrays, you can also use associative arrays to simulate multidimensional arrays. Because an associative array allows an arbitrary string as its index, it is easy to use them to simulate multidimensional arrays—i.e., to look up a value based on more than one index. You could use the following function, for example, to simulate reading a value from a three-dimensional array:

```
function index3(arr, x, y, z)
{
    return arr[x + "," + y + "," + z];
}
```

This example works because it combines the x, y, and z index values into a single, unique string that acts as a property name in the associative array (or object).

8.3 *Array/Object Dual Nature*

Throughout this book, we've been treating objects and arrays as if they were separate data types. This is a useful and reasonable simplification, and you can treat them as separate data types for most of your JavaScript programming. To fully understand the behavior of objects and arrays, however, you have to know the truth: *objects and arrays are the same thing.*

You can verify this with the typeof operator—use it with any array or with any object, and it returns the string "object". Because arrays and objects are the same thing, any object can have numerically indexed array elements, and any array can have named properties:

```
o.prop = "property1"
o[1] = "element1"

a[3] = a[2] + a[1];
a.size = 3;
```

Note, however, that because of the ways arrays and objects are implemented in Navigator 2.0, there are some nonobvious consequences of mixing properties and elements that you must beware of. These, and other features of arrays in Navigator 2.0, are discussed later in this chapter.

8.4 Creating Arrays

Since arrays are the same thing as objects, they can be created in exactly the same way as objects are with the new operator:

```
a = new Object();
a[0] = 1;
a[1] = 2;
    ... etc ...
```

Just as you write custom constructor methods to perform initialization on newly created objects, you can also write your own custom array constructor functions as shortcuts for array initialization. Example 8-1 shows a constructor that creates an array, initializes a size property of the array, and then initializes size elements (starting at 1, rather than 0) to a value of 0. This is useful when you want to know exactly how many elements your array contains, and want to be sure that all elements have a defined value.

Example 8-1: An Array Constructor

```
// The constructor function
function EmptyArray(length)
{
    this.size = length;
    for(var i = 1; i <= length; i++)
        this[i] = 0;
}

// Using the constructor
a = new EmptyArray(32);
```

In Navigator 3.0 and Internet Explorer 3.0, there is a predefined Array() constructor function that you can use to create arrays. You can use this constructor in three distinct ways. The first is to call it with no arguments:

```
a = new Array();
```

This method creates an empty array with no elements. It is like calling new Object(), except that it gives the newly created object (i.e., an array) a length property set to 0.

The second technique is to call the Array() constructor with a single argument, which specifies a length:

```
a = new Array(10);
```

This technique creates an empty array as well, but it sets the length property of the array to the value specified.

The final technique allows you to specify values for the first *n* elements of an array:

```
a = new Array(5, 4, 3, 2, 1, "testing, testing");
```

In this form, the constructor is passed two or more arguments. Each argument specifies an element value and may be of any type. Elements are assigned to the array starting with element 0. The length property of the array is set to the number of arguments that were passed to the constructor.

Remember that the Array() constructor is available only in Navigator 3.0 and later. In 2.0, you must write your own array constructor functions. And, of course, in either 2.0 or 3.0, you can use any object, no matter how you create it, as an array. Bear in mind, though, that there are some significant differences (which we'll explore later) between arrays in Navigator 2.0 and Navigator 3.0, and you must carefully take these into account when backward compatibility with Navigator 2.0 is required.

8.5 *Array Length Property*

As we saw in the previous section, the Array() constructor method automatically initializes a length property for the array you create. When you create an array with this constructor (available only in Navigator 3.0 and later) this length property is automatically updated by JavaScript so that it is always one greater than the largest element number in the array. The following code illustrates this:

```
a = new Array();        // a.length == 0  (no elements defined)
a = new Array(10);      // a.length == 10 (empty elements 0-9 defined)
a = new Array(1,2,3);   // a.length == 3  (elements 0-2 defined)
a[5] = -1;              // a.length == 6  (elements 0,1,2, and 5 defined)
a[49] = 0;              // a.length == 50 (elements 0,1,2,5, and 49 defined)
```

The length property of a Navigator 3.0 array is not read-only. You can set length to a value smaller than its current value; the array will then be shortened to the new length—elements will be truncated from the end of the array, and their values will be lost. If you change the length property so that it is larger than its current value, the array will be made larger—new, undefined, elements will be added at the end to increase it to the newly specified size.

We've said that arrays are the same data type as objects are, and that any object can have array elements. This is true, but in Navigator 3.0, arrays created with the Array() constructor have features that other objects do not have. One of these features is the length property. If you create an object with the Object() constructor (or a constructor you define yourself) you can assign array elements to that object, but that object will not have the special length property described in this section.

Because the `Array()` constructor and the array `length` property are not available in Navigator 2.0, JavaScript programs written for Navigator 2.0 often define custom array constructor functions that attempt to simulate the `length` property. (To avoid confusion with the "real" `length` property of arrays in 3.0, I prefer to name the property `size` in 2.0.) We saw such an array constructor in Example 8-1, and will learn more about arrays in Navigator 2.0 later in this chapter.

8.5.1 The length Property and Sparse Arrays

But what is the point of the `length` property to begin with? One obvious feature is that it allows you to loop through the elements of an array:

```
sum = 0;
for(var i = 0; i < .arr.length; i++)
    sum += arr[i];
```

This technique only works, of course, if the array in question has contiguous elements defined for each index between 0 and `length-1`. Since arrays in JavaScript are associative, sparse arrays, array elements do not have to be defined in contiguous blocks, like they do in C and related languages. For example, consider the code we saw above:

```
a = new Array();
a[5] = -1;
a[49] = 0;
```

These lines of code define an array with two elements, one with index 5 and one with index 49. There are not any elements defined at indexes 0 through 4 and 6 through 48. An array like this with non-contiguous elements is sometimes called a "sparse" array. By contrast, an array with contiguous elements is sometimes called a "dense" array.[*]

When you are programming in JavaScript, you will typically use dense arrays with contiguous elements, if for no other reason than that you probably learned to program with languages that did not directly support sparse arrays.

8.6 Array Methods

In the previous section we saw that—in Navigator 3.0 and Internet Explorer 3.0—arrays created with the `Array()` constructor have a `length` property. In Navigator 3.0, but *not* in IE 3.0, these arrays also support three methods that can be

---

[*] Note though that the terms "sparse" and "dense" may also refer to the underlying implementation of the array, rather than to how you use it. JavaScript's arrays are implemented as sparse arrays, regardless of how you use them in any particular case.

used to manipulate the array elements. These methods will be implemented in a future version of IE.

The `Array.join()` method converts all the elements of the array to a string, and concatenates them, separating them with an optionally specified string passed as an argument to the method. If no separator string is specified, then a comma is used. For example, the following lines of code produce the string "1,2,3":

```
a = new Array(1,2,3);  // Create a new array with these three elements.
s = a.join();          // s == "1,2,3"
```

And the following lines specify the optional separator to produce a slightly different result:

```
a = new Array(1,2,3);
s = a.join(", ");  // s == "1, 2, 3". Note the space after the comma.
```

In some ways, the `Array.join()` method is the reverse of the `String.split()` method which creates an array by breaking a string up into pieces.

The `Array.reverse()` method reverses the order of the elements of an array. It does this "in place"—i.e., it doesn't create a new array with the elements rearranged, but instead rearranges them in the already existing array. For example, the following code, which uses the `reverse()` and the `join()` methods, produces the string "3,2,1":

```
a = new Array(1,2,3);  // a[0] = 1; a[1] = 2; a[2] = 3;
a.reverse();           // now a[0] = 3; a[1] = 2; a[2] = 1;
s = a.join()           // s = "3,2,1"
```

The final array method is `Array.sort()`, which sorts the elements of an array. Like the `reverse()` method, it does this "in place". When `sort()` is called with no arguments, it sorts the array elements in alphabetical order (temporarily converting them to strings, to perform the comparison, if necessary):

```
a = new Array("banana", "cherry", "apple");
a.sort();
s = a.join(", ");  // s == "apple, banana, cherry".
```

You can also pass an argument to the `sort()` method if you want to sort the array elements in some other order. To allow this method to be a fully general sorting algorithm, the optional argument should be a function. This function will be passed two arguments that it should compare. If the first argument should appear before the second in the sorted array, then the function should return a number less than zero. If the first argument should appear after the second in the sorted array, then the function should return a number greater than zero. And if the two values are equivalent (their order is irrelevant), then the function should return 0.

So, for example, to sort array elements into numerical, rather than alphabetical order, you might do the following:

```
a = new Array(33, 4, 1111, 222);
a.sort();                           // alphabetical order: 1111, 222, 33, 4
function numberorder(a,b) {
    return a-b;
}
a.sort(numberorder);                // numerical order: 4, 33, 222, 1111
```

You can probably think of other comparison functions that will sort numbers into various esoteric orders: reverse numerical order, odd numbers before even numbers, etc. The possibilities become more interesting, of course, when the elements you are comparing are objects rather than simple types like numbers or strings.

8.7 *Arrays in Navigator 2.0*

As noted above, the implementation of arrays in Navigator 2.0 is substantially different than that in either Navigator 3.0 or Internet Explorer 3.0. One of the differences we've seen is that there is no Array() constructor in Navigator 2.0, and so you may want to write your own constructor function. Similarly, you may want to manage the value of a length (or size) property yourself.

But the biggest difference between Navigator 2.0 and 3.0 is in how array elements and object properties interact. In both versions of Navigator, arrays and objects are the same basic data type: objects can have array elements, and arrays can have object properties. The difference is that in Navigator 2.0, elements and properties can *overwrite* each other; in Navigator 3.0 they can't.

In Navigator 2.0, a newly defined property takes up the "slot" of the next available array element. Thus after executing the following lines, in the Navigator 2.0 browser, person.name is the same as person[0], and person.address is the same as person[1]:

```
person = new Object();
person.name = "david";
person.address = "somewhere on the internet";
```

If there are already some array elements defined in the object, then a new property takes up the element after the highest element already defined (even if there are undefined elements with lower indexes). So in the following code, in Navigator 2.0, address.zip is the same as address[4]:

```
address = new Object();
address[3] = "Anytown, USA";
address.zip = 22222;
```

The implication of all this is that if you define properties and later set array elements (for example, address[4] = 66666), you may inadvertently be overwriting the value of your properties. This can lead to strange bugs that are difficult to find.

Note that if, for any given object, you use only object properties, or only array elements, then you won't encounter this overlap problem. But, as we've seen, it is common to use a length property (or a size property) in conjunction with arrays. We must be careful to do this correctly. The convention for most Navigator 2.0 JavaScript code is to use array element 0 to hold the length property, and then to begin the array contents themselves with element 1. Thus, in Navigator 2.0 it is common to see array constructors like the one we saw above:

```
function EmptyArray(length)
{
    this.size = length;
    for(var i = 1; i <= length; i++)
        this[i] = 0;
}
```

The crucial feature of this constructor is that it assigns a value to the size[*] property *before* it initializes any of the array elements. Creating this size property uses up element 0 of the array, so the loop initializes the array starting with element 1. If, instead, we had initialized the array and then set the size property, then that property would have been at the end of the array. If we later added more elements to the array, we would overwrite the value of size. Of course, if we know that our array has a fixed size and will never be made larger, then there would be no problem with doing it this way, and it allows us to begin the array with element 0 instead of element 1.

As we've seen, another difference between arrays in Navigator 2.0 and 3.0 is that in Navigator 3.0, arrays created with the Array() constructor have their length property automatically updated when new elements are added to the array. If you need this feature in Navigator 2.0, you'll have to implement it yourself. You can do it with code like this:

```
a[i] = j;
if (i > a.size) a.size = i;
```

Note that this code fragment assumes the array begins with an index of 1, not 0.

Despite all this discussion of the array length property, and the ways to simulate it in Navigator 2.0, don't forget that there are many algorithms and uses for arrays in which a size or length property is not necessary. When this is possible, you

---

[*] We use a size property here instead of length to avoid confusion with Navigator 3.0 arrays that have an automatically updated length property. By using a different name we won't expect the property to be automatically updated.

can simply not bother with a `size` property. If your array has no object properties assigned, you don't have to worry about about overwriting array elements. And when your algorithm does require you to keep track of the size of your array, an obvious alternative to a `size` property is to maintain the array length in a separate variable, independent of the array. This also avoids the problem of properties overwriting elements.

Finally, one further feature of arrays in Navigator 2.0 is that they can be indexed using object notation. Just as object properties can be accessed with the `.` operator and a literal property name or the `[]` operator and a property name expressed as a string, so too can Navigator 2.0 arrays be accessed with either operator. When using the traditional array `[]` operator, the index can be any expression that evaluates to a positive integer. When using the `.` operator, the index must be an integer literal. So, in Navigator 2.0, the expression `a.2` is legal and is equivalent to `a[2]`. Using the `.` operator is not at all recommended—this bizarre feature of the language is deprecated, and has been removed in Navigator 3.0.

8.8 Built-in Arrays

As we'll see later in this book, client-side JavaScript has quite a few built-in arrays. For example, the `elements[]` array of the Form object contains references to the buttons, input fields, and other input elements of an HTML form in a web document. JavaScript provides a `length` property for these built-in arrays in both Navigator 2.0 and Navigator 3.0. It is only user-defined arrays that lack the `length` property in Navigator 2.0.

Certain built-in arrays may also have special behavior. For example, in Navigator 3.0, the `options[]` array of the Select object (an HTML form element) allows you to delete an element simply by setting it to `null`. This is special-case behavior implemented only for this particular array, and is not a general property of arrays. This kind of behavior is documented on a case-by-case basis in this book.

8.9 Array Summary

JavaScript array creation, usage, and compatibility techniques can be confusing. Here are the main points of this chapter in review:

* Arrays and objects are the same thing in JavaScript. Any object can have array elements, and any array can have object properties.

- In Navigator 3.0, there are three methods that can be used to manipulate arrays:

  1. You can can convert an array, and all of its elements into a single string with the `Array.join()` method.

  2. You can reverse the order of elements in an array with the `Array.reverse()` method.

  3. You can sort the elements of an array with the `Array.sort()` method.

- In Navigator 3.0 and Internet Explorer 3.0, array elements and object properties do not overlap and cannot overwrite each other. There is an `Array()` constructor, and arrays created with this constructor have a (read-only in IE 3.0) `length` property that is automatically maintained so that it always contains a value one greater than the largest index of the array.

- In Navigator 2.0, object properties and array elements overlap; when you create a new property, it is as if you added a new array element one higher than the highest existing element. There is no built-in `Array()` constructor, but you can write your own. Also, there is no automatically maintained `length` property, but it is common to reserve element 0 of an array for a `size` property (which you update yourself as the array grows).

- For many algorithms, the size of an array is maintained in a variable externally to an array, and there is no need for a `length` or `size` property.

- All arrays in JavaScript are implemented as associative arrays, and can be "sparse"—i.e., they can contain non-contiguous elements. Usually, though, you'll use arrays as if they were non-associative, fixed-size arrays like those found in C, C++, and Java.

9

Further Topics
in JavaScript

This chapter covers miscellaneous JavaScript topics that would have bogged down previous chapters had they been covered there. Now that you have read through the preceding chapters, and are experienced with the core JavaScript language, you are ready to tackle the more advanced and detailed concepts presented here. In fact, you may prefer to move on to other chapters and learn about the specifics of client-side JavaScript at this point. Do be sure to return to this chapter, however. You will not truly understand the workings of the JavaScript language if you have not read the material in this chapter.

9.1 Automatic Data Type Conversion

We've seen that JavaScript is an untyped language. This means, for example, that we don't have to specify the data type of variable when we declare it. The fact that JavaScript is untyped gives it the flexibility and simplicity that are desirable for a scripting language (although those features come at the expense of rigor, which is important for the longer, more complex programs often written in stricter languages like C and Java). Another feature of JavaScript's flexible treatment of data types is the automatic type conversions that it performs. For example, if you call `document.write()` to output the value of a Boolean value, JavaScript will automatically convert that value to the string `"true"` or the string `"false"`. Similarly, if you write an `if` that tests a string value, JavaScript will automatically convert that string to a Boolean value—to `false` if the string is empty and to `true` otherwise.

The subsections below explain, in detail, all of the automatic data conversions performed by JavaScript.

9.1.1 Conversions to Strings

Of all the automatic data conversions performed by JavaScript, conversions to strings are probably the most common. Whenever a nonstring value is used in a "string context," JavaScript converts that value to a string. A "string context" is anywhere that a string value is expected. Generally, this means arguments to built-in JavaScript functions and methods. As described above, for example, if we pass a Boolean value to document.write(), it will be converted to a string before being output. Similarly, if we pass a number to this method, it will also be converted to a string before output.

Another common "string context" occurs with the + operator. When + is used with numeric operands, it adds them. When it is used with string operands, however, it concatenates them. When one operand is a string, and one is a nonstring, the nonstring operand will first be converted to a string and then the two strings will be concatenated:

```
x = 1 + 2;              // yields 3
x = 'hello' + 'world';  // yields 'helloworld'
x = 1 + '2';            // yields '12'
x = true + '3';         // yields 'true3'
```

Actually, the + operator even works when both operands are of object type: the operands are converted to strings and concatenated. When one operands is an object, and the other is neither an object nor a string, both operands are converted to strings and concatenated:

```
x = window + 1;         // yields '[object Window]1'
x = window + top;       // yields '[object Window][object Window]'
x = window + true;      // yields '[object Window]true'
```

The paragraphs above have described the "string contexts" in which values are converted to strings. Here is exactly how that conversion is performed:

- Numbers are converted to strings in the obvious way: the resulting string contains the digits of the decimal representation of the number. The number 123.45, for example, is converted to the string "123.45".

- The Boolean value true is converted to the string "true", and the value false is converted to the string "false".

- In Navigator, functions are converted to strings which consist of the text of the function definition, including the complete body of the function. Thus, a function defined as follows:

```
function square(x) { return x*x; }
```

is converted to the string:

```
"function square(x) {
    return x*x;
}"
```

The JavaScript code in the function body may be reformatted during this conversion—note the insertion of newlines in the example above. Similarly, any comments in the original function definition will not appear in the resulting string. An interesting feature of the string conversion of a function is that it is guaranteed to be perfectly legal JavaScript code, and is thus may be passed to the eval() method to be reinterpreted (perhaps in some new context). You should not rely on this, however, because Internet Explorer 3.0 does not include the body of a function when it converts it to a string, and this behavior is not likely to change in future versions.

- Objects are converted to strings by calling their toString() method. By default, most objects have a toString() method that specifies at least the type of the object. For example, the Window object window is converted to the string "[object Window]". Similarly, the navigator object converts to the string "[object Navigator]". By default, all user-defined objects convert to the vague string "[object Object]".

  Note that you can override the default toString() method for any object, thereby controlling exactly how the object is converted to a string.

- The null value is converted to the string "null", and the JavaScript undefined value is converted to the string "undefined".

9.1.2 Conversions to Numbers

Just as JavaScript values are automatically converted to strings when used in a "string context," they are automatically converted to numbers when used in a "numeric context." The two numeric contexts are:

- Numeric arguments to built-in functions and methods (arguments to user-defined functions do not have a type defined, so no conversion is performed).

- Operands of various arithmetic, comparison, and other operators.

For example, the following lines of code contain non-numeric values in numeric contexts, and cause automatic conversion to occur:

```
Math.sin("1.45");       // String "1.45" converted to number 1.45
done = sum > "10"       // String "10" converted to number 10
sum = sum + true;       // Boolean value true converted to number 1
total = total - "3";    // String "3" converted to number 3
```

Note, however, that the following line of code does not cause a numeric conversion to occur.

```
total = total + "3"
```

Recall that the + operator adds numbers *and* concatenates strings. Since there is one string operand in this example, JavaScript interprets the operator as the string concatenation operator, rather than the addition operator. Therefore, there is not a numeric context here, and the string is not converted to a number. In fact, just the opposite occurs: the numeric value total occurs in a string context, and therefore is converted to a string.

JavaScript values are converted to numbers according to the following rules:

- If a string contains the decimal representation of an integer or floating-point number, with no trailing non-numeric characters, then the string is converted to that number. If the string does not represent a number, or contains trailing characters that are not part of the number, then the attempt to convert it fails, and JavaScript displays an error message. As a special case, the empty string ("") is converted to the number 0.

- The Boolean value true is converted to the number 1, false to 0.

- null is converted to the number 0.

- Objects are converted to numbers by invoking their valueOf() method, if they have one. If the valueOf() method returns a number, that value is the result of the conversion. If valueOf() returns a string or Boolean value, then that value is converted to a number following the rules above. If the valueOf() method returns some other type, or if no such method exists, then the conversion fails, and JavaScript displays an error message.

- Functions and the undefined value cannot be converted to numbers. Using a function or an undefined value in a numeric context will always cause a error message to be displayed.

9.1.3 Conversions to Booleans

When a JavaScript value is used in a "Boolean context", it is automatically converted to a Boolean value. A "Boolean context" is anywhere that a Boolean value is expected: Boolean arguments to certain built-in methods, the return value from certain event-handlers, and, more commonly, the expressions used by the if statement, the while and for loops, and the conditional (:?) operator.

For example, the following lines of code use the integer i, the string s, and the object o in Boolean contexts, and cause those values to be converted to Boolean values:

```
for(i = 10; i; i--) document.write(messages[i]);
response = s?"yes":"no";
if (o) sum += o.value;
```

In C, there is no Boolean type. Integer values are used instead, and just about any value can implicitly be used in a "Boolean context". In Java, however, there is a Boolean type, and the language does not permit any conversion, implicit or explicit, to Boolean values. This means that you need to be very precise with your if and while statement (for example) in Java. JavaScript—like Java—has a Boolean type, but—like C—it allows just about any type to be used in a Boolean context. If you are a C programmer, you will find the JavaScript Boolean conversions intuitive and convenient. The conversions follow these rules:

- The number 0 is converted to false. All other numbers are converted to true.

- The empty string ("") is converted to false. All other strings are converted to true.

- null is converted to false. Non-null objects are converted to the value true, with one exception: if the object has a valueOf() method, and that method returns false, 0, or the empty string, then the object is converted to false.

- Functions are always converted to the value true.

- Undefined values are converted to false.

9.1.4 Conversions to Objects

Just as JavaScript values are converted to strings, numbers, and Boolean values, when used in the appropriate context, so too are they converted to objects when used in an "object context." This is the most subtle of the automatic conversions, and it is possible to use JavaScript without ever realizing that it is happening. A value is used in an "object context" when you use the . operator to read or write a property of the value or to reference a method of the object. A value is also used in an object context when you use the [] operator to access an array element of the value.

Why would we want to do this? If a value is not already an object, how can it have properties or methods to access, anyway? Consider JavaScript strings, for example. JavaScript defines quite a few methods that can operate on strings. If s is a string, then each of the following lines is legal JavaScript:

```
len = s.length;
document.write(s.bold());
t = s.substring(2,4);
a = s.split(",");
```

A string isn't an object, so why can we treat it like one? Are strings simply a special case supported by JavaScript? Are they a special data type that is half object, half primitive type? No. When a JavaScript string is used in an object context, as the strings in the above example are, they are converted to a String object that represents the same underlying value as the original string did. (Note the capitalization convention: the primitive type is a string, the corresponding object is a String.) The String object defines a length property and quite a few methods that perform various operations on the string.

Strings are the primary example of why and when this sort of automatic conversion to an object data type is necessary. But it is occasionally used with other data types as well. For example, JavaScript will convert a function value to a Function object so that you can access the arguments property, which is an array of arguments passed to the function. Also, a numeric value can be converted to a Number object, which allows you to invoke the toString() method of that object, a method that takes an optional argument to specify what base the number should be converted to.

The rules for automatic conversions to objects are particularly straightforward:

- Strings are converted to String objects.
- Numbers are converted to Number objects.
- Boolean values are converted to Boolean objects.
- Functions are converted to Function objects.
- null and the undefined value cannot be converted to objects, and cause an error message to be displayed if used in an object context.

The conversion of values to objects is handled quite transparently by JavaScript, and it is often not obvious to a casual programmer that the conversion is happening at all. This is for two reasons. First, the converted objects are transient: suppose a string, for example, is converted to a String object, and a method is invoked on that String object. The String object is never saved into a variable, and so it is used once and then is no longer available to the program (it is "garbage collected" so memory is not wasted). This makes it difficult to even obtain an instance of a String object. To do so, we must explicitly convert our string to String object. We can do this in either of two ways:

```
s = new String("hello");
s = new Object("hello");
```

Similarly, we can create Number, Boolean, and Function objects by invoking the `Number()`, `Boolean()`, or `Function()` constructors with our number, Boolean, or function value, or, more generally, by invoking the `Object()` constructor with the value to be converted.

The second reason why conversion to objects is often transparent to programmers is that each of the String, Number, Boolean, and Function objects have `toString()` methods that are invoked when they are used in a string context, and have `valueOf()` methods that are invoked when they are used in numeric, Boolean, or function contexts. Because the data conversion is so completely automatic, it can be difficult to even distinguish between a value and its corresponding object. The `typeof` operator provides one way to distinguish primitive values from objects. When invoked on a primitive value, `typeof` will return one of the strings "string", "number", "boolean", and "function". When invoked on the corresponding object, however, it will return "object":

```
typeof "hello"              // returns "string"
typeof new String("hello")  // returns "object"
```

9.1.5 Conversions to Functions

The only time that JavaScript can convert a value to a function is when a Function object is used in a function context (which occurs when you use the `()` operator to invoke a value.) In this case, the Function object is trivially converted to the primitive function value it represents. Using any value other than a function or a Function object in a function context will cause JavaScript to display an error message.

9.1.6 Data Conversion Summary

While many of the automatic data conversions explained in the subsections above are intuitive, there are so many of them that it can be difficult to keep them all straight. Table 9-1 summarizes each of the possible conversions.

Table 9–1: Automatic Data Type Conversions

Value:	String	Number	Boolean	Object	Function
	Used As:				
non-empty string	-	Numeric value of string, or error	`true`	String object	*error*
empty string	-	0	`false`	String object	*error*
0	`"0"`	-	`false`	Number object	*error*
NaN	`"NaN"`	-	`true`	Number object	*error*
Infinity	`"Infinity"`	-	`true`	Number object	*error*
Negative Infinity	`"-Infinity"`	-	`true`	Number object	*error*
any other number	string value of number	-	`true`	Number object	*error*
true	`"true"`	1	-	Boolean object	*error*
false	`"false"`	0	-	Boolean object	*error*
object or array	`toString()` result, or object type	`valueOf()` result, or *error*	`valueOf()` result, or `true`	-	*error* (unless Function obj)
null	`"null"`	0	`false`	-	*error*
undefined value	`"undefined"`	*error*	`false`	*error*	*error*
function	Complete function text	*error*	`true`	Function object	-

9.2 Explicit Data Type Conversions

The section above described all of the automatic data type conversions performed by JavaScript. Sometimes, however, you will want to explicitly convert a value from one type to another. For example, instead of repeatedly using a number in a string context, and relying on JavaScript to convert it to a string, you might prefer (for efficiency) to convert the number to a string a single time and then repeatedly use the converted value. Or, you might simply prefer to make your data type conversions explicit so that your code is easier to understand.

JavaScript does not have a cast operator, a mechanism often used in C, C++, and Java to convert values from one type to another. To force a conversion in JavaScript, you must generally invoke a function or method. The sections below show how you can do this.

9.2.1 Conversions to and from Objects

We saw in the section on automatic conversions that all objects have a `toString()` method that provides at least a default string conversion for each object type. Similarly, many objects define a `valueOf()` method that returns the primitive type equivalent of the object. Although these methods are invoked automatically under certain appropriate circumstances, there is nothing to prevent you from using them explicitly to convert objects. For example, you might use lines of code like the following to perform explicit conversions of Date objects:

```
message = "Today is: " + today.toString();
elapsed_time = end_time.valueOf() - start_time.valueOf();
```

Also remember that primitive types are automatically converted to objects when used in an object context, so you can invoke the `toString()` method on a primitive type to explicitly convert it to a string. For example:

```
// define one of our functions in a new document in a new window
newwin.document.write('<script>' + myfunc.toString() + '</' + 'script>');
```

Note that because of syntactic constraints in JavaScript, you can't directly invoke the `toString()` method on a numeric literal (although you can on string and Boolean literals). You must enclose the number in parentheses, or must first assign it to a variable:

```
321.toString();          // this is a syntax error
(123).toString();        // this is okay
a = 45; a.toString();    // also okay
true.toString();         // this works fine
```

Although you may less frequently need to do it, you can also explicitly convert primitive values to their corresponding String, Number, Boolean, and Function object values. You can use the constructor methods for each of these object types, or you can simply use the `Object()` constructor instead:

```
func_obj = new Object(my_func);    // these two lines are equivalent
func_obj = new Function(my_func);
```

9.2.2 Converting Numbers to Strings

The number-to-string conversion is probably the one most often performed in JavaScript. Although it usually happens automatically, there are a couple of useful ways to perform this conversion explicitly. Perhaps the simplest is to add the empty string to a number. This forces the number to be converted (because it is used in a string context) and concatenated with nothing:

```
string_value = number + "";
```

Another technique for converting numbers to strings is with the `toString()` method, as we saw above:

```
string_value = number.toString();
```

The `toString()` method of the Number object (numbers are converted to Number objects so that this method can be called) takes an optional argument that specifies a radix, or base, for the conversion. If you do not specify the argument, the conversion will be done in base 10. But you can also convert numbers in other bases (between 2 and 16) as well. For example:

```
binary_string = n.toString(2);
octal_string = "0" + n.toString(8);
hex_string = "0x" + n.toString(16);
```

A shortcoming of JavaScript is that there is no built-in way to convert a number to a string and specify the number of decimal places to be included. This can make it a little difficult to display numbers that represent monetary values, and which have a traditional format. In fact, JavaScript lacks any kind of numeric formatting function, so it is not possible to specify whether exponential notation should be used or not, nor whether leading zeros should be displayed, and so on.

9.2.3 Converting Strings to Numbers

We've seen that strings that represent numbers are automatically converted to actual numbers when used in a numeric context. We can make this conversion explicit by choosing the numeric context we use. Just as we can convert a number to a string by adding the empty string to it, we can convert a string to a number by subtracting zero from it:

```
numeric_value = string_value - 0;
```

We can't add zero, of course, because in that case the + operator would be interpreted as the string concatenation operator.

The trouble with this sort of string-to-number conversion is that it is overly strict. It works only with base-10 numbers, and only when the string contains nothing but leading spaces and numbers, with no trailing characters, not even trailing spaces. To allow more flexible conversions, you can use the parseInt() and parse-Float() functions. These convert and return any number at the beginning of a string, ignoring any trailing non-numbers. parseInt() only parses integers, and parseFloat() parses both integers and floating-point numbers. If a number begins with 0, parseInt() interprets it as an octal number. If it begins with 0x or 0X, parseInt() interprets it as a hexadecimal number.

```
parseInt("3 blind mice");      // returns 3
parseFloat("3.14 meters");     // returns 3.14
parseInt("12.34");             // returns 12
parseInt("077");               // returns 63 (7*8 + 7)
parseInt("0xFF");              // returns 255
```

parseInt() can even take a second argument, which specifies the radix (base) of the number to be parsed. Legal values are between 2 and 36. For example:

```
parseInt("11", 2);             // returns 3 (1*2 + 1)
parseInt("ff", 16);            // returns 255 (15*16 + 15)
parseInt("zz", 36);            // returns 1295 (35*36 + 35)
```

If parseInt() or parseFloat() cannot convert the specified string to a number, they return NaN in Navigator 3.0 (and on Unix platforms in Navigator 2.0). On Navigator 2.0 non-Unix platforms and in Internet Explorer 3.0, these functions return 0 in this case, which makes it impossible to distinguish between the legal string "0" and an a string that does not represent a number. A future version of IE will correctly support the NaN return value.

```
parseInt("eleven");            // returns NaN (or 0)
parseFloat("$72.47");          // returns NaN (or 0)
```

Finally, you can also convert strings to numbers (and to other types) with the eval() method. This method interprets an arbitrary JavaScript expression and returns the result (which may be of any JavaScript type). For example:

```
eval("3.14");                  // returns 3.14
eval("2 * 3.14 * radius");     // returns the result of the multiplication
eval("radius > 3");            // returns true or false
```

Note that you rarely actually need to use `eval()`—generally, your JavaScript expressions occur in JavaScript code itself, not in strings that are later evaluated!

9.2.4 Miscellaneous Conversions

JavaScript does not contain any built-in conversion functions other than those described above. You can write your own JavaScript code to perform certain conversions for you, however. To explicitly convert between Boolean values and numeric values, for example, you could use expressions like the following:

```
b?1:0             // converts a Boolean, b, to a number
(x==0)?false:true // converts a number, x, to a Boolean
```

You may write your own code for custom data conversions. For example, to convert a Boolean value to either the string "yes" or "no", you might use:

```
(reply)?"yes":"no"
```

To convert an arbitrary value to a string, you might write a function like the following, which follows some custom rules:

```
function convert_to_string(x)
{
    if (x == null) return "";
    if (typeof x == "boolean") return x?"on":"off";
    if (typeof x == "function") return "[function]";
    return x.toString();
}
```

9.3 By Value vs. By Reference

In JavaScript, and all programming languages, there are three important ways that you can manipulate a data value. First, you can copy it, by assigning it to a new variable, for example. Second, you can pass it as an argument to a function or method. Third, you can compare it with another value to see if the two values are equal. In order to understand any programming language, you must understand how these three operations are performed in that language.

There are two fundamentally distinct techniques in which data values can be manipulated. These techniques are called "by value" and "by reference." When a value is manipulated "by value" it is the *value* of the datum that matters: in an assignment, a copy of the actual value is made and that copy is stored in a variable or object property or array element; the copy and the original are two totally independent values that are stored separately. When a datum is passed "by value" to a function, a *copy* of the datum is passed to the function; if the function modifies that value, the change affects only the function's copy of the datum—it does not affect the original datum. And when a datum is compared "by value" to another datum, the two distinct pieces of data must represent exactly the same value (which usually means that a byte-by-byte comparison finds them to be equal).

The other way of manipulating a datum is "by reference." With this technique, there is only one actual copy of the datum, and it is references to that datum that are manipulated.[*] When a datum is manipulated "by reference," there is only ever one copy of the actual value. If a value is manipulated "by reference," then variables do not hold that value directly; they only hold references to it. It is these references that are copied, passed, and compared.

So, in an assignment made "by reference," it is the reference to the value that is assigned, not a copy of the value, and not the value itself. After the assignment, the new variable will contain the same reference to the value that the original variable contains. Both references are equally valid, and both can be used to manipulate the value—if the value is changed through one reference, that change will also appear through the original reference. The situation is similar when a datum is passed to a function "by reference:" a reference to the value is passed to the function, and the function can use that reference to modify the value itself; any such modifications will be visible outside the function. And finally, when a datum is compared to another "by reference," the two references are compared to see if they refer to the same unique copy of a value; references to two distinct datums that happen to have the same value (consist of the same bytes) will not be treated as equal.

These are two very different ways of manipulating values, and they have very important implications that you should understand. Table 9-2 summarizes these implications. This discussion of manipulating data "by value" and "by reference" has been a general one: the distinctions apply to all programming languages. The subsections that follow explain how they apply specifically to JavaScript—which data types are manipulated by value and which are manipulated by reference.

---

[*] C programmers, and anyone else familiar with the concept of "pointers," will understand the idea of a "reference" in this context. Note, however, that JavaScript does not support pointers.

Table 9–2: By Value versus By Reference

	By Value	**By Reference**
Copy	The value is actually copied; there are two distinct, independent copies.	Only a reference to the value is copied. If the value is modified through the new reference, that change is also visible through the original reference.
Pass	A distinct copy of the value is passed to the function; changes to it have no effect outside the function.	A reference to the value is passed to the function. If the function modifies the value through the passed reference, the modification is visible outside the function.
Compare	Two distinct values are compared (often byte by byte) to see if they are the same value.	Two references are compared to see if they refer to the same value. Two references to distinct values are not equal, even if the two values consist of the same bytes.

9.3.1 Primitive Types and Reference Types

The basic rule in JavaScript is this: primitive types are manipulated by value, and reference types, as the name suggests, are manipulated by reference. Numbers and Booleans are primitive types in JavaScript—primitive because the consist of nothing more than a small fixed number of bytes, bytes that are very easily manipulated at the low (primitive) levels of the JavaScript interpreter. On the other hand, objects and arrays are reference types. These data types can contain arbitrary numbers of properties or elements, and so can be of arbitrary size, and cannot be so easily manipulated. Since object and array values can become quite large, it doesn't make sense to manipulate these types by value, which could involve the inefficient copying and comparing of large amounts of memory.

What about strings and functions? These types may have arbitrary length, and so it would seem that they would be reference types. In fact, though, they are usually considered to be primitive types in JavaScript, simply for the reason that they are not objects or arrays. Strings and functions do not follow the "primitive types by value and reference types by reference" rule presented above, and will be discussed in a section of their own later in this chapter.

Examples using primitive and reference types are the best way to explore the differences between data manipulation by value and data manipulation by reference.

Study the following examples carefully, paying attention to the comments. First, Example 9-1 copies, passes, and compares numbers. Since numbers are primitive types, this illustrates data manipulation by value.

Example 9-1: Copying, Passing, and Comparing by Value

```
// First we illustrate copy by value.
n = 1;              // variable n holds the value 1
m = n;              // copy by value: variable m holds a distinct value 1

// Here's a function we'll use to illustrate pass-by-value.
// As we'll see, the function doesn't work the way we'd like it to.
function add_to_total(total, x)
{
    total = total + x;  // this line only changes the internal copy of total
}

// Now call the function, passing the numbers contained in n and m by value.
// The value of n is copied, and that copied value is named total within the
// function. The function adds a copy of m to that copy of n. But adding
// something to a copy of n doesn't affect the original value of n outside
// of the function. So calling this function doesn't accomplish anything.
add_to_total(n, m);

// Now, we'll look at comparison by value.
// In the line of code below, the literal 1 is clearly a distinct numeric
// value encoded in the program. We compare it to the value held in variable
// n. In comparison by value, the bytes of the two numbers are checked to
// see if they are the same.
if (n == 1) m = 2;      // n contains the same value as the literal 1
```

Next, consider Example 9-2. This example copies, passes, and compares an object. Since objects are reference types, these manipulations are performed "by reference." The example uses Date objects, which you can read about in the reference section of this book, if necessary.

Example 9-2: Copying, Passing, and Comparing by Reference

```
// Here we create an object representing the date of Christmas, 1996.
// The variable xmas contains a reference to the object, not the object itself.
xmas = new Date(96, 11, 25);

// When we copy by reference, we get a new reference to the original object.
solstice = xmas;      // both variables now refer to the same object value

// Here we change the object through our new reference to it
solstice.setDate(21);

// The change is visible through the original reference, as well.
xmas.getDate();         // returns 21, not the original value of 25
```

Example 9-2: Copying, Passing, and Comparing by Reference (continued)

```
// The same is true when objects and arrays are passed to functions.
// The following function adds a value to each element of an array.
// A reference to the array is passed to the function, not a copy of the array.
// Therefore, the function can change the contents of the array through
// the reference, and those changes will be visible when the function returns.
function add_to_totals(totals, x)
{
    totals[0] = totals[0] + x;
    totals[1] = totals[1] + x;
    totals[2] = totals[2] + x;
}


// Finally, we'll examine comparison by value.
// When we compare the two variables defined above, we find they are
// equal, because the refer to the same object, even though we were trying
// to make them refer to different dates:
(xmas == solstice)               // evaluates to true


// The two variables defined below refer to two distinct objects, both
// of which represent exactly the same date.
xmas = new Date(96, 11, 25);
solstice_plus_4 = new Date(96, 11, 25);


// But, by the rules of "compare by reference," distinct objects not equal!
(xmas != solstice_plus_4)        // evaluates to true
```

Before we leave the topic of manipulating objects and arrays by reference, there is a point about passing values by reference that it is important to get straight. When an object is passed to a function, it is a reference to the object that is passed, not a copy of the object's actual value. As we've seen in Example 9-2 this means that we can modify the object's value through the reference, and these modifications will be visible when the function returns. What we cannot do, and this is where confusion can arise, is modify the reference itself. The function is passed a copy of the reference to the object (in a sense, the reference itself is "passed by value"). If the function changes its copy of the reference, that change does not affect the object value nor the original reference to the object, and the change will not be visible outside of the function. Example 9-3 illustrates this.

Example 9-3: References Themselves Are Passed by Value

```
// This is another version of the add_to_totals() function. It doesn't
// work, through, because instead of changing the array itself, it tries to
// change the reference to the array.
function add_to_totals2(totals, x)
{
    newtotals = new Array(3);
    newtotals[0] = totals[0] + x;
```

Example 9–3: References Themselves Are Passed by Value (continued)

```
    newtotals[1] = totals[1] + x;
    newtotals[2] = totals[2] + x;
    totals = newtotals;  // this line has no effect outside of the function.
}
```

Note that this rule applies not only to pass-by-reference, but also copy-by-reference. You can modify an object through a copy of a reference, but changing the copied reference itself does not affect the object nor the original reference to the object. This is a more intuitive and less confusing case, so we don't illustrate it with an example.

9.3.2 Copying and Passing Strings and Functions

As mentioned in the previous section, strings and functions in JavaScript don't fit neatly into the primitive-type versus reference-type dichotomy. For most purposes, strings and functions are considered primitive types by default—because they are not objects or arrays. If they are primitive types, then by the rules given above, they should be manipulated by value. But since a string can be arbitrarily long, and a function can contain an arbitrary amount of JavaScript code, these types do not have a fixed size, and it would be inefficient to copy, pass, and compare these data types byte by byte.

Since it is unclear whether JavaScript copies and passes strings and functions by value or by reference, we can try to write some JavaScript code to experiment with these data types. If they are copied and passed by reference, then we should be able to modify the contents of a string or function value through a copy of the value or a through a function that takes the value as an argument. When we set out to write the code to perform this experiment and determine whether strings and functions are copied and passed by reference, we run into a major stumbling block: there is no way to modify the contents of a string or a function. We can modify the contents of an object or an array by setting object properties or array elements. But strings and functions are *immutable* in JavaScript—that is, there is no JavaScript syntax, or JavaScript functions, methods, or properties that allow you to change the characters in the string or the code in the function.

Since strings and functions are immutable, our original question is moot: there is no way to tell if strings and functions are passed by value or by reference. Because of efficiency considerations, we can assume that JavaScript is implemented so that strings and functions are passed by reference, but in actuality it doesn't matter, since it has no practical bearing on the code we write.

9.3.3 Comparing Strings and Functions

Despite the fact that we cannot determine whether strings and functions are copied and passed by value or by reference, we can write JavaScript code to determine whether they are compared by value or by reference. Example 9-4 shows the code we might use to make this determination.

Example 9-4: Are Strings and Functions Compared by Value or by Reference?

```
// Determining whether strings are compared by value or reference is easy.
// We compare two clearly distinct strings that happen to contain the same
// characters. If they are compared by value they will be equal, but if they
// are compared by reference, they will not be equal:
s1 = "hello";
s2 = "hell" + "o";
if (s1 == s2) document.write("Strings compared by value");


// Determining whether functions are compared by value or reference is trickier,
// because we cannot define two functions with the same name. Therefore, we
// have to use unnamed functions. Don't feel you have to understand this code.
// We create two distinct functions that contain exactly the same code.
// If JavaScript says these two functions are equal, then functions are
// compared by value, otherwise they are compared by reference.
F = new Function("return 1;"); // F and G are Function objects that contain
G = new Function("return 1;"); //     unnamed function values.
f = F.valueOf();               // convert F and G to the actual function values
g = G.valueOf();
if (f == g)                    // now compare them
    document.write("Functions compared by value");
```

The results of this experiment are surprising. Strings are compared by value, and functions are compared by reference. The fact that strings are compared by value may be counter-intuitive to C, C++, and Java programmers—in those languages, strings are reference types, and you must use a special function or method when you want to compare them by value. JavaScript, however, is a higher-level language, and recognizes that when you compare strings you almost always want to compare them by value. Thus, as a special case, it compares strings by value even though they are (presumably) copied and passed by reference.

The fact that functions are compared by reference is quite reasonable. Since it doesn't make sense to write two separate functions that do exactly the same thing, we never really want to compare functions by value. Comparing functions by reference is far more useful.

9.3.4 Copying Objects with the assign() Method

We've seen above that objects are copied by reference. There is one exception to this rule, however. If the left-hand side of an assignment expression refers to an object, and that object has an `assign()` method, then instead of copying a reference to the right-hand value into the left-hand variable, as usual, the `assign()` method is called instead, with the value of the right-hand side as its argument. You can define this method so that an assignment performs any sort of action you desire. Example 9-5 shows how you can use this feature to override the "copy-by-reference" nature of an object. The `assign()` method is also covered in detail in Chapter 7, *Objects.*[*]

Example 9–5: The assign() Method

```
// This is the function we'll use for the assign() method.
function myassign(rhs) {
    var i;
    for (i in rhs) this[i] = rhs[i];
}

myobject = new Object;        // create an object
myobject.assign = myassign;   // set the custom assign() method on it

// Now, when an object is assigned to "myobject", the properties
// of that object are copied, rather than overwriting the "myobject"
// variable with a reference to the other object.
myobject = my_other_object;

// After the above assignment, myobject and my_other_object still refer
// to two separate objects, but myobject has a copy of each of the
// properties of my_other_object.
```

9.3.5 By Value vs. By Reference: Summary

The sections above have been quite detailed and perhaps somewhat confusing. Table 9-3 summarizes these sections.

---

[*] Note that the `assign()` method is not supported in Internet Explorer 3.0, and may not be supported in future versions of Navigator.

Table 9–3: Data Type Manipulation in JavaScript

	Copied	Passed	Compared
Number	By value	By value	By value
Boolean	By value	By value	By value
Object	By reference (or `assign()` method)	By reference	By reference
Array	By reference (or `assign()` method)	By reference	By reference
String	Immutable (by reference)	Immutable (by reference)	By value
Function	Immutable (by reference)	Immutable (by reference)	By reference

II

Client-Side JavaScript

This part of the book, Chapters 10 through 20, documents JavaScript as it is implemented in web browsers. These chapters introduce a host of new JavaScript objects which represent the web browser and the contents of HTML documents. There are quite a few examples showing typical uses of these new objects. You will find it helpful to study these examples carefully.

10

Client-Side Program Structure

The first part of this book described the core JavaScript language, used in both client- and server-side scripts. Many of the examples we've seen, while legal JavaScript code, had no particular context—they were JavaScript fragments, rather than legal client-side scripts or legal server-side scripts. This chapter provides that context: it explains how JavaScript code can be integrated into HTML files so that it is run by the client web browser.

There are five techniques for including JavaScript code in HTML:

Embedding a JavaScript script between <SCRIPT> and </SCRIPT> tags.
   This is the most common method.

Using the <SCRIPT> tag to refer to a file of JavaScript code.
   This is done by specifying a URL as the value of the SRC attribute, instead of including the JavaScript statements literally between the <SCRIPT> and </SCRIPT> tags. (This is much like including an image on a web page with the <IMG SRC=> tag.) This technique for including external files of JavaScript code into a web page is not available in Navigator 2.0.

Defining event handlers.
   These are function definitions that are invoked by the browser when certain events occur. These event handler functions are defined by specifying JavaScript statements as the value of appropriate attributes within HTML tags. For example, in the <BODY> HTML tag, you can specify arbitrary JavaScript code as the value of the onLoad attribute. This code will be executed when the web page is fully loaded.

Using the special `javascript:` *URL pseudo-protocol.*

You can type these URLs directly into your browser (this doesn't work in Internet Explorer 3.0), or use them as the target of hypertext links in your web documents. When such a link is invoked, the JavaScript code following the `javascript:` protocol identifier will be executed, and the resulting value will be used as the text of the new document.

Embedding code with the JavaScript HTML entity.

This is available in Navigator 3.0 only. Recall that an HTML entity is a code usually representing a special character—either one reserved by HTML or one that does not appear on most keyboards. For example, `&lt;` is an HTML entity that represents the < character. All HTML entities begin with an ampersand and end with a semicolon. The JavaScript entity may contain arbitrary JavaScript statements in curly braces between this ampersand and semicolon. The value of the JavaScript statements becomes the value of the entity. This special JavaScript entity may not be used arbitrarily in HTML; it may only appear within the attribute value of an HTML tag.

The following sections document each of these five JavaScript embedding techniques in more detail. Together, they explain all the ways that JavaScript can be included in web pages—that is, they explain the allowed structure of JavaScript programs on the client side.

10.1 The <SCRIPT> Tag

Client-side JavaScript scripts are part of an HTML file, and are usually coded within the <SCRIPT> and </SCRIPT> tags. Between these tags you may place any number of JavaScript statements, which will be executed in the order they appear as part of the document loading process. (Definitions of JavaScript functions are stored, but they are not executed until they are called.) <SCRIPT> tags may appear in either the <HEAD> or <BODY> of an HTML document.

A single HTML document may contain more than one pair of (non-overlapping) <SCRIPT> and </SCRIPT> tags. These multiple separate scripts will have their statements executed in the order they appear within the document. While separate scripts within a single file are executed at different times during the loading and parsing of the HTML file, they constitute part of the same JavaScript program—functions and variables defined in one script will be available to all scripts that follow in the same file. For example, if you have the following script somewhere in an HTML page:

```
<SCRIPT>var x = 1;</SCRIPT>
```

later on in the same HTML page, you can refer to x, even though it's in a different script block.

The context that matters is the HTML page, not the script block:

```
<SCRIPT>document.write(x);</SCRIPT>
```

Example 10-1 shows a sample HTML file that includes a simple JavaScript program. Note the difference between this example and many of the code fragments shown earlier in the book—this one is integrated with an HTML file and has a clear context in which it runs. Note the use of a LANGUAGE attribute in the <SCRIPT> tag—it will be explained in the following subsection.

Example 10-1: A Simple JavaScript Program in an HTML File

```
<HTML>
<HEAD>
<TITLE>Today's Date</TITLE>
    <SCRIPT LANGUAGE="JavaScript">
    // Define a function for use later on.
    function print_todays_date()
    {
        var d = new Date();  // today's date and time.
        document.write(d.toLocaleString());
    }
    </SCRIPT>
</HEAD>
<BODY>
<HR>The date and time are:<BR><B>
    <SCRIPT LANGUAGE="JavaScript">
    // Now call the function we defined above.
    print_todays_date();
    </SCRIPT>
</B><HR>
</BODY>
</HTML>
```

10.1.1 The LANGUAGE Attribute

The <SCRIPT> tag has an optional LANGUAGE attribute that specifies the scripting language used for the script. This attribute is necessary because there is more than one version of JavaScript, and because there is more than one scripting language that can be embedded between <SCRIPT> and </SCRIPT> tags. By specifying what language a script is written in, you tell a browser whether it should attempt to interpret the script, or whether it is written in a language that the browser doesn't understand, and therefore should be ignored.

If you are writing JavaScript code, you use the LANGUAGE attribute as follows:

```
<SCRIPT LANGUAGE="JavaScript">
    // JavaScript code goes here
</SCRIPT>
```

On the other hand, if you were writing a script in Microsoft's "VBScript" scripting language[*] you would use the attribute like this:

```
<SCRIPT LANGUAGE="VBScript">
    ' VBScript code goes here (' is a comment character like // in JavaScript)
</SCRIPT>
```

When you specify the LANGUAGE="JavaScript" attribute for a script, both Navigator 2.0 and Navigator 3.0 will run the script. There have been quite a few new features added to JavaScript between Navigator 2.0 and 3.0, however, and you may often find yourself writing scripts that simply won't work in Navigator 2.0. In this case, you should specify that the script should only be run by Navigator 3.0 (and browsers that support a compatible version of JavaScript) like this:

```
<SCRIPT LANGUAGE="JavaScript1.1">
    // JavaScript code goes here for Navigator 3.0
    // All this code will be ignored by Navigator 2.0
</SCRIPT>
```

When you set the LANGUAGE attribute to "JavaScript1.1", you inform Navigator 2.0 and Internet Explorer 3.0 that you are using a version of the language that they do not understand. By doing this, you tell these browsers to ignore the <SCRIPT> tags and all the code between them.

JavaScript is, and is likely to remain, the *default* scripting language for the Web. If you omit the LANGUAGE attribute, both Navigator and Internet Explorer default to the value "JavaScript". Nonetheless, because there are now multiple scripting languages available it is a good habit to always use the LANGUAGE attribute to specify exactly what language (or what version) your scripts are written in.

10.1.2 The </SCRIPT> Tag

You may at some point find yourself writing a script that writes a script into some other browser window or frame.[†] If you do this, you'll need to write out a

---

* The language is actually called "Visual Basic Scripting Edition." Obviously, it is a version of Microsoft's Visual Basic language. The only browser that supports it is Internet Explorer 3.0. VBScript interfaces with HTML objects in the same way that JavaScript does, but the core language itself has a different syntax than JavaScript.

† This happens more commonly than you might think; one commonly used feature of JavaScript is the ability to dynamically generate HTML and JavaScript content for display in other browser windows and frames.

</SCRIPT> tag to terminate the script you are writing. You must be careful, though—the HTML parser doesn't know about quoted strings, so if you write out a string that contains the characters "</SCRIPT>" in it, the HTML parser will terminate the currently running script.

To avoid this problem simply break this tag up into pieces, and write it out using an expression like "</" + "SCRIPT>":

```
<SCRIPT>
f1.document.write("<SCRIPT>");
f1.document.write("document.write('<H2>This is the quoted script</H2>')");
f1.document.write("</" + "SCRIPT>");
</SCRIPT>
```

Alternatively, you can escape the / in </SCRIPT> with a backslash:

```
f1.document.write("<\/SCRIPT>");
```

10.2 Including JavaScript Files

In Navigator 3.0 and Internet Explorer 3.0, the <SCRIPT> tag supports a new SRC attribute. The value of this attribute specifies the URL of a file of JavaScript code. It is used like this:

```
<SCRIPT SRC="../../javascript/util.js"></SCRIPT>
```

A JavaScript file is just that—pure JavaScript, without <SCRIPT> tags or any other HTML. A JavaScript file typically has a .js extension, and should be exported by a web server with MIME-type "application/x-javascript". This last point is important, and may require special configuration of your web server in order to successfully use JavaScript files in this way.

The behavior of the <SCRIPT> tag with the SRC attribute specified is exactly as if the contents of the specified JavaScript file appeared directly between the <SCRIPT> and </SCRIPT> tags. Any code that does appear between the open and close <SCRIPT> tags will be ignored by browsers that support the SRC attribute (although it would still be executed by browsers, like Navigator 2.0, that do not recognize the tag). Note that the closing </SCRIPT> tag is required even when the SRC attribute is specified and there is no JavaScript between the <SCRIPT> and </SCRIPT> tags.

Since both Navigator 3.0 and Internet Explorer 3.0 both support the SRC attribute, you cannot assume that any browser that understands the SRC tag also understands JavaScript 1.1. Thus it is a good idea to use the LANGUAGE attribute with the SRC attribute:

```
<SCRIPT LANGUAGE="JavaScript1.1" SRC="../../javascript/util.js"></SCRIPT>
```

Note that the web server that exports the included file also specifies the scripting language that the file contains (although perhaps not the version of the language) by specifying a MIME type for the file.

There are a number of advantages to using the SRC tag:

- It simplifies your HTML files by allowing you to remove large blocks of JavaScript code from them.

- When you have functions or other JavaScript code used by several different HTML files, you can keep it in a single file and read it into each HTML file that needs it. This reduces disk usage, and makes code maintenance much easier.

- When JavaScript functions are used by more than one page, placing them in a separate JavaScript file allows them to be cached by the browser, making them load much more quickly. When JavaScript code is shared by multiple pages, the time savings of caching more than outweigh the small delay required for the browser to open a separate network connection to download the JavaScript file the first time it is requested.

- Because the SRC attribute takes an arbitrary URL as its value, a JavaScript program or web page from one web server can employ code (such as subroutine libraries) exported by other web servers.

10.3 JavaScript and Events

We've seen how JavaScript "scripts" can be embedded into HTML files. The following subsections explain how JavaScript event-handler functions are embedded in HTML files to allow web pages to interact with the user.

10.3.1 The Event-Driven Programming Model

In the old days, computer programs often ran in "batch" mode. This meant that they read a batch of data in, did some computation on that data, and then wrote out the results. Later, with timesharing and text-based terminals, limited kinds of interactivity became possible—the program could ask the user for input, and the user could type in data; the computer could process the data and display the results on-screen.

Nowadays, however, with graphical displays and pointing devices like mouses, the situation is different—programs are generally "event driven," responding to mouse button clicks and keystrokes in a way that depends on the position of the mouse pointer. A web browser is just such a graphical environment, and so client-side JavaScript uses the event-driven programming model.

In order to implement an event-driven program, you must write event-handler functions that take the appropriate actions in response to the user's input. You must also register these event handlers with the system in some way (perhaps just by giving them standard names) so that the system can invoke them at the appropriate times.

10.3.2 Event Handlers in JavaScript

Events do not just occur of their own accord. Generally, they are generated when the user interacts with something in the user interface. When the user interface is an HTML file, as is the case for client-side JavaScript programs, then that "something" will be a HTML object, such as a hypertext link, a button, a drop-down menu or an input field. Since events occur "on" particular objects, it follows that they must be handled "for" those particular objects. Therefore, the logical way to define an event handler is as part of the HTML object to which it responds.

In order to allow us to define JavaScript event handlers as part of HTML object definitions, JavaScript extends HTML by adding new attributes to various HTML tags that define objects. For example, to define an event handler that is invoked when the user clicks on a checkbox in a form, for example, you specify the handler code as an attribute of the HTML tag that defines the checkbox in the form:

```
<INPUT
    TYPE="checkbox"
    NAME="opts"
    VALUE="ignore-case"
    onClick="ignore_case = this.checked;"
>
```

What's of interest to us here is the onClick attribute.[*] The string value of the onClick attribute may contain one or more JavaScript statements. If there is more than one statement, they must be separated from each other with semicolons.[†]

---

[*] The mixed-case capitalization of onClick is a common convention for JavaScript event handlers defined in HTML files. HTML element and attribute names are case-insensitive, but writing "onClick" rather than "ONCLICK" sets off the handlers from standard HTML tags that are, by convention, shown in all capitals.

[†] The statements may not be separated by newlines: while an HTML attribute value normally may contain newlines, this doesn't work with JavaScript.

When the specified event—in this case, a click—occurs on the checkbox the JavaScript code within the string will be executed.

While you can include any number of JavaScript statements within an event-handler definition, a common technique, when more than one or two simple statements are required, is to define the body of an event handler as a function between <SCRIPT> and </SCRIPT> tags, and then to simply invoke this function from the event handler. This keeps most of your actual JavaScript code within scripts and reduces the need to mingle JavaScript and HTML.

Most form elements have one or more event handlers that you can define. Buttons, checkboxes, and radio buttons are among the elements that can specify an onClick handler. Text and Textarea elements can have onChange, onFocus, and onBlur event handlers that are invoked when the user changes the displayed value or when the user gives keyboard focus to, or takes away keyboard focus from, the element. In addition to these HTML form–related event handlers, there are also handlers invoked whenever the user moves the mouse over a hypertext link and whenever a web page is loaded into the browser or unloaded from the browser.

Table 10-1 lists the event handlers defined by all client-side JavaScript objects. The objects themselves will be introduced in some of the following chapters, but this table will, for now, illustrate what a diverse collection of event handlers is supported by JavaScript. Once you've learned about all of the client-side objects supported by JavaScript, this table should serve as a convenient event-handler reference. Note that this table lists event handlers supported by Navigator 3.0; not all those shown are supported by Navigator 2.0 or Internet Explorer 3.0.

Table 10–1: JavaScript Event Handlers

Object	Supported Event Handlers		
Area	onClick()[a]	onMouseOut()	onMouseOver()
Button	onBlur()[b]	onClick()	onFocus()[b]
Checkbox	onBlur()[b]	onClick()	onFocus()[b]
FileUpload	onBlur()	onChange()	onFocus()
Form	onReset()	onSubmit()	
Frame	onLoad()	onUnload()	
Image	onAbort()	onError()	onLoad()
Link	onClick()	onMouseOut()	onMouseOver()
Radio	onBlur()[b]	onClick()	onFocus()[b]
Reset	onBlur()[b]	onClick()	onFocus()[b]

Table 10-1: JavaScript Event Handlers (continued)

Object	Supported Event Handlers				
Select	onBlur()[b]	onChange()	onFocus()[b]		
Submit	onBlur()[b]	onClick()	onFocus()[b]		
Text	onBlur()	onChange()	onFocus()		
Textarea	onBlur()	onChange()	onFocus()		
Window	onBlur()	onError()	onFocus()	onLoad()	onUnload()

a. Not supported in Navigator 3.0 on Windows platforms.
b. Not supported in Navigator 3.0 on Unix platforms.

10.3.3 Event Handlers as Functions

Specifying an event handler as a string within an appropriate HTML tag defines a JavaScript function that is invoked by the browser when the appropriate event occurs. In fact, in Navigator 3.0, event-handler functions are stored as properties of the objects for which they are defined. Thus, if the checkbox defined in the example above was accessible in JavaScript as document.forms[0].opts[2], the event handler defined in the object's HTML tag would be available to JavaScript code as:

```
document.forms[0].opts[2].onclick
```

Note the capitalization of onclick here and recall that JavaScript *is* case-sensitive while HTML is not. Event-handler properties in JavaScript are always all lowercase, even if the corresponding HTML happens to appear in mixed-case or all-caps.

In Navigator 3.0, you can use event-handler properties in the ways you can use any method property. You can use it to invoke the event handler explicitly, to assign the event handler to some other variable or pass it to a function, and even to define or redefine an event handler by assigning an appropriate function to the event-handler property—thereby avoiding the need to define the event handler with a (sometimes long and awkward) string value of an HTML attribute.

10.3.4 Event Handlers in <SCRIPT> Tags

In Internet Explorer, but not in Navigator, there is an alternative syntax for defining event handlers. It involves using new FOR and EVENT attributes to the <SCRIPT> tag to specify code that constitutes an event handler for a named object and a named event. Using this Internet Explorer technique, we could rewrite the checkbox example shown earlier like this:

```
<INPUT TYPE="checkbox" NAME="opts" VALUE="ignore-case">
<SCRIPT FOR="opts" EVENT="onClick">
    ignore_case = this.checked;
</SCRIPT>
```

Note that the value of the FOR attribute must be an object name assigned with the NAME attribute when the object is defined. And the value of the EVENT attribute is the name of the event handler (but not the name of the event itself).

There is a certain elegance to specifying event handlers in this way—it avoids the need to add new JavaScript-specific attributes to all the HTML objects. Nevertheless, since this technique is not supported by Navigator, I do not recommend its use.

10.3.5 Timer Events

There is another type of event, besides those generated through user interaction. These are events generated when specified periods of time have elapsed; they are known as timer events, or "timeouts." Timeouts are important to any JavaScript program that must perform an action on some regular schedule, even when the user is not actively interacting with the browser. Applications of timeouts include clocks and animation.

You use setTimeout() (a method of the Window object) to specify that a timeout should occur a specified number of milliseconds in the future. Timer events do not have predefined event handlers as other types of events do. Instead, the code to be executed when the specified time interval elapses is passed as a string argument to setTimeout(). For example, the following code arranges for a timer event to occur in 1 second (1000 milliseconds). When that timer event occurs, the function show_date_time() will be invoked.

```
// call the show_date_time() function 1 second from now
setTimeout("show_date_time();", 1000);
```

When you register a timeout with code like that above, only one timer event will occur—i.e., the timer event will occur one second in the future; it will not repeat itself every second after that. When you do want a timer that repeats periodically, you simply include code in the "handler" that re-registers the timeout by calling setTimeout() again. This is a useful technique for animation and related tasks. It might be done like this:

```
function animate_status_line_annoyingly()
{
    // Set the Window.status property here,
```

```
        // then arrange to be called later so we can do it again!
        setTimeout("animate_status_line_annoyingly()", 1000);
    }
```

In complex programs you may need to use more than one timeout. This is no problem; JavaScript can keep track of any number of pending timer events. After you have registered a timeout with `setTimeout()`, but before the timer event has actually occurred, you can cancel the timeout with the `clearTimeout()` method. See the reference section of this book for complete detains on `Window.setTimeout()` and `Window.clearTimeout()`.

10.4 *JavaScript in URLs*

Another way that JavaScript code can be included on the client side is in a URL following the `javascript:` pseudo-protocol specifier. This special protocol type specifies that the body of the URL is arbitrary JavaScript code to be interpreted by the JavaScript interpreter. If the JavaScript code in a `javascript:` URL contains multiple statements, the statements must be separated from one another by semicolons. Such a URL might look like the following:

```
javascript:var now = new Date(); "<h1>The time is:</h1>" + now;
```

When the browser "loads" one of these JavaScript URLs, it executes the JavaScript code contained in the URL and displays the "document" referred to by the URL. This "document" is the string value of the last JavaScript statement in the URL. This string will be formatted and displayed just like any other document loaded into the browser.

More commonly, a JavaScript URL will contain JavaScript statements that perform actions but return no value. For example:

```
javascript:alert("Hello World!")
```

When this sort of URL is "loaded," the browser executes the JavaScript code, but, because there is no value to display as the new document, it does not modify the currently displayed document.

Note that in Navigator 3.0, you can use the `void` operator to force an expression to have no value. This is useful when you want to execute an assignment statement, for example, but do not want to display the assigned value in the browser window. (Recall that assignment statements are also expressions, and that they evaluate to the value of the right-hand-side of the assignment.)

The `javascript:` URL can be used anywhere you'd use a regular URL. It is not altogether clear, however, why you'd want to do so. In Navigator, one important use for this syntax is typing it directly into the **Location** field of your browser, where it allows you to try out and test arbitrary JavaScript code without having to get out your editor and create an HTML file containing the code. In fact, Navigator takes this idea even further. As described in Chapter 1, *Introduction to JavaScript*, if you enter the URL javascript: alone, with no JavaScript code following it, Navigator displays a JavaScript interpreter page that allows you to sequentially enter and execute lines of code. Unfortunately, neither of these techniques work in Internet Explorer 3.0.

javascript: URLs can also be used in other contexts. You might use one as the target of a hypertext link, for example. Then when the user clicks on the link, the specified JavaScript code will be executed. Or, if you specify a javascript: URL as the value of the ACTION attribute of a <FORM> tag, then the JavaScript code in the URL will be executed when the user submits the form. In these contexts, the javascript: URL is essentially a substitute for an event-handler. Event handlers and javascript: URLs can often be used essentially interchangeably, and which you choose is basically a stylistic matter.

There are a few circumstances where a javascript: URL can be used with objects that do not support event handlers. For example the <AREA> tag does not support an onClick() event-handler on Windows platforms in Navigator 3.0 (one will be added in the next release, though). So if you want to execute JavaScript code when the user clicks on a client-side image map, you must use a javascript: URL.

Internet Explorer supports the javascript: protocol specifiers for URLs, but does not have a special built-in JavaScript interpreter page. A future version of Explorer will probably also support a vbscript: protocol.

10.5 JavaScript Entities

In Navigator 3.0 and later, JavaScript code may appear in one additional location in a web page. This is in a JavaScript entity within the value of an attribute of an HTML tag. Recall that an HTML entity is a sequence of characters like < that represents a special character like <. A JavaScript entity is similar. It has the following syntax:

```
&{ JavaScript-statements };
```

The entity may contain any number of JavaScript statements, which must be separated from one another by semicolons. It must begin with an ampersand and an open curly bracket and end with a close curly bracket and a semicolon.

Whenever an entity is encountered in HTML, it is replaced with its value. The value of a JavaScript entity is the value of the last JavaScript statement or expression within the entity, converted to a string.

In general, entities can be used anywhere within HTML code. The JavaScript entity, however, is restricted to appear only within the value of HTML attributes. These entities allow you to, in effect, write conditional HTML. Typical usages might look like these:

```
<BODY BGCOLOR="&{favorite_color();};">
<INPUT TYPE="text" NAME="lastname" VALUE="&{defaults.lastname};">
```

10.6 Execution of JavaScript Programs

The previous sections of this chapter have discussed the *structure* of JavaScript programs. This section moves on to discuss how those programs are executed by the JavaScript interpreter. Although it may seem obvious, it is important to understand how and when a web browser executes the JavaScript code embedded in various parts of an HTML file. The subsections below explain how different forms of JavaScript code are executed and also explain the implications that you must be aware of when writing JavaScript programs.

10.6.1 Scripts

JavaScript statements that appear between <SCRIPT> and </SCRIPT> tags are executed in the order that they appear, and, when more than one script appears in a file, those scripts are executed in the order they appear. The same rules apply to scripts included from separate files with the SRC attribute. This much is obvious.

The detail that is not so obvious, but that is important to remember, is that execution of scripts occurs as part of the web browser's HTML parsing process. Thus, if a script appears in the <HEAD> of an HTML document, none of the <BODY> of the document will have been defined yet. This means that the Form, Link, and other JavaScript objects that represent the contents of the document body will not have been created yet and cannot be manipulated by that code. (We'll learn more about these objects in Chapter 12, *Programming with Windows*, and the chapters that follow it, and you can find complete details in the reference section of this book.)

Because JavaScript scripts are evaluated as part of the web browser's HTML parsing, the JavaScript objects that represent parts of the HTML document do not exist until they are parsed, and your scripts should not attempt to manipulate objects that haven't been created yet. For example, you can't write a script that manipulates the contents of an HTML form if the script appears before the form in the

HTML file. There are some other, similar, rules that apply on a case-by-case basis. For example, there are properties of the JavaScript Document object that may be set only from a script in the <HEAD> of an HTML document, before Navigator has begun to parse the document content from the <BODY> section. Any special rules of this sort are documented in this book's reference entry for the affected object or property.

As noted above, scripts that use the SRC attribute to read in an external JavaScript file are executed just as scripts that include their code directly in the file are. What this means is that the HTML parser and the JavaScript interpreter must both stop and wait for the external JavaScript file to be downloaded—scripts cannot be downloaded in parallel as embedded images can. Downloading an external file of JavaScript code, even over a relatively fast modem connection, can cause notice-able delays in the loading and execution of a web page. Of course, once the JavaScript code is cached locally, this problem effectively disappears.

Note that scripts using the Internet Explorer FOR and EVENT tags are not executed following the rules described here—they should rightly be considered event han-dlers, rather than scripts, and are executed in the same way (described below) that more conventionally defined event handlers are.

In Navigator 2.0, there is a notable bug relating to execution of scripts: whenever the web browser is resized, all the scripts within it are re-interpreted.

10.6.2 Functions

Remember that defining a function is not the same as executing it. It is perfectly safe to define a function that manipulates variables that aren't declared yet, or objects that haven't been created yet. You simply must take care that the function is not executed or invoked until the necessary variables, objects, and so on, all exist. We said above that you can't write a script to manipulate an HTML form if the script appears before the form in the HTML file. You can, however, write a script that defines a function to manipulate the form, regardless of the relative location of the script and form. In fact, this is quite a common thing to do. Many JavaScript programs start off with a script at the beginning of the file that does nothing more than define functions that will be used elsewhere further down in the HTML file.

It is also common to write JavaScript programs that use scripts simply to define functions that are later invoked through event handlers. As we'll see in the next section, you must take care in this case to insure two things: first, that all functions are defined before any event handler attempts to invoke them. And second, that event handlers and the functions they invoke do not attempt to use objects that have not been defined yet.

10.6.3 Event Handlers

As we've seen, defining an event handler creates a JavaScript function. These event-handler functions are defined as part of the HTML parsing process, but, like functions defined directly by scripts, event handlers are not executed immediately. Event handler execution is *asynchronous*. Since events occur, in general, when the user interacts with HTML objects, there is no way to predict when an event handler will be invoked. In fact, event handlers may be invoked even before a web page is fully loaded and parsed. This is easier to understand if you imagine a slow network connection—even a half-loaded document may display hypertext links and form elements that the user can interact with, thereby causing event handlers to be invoked before the second half of the document is loaded.

The fact that event handlers are invoked asynchronously has two important implications. First, if your event handler invokes functions, you must be sure that the functions are already defined before the handler calls them. One way to guarantee this is to define all your functions in the <HEAD> of an HTML document. This section of a document will always be completely parsed (and any functions in it defined) before the <BODY> of the document is parsed. Since all objects that define event handlers must themselves be defined in the <BODY>, functions in the <HEAD> are guaranteed to be defined before any event handlers are invoked.

The second implication of the fact that event handlers may be invoked before a document is fully loaded is that you must be sure that event handlers do not attempt to manipulate HTML objects that have not yet been parsed and created. An event handler may always safely manipulate its own object, of course, and also any objects that are defined before it in the HTML file. One strategy is simply to define your web page user interface in such a way that event handlers always refer only to objects defined before they are. For example, if you define a form that contains event handlers only on the **Submit** and **Reset** buttons, then you simply need to place these buttons at the bottom of the form (which is where good UI style says they should go anyway).

In more complex programs, you may not be able to ensure that event handlers will only manipulate objects defined before them, and in these programs you need to take extra care. If an event handler only manipulates objects defined within the same form, it is pretty unlikely that you'll ever have problems. When you start manipulating objects in other forms or in other frames, however, this starts to be a real concern. One technique is to test for the existence of the object you want to manipulate before you manipulate it. You can do this simply by comparing it (and any parent objects) to null. For example:

```
<SCRIPT>
function set_name_other_frame(name)
{
    if (parent.frames[1] == null) return;   // other frame not defined yet
    if (parent.frames[1].document) return;  // document not loaded in it yet
    if (!parent.frames[1].document.myform) return;  // form not defined yet
    if (!parent.frames[1].document.myform.lastname) return; // field not defined

    parent.frames[1].document.myform.name.value = name;
}
</SCRIPT>

<INPUT TYPE="text" NAME="lastname"
       onChange="set_name_other_frame(this.value)";
>
```

Another technique that an event handler can use to ensure that all required objects are defined involves the onLoad() event handler. This event handler is defined in the <BODY> or <FRAMESET> tag of an HTML file and is invoked when the document or frameset is fully loaded. If you set a flag within the onLoad() event handler, then other event handlers can test this flag to see if they can safely run, with the knowledge that the document is fully loaded and all objects it contains are defined. For example:

```
<BODY onLoad="window.loaded = true;">
  <FORM>
    <INPUT TYPE="button" VALUE="Press Me"
           onClick="if (window.loaded != true) return; doit();"
    >
  </FORM>
</BODY>
```

Unfortunately, in Navigator 2.0, documents that contain images and do not contain frames may invoke the onLoad() handler early, and so this technique is not fool-proof. A possible solution is to include a small script at the very *end* of the document and have this script set the necessary flag:

```
    <SCRIPT>window.loaded = true;</SCRIPT>
  </BODY>
</HTML>
```

The following subsection contains more information on the onLoad() event handler, and its partner, the onUnload() handler.

10.6.4 onLoad() and onUnload() Event Handlers

The onLoad() event handler and its partner the onUnload() handler are worth a special mention in the context of execution order of JavaScript programs. Both these event handlers are defined in the <BODY> or <FRAMESET> tag of an HTML file. (No HTML file can legally contain both these tags.) The onLoad() handler is executed when the document or frameset is fully loaded, which means that all images have been downloaded and displayed, all sub-frames have loaded, any Java applets and plug-ins (Navigator) have started running, and so on. The onUnload() handler is executed just before the page is "unloaded", which occurs when the browser is about to move on to a new page. Be aware that when you are working with multiple frames, there is no guarantee of the order in which the onLoad() event handler will be invoked for the various frames, except that the handler for the parent frame will be invoked after the handlers of all its children frames (although this is buggy and doesn't always work correctly in Navigator 2.0).

The onLoad() event handler lets you perform initialization for your web page. And the onUnload() event handler lets you undo any lingering effects of the initialization, or perform any other necessary "clean up" on your page. For example, onLoad() could set the Window.defaultStatus property to display a special message in the browser's status bar. Then the onUnload() handler would restore the defaultStatus property to its default (the empty string) so that the message does not persist on other pages.

10.6.5 JavaScript URL Execution

JavaScript code in a javascript: URL is not executed when the document containing the URL is loaded. It is not interpreted until the browser tries to "load the document" that the URL refers to. This may be when a user types in a JavaScript URL, or, more likely, it is when the user follows a link, clicks on a client-side image map, or submits a form. javascript: URLs are usually equivalent to event handlers, and like event handlers, the code in those URLs can be executed before a document is fully loaded. Thus, you must take the same precautions with javascript: URLs that you take with event handlers to ensure that they do not attempt to reference objects (or functions) that are not yet defined.

10.6.6 JavaScript Entity Execution

Since JavaScript entities are used as the value of HTML attributes, these pieces of JavaScript code are executed during the process of HTML parsing that is done while the document is loading. In fact, since the JavaScript code in an entity produces a value that becomes part of the HTML itself, the HTML parsing process is dependent on the JavaScript interpreter in this case. JavaScript entities can always be replaced by more cumbersome scripts that write the affected HTML tags dynamically. For example, the following line of HTML:

```
<INPUT TYPE="text" NAME="lastname" VALUE="&{defaults.lastname};">
```

can be replaced with these lines:

```
<SCRIPT>
   document.write('<INPUT TYPE="text" NAME="lastname" VALUE="' +
                  defaults.lastname +
                  '">');
</SCRIPT>
```

For all intents and purposes, JavaScript entities are executed just like their equivalent scripts are.

10.7 *JavaScript and Threads*

Since a web browser can display multiple documents at the same time by using multiple windows and frames, and since any of those documents can contain JavaScript code, it is natural to wonder whether more than one script can be running at the same time.

The answer is no. Although Navigator, like most browsers, is multithreaded, JavaScript in Navigator 2.0 and 3.0 is single-threaded: only one script may run at a time. If a script is running, other scripts will not be able to run until it has finished. This is an implementation-dependent feature of Navigator, not something inherent about client-side JavaScript itself. It could be that we will see multithreaded JavaScript in future releases.

Because JavaScript is not multithreaded, scripts and event handlers should be written so that they do only small amounts of computation and return quickly. If a script or event handler runs for more than about a half second, the delay will potentially be noticeable and annoying to the user. If your script runs for even longer than this (say 3 or more seconds) then the browser may appear to have "locked up" or "frozen" and the user may think that it has crashed. Note that Navigator 2.0 and 3.0 do not display the **Stop** button while JavaScript code is running, so there is no way for the user to abort a script that is taking a long time (see the subsection below for an exception, however).

If you need to write a computation-intensive script, one technique is to break it up into small chunks and have each chunk do its computation, and then invoke the next chunk through the `Window.setTimeout()` method. Doing this, even with a 0 millisecond delay, will give Navigator a chance to do any updating it needs to do itself *and will also give scripts from other windows a chance to run.* In other words, as far as the user is concerned, it will look as if JavaScript is multithreaded. See the reference section for more details on the `setTimeout()` method of the Window object.

10.7.1 Infinite Loops in JavaScript

JavaScript is one of the few programming languages in which you cannot write an infinite loop! In order to prevent buggy or malicious code from monopolizing the browser and consuming lots of CPU time,[*] the JavaScript interpreter keeps track of how long a script has run for. When a script seems excessively long, Navigator pops up a dialog box that informs you that a script is still running ("Lengthy JavaScript still running. Continue?"), and gives you the choice of continuing it or aborting it.

Execution time is not measured in absolute time for these purposes, but in the number of branches the JavaScript code makes. Every one million branches, Navigator will ask again if you want to continue running it. For example, a very simple loop like `for(var i = 0;;i++);` will run one million times before Navigator asks you if you want to abort it. More complex loops will run fewer times. The actual time elapsed before Navigator gives you the option of aborting the script depends entirely upon the speed of your computer.

---

[*] When malicious code does this intentionally, it is called a "denial-of-service attack".

11

Windows and the JavaScript Name Space

The interesting features of client-side JavaScript are those that integrate the programming language with the functionality of the browser. Since the most notable function of any web browser is its ability to display HTML text in a window, the Window object is the central, most important object in JavaScript. As we'll see in this chapter, the Window object is also the root of the "object hierarchy"—that is, all other HTML objects in JavaScript are accessed as properties of the Window object, or as properties of those properties. JavaScript HTML objects other than the Window object will be documented in the chapters that follow this one.

11.1 The Implicit Window Reference

In client-side JavaScript, the web browser window is represented by a Window object. This object has methods like `alert()` and `prompt()` that pop up dialog boxes to display messages and get input from the user. It has properties like `location` that specify the URL of the document currently displayed in the window and also allows programs to force the window to load a new document. As further examples, the Window object also has a `status` property that controls the message displayed in the browser status line, and a `history` property that refers to an object which allows programs to move the browser backwards and forwards through the user's browsing history.

While we've named various methods and properties of the Window object, we haven't named the Window object itself yet. ("Window" is the object's type, of course, not a reference to the actual object.) In fact, the Window object simply does not have a name—that is, there is no variable that contains a reference to the object that represents the browser window. The Window object is so central to client-side JavaScript that every JavaScript expression is evaluated in the context of that object. So whenever you use properties like `history` or methods like `alert()`, you implicitly refer to the `history` property of the Window object and the `alert()` method of the Window object. This reference to the window is implicit in all JavaScript expressions.

Having said this much, you may be confused, because you've probably seen JavaScript code that uses expressions like this:

```
window.alert("The URL is: " + window.location);
```

This is how it works: the Window object actually has a property named `window` that refers to itself. Thus, the expressions above are still implicitly evaluated in the context of the Window object. They reference the `window` property, which is simply another reference, explicit this time, to the same Window object. Then these expressions use this explicit reference to refer to the `alert()` method or `location` property. Therefore, using `window` in the above expression is unnecessary, and the following would work just as well.

```
alert("The URL is: " + location);
```

The Window object has another property, `self`, that is a synonym for the `window` property. In some cases, it is useful to use one of these properties to make your code clearer or to disambiguate it. Using these properties is largely a stylistic matter, however. For example, you might find it clearer to rewrite the JavaScript statement above like this:

```
alert("The URL is: " + self.location);
```

There are also a few occasions in which you need an explicit reference to the Window object—if you want to pass it as an argument to a function, for example. The `self` and `window` properties are useful in these cases.

11.2 *Multiple Windows and Explicit Window References*

The difficulty with an implicit window reference is that most web browsers, including Navigator, allow more than one browser window to be open at a time.

Since there can be more than one window, there must be more than one Window object, but the implicit window reference can only refer to one of them. Logically, the implicit reference is a reference to the *current* window—the window that is displaying the HTML document that contains the JavaScript code being executed.

If you want use the properties or methods of a Window object other than the current, implicit, window, you must obtain an explicit reference to it. In general, the only way to obtain an explicit reference to another Window object is to create that Window (and the browser window it represents) yourself. You open a new browser window, and create the Window object that represents it with the open( ) method of the Window object. You might use it like this. (Note that we access it through the window property of the implicit Window object to make more clear what it is we are opening.)

```
var newwin = window.open("sitemap.html", "site_map_window");
```

The first argument to this method is the URL of the document to be displayed in the new window. The second argument is a name for the new window. We'll see what this name can be used for later in this chapter. For now, note that this is not a variable name; you can't refer directly to the new window with this name. There is also a third, optional argument to the Window.open( ) method that specifies the size of the new window, and the features, such as a menubar, toolbar, and so on, that it should contain. See the reference section for full details on this third argument and on the method itself.

The most important feature of the open( ) method is the value it returns. This is the explicit reference to the new Window object that we need. In the line of code above, we store this reference in a variable named newwin. (Note the difference between the name of the variable that contains a reference to the window and the name of the window itself.) With this explicit reference to the new Window object, we can use properties and methods of the new window. For example, to set the text in the new window's status line, we could do this:

```
newwin.defaultStatus = "Site Map. Click map for details.";
```

The code shown above is intended to run in the original window, and use the newwin variable defined in that window to refer explicitly to the newly created window. Any code in the new window (i.e., JavaScript that is part of the *sitemap.html* document displayed in that window) can of course refer to that new window with an implicit reference—for that code, the new window is the "current" window. This raises the question of how code in the new window can refer to the original window, in order to use properties and methods of that Window object. Once again, an explicit reference is needed. In this case, the original

window can provide that explicit reference for the use of the new window. The
code to do so might look like this:

```
// Create a new window.
var newwin = window.open("sitemap.html", "site_map_window");


// Set a property in the new window that contains an explicit reference
// to the original window. There is nothing special about the name "creator";
// we can choose any property name we want.
newwin.creator = self;
```

Code in the new window can use this `creator` property to refer back to the original window:

```
// Code in the new window. Note that we refer to the creator property
// of the new window using the implicit window reference for that window.
creator.alert("Hello old window, this is the new window!");
```

In Navigator 3.0 and Internet Explorer 3.0, the `open()` method automatically creates an `opener` property for the new window that refers back to the window that
opened it. This `opener` property can be used just like the `creator` property in the
example above.

We've seen how we can use the `Window.open()` method to create a new browser
window and obtain an explicit reference to it. The `open()` method also allows us
to obtain an explicit reference to windows that already exist, if we know the name
of that window. We mean here the name of the window itself, of course, not the
name of a variable that refers to the window. This is the name specified by the
second argument to `Window.open()`. In the examples above, we've used the
name "site_map_window". So, if we know that a window by this name already
exists, but we do not have a variable or a property that refers to the Window
object for that window, then we can obtain such a reference like this:

```
// Return a reference to a named window that already exists, or, if it
// doesn't actually exist, then create a window with this name.
site_map = window.open("", "site_map_window");
```

The syntax used here is exactly the same as that we used when creating a window—if you specify the name of window that already exists, the `open()` method
returns a reference to that window rather than creating a new one. On the other
hand, if no window with the specified name exists, then `open()` creates one and
returns a reference to it. Note that in Navigator 3.0 the `open()` sets the `opener`
property of the named window whenever it is called, not only when it is created.
So, this property of a window refers either to the window that created it or to the
window that most recently looked it up by name.

11.2.1 Closing Windows

After all this talk of opening new windows, we should note that the Window object also has a `close()` method. If your program has created and used a new browser window, and that window is no longer needed, then it can close the new window with code like this:

```
window.close(site_map);
```

Or, the new window could close itself when it is no longer needed:

```
window.close(self);
```

Once a window has been closed, you should no longer use any of its properties or methods. (In Navigator 3.0, you may safely test the `closed` property of a closed window—if this property is `true` it lets you know that the window has already been closed and that you should not use any of the other properties.)

Note that you are only allowed to automatically close windows that your code created. If you attempt to close a window that the user opened, your attempt will either fail (in Navigator 2.0) or will pop up a prompt dialog asking the user if the window should really be closed (Navigator 3.0). This prevents malicious coders from creating web pages to lure unsuspecting surfers in and then close their main (and only) browser window!

11.3 Windows and Frames

While Navigator (and other browsers) can display multiple HTML pages in multiple browser windows, it can also display multiple pages within a single window by using *frames*—a feature that allows a single browser window to be divided horizontally or vertically (or both) into individual sections that each display a separate HTML document. Although frames are not strictly windows in their own right, they behave like windows in many ways, and in JavaScript, each frame is represented with a Window object. Thus the Window class can represent both top-level browser windows and frames within a browser window (and frames within other frames, of course).

Each Window object has a `frames[]` array property that contains references to each of the frames (if any) that the window contains. The `frames.length` property specifies the number of frames in the array. Also, each Window object has a `parent` property that refers to the window or frame that contains the object (top-level browser windows have their `parent` property set to themselves). Thus, if a browser window contains two frames, and JavaScript code is running in the first frame, that code refers to the first frame implicitly or with the `self` or `window` properties. To refer to the second frame, that code could use the expression `parent.frames[1]`.

The `top` property is similar to the `parent` property, but differs for frames that are recursively contained within other frames. The `top` property always contains a reference to the top-level browser window that contains the frame, which, in the recursive frames case, is not the same as the parent of the frame. Figure 11-1 illustrates the relationship between frames and windows, and shows a schematic representation of the `frames[]` array, and the `parent`, `top`, `window`, and `self` properties.

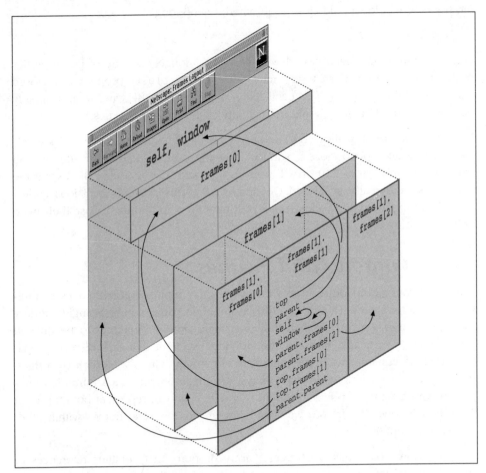

Figure 11-1: Browser windows and frames

Top-level windows and frames have a significantly different representation on the screen, so it would seem that they would have a different representation in JavaScript. As we've seen, however, they are both represented by the Window object, and have the same properties and methods. As it turns out, the practical differences between top-level windows and frames really are quite minor:

- For top-level windows, the `parent` and `top` properties are simply references to the window itself; these properties are really useful only when used with frames, or when used to distinguish a frame from a top-level window; you can check for a top-level window with `if (parent == self)`.

- The `alert()`, `confirm()`, and `prompt()` methods pop up dialog boxes. While these methods may be invoked through any Window object, including those that represent frames, the dialog boxes always appear centered over the top-level window, not over individual frames.

- Setting the `status` or `defaultStatus` properties of a top-level window sets the text that appears in the browser status line. When these properties are set for a frame, the status line only displays the specified text when the mouse is over the frame.

11.4 Window and Frame Names

The second, optional* argument to the `open()` method discussed earlier is a name for the newly created window. By giving a top-level browser window a name, we've seen that you can look up a reference to that window by calling the `open()` method again. But you can also refer to a window by name in another way: by specifying the window name as the value of the `TARGET` attribute of the `<A>`, `<MAP>`, and `<FORM>` tags. What this does is tell the browser where you want the results of activating a link, clicking on an image map, or submitting a form to be displayed. For example, if you have two windows, one named "table_of_contents" and the other named "mainwin", then you might have HTML like the following in the "table_of_contents" window:

```
<A HREF="chapter01.html" TARGET="mainwin">
Chapter 1, Introduction
</A>
```

When the user clicks on this hyperlink, the browser will load the specified URL, but instead of displaying it in the window the link is in, it will display it in the window named "mainwin". If there is no window with the name "mainwin", then clicking on the link will create a new window with that name, and load the specified URL into it.

Since frames are a type of window, frames can also have names that can be used with the `TARGET` attribute. You specify a name for a frame with the `NAME` attribute of the `<FRAME>` tag that creates the frame.

---

* This argument is *not* optional in Internet Explorer 3.0.

There is even another reason to give names to frames. We've seen that every Window object has a `frames[]` array that contains references to each of its frames. This array contains all frames in a window (or frame) whether or not they have names. But if a frame is given a name, then a reference to that frame is also stored in a new property of the parent Window object. The name of that new property is the same as the name of the frame. Therefore, if you create a frame with HTML like this:

```
<FRAME NAME="table_of_contents" SRC="toc.html">
```

Then you can refer to that frame from another, sibling frame with:

```
parent.table_of_contents
```

This makes your code easier to read and understand than using (and relying on) a hardcoded array index as you'd have to do with an unnamed frame:

```
parent.frames[1]
```

Much of the discussion in this section has been about the TARGET attribute and other features of HTML rather than about JavaScript itself. If windows can have names, then it is logical to expect that Window objects have a JavaScript property that contains the window name. This is indeed true. The `name` property of any Window object contains the name of that window. In Navigator 2.0, this property is read-only. In Navigator 3.0, however, you can set this property, thereby changing the name of a window or a frame. One common reason to do this is to set the name of the initial browser window. When Navigator starts up, the initial window has no name, and so it cannot be used with the TARGET attribute. If you set the `name` property of the window, however, you can then use that name in TARGET attributes.

11.5 The JavaScript Name Space

We've said that the Window object is really the most central one in client-side JavaScript. This is because it is the object that defines the *name space* of a program. We saw earlier that every JavaScript expression implicitly refers to the current window. This includes expressions as simple as `window`, which is a reference to a property within the current window that happens to refer to that window itself.

But if every expression refers to the current window, then so does code like this:

```
var i;  // declare a variable i
i = 0;  // assign the variable a value
```

The assignment i = 0 is actually the same as writing

```
window.i = 0;
```

This is an important point to understand about client-side JavaScript: *variables are nothing more than properties of the current window*. (This is not true for local variables declared within a function, however.)

One implication of the fact that variables are properties of the current Window object is that two variables with the same name may be declared in different windows or different frames, and they will not overwrite or conflict with each other.

Another implication is that JavaScript code running in one window or frame may read and write variables declared by code in another window or frame, as long as the first window knows how to refer to the second window.[*] So, if a top-level window has two frames, and code in the first frame does the following:

```
parent.frames[1].i = 3;
```

it is equivalent to code in the second frame doing the following:

```
i = 3;
```

The final implication of the equivalence between variables and window properties is that there is no such thing as a "global variable" in client-side JavaScript—i.e., there are no user-created variables that are global to Navigator as a whole, across all windows and frames. Each variable is defined only within one window.

Recall that the function keyword that defines functions declares a variable just like the var keyword does. Since functions are referred to by variables, they to are defined only within the window in which they are declared. That is, if you define a function in one window, you cannot use it in another, unless you explicitly assign the function to a variable in the other window.

Remember that constructors are also functions, so when you define a class of objects with a constructor function and an associated prototype object, that class is only defined for a single window. (See Chapter 7, *Objects*, for details on constructor functions and prototype objects.) This is true of predefined constructors as well as constructors you define yourself. The String constructor is available in all windows, but that is because all windows automatically are given a property that refers to this predefined constructor function. Just as each window has its own separate reference to the constructor, each window has a separate copy of the prototype object for a constructor. So if you write a new method for manipulating JavaScript strings, and make it a method of the String class by assigning it to the

---

[*] See Chapter 20, *JavaScript Security*, however, for a discussion of a "security hobble" that prevents scripts from one web server from reading values from windows that contain data from other web servers.

`String.prototype` object in the current window, then all strings in that window will be able to use the new method. But the new method will not be accessible to strings defined in other windows.

Bear in mind that this discussion of variables and Window object properties does not apply to variables declared within functions. These "local" variables exist only within the function body and are not accessible outside of the function. Also, note that there is one difference between variables and properties of the current window. This difference is revealed in the behavior of the `for/in` loop. Window properties that were created by variable declarations are not returned by the `for/in` loop, while "regular" properties of the Window are. See Chapter 5, *Statements*, for details.

11.5.1 Variable Scope

We saw above that top-level variables are implemented as properties of the current window or frame object. In Chapter 6, *Functions*, we saw that local variables in a function are implemented as transient properties of the function object itself. From these facts, we can begin to understand variable scoping in JavaScript; we can begin to see how variable names are looked up.

Suppose a function f uses the identifier x in an expression. In order to evaluate the expression, JavaScript must look up the value of this identifier. To do so, it first checks if f itself has a property named x. If so, the value of that property is used; it is an argument, local variable, or static variable assigned to the function. If f does not have a property named x, then JavaScript next checks to see if the window that f is defined in has a property named x, and, if so, it uses the value of that property. In this case x would be a top-level or "global" (to that window) variable. Note that JavaScript looks up x in the window in which f was defined, which may not be the same as the window that is executing the script that called f. This is a subtle but important difference that can arise in some circumstances.

A similar process occurs if the function f uses `document.title` in an expression. In order to evaluate `document.title`, JavaScript must first evaluate `document`. It does this in the same way it evaluated x. First it sees if f has a property named `document`. If not, it checks whether its Window object has such a property. Once it has obtained a value for `document`, it proceeds to look up `title` as a property that object—it does not check the properties of the function or window, in this case, of course. In this example, the code probably refers to the `document` property of the Window object, and if the function inadvertently defined a local variable named `document`, the `document.title` expression might well be evaluated incorrectly.

What we learn from these examples is that identifiers are evaluated in two scopes: the current function, and the window in which the function is defined. In Chapter 5 we saw that the with statement can be used to add additional scopes. When an identifier is evaluated, it is first looked up in the scopes specified by any containing with statements. For example, if a top-level script runs the following code:

```
with(o) {
  document.write(x);
}
```

Then the identifier x is evaluated first in the scope of the object o. If no definition is found in that object's properties, then x is evaluated in the context of the current window. If the same code occurred within a function f then x would be looked up first as a property of o, then as a property of f and finally as a property of the current window.

Recall that with statements can be nested arbitrarily, creating a variable "scope" of any depth. One interesting way to use with is with a window reference:

```
with(parent.frames[1]) {
  ...
}
```

This technique allows code in one window to easily read properties of another window. Another technique that is sometimes of interest is to place the entire body of a function within the block of a with(this) statement. What this does is create a method that evaluates identifiers by looking them up first as properties of the object that it is a method of. Note, however, that such a method would find properties of its object *before* it found its own local variables and arguments, which is unusual behavior!

11.5.1.1 Scope of event handlers

Event handlers are scoped differently than regular functions are. Consider the onChange() event handler of a text input field named t within an HTML form named f. If this event handler wants to evaluate the identifier x, it first uses the scope of any with statements of course, and then looks at local variables and arguments, as we saw above. If the event handler were a standalone function, it would look in the scope of the containing window next and stop there. But because this function is an event handler, it next looks in the scope of the text input element t. If the property x is not defined there, it looks at the properties of the form object f. If f does not have a property named x, JavaScript next checks to see if the Document object that contains the form has a definition of this property. Finally, if no definition of x is found in any of these objects, the containing window is checked.

If all identifiers had unique names, scope would never matter. But identifiers are not always unique, and we have to pay attention to scope. One important case is the `Window.open()` method and the `Document.open()` method. If a top-level script of a regular function calls `open()`, JavaScript's scoping rules will find the `open` property of the Window object and use this method. On the other hand, if an event handler calls `open()`, the scoping rules are different, and JavaScript will find the definition of `open` in the Document object before it finds it in the Window object. The same code may work in different ways depending on its context. The moral of this particular example is to never use the `open()` method without explicitly specifying whether you mean `document.open()` or `window.open()`. Be similarly cautious when using `location`; it, too, is a property of both the Window and Document objects.

Finally, note that if an event handler doesn't call `open()` directly but instead calls a function that calls `open()`, the function does *not* inherit the scope of the event handler that invoked it. The function's scope would be the function itself, and then the window that contains it, so in this case, the `open()` method would be interpreted as the `Window.open()` method, not `Document.open()`.

11.6 *Window and Variable Lifetime*

We've seen earlier that Window objects are the central feature of client-side JavaScript, and that all variables (except those local to functions) are actually properties of a window. Having investigated the scope of variables, we now turn to the lifetime of the Window object, and of the variables it contains. In particular, we want to look at what happens when a window or frame moves from one web page and on to another.

A Window object that represents a top-level browser window exists as long as the window it represents exists. A reference to that Window object remains valid regardless of how many web pages it loads and unloads. The Window object is valid as long as the top-level window is open.[*]

A Window object that represents a frame remains valid as long as the frame remains within the frame or window that contains it. If the containing frame or window loads a new document, then the frames it contains will be destroyed in the process of loading that new document.

This is to say that Window objects, whether they represent top-level windows or frames, are fairly persistent—their lifetimes may be longer than that of the web

---

[*] As we'll see in the next section, a Window object may not actually be destroyed when its window is closed, but references to that window will no longer be of much use.

pages that they contain and display, and longer than the lifetime of the scripts contained in the web pages they display.

When a web page that contains a script is unloaded because the user has pointed the browser on to a new page, the script is unloaded along with the page that contains it. (If the script was not unloaded, a browser might soon be overflowing with various lingering scripts!) But what about the variables defined by the script? Since these variables are actually properties of the Window object that contained the script, you might think that they would remain defined. On the other hand, leaving them defined seems dangerous—a new script that was loaded wouldn't be starting with a clean slate, and in fact, it could never know what sorts of properties (and therefore variables) were already defined.

In fact, all user-defined properties (which includes all variables) are erased whenever a web page is unloaded. The scripts in a freshly loaded document start with no variables defined, and no properties in their Window object, except for the standard properties defined by the system. What this means is that the lifetime of scripts and of the variables they define is the same as the lifetime of the document that contains the script. This is potentially much shorter than the lifetime of the window or frame that displays the document that contains the script.

11.7 Garbage Collection

In any programming language in which you can dynamically create new objects (such as with the new operator in JavaScript) there must be some form of "garbage collection"—a way of reclaiming the memory occupied by objects that are no longer in use. In C and C++, garbage collection is manual—the programmer explicitly decides when to free memory for reuse. In Java, on the other hand, garbage collection is handled automatically—the system can detect when objects are no longer in use and free them appropriately.

JavaScript also supports automatic garbage collection. In Internet Explorer 3.0, garbage collection is implemented in a technically sound way and you don't have to understand any of its details—it is enough to know that when your objects are no longer in use, the memory they occupy will automatically be reclaimed by the system. Navigator 4.0 will also have a perfectly transparent garbage collection scheme like this. Unfortunately, garbage collection in earlier versions of Navigator is less than perfect. In Navigator 3.0, it is pretty good, but requires you to be aware of a couple of issues. In Navigator 2.0, garbage collection is seriously flawed, and you must take a number of steps to avoid crashing the browser! The following subsections provide the details.

11.7.1 Reference Counting in Navigator 3.0

In Navigator 3.0, garbage collection is performed by reference counting. This means that every object (whether a user object created by JavaScript code, or a built-in HTML object created by the browser) keeps track of the number of references there are to it. Recall that objects are assigned by reference in JavaScript, rather than having their complete value copied.

When an object is created and a reference to it is stored in a variable, the object's reference count is 1. When the reference to the object is copied and stored in another variable, the reference count is incremented to 2. When one of the two variables that holds these references is overwritten with some new value, the object's reference count is decremented back to 1. If the reference count reaches zero, then there are no more references to the object, and since there are no references to copy, there can never again be a reference to the object in the program. Therefore, JavaScript knows that it is safe to destroy the object and "garbage collect" the memory associated with it.

This reference-counting scheme has some important implications. (These implications are also true of the Internet Explorer garbage collector, but, as we'll see, they are not true of the garbage collection scheme in Navigator 2.0.) If JavaScript code running in a window creates an object, and a reference to that object is stored in a variable of another window, then that object will continue to exist even after the window that created it is closed, or loads in a different page. The original reference to the object is lost, but since a reference still exists from another window, the object will not be garbage collected.

Perhaps a more surprising implication is that a top-level browser window may be closed by the user or by JavaScript code, but the Window object associated with it may continue to exist. This occurs when a variable in one window contains a reference to the window that is closed. Since there is still a reference to the Window object, that object cannot be garbage collected. Note, however, that many of the methods and properties of a Window object that is closed cannot be meaningfully used. In Navigator 3.0, you should be sure to check the `closed` property (a Boolean value) of any Window object before using its properties or methods, if there is any chance that it could have been closed.

11.7.2 Shortcomings of Garbage Collection by Reference Counting

As you may already be aware, there are some shortcomings to using reference counting as a garbage collection scheme. In fact, some people don't even consider reference counting to be true garbage collection, and reserve that term for algorithms such as "mark-and-sweep" garbage collection. The computer science literature on garbage collection is large and technical, and we won't get into it here. For our purposes it is enough to know that reference counting is a very simple form of garbage collection to implement, and it works fine in many situations. There are situations, however, in which reference counting cannot correctly detect and collect all "garbage", and you need to be aware of these.

The basic flaw with reference counting has to do with cyclical references. If object A contains a reference to object B and object B contains a reference to object A, then a cycle of references exists. A cycle would also exist, for example, if A referred to B, B referred to C, and C referred back to A. In cycles such as these, there is always a reference from within the cycle to every element in the cycle. Thus, even if none of the elements of the cycle has any remaining references, their reference count will never drop below one, and they can never be garbage collected. The entire cycle may be garbage, because there is no way to refer to any of these objects from a program, but because they all refer to each other, a reference-counting garbage collector will not be able to detect and free this unused memory.

This problem with cycles is the price that must be paid for a simple, lightweight, portable garbage collection scheme. The only way to prevent this problem is by manual intervention. If you create code in which A refers to B, B refers to C, and C refers to A, then you must be able to recognize that you've created a cycle, and take steps to force the cycle to be garbage collected when it is no longer needed.

When you know that the objects in your cycle are no longer in use, you can force them to be garbage collected by breaking the cycle. You can do this by picking one of the objects in the cycle and setting the property of it that refers to the next object to null. For example, suppose that A, B, and C are objects that each have a next property, and the value of this property is set so that these objects refer to each other and form a cycle. When these objects are no longer in use, you can break the cycle by setting A.next to null. This means that object B no longer has a reference from A, so its reference count can drop to zero and it can be garbage collected. Once it has been garbage collected, then it will no longer refer to C, so its reference count can drop to zero and it can be garbage collected. Once C is garbage collected, A can be garbage collected.

Note, of course, that none of this can happen if A, B, and C are stored in global variables in a window that is still open, because those variables A, B, and C still refer to the objects. If these were local variables in a function, and you broke their cycle before the function returned, then they could be garbage collected. But if they are stored in global variables, they will remain referenced until the window that contains them closes. In this case, if you want to force them to be garbage collected you must break the cycle and set the variables to `null`:

```
A.next = null;     // break the cycle
A = B = C = null;  // remove the last remaining external references
```

11.7.3 Per-Page Memory Management in Navigator 2.0

The garbage collection scheme in Navigator 2.0 is much simpler than that in Navigator 3.0, and, unfortunately, it is inadequate for the needs of JavaScript programs that use multiple windows and frames. In Navigator 2.0, all objects created by JavaScript code running in any particular window allocate memory from a pool of memory owned by the window. Then, when the window is destroyed, or when the document (containing the JavaScript program) displayed in the window is unloaded, the entire pool of memory is freed at once. No memory is freed until then.

With this garbage collection scheme, all memory allocated by the JavaScript running in a window can be freed in a single stroke. It is a simple and efficient scheme to implement. Unfortunately, it suffers from two major drawbacks.

First, if an object is created in one window, and then a reference to that object is stored in a variable in a second window, that object will be destroyed when the first window moves on to a new page, despite the fact that there is still an active reference to it from the other window. If this other window attempts to use this reference to the destroyed object, an error will result, possibly crashing the browser! This is an especially pernicious problem, because doing something as simple as assigning a string can cause this problem. Consider the following code:

```
newwin = window.open("", "temp_window");
newwin.defaultStatus = "temporary browser window".
```

The `defaultStatus` property is set to a string "owned" by the original window. If that window is closed, the string will be destroyed and the next reference to `defaultStatus` will go looking for a non-existing string.

The second problem with this scheme is that if a window never unloads, the memory associated with it will never be freed. For a page that runs some JavaScript once and then is static, this is not a problem. But consider a page that performs a status-bar animation, for example. If it updates the status bar several times a second for a long time, the memory consumed by that page will grow and grow. Another example occurs with the use of frames. One frame might serve as a navigation window, with controls that allow a user to easily browse a large site in other frames or other windows. These other frames and windows may load and unload pages frequently, freeing memory. But the navigation frame itself remains the same, and the memory associated with it is not freed. Depending on how the event handlers are written, there is a good chance that each time the user interacts with the navigation controls some new string or object will be created, and no memory will ever be freed. Eventually, the browser will run out of memory, and may well crash.

11.7.4 *Workarounds for Navigator 2.0*

It is possible to compensate, somewhat, for these memory management problems in Navigator 2.0. For the problem of memory not being released until the page is unloaded, the solution is simply to be careful about how much memory your scripts consume. If your page loops a lot or does a repetitive animation, look very carefully at the code that is executed over and over, and minimize the number of objects created on each iteration. Similarly, if you write a script that the user may use frequently without ever unloading, be sure to keep careful tabs on your memory usage.

Note that string manipulation is a big memory sink—each time you call a method on a string object, a new string object is generally created for the result. The same is true for string concatenation with the + operator.

For the problem of dangling references from one window to destroyed objects that were owned by another, one solution is to avoid programs that rely on inter-window references. Another solution is to be sure to make copies of all strings and other objects that are passed from one window to another. Suppose that in window 1, you want to set the defaultStatus property of window 2, as we saw earlier. If you do this directly with code in window 1, then window 2 will contain a reference to an object owned by window 1. But, if you call a function in window 2 to do the assignment, and make sure that the function makes a copy of the object, then the object assigned in window 2 will be owned by window 2. You could, for example, ensure that window 2 contains a definition of the following function:

```
function set_string_property(name, value)
{
    // Assign a property to this window, using associative array notation.
    // We add the empty string to the value to force JavaScript to make
    // a copy. If this function is called from another window, we won't
    // own the value string, but by making a copy, we do own the result.
    self[name] = value + "";
}
```

With this function defined, you could then set the property from window 1 with a line like the following:

```
window2.set_string_property("defaultStatus", "temporary browser window");
```

11.8 The JavaScript Object Hierarchy

We've seen that the Window object is the central object of client-side JavaScript. All other client-side objects that radiate out from this center. As we've seen, JavaScript variables are nothing more than properties of the current Window object, and every JavaScript expression is implicitly evaluated in the context of that current window object. Therefore, any other objects in JavaScript can only be referred to through the Window object. For example, every Window object contains a `document` property that refers to the Document object associated with the window. Window objects also contain a `frames[]` array that refers to the Window objects that represent the frames of the original window. So, for example, `document` represents the Document object of the current window, and `frames[1].document` refers to the Document object of the second child frame of the current window.

Objects referred to through the current window or through some other Window object may themselves refer to other objects. For example, every Document object has a `forms[]` array that contains Form objects representing any HTML forms that appear in the document. To refer to one of these forms, you might write:

```
self.document.forms[0]
```

To continue with the same example, each Form object contains a `elements[]` array that contains objects that represent the various HTML form elements (input fields, buttons, etc.) that appear within the form. In extreme cases, you can write code that refers from one object to another and another and end up with expressions as complex as this one:

```
parent.frames[0].document.forms[0].elements[3].options[2].text
```

Because all client-side objects in JavaScript exist as properties of other objects, and because all expressions include an implicit reference to the current Window object, a hierarchy of JavaScript objects exists and that this hierarchy has the current window as its root. Figure 11-2 shows this hierarchy. Study this figure carefully; understanding the HTML object hierarchy and the objects it contains is crucial to successful client-side JavaScript programming.

Note that Figure 11-2 shows only object properties that refer to other objects. Most of the objects shown in the diagram have quite a few more properties than those shown. The notation "3.0" in the figure indicates properties that do not exist in Navigator 2.0. The chapters that follow document each of the objects shown in the

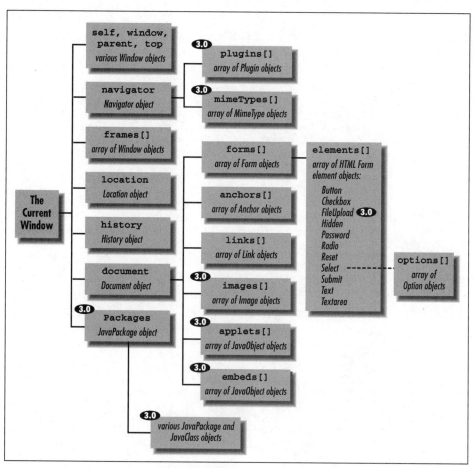

Figure 11–2: The JavaScript object hierarchy

object hierarchy diagram and demonstrate common JavaScript programming techniques that make use those objects. You may want to refer back to Figure 11-2 while reading these chapters.

12

Programming with Windows

Chapter 11, *Windows and the JavaScript Name Space*, discussed implicit and explicit references to windows, window names, window lifetime, variable scope within windows, and other window-related architectural issues in JavaScript. This chapter gets down to fundamentals and describes some practical methods, properties, and techniques for programming with JavaScript windows.

12.1 Simple Dialogs

Three commonly used Window methods are `alert()`, `confirm()`, and `prompt()`. These methods pop up simple dialog boxes. `alert()` displays a message to the user. `confirm()` asks the user to click an **Ok** or **Cancel** button to confirm or abort an operation. And `prompt()` asks the user to enter a string. Sample dialogs produced by these three methods are shown in Figure 12-1, and Example 12-1 shows some typical uses of these methods.

Note that the text displayed by these dialog boxes is plain text, not HTML-formatted text. The only formatting you can do is with spaces, newlines, and various punctuation characters. Adjusting the formatting generally requires trial-and-error. Bear in mind, though, that the dialogs will look different on different platforms and in different browsers, so you can't always count on your formatting to look right on all possible browsers.

The most commonly asked question about these dialog boxes is, "How can I get rid of the 'JavaScript Alert:' message?" There is no way to do this. It is there to prevent you from writing malicious code that spoofs system dialogs and tricks users into doing things that they shouldn't do.

Finally, note that JavaScript code keeps executing when an `alert()` dialog is posted, but both the `confirm()` and `prompt()` methods block—that is, those

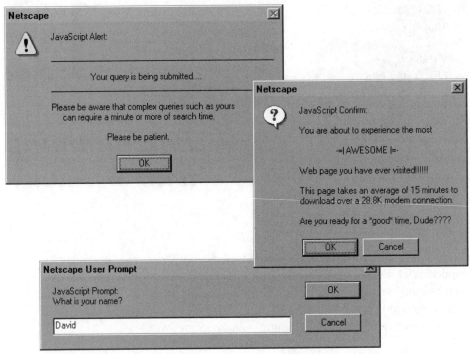

Figure 12-1: alert(), confirm(), and prompt() dialog boxes

methods do not return until the user dismisses the dialog they display. This means
that when you pop one up, your code will stop running and the currently loading
document, if any, will stop loading until the user responds with the requested
input. There is no alternative to blocking for these methods—their return value is
the user's input, so they must wait for the user before they can return.

Example 12-1: Using the alert(), confirm() and prompt() Methods

```
// Here's a function that uses the alert() method to tell the user
// that their form submission will take some time, and that they should
// be patient. It would be suitable for use in the onSubmit() event handler
// of an HTML form.
// Note that all formatting is done with spaces, newlines, and underscores.
function warn_on_submit()
{
    alert("\n_____\n\n" +
          "                   Your query is being submitted....\n"    +
          "_____\n\n" +
          "Please be aware that complex queries such as yours\n"      +
          "      can require a minute or more of search time.\n\n"    +
          "                      Please be patient.");
}
```

Example 12–1: Using the alert(), confirm() and prompt() Methods (continued)

```
// Here is a use of the confirm() method to ask the user if they really
// want to visit a web page that takes a long time to download. Note that
// the return value of the method indicates the user response. Based
// on this response, we reroute the browser to an appropriate page.

var msg = "\nYou are about to experience the most\n\n" +
          "                     -=| AWESOME |=-\n\n" +
          "Web page you have ever visited!!!!!!\n\n" +
          "This page takes an average of 15 minutes to\n" +
          "download over a 28.8K modem connection.\n\n" +
          "Are you ready for a *good* time, Dude????";

if (confirm(msg))
    location.replace("awesome_page.html");
else
    location.replace("lame_page.html");

// Here's some very simple code that uses the prompt() method to get
// a user's name, and then uses that name in dynamically generated HTML.
n = prompt("What is your name?", "");
document.write("<hr><h1>Welcome to my home page, " + n + "</h1><hr>");
```

12.2 Opening and Closing Windows

Earlier in this chapter we learned about the `Window.open()` and `Window.close()` methods that open and close browser windows. As you'll recall, the first argument to the `open()` method specifies a URL to be loaded into the new window, or the empty string if the window should be blank. The second argument is the name for the window. In Navigator, this second argument is optional, but it is required by Internet Explorer 3.0.

The `open()` method also has an optional third argument that we haven't seen yet. This third argument is a string that contains a comma-separated list of "features" for the new window. These "features" specify whether the window will have a menu bar, whether it will display a toolbar, whether it will be resizable, and so on. The features may also specify what the width and height of the window will be. If you do not specify this third argument, you'll get a full-size window will all the standard features. If you do specify the argument, you get only the features you specify. For example, you could use a line like the following to open a 400×300 window with a location field and a status bar:

```
smallwin = window.open("", "small", "location,status,width=400,height=300");
```

The list of available features and complete syntax for the third argument is given in the `Window.open()` reference page.

One common reason to open new browser windows with reduced sizes and reduced feature sets is to create "dialog boxes" that are more complex than those available through `alert()` and related methods. Figure 12-2 shows such a "dialog box" in a small browser window.

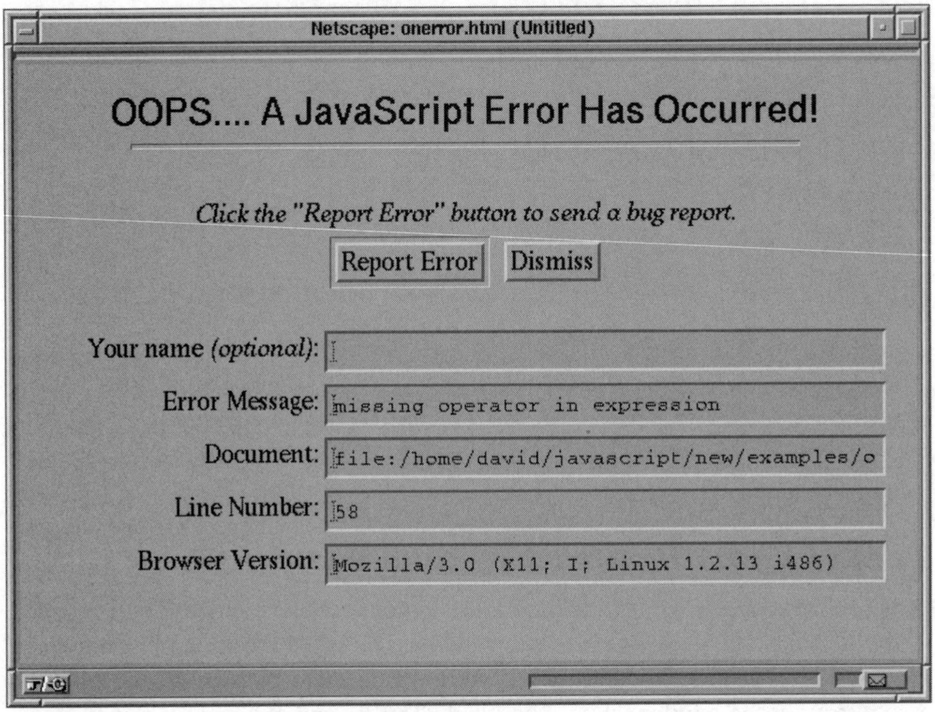

Figure 12–2: Using a browser window as a dialog box

Example 12-2 shows the code used to create the "dialog box" of Figure 12-2. This example is a function that serves as an error handler. This handler is invoked when the JavaScript interpreter detects an error in code it is executing. The function we define here creates a new window and dynamically generates an HTML document containing details about the error and about the platform the error occurred on, using an HTML form designed to be submitted via email (which provides a way for end users to automatically mail bug reports to a program's author).

Example 12–2: Reporting JavaScript Errors with a Secondary Window

```
<script>
// a variable we use to ensure that each error window we create is unique
var error_count = 0;

// Define the error handler. It generates an HTML form so
// the user can report the error to the author.
```

Example 12-2: Reporting JavaScript Errors with a Secondary Window (continued)

```
function report_error(msg, url, line)
{
    var w = window.open("",                        // URL (none specified)
                        "error"+error_count++, // name (force it to be unique)
                        "resizable,status,width=625,height=400"); // features
    var d = w.document;     // We use this variable to save typing!

    // Output an HTML document, including a form, into the new window.
    d.write('<DIV align=center>');
    d.write('<FONT SIZE=7 FACE="helvetica"><B>');
    d.write('OOPS.... A JavaScript Error Has Occurred!');
    d.write('</B></FONT><BR><HR SIZE=4 WIDTH="80%">');
    d.write('<FORM ACTION="mailto:david@ora.com" METHOD=post');
    d.write(' ENCTYPE="text/plain">');
    d.write('<FONT SIZE=3>');
    d.write('<I>Click the "Report Error" button to send a bug report.</I><BR>');
    d.write('<INPUT TYPE="submit" VALUE="Report Error">  ');
    d.write('<INPUT TYPE="button" VALUE="Dismiss" onClick="self.close()">');
    d.write('</DIV><DIV align=right>');
    d.write('<BR>Your name <I>(optional)</I>: ');
    d.write('<INPUT SIZE=42 NAME="name" VALUE="">');
    d.write('<BR>Error Message: ');
    d.write('<INPUT SIZE=42 NAME="message" VALUE="' + msg + '">');
    d.write('<BR>Document: <INPUT SIZE=42 NAME="url" VALUE="' + url + '">');
    d.write('<BR>Line Number: <INPUT SIZE=42 NAME="line" VALUE="' + line +'">');
    d.write('<BR>Browser Version: ');
    d.write('<INPUT SIZE=42 NAME="version" VALUE="'+navigator.userAgent + '">');
    d.write('</DIV></FONT>');
    d.write('</FORM>');
    // Remember to close the document when we're done.
    d.close();

    // Return true from this error handler, so that JavaScript does not
    // display its own error dialog.
    return true;
}


// Before the event handler can take effect, we have to register it
// for a particular window.
self.onerror = report_error;
</script>

<script>
// The following line of code causes the error that creates the dialog
// box shown in the accompanying figure.
self = null;
</script>
```

Example 12-2 demonstrates a number of important techniques for programming with windows. First, of course, it shows how you can create a window with reduced size and few extraneous features. It also shows how this window can close itself when the user clicks the "Dismiss" button. Perhaps most important, it demonstrates the fundamentally important technique of using JavaScript code running in one window to dynamically create an HTML document in another window. It does this using the Document.write() method, of course, and it uses that method to create a relatively complex HTML form in the new window. The details of the form are not particularly important here—we'll study the Form object and form elements in Chapter 17, *Forms and Form Elements*—what is important is the way that the form is dynamically created.

In addition to the above techniques, Example 12-2 also demonstrates the use of the Window.onerror() event handler, and in fact, the example consists primarily of an onerror() event handler. This event handler is new in Navigator 3.0—it is invoked by JavaScript when any sort of error occurs in the JavaScript interpreter. The handler is passed three arguments that specify the error message, the document it occurred in, and the line number it occurred at. It can use these arguments to handle the error any way it chooses. If the handler returns true, as it does in this example, then JavaScript will not display its own error message dialog. Because this event handler is passed arguments, there is no appropriate syntax for defining it as the value of an HTML attribute. For this reason, it must be defined by assigning a function to the onerror property of a window, in the same way that you would define a method of an object.

12.3 The Status Line

At the bottom of every browser window (except for those we open() without it) is a *status line*. This is a location in which the browser can display messages to the user. When you move the mouse over a hypertext link, for example, the browser displays the URL that the link points to. And when you move the mouse over a browser control button, the browser displays a simple "context help" message that explains the purpose of the button. You can also make use of this status line in your own programs—its contents are controlled by two properties of the Window object: status and defaultStatus.

We've just said that browsers display the URL of a hypertext link when you pass the mouse pointer over the link. This is generally the case, but in your excursions through the web, you may have found some links that don't behave this way—links that display some text other than the link's URL. This is done with the status property of the Window object, and the onMouseOver() event handler of hypertext links, as shown in Example 12-3.

Example 12-3: Displaying a Link's Destination in the Status Line

```
<!-- Here's how you set the status line in a hyperlink.
  -- Note that the event handler *must* return true for this to work. -->
Lost? Dazed and confused? Visit the
<A HREF="sitemap.html" onMouseOver="status='Go to Site Map'; return true;">
  Site Map
</A>


<!-- You can do the same thing for client-side image maps.-->
<IMG SRC="images/imgmap1.gif" USEMAP="#map1">
<MAP NAME="map1">
  <AREA COORDS="0,0,50,20" HREF="info.html"
    onMouseover="status='Visit our Information Center'; return true;">
  <AREA COORDS="0,20,50,40" HREF="order.html"
    onMouseOver="status='Place an order'; return true;">
  <AREA COORDS="0,40,50,60" HREF="help.html"
    onMouseOver="status='Get help fast!'; return true;">
</MAP>
```

In Example 12-3 note that the onMouseOver() event handler must return true. This tells the browser that it should not perform its own default action for the event—that is, it should not display the URL of the link in the status line. If you forget to return true, then the browser will overwrite whatever message the handler displayed in the status line with its own URL.

When you move the mouse pointer over a hyperlink, the browser displays the URL for the link, and then erases it when the mouse moves off the hyperlink. The same is true when you use an onMouseOver() event handler to set the Window status property—your custom message will be displayed while the mouse is over the hyperlink, and then will be erased when it moves off the link. Or that is the way it is supposed to work, anyway. In the Windows version of Navigator (but not the Mac or X11 versions), the status line is not automatically cleared when you set the status property from an onMouseOver() event handler. To force it to be erased, you can use the onMouseOut() event handler, like this:

```
<A HREF="sitemap.html"
  onMouseOver="status='Go to Site Map'; return true;"
  onMouseOut="status='';">
  Site Map
</A>
```

The status property is intended for exactly the sort of transient message we saw above. Sometimes, though, you want to display a message that is not so transient in the status line—for example, you might display a welcome message to users visiting your web page, or might display a simple line of help text for novice visitors. To do this, you set the `defaultStatus` property of the Window—this property specifies the default text displayed in the status line. That text will temporarily be replaced with URLs, context help messages, or other transient text when the mouse pointer is over hyperlinks or browser control buttons, but once the mouse moves off of those areas, the default text will be restored.

You might use the `defaultStatus` property like this to provide a friendly and helpful message to real beginners:

```
<SCRIPT>
defaultStatus = "Welcome!  Click on underlined blue text to navigate.";
</SCRIPT>
```

If your web page contained an HTML form, you might change the `defaultStatus` property as the user enters data in the form, in order to to display step-by-step instructions for completing it.

Any time you can programmatically set a value and cause a user-visible change to appear on the screen, the true JavaScript programmer's mind turns immediately to the possibilities of animation—that is of updating a value (that updates the screen) periodically to produce some sort of special effect. In general, animations involving the status bar are gaudy and in very poor taste; shun them!

On the other hand, status bar animation is interesting because it demonstrates important JavaScript programming techniques, including the use of the `Window.setTimeout()` method. Example 12-4 shows a simple status bar animation (that is in good taste). It displays the current time in the status bar, and updates that time once a minute. Because the update only occurs once a minute, this animation does not produce a constant flickering distraction at the bottom of the browser window like so many others do. Note the use of the `setTimeout()` method in this example—it causes JavaScript code to be executed after a specified number of milliseconds elapse. It was first introduced in Chapter 10, *Client-Side Program Structure*. Also note the use of the `onLoad()` event handler to start the clock running. `onLoad()` is an event handler of the Window object, and is specified here as an attribute of the `<BODY>` tag. It was first introduced in Chapter 10.

Example 12-4: A Digital Clock in the Status Line

```
<HTML>
<HEAD>
<SCRIPT>
// This function displays the time in the status line.
// Invoke it once to activate the clock; it will call itself from then on.
function display_time_in_status_line()
{
```

Example 12–4: A Digital Clock in the Status Line (continued)

```
    var d = new Date();             // get current time;
    var h = d.getHours();           // extract hours: 0 to 23
    var m = d.getMinutes();         // extract minutes: 0 to 59
    var ampm = (h >= 12)?"PM":"AM"; // is it am or pm?
    if (h > 12) h -= 12;            // convert 24-hour format to 12-hour
    if (h == 0) h = 12;             // convert 0 o'clock to midnight
    if (m < 10) m = "0" + m;        // convert 0 minutes to 00 minutes, etc.
    var t = h + ':' + m + ' ' + ampm; // put it all together

    defaultStatus = t;              // display it in the status line

    // arrange to do it all again in 1 minute.
    setTimeout("display_time_in_status_line()", 60000); // 60000 ms in 1 minute
}
</SCRIPT>
</HEAD>
<!-- Don't bother starting the clock 'till everything is loaded. The
  -- status line will be busy with other messages during loading, anyway -->
<BODY onLoad="display_time_in_status_line();">
<!-- The HTML document contents go here -->
</BODY>
</HTML>
```

If you write a JavaScript program that performs any sort of lengthy computation, you might decide to use a simple status bar animation to give the user feedback that your program is computing, and is making progress. Without some kind of feedback, there is a danger that the user might think the browser has hung. Unfortunately, this sort of animation won't work. You can update the `defaultStatus` and `status` properties at any time, but your specified text won't actually appear in status line until all the JavaScript code that is running completes. Thus, if you attempt to animate the line to indicate progress during a lengthy computation, none of your updates to the status line will actually appear to the user.

12.4 *Frame Programming Techniques*

In a section above we demonstrated that it is possible to open a new browser window, and to dynamically create a HTML document within that new window. This is a very powerful technique in JavaScript, and it applies not only to new browser windows, but also to frames. In fact, it is much more common to create a web site that uses multiple frames than it is to create one that uses multiple browser windows. The key to successful programming with frames is knowing how to refer to one frame from another. Recall that every Window object (which means every browser window, and every frame within a window or within another frame) has a `frames[]` array, and also `parent`, `top`, `self`, and `window` properties. You might want to refer back to Figure 12-1 to refresh your memory about how each of these properties work.

Once you know how to refer to any frame from any other frame, you can start writing JavaScript programs that work in complex framed documents. Pay careful attention to how you name frames, and be aware of what window any given piece of code is running in. For example, if an event handler in frame A invokes a function that is defined in frame B, the code in that function is running in frame A, not frame B—and if the code wants to refer to frame B, it can't just use the implicit window reference, as it could if it were actually running in frame B. When you encounter complexities like these, it is helpful to give each frame a name, and refer to them by name rather than by number. (Recall that giving a frame a name creates a property with that name in the frame's parent.) When you are working with frames that are nested, at multiple levels, however you may want to create some "global" properties of the top-level browser window that refer to each of the frames in your program, no matter how many levels down they are nested. Then, for example, you can refer to frames with expressions like `top.frameB`, and know that you are referring to the right frame, regardless of what frame the expression is evaluated in. The key here is to create an absolute naming convention for frames rather than using the relative naming convention that JavaScript provides by default.

As we saw in the error handler example, JavaScript code in one window (or frame) can dynamically create an HTML document in another window (or frame). It is a lot harder for JavaScript code to dynamically create a new HTML document in its own window or frame, because doing this generally overwrites the JavaScript code itself! If your web page design calls for one static frame and two frames that have their contents dynamically updated, the static frame can contain the JavaScript code necessary to update the dynamic frames. But what if your design calls for all the frames to be dynamic? A static frame is still required, but the trick here is to create the static frame so that it is invisible! You do this by explicitly creating it at a location that is greater than 100% of the frame width or height. HTML to create such an invisible frame is shown in Example 12-5.

Example 12-5: Creating an Invisible Frame

```
<!-- Create two frames that take up half the screen each, and one that -->
<!-- takes up "all the rest" of the room. The third frame will be -->
<!-- invisible, because it has a height of zero. -->
<frameset rows="50%,50%,*">
<!-- first two frames start out empty, loading no documents -->
<frame name="dynamic_frame_1">
<frame name="dynamic_frame_2">
```

Example 12–5: Creating an Invisible Frame (continued)

```
<!-- invisible frame contains the code that will -->
<!-- dynamically update the others -->
<frame name="invisible_frame" src="program.html">
</frameset>
```

A technique related to dynamically generating frame content is the use of the TAR-GET attribute of <A>, <AREA>, and <FORM> tags. This attribute was discussed earlier in this chapter—it directs the browser to load the URL pointed to by a hyperlink into the named frame or window, or to load the results of form submission into the named frame. This, too, is a very useful way to change the contents of one frame from another frame.

Another HTML technique that is possible with frames in Navigator 3.0 is creating borderless frames. A borderless frame is visible to the user but its border is not. You can use borderless frames when you want an region of the screen that can display HTML content independently of the rest of the page, but which fits "seamlessly" with its neighboring frames. You can create borderless frames with attributes like those shown here. Note that the entire frameset must be borderless, since if one frame is borderless, its adjoining neighbors must be borderless, too:

```
<frameset border=no width=0 rows="10%,*">
  <frame name="banner" src="ad.html">
  <frame name="main" src="content.html">
</frameset>
```

This HTML fragment hints at one possible use of borderless frames: to create "banner" regions at the top (or bottom) of web pages that do not scroll with the main part of the page. These are useful, of course, for company logos, advertisements, and the like.

We'd described how you can use JavaScript running in one frame to dynamically create HTML content for another frame. But in this discussion we have always created the frames themselves with a frameset specified in a static HTML file. Since frames are specified in HTML, there is no reason we cannot create them dynamically as well. Example 12-6 shows how it can be done. This example opens a small new window, dynamically creates four frames in it, and then, using the set-Timeout() method, periodically changes the background color of each frame, creating a simple but colorful animated display, which is pictured in Figure 12-3. The **Stop** button in the original window stops the animation using clearTimeout() and closes the new window using the Window.close() method. This example brings together many of the window and frame programming techniques we've been discussing.

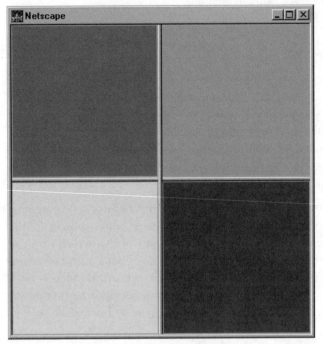

Figure 12-3: A simple animation in dynamically created frames

Example 12-6: Dynamically Creating and Animating Frames

```
<HTML>
<HEAD>
<SCRIPT LANGUAGE="JavaScript1.1">
// open a new window
var n = window.open('', 'f', 'width=400,height=400');

// dynamically create frames in that new window
// note the use of the special about:blank URL to get empty frames
n.document.write('<frameset rows="50%,50%" cols="50%,50%">');
n.document.write('<frame name="f1" src="about:blank">');
n.document.write('<frame name="f2" src="about:blank">');
n.document.write('<frame name="f3" src="about:blank">');
n.document.write('<frame name="f4" src="about:blank">');
n.document.write('</frameset>');

// an array of the colors we cycle through for the animation
colors = new Array("red","green","blue","yellow","white");

// an array of the frames we cycle through (in this order)
windows = new Array(n.f1, n.f2, n.f4, n.f3);
```

Example 12-6: Dynamically Creating and Animating Frames (continued)

```
// the current color and frame counters
var c = 0, f = 0;

// a variable that holds the current timeout id (used to cancel the timeout)
var timeout = null;

// This function sets the "next" frame in the list to the "next" color
// in the list. We call it once to start the animation, and then it
// arranges to invoke itself every quarter second after that.
function change_one_frame()
{
    // dynamically output the HTML necessary to set the background color
    windows[f].document.write('<BODY BGCOLOR="' + colors[c] + '">');
    windows[f].document.close();
    f = (f + 1) % 4;  // increment frame counter
    c = (c + 1) % 5;  // increment color counter

    // arrange to be called again in 250 milliseconds and
    // save the timeout id so that we can stop this crazy thing
    timeout = setTimeout("change_one_frame()", 250);
}
</SCRIPT>
</HEAD>
<!-- start the frame animation when the document is fully loaded -->
<BODY onLoad="change_one_frame();">
<!-- Create a button to stop the animation with clearTimeout() -->
<!-- and close the window with close(). -->
<FORM>
  <INPUT TYPE="button" VALUE="Stop"
     onClick="if (timeout) clearTimeout(timeout); if (!n.closed) n.close();">
</FORM>
</BODY>
</HTML>
```

12.5 *Other Window Programming Techniques*

There are a few miscellaneous useful properties and methods of the Window object. The name, opener, and closed properties were already mentioned briefly earlier in this chapter. The name property specifies the name of a window or frame. In Navigator 3.0 (but not Internet Explorer 3.0), this property can be set, thereby changing the window name, which can be useful in conjunction with the TARGET attribute, for example. The opener property is created when a Navigator

3.0 (or Internet Explorer 3.0) browser window is opened—it refers to the window that most recently called the open() method for the window. closed is another Navigator 3.0 property—it specifies whether a window has already been closed. If so, then your JavaScript code should not make any further use of that window.

The focus() and blur() methods of the Window object transfer keyboard focus to, and away from, the window. If you call focus() on a browser window that is currently obscured on the desktop, it will be brought to the top and made visible. These two methods have corresponding onfocus() and onblur() event handlers that are invoked when a window gains or loses focus. Note that blur() and focus() are not supported for Window objects in Internet Explorer 3.0.

The scroll() method scrolls the contents of a window (or frame), just as if the user had used the window's scrollbars explicitly. The two arguments to this method are the absolute X and Y pixel coordinates that the document should be scrolled to. The document in the window moves so that these coordinates are in the upper-left corner of the window. For example, you can more to the top of a document with:

```
self.scroll(0,0);
```

If you know you are at the top, and want to scroll down 100 pixels, you might write:

```
self.scroll(0,100);
```

Note that the scroll() method is not as useful as it could be because there is no way to find out how big the window is, and there is no way to find out how many pixels tall each line of text is.

Finally, the Window object has a number of other properties, such as document, location and history, and we've seen some of these used in examples in this chapter. These properties, and others like them, simply refer to other HTML objects. These objects, and their methods and properties, are documented in the chapters that follow.

13

The Navigator, Location, and History Objects

The Window object contains references to three objects that contain information about the browser or the browser window itself, rather than information about the contents of the window:

- The Navigator object provides version and configuration information about the browser.

- The Location object specifies the URL currently being displayed, and allows JavaScript code to load new URLs.

- The History object contains information about the URLs that have been previously displayed in the window.

This chapter documents each of these Window-related objects.

13.1 The Navigator, MimeType, and Plugin Objects

The `Window.navigator` property refers to a Navigator object which contains information about the web browser as a whole (such as the version, and the list of data formats it can display). The Navigator object is named after Netscape Navigator, obviously, but it is also supported (although only partially) by Internet Explorer.

The Navigator object has four properties that provide version information about the browser that is running. The `appName` property contains the name of the browser. The `appVersion` property contains information about the version number and platform of the browser. The `userAgent` property contains the string that the browser sends in its USER-AGENT header in HTTP requests. Finally, the `app-CodeName` property contains the "code name" of the browser, which, in general is not particularly useful. Each of these properties is a string in human-readable format, so extracting version information can be a little tricky. See the reference pages for details on the string formats.

In Navigator 3.0, the Navigator object also defines two methods that provide further information about the capabilities of the browser. `javaEnabled()` returns `true` if the browser supports Java, and if it is enabled; otherwise it returns `false`. Similarly, `taintEnabled()` returns `true` if and only if the browser supports a data-tainting security model, and if that model is enabled.

The remaining two properties of the Navigator object are the `mimeTypes[]` array and the `plugins[]` array, which specify the data types that the browser can display and the plug-ins that are installed. These arrays are only available in Navigator 3.0. The subsections below contain more details on these arrays.

13.1.1 Determining Browser Version Information

We saw above that the Navigator object has four properties that contain information about the browser version. This information is useful when you need to work around bugs in particular versions, or make use of special features found in one browser but not another, for example. Unfortunately, it can be a little difficult to access the information in a convenient way. Example 13-1 shows how you can use the Navigator object to determine what browser is being used, what version of that browser, and what platform it is running on. The code in this example stores the information in more convenient properties of a new `browser` object.

Example 13-1: Getting Browser Version Information

```
<SCRIPT>
// Return the version number times 1000. This means that version
// 2.02 would yield 2020, and version 3.0 would yield 3000.
// We multiply because Navigator versions 2.0x convert numbers like
// 2.02 to strings like "2.0199999999875".
function _get_version()
{
    return Math.round(parseFloat(navigator.appVersion) * 1000);
}


// Figure out the OS we are running on, based on the appVersion property.
function _get_os()
{
    if (navigator.appVersion.indexOf("Win95") > 0) return "WIN95";
    else if (navigator.appVersion.indexOf("Win16") > 0) return "WIN31";
    else if (navigator.appVersion.indexOf("Mac") > 0) return "MAC";
    else if (navigator.appVersion.indexOf("X11") > 0) return "UNIX";
```

Example 13-1: Getting Browser Version Information (continued)

```
    else return "UNKNOWN";
}


// Create the object we'll use to store the version information.
var browser = new Object();

// First, check if it is a Netscape browser.
if (navigator.appName.substring(0,8) == "Netscape") {
    // if so, set the name variable appropriately
    browser.name =  "NN";
    // then parse navigator.appVersion to figure out what version
    browser.version = _get_version();
    // Then use appVersion again to determine the OS.
    browser.os = _get_os();
}


// Otherwise, see if it is a Microsoft browser.
//
// If so, we set all the variables directly, because MSIE only has
// one JavaScript-enabled version, and it only runs on one platform.
// We don't use Navigator.appVersion to compute the version number, because
// it returns a Netscape-compatible value of 2.0 rather than the true
// MSIE version number 3.0. We don't use it to compute the OS, because
// MSIE encodes that information with different strings than Navigator
// does, so we can't use the _get_os() function above.
//
// This code will have to be updated when a new version of MSIE is released
// but we'll have to wait and see how MS encodes the information in the
// various Navigator object properties before we can update the code.
else if (navigator.appName.substring(0,9) == "Microsoft") {
    browser.name = "MSIE";
    browser.version = 3000;
    browser.os = "WIN95";
}


// Otherwise, it is some unknown browser that supports JavaScript.
// So we try to guess the browser name, version number and os, assuming
// that this browser stores the information in the same format as Navigator.
else {
    browser.name = navigator.appName;
    browser.version = _get_version();
    browser.os = _get_os();
}


// Now figure out what version of JavaScript is supported by the browser.
// Start by assuming that only version 1.0 is supported.
browser.langlevel = 1000;
</SCRIPT>
```

Example 13-1: Getting Browser Version Information (continued)

```
<SCRIPT LANGUAGE="JavaScript1.1">
// If the browser supports JavaScript 1.1, update the langlevel variable.
browser.langlevel = 1100;
</SCRIPT>

<SCRIPT LANGUAGE="JavaScript1.2">
// If the browser supports JavaScript 1.2, update the langlevel variable.
browser.langlevel = 1200;
</SCRIPT>
```

13.1.2 The MimeType Object

In Navigator 3.0, the `navigator.mimeTypes[]` property is an array of MimeType objects, each of which describe one MIME data format ("text/html", and "image/gif", for example) that the web browser can display (either directly, with an external helper application, or with a plug-in.) The MimeType object itself contains properties that describe the data format.

The `mimeTypes[]` array is indexed numerically, but is also an associative array, indexed by the name of the MIME type. Thus, you can easily check for support of a given data format on the browser:

```
// Check to see if the browser can display MPEG files.
var show_movie = (navigator.mimeTypes["video/mpeg"] != null);
```

If you want to determine whether a given MIME type is supported by a plug-in (instead of a helper application, for example), you can examine the `enabledPlugin` property of the MimeType object. If it is `null`, then no plug-in supports the object. Otherwise, this property refers to a Plugin object that represents the plug-in that is configured to display data of the specified format.

13.1.3 The Plugin Object

In Navigator 3.0, the `navigator.plugins[]` property is an array of Plugin objects, each of which represents one plug-in module that has been installed in the browser. The properties of the Plugin object provide various details about the plug-in. The Plugin object also contains array elements, which are a MimeType objects describing each of data formats supported by that particular plug-in. Note that this array is different than the `navigator.mimeTypes[]` array described above.

You can use the `plugins[ ]` property as an associative array, just as you can the `mimeTypes[ ]` property. This lets you check for the existence of a particular plug-in without having to loop through the array numerically and check every element:

```
// Check to see if the browser has the Shockwave plug-in installed.
var shocked = (navigator.plugins["Shockwave"] != null);
```

13.2 The Location Object

The `location` property of a window is a reference to a Location object, which is a representation of the URL of the document currently being displayed in that window. The `href` property of the Location object is a string that contains the complete text of the URL. Other properties of this object, such as `protocol`, `host`, `pathname`, and `search` specify the various individual parts of the URL. This `search` property of the Location object is an interesting one. It contains any portion of a URL following (and including) a question mark. This is often some sort of "query string", and in general, the question mark syntax in a URL is a technique for embedding arguments in the URL. While these arguments are usually intended for CGI scripts run on a server, there is no reason they cannot also be used in JavaScript-enabled pages. Example 13-2 shows how you can use JavaScript and the Location object to extract arguments embedded within your web page.

Example 13–2: Extracting Arguments from a URL

```
<SCRIPT LANGUAGE="JavaScript1.1">
// location.search has a question mark at the beginning,
// so we call substring() to get rid of it.
var argstr = location.search.substring(1, location.search.length)

// Assuming that the arguments are passed in a comma-separated list, we
// can break them into an array with this line. (Using an ampersand to
// separate arguments is another common URL convention.)
var args = argstr.split(',');

// Now we can use the arguments however we want. This example just
// prints them out. We use the unescape() function in case the arguments
// include escaped characters (like spaces and punctuation) that are
// illegal in URLs. (See escape() and unescape() functions for details.)
for (var i = 0; i < args.length; i++)
    document.write(unescape(args[i]) + "<BR>");
</SCRIPT>
```

In addition to its properties, the Location object can be used as if it were itself a primitive string value. If you read the value of a Location object, you get the same string as you would if you read the `href` property of the object (this is because the Location object has a suitable `toString()` method). What is far more interesting, though, is that you can assign a new URL string to the `location` property of a window. Assigning a URL to the Location object like this has a very important side effect: it causes the browser to load and display the contents of the URL you assign (this side effect occurs because the Location has a suitable assign() method). For example, you might assign a URL to the location property like this:

```
// If Java isn't enabled, go to a page that displays a message
// saying that you can't run this page without Java.
if (!navigator.javaEnabled())
    location = "needsjava.html";
```

As you can imagine, making the browser load specified web pages into windows is a very important programming technique. While you might expect there to be a method you can call to make the browser display a new web page, assigning a URL to the location property of a window is the supported technique to accomplish this. Internet Explorer supports a navigate() method of the Window object to do this, but it is not compatible with Navigator, and therefore should not be used.

Although the Location object does not have a method that serves the same function as assigning a URL directly to the location property of a window, this object does support two methods (in Navigator 3.0). The reload() method reloads the currently displayed page from the web server. The replace() method loads and displays a URL that you specify. But invoking this method for a given URL is different than assigning that URL to the location property of a window. When you call replace(), the specified URL "replaces" the current one in the browser's history list rather than creating a new entry in that history list. Therefore, if you use replace() to overwrite one document with a new one, the **Back** button will not take the user back to the original document, as it would have if you had loaded the new document by assigning to the location property. For web sites that use frames and display a lot of "temporary" pages (perhaps generated by a CGI script) using replace() is often quite useful. By not storing temporary pages in the history list, the **Back** button becomes more useful to the user.

Finally, don't confuse the location property of the Window object, which refers to a Location object, with the location property of the Document object, which is simply a read-only string with none of the special features of the Location object. Document.location is a synonym for Document.URL, which, in Navigator 3.0, is the preferred name for this property (because it avoids the potential confusion). In most cases, document.location is the same as location.href. When there is a server redirect, however, document.location contains the actual URL, as loaded, and location.href contains the URL as originally requested.

13.3 The History Object

The `history` property of the Window object refers to a History object for the window. The History object is an array of the URLs in the browsing history of the window or frame. For a top-level Navigator window, the History object is a representation of the contents of the browser's **Go** menu.

A user's browsing session history is private information and, so for security reasons, there are heavy restrictions on how the History object can be used. In Navigator 3.0, with the data-tainting security model enabled, (see Chapter 20, *JavaScript Security*) the elements of the `history` array are accessible to JavaScript programs. On all other platforms, however, they are never accessible, and the History object is much less useful. In Navigator, the `length` property of the History object can be read, although it is not actually good for much. In Internet Explorer, even this `length` property is hidden for security reasons—querying it always returns 0.

Besides its array elements and `length` property, the History object also supports three methods. The `back()` and `forward()` methods perform the same action as clicking on the **Back** and **Forward** browser buttons. The third method, `go()`, suffers from bugs in Navigator 2.0 and 3.0, and has incompatible behavior in Internet Explorer; it is best avoided. Example 13-3 shows how you might use the `back()` and `forward()` methods of the History object, and also the Location object to add a "navigation bar" to a framed web site. Figure 13-1 shows what it looks like.

Example 13-3: A Navigation Bar Using the History and Location Objects

```
<!-- This file implements a navigation bar, designed to go in a frame at
     the bottom of a window. Include it in a frameset like the following:

        <frameset rows="*,75">
        <frame src="about:blank">
        <frame src="navigation.html">
        </frameset>
-->

<SCRIPT>
// The function is invoked by the Back button in our navigation bar.
function go_back()
{
    // First, clear the URL entry field in our form
    document.navbar.url.value = "";

    // Then use the History object of the main frame to go back.
    parent.frames[0].history.back();
```

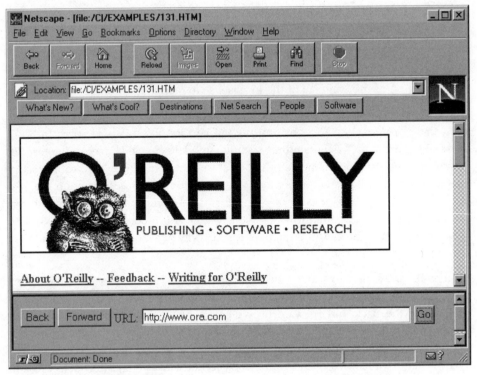

Figure 13-1: A navigation bar

Example 13-3: A Navigation Bar Using the History and Location Objects (continued)

```
    // Wait a second, and then update the URL entry field in the form
    // from the location.href property of the main frame. The wait seems
    // to be necessary to allow the location.href property to get in sync.
    setTimeout("document.navbar.url.value = parent.frames[0].location.href;",
              1000);
}

// This function is invoked by the Forward button in the navigation bar.
// It works just like the one above.
function go_forward()
{
    document.navbar.url.value = "";
    parent.frames[0].history.forward();
    setTimeout("document.navbar.url.value = parent.frames[0].location.href;",
              1000);
}

// This function is invoked by the Go button in the navigation bar, and also
// when the form is submitted (when the user hits the Return key).
function go_to()
```

Example 13-3: A Navigation Bar Using the History and Location Objects (continued)

```
{
    // Just set the location property of the main frame to the URL
    // that the user typed in.
    parent.frames[0].location = document.navbar.url.value;
}
</SCRIPT>

<!-- Here's the form, with event handlers that invoke the functions above -->
<FORM NAME="navbar" onSubmit="go_to(); return false">
<INPUT TYPE="button" VALUE="Back"  onClick="go_back();">
<INPUT TYPE="button" VALUE="Forward"  onClick="go_forward()">
URL:
<INPUT TYPE="text" NAME="url" SIZE=50>
<INPUT TYPE="button" VALUE="Go" onClick="go_to()">
</FORM>
```

14

Documents and Their Contents

14.1 The Document Object

If the Window object, which represents a window or a frame, is the central object in client-side JavaScript, then the Document object, which represents the contents of a window or frame, runs a close second, and is just as commonly used. This object has properties that specify information about the document: the URL, its last-modified date, the URL of the document that linked to it, the colors that it is displayed in. The Document object also has a few methods that allow JavaScript programs to dynamically output text into a document, and to dynamically create new documents from scratch. Finally, the Document object also contains a number of array properties that specify information about the contents of the document. These arrays contain objects that represent the links, anchors, HTML forms, applets, and embedded data contained in the document. These arrays and the objects they contain are very important in JavaScript programming, and will be described in their own sections later in this chapter.

14.1.1 Document Properties

The Document object has a number of properties that correspond to attributes of the <BODY> tag, and which are used to specify the colors that the document is displayed in. The bgColor property, and the BGCOLOR attribute specify the background color of the document. Similarly, the fgColor and the TEXT attribute specify the default color for text in the document. The linkColor property specifies the color of unvisited links, and vlinkColor and alinkColor* specify the

---

* You can set the alinkColor property in Internet Explorer, but it will be ignored, since IE never displays a separate color for activated links.

color of visited links and of activated links (i.e., links currently being clicked on). The `LINK`, `VLINK`, and `ALINK` attributes correspond to these properties.

These color properties of the Document object are read/write properties, but they can only be set before the `<BODY>` tag is parsed. You can set them dynamically with JavaScript code in the `<HEAD>` of a document, or you can set them statically as attributes of the `<BODY>` tag, but you cannot set them elsewhere.

The exception to this rule is the `bgColor` property. You can set this property at any time, and doing so will cause the background color of the browser to change. Unfortunately, on Unix platforms, changing the background color can make the contents of the page disappear (usually until the window is scrolled or otherwise redrawn). Setting the background color can still produce a useful special effect when done with small, empty frames, however.

Each of these color properties has a string value. To set a color, you can use one of the predefined color names listed in Appendix G, *JavaScript and HTML Color Names and Values*, or you can specify the color as red, green, and blue color values, expressed as a string of six hexadecimal digits in the form *"RRGGBB"*.

The Document object also has properties that are somewhat more interesting than these color properties. For the most part, the values of these other properties are derived from the HTML content of the document or from HTML headers supplied by the web server. As we saw in the discussion of the Location object, the Document object has a `location` property (and a `URL` property which is a preferred synonym in Navigator 3.0) that specifies the URL of the document. Because of redirection performed by the web server, this URL may be different than the requested URL.

The `lastModified` property is a string that specifies the date and time of the most recent change to the document. This is a value supplied by some, but not all, web servers. The `referrer` property specifies the URL of the document that contained the hypertext link that the user clicked on to get to the current document. If the current document was loaded by explicitly typing a URL, then this property will be empty. Note that this property is not supported in Internet Explorer 3.0. Finally, the `title` property contains any text that appears between the `<TITLE>` and `</TITLE>` tags in the `<HEAD>` of the document. You cannot use this property, of course, in code that appears before the `<TITLE>` of a document.

A simple use for the `lastModified` property is to automatically include a timestamp in your documents, so that users know whether the information they are seeing is up to date. You can do this by including HTML and JavaScript code like the following at the bottom of all your documents. Note that this code displays the document title and URL as well as its modification date:

```
<HR><FONT SIZE=1>
Document: <I><SCRIPT>document.write(document.title);</SCRIPT></I><BR>
URL: <I><SCRIPT>document.write(document.URL);</SCRIPT></I><BR>
Last Update: <I><SCRIPT>document.write(document.lastModified);</SCRIPT></I>
</FONT>
```

A possible use for the `referrer` property is to save this value in a hidden field of a form on your web page. When the user submits the form (for whatever reason your page contains the form in the first place) you can save this referrer data on the server. This will allow you to analyze what links exist to your page, and also what percentage of hits come through which links. Another use of this property is a trick to prevent unauthorized links to your page from working correctly. For example, if you only want users to be able to get to your page through links in pages from one particular site, you might use code like this at the top of your page:

```
<SCRIPT>
if (document.referrer == "" || document.referrer.indexOf("mysite.com") == -1)
    window.location = "javascript:'You can't get there from here!'";
</SCRIPT>
```

Don't consider this trick to be any kind of serious security measure, of course. Anyone determined to read your pages could simply disable JavaScript in their browser, and then load the page.

14.1.2 The write() Method

Without a doubt, the most important feature of the Document object (and perhaps of client-side JavaScript in general) is the `write()` method, which allows us to dynamically generate web page content from our JavaScript programs. There are several ways that this method can be used. The most obvious is to use it within a script to output HTML into the document that is currently being parsed. This is the way it was used above to display the Document `lastModified` property at the bottom of the web page. Be aware that you can only output HTML to the current document while that document is being parsed. That is, you can only call docu-ment.write() from within <SCRIPT> tags, because these scripts are executed as part of the document parsing process. In particular, if you call document.write() from an event handler, you will end up overwriting the current document (including its event handlers), instead of appending text to it.

Although you can't usefully write to the current document from an event handler, there is no reason you can't write to a document in another window or frame, and doing so can be a very useful technique for multiwindow or multiframe web sites.

For example, JavaScript code in one frame of a multiframe site might display a message in another frame with code like this:

```
<SCRIPT>
parent.frames[0].document.open();
parent.frames[0].document.write("<HRE>Hello from your sibling frame!<HR>");
parent.frames[0].document.close();
</SCRIPT>
```

We previously saw code that dynamically creates an HTML document like this in Example 12-2 and Example 12-6. Recall that to create a new document, we first call the `open()` method of the Document object, then call `write()` any number of times to output the contents of the document, and finally call the `close()` method of the Document object to indicate that we are complete. This last step is important—if you forget to close the document, the browser will not stop the "document loading" animation it displays. Also, the browser may buffer up the HTML you have written, and is not required to display it until you explicitly end the document by calling `close()`.

In contrast to the `close()` call, which is required, the `open()` call is optional. If you call the `write()` method on a document that has already been closed, then JavaScript implicitly opens a new HTML document, as if you called the `open()` method. This explains what happens when you call `document.write()` from an event handler within the same document—JavaScript opens a new document. In the process, however, the current document and its contents, including scripts and event handlers, is discarded. In Navigator 3.0, this causes surprising programming difficulties and unexpected error messages. In Navigator 2.0, it can actually cause the browser to crash. The best rule of thumb is that a document should never call `write()` on itself from within an event-handler.

A couple of final notes about the `write()` method. First, many people do not realize that the `write()` method can take more than one argument. When you pass multiple arguments, they will be output one after another, just as if they had been concatenated. So instead of writing:

```
document.write('Hello, '  + name + " Welcome to my home page!");
```

you can equivalently write:

```
document.write('Hello, ', name, " Welcome to my home page!");
```

The second point to note about the `write()` method is that the Document object also supports a `writeln()` method, which is identical to the `write()` method in every way, except that it appends a newline after outputting its arguments. Since HTML ignores linebreaks, this newline character usually doesn't make a difference, but, as we'll see in a bit, the `writeln()` method can be convenient when working with non-HTML documents.

14.1.3 Flushing Generated Output

When you use the write() method to dynamically generate HTML output, the text you write may not appear in the browser window right away. The contents of your individual write() calls may be buffered up so that they can be written out to the document in larger chunks. Unfortunately, there is no flush() method of the Document object that forces all output to appear. Instead, you must know the necessary tricks to make your output appear.

Calling the close() method is the simplest technique for forcing your output to be displayed, of course. Sometimes, though, you want intermediate output to be displayed, and are not yet ready to close the document you are generating. In this case, there are two techniques for flushing output. In Navigator 3.0, output is flushed whenever a new line is forced in the browser. Thus, if you output a <BR> or <P> or <HR> tag, all the text before that tag will appear. In Internet Explorer 3.0, it is not so easy, however—your output does not appear until the current <SCRIPT> block ends or the current event handler function returns. Thus, for this browser, you may need to break your code up into smaller chunks in order to assure that output is correctly flushed. Note that you can always use setTimeout() to schedule the next "chunk" of code to run in 0 milliseconds. This technique allows control to temporarily return to IE so that it can display any pending output.

N3

IE 3

14.1.4 Non-HTML Documents

When you open a new document with the open() method, the browser assumes that you'll be creating an HTML document. But this is not necessarily the case. Web browsers can display a number of other data formats besides HTML text. When you want to dynamically create and display a document using some other data format, you call the open() method with a single argument, which is the MIME type you desire. Note that while this technique is supported in Navigator 2.0 and 3.0, it does not work in Internet Explorer 3.0—in that browser, any argument passed to open() is ignored.

The MIME type for HTML is "text/html". The most common format other than HTML is plain text, with a MIME type of "text/plain". If you want to use the write() method to output text that uses newlines, spaces, and tab characters for formatting, then you should open the document by passing the string "text/plain" to the open() method. Example 14-1 shows one way you might do this. It implements a debug() function that you can use to output plain-text debugging messages from your scripts into a separate window that appears when needed. Figure 14-1 shows what the resulting window looks like.

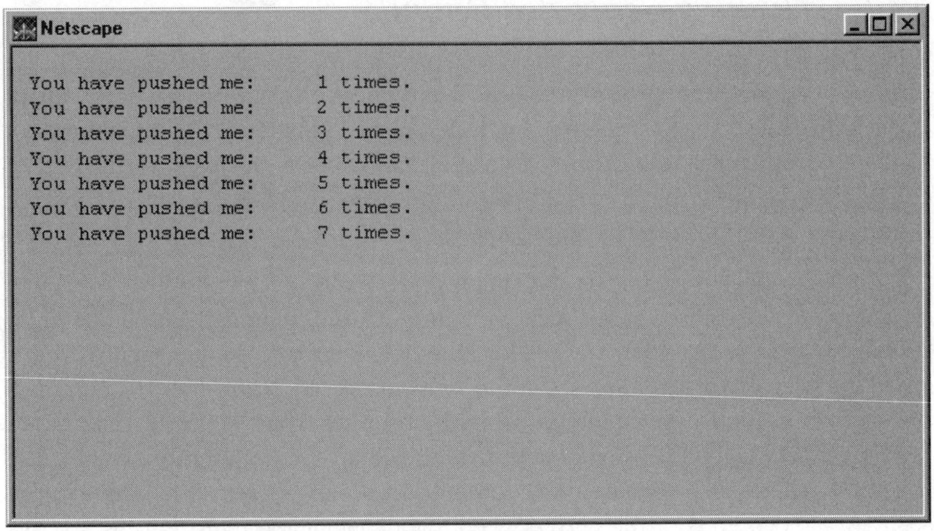

Figure 14-1: A window for plain-text debugging output

Example 14-1: Creating a Plain-Text Document

```
<SCRIPT>
var _console = null;

function debug(msg)
{
    // Open a window the first time we are called, or after an existing
    // console window has been closed.
    if ((_console == null) || (_console.closed)) {
        _console = window.open("","console","width=600,height=300,resizable");
        // open a document in the window to display plain text
        _console.document.open("text/plain");
    }

    _console.document.writeln(msg);
}
</SCRIPT>

<!-- Here's an example of using this script -->
<SCRIPT>var n = 0;</SCRIPT>
<FORM>
<INPUT TYPE="button" VALUE="Push Me"
       onClick="debug('You have pushed me:\t' + ++n + ' times.');">
</FORM>
```

This technique of using non-HTML documents is not limited to plain-text documents, or to textual documents in general. It can also be used with images, for instance. If we open a document and specify the MIME type "image/xbm", for example, then the browser will expect the contents of that document to be an image in XBM format. Because XBM images have an ASCII representation, we can easily write a static XBM image to the document, or even generate a dynamic image on the fly (perhaps using a Java applet to do the image processing, for speed). Example 14-2 shows how you can create an "image/xbm" document with a static XBM image, and also shows how this XBM image can be used for image embedded in an HTML document. Figure 14-2 shows the windows created by the example. This technique would be much more efficient and interesting if it used a compact image format like "image/gif". Unfortunately, this is not possible because GIF images use a binary format that includes NULL characters (i.e., the byte 0) and the current versions of JavaScript cannot output this character.

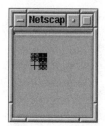  

Figure 14–2: JavaScript-generated images

Example 14–2: Generating XBM Images with JavaScript

```
<SCRIPT>
// This is a long string in XBM image format. It defines an image.
// This is an ASCII format, which means we can easily manipulate it
// in JavaScript, but also means that it is not compact. This is only
// a 22x22 pixel image. The real power of this technique comes, of course
// when we start generating XBM data dynamically at run-time instead of
// using a static string as we do here.
image_text =
"#define plaid_width 22\n" +
"#define plaid_height 22\n" +
"#define plaid_x_hot -1\n" +
"#define plaid_y_hot -1\n" +
"static char plaid_bits[] = {\n" +
"  0x75, 0xfd, 0x3f, 0xaa, 0xfa, 0x3e, 0x75, 0xfd, 0x3f, 0xaa, 0xfa, 0x3e,\n" +
"  0x75, 0xfd, 0x3f, 0xff, 0x57, 0x15, 0x75, 0xfd, 0x3f, 0xaa, 0xfa, 0x3e,\n" +
"  0x75, 0xfd, 0x3f, 0xaa, 0xfa, 0x3e, 0x75, 0xfd, 0x3f, 0x20, 0xa8, 0x2b,\n" +
"  0x20, 0x50, 0x15, 0x20, 0xa8, 0x2b, 0x20, 0x50, 0x15, 0x20, 0xa8, 0x2b,\n" +
"  0xff, 0xff, 0x3f, 0x20, 0xa8, 0x2b, 0x20, 0x50, 0x15, 0x20, 0xa8, 0x2b,\n" +
"  0x20, 0x50, 0x15, 0x20, 0xa8, 0x2b};\n";
```

Example 14-2: Generating XBM Images with JavaScript (continued)

```
// Here we create a new window, open the document, specifying a MIME type of
// image/xbm, and then output the image text. The window will display
// the XBM data we give it.
win1 = window.open("", "win1", "width=100,height=100,resizable");
var d = win1.document;
d.open('image/xbm');
d.write(image_text);
d.close();

// There are also a couple of other ways to use XBM image data that do not
// involve specifying a MIME type when opening the document. Here we
// create a new window, and then use a javascript: URL as the SRC of an
// inline <IMG>. This is an XBM image embedded in a text/html document,
// so we can display text, anchors, etc.
win2 = window.open("", "win2", "width=100,height=100,resizable");
var d = win2.document;
d.open();
d.write('<B>Plaid:</B><BR>');
d.write('<A HREF="javascript:self.close();">');
d.write('<IMG SRC="javascript:opener.image_text" WIDTH=22 HEIGHT=22>');
d.write('</A>');
d.close();

// We can also use the javascript: URL with the BACKGROUND tag of the
// <BODY> tag. XBM is a black-on-white image format, but note how the
// BGCOLOR tag can replace the white background.
win3 = window.open("", "win3", "width=100,height=100,resizable");
var d = win3.document;
d.open();
d.write('<BODY BACKGROUND="javascript:opener.image_text" BGCOLOR="red">');
d.close();
</SCRIPT>
```

14.2 The Link Object

The previous section has described the Document object and some of its important methods and properties. The Document object has a number of other properties that we have not discussed yet. These properties are arrays, each of which contains references to other important JavaScript objects. This and the following sections explain the links[], anchors[], applets[], embeds[], images[], and forms[] properties of the Document object, and the Link, JavaObject, Image, and Form objects those array properties refer to.

The Link object represents a hypertext link in a document, and is created with an <A HREF="*hyperlink*"> HTML tag, or, in Navigator 3.0, with an <AREA> tag within a client-side image map <MAP> tag. The links[] property of the Document object is an array that contains a complete list of hypertext links in the document. The Link object represents the URL of the hypertext link, and contains all of the properties that the Location object does. For example, the href property of a Link object contains the complete text of the URL that is linked to, and the hostname property contains only the hostname portion of that URL. See the reference section for a complete list of these URL-related properties.

One obvious use of the Link object and the links[] array is to write a "web crawler" program. This program would run in one browser window or frame and read web pages into another window or frame (by setting the location property of the Window object). For each page it reads in, it would look through the links[] array and recursively follow them. If carefully written (so it doesn't get caught in infinite recursion or doesn't start going in circles) such a program can, for example, be used to generate a list of all web pages that are accessible from a given starting page, and can be quite useful in web site maintenance. Example 14-3 shows a simple function that can be used to generate a list of all the links in a specified Document object.

Example 14–3: Listing the Links in a Document

```
// Create a new window and list the destinations of all links in document d
// in that window. Note that we use a text/plain document.
function listlinks(d)
{
    var newwin = window.open("", "linklist",
                    "menubar,scrollbars,resizable,width=600,height=300");
    newwin.document.open("text/plain");
    for (var i = 0; i < d.links.length; i++)
        newwin.document.writeln(d.links[i]);
    newwin.document.close();
}
```

Don't expect to search the entire Internet with this technique, however. For security reasons, JavaScript in Navigator 2.0 and Navigator 3.0 is "hobbled" so that it cannot steal data that may be private. The restriction is this: a script running in one window or frame can read properties from other windows or frames only if the contents of the other window or frame were loaded from the same web server as the script. While our "web crawler" program as we've described it above is not a threat to Internet security or privacy, this general security restriction will prevent it from crawling very far beyond the site from which it was loaded. (When the crawler loads a page from a different site, it will appear as if that page simply has no links on it.) See Chapter 20, *JavaScript Security*, for a complete discussion of JavaScript security, including a description of how to partially lift the restriction described here with the `domain` property, or to fully lift it by enabling the data-tainting security model.

More interesting than the URL-related properties of the Link object are the event handlers it supports. We saw the `onMouseOver()` event handler previously in Example 12-3 where it was used with both <A> and <AREA> to change the message in the browser's status line when the mouse moved over the link.

In addition to this `onMouseOver()` event handler, the link object supports two others. The `onClick()` event handler is invoked when the user clicks on a hypertext link. In Navigator 3.0, if this event handler returns `false` then the browser won't follow the link, as it would otherwise. Note that `onClick()` only works for Link objects created with the <A> tag; it should work for those created with the <AREA> tag in a future version of the language.

In Navigator 3.0, both the <A> and <AREA> tags support an `onMouseOut()` event handler. This is simply the opposite of the `onMouseOver()` handler—it is run when the mouse pointer moves off of a hypertext link. If you used `onMouseOver()` to display a message in the status line, you can use `onMouse-Out()` to clear it; as we saw in Chapter 12, *Programming with Windows*, the status line is not automatically cleared, as it should be, on Windows platforms.

Finally, it is worth mentioning that the `href` and other URL properties of the Link object are read/write. Thus, you can write JavaScript programs that dynamically modify the destinations of hypertext links! Example 14-4 is a frivolous piece of JavaScript-enhanced HTML that implements a random hypertext link. It demonstrates each of the features of the Link object that we've considered: the `links[]` array, the use of the Link event handlers, and dynamic setting of the destination of a Link. Note that the example sets the `href` property of the Link, but doesn't bother to read the `href` property of the link it randomly chooses. Instead, it simply relies on the `toString()` method of the Link object to return the URL.

Example 14-4: A Random Hypertext Link

```
<A HREF="about:"
    onMouseOver="status = 'Take a chance... Click me.'; return true;"
    onMouseOut="status = ''"
    onClick="this.href =
            document.links[Math.floor(Math.random()*document.links.length)]"
>
Random Link
</A>
```

14.3 The Anchor Object

Just as a Link object represents a hypertext link, an Anchor object represents a named location within a document which can serve as the target of a hypertext link. Anchors are something like the reverse of Links, and they are treated similarly to Links in HTML and in JavaScript. An anchor is created with the <A> tag, when it is used with the NAME attribute (rather than the HREF attribute, which creates a link). The Document object contains an anchors[] property which is an array of all the Anchors in the document.

There is only one flaw in this analogy between links and anchors: the Anchor object has not been implemented in either JavaScript 1.0 or JavaScript 1.1. So, in Navigator 2.0, Navigator 3.0, and Internet Explorer 3.0, the anchors[] property of the Document object is an array that contains null for each of its elements. The length property of the anchors[] array does work, and you can use it to determine the number of anchors in a given document, although this information may not be of particular use.

The next version of JavaScript will likely contain a useful implementation of the Anchor object.

14.4 The JavaObject Object

The JavaObject object is a JavaScript object that serves as a wrapper around Java objects. It allows JavaScript programs to read and write the public fields of a Java object, and also to invoke the public methods of a Java object. Chapter 19, *Live-Connect: JavaScript and Java*, covers the "LiveConnect" mechanism for communication between Java and JavaScript, and will explain JavaObjects in detail, as well as the JavaArray, JavaClass, and JavaPackage objects.

The reason that JavaObjects are being discussed here is that in Navigator 3.0, the applets[] and embeds[] properties of the Document object are arrays that contain JavaObjects. Elements of the applets[] array are created when a Java applet is included in the document with the <APPLET> tag. Each JavaObject in this array represents the Java Applet object. Similarly, elements of the embeds[] array are created when embedded data are included in the document with the <EMBED> tag. In Navigator, the <EMBED> tag specifies data to be displayed through a plug-in, and the JavaObject objects in the embeds[] array are Java objects provided by the plug-in that allow it to be controlled through a Java-based interface. If a plug-in does not support Java—and many plug-ins currently do not—then the entry in the embeds[] array will be a dummy object with no functionality.

Both the <APPLET> and the <EMBED> tags have optional NAME attributes. If you specify a name for either of these tags, then a property with that specified name will be created in the Document object. The value of this property will be a reference to the JavaObject for the applet or embedded data. Using the NAME attribute in HTML can make your JavaScript code more readable—you can use expressions like document.myapp instead of document.applets[0].

Example 14-5 shows how you might embed a Java applet in a web page with the <APPLET> tag, and then invoke the start() and stop() methods of that applet from JavaScript event handlers.

Example 14-5: Invoking Methods of a Java Applet from JavaScript

```
<APPLET NAME="animation" CODE="Animation.class" WIDTH=500 HEIGHT=200>
</APPLET>
<FORM>
<INPUT TYPE=button VALUE="Start" onclick="document.animation.start()">
<INPUT TYPE=button VALUE="Stop" onclick="document.animation.stop()">
</FORM>
```

The topic of interacting with Java from JavaScript is a broad one, and deserves a chapter on its own. We'll learn more about the JavaObject object and the applets[] and embeds[] arrays in Chapter 19.

15

Saving State with Cookies

The Document object contains property named `cookie` that was not discussed in Chapter 14, *Documents and Their Contents*. On the surface, this property appears to be a simple string value. Surface appearance to the contrary, however, the `cookie` property controls a very important feature of the web browser, and is important enough to warrant a complete chapter of its own.

15.1 An Overview of Cookies

A *cookie* is a small amount of named data stored by the web browser and associated with a particular web page or web site.[*] Cookies serve to give web browsers a "memory", so that they can use data that were input on one page in another page, or so they can recall user preferences or other state variables when the user leaves a page and returns. Cookies were originally designed for CGI programming, and at the lowest level are implemented as an extension to the HTTP protocol. Cookie data is automatically transmitted between web browser and web server so that CGI scripts on the server can read and write cookie values that are stored on the client. As we'll see later in this chapter, client-side JavaScript code can also read and write cookies with the `Document.cookie` property.

`Document.cookie` is a string property that allows you to read, create, modify, and delete the cookie or cookies that apply to the current web page. It can allow you to do all this because the property does not behave like a normal read/write string

---

[*] The name "cookie" does not have a lot of significance, but is not used without precedent. In the obscure annals of computing history, the term "cookie" or "magic cookie" has been used to refer to a small chunk of data, particularly a chunk of privileged or secret data, akin to a password, that proves identity or permits access. Cookies as used in JavaScript are used to save state and can serve to establish a kind of "identity" for a web browser. Cookies in JavaScript do not use any kind of cryptography, and are not secure in any way.

property. You may both read and write the value of `cookie`, but setting the property has the side effect of creating a new cookie for the web page, while reading the property has the side effect of returning a list of all cookies that apply to the web page. Later sections of this chapter explain in detail how to read and write cookie values using the `cookie` property.

In order to use cookies effectively, however, you need to know more about them. First, cookies are transient by default—the values they store last for the duration of the web browser session, but are lost when the user exits the browser. If you want cookies to last beyond a single browsing session, then you specify an expiration date—this will cause the browser to save its cookies in a local file so that it can read them back in. In this case, the cookies values will be saved until the expiration date has past.

The second point that is important to understand about cookies is how they are associated with web pages. By default, a cookie is associated with, and accessible to, the web page that created it and any other web pages in the same directory, or subdirectories of that directory. Sometimes, though, you'll want to use cookie values throughout a multipage web site, regardless of which page creates the cookie. For instance, if the user enters their mailing address in a form on one page, you may want to save that address to use as the default the next time they return to the page, and also use it as the default in another form on another page where they are asked to enter a billing address. To allow this, you specify a *path* for the cookie. Then, any web pages from the same web server that contain that path in their URL will share the cookies. For example, if a cookie's path is set to "/acme", and this cookie is set by the page *http://my.isp.com/acme/catalog/index.html*, then the cookie will also be accessible to the page: *http://my.isp.com/acme/order/ index.html*. If no path were set in this example, then the default path would be "/acme/catalog", and the cookie would not be accessible from the "/acme/order" directory.

By default cookies are only accessible to pages on the same web server from which they were set. Large web sites may want cookies to be shared across multiple web servers, however. For example, the server at *order.acme.com* may need to read cookie values set from *catalog.acme.com*. This is possible if the cookie has a *domain* set. In this example, if the cookie has its domain set to *acme.com*, then it will be available to pages on both of the servers mentioned above, as long as those pages have URLs that match the cookie's path. When setting the domain of a cookie for use across multiple servers, you may often want to set a very generic path like "/". If no domain is set for a cookie, the default is the hostname of web server that serves the page. Note that you cannot set the domain of a cookie to a domain other than the domain of your server.

The third and final point to understand about cookies is that they can be secure or insecure. By default, cookies are insecure, which means that they will be transmitted over a normal, insecure, HTTP connection. If a cookie is marked secure, then it will only be transmitted when the browser and server are connected via HTTPS or another secure protocol.

See Appendix F, *Persistent Client State: HTTP Cookies*, for full technical details on cookies, including their expiration, path, and domain. That appendix contains the actual specification for HTTP cookies, and so contains low-level details that are more suitable to CGI programming than to JavaScript programming. The following sections discuss how you can set and query cookie values in JavaScript, and how you can specify the expiration, path, domain, and security level of a cookie.

15.2 Reading Cookies

When you use the `cookie` property in a JavaScript expression, the value it returns is a string containing all the cookies that apply to the current document. The string is a list of *name=value* pairs separated by semicolons, where *name* is the name of a cookie, and *value* is its string value. You can use the `String.indexOf()` and `String.substring()` methods to determine the value of the named cookie you are interested in. Or, you may find it easier to use `String.split()` to break the string into individual cookies.

Once you have obtained the value of a cookie in this way, you must interpret that value based on whatever format or encoding was used by the creator of that cookie. For example, the cookie might store multiple pieces of information in colon-separated fields. In this case, you would have to use appropriate string methods to extract the various fields of information.

The value of a cookie must not contain any semicolons, commas, or whitespace. Because these are commonly used characters, it is common to use the JavaScript `escape()` function to encode cookie values before storing them, and the `unescape()` function to decode the values after retrieving them.

Note that the `Document.cookie` property provides no way to obtain the domain, path, expiration, or secure fields associated with a cookie.

15.3 Storing Cookies

To associate a temporary cookie value with the current document, simply set the `cookie` property to a string of the form:

```
name=value
```

The next time you read the `cookie` property, the name/value pair you stored will be included in the list of cookies for the document. As noted above, the cookie value may not include semicolons, commas or whitespace. For this reason, you may want to use the JavaScript `escape()` function to encode the value before storing it in the cookie.

A cookie written as described above will last for the current web browsing session, but will be lost when the user exits the browser. To create a cookie that can last across browser sessions, include an expiration date. You can do this by setting the `cookie` property to a string of the form:

```
name=value; expires=date
```

When setting an expiration date like this, *date* should be a date specification in the format written by `Date.toGMTString()`.

Similarly, you can set the path, domain, and secure fields of a cookie by appending strings of the following form to the cookie value before that value is written to the *document*.`cookie` property:

```
; path=path
; domain=domain
; secure
```

To change the value of a cookie, set its value again, using the same name (and the same path and domain, if any) and the new value. To delete a cookie, set it again using the same name, an arbitrary value, and an expiration date that has already passed. Note that the browser is not required to immediately delete expired cookies. In practice, with Netscape, cookie deletion seems to work more effectively if the expiration date is in the relatively distant (several hours or more) past.

15.4 Cookie Limitations

Cookies are intended for infrequent storage of small amounts of data. They are not intended as a general-purpose communication or mechanism; use them in moderation. Note that web browsers are not required to retain more than 300 cookies total, nor more than 20 cookies per web server (for the entire server, not just for your page or site on the server), nor to retain more than 4 kilobytes of data per cookie (both name and value count towards this 4 kilobyte limit). The most restrictive of these is the 20 cookies per server limit, and so it is not a good idea to use a separate cookie for each variable you want to save. Instead, you should try to store multiple state variables within a single named cookie.

15.4.1 Cookies in Internet Explorer 3.0

In Internet Explorer 3.0, the `cookie` property only works for Document objects that were retrieved using the HTTP protocol. Documents retrieved from the local file system or via other protocols such as FTP cannot have cookies associated with them. This limitation will be resolved in a future release of IE.

15.5 Cookie Example

Example 15-1 brings all this discussion of cookies together. This example defines a Cookie class. When you create a Cookie object, you specify a Document object, a name for the cookie, and, optionally, an expiration time, a path, a domain, and whether the cookie should be secure. After creating a Cookie object, you may set arbitrary properties on this object. When you call the `store()` method of the object, these property names and values will be stored as the value of the cookie (a single cookie, not one for each property). Later, when you return to the page, or on another page, you can create a Cookie object with the same name. When you invoke the `load()` method of the object, the cookie value will be read and parsed, and the stored properties will be re-created in the new Cookie object. Finally, if you call the `remove()` method of the Cookie object, the cookie values will be deleted.

This example demonstrates a useful and elegant way to use cookies. The code is somewhat complicated, but is worth studying. You might choose to start at the bottom of the example, so you understand how the Cookie class is used before you start trying to understand how it is defined.

Example 15-1: A Utility Class for Working with Cookies

```
<SCRIPT LANGUAGE="JavaScript1.1">

// The constructor function: creates a cookie object for the specified
// document, with a specified name and optional attributes.
// Arguments:
//   document: the Document object that the cookie is stored for. Required.
//   name:     a string that specifies a name for the cookie. Required.
//   hours:    an optional number that specifies the number of hours from now
//             that the cookie should expire.
//   path:     an optional string that specifies the cookie path attribute.
//   domain:   an optional string that specifies the cookie domain attribute.
//   secure:   an optional Boolean value that, if true, requests a secure cookie.
//
function Cookie(document, name, hours, path, domain, secure)
{
```

Example 15-1: A Utility Class for Working with Cookies (continued)

```
    // All the predefined properties of this object begin with '$'
    // to distinguish them from other properties which are the values to
    // be stored in the cookie.
    this.$document = document;
    this.$name = name;
    if (hours)
        this.$expiration = new Date((new Date()).getTime() + hours*3600000);
    else this.$expiration = null;
    if (path) this.$path = path; else this.$path = null;
    if (domain) this.$domain = domain; else this.$domain = null;
    if (secure) this.$secure = true; else this.$secure = false;
}


// This function is the store() method of the Cookie object.
function _Cookie_store()
{
    // First, loop through the properties of the Cookie object and
    // put together the value of the cookie. Since cookies use the
    // equals sign and semicolons as separators, we'll use colons
    // and ampersands for the individual state variables we store
    // within a single cookie value. Note that we escape the value
    // of each state variable, in case it contains punctuation or other
    // illegal characters.
    var cookieval = "";
    for(var prop in this) {
        // Ignore properties with names that begin with '$' and also methods.
        if ((prop.charAt(0) == '$') || ((typeof this[prop]) == 'function'))
            continue;
        if (cookieval != "") cookieval += '&';
        cookieval += prop + ':' + escape(this[prop]);
    }

    // Now that we have the value of the cookie, put together the
    // complete cookie string, which includes the name, and the various
    // attributes specified when the Cookie object was created.
    var cookie = this.$name + '=' + cookieval;
    if (this.$expiration)
        cookie += '; expires=' + this.$expiration.toGMTString();
    if (this.$path) cookie += '; path=' + this.$path;
    if (this.$domain) cookie += '; domain=' + this.$domain;
    if (this.$secure) cookie += '; secure';

    // Now store the cookie by setting the magic Document.cookie property.
    this.$document.cookie = cookie;
}
```

Example 15-1: A Utility Class for Working with Cookies (continued)

```
// This function is the load() method of the Cookie object.
function _Cookie_load()
{
    // First, get a list of all cookies that pertain to this document.
    // We do this by reading the magic Document.cookie property.
    var allcookies = this.$document.cookie;
    if (allcookies == "") return false;

    // Now extract just the named cookie from that list.
    var start = allcookies.indexOf(this.$name + '=');
    if (start == -1) return false;   // cookie not defined for this page.
    start += this.$name.length + 1;  // skip name and equals sign.
    var end = allcookies.indexOf(';', start);
    if (end == -1) end = allcookies.length;
    var cookieval = allcookies.substring(start, end);

    // Now that we've extracted the value of the named cookie, we've
    // got to break that value down into individual state variable
    // names and values. The name/value pairs are separated from each
    // other with ampersands, and the individual names and values are
    // separated from each other with colons. We use the split method
    // to parse everything.
    var a = cookieval.split('&');  // break it into array of name/value pairs
    for(var i=0; i < a.length; i++)  // break each pair into an array
        a[i] = a[i].split(':');

    // Now that we've parsed the cookie value, set all the names and values
    // of the state variables in this Cookie object. Note that we unescape()
    // the property value, because we called escape() when we stored it.
    for(var i = 0; i < a.length; i++) {
        this[a[i][0]] = unescape(a[i][1]);
    }

    // We're done, so return the success code.
    return true;
}


// This function is the remove() method of the Cookie object.
function _Cookie_remove()
{
    var cookie;
    cookie = this.$name + '=';
    if (this.$path) cookie += '; path=' + this.$path;
    if (this.$domain) cookie += '; domain=' + this.$domain;
    cookie += '; expires=Fri, 02-Jan-1970 00:00:00 GMT';

    this.$document.cookie = cookie;
}
```

Example 15-1: A Utility Class for Working with Cookies (continued)

```
// Create a dummy Cookie object, so we can use the prototype object to make
// the functions above into methods.
new Cookie();
Cookie.prototype.store = _Cookie_store;
Cookie.prototype.load = _Cookie_load;
Cookie.prototype.remove = _Cookie_remove;


//==================================================================
//   The code above is the definition of the Cookie class.
//   The code below is a sample use of that class.
//==================================================================


// Create the cookie we'll use to save state for this web page.
// Since we're using the default path, this cookie will be accessible
// to all web pages in the same directory as this file or "below" it.
// Therefore, it should have a name that is unique among those pages.
// Note that we set the expiration to 10 days in the future.
var visitordata = new Cookie(document, "name_color_count_state", 240);

// First, try to read data stored in the cookie. If the cookie is not
// defined, or if it doesn't contain the data we need, then query the
// user for that data.
if (!visitordata.load() || !visitordata.name || !visitordata.color) {
    visitordata.name = prompt("What is your name:", "");
    visitordata.color = prompt("What is your favorite color:", "");
}

// Keep track of how many times this user has visited the page:
if (visitordata.visits == null) visitordata.visits = 0;
visitordata.visits++;

// Store the cookie values, even if they were already stored, so that the
// expiration date will be reset to 10 days from this most recent visit.
// Also, store them again to save the updated visits state variable.
visitordata.store();

// Now we can use the state variables we read:
document.write('<FONT SIZE=7 COLOR="' + visitordata.color + '">' +
               'Welcome, ' + visitordata.name + '!' +
               '</FONT>' +
               '<P>You have visited ' + visitordata.visits + ' times.');
</SCRIPT>

<FORM>
<INPUT TYPE="button" VALUE="Forget My Name" onClick="visitordata.remove();">
</FORM>
```

16

Special Effects with Images

In Navigator 3.0, the images[] property of the Document object is an array of Image elements, each one representing one of the inline images, created with an <IMG> tag, that is contained in the document. While web browsers have always been able to display images with the <IMG> tag, the addition of the Image object in Navigator 3.0 is a major step forward—it allows programs to dynamically manipulate those images.

16.1 Image Replacement with the Image.src Property

The main feature of the Image object is that its src property is read/write. You can read this property to obtain the URL from which an image was loaded. And more importantly, you can set the src property to make the browser load and display a new image in the same space. In order for this to work, the new image must have the same width and height as the original one.

The ability to dynamically replace one image in a static HTML document with another image opens the door to any number of special effects, from animation, to images that change when clicked on, to "digital clocks" that update themselves in real time. With a bit of thought, you can probably imagine many more potential uses for this technique. In order to make the image replacement technique viable, and in order to make animations and other special effects responsive enough to be useful, we need some way to ensure that the necessary images are loaded into the browser's cache.

16.2 Off-Screen Images and Caching

To force an image to be cached, we create an off-screen image and load the desired image into it. Then, when the image is required on-screen, we know it will be quickly loaded from the cache rather than slowly loaded over the network. Example 16-1 shows code that performs a simple animation using this technique.

Example 16-1: An Animation Using Image Replacement

```
<!-- The image that will be animated. Give it a name for convenience -->
<IMG SRC="images/0.gif" NAME=animation>

<SCRIPT>
// Create a bunch of off-screen images, and get them started
// loading the images we're going to animate.
images = new Array(10);
for(var i = 0; i < 10; i++) {
    images[i] = new Image();              // Create an Image object
    images[i].src = "images/" + i + ".gif";  // tell it what URL to load
}


// Later, when we want to perform our animation, we can use these URLs,
// knowing that they've been loaded into the cache. Note that we perform
// the animation by assigning the URL, not the Image object itself.
// Also note that we call the image by name, rather than as document.images[0].
function animate()
{
    document.animation.src = images[frame].src;
    frame = (frame + 1)%10;
    timeout_id = setTimeout("animate()", 250);  // display next frame later
}
var frame = 0;        // Keep track of what frame of the animation we're on.
var timeout_id = null; // This allows us to stop the animation.
</SCRIPT>

<FORM>                   <!-- Buttons to control the animation -->
  <INPUT TYPE=button VALUE="Start"
        onClick="if (timeout_id == null) animate()">
  <INPUT TYPE=button VALUE="Stop"
        onClick="if (timeout_id) clearTimeout(timeout_id); timeout_id=null;">
</FORM>
```

Example 16-1 demonstrates the important steps involved in creating an off-screen image for image caching. The first step is to create an Image object with the `Image()` constructor. The second step is to assign the URL of the desired image to the `src` property of the newly created Image object. Doing so will cause the browser to start loading the contents of the specified URL, which, unless caching is turned off, will cause the image to be loaded into the cache, even though it is not displayed anywhere.

A confusing detail about the use of off-screen Image objects is that they are not themselves directly used for anything. To perform image replacement with an off-screen Image object, you do *not* assign the Image object directly into the images[] array of the Document object. Instead, you simply set the src property of the desired on-screen image to the URL of the desired image. If this URL has previously been loaded by an off-screen image, then the the desired image should be in the cache and the on-screen image replacement will happen quickly. The off-screen image object is used to force the image to be loaded, but there isn't anything else that you can do with it.

16.3 *Image Event Handlers*

In Example 16-1, our animation does not begin until the user clicks the **Start** button, which allows plenty of time for our images to be loaded into the cache. But what about the more common case in which we want to automatically begin an animation as soon as all the necessary images are loaded? It turns out that images, whether created on screen with an <IMG> tag or off screen with the Image() constructor, have an onLoad() event handler that is invoked when the image is fully loaded. Example 16-2 is an update to the previous example which shows how we could automatically start the animation as soon as the images are loaded.

Example 16–2: An Animation Using the onLoad() Event Handler

```
<!-- The image that will be animated. Give it a name for convenience. -->
<IMG SRC="images/0.gif" NAME=animation>

<SCRIPT>
// Count how many images have been loaded. When we reach 10, start animating.
function count_images() {  if (++num_loaded_images == 10) animate(); }
var num_loaded_images = 0;

// Create the off-screen images and assign the image URLs.
// Also assign an event handler so we can count how many images have been
// loaded. Note that we assign the handler before the URL, because otherwise
// the image might finish loading (e.g., if it is already cached) before
// we assign the handler, and then we'll lose count of how many have loaded!
images = new Array(10);
for(var i = 0; i < 10; i++) {
    images[i] = new Image();                  // Create an Image object
    images[i].onload = count_images;          // assign the event handler
    images[i].src = "images/" + i + ".gif";   // tell it what URL to load
}
```

Example 16-2: An Animation Using the onLoad( ) Event Handler (continued)

```
function animate()  // The function that does the animation.
{
    document.animation.src = images[frame].src;
    frame = (frame + 1)%10;
    timeout_id = setTimeout("animate()", 250);  // display next frame later
}
var frame = 0;          // Keep track of what frame of the animation we're on.
var timeout_id = null; // This allows us to stop the animation.
</SCRIPT>

<!-- Buttons to control the animation. Note that we don't let the user
  -- start the animation before all the images are loaded. -->
<FORM>
  <INPUT TYPE=button VALUE="Start"
       onClick="if (timeout_id==null && num_loaded_images==10) animate()">
  <INPUT TYPE=button VALUE="Stop"
       onClick="if (timeout_id) clearTimeout(timeout_id); timeout_id=null;">
</FORM>
```

In addition to the onLoad( ) event handler, the Image object also supports two others. The onError( ) event handler is invoked when an error occurs during image loading, such as when the specified URL refers to a corrupt image data. The onAbort( ) handler is invoked if the user aborts the image load (for example, by clicking the **Stop** button in the browser) before it has finished. For any image, one (and only one) of these handlers will be called. In addition to these handlers, each Image object also has a complete property. This property is false while the image is loading, and is true once the image has loaded or once the browser has stopped trying to load it. That is, the complete property becomes true once one of the three possible event handlers is invoked.

16.4 Other Image Properties

The Image object has a few other properties as well. Most of them are read-only properties that simply mirror attributes of the <IMG> tag that created the image. The width, height, border, hspace, and vspace properties are read-only integers that specify the size of the image, the width of its border, and the size of its horizontal and vertical margins. These properties are set by the attributes of the IMG tag which share their names.

Finally, the lowsrc property of the Image object mirrors the LOWSRC attribute of the IMG tag. It specifies the URL of an optional image to display when the page is viewed on a low-resolution device. The lowsrc property is a read/write string, like src is, but unlike the src property, setting lowsrc does not cause the browser to load and display the newly-specified low-res image. If you want to perform an animation, or some other special effect, that works with low-resolution images as well as high-resolution, then always remember to update the lowsrc property before you set the src property. If the browser is running on a low-resolution device when you set the src literal, it will load the new lowsrc image instead.

16.5 Image Replacement Example

Because image replacement is such a versatile technique we will end our discussion of the Image object with an extended example. Example 16-3 defines a ToggleButton class that uses image replacement to simulate a graphical checkbox. Because this class uses images that we provide, we can use bolder graphics than those plain-old graphics used by the standard HTML Checkbox object. Figure 16-1 shows how these toggle button graphics could appear on a web page. This is a complex, real-world example, and is worth studying carefully.

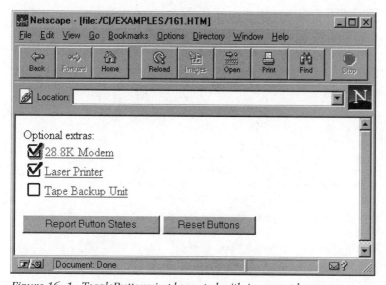

Figure 16–1: ToggleButtons implemented with image replacement

Example 16–3: Implementing a ToggleButton with Image Replacement

```
<SCRIPT LANGUAGE="JavaScript1.1">
// This is the constructor function for our new ToggleButton class.
// Calling it creates a ToggleButton object and outputs the required
// <A> and <IMG> tags into the specified document at the current location.
// Therefore, don't call it for the current document from an event handler.
```

Example 16–3: Implementing a ToggleButton with Image Replacement (continued)

```
// Arguments:
//    document: the Document object the buttons will be created in.
//    checked: a Boolean that says whether the button is initially checked.
//    label:   an optional string that specifies text to appear after the button.
//    onclick: an optional function to be called when the toggle button is
//             clicked. It will be passed a Boolean indicating the new
//             state of the button. You can also pass a string, which will
//             be converted to a function which is passed a Boolean argument
//             named "state".
function ToggleButton(document, checked, label, onclick)
{
    // first time called, document will be false. Ignore this call.
    if (document == null) return;

    // The first time we are called (and only the first time) we have
    // to do some special stuff. First, now that the prototype object
    // is created, we can set up our methods.
    // Second, we've got to load the images that we'll be using.
    // Doing this will get the images in the cache for when we need them.
    if (!ToggleButton.prototype.over) {
        // Initialize the prototype object to create our methods.
        ToggleButton.prototype.over = _ToggleButton_over;
        ToggleButton.prototype.out = _ToggleButton_out;
        ToggleButton.prototype.click = _ToggleButton_click;

        // Now create an array of image objects, and assign URLs to them.
        // The URLs of the images are configurable, and are stored in an
        // array property of this constructor function itself. They will be
        // initialized below. Because of a bug in Navigator, we've got
        // to maintain references to these images, so we store the array
        // in a property of the constructor rather than using a local variable.
        ToggleButton.images = new Array(4);
        for(var i = 0; i < 4; i++) {
            ToggleButton.images[i] = new Image(ToggleButton.width,
                                               ToggleButton.height);
            ToggleButton.images[i].src = ToggleButton.imagenames[i];
        }
    }

    // Save some of the arguments we were passed.
    this.document = document;
    this.checked = checked;

    // Remember that the mouse is not currently on top of us.
    this.highlighted = false;
```

```
    // Save the onclick argument to be called when the button is clicked.
    // If it is not already a function, attempt to convert it
    // to a function that is passed a single argument, named state.
    this.onclick = onclick;
    if (typeof this.onclick == "string")
        this.onclick = new Function("state", this.onclick);

    // Figure out what entry in the document.images[] array the images
    // for this checkbox will be stored at.
    var index = document.images.length;

    // Now output the HTML code for this checkbox. Use <A> and <IMG> tags.
    // The event handlers we output here are confusing, but crucial to the
    // operation of this class. The "_tb" property is defined below, as
    // are the over(), out(), and click() methods.
    document.write(' <A HREF ="" ' +
      'onMouseOver="document.images[' + index + ']._tb.over();return true;" '+
      'onMouseOut="document.images[' + index + ']._tb.out()" '+
      'onClick="document.images[' + index + ']._tb.click(); return false;">');
    document.write('<IMG SRC="' + ToggleButton.imagenames[this.checked+0] +'"'+
                   ' WIDTH=' + ToggleButton.width +
                   ' HEIGHT=' + ToggleButton.height +
                   ' BORDER=0 HSPACE=0 VSPACE=0 ALIGN="absmiddle">');
    if (label) document.write(label);
    document.write('</A>');

    // Now that we've output the <IMG> tag, save a reference to the
    // Image object that it created in the ToggleButton object.
    this.image = document.images[index];

    // And also make a link in the other direction: from the Image object
    // to this ToggleButton object. Do this by defining a "_tb" property
    // in the Image object.
    this.image._tb = this;
}


// This becomes the over() method.
function _ToggleButton_over()
{
    // Change the image, and remember that we're highlighted.
    this.image.src = ToggleButton.imagenames[this.checked + 2];
    this.highlighted = true;
}
```

Example 16–3: Implementing a ToggleButton with Image Replacement (continued)

```
// This becomes the out() method.
function _ToggleButton_out()
{
    // Change the image, and remember that we're not highlighted.
    this.image.src = ToggleButton.imagenames[this.checked + 0];
    this.highlighted = false;
}


// This becomes the click() method.
function _ToggleButton_click()
{
    // Toggle the state of the button, change the image, and call the
    // onclick method, if it was specified for this ToggleButton.
    this.checked = !this.checked;
    this.image.src = ToggleButton.imagenames[this.checked+this.highlighted*2];
    if (this.onclick) this.onclick(this.checked);
}


// Initialize static class properties that describe the checkbox images. These
// are just defaults. Programs can override them by assigning new values.
// But the should only be overridden *before* any ToggleButtons are created.
ToggleButton.imagenames = new Array(4);              // create an array
ToggleButton.imagenames[0] = "togglebutton0.gif";  // the unchecked box
ToggleButton.imagenames[1] = "togglebutton1.gif";  // the box with a check mark
ToggleButton.imagenames[2] = "togglebutton2.gif";  // unchecked but highlighted
ToggleButton.imagenames[3] = "togglebutton3.gif";  // checked and highlighted
ToggleButton.width = ToggleButton.height = 25;      // size of all images
</SCRIPT>


<!-- Here's how we might use the ToggleButton class. -->
Optional extras:<BR>
<SCRIPT LANGUAGE="JavaScript1.1">
// Create the buttons
var tb1 = new ToggleButton(document, true, "28.8K Modem<BR>");
var tb2 = new ToggleButton(document, false, "Laser Printer<BR>");
var tb3 = new ToggleButton(document, false, "Tape Backup Unit<BR>");
</SCRIPT>


<!-- Here's how we can use the ToggleButton objects from event handlers. -->
<FORM>
<INPUT TYPE="button" VALUE="Report Button States"
        onClick="alert(tb1.checked + '\n' + tb2.checked + '\n' + tb3.checked)">
<INPUT TYPE="button" VALUE="Reset Buttons"
        onClick="if (tb1.checked) tb1.click();
                 if (tb2.checked) tb2.click();
                 if (tb3.checked) tb3.click();">
</FORM>
```

16.6 Other Image Techniques

There are some other techniques for programming with images besides those that use the Image object discussed here. We saw one, the dynamic generation of XBM images, in Chapter 14, *Documents and Their Contents.* There is another technique that can be useful when dynamically generating documents (in another window or frame) that contain images. Bear in mind that if the image you supply does not match the WIDTH and HEIGHT specified in the <IMG> tag, the browser will stretch the image as necessary. This can be useful, for example if you want to use an image as a graphical horizontal rule: you can supply an image that is only one pixel wide (that will thus load quickly), and rely on the browser to stretch it horizontally for you to any desired length.

Similarly, when you want to include rectangles of a solid color in a document, you can use an image that is just one pixel by one pixel in size, and stretch it to any desired dimensions. This technique can be used, for example, to dynamically generate bar charts and histograms in documents by using JavaScript to dynamically generate IMG tags that stretch a given image to the appropriate sizes.

You can play a related trick (that does not involve JavaScript) with the background image for a document (specified by the BACKGROUND attribute of the <BODY> tag). The browser uses this image as a tile to fill the entire background. Suppose you want your documents to have a vertical bar or border along their left edge. If you create a narrow borderless vertical frame in the window, then you can specify a background image that has the desired width and is only a few pixels tall. The browser will fill the frame with repeating copies of this image, which will produce the vertical bar you're looking for.

17

Forms and Form Elements

As we've seen in examples throughout this book, the use of HTML forms is basic to almost all web programs, whether implemented with CGI, JavaScript, or a combination of the two. This chapter explains the details of programming with forms in JavaScript. It is assumed that you already are at least somewhat familiar with the creation of HTML forms and with the input elements that they contain. If not, you may want to refer to a good book on HTML.[*] In addition, the reference section of this book lists the HTML syntax as well as JavaScript syntax for forms and form elements; you may find these listings helpful as well.

17.1 Forms in CGI and JavaScript

If you are already familiar with CGI programming using HTML forms, you may find that things are done somewhat differently when forms are used with JavaScript. In the CGI model, a form, and the input data it contains is "submitted"—sent to the web server—all at once. The emphasis is on processing a complete "batch" of input data and dynamically producing a new web page in response. With JavaScript, the programming model is quite different. In JavaScript programs, the emphasis is not on form submission and processing but instead on event handling. Forms and the input elements they contain each have event handlers that JavaScript can use to respond to user interactions with a form. If the user clicks on a checkbox, for example, a JavaScript program can receive notification through an event handler, and might respond by changing the value displayed in some other element of the form.

---

[*] Such as *HTML: The Definitive Guide*, by Chuck Musciano and Bill Kennedy, published by O'Reilly & Associates.

With CGI programs, an HTML form can't be useful unless it has a **Submit** button (or unless it has only a single text input field and allows the user to strike the **Return** key as a shortcut for submission). With JavaScript, on the other hand, a Submit button is never necessary (unless the JavaScript program is working with a cooperating CGI program, of course). With JavaScript, your forms can have any number of push-buttons with event handlers that perform any number of actions when clicked. In previous chapters, we've seen some of the possible actions that such a button can trigger: replacing one image with another, using the location property to load and display a new web page, opening a new browser window, or dynamically generating a new HTML document in another window or frame. As we'll see later in this section, a JavaScript event handler can even trigger a form to be submitted.

As we've seen in examples throughout this book, event handlers are almost always the central element of any interesting JavaScript program. And the most commonly used event handlers (excluding the event handlers of the Link object) are used with forms or form elements. The following subsections introduce the JavaScript Form object, and the various JavaScript objects that represent form elements. The section concludes with an example that illustrates how you can use JavaScript to validate user input on the client before submitting it to a CGI program running on the web server.

17.2 The Form Object

The JavaScript Form object represents an HTML form. Forms are always found as elements of the `forms[]` array, which is a property of the Document object. Forms appear in this array in the order that they appear within the document. Thus, `document.forms[0]` refers to the first form in a document, and you can refer to the last form in an document with:

```
document.forms[document.forms.length]
```

The most interesting property of the Form object is the `elements[]` array, which contains JavaScript objects (of various types) that represent the various input elements of the form. Again, elements appear in this array in the order that they appear in the document. So `document.forms[1].elements[2]` refers to the third element of the second form in the document of the current window.

The remaining properties of the Form object are of less importance. They are `action`, `encoding`, `method`, and `target`, and they correspond directly to the `ACTION`, `ENCODING`, `METHOD`, and `TARGET` attributes of the `<FORM>` tag. These properties and attributes are all used to control how form data is submitted to the web server, and where the results are displayed, and they are therefore only useful when the form actually will be submitted to a CGI script. See the reference section for an explanation of the properties, or see a book on HTML or CGI programming[*] for a thorough discussion of the attributes. What is worth noting here is that these Form properties are all read/write strings in Navigator 2.0 and 3.0, so a JavaScript program can dynamically set their values in order to change the way the form is submitted. Unfortunately, while you *can* set the value of these properties in Internet Explorer 3.0, any values you set will be ignored.

In the days before JavaScript, forms were submitted with a special-purpose **Submit** button, and the form elements had their values reset with a special-purpose **Reset** button. The JavaScript Form object, however, supports two methods, submit() and (in Navigator 3.0) reset(), which serve this same purpose. Invoking the submit() method of a Form submits the form, exactly as if the user had clicked on a **Submit** button, and invoking reset() resets the form elements, exactly as if the user had clicked on a **Reset** button.

To accompany the submit() and reset() methods, the Form object provides the onSubmit() event handler to detect form submission, and (in Navigator 3.0) the onReset() event handler to detect form resets. The onSubmit() handler is invoked just before the form is submitted, and can cancel the submission by returning false. This provides an opportunity for a JavaScript program to check the user's input for errors to avoid submitting incomplete or invalid data over the network to a CGI program. We'll see an example of doing this at the end of this section.

The onReset() event handler is similar to the onSubmit() handler. It is invoked just before the form is reset, and may prevent the form elements from being reset by returning false. This allows a JavaScript program to ask for confirmation of the reset, which can be a good idea when the form is long or detailed. You might request this sort of confirmation with an event handler like the following (recall that onReset() requires Navigator 3.0):

```
<FORM...
    onReset="return confirm('Really erase ALL data and start over?')"
>
```

---

[*] Such as *CGI Programming on the World Wide Web*, by Shishir Gundavaram, published by O'Reilly & Associates.

17.3 Form Elements

As noted above, every Form object has an `elements[]` property, which is an array of the JavaScript objects that represent the input elements contained in the form. There are quite a few possible HTML form elements and corresponding JavaScript objects. They are listed in Table 17-1 and pictured in Figure 17-1. The HTML (and JavaScript) code that generated that figure is listed in Example 17-1. For comparison, Figure 17-2 shows the same form elements, as they appear in a different operating system. You can find out more about these JavaScript objects in the reference section of this book, but you may want to refer to an HTML book for complete details on the HTML tags and attributes used to create these form elements.

Table 17-1: HTML Form Elements

Object	HTML Tag	type Property	Description and Events
Button	`<INPUT TYPE=button>`	"button"	A push-button; `onClick()`.
Checkbox	`<INPUT TYPE=checkbox>`	"checkbox"	A toggle-button without radio-button behavior; `onClick()`.
FileUpload	`<INPUT TYPE=file>`	"file"	An input field for entering the name of a file to upload to the web server; `onChange()`.
Hidden	`<INPUT TYPE=hidden>`	"hidden"	Data submitted with the form but not visible to the user; no event handlers.
Option	`<OPTION>`	*none*	A single item within a Select object; event handlers are on Select object, not individual Option objects.
Password	`<INPUT TYPE=password>`	"password"	An input field for password entry—typed characters are not visible; `onChange()`.
Radio	`<INPUT TYPE=radio>`	"radio"	A toggle-button with radio behavior—only one selected at a time; `onClick()`.
Reset	`<INPUT TYPE=reset>`	"reset"	A push-button that resets a form; `onClick()`.
Select	`<SELECT>`	"select-one"	A list or drop-down menu from which one item may be selected; `onChange()`. See also Option object.

Table 17–1: HTML Form Elements (continued)

Object	HTML Tag	type Property	Description and Events
Select	`<SELECT MULTIPLE>`	"select-multiple"	A list from which multiple items may be selected; `onChange()`. See also Option object.
Submit	`<INPUT TYPE=submit>`	"submit"	A push-button that submits a form; `onClick()`.
Text	`<INPUT TYPE=text>`	"text"	A single-line text entry field; `onChange()`.
Textarea	`<TEXTAREA>`	"textarea"	A multiline text entry field; `onChange()`.

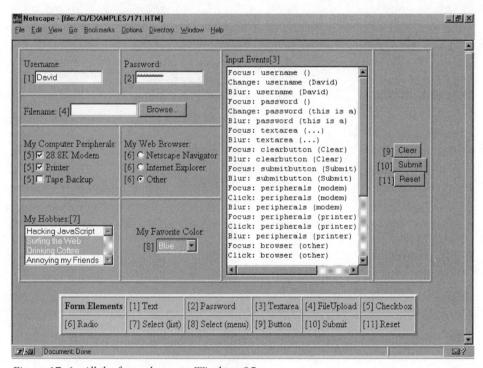

Figure 17–1: All the form elements, Windows 95

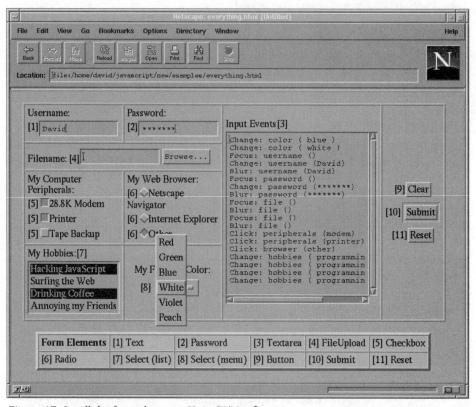

Figure 17-2: All the form elements, Unix (X/Motif)

Example 17-1: An HTML Form Containing All Form Elements

```
<FORM NAME="everything">  <!-- A one-of-everything HTML form... -->
 <TABLE BORDER CELLPADDING=5>   <!-- ...in a big HTML table. -->
   <TR>
     <TD>Username:<BR>[1]<INPUT TYPE=text NAME="username" SIZE=15></TD>
     <TD>Password:<BR>[2]<INPUT TYPE=password NAME="password" SIZE=15></TD>
     <TD ROWSPAN=4>Input Events[3]<BR>
       <TEXTAREA NAME="textarea" ROWS=20 COLS=28></TEXTAREA></TD>
     <TD ROWSPAN=4 ALIGN=center VALIGN=center>
       [9]<INPUT TYPE=button VALUE="Clear" NAME="clearbutton"><BR>
       [10]<INPUT TYPE=submit NAME="submitbutton" VALUE="Submit"><BR>
       [11]<INPUT TYPE=reset NAME="resetbutton" VALUE="Reset"></TD></TR>
   <TR>
     <TD COLSPAN=2>Filename: [4]<INPUT TYPE=file NAME="file" SIZE=15></TD></TR>
   <TR>
     <TD>My Computer Peripherals:<BR>
       [5]<INPUT TYPE=checkbox NAME="peripherals" VALUE="modem">28.8K Modem<BR>
       [5]<INPUT TYPE=checkbox NAME="peripherals" VALUE="printer">Printer<BR>
       [5]<INPUT TYPE=checkbox NAME="peripherals" VALUE="tape">Tape Backup</TD>
```

Example 17-1: An HTML Form Containing All Form Elements (continued)

```
     <TD>My Web Browser:<BR>
       [6]<INPUT TYPE=radio NAME="browser" VALUE="nn">Netscape Navigator<BR>
       [6]<INPUT TYPE=radio NAME="browser" VALUE="ie">Internet Explorer<BR>
       [6]<INPUT TYPE=radio NAME="browser" VALUE="other">Other</TD></TR>
    <TR>
      <TD>My Hobbies:[7]<BR>
        <SELECT multiple NAME="hobbies" SIZE=4>
          <OPTION VALUE="programming">Hacking JavaScript
          <OPTION VALUE="surfing">Surfing the Web
          <OPTION VALUE="caffeine">Drinking Coffee
          <OPTION VALUE="annoying">Annoying my Friends
        </SELECT></TD>
      <TD align=center valign=center>My Favorite Color:<BR>[8]
        <SELECT NAME="color">
          <OPTION VALUE="red">Red          <OPTION VALUE="green">Green
          <OPTION VALUE="blue">Blue         <OPTION VALUE="white">White
          <OPTION VALUE="violet">Violet  <OPTION VALUE="peach">Peach
        </SELECT></TD></TR>
 </TABLE>
</FORM>

<DIV ALIGN=center>         <!-- Another table--the key to the one above. -->
  <TABLE BORDER=4 BGCOLOR=pink CELLSPACING=1 CELLPADDING=4>
    <TR>
      <TD ALIGN=center><B>Form Elements</B></TD>
      <TD>[1] Text</TD>  <TD>[2] Password</TD>  <TD>[3] Textarea</TD>
      <TD>[4] FileUpload</TD> <TD>[5] Checkbox</TD></TR>
    <TR>
      <TD>[6] Radio</TD>  <TD>[7] Select (list)</TD>
      <TD>[8] Select (menu)</TD>  <TD>[9] Button</TD>
      <TD>[10] Submit</TD>  <TD>[11] Reset</TD></TR>
  </TABLE>
</DIV>

<SCRIPT LANGUAGE="JavaScript1.1">
// This generic function appends details of an event to the big Textarea
// element in the form above. It will be called from various event handlers.
function report(element, event)
{
    var t = element.form.textarea;
    var name = element.name;
    if ((element.type == "select-one") || (element.type == "select-multiple")){
        value = " ";
        for(var i = 0; i < element.options.length; i++)
            if (element.options[i].selected)
                value += element.options[i].value + " ";
    }
```

Example 17-1: An HTML Form Containing All Form Elements (continued)

```
    else if (element.type == "textarea") value = "...";
    else value = element.value;
    var msg = event + ": " + name + ' (' + value + ')\n';
    t.value = t.value + msg;
}


// This function adds a bunch of event handlers to every element in a form.
// It doesn't bother checking to see if the element supports the event handler,
// it just adds them all. Note that the event handlers call report() above.
function addhandlers(f)
{
    for(var i = 0; i < f.elements.length; i++) {
        var e = f.elements[i];
        e.onclick = new Function("report(this, 'Click')");
        e.onchange = new Function("report(this, 'Change')");
        e.onfocus = new Function("report(this, 'Focus')");
        e.onblur = new Function("report(this, 'Blur')");
        e.onselect = new Function("report(this, 'Select')");
    }


    // Special case handlers for the buttons:
    f.clearbutton.onclick =
        new Function("this.form.textarea.value=''; report(this, 'Click');");
    f.submitbutton.onclick =
        new Function("report(this, 'Click'); return false");
    f.resetbutton.onclick =
        new Function("this.form.reset(); report(this, 'Click'); return false");
}
// Activate our form by adding all possible event handlers!
addhandlers(document.everything);
</SCRIPT>
```

While specific details about the JavaScript form element objects can be found on their respective reference pages, there are some features that all form element objects share. One obvious similarity is that (almost) all form element objects define event handlers that are invoked when the user interacts with them. The important ones are usually called onClick() or onChange(), depending on the type of object. The event handlers supported by each form element are listed in the fourth column of Table 17-1.

In addition to the event handlers shown in the table, all form elements (except the Hidden element) in Navigator 3.0 also support the onBlur() and onFocus() event handlers, which are invoked when the elements lose or gain the keyboard input focus, respectively. Unfortunately, on Unix platforms, these event handlers only work correctly for those form elements that involve text entry: Text, Textarea, Password and FileUpload. In addition to the onBlur() and onFocus() event handlers, all form elements in Navigator 3.0 also have corresponding blur() and focus() methods that remove input focus from an element and restore it. Again, on Unix platforms, these methods have no effect except on the text-input form elements.

Another similarity between form element objects is that, in Navigator 3.0, all of them have a type property that identifies what type of element they are. The third column of Table 17-1 specifies the value of this property for each object. Because the elements[] array of the Form object contains various types of form element objects, the type property allows you to loop through the elements[] array and operate on the form objects it contains in ways that depending on their type. We'll see this done in Example 17-2, later in the chapter. Note that Internet Explorer 3.0 does not support the type property.

All form element objects also have (in both Navigator 3.0 and Navigator 2.0) a form property. This is simply a reference to the Form object that contains the element. This property provides a useful way for form objects to refer to other form objects from their event handlers. Within a form element event handler, the this keyword refers to the element object itself. This means that this.form always refers to the containing form. And therefore, any event handler in a form can refer to sibling objects in the same form with expressions like this:

```
this.form.elements[4]
```

17.4 Form Element Names and Values

Two other properties shared by all form element objects are name and value. When a form is submitted, the user's input data is passed to the web server in the form of name/value pairs, and these properties specify the name under which each element's data is submitted and the value that is submitted for that element. The name property is a read-only string; its value is specified by the NAME attribute of the HTML tag that defined the form element. This NAME attribute is optional, but data from an element cannot be submitted unless a it is specified. In the next subsection, we'll see another use of the NAME attribute.

The value property is similar to the name property. This property is a read/write string for all form element objects, and it contains the data that is transferred over the network when the form is submitted. The initial value of the value property is, logically enough, usually specified by the VALUE attribute of the HTML tag that defined the form element. For some objects, however, the initial value is specified in some other way.

The `value` property contains a string value for all form elements. Because of the automatic data conversion performed by Navigator, you can assign a value or object of any type to the `value` property and it will automatically be converted to a string. Unfortunately, a limitation in Internet Explorer 3.0 does not allow objects to be assigned to the `value` property. In order to do this you must explicitly convert the object to a string; you cannot rely on automatic conversion as you can with Navigator. Thus, if you wanted to display the current date and time in an input field of a form, the following code would not work in IE 3.0:

```
today = new Date();
document.myform.date.value = today;
```

The easiest way to explicitly convert the `today` object to a string is to add it to the empty string, so the following code would work in IE 3.0:

```
today = new Date();
document.myform.date.value = "" + today;
```

Not all uses of the `value` property are obvious at the first glance. For Text and TextArea objects, the `value` property is simply the string contained in the input field. Setting the `value` property of these objects changes the text that those input fields display. For Button, Reset, and Submit objects, however, the `value` property contains is the text that is displayed by the push-button. Although the property is read/write, changing it will not change the text that appears in the button (at least not on all platforms). Also, the `value` of Button and Reset objects is never actually submitted with the form that contains them. (The value of a Submit object is submitted only when that Submit object was the one that caused the form to be submitted—this allows a CGI script to determine how the form was submitted in cases where there is more than one way to do so.)

The `value` property for Checkbox and Radio objects is also a little bit tricky. Since these objects represent toggle buttons in an HTML form, you might expect their `value` property to indicate the state of the button—i.e., to be a Boolean value that indicates whether the toggle button is checked or not. In fact, though, it is the `checked` property of these objects that indicates what state they are in. The `value` property, as always, is the string value that is submitted with the form if the Checkbox or Radio object is checked when the form is submitted. It should be set to some string that is meaningful to the CGI script that will receive the form submission.

The Select object is another unusual case. It displays a list or drop-down menu of options and allows the user to select one or more of them. These options are not specified by the `<SELECT>` tag, but by a separate `<OPTION>` tag, so it turns out that the Select object actually has no `value` property, and is an exception to the rule above that all form element objects have a property by this name. Since the VALUE attribute belongs to the <OPTION> tag, the value property belongs to the Option object. Now, you might expect that, like the Text and Button objects, the value property of the Option object would specify the text that is displayed to the user in the list or drop-down menu. In fact, though, this is not how it is done. The text displayed for an Option is meant to be a verbose, human-readable string, and this is not ideal for processing by a CGI script. The text property of the Option object specifies the string that the user sees, and the value property specifies the (usually terser) string submitted if the option is selected when the form is submitted.

17.4.1 The Select and Option objects

While we are discussing the Select and Option objects, it should be noted that these differ in a number of ways form other form element objects. First, note that the Option object is not itself a form element—it is an object contained by a Select object. The Select object is the only form element object that contains other objects. They are contained in its options[] array, so you may end up referring to individual Option objects with very long expressions like the following:

```
document.forms[0].elements[1].options[2]
```

The second unique feature of the Option object is that, in Navigator 3.0, they can be dynamically created at run-time. Option objects are created with the Option() constructor function, and can be added to the options[] array of a Select object by simple assignment. This options[] property has several special behaviors itself—if you decrease the value of options.length options will be deleted from the end of the list or drop-down menu displayed by the Select object. Similarly, if you set one of the entries in the options[] array to null, that option will be removed from the list or menu, and the elements following it in the array will be moved down one to fill up the newly vacated array element. For full details, see the Select and Option objects, and their properties in the reference section of this book.

17.5 Naming Forms and Form Elements

As we saw above, all form elements have a NAME attribute that must be set in their HTML tags, if the form is to be submitted to a CGI script. While form submission is not generally of interest to JavaScript programs, there is another useful reason to specify this NAME tag; we'll explain it below.

The <FORM> tag also has a NAME attribute that you can set. This attribute has nothing to do with form submission. It exists for the convenience of JavaScript programmers. If the NAME attribute is defined in a <FORM> tag, then when the Form object is created for that form, it will be stored as an element in the forms[] array of the Document object, as usual, but it will also be stored in its own personal property of the Document object. The name of this newly defined property is the value of the NAME attribute. Thus, if you define a form with HTML like this:

```
<FORM NAME="questionnaire">
   ...
</FORM>
```

Then you can refer to that form as:

```
document.questionnaire
```

Often, you'll find this more convenient than the array notation:

```
document.forms[2]
```

Note that the <IMG>, <APPLET>, and <EMBED> tags all also have NAME attributes that work the same way as the NAME attribute of <FORM>. But with forms, this style of naming goes a step further, because all of the elements contained within a form have NAME attributes. When you give a form element a NAME attribute, you create a new property of the Form object that refers to that element. The name of this property is the value of the attribute, of course. Thus, you can refer to an element named "zipcode" in a form named "address" as:

```
document.address.zipcode
```

With reasonably chosen names, this syntax is much more elegant than the alternative which relies on hard-coded array indices:

```
document.forms[1].elements[4]
```

In HTML forms that use Checkbox and Radio elements, it is common practice to give each of a set of related elements the same name. For example, if a form contains a number Radio buttons that allow the user to indicate their favorite web browser, then each of these buttons might be given the name "favorite". The VALUE property of one button might be "nn", and the value of another might be "ie". When the form is submitted, a string like "favorite=mosaic" will be sent to indicate the user's selection. Using the same name for multiple elements is not a problem in this case because only one of those elements can be selected at a time, so only one value can be submitted with that name.

When more than one element in a form has the same NAME attribute, JavaScript simply places those elements into an array using the specified name. So, if the Radio objects in the example above were part of our form named "questionnaire", then you could refer to them with expressions like these:

```
document.questionnaire.favorite[0]
document.questionnaire.favorite[1]
```

17.6 Form Verification Example

We'll close our discussion of forms with an extended example that demonstrates several of the concepts we've been talking about. Example 17-2 shows how you might use the onSubmit() event handler of the Form object to perform input validation to notify the user and prevent the form from being submitted when it contains missing or invalid data. After studying this example, you may want to turn back to Example 1-3, the forms programming example with which we began this book. The code of that example will probably make more sense now that you are a JavaScript expert!

Example 17-2 defines a verify() function suitable for use as a generic form validator. It checks for empty non-optional fields, and can also check that numeric values are in fact numeric and that they fall within a specified numeric range. This verify() function relies on the type property of form elements to determine which elements are which, and also relies on additional user-defined properties to distinguish optional fields from required fields and to specify the allowed range for numeric fields. Note also how it reads the value property of input fields, and uses the name property of those fields when reporting errors. Figure 17-3 shows an example form using this verification scheme, and the error message that is displayed when the user attempts to submit the form before correctly filling it in.

Example 17-2: Performing Form Validation

```
<SCRIPT LANGUAGE="JavaScript1.1">
// A utility function that returns true if a string contains only
// whitespace characters.
function isblank(s)
{
    for(var i = 0; i < s.length; i++) {
        var c = s.charAt(i);
        if ((c != ' ') && (c != '\n') && (c != '\t')) return false;
    }
    return true;
}


// This is the function that performs form verification. It will be invoked
// from the onSubmit() event handler. The handler should return whatever
// value this function returns.
function verify(f)
{
    var msg;
    var empty_fields = "";
    var errors = "";
```

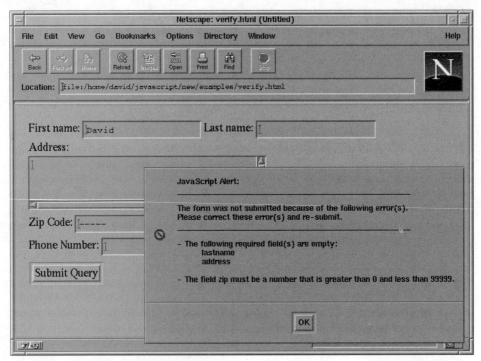

Figure 17-3: A form that failed validation

Example 17-2: Performing Form Validation (continued)

```
// Loop through the elements of the form, looking for all
// text and textarea elements that don't have an "optional" property
// defined. Then, check for fields that are empty and make a list of them.
// Also, if any of these elements have a "min" or a "max" property defined,
// then verify that they are numbers and that they are in the right range.
// Put together error messages for fields that are wrong.
for(var i = 0; i < f.length; i++) {
    var e = f.elements[i];
    if (((e.type == "text") || (e.type == "textarea")) && !e.optional) {
        // first check if the field is empty
        if ((e.value == null) || (e.value == "") || isblank(e.value)) {
            empty_fields += "\n           " + e.name;
            continue;
        }

        // Now check for fields that are supposed to be numeric.
        if (e.numeric || (e.min != null) || (e.max != null)) {
            var v = parseFloat(e.value);
            if (isNaN(v) ||
                ((e.min != null) && (v < e.min)) ||
                ((e.max != null) && (v > e.max))) {
```

Example 17-2: Performing Form Validation (continued)

```
                        errors += "- The field " + e.name + " must be a number";
                        if (e.min != null)
                            errors += " that is greater than " + e.min;
                        if (e.max != null && e.min != null)
                            errors += " and less than " + e.max;
                        else if (e.max != null)
                            errors += " that is less than " + e.max;
                        errors += ".\n";
                    }
                }
            }
        }

        // Now, if there were any errors, then display the messages, and
        // return true to prevent the form from being submitted. Otherwise
        // return false.
        if (!empty_fields && !errors) return true;

        msg  = "_____\n\n"
        msg += "The form was not submitted because of the following error(s).\n";
        msg += "Please correct these error(s) and re-submit.\n";
        msg += "_____\n\n"

        if (empty_fields) {
            msg += "- The following required field(s) are empty:"
                    + empty_fields + "\n";
            if (errors) msg += "\n";
        }
        msg += errors;
        alert(msg);
        return false;
}
</SCRIPT>


<!------------------------------------------------------------------------
    Here's a sample form to test our verification with. Note that we
    call verify() from the onSubmit() event handler, and return whatever
    value it returns. Also note that we use the onSubmit() handler as
    an opportunity to set properties on the form objects that verify()
    will use in the verification process.
------------------------------------------------------------------------>
<FORM onSubmit="
    this.firstname.optional = true;
    this.phonenumber.optional = true;
    this.zip.min = 0;
    this.zip.max = 99999;
    return verify(this);
">
```

Example 17-2: Performing Form Validation (continued)

```
First name: <INPUT TYPE=text NAME="firstname">
Last name: <INPUT TYPE=text NAME="lastname"><BR>
Address:<BR><TEXTAREA NAME="address" ROWS=4 COLS=40></TEXTAREA><BR>
Zip Code: <INPUT TYPE=text NAME="zip"><BR>
Phone Number: <INPUT TYPE=text NAME="phonenumber"><BR>
<INPUT TYPE=submit>
</FORM>
```

18

Compatibility Techniques

JavaScript, like Java, is one of a new breed of "platform-independent" languages. That is, you can develop a program in JavaScript, and expect to run it unchanged in a JavaScript-enabled web browser running on any type of computer with any type of operating system. Though this is the ideal, we live in an imperfect world, and have not yet reached that state of perfection.

There are, and probably always will be, compatibility problems that we JavaScript programmers must bear in mind. The one fact that we must always remember is that it is a heterogeneous net out there. Your JavaScript programs will be run on many different platforms, using browsers from possibly many different vendors, and for any given browser, using various versions of the browser. This can be difficult to remember for those of us who come from the non-portable past when programs were developed on a platform-specific basis. Remember: it doesn't matter what platform we develop a program on. It may work fine on that platform, but the real test is whether it works fine (or fails gracefully) on *all* platforms.

The compatibility issues to be aware of fall into two broad categories: platform, browser, and version-specific features or bugs, and language-level incompatibilities, including the incompatibility of JavaScript with non-JavaScript browsers. This chapter discusses techniques for coping with compatibility issues in both of these areas. If you've worked your way through all the previous chapters in this book, you are probably an expert JavaScript programmer, and you may already be writing serious JavaScript programs. Don't release those programs on the Internet (or onto a heterogeneous intranet) before you've read this chapter, though!

18.1 Platform, Browser, and Version-Specific Compatibility

When developing production-quality JavaScript code, testing and knowledge of platform-specific incompatibilities are your chief allies. If you know, for example, that Navigator 2.0 on Macintosh platforms always gets the time wrong by about an hour, then you can take steps to deal with this. If you know that Windows platforms do not automatically clear your setting of the status line when the mouse moves off of a hypertext link, then you can provide an appropriate event handler to explicitly clear the status line. If you know that Internet Explorer 3.0 uses ActiveX to communicate with java applet while Navigator uses Netscape's LiveConnect mechanism, you can write a page that uses the appropriate mechanism depending on the browser currently in use.

Knowledge of existing incompatibilities is crucial to writing compatible code, and you'll probably find Appendix B, *Known Bugs*, Appendix C, *Differences between Navigator 2.0 and 3.0*, and Appendix D, *JavaScript Incompatibilities in Internet Explorer 3.0*, quite helpful in this area. Once you have identified an area of incompatibility, there are a number of basic approaches you can take to coping with it. They are described in the following subsections.

18.1.1 The Least-Common-Denominator Approach

One technique for dealing with incompatibilities is to avoid them like the plague. For example, the Date object is notoriously buggy in Navigator 2.0. If you want Navigator 2.0 users to be able to use your programs, then you can simply avoid relying upon the Date object altogether.

As another example, Navigator 3.0 and Internet Explorer 3.0 both support the `opener` property of the Window object, but Navigator 2.0 does not. The least-common-denominator approach says that you should not use this property. Instead, you can create an equivalent property of your own whenever you open an new window:

```
newwin = window.open("", "new", "width=500, height=300");
newwin.creator = self;
```

If you consistently set a `creator` property of a new window, then you can rely on it instead of the non-portable `opener` property.

With this technique you use only features that are known to work everywhere. It doesn't allow you to write cutting-edge programs or push the envelope, but it results in very portable, safe programs that can serve a lot of important functions.

18.1.2 Defensive Coding

With the "defensive coding" approach to compatibility you write code that contains platform-independent workarounds for platform-specific incompatibilities. For example, if you set the `status` property of a Window object from the `onMouseOver()` event handler to display a custom message in the status line, the status line will be cleared when you move the mouse off the hyperlink on all platforms except the crucial Windows platform. To correct for this, you might just get into the habit of including an `onMouseOut()` event handler to clear the status line.

To return to the example of the `opener` property from above, the defensive coding approach to compatibility does not discard the property altogether, but does insert a workaround to take care of platforms that do not support the property:

```
newwin = window.open("", "new", "width=500, height=300");
if (!newwin.opener) newwin.opener = self;
```

Note how we tested for the existence of the `opener` property above. The same technique works to test for the existence of methods. For example, the `split()` method of the String object only exists for JavaScript 1.1 implementations, so using defensive coding we would write our own version of this function that works for JavaScript 1.0 and JavaScript 1.1. But for efficiency we'd like to use the fast built-in method on those platforms that do support it. Our platform-independent code to `split()` a string might end up looking like this:

```
if (s.split)  // if method exists, use it
    a = s.split(":");
else          // otherwise, use our alternative implementation
    a = mysplit(s, ":");
```

Defensive coding using platform-independent workarounds is a useful and practical approach to incompatibilities. It relies on being able to come up with appropriate platform-independent workarounds, such as the following ingenious workaround for the Navigator 2.0 Macintosh date-skew bug, invented by Bill Dortch:

```
function FixDate(d)
{
    // Create a new Date(0) to detect any skew, and subtract it.
    d.setTime(d.getTime - (new Date(0)).getTime())
}
```

Sometimes, though, you won't be able to develop a platform-independent workaround and will have to take a more aggressive, platform-specific, approach to incompatibilities.

18.1.3 Platform-Specific Workarounds

When the least-common denominator and defensive coding approaches to incompatibilities won't work, you may find yourself having to create platform-specific workarounds. Recall from Chapter 13, *The Navigator, Location, and History Objects*, that the `navigator` property of the Window object provides information about the vendor and version of the browser and about the platform it is running on. You can use this information to insert code that is very platform-specific into your program. You might use this approach to distinguish between Navigator and Internet Explorer, for example, when working with Java applets or data embedded with the `<EMBED>` tag.

Another example of a platform-specific workaround might involve the `bgColor` property of the Document object. On Windows and Mac platforms, you can set this property at run time to change the background color of a document. Unfortunately, when you do this on Unix platforms, the color changes, but the document contents temporarily disappear. If you wanted to create a special effect using a changing background color, you could use the Navigator object to test for Unix platforms and simply skip the special effect for those platforms.[*] The code could look like this:

```
if (navigator.appVersion.substring("X11") == -1) // if not a Unix platform
    fade_bg_color();                              // then do the special effect
```

18.1.4 Ignore the Problem

An important question to ask when considering any incompatibility is "how important is it?" If the incompatibility is a minor or cosmetic one, or affects a browser or platform that is not widely used, or only affects an out-of-date version of a browser, then you might simply decide to ignore the problem and let the users affected by it cope with it on their own.

For example, earlier we suggested defining an `onMouseOut()` event handler to correct for the fact that Navigator 2.0 and 3.0 for Windows do not correctly clear the status line. Unfortunately, the `onMouseOut()` event handler does not exist in Navigator 2.0, so this workaround won't work for that platform. If you expect your application to have a lot of users who use Navigator 2.0 on Windows, and you think that it is really important to get that status line cleared, then you'll have to develop some other workaround. For example, you could use `setTimeout()` in your `onMouseOver()` event handler to arrange for the status line to be cleared in two seconds. But this solution brings problems with it—what if the mouse is still

---

[*] It's okay; we Unix users are accustomed to missing out on all the fun!

over the hypertext link and the status line shouldn't be cleared in two seconds—and a simpler approach in this case might really be to ignore the problem.

18.1.5 Fail Gracefully

Finally, there are some incompatibilities that cannot be ignored and that cannot be worked around. In this case, your programs should work correctly on all platforms, browsers, and versions that provide the needed features, and should fail gracefully on all others. Failing gracefully means recognizing that the required features are not available and informing the user that they will not be able to use your JavaScript program.

For example, the image replacement technique we saw in Chapter 16, *Special Effects with Images*, does not work in Navigator 2.0 or Internet Explorer 3.0, and there is really no workaround that can simulate it. Therefore, we should not even attempt to run the program on those platforms—instead we should politely notify the user of the incompatibility.

Failing gracefully can be harder than it sounds. Much of the rest of this chapter explains techniques for doing so.

18.2 Compatibility with Non-JavaScript Browsers

When a user without a JavaScript-capable browser visits your web pages, they obviously won't be able run your JavaScript programs. Therefore, your JavaScript scripts should fail gracefully when read into browsers that do not understand JavaScript. There are two components to this. First, they must not simply format and display your entire JavaScript program as if it was HTML text. And second, they should display a message informing the visitor that their browser cannot correctly handle the page. You can do both of these things with some carefully placed comments.

18.2.1 Hiding Scripts from Old Browsers

Web browsers that support JavaScript will execute the JavaScript statements that appear between the <SCRIPT> and </SCRIPT> tags. Browsers that don't support JavaScript, but that recognize the <SCRIPT> tag, will simply ignore everything between <SCRIPT> and </SCRIPT>. This is as it should be. Other, older browsers, however (and there are a lot of them), do not recognize the <SCRIPT> and </SCRIPT> tags, and so they ignore the tags themselves, and treat all the

JavaScript between them as text to be displayed. Users of old browsers cannot run your JavaScript programs, and this should be punishment enough—they should not also have to look at your code!

In order to prevent this, you enclose the body of your scripts within an HTML comment, using the format shown in Example 18-1.

Example 18-1: A Script Hidden from Old Browsers

```
1   <SCRIPT LANGUAGE="JavaScript">
2   <!-- begin HTML comment that hides the script
3             .
4             . JavaScript statements go here
5             .
6   // end HTML comment that hides the script -->
7   </SCRIPT>
```

Browsers that do not understand the <SCRIPT> and </SCRIPT> tags simply ignore them. Thus, lines 1 and 7 in Example 18-1 have no effect on these browsers. They'll ignore lines 2 through 6 as well, because the first four characters on line 2 begin an HTML comment, and the last three characters on line 6 end that comment—everything between is ignored by the HTML parser.

This script-hiding technique also works for browsers that *do* support JavaScript. Lines 1 and 7 indicate the beginning and ending of a script. As noted in Chapter 2, *Lexical Structure*, JavaScript-enabled web browsers recognize the HTML comment opening string <!--, but treat it as a single-line comment. Thus, a browser with JavaScript support treats line 2 as a single-line comment. Similarly, line 6 begins with the // single-line comment string, so that line is ignored by JavaScript-enabled browsers as well. This leaves lines 3 through 5, which are executed as JavaScript statements.

While it takes a little getting used to, this simple and elegant mix of HTML and JavaScript comments do exactly what we need—prevent JavaScript code from being displayed by browsers that do not support JavaScript. You should get in the habit of using these comments with all your scripts. The comments need not be as verbose as this, of course. It is common to see scripts that look like this:

```
<SCRIPT LANGUAGE="JavaScript">
<!-- begin hiding
   document.write(new Date());
// end hiding -->
</SCRIPT>
```

It is also common to strip the English text out of the comments:

```
<SCRIPT LANGUAGE="JavaScript">
<!--
  document.write(new Date());
// -->
</SCRIPT>
```

When writing very short scripts, you can even compress them by removing some of the line breaks:

```
<SCRIPT LANGUAGE="JavaScript"> <!--
  document.write(new Date());
// --> </SCRIPT>
```

And even the following is legal:

```
<SCRIPT LANGUAGE="JavaScript"> <!--
  document.write(new Date()); // --> </SCRIPT>
```

The only rule to hiding JavaScript code with an HTML comment is that there must be a line break after the `<!--` that opens the comment. Remember that this functions as a JavaScript comment, and comments out the remainder of the line. So the JavaScript interpreter won't run any code that follows it.

This commenting technique has solved the problem of hiding our JavaScript code from browsers that can't run it. The next step in failing gracefully is to display a message to the user letting them know that the page cannot run. The next subsection shows how to accomplish this.

18.2.2 Notifying Users of Old Browsers

In order to inform users of old browsers that their browser cannot successfully run the JavaScript programs on a web page we need some technique for displaying a message on an old browser but not displaying it on a JavaScript-capable browser. This would be easy if we could use a JavaScript `if` statement and the `document.write()` method to display the message, but of course we can't do this if the browser doesn't understand JavaScript in the first place. So instead we again rely on HTML comments and take advantage of the fact that JavaScript treats HTML comments differently than HTML does.

JavaScript treats the `<!--` sequence that begins an HTML comment as a single-line comment like `//`. This means that the following text is commented out in both HTML and in JavaScript:

```
<!-- This text is commented out in HTML and JavaScript -->
```

JavaScript doesn't recognize the `-->` closing comment and doesn't care where it occurs, however, so the following text is commented out in JavaScript but not in HTML:

```
<!-- --> This text is commented out in JavaScript, but not in HTML.
```

Herein lies the secret to displaying messages on non-JavaScript browsers but not on JavaScript-enabled browsers. Example 18-2 shows what our JavaScript scripts might look like with our JavaScript code hidden from the HTML parser, as above, and with our HTML messages hidden from the JavaScript interpreter.

Example 18-2: Displaying a Message on Non-JavaScript Browsers

```
<SCRIPT LANGUAGE="JavaScript">
<!-- The message below will only display on non-JavaScript browsers -->
<!-- --> <HR><H1>This Page Requires JavaScript</H1>
<!-- --> Your web browser is not capable of running JavaScript programs,
<!-- --> so you will not be able to use this page. Please consider
<!-- --> upgrading to the latest version of either Netscape Navigator
<!-- --> or Microsoft Internet Explorer.
<!-- --> <HR>
<!-- This HTML comment hides the script from non-JavaScript browsers
    .
    . JavaScript code goes here
    .
// This JavaScript comment is also the end of the HTML comment above. -->
</SCRIPT>
```

18.2.3 Hiding Scripts from Really Old Browsers

One flaw in the script-hiding scheme described above is that some older web browsers recognize the `<!--` string to begin a comment, but then end the comment with a `>` character alone, instead of looking for a complete `-->` string. This means that if the `>` character appears anywhere within your JavaScript code, either in a string, or as one of the `>`, `>=`, `>>` or `>>>` operators, then the HTML parser for these older browsers will close the comment, and will treat the rest of your script as HTML text to be formatted and displayed.

There are two possible solutions to this problem. The first is to ignore it. Maybe being forced to look at your JavaScript code will encourage users of these really old browsers to upgrade to one that supports the correct HTML comment syntax! Unfortunately, the Lynx browser, prior to version 2.6, is one of the ones that has the problem. This browser for text only terminals fills an important niche, and there are quite a few copies in use. In version 2.6, comment syntax is no longer an issue for Lynx, because it now correctly recognizes the `<SCRIPT>` tag and ignores anything between it and `</SCRIPT>`.

The only other solution to this problem is somewhat tedious and not entirely satisfactory. Since the problem is with the ">" character appearing in your JavaScript code, the solution is to make sure that that character does not appear, at least not in its unescaped form. You can do this with the following rules:

- Anywhere > appears within a string, replace it with the characters \076—this tells JavaScript to use the character with the same encoding as the > character.

- Replace expressions of the form (a > b) with the equivalent (b <= a).

- Replace expressions of the form (a >= b) with the equivalent (b < a).

- Replace the >> and >>> operators with division by the appropriate power of 2, and with appropriate sign manipulation. Fortunately, these operators are rarely used; if you ever need to use them, you'll understand them well enough to figure out the correct replacement.

- Do not try to replace the > character with the HTML escape >. The HTML parser recognizes this string, but the JavaScript interpreter doesn't.

18.2.4 Falling Back to a Non-JavaScript Page

Sometimes, if a browser cannot run the scripts in one web page, you'd like to have it load some other page that does not use JavaScript. This page might be a CGI-based version of your program, for example, or it might simply contain static HTML content, formatted in a way that does not rely on embedded JavaScript.

Loading an alternate page would be easy if we could use JavaScript, but obviously, we can't. What we can do, however, instead of "falling back" on a non-JavaScript page is turn things around and "skip ahead" to a JavaScript page if JavaScript *is* supported. That is, we load the non-JavaScript page by default. This page will actually contain a short script. If the script runs, then JavaScript is supported, and the script uses the Location object to read in the JavaScript version of the page. Example 18-3 shows an example HTML document using this technique.

Example 18–3: Loading a JavaScript-Based Page Only if JavaScript Is Supported

```
<HEAD>
<SCRIPT LANGUAGE="JavaScript">    <!-- hide script
location = "my_js_home_page.html";      // stop hiding -->
</SCRIPT>
<TITLE>My Home Page (Non-JavaScript Version)</TITLE>
</HEAD>
<BODY>

      .
      .  Arbitrary, non-JavaScript HTML goes here
      .

</BODY>
```

You can even automate this process. If every non-JavaScript web page in a directory has a JavaScript equivalent in a subdirectory named "js/", then you might use code like this at the top of a non-JavaScript page to load in the equivalent when JavaScript is supported:

```
<SCRIPT>                        <!-- hide script
  var path = location.path;
  var filename = path.substring(path.lastIndexOf("/")+1, path.length);
  location = "js/" + filename;  // stop hiding -->
</SCRIPT>
```

There is one shortcoming to the technique shown here. If the user loads a non-JavaScript page in a JavaScript-capable browser, the short initial script will take them to the full JavaScript page. This is what we want. But when they click on the browser's **Back**, they'll move to the non-JavaScript page, and the script there will send them forward again! In effect, this technique breaks the **Back** button. With Navigator 3.0, the workaround is to use the `replace()` method of the Location object rather than assigning directly to the `location` property. So you should replace the code above with this:

```
<SCRIPT>                        <!-- hide script
  var path = location.path;
  var filename = "js/" + path.substring(path.lastIndexOf("/")+1, path.length);
  if (location.replace) location.replace(filename)
  else location = filename;     // stop hiding -->
</SCRIPT>
```

18.3 Compatibility with JavaScript 1.0 Browsers

The previous section discussed compatibility techniques that are useful when JavaScript 1.0 (or JavaScript 1.1) code is loaded into a browser that does not support JavaScript. This section discusses techniques you can use when JavaScript 1.1 code is loaded into browsers that only support JavaScript 1.0. The basic goals are the same: we need to prevent the code from being interpreted by browsers that don't understand it, and we need to display a special message on those browsers that informs the user that their browsers can't run the scripts on the page.

18.3.1 The LANGUAGE Attribute

The first goal is easy. As we saw in Chapter 10, *Client-Side Program Structure*, we can prevent a JavaScript 1.0 browser from attempting to run code that requires

JavaScript 1.1 by setting the LANGUAGE attribute of the <SCRIPT> tag appropriately. It looks like this:

```
<SCRIPT LANGUAGE="JavaScript1.1">
<!-- Hide from non-JavaScript browsers
        .
      .  JavaScript 1.1 code goes here
        .
// Done hiding -->
</SCRIPT>
```

Note that we still have to use our trick with HTML comments to prevent old non-JavaScript browsers from formatting our JavaScript code as HTML.

Note that the use of the LANGUAGE attribute is a perfectly general technique. When the next version of JavaScript (presumably known as "JavaScript1.2") arrives, we'll be able to prevent JavaScript 1.0 and JavaScript 1.1 browsers from interpreting 1.2–level code by specifying LANGUAGE="JavaScript1.2".

18.3.2 *<NOSCRIPT>*

Hiding our JavaScript 1.1 code from browsers that can't understand it was easy. It turns out that gracefully displaying a message on all browsers that don't understand our JavaScript 1.1 code is not nearly so straightforward. When we wanted to display a message for non-JavaScript browsers that couldn't run our JavaScript 1.0 code used the comment trick shown in Example 18-2. This technique will still work when our JavaScript 1.1 code is read by non-JavaScript browsers, but it won't work when that code is read by JavaScript 1.0 browsers.

The <NOSCRIPT> and </NOSCRIPT> tags provide a partial solution. These tags were introduced by Netscape in Navigator 3.0. The intent of these tags is that anything between them will be ignored on a script-capable browser and will be displayed on a script-incapable browser. This is a simple, obvious idea, but the implementation isn't quite right. Since these tags were introduced in Navigator 3.0, Navigator 2.0 does not know about them, and so it ignores them and displays any HTML that appears between them. Navigator 3.0, on the other hand knows about these tags, and since it is a JavaScript-enabled browser it ignores all the HTML between the tags. What this means is that <NOSCRIPT> and </NOSCRIPT> provide us a way to display a message on Navigator 2.0 (a JavaScript 1.0 browser) that does not appear on Navigator 3.0 (a JavaScript 1.1 browser). Example 18-4 shows how you might use these tags to display a message when our JavaScript 1.1 code could not be run.

Example 18-4: Displaying a Message with <NOSCRIPT>

```
<HTML>
<HEAD><TITLE>My Cool JavaScript 1.1 Page</TITLE></HEAD>
<BODY>
<H1>My Cool JavaScript 1.1 Page</H1>

<NOSCRIPT>
    <!-- This message will be displayed by Navigator 2.0 and -->
    <!-- by non-JavaScript browsers -->
    <HR><I>
    This page depends heavily on JavaScript 1.1.<BR>
    Since your browser doesn't seem support that version of
    JavaScript, you're missing out on a lot of cool stuff!
    </I><HR>
</NOSCRIPT>
<SCRIPT LANGUAGE="JavaScript1.1"> <!--
    // My Cool JavaScript 1.1 code goes here
// --></SCRIPT>
</BODY></HTML>
```

Unfortunately, this <NOSCRIPT> technique is not entirely adequate. Since Navigator 2.0 does not recognize <NOSCRIPT>, this tag does not serve to distinguish JavaScript-enabled browsers from non-JavaScript browser. In the example above, we use it to distinguish JavaScript 1.1 browsers from JavaScript 1.0 browsers and from non-JavaScript browsers. But this use isn't correct either. It turns out that Internet Explorer 3.0 recognizes <NOSCRIPT>, and since it supports scripting, even JavaScript 1.0 scripting, it ignores everything between <NOSCRIPT> and </NOSCRIPT>. While this is the technically correct thing to do, the incompatibility between Navigator and Internet Explorer renders the <NOSCRIPT> tag practically useless. What this means is that the message shown in Example 18-4 will be displayed, as desired, in Navigator 2.0 and in non-JavaScript browsers, but it will not be displayed by Internet Explorer.

There is another problem with <NOSCRIPT> as well. It is not a general-purpose mechanism. When JavaScript 1.2 is out, there will no way to use <NOSCRIPT> to display a message on all browsers that do not support that version of the language.

18.3.3 Failing Gracefully the Hard Way

Since <NOSCRIPT> doesn't do quite what we want we have to be more explicit in displaying our messages. We'll revert to using HTML comments to display our failure message on non-JavaScript browsers, and we'll use JavaScript 1.0 to display a message on JavaScript-enabled browsers that do not support JavaScript 1.1. Example 18-5 shows how we do it.

Example 18–5: Displaying a Message for Browsers That Do Not Support JavaScript 1.1

```
<!-- Set a variable to determine what version of JavaScript we support -->
<!-- This technique can be extended to any number of language versions -->
<SCRIPT LANGUAGE="JavaScript"> <!--
  _version = 10; // --> </SCRIPT>
<SCRIPT LANGUAGE="JavaScript1.1"> <!--
  _version = 11; // --> </SCRIPT>
<SCRIPT LANGUAGE="JavaScript1.2"> <!--
  _version = 12; // --> </SCRIPT>

<!-- If the version is not high enough, display a message -->
<!-- This version of the message appears for JavaScript 1.0 browsers -->
<SCRIPT LANGUAGE="JavaScript"> <!--
  if (_version < 11) {
    document.write('<HR><H1>This Page Requires JavaScript 1.1</H1>');
    document.write('Your JavaScript 1.0 browser cannot run this page.<HR>');
  }
// --> </SCRIPT>

<SCRIPT LANGUAGE="JavaScript1.1">
<!-- This version of the message will appear on non-JavaScript browsers -->
<!-- --> <HR><H1>This Page Requires JavaScript 1.1</H1>
<!-- --> Your non-JavaScript browser cannot run this page.<HR>
<!--  Start hiding the actual program code

      . The actual JavaScript 1.1 code goes here.

// Done hiding -->
</SCRIPT>
```

While the technique shown in Example 18-5 is not nearly so elegant as the <NOSCRIPT> solution, the important points to note are that it works correctly with Internet Explorer, and that it is extensible for future versions of the language. That is, this technique will allow you to display messages on JavaScript 1.0, JavaScript 1.1, and non-JavaScript browsers when you write code that only works for JavaScript 1.2.

18.3.4 Loading a New Page for Compatibility

In Example 18-3 we saw how you could use the Location object to read in a JavaScript-based page if JavaScript is supported, and otherwise simply use a non-JavaScript page. You can obviously use this same technique to load a JavaScript 1.1 page from a default JavaScript 1.0 page, or vice versa.

If we take this idea a couple of steps further, we can come up with some interesting variations. Example 18-6 shows one such variation. It is a short program that tests whether JavaScript 1.1 is supported. If so, it uses the `Location.replace()` method to load in a JavaScript 1.1 page (recall that using `replace()` prevents the **Back** button from breaking). If JavaScript 1.1 is not supported, it displays a message saying so on either a JavaScript 1.0 browser or a non-JavaScript browser.

Example 18-6: A Web Page to Test for JavaScript Compatibility

```
<!-- This script jumps to a new page if JavaScript 1.1 is supported -->
<!-- it also set a flag that we can test for below so we don't display -->
<!-- the message during the time the browser is loading the new file -->
<SCRIPT LANGUAGE="JavaScript1.1"> <!--
location.replace(location.search.substring(1)); self.loading = true;
// --> </SCRIPT>


<!-- Otherwise we display a message, either in HTML or with JavaScript 1.0 -->
<SCRIPT LANGUAGE="JavaScript">
<!-- --> <HR><H1>This Page Requires JavaScript 1.1</H1>
<!-- --> Your non-JavaScript browser cannot run this page.<HR>
<!--
  if (!self.loading) {
    document.write('<HR><H1>This Page Requires JavaScript 1.1</H1>');
    document.write('Your JavaScript 1.0 browser cannot run this page.<HR>');
  }
// -->
</SCRIPT>
```

The most interesting thing about this example is that it is a generic one—the name of the JavaScript 1.1 file to be loaded is encoded in the search portion of the original URL, and that file will be loaded only if JavaScript 1.1 is supported. Thus if the file in this example had the name `testjs11.html`, then you could use it in URLs like the one shown in this hyperlink:

```
<A HREF="http://my.isp.net/~david/utils/testjs11.html?../js/cooljs11.html">
Visit my cool JavaScript 1.1 page!
</A>
```

The other thing to note about Example 18-6 is that (at least with Navigator 3.0) calling `Location.replace()` starts a new page loading but does not immediately stop the current page from executing. Therefore, this example has to set a flag when it starts loading the specified JavaScript 1.1 page. If this flag is set, then the JavaScript 1.0 code in the example will not display the message. If it didn't do this, the message would briefly flash on the screen before the JavaScript 1.1 page was loaded. For this same reason the example can't simply display the compatibility message in a normal HTML `<BODY>`.

18.3.5 Included Files and Compatibility with Navigator 2.0

As we saw in Chapter 10, Navigator 3.0 can use the SRC attribute of the <SCRIPT> tag to refer indirectly to a file of JavaScript code rather than having that code appear directly in the HTML file. This is a very useful thing to do for a number of reasons, including modularity, ease of code maintenance and reuse, and caching efficiency on the client-side.

The use of the SRC attribute also makes it somewhat easier to fail gracefully and display a message. Example 18-7 shows how. This example relies on the fact that a JavaScript 1.0 browser doesn't understand the SRC attribute and tries to execute the code between the <SCRIPT> and </SCRIPT> tags.

Example 18-7: Displaying a Failure Message When Using <SCRIPT SRC=>

```
<SCRIPT LANGUAGE="JavaScript" SRC="../javascript/util.js">
<!-- This is the message for non-JavaScript browsers -->
<!-- --> <H1>Sorry, this page requires Netscape Navigator 3.0</H1>
<!-- code for Navigator 2.0 browsers here
document.write("<H1>Sorry, this page requires Navigator 3.0.</H1>");
// --></SCRIPT>
```

There are so many good reasons to use the SRC attribute that you may find yourself wanting to use it even when you are trying to maintain compatibility with JavaScript 1.0. In order to do this, you'll have to maintain two separate versions of your web page, one that works with JavaScript 1.1 and one that works with JavaScript 1.0. The default page will assume JavaScript 1.1 support and will load the JavaScript code with the SRC attribute. If that attribute is not recognized, then this default page must arrange to load in the other version of the page which has JavaScript 1.0 code explicitly included in it. You can do this with a variation on code we saw earlier in this chapter. Example 18-8 shows what it will look like.

Example 18-8: Load an Alternate Page When <SCRIPT SRC=> Fails

```
<!-- Try to load the JavaScript code with SRC. -->
<SCRIPT SRC="../javascript/utils.js"> <!--
// if the SRC attribute is not recognized, then this code will load
// a compatible version of the page that does not use SRC. The new
// page will have the same name but will be in a directory named "compat/"
var path = location.path;
var filename = path.substring(path.lastIndexOf("/")+1, path.length);
location = "compat/" + filename;
// --></SCRIPT>
```

Note that, as we've seen, techniques like this one that rely on assigning a new URL to the `location` property break the **Back** button of the browser. Also note that server-side includes (SSI) provide an easy way to maintain the two separate versions of a web page required by this technique. One file uses the `SRC` attribute to read in its JavaScript code on the client side, and the other uses a server-side include to read in the JavaScript code on the server side.

18.4 Compatibility Through CGI Scripts

When your web application includes the use of CGI scripts, another approach to all forms of JavaScript compatibility is to use a CGI script on your web server to generate all the JavaScript code used in your application. Then, this script can inspect the `User-Agent` field of the HTTP request header. This allows it to determine exactly what browser the user is running and generate customized JavaScript code that is known to work correctly on that browser. And if the CGI script detects that the user's browser does not support JavaScript, it can generate web pages that do not require JavaScript at all. The only drawback to this approach is that the CGI script cannot detect when a user has disabled JavaScript support in their browser.

Using a CGI script is also an ideal way to handle the `SRC` attribute of the `<SCRIPT>` tag. If the CGI script detects a browser that supports this attribute, it can trivially generate a web page that simply contains a reference to its JavaScript code. For other browsers, it can include that JavaScript code literally into the web page.

The `Navigator.userAgent` property contains the string that a browser sends as its `User-Agent` HTTP header. See the reference page for this property for more information. Note that writing CGI scripts is well beyond the scope of this book. For more information on doing so, see *CGI Programming on the World Wide Web* by Shishir Gundavaram, published by O'Reilly & Associates.

19

LiveConnect: JavaScript and Java

Navigator 3.0 opens up a tremendous new set of programming possibilities by allowing JavaScript to communicate with the Java virtual machine running in the browser. Netscape's name for this new JavaScript-to-Java and Java-to-JavaScript communication facility is "LiveConnect." This chapter explains how LiveConnect works, and how you can use it in your programs.

Note that Internet Explorer 3.0 does not support LiveConnect. Instead, it treats Java applets as ActiveX objects and allows them to be scripted through that mechanism. Doing so is described briefly at the end of this chapter.

To use LiveConnect, you'll need to understand Java programming. This chapter assumes you have at least a basic familiarity with Java (see *Java in a Nutshell*, by David Flanagan, and *Exploring Java*, by Patrick Niemeyer and Joshua Peck, both published by O'Reilly).

19.1 Overview of LiveConnect

LiveConnect is the mechanism that allows JavaScript and Java to work together. Using LiveConnect, all of the following are possible:

- JavaScript programs can interact with the standard Java system classes built-in to the browser.

- JavaScript programs can interact with Java applets, both reading and writing public fields of the applet and invoking public methods of the applet.

- JavaScript programs can interact with Java-enabled Navigator plug-ins in the same way.

- Applets and Java-enabled plug-ins can interact with JavaScript, reading and writing JavaScript object properties and array elements, and invoking JavaScript functions.

The surprising thing about LiveConnect is how easy it makes it to accomplish these difficult things. LiveConnect automatically handles all the required communication and data type conversion that must take place to allow Java and JavaScript to work together. LiveConnect is an underlying communication framework that opens up all sorts of possibilities for communication among JavaScript programs, Java applets, and Java-enabled plug-ins. LiveConnect can be thought of as the glue that ties these things together. Figure 19-1 illustrates this.

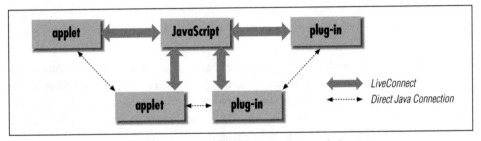

Figure 19–1: LiveConnect glues together JavaScript, applets, and plug-ins

19.2 LiveConnect Data Types

In order to understand how LiveConnect does its amazing job of connecting JavaScript to Java, you've got to understand the five JavaScript data types that Live-Connect uses. (There is also a Java data type that LiveConnect uses to connect Java back to JavaScript; we'll learn about that Java class later in this chapter.) The following subsections explain these JavaScript data types. Once we've explored these LiveConnect fundamentals, the following sections will show how we can actually use LiveConnect to connect JavaScript to Java.

19.2.1 The JavaPackage Object

The JavaScript JavaPackage object represents a Java package, which is a collection of related Java classes. The properties of a JavaPackage are the classes that the package contains (classes are represented by the JavaClass object, which we'll see later), as well as any other packages that the package contains. A restriction on the JavaPackage object is that you cannot use a JavaScript `for/in` loop to obtain a complete list of all packages and classes that a JavaPackage contains. The reason for this restriction will become clear in a moment.

All JavaPackage objects are contained within a parent JavaPackage, and the Window property named `Packages` is a top-level JavaPackage that serves as the root of this package hierarchy. It has `java`, `sun`, and `netscape` properties, which are JavaPackage objects that represent the various hierarchies of Java classes that are included with Navigator. For example, the JavaPackage `Packages` contains the JavaPackage `Packages.java`, which contains the JavaPackage `Packages.java.awt`. For convenience, every Window object has `java`, `sun`, and `netscape` properties which are shortcuts to `Packages.java`, `Packages.sun`, and `Packages.netscape`. Thus, instead of typing `Packages.java.awt`, you can simply use `java.awt`.

To continue with the example, `java.awt` is a JavaPackage object that contains JavaClass objects like `java.awt.Button`, which represents the *java.awt.Button* class. But it also contains yet another JavaPackage object, `java.awt.image` which represents the *java.awt.image* package in Java.

As you can see, the property naming scheme for the JavaPackage hierarchy mirrors the naming scheme for Java packages. Note that there is one big difference between the JavaPackage object and actual Java packages. Packages in Java are collections of classes, not collections of other packages. That is, *java.lang* is the name of a Java package, but *java* is not. So the JavaPackage object named `java` does not actually represent a package in Java, but is simply a convenient placeholder in the package hierarchy for other JavaPackage objects that do represent real Java packages.

On many systems, Java classes are installed in files in a directory hierarchy that corresponds to the package name. For example, the *java.lang.String* class is stored in the file *java/lang/String.class* in my Java implementation from Sun. In other implementations, notably that from Netscape, the class files are actually stored in a large uncompressed zip file. The directory hierarchy is still there, encoded in the file; it is just not visible on the surface. Therefore, instead of thinking of the Java-Package object as representing a Java package, you may find it clearer to consider it as representing a directory in the Java class hierarchy.

As we've said above, a JavaPackage object contains properties for each of the packages and classes it contains. If you think of a JavaPackage as representing a directory in the Java class directory hierarchy, then the properties of the JavaPackage are the contents of the directory. Each subdirectory of the directory becomes a

JavaPackage property, with the package name matching the subdirectory name. Each file in the directory becomes a JavaClass property, with the property name matching the file name, after the *.class* extension is stripped off. When viewed in this way, it is easy to understand why the JavaPackage object does not allow the for/in loop to list all of its properties—those properties actually correspond to directory contents, and they are not actually looked up and created until they are first used. Thus, a for/in loop will only find those properties of a JavaPackage object that have already been used at least once by the program.

19.2.2 The JavaClass Object

The JavaClass object is a JavaScript representation of a Java class. A JavaClass object does not have any properties of its own—all of its properties represent (and have the same name as) the public static fields and methods of the represented Java class. These public static fields and methods are sometimes called *class fields* and *class methods* to indicate that they are associated with an object class rather than an object instance. Unlike the JavaPackage object, the JavaClass object does allow the use of the for/in loop to enumerate its properties. Note that the JavaClass object does not have properties representing the *instance* fields and methods of a Java class—individual instances of a Java class are represented by the JavaObject object, which will be documented below.

As we saw above, JavaClass objects are contained in JavaPackage objects. For example, java.lang is a JavaPackage that contains a System property. Thus java.lang.System is a JavaClass object, representing the Java class *java.lang.System*. This JavaClass object, in turn, has properties such as out and in that represent static fields of the *java.lang.System* class. You can use JavaScript to refer to any of the standard Java system classes in this same way. The *java.lang.Double* class is named java.lang.Double (or Packages. java.lang.Double) in JavaScript, for example, and the *java.awt.Button* class is java.awt.Button.

Another way to obtain a JavaClass object in JavaScript is to use the getClass() function. Given any JavaObject, you can obtain a JavaClass that represents the class of that Java object by passing the JavaObject to getClass().

Once you have a JavaClass object, there are several things you can do with it. The JavaClass object implements the LiveConnect functionality that allows JavaScript programs to read and write the public static fields of Java classes, and to invoke the public static methods of Java classes. For example, java.lang.System is a JavaClass. We can read the value of a static field of this class like this:

```
var java_console = java.lang.System.out;
```

Similarly, we might invoke a static method of this class with a line like this one:

```
var java_version = java.lang.System.getProperty("java.version");
```

Recall that Java is a typed language—all fields and method arguments have types. If you attempt to set a field or pass an argument of the wrong type, you will cause a JavaScript error.

There is one more important feature of the JavaClass object. You can use it with the JavaScript new operator to create new instances of Java classes—i.e., to create JavaObject objects. The syntax for doing so is just as it is in JavaScript (and just as it is in Java):

```
var d = new java.lang.Double(1.23);
```

Finally, having created a JavaObject in this way, we can return to the getClass() function and show an example of its use:

```
var d = new java.lang.Double(1.23);   // Create a JavaObject.
var d_class = getClass(d);            // Obtain the JavaClass of the JavaObject.
if (d_class == java.lang.Double) ...; // This comparison will be true.
```

When working with standard system classes like this, you can usually just use the name of the system class directly rather than calling getClass(). The function is more useful to obtain the class of other non-system objects, such as applet instances.

19.2.3 The JavaObject Object

The JavaObject object is a JavaScript object that represents a Java object (that is, it represents an instance of a Java class). The JavaObject object is, in many ways, analogous to the JavaClass object. Like JavaClass, a JavaObject object has no properties of its own—all of its properties represent (and have the same names as) the public instance fields and public instance methods of the Java object it represents. Like JavaClass, you can use a JavaScript for/in loop to enumerate all properties of a JavaObject object. The JavaObject object implements the LiveConnect functionality that allows us to read and write the public instance fields and invoke the public methods of a Java object.

For example, if d is a JavaObject that, as above, represents an instance of the *java.lang.Double* class, then we can invoke a method of that Java object with JavaScript code like this:

```
n = d.doubleValue();
```

Similarly, we saw above that the *java.lang.System* class has a static field *out*. This field refers to a Java object of class *java.io.PrintStream*. In JavaScript, we can refer to the corresponding JavaObject as:

```
java.lang.System.out
```

And we can invoke a method of this object like this:[*]

```
java.lang.System.out.println("Hello world!");
```

The JavaObject object also allows us to read and write public instance fields of the Java object it represents. Neither the *java.lang.Double* class or the *java.io.PrintStream* class used in the examples above has any public instance fields, however. But suppose we use JavaScript to create an instance of the *java.awt.Rectangle* class:

```
r = new java.awt.Rectangle();
```

Then we can read and write its public instance fields with JavaScript code like the following:

```
r.x = r.y = 0;
r.width = 4;
r.height = 5;
var perimeter = 2*r.width + 2*r.height;
```

The beauty of LiveConnect is that it allows a Java object, r, to be used just as if it were a JavaScript object. Some caution is required, however: r is a JavaObject, and does not behave identically to regular JavaScript objects. The differences will be detailed later. Also, remember that unlike JavaScript, the fields of Java objects and the arguments of its methods are typed. If you do not specify JavaScript values of the correct types, you will cause a JavaScript error.

19.2.4 The JavaMethod Object

The JavaMethod object represents a Java method. In the sections above, we've said that the JavaClass and JavaObject objects provide the LiveConnect functionality that allows JavaScript programs to invoke public class methods and public instance methods. In fact, that claim was an over-simplification. The JavaClass and

---

[*] The output of this line of code doesn't appear in the web browser itself, but in the "Java Console." Select **Show Java Console** in the **Options** menu to make the console visible.

JavaObject objects contain properties that have the same names as the class and instance fields and the class and instance methods of a Java class or object. The properties that represent fields allow us to read and write class and instance fields. The properties that represent methods, on the other hand, simply contain JavaMethod objects, and it is these JavaMethod objects that actually implement the LiveConnect functionality that lets us invoke Java class and instance methods.

So, when we write lines of JavaScript code like this one:

```
java.lang.System.out.println("Hello world!");
```

What is actually happening can be made clearer with code like this:

```
var println_method = java.lang.System.out.println;
println_method("Hello world!");
```

The LiveConnect functionality provided by the JavaMethod object is substantial. Consider the following JavaScript code:

```
var r = java.awt.Rectangle(0, 0, 10, 10);   // a 10x10 square at (0,0)
var i = r.inside(5,5);                        // is the point (5,5) inside?
```

In order to run this code, LiveConnect must convert the two JavaScript numeric arguments to the Java `int` type. Then it must invoke the Java method, passing these converted values. Finally, it must take the return value, a Java `boolean`, and convert it to a JavaScript Boolean value and return it. This conversion is completely transparent to the JavaScript programmer, which is what makes LiveConnect so powerful.

JavaMethod objects behave much like regular JavaScript functions, with a few important differences. Java methods, unlike JavaScript functions, expect a fixed number of arguments of a fixed type. If you pass the wrong number or wrong type of arguments, you will cause a JavaScript error. There is a more subtle difference between Java methods and JavaScript functions as well. When a JavaScript function is assigned to an object property, it becomes a method, and is passed a reference to that object as the value of the `this` keyword. Thus, a JavaScript function may behave differently depending upon which object it is assigned as a property of. This is not true of JavaMethod object—they are invoked in the context of a Java object, and they carry that context with them. A JavaMethod will behave the same regardless of what JavaScript object it is a property of.

19.2.5 The JavaArray Object

The final LiveConnect datatype for JavaScript is the JavaArray object. As you might expect by now, this object represents a Java array, and provides the LiveConnect functionality that allows JavaScript to read the elements of a Java array. Like JavaScript arrays (and like Java arrays), a JavaArray object has a `length` property that specifies the number of elements it contains. The elements of a JavaArray object are read with the standard JavaScript `[]` array index operator. They can also be enumerated with the `for/in` loop. You can also use JavaArray objects to access multidimensional arrays (actually arrays of arrays) just as you would in JavaScript or in Java.

For example, suppose we create an instance of the *java.awt.Polygon* class:

```
p = new java.awt.Polygon();
```

Then the JavaObject p has properties `xpoints` and `ypoints` which are JavaArray objects representing Java arrays of integers. (We know the names and types of these properties because we looked up the documentation for *java.awt.Polygon* in a Java reference manual.) We can use these JavaArray objects to them to randomly initialize the Java polygon with code like this:

```
for(int i = 0; i < p.xpoints.length; i++)
    p.xpoints[i] = Math.round(Math.random()*100);
for(int i = 0; i < p.ypoints.length; i++)
    p.ypoints[i] = Math.round(Math.random()*100);
```

19.3 *LiveConnect Data Conversion*

Java is a strongly typed language with a relatively large number of data types. JavaScript is an untyped language with a relatively small number of types. Because of these major structural differences in the two languages, one of the central responsibilities of LiveConnect is data conversion. When JavaScript sets a Java class or instance field or passes an argument to a Java method, a JavaScript value must be converted to an equivalent Java value. And when JavaScript reads a Java class or instance field or obtains the return value of Java method, that Java value must be converted into a compatible JavaScript value.[*]

Figure 19-2 and Figure 19-3 illustrate how data conversion is performed when JavaScript writes Java values and when it reads them.

Notice the following points about the data conversions illustrated in Figure 19-2.

- JavaScript numbers can be converted to any of the primitive Java numeric types. The actual conversion performed will depend, of course, on the type of the Java field being set or method argument being passed. Note that you can

---

[*] In addition, data conversion must also happen when Java reads or writes a JavaScript field or invokes a JavaScript method. These conversions are done differently, however, and will be described later in the chapter when we explain how to use JavaScript from Java. For now, we're only considering the data conversion that happens when JavaScript code interacts with Java, not the other way around.

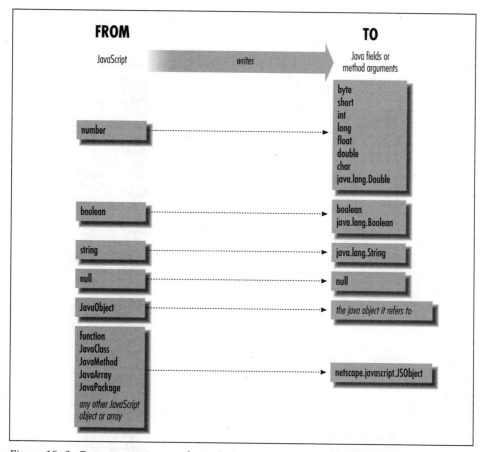

Figure 19–2: Data conversions performed when JavaScript writes Java values

lose precision doing this, for example, when you pass a large number to a Java field of type `short`, or when you pass a floating-point value to a Java integral type.

- JavaScript numbers can also be converted to instances of the java class *java.lang.Double*, but not to instances of related classes such as *java.lang.Integer* or *java.lang.Float*.

- JavaScript does not have any representation for character data, so JavaScript numbers may also be converted to the Java primitive `char` type.

- A JavaObject in JavaScript is "unwrapped" when passed to Java, and is converted to the Java object it represents. Note, however, that JavaClass objects in JavaScript are not converted to Java instances of *java.lang.Class*, as might be expected.

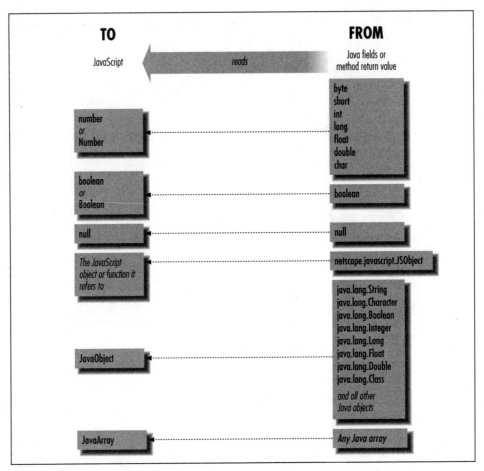

Figure 19-3: Data conversions performed when JavaScript reads Java values

Also notice these points about the conversions illustrated in Figure 19-3.

- Since JavaScript does not have a type for character data, the Java primitive char type is converted to a JavaScript number, and not a string, as might be expected.

- The figure shows that Java numbers are returned either as primitive JavaScript numbers or as a JavaScript Number object. Similarly, Java boolean values are returned as primitive JavaScript Booleans or as JavaScript Boolean objects. Which is returned depends on whether the value read is a Java field or the return value of a Java method. The discrepancy will be explained in a subsection later in the chapter.

- Java instances of *java.lang.Double*, *java.lang.Integer*, and similar classes are not converted to JavaScript numbers. Like all Java objects, they are converted to JavaObject objects in JavaScript.

- Java strings are instances of *java.lang.String*, so like other Java objects they are converted to JavaObject objects rather than to actual JavaScript strings.

- Any type of Java array is converted to a JavaArray object in JavaScript. Note, however, that Java instances of *java.lang.Class* are not converted to a Java-Class object—like other Java objects, they are converted to a JavaObject.

19.3.1 Wrapper Objects

In addition to the note above, there is a very important concept that must be made clear in order for you to fully understand Figure 19-2 and Figure 19-3. This is the idea of "wrapper" objects. While conversions between most JavaScript and Java primitive types are possible, conversions between object types are not, in general, possible. This is why LiveConnect defines the JavaObject object in JavaScript—it represents a Java object that cannot be directly converted to a JavaScript object. In a sense, a JavaObject is a JavaScript "wrapper" around a Java object. When JavaScript reads a Java value (a field or the return value of a method), Java objects are "wrapped" and JavaScript sees a JavaObject.

A similar thing happens when JavaScript writes a JavaScript object into a Java field or passes a JavaScript object to a Java method. There is no way to convert the JavaScript object to a Java object, so the object gets wrapped. Just as the JavaScript wrapper for a Java object is a JavaObject, the Java wrapper for a JavaScript object is the Java class *netscape.javascript.JSObject*.

It gets interesting when these wrapper objects are passed back. If JavaScript writes a JavaObject into a Java field or passes it to Java method, then LiveConnect first "unwraps" the object, converting the JavaObject back into the Java object that it represents. And similarly, if JavaScript reads a Java field or gets the return value of a Java method that is an instance of *netscape.javascript.JSObject*, then that JSObject is also unwrapped to reveal and return the original JavaScript object.

19.3.2 Java Field Values versus Method Return Values

In Navigator 3.0, LiveConnect returns slightly different data types when a value is read from a Java field than it does when the same value is read as the return value of a Java method. Figure 19-3 shows that all Java primitive numeric types and instances of *java.lang.Double* are returned as primitive JavaScript numbers or as

Number objects. When the numeric return value of a method is read, it is returned as a primitive JavaScript number. But when a numeric value is read from a field, it is returned as a Number object.

Recall that Number objects in JavaScript behave almost the same, but not exactly, as primitive JavaScript numbers. One important difference is that Number objects, like all JavaScript objects, use the + operator for string concatenation rather than addition. So code like the following can yield unexpected results:

```
var r = new java.awt.Rectangle(0,0,5,5);
var w = r.width;        // This is a Number object, not a primitive number.
var new_w = w + 1;      // Oops! new_w is now "51", not 6, as expected.
```

To work around this problem, you can explicitly call the valueOf() method to convert a Number object to its corresponding numeric value. For example:

```
var r = new java.awt.Rectangle(0,0,5,5);
var w = r.width.valueOf(); // Now we've got a primitive number.
var new_w = w + 1;         // This time, new_w is 6, as desired.
```

You can also force a Number object to a primitive number by using it in a numeric context (but not the + operator) by subtracting zero, for example. So in the above example we could also have done this:

```
var w = r.width - 0;     // Now we've got a primitive number.
```

The same discrepancy occurs when Java primitive Boolean values and instances of *java.lang.Boolean* are read from Java fields—they are returned as JavaScript Boolean objects even though the same Java value would have been returned as a primitive Boolean value if it had been the return value of a method. You can work around this with the valueOf() method, as above.

Finally, when Java objects are read from Java fields (but not when they are read as the return value of a Java method), the returned value behaves in all respects like a JavaObject, except that passing it to the getClass() function fails with an error: "getClass expects a Java object argument". To work around this problem, to obtain a JavaObject object that getClass() recognizes as such, you can use code like the following:

```
var o = java.lang.System.out;    // This should be a JavaObject
var c = getClass(o);             // ...but this causes an error.
var p = new Object(o);           // This is the workaround
var c = getClass(p);             // ...this works now.
```

The fact that values are returned differently when read from a field than when read as method return values is not exactly a bug in LiveConnect; it is more of a misfeature, and it is one that the designers of LiveConnect may not be able to correct in future versions of Navigator. It stems from a subtle incompatibility between Java and JavaScript. In Java methods are not data types as they are in JavaScript, so it is perfectly legal to define a method that has the same name as a field. JavaScript, however, allows us to treat methods, including Java methods, as variables that we can manipulate, and so it is not possible to use the same name for a JavaScript property and a method.

We run into a problem when we try to use a Java class has a field and a method by the same name. Suppose that a JavaObject o refers to an instance of such a class, and the name shared by the field and the method is f. Then the JavaScript expression o.f is ambiguous; JavaScript does not know whether we are referring to the method or the field. Consider this code:

```
var ambiguous = o.f;      // Is it a JavaMethod or JavaObject?
                          // It depends on how we use it in the future!
ambiguous();              // Hmm...we must have meant the method.
s += ambiguous;           // In this case, we must have meant the field.
```

The variable ambiguous really can't have a value until it is used in a context that makes it clear what value it is supposed to have. The way this ambiguity is resolved is that ambiguous is implemented as an internal object of a type known as a JavaSlot. Only when it is clear what context the "slot" is being used in is this value converted to the appropriate type.

Notice that this ambiguity only arises when reading Java fields; there is no possibility of it when reading the return values of Java methods. Thus the differences the way values are read arises from the JavaSlot conversion process when Java field values are read.

19.4 *JavaScript Conversion of JavaObjects*

Having worked your way through that dense data conversion section above you may have hoped that we were through with the topic of data conversion. But there is more to be discussed. It has to do with how JavaScript converts JavaObjects to various JavaScript primitive types. Notice in Figure 19-3 that quite a few Java data types, including Java strings (instances of *java.lang.String*) are converted to JavaObject objects in JavaScript rather than being converted to actual JavaScript primitive types, such as strings. This means that when you use LiveConnect, you'll commonly be working with JavaObject objects.

Refer back to Table 9-1. You may also want to re-read the section of Chapter 9, *Further Topics in JavaScript*, that Table 9-1 is contained in. The table shows how various JavaScript data types are converted when used in various "contexts." For example, when a number is used in a string context, it is converted to a string. And when an object is used in a Boolean context, it is converted to the value `false` if it is `null` and `true` otherwise. These conversion rules don't apply to JavaObject objects. JavaObject objects are converted using their own rules, as follows:

- When a JavaObject is used in a numeric context, it is converted to a number by invoking the `doubleValue()` method of the Java object it represents. If the Java object does not define this method, a JavaScript error occurs.

- When a JavaObject is used in a Boolean context, it is converted to a Boolean value by invoking the `booleanValue()` method of the Java object it represents. If the Java object does not define this method, a JavaScript error occurs.

- When a JavaObject is used in a string context, it is converted to a string value by invoking the `toString()` method of the Java object it represents. All Java objects define or inherit this method, so this conversion always succeeds.

- When a JavaObject is used in a function context, a JavaScript error occurs.

- When a JavaObject is used in an object context, no conversion is necessary, since it is already a JavaScript object.

Because of these different conversion rules, and for other reasons as well, JavaObjects behave differently than other JavaScript objects, and there are some common pitfalls that you need to beware of. First, it is not uncommon to work with a JavaObject that represents an instance of a *java.lang.Double* or some other numeric object. In many ways, such a JavaObject will behave like a primitive number value, but be careful when using the + operator. When you use a JavaObject (or any JavaScript object) with +, it constitutes a string context, and the object is converted to a string for string concatenation, instead of being converted to a number for addition.

When we described this same problem above when working with a Number object, we said that the workaround was to explicitly call `valueOf()` to convert the Number to a primitive number. Because of another difference between JavaObjects and other JavaScript objects, this workaround doesn't work in this case. Recall that the JavaObject object has no properties of its own; all of its properties represent fields and methods of the Java object it represents. This means that JavaObjects don't even have the `valueOf()` method recommended above! So when you've got a JavaObject representing an instance of *java.lang.Double*, or something similar, you'll have to call the `doubleValue()` method when you need to force it to a primitive value.

Another difference between JavaObjects and other JavaScript data types is that JavaObjects can only be used in a Boolean context if they define a `boolean-Value()` method. Suppose `button` is a JavaScript variable that may contain `null` or may hold a JavaObject that represents an instance of the *java.awt.Button* class. If you want to check whether the variable contains null, you might write code like this, out of old habit:

```
if (!button) { ... }
```

If button is null, this will work fine. But if button actually contains a JavaObject representing a *java.awt.Button* instance, then LiveConnect will try to invoke the booleanValue() method. When it discovers that the *java.awt.Button* class doesn't define one, it will cause a JavaScript error. The workaround in this case is to be explicit about what you are testing for, to avoid using the JavaObject in a Boolean context:

```
if (button != null) { ... }
```

This is a good habit to get into, in any case, since it makes your code easier to read and understand.

19.5 *Scripting Java with JavaScript*

Now that we've discussed the JavaScript data types used by LiveConnect, and the data conversions that go on when JavaScript reads and writes Java data values, we can begin to discuss some of the practical applications of LiveConnect. Bear in mind, while reading this section, that we have still only discussed half of LiveConnect—the half that allows JavaScript to work with Java. The portions of LiveConnect that allow a Java applet to use JavaScript will be documented later.

19.5.1 *Using the Java System Classes*

All of the LiveConnect examples presented so far in this chapter have made use of Java classes from the standard Java libraries from Sun. There is not a whole lot of interesting things you can do with an instance of *java.ang.Double*, but we have seen some interesting uses of the *java.lang.System* class, for example.

LiveConnect gives us the capability to create new instances of Java classes, to set and query fields of classes and their instances, and to invoke methods of classes or instances. Using these capabilities, there are some interesting things we can do with the "built-in" or "system" classes that are installed with Navigator. Note also, that there are some things that we cannot do. LiveConnect does not give us the capability to define new Java classes or subclasses from within JavaScript, nor does it give us the ability to create Java arrays. Also, the things we can do with the standard Java classes are restricted for security reasons. A JavaScript program cannot use the *java.io.File* class, for example, because that would give it the power to read, write, and delete files on the host system—exactly the capabilities needed for Internet "viruses". Because of security issues like this one, JavaScript can use Java only in those ways that untrusted applets can.

Example 19-1 shows JavaScript code that uses standard Java classes (the JavaScript code looks almost identical to Java code, in fact) to pop up a window and display some text. The results are shown in Figure 19-4.

Example 19–1: Scripting the Built-in Java Classes

```
var f = new java.awt.Frame("Hello World");
var ta = new java.awt.TextArea("hello, world", 5, 20);
f.add("Center", ta);
f.pack();
f.show();
```

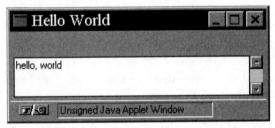

Figure 19–4: A Java window created from JavaScript

Example 19-1 shows how it is possible to use JavaScript to create simple Java user interfaces. But while this technique of creating and popping up a Java window from JavaScript seems like it could lead to much more complex examples of Java user interfaces and graphics drawn from JavaScript, it is not actually so easy. Live-Connect allows us only to call methods in classes and objects. It does not define any way to subclass Java objects or define Java methods, and both of these techniques are required in Java to be able to handle events (such as button presses). Thus, in general, you can only use JavaScript to create static Java programs, not Java programs that *interact* with a user. This may change in the future, however— both the JDK 1.1 version of the AWT user-interface library from Sun and the Internet Foundation Classes (IFC) library from Netscape make it easier to define event handlers, and may make it possible to connect Java user-interfaces to JavaScript functions that handle user interaction.

19.5.2 Interacting with Applets

We saw in Chapter 14, *Documents and Their Contents*, that the Document object has an applets[] property which is an array containing JavaObject objects, one for each Java applet in the document. The JavaObject objects in this array represent the Java object of each applet—this will always be an instance of some subclass *java.applet.Applet*. Because LiveConnect exposes the Java object for each applet on a web page, you can freely read and write public fields of the applet and just as freely invoke public methods of the applet.

Example 19-2 shows some simple HTML that embeds an applet in a web page and includes buttons that start and stop the applet by using LiveConnect to invoke the applet's start( ) and stop( ) methods.

Example 19-2: Controlling an Applet with JavaScript

```
<!-- Here's the applet -->
<APPLET NAME="animation" CODE="Animation.class" WIDTH=500 HEIGHT=200>
</APPLET>

<!-- And here are the buttons that start and stop it. -->
<FORM>
<INPUT TYPE=button VALUE="Start" onclick="document.animation.start()">
<INPUT TYPE=button VALUE="Stop" onclick="document.animation.stop()">
</FORM>
```

There are a couple of points to note about this example. First, the <APPLET> tag is given a NAME attribute, and the value of that attribute becomes the name of a property in the document object. We've seen this technique before with the <FORM> and <IMG> tags; in this case it allows us to refer to applets by names such as document.animation instead of numbers such as document.applets[0].

The second point to note about this example is that it calls the start( ) and stop( ) methods of the applet—these are standard methods that all applets define; they are the methods that the browser itself calls to start and stop the applet. But you needn't stop at calling the standard methods of the Java *Applet* class. If your applet defines other methods of its own, you can call any of these as well.[*] If you were working with a full-featured animation applet, for example, you might define an HTML form to serve as a complete control panel for the animation, with **Fast-Forward** and **Reverse** buttons, an input field for specifying speed, and so on. The buttons in this control panel could then control the applet by invoking special-purpose methods, such as fast_forward( ), provided by the applet.

Another possibility to bear in mind is that you can write passive applets that take no action on their own, but exist simply to serve your JavaScript code. An applet might define various utility functions for popping up dialog boxes that are more

---

[*] In fact, it is safer and more portable to call your own custom methods than to call those that are intended to be called by the browser.

complex than those provided by the `alert()`, `confirm()`, and `prompt()` methods, for example.

19.5.3 Working with Plug-Ins

Just as the `applets[]` array of the Document object contains JavaObjects that represent the applets embedded in a document with the `<APPLET>` tag, the `embeds[]` array of the Document object contains JavaObjects that represent data embedded in a web page with the `<EMBED>` tag. This is data that is intended to be displayed by a Navigator plug-in. Do not confuse the `Document.embeds[]` array with the `Navigator.plug-ins[]` array. The first contains objects that represent a single piece of embedded data, and the second contains Plugin objects that represent the actual plug-ins that are installed in Navigator to display embedded data.

The JavaObject objects in the `embeds[]` array are all instances of some subclass of the *netscape.plugin.Plugin* class. Each Java-enabled plug-in defines its own subclass of *netscape.plugin.Plugin*, and creates an instance of that subclass for each piece of embedded data (each `<EMBED>` tag) that it displays. The purpose of these *netscape.plugin.Plugin* subclasses is to define an API through which Java applets and JavaScript programs can control the behavior of a plug-in, or of a particular instance of a plug-in.

Because the objects in the `embeds[]` array are provided by plug-ins, the properties and methods of any of these objects will depend on the particular plug-in in use. In general, you'll have to read the vendor's documentation for any given plug-in to determine how to control it through LiveConnect. If the plug-in that is displaying the data is not Java-enabled, then the corresponding object in the `embeds[]` array will be a JavaObject that represents a dummy Java object with no functionality.

Example 19-3 shows how you might use the LiveAudio plug-in (bundled with Navigator 3.0 on most platforms) and LiveConnect to automatically play a sound when the user clicks a button and when the mouse passes over a hyperlink. The example relies upon the `play()` method of the *netscape.plugin.Plugin* instance provided by the LiveAudio plug-in. This method, and many others, are detailed by Netscape in their LiveAudio documentation.

Example 19-3: Controlling a Plug-In from JavaScript

```
<!-- Here we embed some sounds in the browser, with attributes to -->
<!-- specify that they won't be played when first loaded. In this -->
<!-- example, we use sounds found locally on Windows 95 platforms. -->
<EMBED SRC="file:///C|/windows/media/Tada.wav" HIDDEN=true AUTOSTART=false>
<EMBED SRC="file:///C|/windows/media/Ding.wav" HIDDEN=true AUTOSTART=false>
<EMBED SRC="file:///C|/windows/media/The Microsoft Sound.wav"
       HIDDEN=true AUTOSTART=false>
```

Example 19–3: Controlling a Plug-In from JavaScript (continued)

```
<!-- Here are some buttons that play those sounds. Note the use of the -->
<!-- embeds[] array and the play() method invoked through LiveConnect. -->
<FORM>
<INPUT TYPE=button VALUE="Play Sound #1" onClick="document.embeds[0].play()">
<INPUT TYPE=button VALUE="Play Sound #2" onClick="document.embeds[1].play()">
<INPUT TYPE=button VALUE="Play Sound #3" onClick="document.embeds[2].play()">
</FORM>


<!-- Here's a hypertext link that plays a sound when the user passes over -->
<A HREF="" onMouseOver="document.embeds[0].play()">Click Me</A>
```

Although the objects in the embeds[] array are all instances of subclasses of *netscape.plugin.Plugin,* there is one method that all subclasses share which you may find useful in your JavaScript code. The isActive() method returns true if the specified Plugin object is still active and false if it is not. Generally, a plug-in will only become inactive if it was on a page that is no longer displayed. This situation can only arise when you store references to the embeds[] array of one window in JavaScript variables of another window.

19.6 Using JavaScript from Java

Having explored how to control Java from JavaScript code, we now turn to the opposite problem: how to control JavaScript from Java code. This control is accomplished primarily through the *netscape.javascript.JSObject* class. Just as a JavaObject is a JavaScript wrapper around a Java object, so a JSObject is a Java wrapper around a JavaScript object.

19.6.1 The JSObject Class

All Java interactions with JavaScript are performed through a single interface—the *netscape.javascript.JSObject* class. An instance of this class is a wrapper around a single JavaScript object. The class defines methods that allow you to read and write property values and array elements of the JavaScript object, and to invoke methods of the object. A synopsis of this class appears in the code Example 19-4.

Example 19–4: Synopsis of the netscape.javascript.JSObject Class

```
public final class JSObject extends Object {
    // static method to obtain initial JSObject for applet's browser window
    public static JSObject getWindow(java.applet.Applet applet);
    public Object getMember(String name);          // read object property
    public Object getSlot(int index);              // read array element
    public void setMember(String name, Object value);   // set object property
    public void setSlot(int index, Object value);       // set array element
    public void removeMember(String name);         // delete property
```

Example 19-4: Synopsis of the netscape.javascript.JSObject Class (continued)

```
public Object call(String methodName, Object args[]); // invoke method
public Object eval(String s);                          // evaluate string
public String toString();                              // convert to string
protected void finalize();
}
```

Because all JavaScript objects appear in a hierarchy rooted at the current browser window, JSObjects must also appear in a hierarchy. In order for a Java applet to interact with any JavaScript objects, it must first obtain a JSObject that represents the browser window (or frame) in which the applet appears. The JSObject class does not define a constructor method, so we cannot simply create an appropriate JSObject. Instead, we must call the static getWindow() method. When passed a reference to an applet itself, this method returns a JSObject that represents the browser window that contains that applet. Thus, every applet that interacts with JavaScript will include a line that looks something like this

```
JSObject jsroot = JSObject.getWindow(this);  // "this" is the applet itself
```

Having obtained a JSObject that refers to the "root" window of the JavaScript object hierarchy, you can use instance methods of the JSObject to read the values of properties of the JavaScript object that it represents. Most of these properties have values that are themselves JavaScript objects, and so you can continue the process and read their properties as well. The JSObject getMember() method returns the value of a named property, and the getSlot() method returns the value of a numbered array element of the specified JavaScript object. You might use these methods as follows:

```
import netscape.javascript.JSObject;  // this must be at the top of the file
    ...
JSObject jsroot = JSObject.getWindow(this);                 // self
JSObject document = (JSObject) jsroot.getMember("document"); // .document
JSObject applets = (JSObject) document.getMember("applets"); //    .applets
Applet applet0 = (Applet) applets.getSlot(0);               //       [0]
```

Note two things about this code fragment above. First, that getMember() and getSlot() both return a value of type Object, which generally must be cast to some more specific value, such as a JSObject. Second, that the value read from "slot" 0 of the applets array can be cast to an Applet, rather than a JSObject. This is because the elements of the JavaScript applets[] array are JavaObject objects that represent Java Applet objects. When Java reads a JavaScript JavaObject, it "unwraps" that object and returns the Java object (in this case an Applet) that it contains. The data conversion that occurs through the JSObject interface will be documented later in this section.

The JSObject class also supports methods for setting properties and array elements of JavaScript objects. setMember() and setSlot() are analogous to the getMember() and getSlot() methods we've already seen. These methods set the value of a named property or a numbered array element to a specified value. Note, however, that the value to be set must be a Java Object. This means that you can set JavaScript properties to values of types such as Applet, String, and JSObject, but you cannot set them to boolean, int, or double. Instead of setting properties or array elements to primitive Java values, you must use their corresponding Java object types, such as Boolean, Integer, and Double. Finally, on a related not, the removeMember() method allows you to delete the value of a named property from a JavaScript object.

Besides reading and writing properties and array elements from JavaScript objects, the JSObject class also allows you to invoke methods of JavaScript objects. The JSObject call() method invokes a named method of the specified JavaScript object, and passes a specified array of Java objects as arguments to that method. As we saw when setting JavaScript properties, note that it is not possible to pass primitive Java values as arguments to a JavaScript method; instead you must use their corresponding Java object types. For example, you might use the call() method in Java code like the following to open a new browser window:

```
public JSObject newwin(String url, String window_name)
{
    Object[] args = { url, window_name };
    JSObject win = JSObject.getWindow(this);
    return (JSObject) win.call("open", args);
}
```

The JSObject has one more very important method: eval(). This Java method of the JSObject works just like the JavaScript method of the JavaScript Object type—it executes a string that contains JavaScript code. You'll find that using eval() is often much easier than using the various other methods of the JSObject class. One reason is that it can be much simpler to use. Another is that since all the code is passed as a string, you can use a string representation of the data types you want, and do not have to convert Java primitive types to their corresponding object types. For example, compare the following two lines of code that set properties of the main browser window:

```
jsroot.setMember("i", new Integer(0));
jsroot.eval("self.i = 0");
```

The second line is obviously easier to understand. As another example, consider the following use of eval():

```
JSObject jsroot = JSObject.getWindow(this);
jsroot.eval("parent.frames[1].document.write('Hello from Java!')");
```

To do the equivalent without the `eval()` method is a lot harder:

```
JSObject jsroot = JSObject.getWindow(this);
JSObject parent = (JSObject) jsroot.getMember("parent");
JSObject frames = (JSObject) parent.getMember("frames");
JSObject frame1 = (JSObject) frames.getSlot(1);
JSObject document = (JSObject) frame1.getMember("document");
Object[] args = { "Hello from Java!" };
document.call("write", args);
```

19.6.2 Using JSObjects in Applets

Example 19-5 shows the `init()` method of an applet that uses LiveConnect to interact with JavaScript.

Example 19-5: Using JavaScript from an Applet Method

```
import netscape.javascript.*

public void init()
{
    // get the JSObject representing the applet's browser window.
    JSObject win = JSObject.getWindow(this);

    // Run JavaScript with eval(). Careful with those nested quotes!
    win.eval("alert('The CPUHog applet is now running on your computer. " +
            "You may find that your system slows down a bit.');");
}
```

In order to use any applet you must compile it and then embed it in an HTML file. When the applet interacts with JavaScript, special instructions are required for both of these steps.

19.6.2.1 Compiling applets that use the JSObject class

Any applet that interacts with JavaScript uses the *netscape.javascript.JSObject* class. In order to compile these applets, therefore, your Java compiler must know where to find a definition of this class. Because the class is defined and shipped by Netscape and not by Sun, the *javac* compiler from Sun does not know about it. This section explains how to enable your compiler to find this required class. If you are not using the JDK from Sun, then you may have to do something a little different—see the documentation from the vendor of your Java compiler or Java development environment.

The basic approach to tell the JDK compiler where to find classes is to set the CLASSPATH environment variable. This environment variable specifies a list of directories and zip files that the compiler should search for class definitions (in addition to its standard directory of system classes). Navigator 3.0 stores its class definitions in a file named java_30. The exact location of this file depends on what platform you use and also on how and where you installed the browser files. On a Unix system, the full path to this file will depend on where you installed Navigator, but will typically be something like:

```
/usr/local/lib/netscape/java_30
```

On a Windows 95 system, the path will also depend on where you chose to install Navigator, but it will usually be something like:

```
C:\ProgramFiles\Netscape\Navigator\Program\Java\Classes\Java_30
```

You may have to search a bit to locate this file on your system.

The java_30 file, wherever it is located, is an uncompressed zip file of all the Java classes Navigator needs. The *javac* compiler can extract classes from zip files, and so you can tell the compiler where to find the *netscape.javascript.JSObject* class with lines like the following. For Unix systems:

```
setenv CLASSPATH .:/usr/local/lib/netscape/java_30
```

And for Windows 95 systems:

```
set CLASSPATH=.;C:\Program Files\Netscape\Navigator\Program\Java\Classes\Java_30
```

If this does not work for you, you may need to extract the netscape/ directory from the java_30 zip file, and install this directory somewhere like /usr/local/lib/netscape_classes. Then, you can include this unzipped directory in your CLASSPATH environment variable.

19.6.2.2 The MAYSCRIPT attribute

There is one further requirement before you can run an applet that interacts with JavaScript. As a security precaution, applets are not allowed to use JavaScript unless the web page author (who may be different than the applet author) explicitly gives the applet permission to do so. To give this permission, you must include the new MAYSCRIPT attribute in an applet's <APPLET> tag in the HTML file.

Example 19-5 showed a fragment of an applet that used JavaScript to display an alert dialog box. Once you have successfully compiled this applet, you might include it in an HTML file with HTML code like the following:

```
<APPLET code="CPUHog.class" width=300 height=300 MAYSCRIPT></APPLET>
```

If you do not remember to include the MAYSCRIPT tag, the applet will not be allowed to interact with JavaScript.

19.6.2.3 A complete example

Example 19-6 shows a complete example of a Java class that uses LiveConnect and
the JSObject class to communicate with JavaScript. The class is a subclass of
java.io.OutputStream, and is used to allow a Java applet to write HTML text into a
newly created web browser window. An applet might want to do this because it
provides a way to display formatted text, which is difficult to do with Java itself.
Another important reason that an applet might want to display its output in a
browser window is that this gives the user the ability to print the output or save it
to a file, which are capabilities that applets themselves do not have.

Example 19-6: An OutputStream for Displaying HTML in a Browser Window

```
import netscape.javascript.JSObject;    // these are the classes we'll use
import java.applet.Applet;
import java.io.OutputStream;


// an output stream that sends HTML text to a newly created web browser window
public class HTMLOutputStream extends OutputStream
{
    JSObject main_window;        // the initial browser window
    JSObject window;             // the new window we create
    JSObject document;           // the document of that new window
    static int window_num = 0;   // used to give each new window a unique name


    // To create a new HTMLOutputStream, you must specify the applet that
    // will use it (this specifies a browser window) and the desired size
    // for the new window.
    public HTMLOutputStream(Applet applet, int width, int height)
    {
        // get main browser window from the applet with JSObject.getWindow()
        main_window = JSObject.getWindow(applet);
        // use JSObject.eval() to create a new window
        window = (JSObject)
            main_window.eval("self.open('','" +
                        "'HTMLOutputStream" + window_num++ + "','" +
                        "'menubar,status,resizable,scrollbars," +
                        "width=" + width + ",height=" + height + "')");
        // use JSObject.getMember() to get the document of this new window
        document = (JSObject) window.getMember("document");
        // Then use JSObject.call() to open this document.
        document.call("open", null);
    }


    // This is the write() method required for all OutputStream subclasses.
    public void write(byte[] chars, int offset, int length)
    {
        // create a string from the specified bytes
        String s = new String(chars, 0, offset, length);
```

Example 19–6: An OutputStream for Displaying HTML in a Browser Window (continued)

```
        // store the string in an array for use with JSObject.call()
        Object[] args = { s };
        // check to see if the window has been closed
        boolean closed = ((Boolean)window.getMember("closed")).booleanValue();
        // if not, use JSObject.call() to invoke document.write()
        if (!closed) document.call("write", args);
    }
    // Here are two variants on the above method, also required.
    public void write(byte[] chars) { write(chars, 0, chars.length); }
    public void write(int c) { byte[] chars = {(byte)c}; write(chars, 0, 1); }

    // When the stream is closed, use JSObject.call() to call Document.close
    public void close() { document.call("close", null); }

    // This method is unique to HTMLOutputStream. If the new window is
    // still open, use JSObject.call() to invoke Window.close() to close it.
    public void close_window()
    {
        boolean closed = ((Boolean)window.getMember("closed")).booleanValue();
        if (!closed) window.call("close", null);
    }
}
```

19.6.3 Data Conversion

At the beginning of this chapter we described the rules by which value are converted when JavaScript reads and writes Java fields and invokes Java methods. Those rules explained how the JavaScript JavaObject, JavaArray, JavaClass, and JavaMethod objects convert data, and they apply only to the case of JavaScript manipulating Java. When Java manipulates JavaScript, the conversion is performed by the Java JSObject, and the conversion rules are different. Figure 19-5 and Figure 19-6 illustrate this conversion.

The point to remember when studying these figures is that Java can only interact with JavaScript through the API provided by the JSObject class. This class allows only Java objects, not primitive values, to be written to JavaScript, and allows only Java objects to read from JavaScript. When writing JavaScript functions that will be invoked from Java, bear in mind that the arguments passed by Java will either be JavaScript objects from unwrapped Java JSObjects, or they will be JavaObjects. As we saw earlier in this chapter, JavaObjects behave somewhat differently than other types. For example, an instance of *java.lang.Double* behaves differently than a primitive JavaScript number or even a JavaScript Number object. The same caution applies when you are working with JavaScript properties that will have their values set by Java.

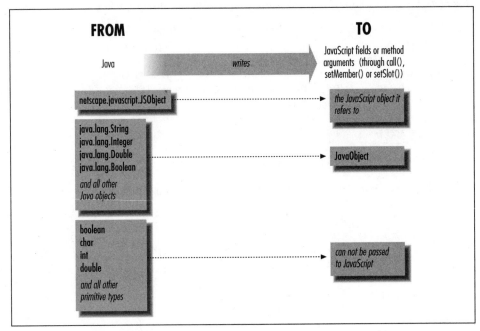

Figure 19-5: Data conversions performed when Java writes JavaScript values

Keep in mind that one way to avoid the whole issue of data conversion is to use the eval() method of the JSObject class whenever your Java code wants to communicate with JavaScript. In order to do this, your Java code must convert all method arguments or property values to string form. Then the string to be evaluated can be passed unchanged to JavaScript, which can convert the string form of the data to the appropriate JavaScript data types.

19.7 Working with Java in Internet Explorer

Internet Explorer 3.0 does not support LiveConnect. Instead, it treats Java applets as ActiveX objects and allows JavaScript to interact with them through that mechanism. This gives Internet Explorer some, but not all, of the capabilities of LiveConnect.

19.7.1 Interacting with Applets

Internet Explorer 3.0 can invoke the public methods of Java applets and can read and write the values of public fields of Java applets, in much the same way that Navigator 3.0 can. Although the underlying mechanism is different, the basic syntax is the same:

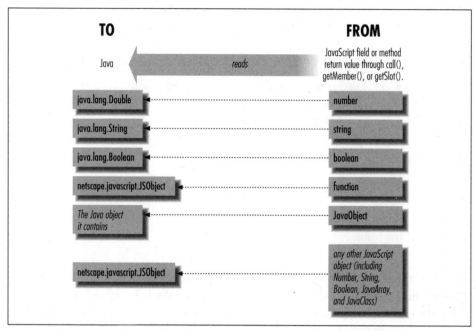

Figure 19–6: Data conversions performed when Java reads JavaScript values

```
document.appletname.property
document.appletname.method(...)
```

The data conversion that occurs when Internet Explorer passes values back and forth to Java follows ActiveX's rules, and is not documented here.

There are a couple of restrictions on IE 3.0 interactions with applets. First, note that it does not support the applets[] array of the Document object. So if you want to read or write properties or invoke methods of an applet, you must call the applet by name, and you must assign a name to the applet with the NAME attribute of the <APPLET> tag.

Second, note the Internet Explorer can only read and write properties and invoke methods of the applet object itself. IE does not have an equivalent to the LiveConnect JavaObject object, so if an applet has a property that refers to some other Java object, IE cannot read and write properties or invoke methods of that other object. To work around this shortcoming, you simply need to be sure that all functionality you need to access from JavaScript is implemented as a method of the applet, even if some of those methods do nothing more than invoke a method of some other object.

Third, Internet Explorer can only invoke the public *instance* methods of an applet. It has no mechanism for invoking with Java class methods.

19.7.2 *Interacting with Plug-Ins and System Classes*

Internet Explorer 3.0 can install and use Navigator plug-ins, but it does not allow JavaScript to interact with them in the way that Navigator does. Similarly, it does not have JavaPackage or JavaClass objects, and so has no way to read or write properties of system classes, invoke methods of system classes or create instances of system classes.

19.7.3 *Calling JavaScript from Applets*

Internet Explorer does not support the *netscape.javascript.JSObject* class, and does not allow Java applets to invoke JavaScript methods or read and write JavaScript properties.

Microsoft's ActiveX technology does allow Java applets in IE to interact with OLE objects embedded in a web page, as long as the applet is compiled so that it supports the desired object and as long as JavaScript passes a reference to the OLE control to the applet. Once JavaScript has told the applet where it can find the OLE control, any interaction occurs directly between the applet and the OLE object, without the intervention of JavaScript. This differs from the LiveConnect model in which an applet can use JavaScript as an intermediary to control any arbitrary applet or plug-in without special compilation being required to enable direct communication between the first applet and the other applet or plug-in.

19.8 *Summary*

LiveConnect allows JavaScript and Java to cooperate through two fairly separate and symmetrical systems. In JavaScript, the JavaPackage, JavaClass, JavaObject, JavaArray, and JavaMethod objects all allow JavaScript to read and write Java properties and arrays and to invoke Java methods. In Java, the *netscape.javascript.JSObject* class allows Java programs to read and write properties of JavaScript objects and elements of JavaScript arrays, to invoke JavaScript functions, and evaluate strings of JavaScript code. The following two subsections summarize these two halves of LiveConnect.

19.8.1 *JavaScript to Java*

- The JavaClass, JavaObject, JavaArray, and JavaMethod objects allow transparent communication between JavaScript and Java—they handle data conversion and all the tricky behind-the-scenes work.

- The data conversions performed when JavaScript reads and writes Java values are illustrated in Figure 19-2 and Figure 19-3.

- Most Java objects are converted to JavaScript JavaObject objects. JavaObjects behave differently than other JavaScript objects, and need to be handled with care. In particular, JavaObjects are converted to numeric, Boolean and string values differently than other JavaScript types are.

- You can use the JavaPackage objects referred to by the Window properties `Packages`, `java`, `sun`, and `netscape` to obtain a JavaClass object for any of the standard classes built in to Navigator. The JavaClass object allows you to read and write static properties and invoke static methods of a class.

- You can use the `new` operator on a JavaClass object to create a new Java object and a JavaScript JavaObject wrapper for it. You can use this JavaObject to read and write instance fields and invoke instance methods.

- You can use the `getClass()` function to obtain a JavaClass object corresponding to the Java class of a JavaObject object.

- You can "script" Java directly from JavaScript simply by working with the predefined classes. But this technique is limited—no significant user interaction with a "scripted" Java program is possible.

- You can also use the `document.applets[]` array and the JavaObject objects it contains to interact with applets. Manipulating the fields and methods of a custom-written applet allows a richer set of possibilities than simply scripting with the basic Java classes.

- You can use the `document.embeds[]` array and the JavaObjects it contains to interact with the plug-ins that are displaying embedded data in the document. You can control plug-ins through vendor-specific Java APIs.

19.8.2 Java to JavaScript

- The *netscape.javascript.JSObject* class is the Java equivalent of the JavaScript JavaObject class. It handles data conversion and all the behind-the-scenes work to allow Java code to communicate with JavaScript.

- The data conversions performed when Java reads and writes JavaScript data are illustrated in Figure 19-5 and Figure 19-6.

- The `getMember()` and `getSlot()` methods of a JSObject allow Java to read JavaScript object properties and array elements.

- The `setMember()` and `setSlot()` methods allow Java to set the value of JavaScript object properties and array elements.

- The `call()` method of a JSObject allows Java to invoke JavaScript functions.

- The `eval()` method of a JSObject allows Java to pass an arbitrary string of JavaScript code to the JavaScript interpreter for execution. This method is often easier to use than the other JSObject methods.

- An applet that uses the JSObject class must import it with an `import` statement. To compile the applet, the `CLASSPATH` environment variable must be set to include the Java classes supplied by Netscape.

- In order to interact with JavaScript, an applet must be embedded in an HTML document with an `<APPLET>` tag that includes the `MAYSCRIPT` attribute.

20

JavaScript Security

Because of the wide-open nature of the Internet, security is an important issue. This is particularly true with the introduction of languages like Java and JavaScript, because they allow executable content to be embedded in otherwise static web pages. Since loading a web page can cause arbitrary code to be executed on your computer, stringent security precautions are required to prevent malicious code from doing any damage to your data or your privacy. This chapter discusses Internet security issues related to JavaScript. Note that this chapter does *not* cover any of the many other issues involved in web security, such as the authentication and cryptography technologies used to keep the contents of web documents and HTML forms private while they traverse the Web.

20.1 JavaScript and Security

JavaScript's first line of defense against malicious code is that the language simply doesn't support certain capabilities. For example, client-side JavaScript does not provide any way to read, write, create, delete, or list files or directories on the client computer. Since there is no File object, and no file access functions, a JavaScript program obviously cannot delete a user's data, or plant viruses on the user's system, for example.

Similarly, client-side JavaScript has no networking primitives of any type. A JavaScript program can load URLs and send HTML form data to web servers and CGI scripts, but it cannot establish a direct connection to any other hosts on the network. This means, for example, that a JavaScript program cannot use a client's machine as a attack platform from which to attempt to crack passwords on other machines. (This would be a particularly dangerous possibility if the JavaScript program has been loaded from the Internet, through a firewall, and then could attempt to break into the intranet protected by the firewall.)

While the JavaScript language itself provides this basic level of security against the most egregious attacks, there are other security issues that remain. Primarily these are privacy issues—JavaScript programs must not be allowed to export information about the user of a browser when that information is supposed to be private.

When you browse the Web, one of the pieces of information you are consenting to release about yourself is the web browser that you use: it is a standard part of the HTTP protocol that a string identifying your browser, version, and vendor is sent with every request for a web page. This information is public, as is the IP address of your Internet connection, for example. But other information should not be public. This includes your email address, for example, which should not be released unless you choose to do so by sending an email message or authorizing an automated email message to be sent under your name.

Similarly, your browsing history (what sites you've already visited) and the contents of your bookmarks list should remain private. Because your browsing history and bookmarks say a lot about your interests, this is information that direct marketers and others would pay good money for, so that they can more effectively target sales pitches to you. Because this information is so valuable, you can be sure that if a web browser or JavaScript allowed this private information to be stolen, someone would be stealing it every time you visited their site. Once stolen, it would be on the market only nanoseconds later. Most users of the Web would be uncomfortable with the idea that any site they visit could find out that they are cat fanciers who are interested in women's footwear and the Sierra Club.

Even assuming that we have no embarrassing fetishes to hide, there are plenty of good reasons to be concerned about data privacy. One such reason is a pragmatic concern about receiving electronic junk mail and the like. Another is a very legitimate concern about keeping secrets. We don't want a JavaScript program to be able to start examining data behind our corporate firewall or to upload our passwords file to its web server, for example. At a more general level, we might desire that our private data be protected simply because we believe that individuals should have control over the ways that their personal data is collected and used.

Navigator and other browsers already have the ability to establish secure communication channels on the Web so that the information transferred back and forth between web server and web client remains private. By turning static HTML into dynamic programs, JavaScript opens the door to unethical web pages that steal private information and send it (through secure or insecure channels) back to the web server. It is this possibility that JavaScript must defend against. The remainder of this chapter explains how JavaScript does this, and also documents cases where it has failed to do it.

20.2 Security Holes and Security Hobbles

The approach to JavaScript security in Navigator 2.0 and 3.0 has been to first identify security holes through which private information could be exported, and then to plug those holes. Typically, security holes are plugged by implementing a "security hobble"—i.e., by restricting or "hobbling" the capabilities of JavaScript so that the hole cannot be exploited. For example, the History object in client-side JavaScript is an array of the URLs that the user has previously visited during the current browsing session. Because this information is private, JavaScript has been hobbled so that it cannot access the elements of this array. Because of this hobble, we are left with a History object that supports only forward(), back(), and go() methods.

The problem with an identify-and-patch approach is that it can be difficult to identify security holes, and that there is no way of knowing when you've found all possible holes. A web browser is a complex thing, and JavaScript is a powerful scripting language. In Navigator 2.0 and 2.0.1, these two facts intersected to produce a number of security holes that had not been patched. For example, in Navigator 2.0, a JavaScript program could open a new window to display the special about:cache URL. Then it could read the links[] array of the document of that window to obtain information about cached files (and hence browsing history) of the client browser. This information could be placed in hidden fields of an HTML form and submitted to the web server without the user's knowledge. The about:cache URL could be displayed in a window so small that the user wouldn't notice it, or it could even be displayed in an invisible frame (i.e., one with zero height). A similar attack used the file:/// URL to discover the contents of the root directory of the client's system, and could recursively proceed to determine the client's entire directory structure.

Another attack, one that was undoubtedly exploited to some extent on the Internet, allowed a JavaScript program to automatically send email to any desired address whenever the user visited a web page. What this does, of course, is steal the email address of everyone who visits a page. This attack was accomplished by using the submit() method of the Form object to automatically submit an empty (and invisible) HTML form to a mailto: URL.

Not all security holes in Navigator 2.0 and 2.0.1 were the result of unforeseen interactions between the features of JavaScript and the rest of Navigator. Some were just bugs, plain and simple. For example, one bug allowed a web page to leave JavaScript code behind after it was unloaded. This code could do anything it wanted to. It could violate security by checking the URL of the document currently being viewed once every second and sending that information off to a web server or email address. Instead of publicizing a user's browsing history, this security hole publicized a user's browsing future!

Another serious bug-induced security hole was related to a bug in the security hobble for the FileUpload form element. JavaScript is hobbled so that it is not allowed to set the filename that appears in the FileUpload element. If it could set it, it would clearly be trivial to send the contents of any file on the client's computer (a password file, perhaps) across the network to a web server, an obviously grave breach of security. Unfortunately, there the hobble that prevented this was not sufficient, and there was a straightforward trick that would allow a JavaScript program to specify what file was to be uploaded. Fortunately, this trick was not publicized, and a new version of Navigator, with this bug fixed, was quickly released.*

Many of the security holes discovered in Navigator 2.0 were patched with hobbles in Navigator 2.0.1, and Netscape even added the option to disable JavaScript entirely (the ultimate hobble) in this version of the browser. Unfortunately, a new crop of holes were discovered almost as soon as 2.0.1 was released. Because of the continuing problem with security holes, and because of the resulting bad press, Netscape soon released Navigator 2.0.2, which fixed all known security-related bugs and implemented a very general hobble that would, hopefully, spell an end to security holes. With this hobble implemented, a JavaScript program is not allowed to read the properties of any window (or frame) or the properties of any objects within a window if the contents of that window were loaded from a different web server than the JavaScript program itself. This hobble rules out a whole class of security holes. It means that a program cannot open a new window to display about:cache, file:///, or some other URL and extract information from that URL. This hobble is particularly important when a corporate firewall is in use—it prevents a script loaded from the Internet from opening a new window and going browsing in a private intranet.

The bug fixes and the mega-hobble in Navigator 2.0.2 were included in Navigator 3.0 and appear to have been quite effective at patching security holes—there has been a long spell without any new ones being discovered. Unfortunately a new hole has recently been discovered. The hobble that was inserted to prevent automatic submission of a form to a mailto: URL only worked for certain form encodings and methods. Embarrassingly for Netscape, it turns out that other combinations of form submission methods and encodings still allow a form to be

---

* For more information on this and other Netscape 2.0 and 2.0.1 security holes, see the "JavaScript Problems I've Discovered" web pages by John Robert LoVerso of the OSF Research Institute at *http://www.osf.org/˜loverso/javascript.*

automatically submitted without user confirmation, effectively stealing the user's email address. By the time this book is published, the hobble will have been strengthened, and this security hole will have been patched (for good this time, we hope) in Navigator 3.0.1.

20.2.1 Security Hobbles in Navigator 3.0

The following is a complete list of security hobbles in Navigator 3.0.1. While not all earlier versions of Navigator implement all of these hobbles, you should assume that they are all in place, if you want your code to be portable to the latest versions of Navigator. If you are yourself worried about private information being exported through security holes, then you should of course upgrade to the most recent version of Navigator that has all of these hobbles implemented.

- The History object does not allow access to its array elements or to its `next`, `previous`, or `current` properties that contain URLs that the browser has previously visited. These URLs are private information and scripts are not allowed to access them because they could otherwise export them through an HTML form.

- The `value` property of the Password object does not contain the user's input to that Password field. The user's input is submitted with the form, but is hidden from the script. A script can read and write the `value` property, but cannot affect the value displayed in the field nor obtain the user's actual input to that field. In theory, if a user trusts a CGI script with their password, they should also trust a script from the same site with it, but because passwords are such sensitive information, access is limited on a "need to know" basis. Since JavaScript does not "need to know" the value of a password intended for a CGI script, it is not allowed to know.

- The `value` property of the FileUpload object is read-only. If this property could be set by JavaScript, a script could set it to any desired filename and cause the form to upload the contents of any specified file (such as a password file) to the server. There was a flaw in this hobble in Navigator 2.0.1 which allowed malicious scripts to upload arbitrary files. The hobble has been strengthened and correctly implemented in 2.0.2 and later versions.

- A form that is to be submitted to a `mailto:` URL cannot be submitted without the user's explicit approval. If this were not the case, then a script could steal the user's email address by submitting an empty form automatically through the `Form.submit()` method or by tricking the user into clicking on a **Submit** button. Prior to Navigator 3.0.1, this hobble was only partially implemented— user confirmation for `mailto:` forms was only required when the form was submitted with the POST method and the default encoding type. In 3.0.1, confirmation is required for all `mailto:` form submissions.

- JavaScript cannot read properties of a window if the contents of that window were loaded from a different server than the JavaScript code being run. A "different server" is any server on a different host, or a server on the same host using a different protocol. This prevents scripts from one site from stealing any kind of information from other sites (which might be behind firewalls, for example).

- A JavaScript program cannot run for a very long time without periodic user confirmation that it should continue. After every one million "branches" (i.e., if statements and loop iterations) that the JavaScript interpreter executes, it pops up a dialog notifying the user that the script is still running and asks if it should continue to execute it. This helps prevent JavaScript programs from using a client machine as a computation server, or from attempting a "denial of service" attack by locking up the browser or slowing it down so much as to be unusable. Note, however, that this doesn't help all that much. One trivial denial-of-service attack simply involves repeatedly popping up dialog boxes with alert().

- A JavaScript program cannot close a browser window without user confirmation unless it opened the window itself. This prevents malicious scripts from calling self.close() to close the user's browsing window, thereby causing Navigator to exit. There is one exception to this hobble. The first page loaded when Navigator starts up is allowed to close the initial browsing window. This exception enables power users to create home pages that close the default browsing window and open one or more custom windows.

20.2.2 *Security in Internet Explorer*

Since Internet Explorer 3.0 has not been around as long and is not used as commonly as Navigator, it has not been subjected to such intense scrutiny, as Netscape's browser was. Thus, while IE does not have a history of security holes its implementation of JavaScript, there may yet be holes discovered.

The one known JavaScript security hole in Internet Explorer is a major one. IE does not contain the security hobble described above which prevents a script from one URL from reading the properties of a script from another URL. This means, for example, that if you use IE on Windows 95, a script could load the contents of a URL like *file:///C\Windows\StartMenu* into a hidden frame, and then examine the links[] array of that frame to determine what programs you have installed in your Windows start menu. This private information might then be submitted in a hidden field of some innocuous looking form.

20.3 The domain Property

As we've seen, Navigator 2.0.2 and later implement a very general security hobble intended to blanket an entire category of security holes: scripts from one server cannot read properties of windows or documents from another server. This is quite a severe restriction, and poses problems for large web sites that use more than one server. For example, a script from *home.netscape.com* might legitimately want to read properties of a document loaded from *developer.netscape.com*. While this seems like a reasonable and secure thing to do, the hobble does not allow it.

In order to support large web sites of this sort, Navigator 3.0 slightly relaxes the security hobble by introducing the domain property of the Document object. Internet Explorer 3.0 does not implement this property, but, as noted above, it also does not implement the problematic security hobble. By default, the domain property is the same as the hostname of the web server from which the document was loaded. You can set this property, but only to a string that is a valid domain suffix of itself. Thus, if domain is the string "home.netscape.com", you can set it to the string "netscape.com", but not to "home.netscape" or "cape.com", and certainly not to "microsoft.com".

If two windows contain scripts that both set their domain to the same value, then the security hobble will be relaxed for these two windows and in each of windows may read properties from the other.

20.4 The Data-Tainting Security Model

The security model adopted by Navigator 2.0 and 3.0 is functional, but suffers from a number of problems. As we've seen, the "identify and hobble" approach is not very good at identifying security holes in the first place, and in a complex system like Navigator plus JavaScript, security holes can be difficult to find. Furthermore, hobbling JavaScript reduces the functionality available to developers. Some hobbles, while essential for security, end up breaking perfectly good scripts that pose no security threat and that ran correctly on earlier versions of the browser.

The hobble that prevents one script from reading the contents of a window from another server is a particularly draconian example. This hobble means that I cannot write a debugger program in JavaScript and post it on my web site for other developers to use on their own JavaScript programs. Developers would have to go through the extra step of downloading the debugging script and installing it on their own site, so that it can successfully examine the properties of the documents to be debugged. Similarly, this hobble prevents the creation of JavaScript programs that "crawl" the Web, recursively following links from a given starting page.

Because of the problems with hobbles, and with the theoretical underpinnings of security through hobbling, the developers at Netscape have created an entirely new security model. This new model is experimental in Navigator 3.0, and may be enabled by the end user through a procedure outlined later in this section. The new security model is theoretically much stronger, and should be a big advance for JavaScript security if it is enabled by default in Navigator 4.0. The following subsections explain this new model. Be aware in advance that this is a confusing model and can be difficult to understand.

20.4.1 Data Tainting in Theory

Let's back up a bit and reconsider the security problem we are worried about in the first place. For the most part, the problem is that private data may be sent across the Web by malicious JavaScript programs. The hobbling approach to security generally patches this problem by preventing JavaScript programs from accessing private data. Unfortunately, this approach rules out non-malicious JavaScript programs that would like to use that private data without exporting it. One such program, for example, might be a navigation aid that generates a list of all the links from a web page and displays them in a separate window or frame.

Instead of preventing scripts from reading private data, a better approach would be to prevent them from exporting it, since this is what we are trying to prevent in the first place. If we could do this, then we could lift most of the hobbles that were detailed in the sections above. (We'd still need some hobbles, to prevent a program from closing windows it didn't open, for example.) Unfortunately, preventing the export of private data can be tricky to do, because not only must we prevent a script from exporting private data directly, be we must also prevent it from exporting data derived, in any way, from private data. If you think through the implications, you can see that keeping track of the data that must not be exported could be a very difficult proposition.

This is where the concept of data tainting comes in. The idea is that all JavaScript data values are given a flag. This flag indicates if the value is "tainted" (private) or not. Tainted values will be allowed to be exported only in certain very restricted ways. Untainted values can be exported arbitrarily. But any value, regardless of taint, can be manipulated by the program, which is a big improvement over the heavy-handed measures required by the hobbling approach. As the term "tainted" implies, any data derived from tainted data will itself be tainted. If a tainted string is added to a non-tainted string, the resulting string is tainted. If a tainted value is passed to a function, then the return value of the function is tainted. If a string is tainted, then any substring of the string is also tainted.

Theoretically, the data-tainting model is a strong one, and it has been proven practical in the Perl programming language. With a careful and rigorous implementation of tainting, Navigator will be able to prevent private data, or any modified version of private data from being incorrectly exported by a JavaScript program. Because data tainting is a uniform security model that covers all possible exports of data, we can also trust its security much further than we would trust the "identify a hole and patch it with a hobble" model.

20.4.2 Data Tainting in JavaScript

To really understand the data-tainting security model in JavaScript, you must understand what the taint flag indicates. In fact, this "flag" is better described as an "accumulator" because there are many possible types of taint, and any value can be tainted in more than one way. Entries in the history array, for example, are tainted in a way that indicates "this is private data and must not be exported in any way." On the other hand, in a document loaded from *server.xyz.com* data values in an HTML form are tainted in a way that indicates "this data belongs to *server.xyz.com*, and it must not be exported anywhere except to that server". When taint propagates from a tainted value to a derived value, this meaning propagates with it, of course.

As we can see, tainting does not prevent all tainted data from being exported; it merely prevents it from being exported to a server that does not already "own" it. Furthermore, tainting does not even absolutely prevent data from being sent where it shouldn't be; it only prevents it from automatically being sent there. Whenever an attempt to export data violates the tainting rules, the user will be prompted with a dialog box asking them whether the export should be allowed. If they so choose, they can allow the export.

Consider how this might work. If a malicious script tries to export the URLs contained in the History object, JavaScript will see that these values are tainted in a way that does not allow them to be exported in any way, and will not allow the export. On the other hand, when a web page contains an HTML form, the user input values will be tainted in such a way that allows them to be exported back to the server form which the form was loaded. But if a malicious script running in another window attempts to spy on that HTML form and makes copies of the user's input, those copied values will still carry a taint value that identifies them as belonging to their original server. If the malicious scripts attempts to export them to its own malicious server, the attempt will fail because the taint values indicate that that server does not own that data.

It is not only data values that can carry taint. JavaScript functions and methods can carry taint as well. If a function or method is tainted, then its return value will automatically be tainted, regardless of the taintedness of its arguments. For example, the `toString()` method of the Location object and of the Text and Textarea objects are tainted because these methods return data that is private.

Functions are actually just another datatype in JavaScript, so it is not surprising that they can carry taint. What is surprising is that JavaScript programs themselves can become tainted. If a tainted value is used in an expression that is tested as part of an `if`, `while` or `for` statement, then the script itself must carry taint. If not, it would be easy to "launder" taint from a value with code like the following:

```
// b is a tainted Boolean value that we want to export
if (b == true) newb = true;
else newb = false;
// Now newb has the same value as b, but is not tainted, so we could
// export it if this script itself did not become tainted in the process.
```

When a script becomes tainted, the window that contains it "accumulates" the same taint values, with the same meanings, that data values do. If a window carries taint, it will not be allowed to export data to a server unless the script's taint code and the data's taint code both indicate that they belong to the server.

In addition to understanding the different types of taint that are possible, you should also understand just what is meant by "exporting" data. In general terms, this means sending data over the Net. In practical terms, it occurs when a form is submitted in any way, or when a new URL is requested in any way. It is obvious that form submission exports data, but is less obvious that requesting a new document exports data. Bear in mind though that arbitrary data can be encoded into a URL following a question mark or hash sign (#). Also, the file and path of a URL can encode information.

While the data-tainting model is relatively straightforward on the surface, a working implementation requires careful attention to detail. JavaScript propagates taint through the strings of code passed to the `eval()` and `setTimeout()` functions, for example, so that you cannot untaint a value simply by converting it to a string of JavaScript code and executing that code later. Similarly, JavaScript propagates taint through the `document.write()` method so that a script can't launder tainted values by writing them out into a new script in a new window. For the same reason, JavaScript propagates taint through `javascript:` URLs, and prevents tainted strings from being stored in cookies. JavaScript also prevents data from being laundered through LiveConnect. In Navigator 3.0, this happens in a heavy-handed way: all data retrieved from Java is automatically tainted.

20.4.3 Enabling Data Tainting in Navigator 3.0

As noted above, the data-tainting security model is experimental in Navigator 3.0, and is not enabled by default. It is expected to be the default security model in version 4.0 of Navigator, however. If you want to try using data tainting with Navigator 3.0, you must enable it by setting an environment variable before starting Navigator. On Unix systems, do this with the following command in *csh*:

```
setenv NS_ENABLE_TAINT 1
```

On Windows platforms, enable taint with a set command in the *autoexec.bat* file or in NT user settings:

```
set NS_ENABLE_TAINT=1
```

And on the Macintosh, use the resource editor to edit the resource with type "Envi" and number 128 in the Netscape application. Modify this resource by removing the two slashes (//) before the NS_ENABLE_TAINT at the end of the string.

Note that if you enable this security model, you may find that many more scripts than you expect produce taint violations, and you'll spend a lot of time responding to dialogs that ask you to confirm form submissions or new page requests. One of the main reasons that tainting was not enabled in Navigator 3.0 was that the user interface to support it well was not yet ready. Thus, for Navigator 4.0, we can hope to see a smoother UI that does not ask as many questions.

20.4.4 Values Tainted by Default

Table 20-1 lists the object properties and methods that are tainted by default. The taint() and untaint() functions that will be introduced below allow you to modify these defaults.

Table 20-1: JavaScript Properties and Methods That Are Tainted by Default

Object	Tainted Properties and Methods
Document	cookie, domain, forms[], lastModified, links[], location, referrer, title, URL
Form	action
All Form input elements: Button, Checkbox, FileUpload, Hidden, Password, Radio, Reset, Select, Submit, Text, Textarea	checked, defaultChecked, defaultValue, name, selectedIndex, toString(), value

Table 20–1: JavaScript Properties and Methods That Are Tainted by Default (continued)

Object	Tainted Properties and Methods
History	`current`, `next`, `previous`, `toString()`, all array elements[a]
Location, Link, Area	`hash`, `host`, `hostname`, `href`, `pathname`, `port`, `protocol`, `search`, `toString()`
Option	`defaultSelected`, `selected`, `text`, `value`
Window	`defaultStatus`, `status`

a. Note that History properties belong to the browser, not the server, and thus have a different taint value.

20.4.5 The taint() and untaint() Functions

Table 20-1 shows the object properties and methods that are tainted by default in Navigator 3.0. This list is not the final word on tainting. If a script would like to prevent other data it owns from being exported, it may taint that data with the `taint()` method. Similarly, if a script would like to relax the data-tainting rules in order to allow information it owns to be exported more freely, it can remove its taint from a value with the `untaint()` method.

There are some important things to note about these functions. First, both `taint()` and `untaint()` return a tainted or untainted copy of primitive vales or a tainted or untainted *reference* to objects and arrays. In JavaScript, taint is carried by references to objects, not by the objects themselves. So when you untaint an object, what you are really doing is untainting a reference to that object, not the object itself. The object's value may be exported through the untainted reference but not through the tainted reference.

The second point to note is that a script can use `untaint()` only to remove its own taint from a value. If a value X carries taint that identifies it as owned by server A, then a script running in a document from server B may call `untaint()` on value X but will not succeed in removing server A's taint, and will not be able to export that value to server B.

Finally, if `taint()` and `untaint()` are called with no argument, then they add and remove taint from the script rather than from a particular object. Again, a script can only remove its own taint from itself: if a script from server A has tainted itself by examining tainted data owned by server B, then server A cannot remove that taint from itself.

III

Reference

This part of the book is a complete reference to all of the objects, properties, functions, methods, and event handlers in client-side JavaScript and in the core JavaScript language. The first few pages of this part explain how to use this reference and provide a table of contents for it.

JavaScript Reference

This section of the book is a complete reference for all JavaScript objects, properties, constants, arrays, functions, methods, and event handlers. It even includes documentation for the Java class *netscape.javascript.JSObject*, which is used by LiveConnect to allow Java applets to communicate with JavaScript.

How to Find the Reference Page You Want

The reference section is arranged alphabetically; all properties, methods, and event handlers are alphabetized by their full name, which includes the name of the object of which they are a part. For example, if you want the `write()` method of the Document object, look up "Document.write", not just "write".

JavaScript defines some global variables, such as `navigator` and `Packages`, which, strictly speaking, are properties of the Window object. They are never used this way, however, and so these few "globals" are alphabetized without the "Window." prefix. Note, however that other properties, methods, and event handlers of the Window object, such as `location`, `alert()`, and `onload()` *are* documented as part of the Window object. Thus you should look these up as "Window.location", "Window.alert()", and "Window.onload()".

Sometimes you may need to look up a method or property without knowing what object it is part of. Or you may not be able to find a reference page where you expect it. The table of contents that follows will help you with this. The left column lists the names of all objects, functions, properties, methods, and event handlers in JavaScript, and the right column gives the full name of the reference page on which documentation can be found. Note that some property, method, and event-handler names are used by more than one object. So, for example, if you look up the `toString()` method in the table, you find several reference pages that document different objects' implementations of that method.

Table of Contents

For	See
clearTimeout()	Window.clearTimeout()
click()	Element.click()
close()	Document.close()
	Window.close()
closed	Window.closed
complete	Image.complete
confirm()	Window.confirm()
constructor	Object.constructor
cookie	Document.cookie
cos()	Math.cos()
current	History.current
Date	Date
defaultChecked	Checkbox.defaultChecked
	Element.defaultChecked
	Radio.defaultChecked
defaultSelected	Option.defaultSelected
defaultStatus	Window.defaultStatus
defaultValue	Element.defaultValue
description	MimeType.description
	Plugin.description
Document	Document
document	Window.document
domain	Document.domain
E	Math.E
Element	Element
elements[]	Form.elements[]
embeds[]	Document.embeds[]
enabledPlugin	MimeType.enabledPlugin
encoding	Form.encoding
escape()	escape()
eval()	JSObject.eval()
	Object.eval()
	eval()
exp()	Math.exp()
fgColor	Document.fgColor
filename	Plugin.filename
FileUpload	FileUpload
fixed()	String.fixed()
floor()	Math.floor()
focus()	Element.focus()

For	See
focus() *(cont.)*	Window.focus()
fontcolor()	String.fontcolor()
fontsize()	String.fontsize()
Form	Form
form	Element.form
forms[]	Document.forms[]
forward()	History.forward()
Frame	Frame
frames[]	Window.frames[]
Function	Function
getClass()	getClass()
getDate()	Date.getDate()
getDay()	Date.getDay()
getHours()	Date.getHours()
getMember()	JSObject.getMember()
getMinutes()	Date.getMinutes()
getMonth()	Date.getMonth()
getSeconds()	Date.getSeconds()
getSlot()	JSObject.getSlot()
getTime()	Date.getTime()
getTimezoneOffset()	Date.getTimezoneOffset()
getWindow()	JSObject.getWindow()
getYear()	Date.getYear()
go()	History.go()
hash	URL.hash
height	Image.height
Hidden	Hidden
History	History
history	Window.history
host	URL.host
hostname	URL.hostname
href	URL.href
hspace	Image.hspace
Image	Image
images[]	Document.images[]
index	Option.index
indexOf()	String.indexOf()
isNaN()	isNaN()
italics()	String.italics()
java	Packages.java

For	See
java *(cont.)*	java
JavaArray	JavaArray
JavaClass	JavaClass
javaEnabled()	Navigator.javaEnabled()
JavaMethod	JavaMethod
JavaObject	JavaObject
JavaPackage	JavaPackage
join()	Array.join()
JSObject	JSObject
lastIndexOf()	String.lastIndexOf()
lastModified	Document.lastModified
length	Array.length
	History.length
	JavaArray.length
	Select.length
	String.length
	Window.length
Link	Link
link()	String.link()
linkColor	Document.linkColor
links[]	Document.links[]
LN10	Math.LN10
LN2	Math.LN2
Location	Location
location	Document.location
	Window.location
log()	Math.log()
LOG10E	Math.LOG10E
LOG2E	Math.LOG2E
lowsrc	Image.lowsrc
Math	Math
max()	Math.max()
MAX_VALUE	Number.MAX_VALUE
method	Form.method
MimeType	MimeType
mimeTypes[]	Navigator.mimeTypes[]
min()	Math.min()
MIN_VALUE	Number.MIN_VALUE
name	Element.name
	Image.name

For	See
name *(cont.)*	`Plugin.name`
	`Window.name`
`NaN`	`Number.NaN`
`navigate()`	`Window.navigate()`
`Navigator`	`Navigator`
`navigator`	`navigator`
`NEGATIVE_INFINITY`	`Number.NEGATIVE_INFINITY`
`netscape`	`Packages.netscape`
	`netscape`
`next`	`History.next`
`Number`	`Number`
`Object`	`Object`
`onabort()`	`Image.onabort()`
`onblur()`	`Element.onblur()`
	`Window.onblur()`
`onchange()`	`Element.onchange()`
	`FileUpload.onchange()`
	`Password.onchange()`
	`Select.onchange()`
	`Text.onchange()`
	`Textarea.onchange()`
`onclick()`	`Button.onclick()`
	`Checkbox.onclick()`
	`Element.onclick()`
	`Link.onclick()`
	`Radio.onclick()`
	`Reset.onclick()`
	`Submit.onclick()`
`onerror()`	`Image.onerror()`
	`Window.onerror()`
`onfocus()`	`Element.onfocus()`
	`Window.onfocus()`
`onload()`	`Image.onload()`
	`Window.onload()`
`onmouseout()`	`Link.onmouseout()`
`onmouseover()`	`Link.onmouseover()`
`onreset()`	`Form.onreset()`
`onsubmit()`	`Form.onsubmit()`
`onunload()`	`Window.onunload()`
`open()`	`Document.open()`

For	See
open() *(cont.)*	Window.open()
opener	Window.opener
Option	Option
options[]	Select.options[]
Packages	Packages
parent	Window.parent
parse()	Date.parse()
parseFloat()	parseFloat()
parseInt()	parseInt()
Password	Password
pathname	URL.pathname
PI	Math.PI
Plugin	Plugin
plugins	Document.plugins
plugins[]	Navigator.plugins[]
port	URL.port
POSITIVE_INFINITY	Number.POSITIVE_INFINITY
pow()	Math.pow()
previous	History.previous
prompt()	Window.prompt()
protocol	URL.protocol
prototype	Function.prototype
Radio	Radio
random()	Math.random()
referrer	Document.referrer
refresh()	Navigator.plugins.refresh()
reload()	Location.reload()
removeMember()	JSObject.removeMember()
replace()	Location.replace()
Reset	Reset
reset()	Form.reset()
reverse()	Array.reverse()
round()	Math.round()
scroll()	Window.scroll()
search	URL.search
Select	Select
select()	Element.select()
selected	Option.selected
selectedIndex	Select.selectedIndex
self	Window.self

For	See
setDate()	Date.setDate()
setHours()	Date.setHours()
setMember()	JSObject.setMember()
setMinutes()	Date.setMinutes()
setMonth()	Date.setMonth()
setSeconds()	Date.setSeconds()
setSlot()	JSObject.setSlot()
setTime()	Date.setTime()
setTimeout()	Window.setTimeout()
setYear()	Date.setYear()
sin()	Math.sin()
small()	String.small()
sort()	Array.sort()
split()	String.split()
sqrt()	Math.sqrt()
SQRT1_2	Math.SQRT1_2
SQRT2	Math.SQRT2
src	Image.src
status	Window.status
strike()	String.strike()
String	String
sub()	String.sub()
Submit	Submit
submit()	Form.submit()
substring()	String.substring()
suffixes	MimeType.suffixes
sun	Packages.sun
	sun
sup()	String.sup()
taint()	taint()
taintEnabled()	Navigator.taintEnabled()
tan()	Math.tan()
target	Form.target
	Link.target
Text	Text
text	Option.text
Textarea	Textarea
title	Document.title
toGMTString()	Date.toGMTString()
toLocaleString()	Date.toLocaleString()

For	See
toLowerCase()	String.toLowerCase()
top	Window.top
toString()	Boolean.toString()
	Function.toString()
	JSObject.toString()
	Number.toString()
	Object.toString()
toUpperCase()	String.toUpperCase()
type	Element.type
	MimeType.type
	Select.type
unescape()	unescape()
untaint()	untaint()
URL	Document.URL
	URL
userAgent	Navigator.userAgent
UTC()	Date.UTC()
value	Button.value
	Checkbox.value
	Element.value
	FileUpload.value
	Hidden.value
	Option.value
	Password.value
	Radio.value
	Reset.value
	Submit.value
	Text.value
	Textarea.value
valueOf()	Object.valueOf()
vlinkColor	Document.vlinkColor
vspace	Image.vspace
width	Image.width
Window	Window
window	Window.window
write()	Document.write()
writeln()	Document.writeln()

How to Read the Reference Pages

Once you've found the reference page you're looking for, you shouldn't have much difficulty obtaining the information you need from it. Still, however, you'll be able to make better use of this reference section if you understand how the reference pages are written and organized. The very first reference page is titled "Sample Entry"; it explains the structure of each reference pages and tells you where to find various types of information within the pages. Do be sure to read this page before diving in to the reference section.

Sample Entry — how to read these reference pages

Title and Description

Every reference page begins with a title and one-line description like those above. They are useful to help you find the page you are looking for. The title usually consists of two words. The first is the name of the reference page, and the second is the type of reference page. For example, the reference page for the Date object is titled "Date Object". The reference page for the getDay() method of the Date object is "Date.getDay() Method". Similarly, the title of the reference page for the frames[] array property of the Window object is "Window.frames[] Property". The title of the page documenting the Button element of an HTML form is "Button Element", and you'll also find reference pages with titles that include the types "Function" (functions that are not methods), "Handler" (event handlers) and "Constant" (read-only properties that always have the same value).

Availability

Because slightly different versions of JavaScript run on Navigator 2.0 and 3.0 and on Internet Explorer 3.0, each reference page begins with an "Availability" section. This section specifies exactly which platforms the object, method, property, function, or event handler is available on. You can assume that anything available in one version of a browser is also available in later versions. For example, an objects available in Navigator 2.0 is also available in Navigator 3.0. Similarly, you can assume that methods, properties, etc., that are available in Navigator 3.0 and Internet Explorer 3.0 will also be available in Navigator 4.0 and Internet Explorer 4.0.

The availability section will occasionally note other things as well. If something is particularly buggy, or if it is deprecated (i.e., if its use is discouraged), that will be noted in this section as well.

Synopsis

The next section of every page is a synopsis of how you use the object, method, property, function, or event handler in your actual code. For example, the synopsis for the Form object is:

```
document.form_name
document.forms[form_number]
```

This synopsis shows two different ways of referring to a Form object. The italic font indicates text that is to be replaced with something else. *form_name* would be replaced with the name of a form, and `form_number` would be replaced with the index of the form in the `forms[]` array. Similarly, `document` would be replaced in these synopses with a reference to a Document object. By looking up the synopsis of the Document object, we discover that it also has two forms:

```
document
window.document
```

That is, we can replace `document` with the literal `document`, or with `window.document`. If we choose the latter, then we'll need to look up the Synopsis of the Window object to find out how to refer to a Window—that is, to find out what to replace `window` with.

Arguments

If the reference page describes a function or method, then the Synopsis is followed by an Arguments subsection, which describes the arguments to the function or method. For some object types, such as the Date object, the Synopsis section is replaced by a "Constructor" section. The Constructor section is also followed by this Arguments subsection.

`arg1`	The arguments are described in a list here. This is the description for argument `arg1`, for example.
`arg2`	And this is the description for argument `arg2`.

Returns

Because functions, methods, and constructors have return values as well as arguments, the Arguments subsection is followed by a Returns subsection, which explain the return value of the function, method, or constructor.

Properties

If the reference page documents an object, then the Properties section lists the properties the object supports, and provides short explanations of each. Each property will also have a complete reference page of its own. For example, the reference page for the Document object lists the `lastModified` property in this section, and gives a brief explanation of it. But the property is fully documented in the `Document.lastModified` reference page. The property listing looks like this:

`prop1`	This is a summary of property `prop1`, including the type of the property, its purpose or meaning, and whether it is read-only or read/write.
`prop2`	This is the same for `prop2`.

Methods

Reference pages for objects that define methods include a Methods section. It is just like the Properties section, except that it documents methods instead of properties.

Event Handlers

Some objects define event handlers in addition to properties and methods. They are listed and briefly described in this section.

HTML Syntax

A number of JavaScript objects have analogs in HTML. The reference pages for these objects include a section that shows the annotated HTML syntax that is used to create one of the JavaScript objects. For example, the reference page for the Button form element has the following in its "HTML Syntax" section:

```
<INPUT
  TYPE="button"        specifies that this is a button
  VALUE="label"        the text that is to appear within the button
                       specifies the value property
. [ NAME="name" ]      a name that can later be used to refer to the button
                       specifies the name property
  [ onClick="handler" ] JavaScript statements to be executed when the button is clicked
>
```

Description

Each reference page contains a section named "Description." This is the basic description of whatever it is that is being documented, the heart of the reference page. Unfortunately, on some of the more complex pages you have to read through quite a bit of synopsis, syntax, and lists of properties, methods, and event handlers before you get to it.

For some pages this section is no more than a short paragraph. On others it may occupy a page or more.

Usage

Some pages have a Usage section in addition to the Description section. When this section appears, be sure to pay attention to it. It describes common techniques for using the function, object, property or whatever, or it contains cautions that you should be aware of when using it.

Example

Some pages follow the Description and Usage information with an example showing a typical usage. Most pages do not contain examples—you'll find those in the main body of the text instead.

Bugs

When the topic of the page doesn't work quite right, this section describes the bugs. Appendix B also contains a complete listing of common JavaScript bugs.

See Also

Finally, every reference page concludes with cross-references to related reference pages that may be of interest. Sometimes reference pages also refer back to one of the main chapters of the book.

alert( ) Method — see Window.alert( )

Anchor Object — the target of a hypertext link

Availability

Implemented but nonfunctional in Navigator 2.0, 3.0, and Internet Explorer 3.0

Synopsis

```
document.anchors.length
document.anchors[i]
```

HTML Syntax

An Anchor object is created by any standard HTML <A> tag that contains a <NAME> attribute:

```
<A
  NAME="anchor_name"                    links may refer to this anchor by this name
  [ HREF=URL ]                          an anchor may also be a link
  [ TARGET="window_name" ]              links may refer to other windows
>
link text
</A>
```

Description

An "anchor" is a named location within an HTML document. Anchors are created with the NAME attribute of the <A> tag. The JavaScript Document object has an anchors[] array property that should contain references to each of the anchors in the document. Unfortunately, in Navigator 2.0 and 3.0 and in Internet Explorer 3.0, the elements of this array always contain null. The problem is that the Anchor object has not yet been implemented. A future version of the language should contain an actual working Anchor object, and the anchors[] array will be filled in with references to appropriate Anchor objects.

Note that the <A> tag used to create anchors is also used to create hypertext links. Although hypertext links are often called "anchors" in HTML parlance, they are represented in JavaScript with the Link object, not with the Anchor object.

See Also

Document.anchors[], Link

Applet Object — see Document.applets[] and JavaObject

Area Object — a hypertext link in a client-side image map

Availability

Navigator 3.0

Synopsis

```
document.links[]
document.links.length
```

HTML Syntax

An Area object is created by an <AREA> tag within a client-side image map:

```
<MAP NAME="map_name">
    <AREA SHAPE="area_shape"
        COORDS=coordinates
        HREF="url"                          the destination of the link
        [ TARGET="window_name" ]            where the new document should be displayed
        [ onClick="handler" ]               invoked when area is clicked
        [ onMouseOver="handler" ]           invoked when mouse is over area
        [ onMouseOut="handler" ]            invoked when mouse leaves area
    >
        . . .
    </MAP>
```

Description

The Area object represents a hypertext link created with the <AREA> tag within a client-side image map. JavaScript does not distinguish between hypertext links created with the <AREA> tag and those created with the <A> tag, however, and the Area object is actually the same thing as the Link object. All hypertext links, regardless of what HTML tag creates them, are represented by Link objects stored in the links[] array of the Document object that contains them.

There are only two differences between hypertext links created with the <AREA> tag and those created with the <A> tag. The first is that links in image maps are not recognized by Navigator 2.0 and Internet Explorer—those browsers only recognize links created with the <A> tag. The second difference is simply a bug: the onClick() event handler of the <AREA> tag doesn't work on Windows platforms in Navigator 3.0.

See Link for a listing and description of the properties and event handlers of hypertext links.

See Also

Link, Location, URL

Array Object — built-in support for arrays

Availability

Navigator 3.0, Internet Explorer 3.0; arrays are available in Navigator 2.0, but the Array object class that supports them is not.

Constructor

```
new Array()
new Array(size)
new Array(element0, element1, ..., elementn)
```

Arguments

size   The desired number of elements in the array. The returned array will have its length field set to *size*.

element0, ...elementn

An argument list of two or more arbitrary values. When the Array() constructor is invoked with these arguments, the newly created array will be initialized with the specified argument values as its elements, and its length field set to the number of arguments.

Returns

The newly created and initialized array. When Array() is invoked with no arguments, the returned array will have a length field of 0.

Properties

length   A read/write integer specifying the number of elements in the array, or, when the array does not have contiguous elements, a number one larger than the index of the last element in the array.

Methods

join   Convert all array elements to strings and concatenate them.

reverse   Reverse, in place, the order of the elements of an array.

sort   Sort, in place, the elements of an array.

Description

Arrays are a basic syntactic feature of JavaScript. All JavaScript objects, regardless of their type, may be used as arrays. The dual nature of arrays and objects is discussed in Chapter 8, along with full details on the JavaScript syntax for reading and setting array elements.

The Array is a new object type, added in Navigator 3.0, which, along with the usual array capabilities that all JavaScript objects have, also provides additional array functionality: a constructor function for initializing arrays, an automatically updated length field that stores the size of the array, and join(), reverse(), and sort() methods that manipulate the elements of an array. See the individual reference pages for details.

See Also

Object, Chapter 8

Array.join() Method — concatenate the elements of an array

Availability

Navigator 3.0

Synopsis

```
array.join()
array.join(separator)
```

Arguments

separator   An optional character or string used to separate one element of the array from the next in the returned string. If this argument is omitted, the empty string is used.

Returns

The string that results from converting each element of *array* to a string, and then concatenating them together, with the *separator* string between elements.

Description

join() converts each of the elements of an array to a string, and then concatenates those strings, inserting the specified *separator* string between the elements. It returns the resulting string.

Usage

You can perform the opposite direction—split a string up into array elements—with the split() method of the String object.

Example

```
a = new Array(1, 2, 3, "testing");
s = a.join("+");          s is the string "1+2+3+testing"
```

See Also

Array, String.split()

Array.length Property — the size of an array

Availability

Navigator 3.0, Internet Explorer 3.0

Synopsis

```
array.length
```

Description

The length property of an array is always one larger than the highest element defined in the array. For traditional "dense" arrays that have contiguous elements and begin with element 0, the length property specifies the number of elements in the array.

The length property of an array is initialized when the array is created with the Array() constructor method. Adding new elements to an array updates the length, if necessary:

```
a = new Array();                      a.length initialized to 0
b = new Array(10);                    b.length initialized to 10
c = new Array("one", "two", "three"); c.length initialized to 3
```

```
c[3] = "four";                    c.length updated to 4
c[10] = "blastoff";               c.length becomes 11
```

Note that all JavaScript objects can be used as arrays, but only those created with the `Array()` constructor have an automatically created and updated `length` property.

You can set the value of the `length` property to change the size of an array. If you set `length` to be smaller than its previous value, then the array will be truncated, and elements at the end will be lost. If you set `length` to be larger than its previous value, then then the array will become bigger, and the new elements added at the end of the array will have the special JavaScript undefined value.

Usage

The `Array()` constructor and `length` field were added to JavaScript in Navigator 3.0. Some Navigator 2.0 programs attempt to simulate a `length` field by setting it in the array constructor methods they write. Note, however, that the `length` field is not automatically updated as elements are added to the array. Nor can it grow or shrink the array when its value is set.

See Also

Array, Chapter 8

Array.reverse() Method — reverse the elements of an array

Availability

Navigator 3.0

Synopsis

```
array.reverse()
```

Arguments

None.

Returns

Nothing.

Description

The `reverse()` method of an Array object reverses the order of the elements of an array. It does this "in place"—i.e., it rearranges the elements of the specified *array*, without creating a new array. If there are multiple references to *array*, then the new order of the array elements will be visible through all references.

Example

```
a = new Array(1, 2, 3);           a[0] == 1, a[2] == 3;
a.reverse();                      now a[0] == 3, a[2] == 1;
```

See Also
Array, Array.sort()

Array.sort() Method — sort the elements of an array

Availability
Navigator 3.0

Synopsis
```
array.sort()
array.sort(orderfunc)
```

Arguments
orderfunc   An optional function used to specify the sorting order.

Returns
Nothing.

Description
The sort() method sorts the elements of *array* in place—i.e., no copy of the array is made. If sort() is called with no arguments, then the elements of the array are arranged in alphabetical order (more precisely: the order determined by the character encoding). To do this, elements are first converted to strings, if necessary, so that they can be compared.

If you want to sort the array elements in some other order, you must supply a comparison function that compares two values and returns a number indicating their relative order. The comparison function should take two arguments, *a* and *b*, and should:

- Return a value less than zero if, according to your sort criteria, *a* is "less than" *b*, and should appear before *b* in the sorted array.

- Return zero if *a* and *b* are equivalent for the purposes of this sort.

- Return a value greater than zero if *a* is "greater than" *b* for the purposes of the sort.

The example section shows how you might write a comparison function to sort an array of numbers in numerical, rather than alphabetical order.

Example
The following code shows how you can write an ordering function and use it to sort an array:

```
// An ordering function for a numerical sort
function numberorder(a, b) { return a - b; }

a = new Array(33, 4, 1111, 222);
a.sort();            // Alphabetical sort: 1111, 222, 33, 4
a.sort(numberorder); // Numerical sort: 4, 33, 222, 1111
```

See Also
Array, Array.reverse( )

assign( ) Method — see Object.assign( )

blur( ) Method — see Window.blur( )

Boolean Object — support for Boolean values

Availability
Navigator 3.0

Constructor
```
new Boolean(value)
```

Arguments
value   The value to be held by the Boolean object. This argument will be converted to a Boolean value, if necessary. The values 0, null and the empty string " " are all converted to false. All other values, including the string "false", are converted to true.

Returns
The newly created Boolean object.

Methods
toString( )   Return "true" or "false", depending on the Boolean value represented by the Boolean object.

valueOf( )   Return the Boolean value represented by the Boolean object.

Description
Boolean values are a fundamental data type in JavaScript. The Boolean object is an object wrapper around the Boolean value. This Boolean object type exists solely to provide a toString( ) method to convert Boolean values to strings. When the toString( ) method is invoked to convert a Boolean value to a string (and it is often invoked implicitly by JavaScript) JavaScript internally converts the Boolean value to a transient Boolean object, on which the method can be invoked.

You can create Boolean objects that are not transient by calling the Boolean( ) constructor method. One reason you might occasionally want to do so is to force a conversion of another value to a Boolean value. Having created a Boolean object, you can use it freely wherever JavaScript expects a primitive Boolean value—JavaScript will automatically invoke the valueOf( ) method to return the primitive value of the Boolean object.

See Also
Object

Boolean.prototype Property — see Function.prototype

Boolean.toString() Method — convert a Boolean value to a string

Availability

Navigator 3.0

Synopsis

```
b.toString()
```

Arguments

None.

Returns

The string "true" or "false", depending on the value of the Boolean variable or Boolean object *b*.

See Also

Boolean, Object.toString()

Boolean.valueOf() Method — see Object.valueOf()

Button Element — a graphical pushbutton

Availability

Navigator 2.0, Internet Explorer 3.0; enhanced in Navigator 3.0

Synopsis

```
form.button_name
form.elements[i]
```

Properties

form   A read-only reference to the Form object that contains the Button.

name   A read-only String, set by the HTML NAME attribute, that specifies the name of the button.

type   A read-only string that specifies the type of this form element. For Button elements, it has the value "button". Available in Navigator 3.0 and later.

value   A read-only String property, specified by the HTML VALUE attribute, which specifies the value displayed in the Button element.

Methods

blur()   Remove keyboard focus from the button.

click()   Simulate a click on the button.

focus()   Give keyboard focus to the button.

Event Handlers

onblur()   Invoked when the button loses keyboard focus.

onclick()   Invoked when the button is clicked.

onfocus()   Invoked when the button is given keyboard focus.

HTML Syntax

A Button element is created with a standard HTML <INPUT> tag, with the addition of the onClick attribute:

```
<FORM>
   ...
  <INPUT
    TYPE="button"                 specifies that this is a button
    VALUE="label"                 the text that is to appear within the button
                                  specifies the value property
    [ NAME="name" ]               a name that can later be used to refer to the button
                                  specifies the name property
    [ onClick="handler" ]         JavaScript statements to be executed when the button
                                  is clicked
  >
   ...
</FORM>
```

Description

The Button element represents a graphical push button in a form within an HTML document. The value property contains the text that is displayed by the button. The name property is a name by which the button may be referred to. The onClick event handler is invoked when the user clicks on the button.

Usage

Use a Button element whenever you want to allow the user to trigger some action on your web page. You can sometimes use a Link object for the same purpose, but unless the desired action is to follow a hypertext link, a Button is a better choice than a Link, because it makes it more explicit to the user that there is something to be triggered.

Note that the Submit and Reset elements are types of Buttons that submit a form and reset a form's values. Often these default actions are sufficient for a form, and you do not need to create any other types of buttons.

Example

```
<FORM name="form1">
   <INPUT type="button"
       name="press_me_button"
       value="Press Me"
```

```
        onClick="name = prompt('What is your name?',")"
    >
</FORM>
```

See Also

Element, Form, Reset, Submit

Button.blur() Method — see Element.blur()

Button.click() Method — see Element.click()

Button.focus() Method — see Element.focus()

Button.form Property — see Element.form

Button.name Property — see Element.name

Button.onblur() Handler — see Element.onblur()

Button.onclick() Handler — invoked when a Button is clicked

Availability

Navigator 2.0, Internet Explorer 3.0

Synopsis

```
<INPUT TYPE="button"    a definition of the handler
       VALUE="button-text"
       onClick="handler-statements">

button.onclick          a reference to the handler
button.onclick();        an explicit invocation of the handler
```

Description

onclick() is an event handler invoked when the user clicks on a button. A button's onclick() handler is defined by the onClick attribute of the HTML <INPUT> tag. The value of this attribute may be any number of JavaScript statements, separated by semi-colons; these statements will be executed when the user clicks on the button.

See Also

Button

Button.onfocus( ) Handler — see Element.onfocus( )

Button.type Property — see Element.type

Button.value Property — the text that appears in a Button

Availability

Navigator 2.0, Internet Explorer 3.0

Synopsis

```
button.value
```

Description

`value` is a read-only string property of the Button object. It contains the text that appears in the button. The value of this property is specified by the `VALUE` attribute of the HTML `<INPUT>` tag that creates the button.

See Also

Button

Checkbox Element — a graphical checkbox

Availability

Navigator 2.0, Internet Explorer 3.0; enhanced in Navigator 3.0

Synopsis

A single Checkbox element with a unique name may be referenced in any of these ways:

```
form.checkbox_name
form.elements[i]
```

When a form contains a group of checkboxes with the same name, they are placed in an array, and may be referenced as follows:

```
form.checkbox_name[j]
form.checkbox_name.length
form.elements[i][j]
form.elements[i].length
```

Properties

checked   A read/write Boolean value that specifies whether the button is checked or not.

defaultChecked
              A read-only Boolean that specifies the initial state of the checkbox. May be specified with the HTML `CHECKED` attribute.

form   A read-only reference to the Form object that contains the Checkbox.

name   A read-only String, set by the HTML NAME attribute, that specifies the name of the Checkbox.

type   A read-only string that specifies the type of this form element. For Checkbox elements, it has the value "checkbox". Available in Navigator 3.0 and later.

value   A read/write String, initially set by the HTML VALUE attribute, which specifies the value returned by the Checkbox if it is selected when the form is submitted.

Methods

blur()   Remove keyboard focus from the checkbox.

click()   Simulate a click on the checkbox.

focus()   Give keyboard focus to the checkbox.

Event Handlers

onblur()   Invoked when the checkbox loses keyboard focus.

onclick()   Invoked when the checkbox is clicked.

onfocus()   Invoked when the checkbox is given keyboard focus.

HTML Syntax

A Checkbox element is created with a standard HTML <INPUT> tag, with the addition of the new onClick attribute. Multiple Checkbox elements are often created in groups by specifying multiple <INPUT> tags which have the same NAME attribute.

```
<FORM>
    ...
    <INPUT
      TYPE="checkbox"              specifies that this is a checkbox
      [ NAME="name" ]              a name that can later be used to refer to this checkbox
                                   or to the group of checkboxes with this name
                                   specifies the name property
      [ VALUE="value" ]            the value returned when this checkbox is selected
                                   specifies the value property
      [ CHECKED ]                  specifies that the checkbox is initially checked
                                   specifies the defaultChecked property
      [ onClick="handler" ]        JavaScript statements to be executed
    >                              when the checkbox is clicked
    label                          the HTML text that should appear next to the checkbox
    ...
</FORM>
```

Description

The Checkbox element represents a single graphical checkbox in a HTML form. Note that the text that appears next to the checkbox is not part of the Checkbox element itself, and must be specified externally to the Checkbox's HTML <INPUT> tag.

The onClick event handler allows you to specify JavaScript code to be executed when the Checkbox is checked or unchecked.

You can examine the checked property to determine the state of the Checkbox, and you can also set this property to check or "uncheck" the Checkbox. Note that setting checked changes the graphical appearance of the Checkbox, but does not invoke the onClick event handler.

It is good programming style to specify the NAME attribute for a Checkbox, and is mandatory if the checkbox is part of a form that will submit data to a CGI script running on a web server. Specifying a NAME attribute sets the *name* property, and also allows you to refer to the Checkbox by name (instead of as a member of the form elements array) in your JavaScript code, which makes the code more modular and portable.

For example, if the NAME attribute of a checkbox in form f is "opts", then f.opts refers to the Checkbox element. Checkbox elements are often used in related groups, however, and each member of the group is given the same NAME attribute (the shared name defines the members of the group). In this case, JavaScript places each Checkbox element in the group in an array, and the array is given the shared name. If, for example, each of a group of Checkboxes in form f has its NAME attribute set to "opts", then f.opts is an array of Checkbox elements, and f.opts.length is the number of elements in the array.

Unfortunately, in Navigator 2.0, there is a bug in how Checkbox elements in a group are assigned to an array. See the Bugs section later for details.

You can set the VALUE attribute or the value property of a Checkbox to specify the string that will be passed to the server if the Checkbox is checked when the form is submitted. For a single checkbox, used alone, the default value of "on" is usually adequate. When multiple checkboxes with the same name are used, each should specify a distinct value so that a list of values from selected checkboxes can be passed to the server.

Usage

Checkbox elements can be used to present the user with one or more options. This element type is suitable for presenting non-mutually exclusive choices. Use the Radio element for mutually exclusive lists of options.

Bugs

As described above, when a group of Checkbox elements share the same NAME attribute, JavaScript assigns them to an array that bears that name. Unfortunately, there is a bug in this process in Navigator 2.0: if the Checkbox elements do not have event handlers specified with the onClick attribute, then they are assigned to the array in reverse order. This is counter-intuitive, and is an incompatibility with Navigator 3.0 in which the bug is fixed.

The workaround is to always assign an event handler, if only a dummy one, to your Checkbox elements that will be manipulated with JavaScript. You can do this by including onClick="0" in the <INPUT> tag for each Checkbox element you define. With this workaround, you can ensure that the elements will be assigned to the array in the same order in Navigator 2.0 and Navigator 3.0.

See Also

Element, Form, Radio

Checkbox.blur( ) Method — see Element.blur( )

Checkbox.checked Property — whether a Checkbox is checked

Availability

Navigator 2.0, Internet Explorer 3.0

Synopsis

```
checkbox.checked
```

Description

`checked` is a read/write Boolean property of the Checkbox object. If the Checkbox is checked, then the `checked` property is `true`. If the Checkbox is not checked, then `checked` is `false`.

If you set `checked` to `true`, then the Checkbox will appear checked. Similarly, if you set this property to `false`, the Checkbox will appear unchecked. Note that setting the `checked` property does not cause the Checkbox's `onClick` event handler to be invoked.

See Also

Checkbox

Checkbox.click( ) Method — see Element.click( )

Checkbox.defaultChecked Property — initial state of a Checkbox

Availability

Navigator 2.0, Internet Explorer 3.0

Synopsis

```
checkbox.defaultChecked
```

Description

`defaultChecked` is a read-only Boolean property of the Checkbox object. It is `true` if the Checkbox is initially checked—i.e., if the `CHECKED` attribute appears in the Checkbox's HTML `<INPUT>` tag. If this tag does not appear, then the Checkbox is initially unchecked, and `defaultChecked` is `false`.

Usage

You can use the `defaultChecked` property to reset a Checkbox back to its default state. You might do this when the user selects a **Reset** button in a form, for example. You can reset a Checkbox with the following function:

```
function resetCheckbox(checkbox) {
    if (checkbox.defaultChecked) checkbox.checked = true;
    else checkbox.checked = false;
}
```

See Also

Checkbox

Checkbox.focus( ) Method — see Element.focus( )

Checkbox.form Property — see Element.form

Checkbox.name Property — see Element.name

Checkbox.onblur( ) Handler — see Element.onblur( )

Checkbox.onclick( ) Handler — invoked when a Checkbox is selected

Availability

Navigator 2.0, Internet Explorer 3.0

Synopsis

```
<INPUT TYPE="checkbox" a definition of the handler
        onClick="handler-statements">
```

```
checkbox.onclick          a reference to the handler
checkbox.onclick();       an explicit invocation of the handler
```

Description

onclick() is an event handler invoked when the user clicks on a Checkbox. This event handler is defined by the onClick attribute of the HTML <INPUT> tag that defines the Checkbox. The value of this attribute may be any number of JavaScript statements, separated by semicolons; these statements will be executed when the user clicks on (i.e., checks or unchecks) the Checkbox.

See Also

Checkbox

Checkbox.onfocus( ) Handler — see Element.onfocus( )

Checkbox.type Property — see Element.type

Checkbox.value Property — value returned when form is submitted

Availability

Navigator 2.0, Internet Explorer 3.0

Synopsis

```
checkbox.value
```

Description

value is a read/write string property of the Checkbox object. It specifies the text that is passed to the web server if the Checkbox is checked when the form is submitted. The initial value of value is specified by the VALUE attribute of the Checkbox's HTML <INPUT> tag. If no VALUE attribute is specified, then the default value string is "on".

Usage

Note that the value field does not specify whether or not the Checkbox is selected; the checked property specifies the current state of the Checkbox.

When defining a group of related checkboxes that share the same name, it is important that each be given a distinct value attribute.

See Also

Checkbox

clearTimeout( ) Method — see Window.clearTimeout( )

close( ) Method — see Window.close( )

closed Property — see Window.closed

confirm( ) Method — see Window.confirm( )

Date Object — manipulate dates and times

Availability

Navigator 2.0, Internet Explorer 3.0

Constructor

To create a Date object, use one of the following five syntaxes:

```
new Date();
new Date(milliseconds);
new Date(datestring);
new Date(year, month, day);
new Date(year, month, day, hours, minutes, seconds)
```

With no arguments, the Date() constructor creates a Date object set to the current date and time. Otherwise, the arguments to Date() specify the date, and, optionally, the time for the new object. Note that in the third through fifth syntaxes above, the specified times are interpreted as local times, not Greenwich Mean Time (GMT) times.

Date() can also be used as a function instead of a constructor. When invoked without the new operator, and without any arguments, Date() does not create a Date object but instead returns a string that represents the current date and time for the local time zone. Calling Date() without the new operator is equivalent to using it with the new operator to create a Date object and then using the toString() method of that object to convert the date to a string.

When used as a constructor, the arguments to Date(), are the following:

Arguments

milliseconds

The number of milliseconds between the desired date and midnight GMT on January 1st, 1970. For example passing the argument 5000 would create a date that represents five seconds past midnight on 1/1/70.

datestring A single argument that specifies the date and, optionally, the time as a String. The string should have the format *month day, year hours:minutes:seconds* where *month* is the English name of the month, and hours are specified in 24-hour format. For example:

```
new Date("December 31, 1999 23:59:59");
```

The seconds field or the entire time specification may be omitted from this format.

year   The year, in four-digit format. For example, specify 2001 for the year 2001. For years within the 20th century, you can also subtract 1900 and specify the date in two-digit format. For example, you could specify 97 for the year 1997.

month   The month, specified as an integer from 0 (January) to 11 (December)

day   The day of the month, specified as an integer from 1 to 31. Note that this argument uses 1 as its lowest value, while other arguments use 0 as their lowest value.

hours   The hour, specified as an integer from 0 (midnight) to 23 (11 p.m.).

minutes   The minutes in the hour, specified as an integer from 0 to 59.

seconds   The seconds in the minute, specified as an integer from 0 to 59.

Returns

The newly created Date object.

Methods

Once a Date object is created by using `Date()` as a constructor in any of the forms shown above, any of the following methods can be used to operate on the Date object. Note that unlike most JavaScript objects, the Date object has no properties that can be read and written directly; instead, all access to date and time fields is done through these methods.

`getDate( )`   Return the day of the month of a Date object.

`getDay( )`   Return the day of the week of a Date object.

`getHours( )`   Return the hours field of a Date object.

`getMinutes( )`
                  Return the minutes field of a Date object.

`getMonth( )`   Return the month field of a Date object.

`getSeconds( )`
                  Return the seconds field of a Date object.

`getTime( )`   Return the internal, millisecond representation of a Date object.

`getTimezoneOffset( )`
                  Return the time zone difference, in minutes, between this date and GMT.

`getYear( )`   Return the year field of a Date object.

`parse( )`   Parse a string representation of a date, and return it in millisecond format.

`setDate( )`   Set the day of the month field of a Date object.

`setHours( )`   Set the hour field of a Date object.

`setMinutes( )`
                  Set the minutes field of a Date object.

`setMonth( )`   Set the month field of a Date object.

`setSeconds( )`
                  Set the seconds field of a Date object.

`setTime( )`   Set the fields of a Date object using the millisecond format.

`setYear( )`   Set the year field of a Date object.

`toGMTString( )`
                  Convert a Date to a string, using the GMT time zone.

`toLocaleString( )`
                  Convert a Date to a string, using the local time zone.

`UTC( )`   Convert a numeric date and time specification to millisecond format.

Description

The Date object is a datatype built into the JavaScript language. Unlike most other JavaScript object types, the Date object does not represent any HTML construct in the current document. Instead, it is an independent object that can be created and manipulated freely by JavaScript code. Date objects are created with the new Date() syntax shown in the Constructor section above.

Note that when the Date() constructor is used without the new operator, and is called with no arguments, it does not create a Date object but instead simply returns a string containing the current date and time in the local time zone. Calling Date() in this way is equivalent to creating a Date object to represent the current date and time and then calling the toString() method of that object:

```
(new Date()).toString()
```

Once a Date object is created, there are a number of methods that allow you to operate on it. Most of the methods simply allow you to get and set the year, month, day, hour, minute, and second fields of the object. The toGMTString() and toLocaleString() methods convert dates to human-readable strings. getTime() and setTime() convert to and from the internal representation of the Date object—the number of milliseconds since midnight (GMT) on January 1st, 1970. In this standard "millisecond format", a date and time are represented by a single integer, which makes date arithmetic particularly easy.

Most of the Date object methods are invoked through an instance of the Date object. For example:

```
d = new Date();  // get today's date and time
system.write('Today is: " + d.toLocaleString());  // and print it out
```

There are two functions, however, that have Date in their name, but are not methods, and do not operate on a Date object. These functions, Date.parse() and Date.UTC(), are useful for converting dates to millisecond format. Note though that they do not use the Date object, and are therefore not invoked through a Date object.

Usage

Because JavaScript code may be run on machines all over the world, you need to pay attention to time zone differences. The syntax for creating Date objects shown above assumes that date and time values are specified in local time. While this is appropriate in some cases, there are many cases when it is not. When your code must work the same independently of the time zone in which it is run, you should specify all your hardcoded dates in the GMT (or UTC) time zone. You can then use the Date.UTC() method to convert these date specifications to a time zone–independent number of milliseconds. You can then use this number of milliseconds directly, or can use it to create a Date object.

Bugs

In Navigator 2.0, the Date object has quite a few bugs and is almost unusable. On Macintosh platforms, the time returned is off by an hour. There appears to be something wrong with the Navigator implementation of Date.toGMTString. On all platforms, time zones are not handled well, and prior to version 2.0.2, there are difficulties handling daylight savings time. A side effect of this is that Navigator 2.0 and 2.0.1 cannot correctly determine whether a document on a server is newer than the cached version and so the Reload button does not always work correctly.

You can usually use the Date object to print out the current date, and you can use it to compute the interval (in milliseconds) between two dates or times in the same time zone, but you should probably not attempt more sophisticated uses of it than that.

Example

The most common use of the Date object (and probably the only particularly interesting use) is to subtract the millisecond representations of the current time from some other time to determine the difference between the two times. The following example shows two such uses:

```
<SCRIPT language="JavaScript">
today = new Date();              make a note of today's date
christmas = new Date();          get a date with the current year
christmas.setMonth(11);          set the month to December...
christmas.setDate(25);           ...and the day to the 25th

// If Christmas hasn't already passed, compute the number of
// milliseconds between now and Christmas, then convert this
// to a number of days and print a message.
if (today.getTime() < christmas.getTime()) {
    difference = christmas.getTime() - today.getTime();
    difference = Math.floor(difference / (1000 * 60 * 60 * 24));
    document.write('Only ' + difference + ' days until Christmas!<P>');
}
</SCRIPT>
```

    ... rest of HTML document here ..

```
<SCRIPT language="JavaScript">
// Here we use Date objects for timing. We divide by 1000
// to convert milliseconds to seconds. We could divide
// further to convert to minutes, hours or days.
now = new Date();
document.write('<P>It took ' +
    (now.getTime()-today.getTime())/1000 +
    'seconds to load this page.');
</SCRIPT>
```

See Also

Date.parse( ), Date.UTC( )

Date.getDate( ) Method — return the day of the month

Availability

Navigator 2.0, Internet Explorer 3.0

Synopsis

```
date.getDate()
```

Arguments

None.

Returns

The day of the month of the specified Date object *date*. Return values are between 1 and 31.

See Also

Date, Date.setDate()

Date.getDay() Method — return the day of the week

Availability

Navigator 2.0, Internet Explorer 3.0

Synopsis

```
date.getDay()
```

Arguments

None.

Returns

The day of the week of the specified Date object *date*. Return values are between 0 (Sunday) and 6 (Saturday).

See Also

Date

Date.getHours() Method — return the hours field of a Date

Availability

Navigator 2.0, Internet Explorer 3.0

Synopsis

```
date.getHours()
```

Arguments

None.

Returns

The hours field of the specified Date object *date*. Return values are between 0 (midnight) and 23 (11 pm).

See Also

Date, Date.setHours( )

Date.getMinutes( ) Method — return the minutes field of a Date

Availability

Navigator 2.0, Internet Explorer 3.0

Synopsis

```
date.getMinutes( )
```

Arguments

None.

Returns

The minutes field of the specified Date object *date*. Return values are between 0 and 59.

See Also

Date, Date.setMinutes( )

Date.getMonth( ) Method — return the month of a Date

Availability

Navigator 2.0, Internet Explorer 3.0

Synopsis

```
date.getMonth( )
```

Arguments

None.

Returns

The month field of the specified Date object *date*. Return values are between 0 (January) and 11 (December).

See Also

Date, Date.setMonth( )

Date.getSeconds( ) Method — return the seconds field of a Date

Availability

Navigator 2.0, Internet Explorer 3.0

Synopsis

```
date.getSeconds()
```

Arguments

None.

Returns

The seconds field of the specified Date object *date*. Return values are between 0 and 59.

See Also

Date, Date.setSeconds( )

Date.getTime( ) Method — return a Date in milliseconds

Availability

Navigator 2.0, Internet Explorer 3.0

Synopsis

```
date.getTime()
```

Arguments

None.

Returns

The millisecond representation of the specified Date object *date*. That is, this method returns the number of milliseconds between midnight (GMT) on 1/1/1970 and the date and time specified by *date*.

Usage

getTime( ) converts a date and time to a single integer. This is useful when you want to compare two Date objects or to determine the time elapsed between two dates.

Date.parse( ) and Date.UTC( ) allow you to convert a date and time specification to millisecond representation without going through the overhead of first creating a Date object.

See Also

Date, Date.parse( ), Date.setTime( ), Date.UTC( )

Date.getTimezoneOffset( ) Method — determine the offset from GMT

Availability

Navigator 2.0, Internet Explorer 3.0

Synopsis

```
date.getTimezoneOffset()
```

Arguments

None.

Returns

The difference, in minutes, between Greenwich Mean Time (GMT) and the local time.

Description

getTimezoneOffset() returns the number of minutes difference between the GMT or UTC time zone and the local time zone. In effect, this function tells you what time zone the JavaScript code is running in. The return value is measured in minutes, rather than hours, because some countries have time zones that are not at even one-hour intervals.

getTimezoneOffset() is invoked through a Date object. Note, however, that it doesn't actually reference the Date object, and so it ought to be an independent function instead of a method.

See Also

Date

Date.getYear() Method — return the year field of a Date

Availability

Navigator 2.0, Internet Explorer 3.0

Synopsis

```
date.getYear()
```

Arguments

None.

Returns

The year field of the specified Date object *date*.

Description

getYear() returns the year field of a specified Date object. The format that this year is returned in requires additional explanation, however. In Navigator 2.0 and 3.0, the return return value of this method is the year minus 1900 for dates between the years 1900 and 1999. For example, if *date* represents a date in 1997, then the return value would be 97. On the other hand, for dates in years prior to 1900 or after 1999, getYear() returns the year itself in Navigator 2.0 and 3.0. For example, if *date* represents a date in 2000, the method returns 2000 on Navigator platforms.

Internet Explorer 3.0 always returns the year minus 1900, however, so getYear() on this platform would return 85 to represent 1985, 100 to represent the year 2000 and 110 to represent 2010. IE 3.0 cannot represent years prior to 1970, so these return values are never negative numbers.

To work around these strange and incompatible return values, you should replace
getYear() with a function like the following:

```
function getFullYear(d)              returns the correct year for any year after 1000
{
    var y = d.getYear();
    if (y < 1000) y += 1900;
    return y;
}
```

Bugs

The disparity in return values between dates in the twentieth and twenty-first centuries in
Navigator is bizarre, and, if not carefully taken into account may be the source of "millen-
nium bugs" in your code. The incompatibility between platforms makes this method especially annoying to use.

See Also

Date, Date.setYear()

Date.parse() Function — parse a date/time string

Availability

Navigator 2.0, Internet Explorer 3.0

Synopsis

```
Date.parse(date)
```

Arguments

date   A string containing the date and time to be parsed.

Returns

The number of milliseconds between the specified date and time and midnight, January 1st, 1970, GMT.

Description

Date.parse() is a function with a name that begins with "Date". It is related to the Date
object, but it is not a method of the Date object, and is not invoked on a Date object. It is
always invoked as Date.parse(), not as date.parse() on some Date object date.

Date.parse() takes a single string argument. It parses the date contained in this string and
returns it in millisecond format, which can be used directly, or used to create a new Date
object, or to set the date in an existing Date object with Date.setTime().

Date.parse() understands the IETF standard date format used in email and other Internet
communications. Dates in this format look like this:

```
Wed, 8 May 1996 17:41:46 -0400
```

This is the format written by the Date.toGMTString() method. Date.parse() can also
parse dates in this format from which the day of the week, the time zone, the seconds or

the complete time specification have been omitted. It also understands the GMT time zone, and the standard abbreviations for the time zones of the United States.

Bugs

In Navigator 2.0, prior to 2.0.2, this function cannot correctly parse time zone information.

See Also

Date, Date.setTime(), Date.toGMTString(), Date.UTC()

Date.prototype Property — see Function.prototype

Date.setDate() Method — set the day of the month

Availability

Navigator 2.0, Internet Explorer 3.0

Synopsis

```
date.setDate(day_of_month)
```

Arguments

day_of_month
> A number between 1 and 31 that is set as the day of the month in the Date object *date*.

Returns

Nothing.

See Also

Date, Date.getDate()

Date.setHours() Method — set the hours field of a Date

Availability

Navigator 2.0, Internet Explorer 3.0

Synopsis

```
date.setHours(hours)
```

Arguments

hours   An integer between 0 (midnight) and 23 (11pm) that is set as the hours value for the Date object *date*.

Returns

Nothing.

See Also

Date, Date.getHours( )

Date.setMinutes( ) Method — set the minutes field of a Date

Availability

Navigator 2.0, Internet Explorer 3.0

Synopsis

```
date.setMinutes(minutes)
```

Arguments

minutes   An integer between 0 and 59, that is set as the minutes value in the Date object *date*.

Returns

Nothing.

See Also

Date, Date.getMinutes( )

Date.setMonth( ) Method — set the month field of a Date

Availability

Navigator 2.0, Internet Explorer 3.0

Synopsis

```
date.setMonth(month)
```

Arguments

month   An integer between 0 (January) and 11 (December) that is set as the month value for the Date object *date*.

Returns

Nothing.

See Also

Date, Date.getMonth( )

Date.setSeconds() Method — set the seconds field of a Date

Availability

Navigator 2.0, Internet Explorer 3.0

Synopsis

```
date.setSeconds(seconds)
```

Arguments

seconds   An integer between 0 and 59 that is set as the seconds value for the Date object `date`.

Returns

Nothing.

See Also

Date, Date.getSeconds()

Date.setTime() Method — set a Date in milliseconds

Availability

Navigator 2.0, Internet Explorer 3.0

Synopsis

```
date.setTime(milliseconds)
```

Arguments

milliseconds

     The number of milliseconds between the desired date and time and midnight GMT on January 1st, 1970. Representing a date in this millisecond format makes it independent of time zone.

Returns

Nothing.

See Also

Date, Date.getTime()

Date.setYear() Method — set the year field of a Date

Availability

Navigator 2.0, Internet Explorer 3.0

Synopsis

`date.setYear(year)`

Arguments

year   An integer which is set as the year value for the Date object *date*. Usually, you should use four-digit format for year specifications. For example, specify 2001 for the year 2001. For years within the 20th century, you can also subtract 1900 and specify the date in two-digit format. For example, you could specify 97 for the year 1997.

Returns

Nothing.

See Also

Date, Date.getYear( )

Date.toGMTString( ) Method — convert a date to a string

Availability

Navigator 2.0, Internet Explorer 3.0

Synopsis

`date.toGMTString()`

Arguments

None.

Returns

A string representation of the date and time specified by the Date object *date*. The date is converted from the local time zone to the GMT time zone before being converted to a string.

Description

`toGMTString( )` converts a date to a string using the GMT time zone. The format of the returned string is platform dependent, but usually it will appear something like this:

```
Tue, 02 Apr 1996 02:04:57 GMT
```

See Also

Date, Date.parse( ), Date.toLocaleString( )

Date.toLocaleString() Method — convert a Date to a string

Availability

Navigator 2.0, Internet Explorer 3.0

Synopsis

```
date.toLocaleString()
```

Arguments

None.

Returns

A string representation of the date and time specified by the Date object `date`. The date and time are represented in the local time zone.

Usage

`toLocaleString()` converts a date to a string, using the local time zone. This method also uses local conventions for date and time formatting, so the format may vary widely platform to platform, and also country to country. This method returns a string formatted in what is likely the user's preferred date and time format. Because the format may vary widely, this method is not useful when the date string must be passed to a CGI script or otherwise machine processed.

Use `Date.toGMTString()` to convert a date to a string using the GMT time zone and a more standard format.

See Also

Date, Date.parse( ), Date.toGMTString( )

Date.UTC() Function — convert a date specification to milliseconds

Availability

Navigator 2.0, Internet Explorer 3.0

Synopsis

```
Date.UTC(year, month, day [, hours [, minutes [, seconds]]]);
```

Arguments

`year`	The year minus 1900. For example, specify 96 for the year 1996.
`month`	The month, specified as an integer from 0 (January) to 11 (December)
`day`	The day of the month, specified as an integer from 1 to 31. Note that this argument uses 1 as its lowest value, while other arguments use 0 as their lowest value.
`hours`	The hour, specified as an integer from 0 (midnight) to 23 (11 p.m.). This argument may be omitted if `minutes` and `seconds` are also omitted.

minutes	The minutes in the hour, specified as an integer from 0 to 59. This argument may be omitted if *seconds* is also omitted.
seconds	The seconds in the minute, specified as an integer from 0 to 59. This argument may be omitted.

Returns

The number of milliseconds between midnight on January 1st, 1970, UTC and the time specified (also in UTC) by the arguments.

Description

Date.UTC() is a function with a name that begins with "Date". It is related to the Date object, but it is not a method of the Date object, and is not invoked on a Date object. It is always invoked as Date.UTC(), not as *date*.UTC() on some Date object *date*.

The arguments to Date.UTC() specify a date and time, and are understood to be in UTC (Universal Coordinated Time)—i.e., they are in the GMT time zone. The specified UTC time is converted to the millisecond format, which can be used by the Date() constructor method, and by the Date.setTime() method.

Usage

The Date() constructor method can accept date and time arguments identical to those that Date.UTC() accepts. The difference is that the Date() constructor assumes local time, while Date.UTC() assumes UTC. To create a Date object using a UTC time specification, you can use code like this:

```
d = new Date(Date.UTC(96, 4, 8, 16, 30));
```

Bugs

In Navigator 2.0, Date.UTC() does not compute the correct number of milliseconds.

See Also

Date, Date.parse(), Date.setTime()

---

defaultStatus Property — see Window.defaultStatus

---

document Property — see Window.document

Document Object — the currently displayed HTML document

Availability

Navigator 2.0, Internet Explorer 3.0; enhanced in Navigator 3.0

Synopsis

```
window.document
document
```

An instance of the Document object is stored in the document field of the Window object. As a special case, when referring to the Document object of the current window (i.e., the window in which the JavaScript code is executing), you can omit the `window` reference, and simply use `document`.

Properties

`alinkColor`   A string that specifies the color of activated links. May be set in the document <HEAD> or through the `ALINK` <BODY> attribute.

`anchors[ ]`   An array of Anchor objects; one for each hypertext target in the document.

`anchors.length`
    A read-only integer specifying the number of elements in the `anchors[ ]` array.

`applets[ ]`   An array of Java objects, one for each <APPLET> that appears in the document. Navigator 3.0 and higher.

`applets.length`
    A read-only integer specifying the number of elements in the `applets[ ]` array. Navigator 3.0 and higher.

`bgColor`   A string that specifies the background color of the document. Initially set through the `BGCOLOR` <BODY> attribute.

`cookie`   A string, which is the value of a cookie associated with this document.

`domain`   A string that specifies the Internet domain from which the document is from. This property is used for security purposes. Navigator 3.0 and higher.

`embeds[ ]`   An array of Java objects, one for each <EMBED> tag that appears in the document. Navigator 3.0 and higher.

`embeds.length`
    A read-only integer that specifies the number of elements in the `embeds[ ]` array. Navigator 3.0 and higher.

`fgColor`   A string that specifies the color of document text. May be set in the document <HEAD> or through the `TEXT` <BODY> attribute.

`forms[ ]`   An array of Form objects, one for each <FORM> that appears in the document.

`forms.length`
    A read-only integer specifying the number of elements in the `forms[ ]` array.

`images[ ]`   An array of Image objects, one for each image embedded in the document with the <IMG> tag. Navigator 3.0 and higher.

`images.length`
    The number of elements in the `images[ ]` array.

`lastModified`
    A read-only string that specifies the date of the most recent change to the document (as reported by the web server).

linkColor   A string that specifies the color of unvisited links in the document. May be set in the document <HEAD> or through the LINK <BODY> attribute.

links[]   An array of Link objects, one for each hypertext link in the the document.

links.length

A read-only integer specifying the number of elements in the links[] array.

location   A synonym for the URL property. Not the same as the Location object *window*.location.

plugins[]   A synonym for the embeds[] array. Navigator 3.0 and higher.

plugins.length

The number of elements in the plugins[] or embeds[] array. Navigator 3.0 and higher.

referrer   A read-only string that specifies the URL of the document that contained the link that referred to the current document.

title   A read-only string that specifies the <TITLE> of the document.

URL   A read-only string that specifies the URL of the document.

vlinkColor A string that specifies the color of visited links. May be set in the document <HEAD> or through the VLINK <BODY> attribute.

Methods

clear()   A method that erases the contents of the document. This method is deprecated in Navigator 3.0.

close()   A method that closes a document stream opened with the open() method.

open()   A method that opens a stream to which document contents may be written.

write()   A method that inserts the specified string or strings into the document currently being parsed, or into a document stream opened with open().

writeln()   A method identical to write(), except that it appends a newline character to the output.

Event Handlers

onload   An event handler invoked when the document is fully loaded, specified by the onLoad attribute of <BODY>. Although this event handler is specified as an attribute of the <BODY> tag, it is a property of the Window object, not the Document object. See Window.onload() for details.

onunload   An event handler invoked when the document is unloaded, specified by the onUnload attribute of <BODY>. Although this event handler is specified as an attribute of the <BODY> tag, it is a property of the Window object, not the Document object. See Window.onunload() for details.

HTML Syntax

The Document object obtains values for a number of its properties from attributes of the HTML <BODY> tag. Also, the HTML contents of a document appear within the <BODY> and </BODY> tags.

```
<BODY
  [ BACKGROUND="imageURL" ]      a background image for the document
  [ BGCOLOR="color" ]            a background color for the document
  [ TEXT="color" ]              the foreground color the document's text
  [ LINK="color" ]              the color for unvisited links
  [ ALINK="color" ]             the color for activated links
  [ VLINK="color" ]             the color for visited links
  [ onLoad="handler" ]          JavaScript to run when the document is loaded
  [ onUnload="handler" ]        JavaScript to run when the document is unloaded
>

    HTML document contents go here.

</BODY>
```

Description

The Document object represents the HTML document displayed in a browser window or frame. The properties of this object provide details about many aspects of the document, from the colors of the text, background, and anchors, to the date on which the document was last modified. The Document object also contains a number of arrays that describe the contents of the document. The links[] array contains one Link object for each hypertext link in the document. Similarly, the applets[] array contains one object for each Java applet embedded in the document, and the forms[] array contains one Form object for each HTML form that appears in the document.

The write() method of the Document object is especially notable. When invoked in scripts that are run while the document is loading, you can call document.write() to insert dynamically generated HTML text into the document.

See Chapter 14 for an overview of the Document object, and of many of the other JavaScript objects that it refers to. See the individual reference pages for full documentation for each of the properties and methods of this object.

See Also

Form, Window, Chapter 14

Document.alinkColor Property — the color of activated links

Availability

Navigator 2.0; implemented but nonfunctional in Internet Explorer 3.0

Synopsis

```
document.alinkColor
```

Description

alinkColor is a string property that specifies the color of activated links in *document*. This color is displayed between the times that the user presses and releases the mouse button over the link. Note that this property exists, but has no effect in Internet Explorer 3.0. This is because the Internet Explorer user-interface never displays a special color when links are activated.

The activated link color can be specified through the ALINK attribute in the <BODY> HTML tag, and the alinkColor property will contain the specified value. The color may also be specified by assigning a value to alinkColor directly, but this may only be done in the <HEAD> of the document, before the <BODY> tag is parsed.

Colors are specified either as one of the standard color names recognized by JavaScript, or as red, green, and blue color values, expressed as a string of six hexadecimal digits in the form "RRGGBB".

See Also

Document, Document.bgColor, Document.fgColor, Document.linkColor, Document.vlinkColor, Appendix G

Document.anchors[] Property — the Anchors in a document

Availability

Implemented but nonfunctional in Navigator 2.0, 3.0, and Internet Explorer 3.0

Synopsis

```
document.anchors
document.anchors.length
```

Description

The anchors property is an array of Anchor objects, one for each anchor that appears in *document*. An anchor is a named position within the document, which can serve as the target of a hypertext link. The anchors[ ] array has anchors.length elements, numbered from zero to anchors.length-1.

This property has not yet been fully implemented; see the Anchor object for more information.

Do not confuse anchors with hypertext links, which are represented, in JavaScript, by the Link objects in the Document.links[ ] array.

See Also

Anchor, Document, Document.links[], Link

Document.applets[] Property — the applets in a document

Availability

Navigator 3.0

Synopsis

```
document.applets
document.applets.length
```

Description

The applets[] property of the Document object is an array of JavaObject objects, one for each applet that appears in the document. Each JavaObject in the array refers to the Java object for an applet. You can use the JavaObject to read and write all public variables in the applet, and can invoke all of the applet's public methods.

If an <APPLET> tag has a NAME attribute, then the applet may also be referred to by using the name as a property of document or as an index into the applets array. Thus, if the first applet in a document has NAME="animator", then you can refer to it in any of these three ways:

```
document.applets[0]
document.animator
document.applets["animator"]
```

See Also

JavaObject, Chapter 19

Document.bgColor Property — the document background color

Availability

Navigator 2.0, Internet Explorer 3.0

Synopsis

```
document.bgColor
```

Description

bgColor is a string property that specifies the background color of *document*.

The document text color can be set through the BGCOLOR attribute in the <BODY> HTML tag, and the bgColor property will contain the specified value. The background color may also be specified by assigning a value to bgColor directly. Unlike the other color properties, bgColor can be set at any time. Unfortunately, in Navigator 2.0, setting bgColor is buggy.

Colors are specified either as one of the standard color names recognized by JavaScript, or as red, green, and blue color values, expressed as a string of six hexadecimal digits in the form "*RRGGBB*".

Usage

When setting one color property for a Document, you should probably set the other color properties to match. Be careful when specifying color values; it is far easier to end up with a garish web page than it is to choose a palette of harmonious colors. In general, the default colors are a safe choice, and may also reflect the end user's color preferences.

Note that the background of a document may also be set to an image with the BACKGROUND attribute of the HTML <BODY> tag.

See Also

Document, Document.alinkColor, Document.fgColor, Document.linkColor, Document.vlinkColor, Appendix G

Document.clear() Method — clear a document

Availability

deprecated; do not use

Synopsis

```
document.clear()
```

Arguments

None.

Returns

Nothing.

Description

`document.clear()` temporarily erases the specified *document* (i.e., it clears the window or frame that contains *document*). This method does not actually remove the contents of the document, and if the window is covered and then uncovered, for example, the document will be redrawn. This is unusual and generally undesirable behavior, and the use of the `clear()` method is not recommended.

Furthermore, Internet Explorer 3.0 defines this function in an compatible way. On that platform, the `clear()` method is simply a synonym for `Document.open()`.

The `clear()` method will be removed from JavaScript in a future version of the language. When you want to use JavaScript to delete the current document and begin a new one, you should first call the `close()` method for the current document, then call the `open()` method to open a new document, and then use the `write()` and `writeln()` methods to write out the contents of the new document. When you are writing HTML text, you can omit the call to `open()`—a new `text/html` document will be automatically opened if you call `write()` or `writeln()` without first calling `open()`.

See Also

Document, Document.close(), Document.open(), Document.write()

Document.close() Method — close an output stream

Availability

Navigator 2.0, Internet Explorer 3.0

Synopsis

```
document.close()
```

Arguments

None.

Returns

Nothing.

Description

This method displays any output to *document* that has been written but not yet displayed, and closes the output stream to *document*. When generating complete HTML pages with `Document.write()`, you should invoke `Document.close()` when you reach the end of the page.

After *document*`.close()` has been called, if any further output is written to *document* (e.g., with *document*`.write()`) then the document will be implicitly cleared and reopened, erasing all the output that was written prior to calling the `close()` method.

See Also

Document, Document.clear( ), Document.open( ), Document.write( )

Document.cookie Property — the cookie(s) of the document

Availability

Navigator 2.0, partial support in Internet Explorer 3.0

Synopsis

```
document.cookie
```

Description

`cookie` is a string property that allows you to read, create, modify, and delete the cookie or cookies that apply to the current document. A *cookie* is a small amount of named data stored by the web browser. It serves to give web browsers a "memory", so that they can use data input on one page in another page, or so they can recall user preferences across web browsing sessions. Cookie data is automatically transmitted between web browser and web server when appropriate, so that CGI scripts on the server end can read and write cookie values. Client-side JavaScript code can also read and write cookies with this property. For a more complete discussion of cookies, see Netscape's cookie specification at *http://home.netscape.com/newsref/std/cookie_spec.html*.

Internet Explorer 3.0 supports the `cookie` property only when the document was retrieved via the HTTP protocol. Documents retrieved from the local file system, or via other protocols such as FTP and Gopher cannot utilize cookies. This limitation will be removed in a future version of Internet Explorer.

The `Document.cookie` property does not behave like a normal read/write property. You may both read and write the value of of `Document.cookie`, but the value you read from this property will, in general, not be the same as the value you write. The following subsections explain how to read and write cookie values.

Reading Cookie Values

When you use the `cookie` property in a JavaScript expression, the value it returns is a string containing all the cookies that apply to the current document. The string is a list of *name=value* pairs separated by semicolons, where *name* is the name of a cookie, and *value* is its string value. You can use the `String.indexOf()` and `String.substring()` methods to determine the value of the named cookie you are interested in.

Once you have obtained the value of a cookie in this way, you must interpret that value based on whatever format or encoding was used by the creator of that cookie. For example, the cookie might store multiple pieces of information in colon-separated fields. In this case, you would have to use appropriate string methods to extract the various fields of information.

The value of a cookie must not contain any semicolons, commas, or whitespace. Because these are commonly used characters, it is common to use the JavaScript `escape()` function to encode cookie values before storing them, and the `unescape()` function to decode the values after retrieving them.

Note that the `Document.cookie` field provides no way to obtain the domain, path, expiration, or secure fields associated with a cookie.

Storing Cookies

To associate a temporary cookie value with the current document, simply set *document*.`cookie` to a string of the form *name=value*. The next time you read *document*.`cookie`, the *name* and *value* pair will be included in the list of cookies for the document. As noted above, the cookie value may not include semicolons, commas or whitespace. For this reason, you may want to use the JavaScript `escape()` function to encode the value before storing it in the cookie.

A cookie written as described above will last for the current web browsing session, but will be lost when the user exits the browser. To create a cookie that can last across browser sessions, include an expiration date. You can do this by setting *document*.`cookie` to a string of the form:

```
name=value; expires=date
```

date should be a date specification in the format written by `Date.toGMTString()`.

Similarly, you can set the path, domain, and secure fields of a cookie by appending strings of the following form to the cookie value before that value is written to the *document*.`cookie` property. (See *http://home.netscape.com/newsref/ std/cookie_spec.html* for more information about the meaning of the path, domain, and secure fields of a cookie.)

```
; path=path
; domain=domain
; secure
```

To change the value of a cookie, set its value again, using the same name (and the same path and domain, if any) and the new value.

To delete a cookie, set it again using the same name, path and domain, an arbitrary value, and an expiration date that has already passed. Note that the browser is not required to immediately delete expired cookies. In practice, with Netscape Navigator, cookie deletion seems to work more effectively if the expiration date is in the relatively distant (several hours or more) past.

Usage

Cookies are intended for infrequent storage of small amounts of data. They are not intended as a general-purpose communication or programming mechanism; use them in moderation. Note that web browsers are not required to retain the value of more than 20 cookies per web server (for the entire server, not just for your site on the server), nor to retain a cookie *name/value* pair more than 4 kilobytes in length.

Bugs

In Internet Explorer 3.0, cookies and the `cookie` property only work for documents retrieved via the HTTP protocol.

See Also

Chapter 15

Document.domain Property — the security domain of a document

Availability

Navigator 3.0

Synopsis

```
document.domain
```

Description

The `domain` property of the Document object is used for security purposes when the data-tainting security model is not enabled. Under the non-tainting "default" model, a script running in one window is not allowed to read properties of another window unless that window comes from the same web server as the host. This causes problems for large web sites that use multiple servers. For example, a script on the host *www.yahoo.com* might want to be able to share properties with a script from the host *search.yahoo.com*.

The `domain` property helps to address this problem. Initially, this string property contains the hostname of the web server from which the document was loaded. You can set this property, but only in a very restricted way: it can only be set to a domain suffix of itself. For example, a script loaded from *search.yahoo.com* could set its own `domain` property to "yahoo.com". If a script from *www.yahoo.com* is running in another window, and it also sets its `domain` property to "yahoo.com", then these two scripts will be able to share properties, even though they did not originate on the same server.

Note, however, that a script from *search.yahoo.com* can't set its `domain` property to "search.yahoo". And, importantly, a script from *snoop.direct_market.com* cannot set its `domain` to "yahoo.com" to determine, for example, what search keywords you use.

See Also

Document, Chapter 20

Document.embeds[] Property — embedded objects in a document

Availability

Navigator 3.0

Synopsis

```
document.embeds[i]
document.embeds.length
document.embed-name
```

Description

The embeds property of the Document object is an array of JavaObjects, each of which represents one embedded object in the document. Objects or data are embedded in an HTML page with the <EMBED> tag, and embedded objects are displayed, in Navigator at least, with plug-ins. For Java-enabled plug-ins, the JavaObjects in the embeds[] array allow you to interact with the plug-in that is displaying the embedded object. For plug-ins that are not Java-enabled, the JavaObject in embeds[] is a dummy object, and you cannot do anything with it.

Note that the contents of this array are JavaObject objects, not Plugin objects, as you might expect. The Plugin object and the Navigator.plugins[] array simply provides information about installed plug-ins. The Document.embeds[] array allows control over the plug-ins and access to the data those plug-ins are displaying. The fields and methods of the JavaObject objects provided by in the embeds[] array vary from plug-in to plug-in, and documentation will be supplied by the plug-in manufacturers.

If the <EMBED> tag of an embedded object contains the NAME attribute to specify a name, then a reference to the JavaObject for that embedded object will also be available as a property of the Document. The name of this Document property will be the name of the embedded object—i.e., the value of the NAME attribute.

See Also

Document, JavaObject, Navigator, Plugin, Chapter 19

Document.fgColor Property — the default text color

Availability

Navigator 2.0, Internet Explorer 3.0

Synopsis

```
document.fgColor
```

Description

fgColor is a string property that specifies the default color of text in *document*. This default color is used for all text in the document except hypertext links and text with an alternate color specified through the COLOR attribute of the HTML <FONT> tag.

The document text color can be set through the TEXT attribute in the <BODY> HTML tag, and the fgColor property will contain the specified value. The default color may also be specified by assigning a value to fgColor directly, but this may only be done in the <HEAD> of the document, before the <BODY> tag is parsed.

Colors are specified either as one of the standard color names recognized by JavaScript, or as red, green, and blue color values, expressed as a string of six hexadecimal digits in the form "*RRGGBB*".

See Also

Document, Document.alinkColor, Document.bgColor, Document.linkColor, Document.vlinkColor, Appendix G

Document.forms[] Property — the Forms in a document

Availability

Navigator 2.0, Internet Explorer 3.0

Synopsis

```
document.forms
document.forms.length
```

Description

The forms property is an array of Form objects, one for each HTML form that appears in *document*. The forms[] array has forms.length elements, numbered from zero to forms.length-1.

See the Form object for more information.

See Also

Document, Form

Document.images[] Property — the images embedded in a document

Availability

Navigator 3.0

Synopsis

```
document.images[i]
document.images.length
document.image-name
```

Description

The images property of the Document object is an array of Image objects, one for each image that is embedded in the document with the HTML <IMG> tag.

If the NAME attribute is specified in the <IMG> tag for an Image, then a reference to that image will also be stored in a property of the Document object. This property will have the same name as the image. So if an image has a NAME="toggle" attribute, then you can refer to the image with document.toggle.

See Also

Document, Image

Document.lastModified Property — modification date of a document

Availability

Navigator 2.0, Internet Explorer 3.0

Synopsis

```
document.lastModified
```

Description

`lastModified` is a read-only string property that contains the date and time at which *document* was most recently modified. This data is derived from HTTP header data sent by the web server. The web server generally obtains the last-modified date by examining the modification date of the file itself.

Web servers are not required to provide last-modified dates for the documents they serve. When a web server does not provide a last modification date, JavaScript assumes 0, which translates to a date of January 1st, 1970, GMT. The following example shows how you can test for this case.

Example

It is a good idea to let readers know how recent the information you provide on the Web is. You can include an automatic time stamp in your documents by placing the following script at the end of each HTML file. By doing this you do not need to update the modification time by hand each time you make a change to the file. Note that this script tests that the supplied date is a valid one before displaying it.

```
<SCRIPT>
if (Date.parse(document.lastModified) != 0)
    document.write('<P><HR><SMALL><I>Last modified: '
                    + document.lastModified
                    + '</I></SMALL>');

</SCRIPT>
```

See Also

Document, Document.location, Document.referrer, Document.title

---

Document.linkColor Property — the color of unfollowed links

Availability

Navigator 2.0, Internet Explorer 3.0

Synopsis

```
document.linkColor
```

Description

`linkColor` is a string property that specifies the color of unvisited links in *document*. All hypertext links in the document are displayed in this color, except for those that have already been followed or visited.

The link color can be specified through the `LINK` attribute in the `<BODY>` HTML tag, and the `linkColor` property will contain the specified value. The color may also be specified by assigning a value to `linkColor` directly, but this may only be done in the `<HEAD>` of the document, before the `<BODY>` tag is parsed.

Colors are specified either as one of the standard color names recognized by JavaScript, or as red, green, and blue color values, expressed as a string of six hexadecimal digits in the form `"RRGGBB"`.

See Also

Document, Document.alinkColor, Document.bgColor, Document.fgColor, Document.vlinkColor, Appendix G

Document.links[] Property — the Link objects in a document

Availability

Navigator 2.0, Internet Explorer 3.0

Synopsis

```
document.links
document.links.length
```

Description

The `links` property is an array of Link objects, one for each hypertext link that appears in *document*. The `links[]` array has `links.length` elements, numbered from zero to `links.length-1`.

See the Link object for more information.

See Also

Anchor, Document, Document.anchors[], Link

Document.location Property — the URL of the current document

Availability

Navigator 2.0, Internet Explorer 3.0;
deprecated in Navigator 3.0—use Document.URL instead

Synopsis

```
document.location
```

Description

In Navigator 2.0 and Internet Explorer 3.0, `location` is a read-only string property that contains the complete URL of the current *document*. The `document.location` property of a document is usually equal to the `location.href` of a window on these platforms. These two properties are not always equal, however, because the the `location` property of the Document object may be modified through URL redirection—`Window.location` contains the requested URL and `Document.location` specifies the actual URL of the retrieved document.

In Navigator 3.0, the location property of the Document object is a read-only reference to the same Location object referred to by the `location` property of the Window object. That is, in Navigator 3.0, `window.location` is always equal to `document.location`. Navigator 3.0 also introduces the `URL` property of the Document object. That new property behaves the same way as the `location` property did prior to Navigator 3.0—it is a string that contains the possibly redirected URL of the document.

While this is a fairly major change made in Navigator 3.0, it should not break many scripts. Because the Location object has a `toString()` method, the `document.location` property in Navigator 3.0 can be treated as if it were a string, just as it was in Navigator 2.0.

See Also

Document, Document.URL, Window.location

Document.open() Method — begin a new document

Availability

Navigator 2.0, partial support in Internet Explorer 3.0

Synopsis

```
document.open()
document.open(mimetype)
```

Arguments

mimetype   An optional string argument that specifies the type of data to be written to and display in *document*. The value of this argument should be one of the standard MIME types that the browser understands ("text/html", "text/plain", "image/gif", "image/jpeg", "image/x-bitmap" for Navigator) or some other MIME type that can be handled by an installed plug-in. If this argument is omitted, it is taken to be "text/html". This argument is ignored by Internet Explorer 3.0, which always assumes a document of type "text/html".

Returns

Nothing.

Description

The `document.open()` method opens a stream to *document*, so that subsequent `document.write()` calls can append data to the document. The optional *mimetype* argument specifies the type of data to be written, and tells the browser how to interpret that data. Note, however that Internet Explorer 3.0 does not support the *mimetype* argument and always assumes documents of HTML text.

If there is any existing document displayed when the `open()` method is called, it will be automatically cleared by the call to `open()` or by the first call to `write()` or `writeln()`.

After opening a document with `open()` and writing data to it with `write()`, you should complete the document by calling `close()`.

Usage

You will usually call `Document.open()` with no argument, to open an HTML document. Occasionally, a "text/plain" document is useful; for example for a pop-up window of debugging messages.

See Also

Document, Document.clear(), Document.close(), Document.write()

Document.plugins Property — embedded objects in a document

Availability

Navigator 3.0

Synopsis

```
document.plugins[i]
document.plugins.length
document.embedded-object-name
```

Description

The `plugins` property of the Document object is a synonym for the `embeds` property. Both properties refer to an array of JavaObjects that represent embedded data being displayed by a plug-in.

The `embeds` property is the preferred way to access this array, since it avoids confusion with the `Navigator.plugins[]` array, which is totally different than the array `Document.plugins[]`. See `Document.embeds[]` for full details.

See Also

Document, Document.embeds[]

Document.referrer Property — the URL of the linked-from document

Availability

Navigator 2.0; implemented but nonfunctional in Internet Explorer 3.0

Synopsis

```
document.referrer
```

Description

`referrer` is a read-only string property that contains the URL of the document from which the current *document* was reached. For example, if the user follows a link in document A to document B, then in document B, the `Document.referrer` property contains the URL of document A. On the other hand, if the user types the URL of document B directly and does not follow any link to get there, then the `Document.referrer` property for document B will be an empty string.

See Also

Document, Document.lastModified, Document.location, Document.title

Document.title Property — the title of a document

Availability

Navigator 2.0, Internet Explorer 3.0

Synopsis

```
document.title
```

Description

`title` is a read-only string property that specifies the title of the current *document*. The title is any text that appears within `<TITLE>` and `</TITLE>` tags in the `<HEAD>` of the document.

See Also

Document, Document.lastModified, Document.location, Document.referrer

Document.URL Property — the URL of the current document

Availability

Navigator 2.0; enhanced in Navigator 3.0

Synopsis

```
document.URL
```

Description

`URL` is a read-only string property that contains the complete URL of the current *document*. `document.URL` is usually equal to `window.location.href` for the *window* that contains *document*. These two are not always equal, however, because the `Document.URL` property may be modified through URL redirection—`Window.location` contains the requested URL, and `Document.URL` specifies the actual URL where it was found.

The `Document.location` property is a synonym for the `Document.URL` property. The `URL` property is the preferred one, because it is less likely to be confused with the Window object's `location` property. Note, however, that in Navigator 2.0, the `URL` property does not appear in `for/in` loops run over Document objects. Also, the `URL` property is not supported by Internet Explorer 3.0.

Usage

Some web authors like to include the URL of a document somewhere within the document, so that, for example, if the document is cut-and-pasted to a file, or printed out, there will still be a reference to where it can be found online. The following script, when appended to a document will automatically add the document's URL. (Unfortunately, in Netscape 2.0, text such as this generated by JavaScript won't appear in printouts, which defeats an important purpose of including the location in the first place.)

```
<script>
document.write('<P><HR><SMALL><I>URL: ' + document.URL
    + '</I></SMALL>');
</script>
```

See Also

Document, Document.lastModified, Document.location, Document.referrer, Document.title, Location, Window.location

---

Document.vlinkColor Property — the color of visited links

Availability

Navigator 2.0, Internet Explorer 3.0

Synopsis

```
document.vlinkColor
```

Description

`vlinkColor` is a string property that specifies the color of visited links in *document*. This color is displayed for links that the user has already followed, i.e., those that reference a URL that the user has already visited.

The visited link color can be specified through the `VLINK` attribute in the `<BODY>` HTML tag, and the `vlinkColor` property will contain the specified value. The color may also be specified by assigning a value to `vlinkColor` directly, but this may only be done in the `<HEAD>` of the document, before the `<BODY>` tag is parsed.

Colors are specified either as one of the standard color names recognized by JavaScript, or as red, green, and blue color values, expressed as a string of six hexadecimal digits in the form `"RRGGBB"`.

See Also

Document, Document.alinkColor, Document.bgColor, Document.fgColor, Document.linkColor, Appendix G

Document.write() Method — append data to a document

Availability

Navigator 2.0, Internet Explorer 3.0

Synopsis

```
document.write(value, ... )
```

Arguments

value   An arbitrary JavaScript value that is to be appended to `document`. If the value is not a string, it is converted to one before being appended.

. . .   Any number (zero or more) of additional values to be appended (in order) to `document`.

Returns

Nothing.

Description

`document`.write() appends each of its arguments, in order, to `document`. String values are appended as is. Numeric values are converted to a string representation, and Boolean values are appended as either the string "true" or the string "false". Object values are converted to strings by invoking their `toString()` method.

Document.write() is usually used in one of two ways. The first is when it is invoked on the current document within a <SCRIPT> tag or within a function that is executed while the document is still being parsed. In this case, the write() method writes its HTML output as if that output appeared literally in the file, at the location of the code that invoked the method.

The second way that Document.write() is commonly used is to dynamically generate the contents of documents other than that of the current window. In this case, the target document is never in the process of being parsed, and so the output cannot appear "in place" as it does in the case described above. In order for write() to output text into a document, that document must be "open." You can open a document by explicitly calling the Document.open() method, if you choose. In most cases this is unnecessary, however, because when write() is invoked on a document that is "closed," it implicitly opens the document. When a document is opened, any contents that previously appeared in that document are discarded and replaced with a blank document.

Once a document is open, Document.write() can append any amount of output to the end of the document. When a new document has been completely generated by this technique, the document should be closed by calling Document.close(). Note that although the call to open() is usually optional, the call to close() is never optional.

The results of calling Document.write() may not be immediately visible in the targeted web browser window or frame. This is because a web browser may buffer up data to output in larger chunks. Calling Document.close() is the only way to explicitly force all buffered output to be "flushed" and displayed in the browser window. In Navigator 2.0 and 3.0, however, output will be flushed whenever a line break occurs in the output. So for example, outputting the HTML tags <BR>, <HR>, or <P> would force Navigator to display all pending output. This technique does not work in Internet Explorer 3.0, however. In that browser, output is not "flushed" until the enclosing <SCRIPT> tag or event handler function terminates.

Document.write() can also be used in a third way, but only with extreme caution. When an event handler invokes write() on the current document (i.e., the document of which the event handler is a part), the document must first be opened, as we saw above. But opening a document discards any current contents, including any JavaScript code and function definitions. This means that the event handler calling document.write() on its own document cannot rely on any JavaScript functions defined in that document. In general, this technique is best avoided. If you want to dynamically generated documents without having multiple frames or windows visible, it is often easiest to use an invisible frame (one with zero height, for example) to hold the JavaScript code that does the document generation.

See Also

Document, Document.close(), Document.open(), Document.writeln(), Chapter 14

Document.writeln() Method — append data and newline to a document

Availability

Navigator 2.0, Internet Explorer 3.0

Synopsis

```
document.writeln(value, . . . )
```

Arguments

value   An arbitrary JavaScript value that is to be appended to *document*. If the value is not a string, it is converted to one before being appended.

. . .   Any number (zero or more) of additional values to be appended (in order) to *document*.

Returns

Nothing.

Description

Document.writeln() behaves just like Document.write() except that after appending all of its arguments to *document*, it also appends a newline character. See Document.write() for more information on this method.

Newline characters are not usually displayed in HTML documents, so in general, it is only useful to use Document.writeln() when writing text to appear in a <PRE> or <XMP> environment, or when writing to a document opened with a mime type of "text/plain".

See Also

Document, Document.clear( ), Document.close( ), Document.open( ), Document.write( )

Element Object — a form element

Availability

Navigator 2.0, Internet Explorer 3.0; enhanced in Navigator 3.0

Synopsis

```
form.elements[i]
form.name
```

Properties

checked
: A read/write Boolean that indicates the selection state of form elements that can appear "checked" or "unchecked."

defaultChecked
: A read-only Boolean that specifies the default state of a form element that can be "checked." This value is specified by the CHECKED attribute of the HTML tag that creates the element, and its value is used when the form is reset.

defaultValue
: A read-only string that specifies the default value for a form element. For elements that display text, this property specifies the initial value displayed, and the value displayed after the form is reset. This property corresponds to the HTML VALUE attributed.

form
: A read-only reference to the Form object that contains this element.

length
: For the Select form element, this property specifies the number of options or choices (each represented by an Option object) that are contained within the options[] array of the element.

name
: A read-only string, specified by the HTML NAME attribute, that specifies the name of this element. This name may be used to refer to the element, as shown in the synopsis above.

options[]
: For the Select form element, this array contains Option objects that represent the options or choices displayed by the Select object. The number of elements in the array is specified by the length property of the Select element.

selectedIndex
: For the Select form element, this integer specifies which of the options displayed by the Select object is currently selected. In Navigator 3.0, this property is read/write. In Navigator 2.0 and Internet Explorer 3.0, it is read-only.

type
: A read-only string property, available in Navigator 3.0, that specifies the type of the form element.

value   A string property that specifies the value to be sent to the server for this element when the form that contains it is submitted.

Methods

blur( )   Remove keyboard focus from the element.

click( )   Simulate a mouse-click on the form element.

focus( )   Give keyboard focus to the element.

select( )   For form elements that display editable text, select the text that appears in the element.

Event Handlers

onblur( )   Invoked when the user takes keyboard focus away from the element.

onchange( )   For form elements that are not buttons, this event handler is invoked when the user enters or selects a new value.

onclick( )   For form elements that are buttons, this event handler is invoked when the user clicks or selects the button.

onfocus( )   Invoked when the user gives keyboard focus to the element.

Description

Form elements are stored in the elements[] array of the Form object. The contents of this array are Element objects, which represent the individual buttons, input fields and other controls that appear within the form. Strictly speaking, all elements within a form are represented by Element objects. It is often more convenient, however, to consider these object to have the type of the form element they represent. Thus, in this book we often refer to Button objects, Text objects, Select objects, and so on. This reference page describes the general behavior of form elements. Specific behaviors for form elements are described on their own pages.

The Element object defines quite a few properties, methods, and event handlers, but not all of them are functional for each type of form element. For example, the Button object triggers the onclick( ) event handler, but not the onchange( ) handler, while the Text object triggers onchange( ) but not onclick( ). The following figure shows all of the form elements and the properties associated with them.

In general, there are two broad categories of form elements. The first is the buttons: Button, Checkbox, Radio, Reset, and Submit. These elements have an onclick( ) event handler, but not an onchange( ) handler. Similarly, they respond to the click( ) method but not the select( ) method. The second category are those elements that display text: Text, Textarea, Password and FileUpload. These elements have an onchange( ) event handler rather than an onclick( ) handler, and respond to the select( ) method but not the click( ) method.

The Select and Hidden elements are special, and do not fall into either of the above two categories. The Select element uses several properties of the Element object not used by any other objects, and, surprisingly does not use the value property—values for this object are supplied by the Option objects it contains. Finally, the Hidden element has no on-screen representation, so it does not have any event handlers nor does it respond to any methods.

ELEMENT	PROPERTY	checked	defaultChecked	defaultValue	form	length	name	options	selectedIndex	type	value	blur()	click()	focus()	select()	onblur()	onchange()	onclick()	onfocus()
Button					•		•			•	•	•	•	•		•		•	•
Checkbox		•	•		•		•			•	•	•	•	•		•		•	•
Radio		•	•		•		•			•	•	•	•	•		•		•	•
Reset					•		•			•	•	•	•	•		•		•	•
Submit					•		•			•	•	•	•	•		•		•	•
Text				•	•		•			•	•	•		•	•	•	•		•
Textarea				•	•		•			•	•	•		•	•	•	•		•
Password				•	•		•			•	•	•		•	•	•	•		•
FileUpload				•	•		•			•	•	•		•	•	•	•		•
Select					•	•	•	•	•	•		•		•		•	•		•
Hidden					•		•			•	•								

Figure: Form elements and their available properties

Bugs

Unfortunately, the behavior of form elements varies on different platforms, at least in Navigator 2.0 and Navigator 3.0 (Internet Explorer 3.0 only runs on one platform). On Unix platforms, which run the X11 window system, only the text-entry form elements participate in keyboard navigation, and so the button elements and the Select element do not respond to the blur() and focus() methods nor do they invoke the onblur() and onfocus() event handler. Also, on Unix systems, the Text element is the only one that responds to the select() method. On Windows platforms, on the other hand, all form elements are fully "wired in," and they all respond as noted in the table.

See Also

Button, Checkbox, FileUpload, Form, Hidden, Password, Radio, Reset, Select, Submit, Text, Textarea

---

Element.blur() Method — remove keyboard focus from a form element

Availability

Navigator 2.0, Internet Explorer 3.0

Synopsis

```
element.blur()
```

Arguments

None.

Returns

Nothing.

Description

The `blur()` method of a form element removes keyboard focus from that element without invoking the `onblur()` event handler; it is essentially the opposite of the `focus()` method. The `blur()` method does not transfer keyboard focus anywhere, however, so the only time that it is actually useful to call this method is directly before you plan to transfer keyboard focus elsewhere with the `focus()` method, when you don't want the `onblur()` event handler to be triggered. That is, by removing focus explicitly from the element, you won't be notified when it is removed implicitly by a `focus()` call on another element.

In fact, because it is poor user-interface design to remove keyboard focus without transferring it somewhere else, Internet Explorer 3.0 does not actually remove keyboard focus when you call `blur()`. Instead, on this platform, calling `blur()` on a form element simply puts that element in a special state so that it won't trigger its `onblur()` event handler when focus actually is transferred somewhere else (either by the program or by the user.) Since this is the only reasonable use for `blur()` anyway, this incompatibility should not be a problem.

All form elements other than Hidden support the `blur()` method. Unfortunately, not all platforms support keyboard navigation equally well. In Navigator 2.0 and 3.0 for Unix platforms, the `blur()` method is only functional for those form elements that display text: Text, Textarea, Password and FileUpload.

See Also

Element, Element.focus() , Element.onblur()

Element.checked Property — whether a Checkbox or Radio element is checked

Availability

Navigator 2.0, Internet Explorer 3.0

Synopsis

```
element.checked
```

Description

The `checked` property is a read/write Boolean that specifies whether a Checkbox or Radio form element is currently checked or not. You can set the state of these button elements by setting the value of this property. This property is not used by other form elements.

See Also

Checkbox, Element, Radio

Element.click() Method — simulate a mouse click on a form element

Availability

Navigator 2.0, Internet Explorer 3.0

Synopsis

```
element.click()
```

Arguments

None.

Returns

Nothing.

Description

The click() method of a form element simulates a mouse click on the form element, but does not invoke the onclick() event handler of the element.

The click() method is not often useful. Because it does not invoke the onClick() event handler, it is not useful to call this method on Button elements—they don't have any behavior other than that defined by the onClick() handler. Calling click() on a Submit or Reset element will submit or reset a form, but this can be more directly achieved with the submit() and reset() method of the Form object itself.

You can call click() on Radio and Checkbox elements to check or uncheck those buttons, but it is generally easier to simply set the checked property of those elements. Furthermore, click() does not work for these elements in Navigator 2.0 or 3.0 on Unix platforms.

On Windows (but not Unix) platforms, you can even call click() for Select elements, but doing so does not accomplish much. For Select objects implemented as drop-down menus, for example click() will cause the menu to drop down, but does not actually select an item from the menu. It is poor user-interface design to do this sort of thing—the user should always be in control of the form elements.

Finally, the click() method is *not* defined for the text input form elements: Text, Textarea, Password and FileUpload.

See Also

Element

Element.defaultChecked Property — a Checkbox or Radio element's default status

Availability

Navigator 2.0, Internet Explorer 3.0

Synopsis

```
element.defaultChecked
```

Description

The defaultChecked property is a read-only Boolean value that specifies whether a Checkbox or Radio element is checked by default. This property has no meaning for other form elements. This property corresponds to the CHECKED attribute in the HTML <INPUT> tag that created the form element. If CHECKED was present then defaultChecked will be true. Otherwise, defaultChecked will be false.

The defaultChecked property is used to restore the Checkbox or Radio element to its default value when the form is reset.

See Also

Checkbox, Element, Radio

Element.defaultValue Property — the default text displayed in an element

Availability

Navigator 2.0, Internet Explorer 3.0

Synopsis

    element.defaultValue

Description

The defaultValue property of a form element specifies the initial text that appears in the form element, and the value that is restored to that element when the form is reset. This property is only used by the Text, Textarea, and Password elements. It is not used by the FileUpload element for security reasons. For Checkbox and Radio elements the equivalent property is defaultChecked.

See Also

Element, Password, Text, Textarea

Element.focus() Method — give keyboard focus to a form element

Availability

Navigator 2.0, Internet Explorer 3.0

Synopsis

    element.focus()

Arguments

None.

Returns

Nothing.

Description

The focus() method of a form element transfers keyboard focus to that element without calling the onfocus() event handler. That is, it makes the element the active one with respect to keyboard navigation and keyboard input. Thus, if you call focus() for a Text element, then any text the user types will appear in that text element. Or, if you call focus() for Button element, then the user will be able to invoke that button from the keyboard.

All form elements, except the Hidden element support the focus() method. Unfortunately, not all platforms support keyboard navigation equally well. In Navigator 2.0 and 3.0 for Unix platforms, the focus() method is only functional for those form elements that display text: Text, Textarea, Password and FileUpload.

See Also

Element, Element.blur( ), Element.onfocus( )

Element.form Property — the Form containing the element

Availability

Navigator 2.0, Internet Explorer 3.0

Synopsis

```
element.form
```

Description

The form property of a form element is a read-only reference to the Form object that contains the specified element.

The form property allows the event handlers of one form element to easily refer to "sibling" elements in the same form. When an event handler is invoked, the this keyword refers to the form element for which it was invoked. Thus, an event handler can use the expression this.form to refer to the form that contains it. From there, it can refer to sibling elements by name, or it can use the elements[] array of the Form object to refer to them by number.

See Also

Element, Form

Element.length Property — see Select.length

Element.name Property — the name of a form element

Availability

Navigator 2.0, Internet Explorer 3.0

Synopsis

`element.name`

Description

`name` is a read-only string property of every form element. The value of this property is set by the `NAME` attributes of the HTML `<INPUT>` tag that defines the form element.

The name of a form element is used for two purposes. First, it is used when the form is submitted. Data for each element in the form is usually submitted in the format:

`name=value`

where `name` and `value` are encoded as necessary for transmission. If a name is not specified for a form element, then the data for that element cannot be meaningfully submitted to a web server.

The second use of the `name` property is to refer to a form element in JavaScript code. The name of an element becomes a property of the form that contains the element. The value of this property is a reference to the element. For example, if `address` is a form that contains a text input element with the name `zip`, then `address.zip` refers to that text input element.

With Radio and Checkbox form elements, it is common to define more than one related object, each of which have the same `name` property. In this case, data is submitted to the server with this format:

`name=value1,value2,...,valuen`

Similarly, in JavaScript, each of the elements that shares a name becomes an element of an array with that name. Thus if four Checkbox objects in the form `order` share the name "options," then they are available in JavaScript as elements of the array `order.options[ ]`.

Bugs

In Navigator 2.0, when multiple form elements are given the same name and placed in an array, they will only be placed in the array in the expected source order if they all define an event handler, even a dummy event handler that does nothing. If none of the elements define event-handlers, then they will be inserted into the array in reverse order. If some define event handlers and others don't, the order will be less predictable. In cases where array order actually matters, the workaround to this bug is to define dummy event handlers as needed.

See Also

Element

Element.onblur() Handler — invoked when a form element loses focus

Availability

Navigator 2.0, Internet Explorer 3.0

Synopsis

> `element.onblur`

Description

The `onblur()` event handler of a form element is invoked by the web browser when the user transfers keyboard focus away from that form element. Calling `blur()` to remove focus from an element does not invoke `onblur()` for that object. Note, however, that calling `focus()` to transfer focus to some other element will cause the `onblur()` event handler to be invoked for whatever element currently has the focus.

The `onblur()` event handler is a function defined through the `onBlur` attribute of the HTML tag that defined the form element. The value of this attribute is a string that may contain any number of JavaScript statements, separated by semicolons. In Navigator 3.0, the `onblur()` event handler may also be defined by assigning a function directly to the `onblur` property of an element.

The `onblur()` event handler is available for all form elements except the Hidden element. For Navigator 2.0 and 3.0 on Unix platforms, however, it is only invoked for the text-entry elements: Text, Textarea, Password and FileUpload. Note that in Navigator 3.0, the Window object also defines an `onblur()` event handler.

See Also

Element, Element.onchange(), Element.onclick(), Element.onfocus(),

---

Element.onchange() Handler — invoked when a form element's value changes

Availability

Navigator 2.0, Internet Explorer 3.0

Synopsis

> `element.onchange`

Description

The `onchange()` event handler of a form element is invoked by the web browser when the user changes the value displayed by a form element. Such a change may be an edit to the text displayed in Text, Textarea, Password, or FileUpload elements, or the selection or deselection of an option in a Select element. Note that this event handler is only invoked when the user makes such a change—it is not invoked if a JavaScript program changes the value displayed by an element.

Also note that the `onchange()` handler is not invoked every time the user enters or deletes a character in a text-entry form element. `onchange()` is not intended for that type of character-by-character event handling. Instead, `onchange()` is invoked when the user's edit is complete. The user assumes that the edit is complete when keyboard focus is moved to some other element—for example, when the user clicks on the next element in the form.

The `onchange()` event handler is a function defined through the `onchange` attribute of the HTML tag that defined the form element. The value of this attribute is a string that may contain any number of JavaScript statements, separated by semicolons. In Navigator 3.0, the `onchange()` event handler may also be defined by assigning a function directly to the `onchange` property of a form element.

The onchange() event handler is not used by the Hidden element, or by any of the button elements. Those elements, Button, Checkbox, Radio, Reset, and Submit use the onclick() event handler instead.

See Also

Element, Element.onblur( ), Element.onclick( ), Element.onfocus( )

Element.onclick() Handler — invoked when a form element is clicked

Availability

Navigator 2.0, Internet Explorer 3.0; enhanced in Navigator 3.0

Synopsis

```
element.onclick
```

Description

The onclick() event handler of a form element is invoked by the web browser when the user clicks on the element. Note, however, that it is not invoked when JavaScript calls the click() method of an element.

The onclick() event handler is a function defined through the onClick attribute of the HTML tag that defined the form element. The value of this attribute is a string that may contain any number of JavaScript statements, separated by semicolons. In Navigator 3.0, the onclick() event handler may also be defined by assigning a function directly to the onclick property of an element.

Only form elements that are buttons invoke the onclick() event handler. These are the Button, Checkbox, Radio, Reset and Submit elements. Other form elements use the onchange() event handler instead of onclick().

Note that the Reset and Submit elements perform a default action when clicked: they reset and submit, respectively, the form that they are a part of. You can use the onclick() event handlers of each of these elements to perform actions in addition to these default actions. In Navigator 3.0, you can also prevent these default actions from occurring by returning false. That is, if the onclick() handler of a Reset button returns false, then the form will not be reset, and if the onclick() handler of a Submit button returns false, then the form will not be submitted. Note that you do similar things with the onsubmit() and onreset() event handlers of the Form object itself.

Finally, note that Link object also defines an onclick() event handler.

See Also

Element, Element.onblur( ), Element.onchange( ), Element.onfocus( )

Element.onfocus() Handler — invoked when a form element gains focus

Availability

Navigator 2.0, Internet Explorer 3.0

Synopsis

```
element.onfocus
```

Description

The onfocus() event handler of a form element is invoked by the web browser when the user transfers the keyboard focus to that element. Note that it is not invoked when focus is programmatically transfered with the focus() method.

The onfocus() event handler is a function defined through the onFocus attribute of the HTML tag that defined the element. The value of this attribute is a string that may contain any number of JavaScript statements, separated by semicolons. In Navigator 3.0, the onfocus() event handler may also be defined by assigning a function directly to the onfocus property of the element.

The onfocus() event handler is available for all form elements except the Hidden element. For Navigator 2.0 and 3.0 on Unix platforms, however, it is only invoked for the text-entry elements: Text, Textarea, Password and FileUpload. Note that in Navigator 3.0, the Window object also defines an onfocus() event handler.

See Also

Element, Element.onblur(), Element.onchange(), Element.onclick()

Element.options[] Property — see Select.options[]

Element.select() Method — select the text in form element

Availability

Navigator 2.0, Internet Explorer 3.0

Synopsis

```
element.select()
```

Arguments

None.

Returns

Nothing.

Description

The select() method selects the text displayed in a Text, Textarea, Password, or File-Upload element. The effects of selecting text may vary from platform to platform, but typically invoking this method produces the same effect as if the user had dragged the mouse across all the text in the specified Text object. On most platforms, this produces the following effects:

- The text is highlighted, often displayed with colors reversed.

- If the text remains selected the next time the user types a character, then the selected text will be deleted and replaced with the newly typed character.

- The text becomes available for cut-and-paste.

The user can usually deselect text by clicking in the Text object or by moving the cursor. Once deselected, the user can add and delete individual characters without replacing the entire text value.

Usage

Selecting a string in a Text object like this can be useful when you want to allow the user to accept the string as it is or to replace it entirely and enter a new value from scratch.

Bugs

On Unix platforms in Navigator 2.0 and 3.0, the `select()` method only works for the Text element, and not for the Textarea, Password or FileUpload elements.

See Also

Element

Element.selectedIndex Property — see Select.selectedIndex

Element.type Property — the type of a form element

Availability

Navigator 3.0

Synopsis

```
element.type
```

Description

`type` is a read-only string property of all form elements. It specifies the type of the form element. The value of this property for each possible form element is given in the following table.

Note that the Select element has two possible `type` values, depending on whether it allows single or multiple selection. Also note, that unlike all other element properties, `type` is not available in Navigator 2.0 or Internet Explorer 3.0.

Object Type	HTML Tag	type Property
Button	`<INPUT TYPE=button>`	"button"
Checkbox	`<INPUT TYPE=checkbox>`	"checkbox"
FileUpload	`<INPUT TYPE=file>`	"file"
Hidden	`<INPUT TYPE=hidden>`	"hidden"

Object Type	HTML Tag	type Property
Password	`<INPUT TYPE=password>`	"password"
Radio	`<INPUT TYPE=radio>`	"radio"
Reset	`<INPUT TYPE=reset>`	"reset"
Select	`<SELECT>`	"select-one"
Select	`<SELECT MULTIPLE>`	"select-multiple"
Submit	`<INPUT TYPE=submit>`	"submit"
Text	`<INPUT TYPE=text>`	"text"
Textarea	`<TEXTAREA>`	"textarea"

See Also

Element

Element.value Property — value displayed or submitted by a form element

Availability

Navigator 2.0, buggy in Internet Explorer 3.0

Synopsis

    element.value

Description

`value` is a read/write string property of all form elements. It specifies the value that is displayed by the form element and/or submitted for the element when the form is submitted. The `value` property of the Text element, for example, is the user's input, which is also the value submitted with the form. For the Checkbox object, on the other hand, the `value` property specifies a string that is not displayed, but which will be submitted with the form if the Checkbox element is checked when the form is submitted.

The initial value of the `value` property is specified by the `VALUE` attribute of the HTML tag that defines the form element.

For Button, Submit, and Reset objects, the `value` property specifies the text to appear within the button. On some platforms, changing the `value` property of these elements will actually change the text displayed by the buttons on-screen. This does not work on all platforms, however, and is not an advisable technique because changing the label of a button may change the size of the button, and cause it to overlap and obscure other portions of the document.

The Select element has a `value` property, like all form elements, but does not use it. Instead, the value submitted by this element is specified by the `value` property of the Option objects it contains.

In Navigator 2.0 and Internet Explorer 3.0, the `value` property of the Password object is nonfunctional for security purposes. It can be read and written, but this has no bearing on the value entered by the user, or submitted with the form. In Navigator 3.0, when the data-tainting security model is enabled, the `value` property does actually contain the user's input to this element.

A limitation of Internet Explorer 3.0 only allows strings to be assigned to the `value` property of HTML form elements. If you want to assign objects to this property, you must explicitly convert them to strings by, for example, adding the empty string to them. Thus, to display the current date and time in a text field, Internet Explorer requires code like this:

```
var today = new Date();
document.forms[0].elements[1].value = "" + today;
```

Bugs

Internet Explorer 3.0 does not automatically convert objects to strings when they are assigned to this property; you must explicitly perform that conversion yourself.

See Also

Element, Element.name

Embed Object — see Document.embeds[] and JavaObject

---

escape() Function — encode a string for transmission

Availability

Navigator 2.0, Internet Explorer 3.0

Synopsis

```
escape(s)
```

Arguments

s   The string that is to be "escaped" or encoded.

Returns

An encoded copy of s.

Description

The `escape()` function is a built-in part of JavaScript; it is not a method of any object.

`escape()` creates and returns a new string that contains an encoded version of s. The string s itself is not modified.

The string is encoded as follows: all spaces, punctuation, accented characters, and any other characters that are not ASCII letters or numbers are converted to the form %*xx*, where *xx* is two hexadecimal digits that represent the ISO-8859-1 (Latin-1) encoding of the character. For example, the ! character has the Latin-1 encoding of 33, which is 21 hexadecimal, so `escape()` replaces this character with the sequence %21. Thus the expression:

```
escape("Hello World!");
```

yields the string:

```
Hello%20World%21
```

The purpose of the escape() encoding is to ensure that the string is portable to all computers, and transmittable across all networks, regardless of the character encodings the computers or networks support (as long as they support ASCII, however).

The encoding performed by escape() is like the standard URL-encoding used to encode query strings and other portions of a URL that might include spaces, punctuation, or characters outside of the standard ASCII character set. The only difference is that in the URL encoding, spaces are replaced with a '+' character, while escape() replaces spaces with the %20 sequence.

Usage

Use the unescape() function to decode a string encoded with escape().

A common use of escape() is to encode cookie values, which have restrictions on the punctuation characters they may contain. See Document.cookie.

See Also

String, unescape()

---

eval() Function — execute JavaScript code from a string

Availability

Navigator 2.0, Internet Explorer 3.0; changed in Navigator 3.0

Synopsis

```
eval(code)
```

Arguments

code   A string that contains the JavaScript expression to be evaluated or the statements to be executed.

Returns

The value of the evaluated *code*, if any.

Description

The eval() function of Navigator 2.0 has been changed to a method of Object in Navigator 3.0. See Object.eval() for complete details.

See Also

Object.eval()

FileUpload Element — a file upload field for form input

Availability

Navigator 2.0, Internet Explorer 3.0

Synopsis

```
form.name
form.elements[i]
```

Properties

form   A read-only reference to the Form object that contains the FileUpload element.

name   A read-only string, set by the HTML NAME attribute, that specifies the name of the FileUpload element. This is also the *element_name* that can be used to reference the FileUpload element as a property of its form.

type   A read-only string that specifies the type of this form element. For FileUpload elements, it has the value "file." Available in Navigator 3.0 and later.

value   A read-only string that specifies the value contained in the input field (which is also the value sent to the server when the form is submitted.) In Navigator 2.0, this field is always blank. In Navigator 3.0 any filename specified by the user may be read, but the property still may not be set.

Methods

blur()   Remove the keyboard focus from the FileUpload element.

focus()   Set the keyboard focus to the FileUpload element. When focus is set, all keystrokes are automatically entered into this element.

select() Highlight all the text in the FileUpload element, and enter a special mode so that future input replaces the highlighted text.

Event Handlers

onblur()   Invoked when a user action causes the FileUpload element to lose the keyboard focus.

onchange() Invoked when the user changes the value in the FileUpload element and moves the keyboard focus elsewhere. This event handler is not invoked for every keystroke in the FileUpload element, but only when the user completes an edit.

onfocus()   Invoked when a user action causes the FileUpload element to gain the keyboard focus.

HTML Syntax

A FileUpload element is created with a standard HTML <INPUT> tag, with the addition of optional attributes for event handlers:

```
<FORM ENCTYPE="multipart/form-data"
      METHOD=post>                    required attributes

   ...
  <INPUT
    TYPE"file"                        specifies that this is a FileUpload element
    [ NAME="name" ]                   a name that can later be used to refer to this element
                                      specifies the name property
    [ SIZE=integer ]                  how many characters wide the element is
```

```
    [ MAXLENGTH=integer ]                  max allowed number of input characters
    [ onBlur="handler" ]                   the onblur( ) event handler
    [ onChange="handler" ]                 the onchange( ) event handler
    [ onFocus="handler" ]                  the onfocus( ) event handler
>

    . . .
```

Description

The FileUpload element represents a file upload input element in a form. In many respects, this input element is much like the Text element. On the screen, it appears like a text input field, with the addition of a **Browse** . . . button that opens a directory browser. Entering a filename into a FileUpload element (either directly or through the browser) will cause Netscape to submit the contents of that file along with the form. For this to work, the form must use "multipart/form-data" encoding and the POST method.

The FileUpload element does not have a `defaultValue` property, and does not recognize the `VALUE` HTML attribute to specify an initial value for the input field. Similarly, the `value` property of the FileUpload element is read-only. Only the user may enter a filename; JavaScript may not enter text into the FileUpload field in any way. This is to prevent malicious JavaScript programs from uploading arbitrary files (such as password files) off of the user's machine.

See Also

Element, Form, Text

FileUpload.blur( ) Method — see Element.blur( )

FileUpload.focus( ) Method — see Element.focus( )

FileUpload.form Property — see Element.form

FileUpload.name Property — see Element.name

FileUpload.onblur( ) Handler — see Element.onblur( )

FileUpload.onchange( ) Handler — invoked when input value changes

Availability

Navigator 2.0, Internet Explorer 3.0

Synopsis

```
<INPUT TYPE=file
       onChange="handler-statements" . . . >    a definition of the handler
    fileupload.onchange                         a reference to the handler
    fileupload.onchange();                       an explicit invocation of the handler
```

Description

The `FileUpload.onchange()` event handler is defined by the `onChange` attribute of the `<INPUT>` HTML tag that defines the FileUpload object. The value of this attribute may be any number of JavaScript statements, separated by semicolons; these statements will be executed whenever the user changes the value in the input field and then "commits" those changes by moving keyboard focus elsewhere (i.e., by clicking the mouse elsewhere or by typing the **Tab** or **Return** keys). This handler is intended to process a complete change to the input value, and therefore is not invoked on a keystroke-by-keystroke basis.

Note that in Navigator 2.0, the user's input into a FileUpload object is entirely hidden from JavaScript, so the `onchange()` event handler is of limited use. In Navigator 3.0, the `FileUpload.value` property may be read but not written.

See Also

FileUpload, FileUpload.blur( ), FileUpload.focus( ), FileUpload.onblur( )

FileUpload.onfocus() Handler — see Element.onfocus( )

FileUpload.select() Method — see Element.select( )

FileUpload.type Property — see Element.type

FileUpload.value Property — filename selected by the user

Availability

Navigator 3.0

Synopsis

```
fileupload.value
```

Description

`value` is a read-only string property of the FileUpload object. It specifies the filename entered by the user into the FileUpload object. The user may enter a filename either by typing it directly or by using the directory browser associated with the FileUpload object.

To prevent malicious programs from uploading arbitrary files from the client, this property may not be set by JavaScript code. Similarly, the `VALUE` attribute of the `<INPUT>` tag does not specify a default value for this property.

In Navigator 2.0, reading the `value` property will always return the empty string.

See Also

FileUpload

focus() Method — see Window.focus()

Form Object — an HTML input form

Availability

Navigator 2.0, Internet Explorer 3.0

Synopsis

```
document.form_name
document.forms[form_number]
document.forms.length
```

Properties

action   A read/write string specifying the URL to which the form is to be submitted. Initially specified by the ACTION attribute.

elements[]   An array of input elements that appear in the form. Each element is a Button, Checkbox, Hidden, Password, Radio, Reset, Select, Submit, Text, or Textarea object.

elements.length
              The number of items in the elements[] array.

encoding   A read/write string that specifies the encoding method used for form data. Initially specified by the ENCTYPE attribute. The default encoding of "application/x-www-form-urlencoded" is almost always appropriate.

method   A read/write string that specifies the technique for submitting the form. It should have the value "get" or "post". Initially specified by the METHOD attribute.

target   A read/write string that specifies the name of the frame or window in which the results of submitting a form should be displayed. Initially specified by the TARGET attribute. The special names "_top", "_parent", "_self", and "_blank" are also supported for the target property and the TARGET attribute.

Methods

reset()   Reset each of the input elements of the form to their default values.

submit()   Submit the form.

Event Handlers

onreset()   An event handler invoked just before the elements of the form are reset. Specified by the onReset attribute.

onsubmit()   An event handler that is invoked just before the form is submitted. Specified by the onSubmit attribute. This event handler allows form entries to be validated before being submitted.

HTML Syntax

A Form object is created with a standard HTML <FORM> tag. JavaScript adds the optional onReset and onSubmit event-handler attributes to this tag. The form contains any input elements created with the <INPUT> tag between <FORM> and </FORM>.

```
<FORM
     [ NAME="form_name" ]            used to name the form in JavaScript
     [ TARGET="window_name" ]       the name of the window for responses
     [ ACTION="url" ]               the URL to which the form is submitted
     [ METHOD=(GET|POST) ]          the method of form submission
     [ ENCTYPE="encoding" ]         how the form data is encoded
     [ onReset="handler" ]          a handler invoked when form is reset
     [ onSubmit="handler" ]         a handler invoked when form is submitted
>
                                    form text and <INPUT> tags go here
</FORM>
```

Description

The Form object represents an HTML <FORM> in a document. Each form in a document is represented as an element of the Document.forms[] array. Named forms are also represented by the *form_name* property of their document, where *form_name* is the name specified in the NAME attribute of the <FORM> tag.

The elements of a form (buttons, input fields, check boxes, and so on) are collected in the Form.elements[] array. Named elements, like named forms, can also be referenced directly by name—the element name is used as a property name of the Form object. Thus, to refer to a Text object element named "phone" within a form named "questionnaire," you might use the JavaScript expression:

```
document.questionnaire.phone
```

See the descriptions of the Form properties and methods for more information about this object.

See Also

Button, Checkbox, Element, FileUpload, Hidden, Password, Radio, Reset, Select, Submit, Text, Textarea

---

Form.action Property — the URL for form submission

Availability

Navigator 2.0; implemented but nonfunctional in Internet Explorer 3.0

Synopsis

```
form.action
```

Description

`action` is a read/write string property of the Form object. It specifies the URL to which the form data will be sent when the form is submitted. The initial value of this property is specified by the `ACTION` attribute of the `<FORM>` HTML tag. Usually, this URL specifies a CGI script, although it can also be a `mailto:` address.

You can set this property in Internet Explorer 3.0, but doing so will have no effect on how the form is submitted.

See Also

Form

Form.elements[] Property — the input elements of the form

Availability

Navigator 2.0, Internet Explorer 3.0

Synopsis

```
form.elements[i]
form.elements.length
```

Description

`form.elements` is an array of the form input objects in `form`. The array has `elements.length` items in it. These items may be of any of the form input element types: Button, Checkbox, Hidden, Password, Radio, Reset, Select, Submit, Text, and Textarea. These form input objects appear in the array in the same order that they appear in the HTML source code for the form.

Usage

If an item in the `form.elements[]` array has been given a name with the `NAME="name"` attribute of its HTML `<INPUT>` tag, then that item's name becomes a property of `form`, and this property refers to the item. Thus, it is possible to refer to input objects by name instead of by number:

refer to its value as form.name.value

```
form.name
```

Usually, referring to elements by name is easier, and it is therefore a good idea to specify the `NAME` attribute for all form elements.

See Also

Button, Checkbox, Element, Form, Hidden, Password, Radio, Reset, Select, Submit, Text, Textarea

Form.encoding Property — the encoding of form data

Availability

Navigator 2.0; implemented but nonfunctional in Internet Explorer 3.0

Synopsis

```
form.encoding
```

Description

`encoding` is a read/write string property of the Form object. It specifies how form data is encoding for transmission when the form is submitted. The initial value of this property is specified by the `ENCTYPE` attribute of the `<FORM>` tag. The default value is "application/x-www-form-urlencoded", which is sufficient for almost all purposes. Other values may sometimes be necessary. For example, a value of "text/plain" is convenient when the form is being submitted by email to a `mailto:` URL. See O'Reilly's book *CGI Programming on the World Wide Web*, by Shishir Gundavaram, for further information.

You can set this property in Internet Explorer 3.0, but doing so will have no effect on how the form is encoded.

See Also

Form

Form.method Property — the submission method for the form

Availability

Navigator 2.0; implemented but nonfunctional in Internet Explorer 3.0

Synopsis

```
form.method
```

Description

`method` is a read/write string property of the Form object. It specifies the method by which form data is submitted. The initial value of this property is specified by the `METHOD` attribute of the `<FORM>` tag. The two legal values are `GET` and `POST`.

The `GET` method is the default. It is usually used for form submissions such as database queries that do not have side effects. With this method, the encoded form data is appended to the URL specified by the `Form.action` property. CGI scripts receiving a form submitted by this method generally read the form data from the `QUERY_STRING` environment variable.

The `POST` method is appropriate for form submissions, such as additions to databases, that have side effects. With this method, encoded form data is sent in the HTTP request body, and is available to CGI scripts that read from the standard input stream.

Consult *CGI Programming on the World Wide Web* if you are not sure which method to use or how to write a CGI script to receive data submitted from a form.

You can set this property in Internet Explorer 3.0, but doing so will have no effect on how the form is submitted.

See Also

Form

Form.onreset() Handler — invoked when a form is reset

Availability

Navigator 3.0

Synopsis

```
<FORM
    onReset="handler-statements"     a definition of the handler
      ...attributes...               other attributes here
>

form.onreset                         a reference to the handler
form.onreset();                      an explicit invocation of the handler
```

Description

onreset() is an event handler of the Form object, and is invoked when the form is reset, either through the Form.reset() method or when the user clicks on a Reset button.

This event handler is defined by the onReset attribute of the <FORM> tag that defines a form. The value of this attribute may be any number of JavaScript statements, separated by semicolons; these statements will be executed when the form is submitted.

If the onreset() handler returns false, then the elements of the form will not be reset.

Example

You could use the following event-handler to ask the user to confirm that they really want to reset the form:

```
<FORM ...
    onReset="return confirm('Really erase all entered data?')"
>
```

See Also

Form, Form.onsubmit(), Form.reset()

Form.onsubmit() Handler — invoked when a form is submitted

Availability

Navigator 2.0, Internet Explorer 3.0

Synopsis

```
<FORM
    onSubmit="handler-statements"    a definition of the handler
      ...attributes...               other attributes here
>
form.onsubmit                        a reference to the handler
form.onsubmit();                     an explicit invocation of the handler
```

Description

onsubmit( ) is an event handler which is invoked when the form it is associated with is submitted, either when the user clicks a Submit button object, or when the submit( ) method is called for the form. This event handler is defined by the onSubmit attribute of the <FORM> tag that defines a form. The value of the attribute may be any number of JavaScript statements, separated by semicolons; these statements will be executed when the form is submitted.

A typical use of the onsubmit( ) event handler is to check that the user's input is valid before sending it over the network to a server. If the data is not valid, the onsubmit( ) handler may cancel form submission by returning the value false. If the handler returns any other value, or returns no value at all then the form will be submitted normally.

Usage

Whenever you use the onsubmit( ) event handler to cancel the submission of a form, you should be sure to notify the user why the submission was canceled, so that they can correct the problem. Window.alert( ) is a useful way to provide this information to the user.

See Also

Form, Form.submit( )

Form.reset( ) Method — reset the elements of a form

Availability

Navigator 3.0

Synopsis

```
form.reset( )
```

Arguments

None.

Returns

Nothing.

Description

The reset( ) method resets the specified form, restoring each element of the form to its default value, exactly as if a Reset button had been pressed by the user. The form's onreset( ) event handler is first invoked, and may prevent the reset from occurring by returning the value false.

See Also

Form, Form.onreset( )

Form.submit() Method — submit a form

Availability

Navigator 2.0, Internet Explorer 3.0

Synopsis

```
form.submit()
```

Arguments

None.

Returns

Nothing.

Description

The submit() method submits the specified *form*, almost as if a **Submit** button had been pressed by the user. The form is submitted as specified by the action, method and encoding properties of *form* (or the ACTION, METHOD, and ENCTYPE attributes of the <FORM> tag), and the results are displayed in the window or frame specified by the target property or the TARGET attribute.

The one important difference between the submit() method and form submission by the user is that the onsubmit() event handler is not invoked when submit() is called. If you use onsubmit() to perform input validation, for example, you'll have to do that validation explicitly before calling submit().

Usage

It is more common to use a **Submit** button to allow the user to submit the form than it is to call the submit() method yourself.

See Also

Form, Form.onsubmit(), Submit

Form.target Property — the window for form results

Availability

Navigator 2.0; implemented but nonfunctional in Internet Explorer 3.0

Synopsis

```
form.target
```

Description

target is a read/write string property of the Form object. It specifies the name of the frame or window in which the results of the submission of *form* should be displayed. The initial value of this property is specified by the TARGET attribute of the <FORM> tag. If unset, the default is for form submission results to appear in the same window as the form.

Note that the value of target is the *name* of a frame or window, not the actual frame or window itself. The name of a frame is specified by the NAME attribute of the <FRAME> tag. The name of a window is specified when the window is created with a call to the

`Window.open()` method. If `target` specifies the name of a window that does not exist, then Navigator will automatically open a new window to display the results of form submission, and any future forms with the same `target` name will use the same newly created window.

Four special target names are supported. The target named `"_blank"` specifies that a new, empty browser window should be created and used to display the results of the form submission. The target `"_self"` is the default; it specifies that the form submission results should be displayed in the same frame or window as the form itself. The target `"_parent"` specifies that the results should be displayed in the parent frame of the frame that contains the form. Finally, the `"_top"` target specifies that the results should be displayed in the topmost frame—i.e., that all frames should be removed, and the results should occupy the entire browser window.

You can set this property in Internet Explorer 3.0, but doing so will have no effect on the actual target of the form.

See Also

Form, Link.target

Frame Object — a type of Window object

Availability

Navigator 2.0, Internet Explorer 3.0

Synopsis

```
window.frames[i]
window.frames.length
frames[i]
frames.length
```

Description

Though the Frame object is sometimes referred to, there is, strictly speaking, no such object. All frames within a browser window are instances of the Window object, and they contain the same properties and support the same methods and event handlers as the Window object does. See the Window object, and its properties, methods, and event handlers for details.

There are a few practical differences between Window objects that represent top-level browser windows, and those that represent frames within a browser window, however:

- When the `defaultStatus` property is set for a frame, the specified status message is only visible when the mouse is within that frame.

- The `top` and `parent` properties of a top-level browser window always refer to the top-level window itself. These properties are only really useful for frames.

- The `close()` method is not useful for Window objects that are frames.

See Also
Window

---

frames[] Property — see Window.frames[]

Function Object — a JavaScript function

Availability
Navigator 2.0, Internet Explorer 3.0; enhanced in Navigator 3.0

Synopsis

```
function functionname(argname1 [, ... argname_n])
{
     body
}
```

Constructor

```
new Function([argname1 [, ..., argname_n]], body) Navigator 3.0 only
```

Arguments

argname1, ..., argname_n
> Any number of string arguments, each one of which names one argument of the Function object being created.

body
> A string that specifies the body of the function. It may contain any number of JavaScript statements, separated with semicolons.

Returns

The newly created Function object.

Properties

arguments[ ] An array of arguments that were passed to the function.

arguments.length
> The number of elements in the arguments[ ] array.

caller
> A reference to the Function object that invoked this this one, or null if the function is invoked at the top level.

prototype
> An object which, for constructor functions, defines properties and methods that will be shared by all objects created with that constructor function.

Methods

toString() Return a string representation of the function.

Description

A function is a fundamental data type in JavaScript. Chapter 6, explains how to define and use functions. The Function object is an object wrapper around the basic function data type; this object type exists so that functions can have properties and methods associated with them. When a function value is used in an "object context"—i.e., when you attempt to invoke a method or read a property of a function, JavaScript internally converts the function value into a temporary Function object, so that the method can be invoked or the property value read.

In Navigator 3.0, you can also use the `Function()` constructor method shown above to create your own Function objects. Functions defined in this way are sometimes called "anonymous" functions, because they are not given a name when they are created. Chapter 6 discusses the definition and use of anonymous functions. Just as JavaScript converts from a function value to a Function object whenever necessary, so it will convert from a Function object (created with the `Function()` constructor) to a function value whenever you use the object in a function value context—i.e., whenever you invoke it with the `()` operator. This conversion from Function object to function value is done by the `valueOf()` method.

The `arguments[]` and `caller` properties of the Function object are unusual because they may only be accessed from within the body of a function. That is, they are only defined for a Function object while that function is being executed. There is no special keyword in JavaScript that refers to the currently executing function, so you must refer to Function objects by name. For example:

```
function myfunc()
{
    if (myfunc.arguments.length == 0) return;
        . . .
}
```

Because JavaScript is loosely typed language, it does not care what number or type of arguments you pass to a function, even if you provided argument names when you defined the function. The `arguments[]` property is an array containing whatever arguments were passed to the function. You can use this array to implement functions that can handle any number of arguments correctly.

The `caller` property refers to the function that called this one. You can print out the `caller` for debugging purposes, and you can even use this property to invoke the calling function—creating a strange sort of recursion.

Note that the `arguments` property is actually just a reference to the Function object itself. Therefore, instead of typing *function*.arguments[i] and *function*.arguments.length you can just use *function*[i] and *function*.length. Although using the `arguments` property is unnecessary, it often makes for clearer code, and is the officially supported way to access function arguments.

Finally, the `prototype` property of the Function object is a very powerful one. It refers to a "prototype" object from which other objects "inherit" properties and methods. When a function is used as a constructor function, any objects created with that constructor will inherit the properties and methods defined in the `prototype` object of the constructor. Prototype objects and the `prototype` property are discussed in Chapter 7.

See Also

Object, Chapter 6, Chapter 7

Function.arguments[] Property — arguments passed to a function

Availability

Navigator 2.0, Internet Explorer 3.0

Synopsis

```
function.arguments[i]
function.arguments.length
```

Description

The `arguments` property of a Function object is an array of the arguments that are passed to a function. `arguments.length` specifies the number of elements in the array. JavaScript allows any number and any type of arguments to be passed to a function, and the `arguments[]` array allows you to write functions that can gracefully accept a variable number of arguments.

If the function was defined with n argument names, then the first n elements in the `arguments[]` array may also be referenced through the defined argument names.

See Function for more details on the use of this property.

See Also

Function

Function.caller Property — the function that called this one

Availability

Navigator 2.0, Internet Explorer 3.0

Synopsis

```
function.caller
```

Description

The `caller` property of a Function object is a reference to the function that invoked the current one. If the function was invoked from the top level of a JavaScript program, then `caller` will be `null`. This property may only be used from within the function, i.e., the `caller` property is only defined for a function while that function is executing.

See Function for more information.

See Also

Function

Function.prototype Property — the prototype for a class of objects

Availability

Navigator 3.0, Internet Explorer 3.0

Synopsis

```
function.prototype
```

Description

The `prototype` property of a function is only useful when the function is used as a constructor function. It refers to an object, which is initially empty—i.e., has no properties or methods defined.

The `prototype` object serves as a prototype for an entire class of objects. This is because any objects created through a constructor function will "inherit" the properties and methods defined in that prototype. This "inheritance" is done in a way that does not consume any memory in the inheriting object. When you use a property or invoke a method in the context of an inheriting object, the object's own properties and methods are first checked. If the property or method you specified is not found there, JavaScript then checks the properties and methods of the prototype object. This means that when you add properties to a prototype object, those properties will immediately appear to have been added to any existing instances of the corresponding object type.

Note that prototypes are not shared across windows. If you add a method to the `String.prototype` object in one window, then all strings in that window will have access to this new method. Strings defined in other windows, however, will not see the new method.

In Navigator 3.0, a prototype object is not created for a constructor function until the constructor is used to create an object for the first time. Thus, in Navigator 3.0, you must create and discard a dummy object with a constructor function before you can assign values to the constructor's prototype object. This is not necessary in Internet Explorer 3.0.

The title of this page is "Function.prototype". Note that there are two possible meanings for this title. The first, and the intended one, is that this page documents the `prototype` property shared by all Function objects. But note that all constructor functions have a `prototype` property and `Function()` is a constructor function. Therefore, this page could also be documenting the `prototype` property of the `Function()` constructor. In a sense it is: you can add new properties or methods to all JavaScript Function objects by setting those properties and methods in the `Function.prototype` object.

Usage

Prototypes are one of the main techniques for defining the features of an object type or "class" in JavaScript. They are particularly useful in providing methods and constants for use with a whole class of objects. They are also useful for defining properties with default values which individual objects may optionally override.

The prototype object can also be used to add new properties or methods to many predefined JavaScript object types as well, as the following example shows.

Example

The following code shows how you could add a new method to the String object type by specifying the method on the `prototype` object:

```
// Define a function
function String_output(d) { d.write(this); }
// Set it as a method in the String.prototype object
String.prototype.output = String_output;
// Use it like this
"Hello World!".output(document);
```

In Navigator 3.0, this code makes the new `output()` method available for all strings in the current window. In Internet Explorer 3.0, however, it only makes the method available for String objects, not primitive strings. This misfeature will be fixed in a future release.

As another example, consider the Window object. It has a `top` property that refers to the top-level web browser window. Suppose you wanted *all* objects in your JavaScript application to contain a reference to this top-level window. You could implement this with a single line of code:

```
Object.prototype.top = self.top;
```

After executing this code, any JavaScript object (all current and future objects) that does not already have a `top` property will now have one, and it will refer to the top-level window `self.top`.

Bugs

Navigator 3.0 requires a constructor to be used once before anything can be assigned to its prototype object. Internet Explorer 3.0 does not allow primitive strings to use methods or properties defined in `String.prototype`. Similarly, Internet Explorer 3.0 does not support prototype objects for the Boolean, Number, and Function objects.

See Also

Chapter 7

Function.toString() Method — convert a function to a string

Availability

Navigator 2.0, Internet Explorer 3.0

Synopsis

```
function.toString()
```

Arguments

None.

Returns

A string that represents the function.

Description

The toString() method of the Function object converts a function to a string. In Navigator 2.0 and 3.0, it returns a string of valid JavaScript code—code that includes the function keyword, argument list, the complete body of the function, and so on. In Internet Explorer 3.0, the toString() method returns a string that identifies the function but that does not include the JavaScript code that constitutes the function.

See Also

Function, Object.toString()

getClass() Function — return the JavaClass of a JavaObject

Availability

Navigator 3.0

Synopsis

```
getClass(javaobj)
```

Arguments

javaobj   A JavaObject object.

Returns

The JavaClass object of javaobj.

Description

getClass() is a function that takes a JavaObject object (javaobj) as an argument. It returns the JavaClass object that JavaObject. That is, it returns the JavaClass object that represents the Java class of the Java object represented by the specified JavaObject.

Usage

Don't confuse the JavaScript getClass() function with the *getClass* method of all Java objects. Similarly, don't confuse the JavaScript JavaClass object with the Java *java.lang.Class* class.

Consider the Java rectangle object created with the following line:

```
var r = new java.awt.Rectangle();
```

r is a JavaScript variable that holds a JavaObject object. Calling the JavaScript function get-Class() returns a JavaClass object that represents the *java.awt.Rectangle* class:

```
var c = getClass(r);
```

You can see that this is so by comparing this JavaClass object to java.awt.Rectangle:

```
if (c == java.awt.Rectangle) ...
```

The Java getClass() method is invoked differently and performs an entirely different function:

```
c = r.getClass();
```

After executing the above line of code, c is a JavaObject that represents a *java.lang.Class* object. This *java.lang.Class* object is a Java object that is a Java representation of the *java.awt.Rectangle* class. See your Java documentation for details on what you can do with the *java.lang.Class* class.

To summarize, you can see that the following expression will always evaluate to true, for any JavaObject o:

```
(getClass(o.getClass()) == java.lang.Class)
```

See Also

java, JavaArray, JavaClass, JavaObject, JavaPackage, Packages, Chapter 19

Hidden Element — hidden data for client/server communication

Availability

Navigator 2.0, Internet Explorer 3.0; enhanced in Navigator 3.0

Synopsis

```
form.name
form.elements[i]
```

Properties

form
: A read-only reference to the Form object that contains the Hidden element.

name
: A read-only string, set by the HTML NAME attribute, that specifies the name of the Hidden element. This is also the *name* that can be used to reference the Hidden element as a property of its form.

type
: A read-only string that specifies the type of this form element. For Hidden elements, it has the value "hidden." Available in Navigator 3.0 and later.

value
: A read/write string, initially set by the HTML VALUE attribute, which specifies arbitrary data to be transmitted to the server when the form is submitted. This data is never visible to the user.

HTML Syntax

A Hidden element is created with a standard HTML <INPUT> tag:

```
<FORM>
   ...
  <INPUT
    TYPE="hidden"        specifies that this is a Hidden element
    [ NAME="name" ]      a name that can later be used to refer to this element
                         specifies the name property
    [ VALUE="value" ]    the value transmitted when the form is submitted
                         specifies the initial value of the value property
  >
```

```
    . . .
</FORM>
```

Description

The Hidden element is an invisible form element that allows arbitrary data to be transmitted to the server when the form is submitted. You can use a Hidden element when you want to transmit additional information, besides the user's input data, to the server.

When an HTML document is generated on-the-fly by a server, another use of Hidden form elements is to transmit data from the server to the client for later processing by JavaScript on the user's side. For example, the server might transmit raw data to the client in a compact machine readable form by specifying the data in the VALUE attribute of a Hidden element or elements. On the client side, a JavaScript program (transmitted along with the data or in another frame) could read the value property of the Hidden element or elements and process, format, and display that data in a less compact human-readable (and perhaps user-configurable) format.

Hidden elements can also be useful for communication between CGI scripts, even without the intervention of JavaScript on the client side. In this usage, one CGI script generates a dynamic HTML page containing hidden data, which is then submitted back to a second CGI script. This hidden data can communicate state information, such as the results of submission of a previous form.

Usage

Cookies can also be used to transmit data from client to server. An important difference between hidden form elements and cookies, however, is that cookies are persistent on the client side.

See Also

Element, Form, Document.cookie

Hidden.form Property — see Element.form

Hidden.name Property — see Element.name

Hidden.type Property — see Element.type

Hidden.value Property — arbitrary data submitted with a form

Availability

Navigator 2.0, Internet Explorer 3.0

Synopsis

```
hidden.value
```

Description

value is a read/write string property of the Hidden object. It specifies arbitrary data that is passed to the web server when the form containing the Hidden object is submitted. The initial value of value is specified by the VALUE attribute of the <INPUT> tag that defines the Hidden object. See Hidden for a description of how this property can be used.

See Also

Hidden

history Property — see Window.history

History Object — the URL history of the browser

Availability

Navigator 2.0, Internet Explorer 3.0; enhanced in Navigator 3.0 when data tainting is enabled

Synopsis

```
window.history
frame.history
history
```

Properties

current   A string that specifies the URL of the current document. Only available with data tainting enabled in Navigator 3.0.

length   The number of URLs that are saved in the History object.

next   A string that specifies the URL of the document after this one in the history list. Only available with data tainting enabled in Navigator 3.0.

previous   A string that specifies the URL of the document before this one in the history list. Only available with data tainting enabled in Navigator 3.0.

Methods

back( )   Go backwards to a previously visited URL.

forward( )   Go forward to a previously visited URL.

go( )   Go to a previously visited URL.

toString( )   Return an HTML-formatted table containing the window's browsing history. Only available with data tainting enabled in Navigator 3.0.

Description

The History object is a read-only array of strings that specify the URLs that have been previously visited by the browser. The contents of this array are equivalent to the URLs listed in Navigator's **Go** menu. For security and privacy reasons, the contents of the array are not available to JavaScript in Navigator 2.0, or in Navigator 3.0 when the data-tainting security model is not enabled.

In Navigator 2.0, and Navigator 3.0 without data tainting enabled, JavaScript can use the `length` property to determine the number of entries on the History object's URL list, and can use the `back()`, `forward()` and `go()` methods to cause the browser to revisit any of the URLs in the array, but it cannot directly or indirectly read the URLs stored in the array.

In Navigator 3.0 and later, when the data-tainting security model is enabled, the elements of the array are available and may be read (but not changed). Also, the `current`, `next`, and `previous` properties are available. These properties are strings that specify the URL of the current document, and the URLs of the documents that precede and follow it in the history array. Finally, enabling data tainting also makes the `toString()` method of the History object functional. This method returns a string of HTML text. When this string is formatted by a browser (i.e., written with `document.write()`), it displays the browser history as a table of URLs, each with an appropriate hyperlink.

Usage

You can use the History object to implement your own **Forward** and **Back** buttons, or other navigation controls, within a window. This is most often useful for sites that use frames. With data tainting enabled, more sophisticated navigation aids are possible.

Example

With or without data tainting, you can use the `back()`, `forward()`, and `go()` methods of the History object. The following line performs the same action as clicking the **Back** button:

```
history.back();
```

The following performs the same action as clicking the **Back** button twice:

```
history.go(-2);
```

With data tainting enabled, you can access the history object as an array and read URLs directly. The first URL displayed by the current window is:

```
history[0]
```

The last URL displayed by that window is:

```
history[history.length-1]
```

The currently displayed URL is:

```
history.current
```

And the URLs of the documents before and after that one in the history array are:

```
history.previous
history.next
```

See Also

Location

History.back() Method — return to the previous URL

Availability

Navigator 2.0, Internet Explorer 3.0

Synopsis

```
history.back()
```

Arguments

None.

Returns

Nothing.

Description

back() causes the window or frame to which the History object belongs to revisit the URL (if any) that was visited immediately before the current one. Calling this method has the same effect as a user's click on the Navigator **Back** button. It is also equivalent to:

```
history.go(-1);
```

See Also

History, History.forward(), History.go()

History.current Property — the URL of the currently displayed document

Availability

Navigator 3.0, when data tainting is enabled

Synopsis

```
history.current
```

Description

The current property of the History object is a read-only string that contains the URL of the current document.

See Also

History

History.forward() Method — visit the next URL

Availability

Navigator 2.0, Internet Explorer 3.0

Synopsis

```
history.forward()
```

Arguments

None.

Returns

Nothing.

Description

forward() causes the window or frame to which the History object belongs to revisit the URL (if any) that was visited immediately after the current one. Calling this method has the same effect as a user's click on the Navigator **Forward** button. It is also equivalent to:

```
history.go(1);
```

Note that if the user has not used the **Back** button or the **Go** menu to move backwards through the history, and if JavaScript has not invoked the History.back() or History.go() methods, then the forward() method will have no effect, because the browser is already at the end of its list of URLs and there is no URL to go forward to.

See Also

History, History.back(), History.go()

History.go() Method — revisit a URL

Availability

Buggy in Navigator 2.0 and 3.0, partially implemented in Internet Explorer 3.0

Synopsis

```
history.go(relative_position)
history.go(target_string)        buggy in 2.0
```

Arguments

relative_position

> The relative position in the History list of the URL to visit. In Internet Explorer 3.0, this argument must be 1, 0, or -1.

target_string

> A substring of the URL to be visited. This version of the go() method is buggy in Navigator 2.0 and not implemented in Internet Explorer 3.0.

Returns

Nothing.

Description

The first form of the History.go() method takes an integer argument and causes the browser to visit the URL that is the specified number of positions distant in the history list maintained by the History object. Positive arguments move the browser forward through the list and negative arguments move it backwards. Thus, calling history.go(-1) is equivalent to calling history.back(), and, in Navigator, produces the same effect as a user click on the **Back** button. Similarly, history.go(3) revisits the same URL that would be visited by calling history.forward() three times. Calling go() with an argument of 0 causes the current page to be reloaded (although in Navigator 3.0, the Location.reload() provides a better way of doing this). This form of the method is buggy in multiframe documents in Navigator 3.0, and in Internet Explorer, it can only be called with the values 1, 0, and -1.

The second form of the History.go() method takes a string argument. It is supposed to make the browser revisit the first (i.e., most recently visited) URL that contains the specified string. Unfortunately, in Navigator 2.0, this form of the method is buggy and may cause the browser to crash. This form of the method is not implemented in Internet Explorer 3.0.

Because of the various bugs and incompatibilities in this method, it is best avoided. Use the back() and forward() methods instead.

Bugs

This method does not work correctly in multiframe documents in Navigator 3.0, and may crash Navigator 2.0 when called with a string argument. Its behavior in Internet Explorer 3.0 is incompatible with Navigator 2.0.

See Also

History, History.back( ), History.forward( )

History.length Property — number of elements in history array

Availability

Navigator 2.0, implemented but nonfunctional in Internet Explorer 3.0

Synopsis

```
history.length
```

Description

The length property specifies the number of elements there are in the *history* object. This value is usually only useful in Navigator 3.0 when the data-tainting security model is implemented, and the actual array of URLs is accessible through the History object.

In Internet Explorer 3.0, the length property always returns 0.

See Also

History

History.next Property — the URL of the next document in the history array

Availability

Navigator 3.0, when data tainting is enabled

Synopsis

```
history.next
```

Description

The `next` property of the History object is a read-only string that contains the URL of the document after the current one in the history array.

See Also

History, History.previous

History.previous Property — the URL of the previous document in the history array

Availability

Navigator 3.0, when data tainting is enabled

Synopsis

```
history.previous
```

Description

The `previous` property of the History object is a read-only string that contains the URL of the document before the current one in the history array.

See Also

History, History.next

Image Object — an embedded image in an HTML document

Availability

Navigator 3.0

Synopsis

```
document.images[i]
document.images.length
document.image-name
```

Constructor

```
new Image([width, height]);
```

Arguments

width, height
> An optionally specified width and height for the image.

Returns

A newly created Image object.

Properties

border
> A read-only integer that specifies the width, in pixels, of the border around an image. Its value is set by the BORDER attribute.

complete
> A read-only Boolean that specifies whether the image is completely loaded yet.

height
> A read-only integer that specifies the height, in pixels, of the image. Its value is set by the HEIGHT attribute.

hspace
> A read-only integer that specifies the amount of extra horizontal space, in pixels, inserted on the left and right of the image. Its value is set by the HSPACE attribute.

lowsrc
> A read/write string that specifies the URL of an alternate image, suitable for display at low resolutions. Its initial value is set by the LOWSRC attribute.

name
> A read-only string, specified by the HTML NAME attribute, that specifies the name of the image. When an image is given an name with the NAME attribute, a reference to the image is placed in the *image-name* property, in addition to being placed in the document.images[ ] array.

src
> A read/write string that specifies the URL of the image to be displayed. Its initial value is set by the SRC attribute.

vspace
> A read-only integer that specifies the amount of extra vertical space, in pixels, inserted above and below the image. Its value is set by the VSPACE attribute.

width
> A read-only integer that specifies the width, in pixels, of the image. Its value is set by the WIDTH attribute.

Event Handlers

onabort
> Invoked if the user aborts the download of an image.

onerror
> Invoked if an error occurs while downloading the image.

onload
> Invoked when the image successfully finishes loading.

HTML Syntax

The Image object is created with a standard HTML <IMG> tag, with the addition of event handlers. Some <IMG> attributes have been omitted from the following syntax, because they are not used by or accessible from JavaScript.

```
<IMG SRC="url"                          the image to display
     WIDTH=pixels                       the width of the image
     HEIGHT=pixels                      the height of the image
     [ NAME="image_name" ]              a property name for the image
     [ LOWSRC="url" ]                   alternate low-resolution image
     [ BORDER=pixels ]                  width of image border
     [ HSPACE=pixels ]                  extra horizontal space around image
     [ VSPACE=pixels ]                  extra vertical space around image
     [ onLoad=handler ]                 invoked when image fully loaded
     [ onError=handler ]                invoked if error in loading
     [ onAbort=handler ]                invoked if user aborts load
>
```

Description

The Image objects in the `document.images[]` array represent the images embedded in an HTML document using the <IMG> tag. Most of the properties of this object are currently read-only. The `src` and `lowsrc` properties are exceptions, however. Usually, the `src` (and perhaps `lowsrc`) properties are set once, when the Image object is created from HTML. But these properties may also be set dynamically. When you set the `src` property, the browser will load the image specified by the new value of the `src` property, or by the `lowsrc` property, if specified, for low-resolution monitors. Note that if you want to use the `lowsrc` property, you must set it *before* you set the `src` property, because setting the `src` property starts the download of the new image.

You can dynamically create Image objects in your JavaScript code using the `Image()` constructor function. Note that this constructor method does not have an argument to specify the image to be loaded. As with images created from HTML, you tell Navigator to load an image by setting the `src` property of any images you create explicitly. There is no way to display an Image object in the web browser. All you can do is force the Image object to download an image by setting the `src` property. This is useful, however, because it loads an image into the browser's cache. Later, if that same image URL is specified for one of the images in the `images[]` array, it will be preloaded, and will be displayed quickly. You might do this with lines like the following:

```
document.images[2].src = preloaded_image.src;
document.toggle_image.src = toggle_off.src;
```

Usage

Setting the `src` property of an Image object can be used to implement simple animations in your web pages. It is also an excellent technique for changing the graphics on a page as the user interacts with the page. For example, you might create your own "submit" button using an image and a hypertext link. The button would start out with a "disabled" graphic and remain that way until the user had correctly entered all the required information into the form, at which point the graphic would change, and the user would be able to submit the form.

See Also

Document

Image.border Property — border width of an image

Availability

Navigator 3.0

Synopsis

`image.border`

Description

The `border` property of the Image object is a read-only integer that specifies the width, in pixels, of the border the browser places around images that are hypertext links. The value of this property is specified by the `BORDER` attribute of the `<IMG>` HTML tag.

See Also

Image

Image.complete Property — whether an image load is complete

Availability

Navigator 3.0

Synopsis

`image.complete`

Description

The `complete` property is a read-only Boolean value that specifies whether an image is completely loaded, or, more accurately, whether the browser has completed its attempt to load the image. If an error occurs during loading, or if the load is aborted, the `complete` property will still be set to `true`.

See Also

Image, Image.onabort( ), Image.onerror( ), Image.onload( )

Image.height Property — the height of an image

Availability

Navigator 3.0

Synopsis

`image.height`

Description

The `height` property of the Image object is a read-only integer that specifies the height of `image`. It is set by the `HEIGHT` attribute of the `<IMG>` HTML tag.

The `HEIGHT` attribute is optional in HTML, but including it greatly improves the layout time of your pages. Also, because of a bug, in Navigator 2.0 all images in a page that contains JavaScript must have `WIDTH` and `HEIGHT` attributes specified (even though the `Image` object is not available in 2.0).

See Also

Image

Image.hspace Property — horizontal padding for an image

Availability

Navigator 3.0

Synopsis

`image.hspace`

Description

The hspace property of the Image object is a read-only integer that specifies the number of extra blank pixels that will appear to the left and right of the image in the browser window. The value of this property is specified by the HSPACE attribute of the <IMG> tag.

See Also

Image

Image.lowsrc Property — alternate image for low-resolution displays

Availability

Navigator 3.0

Synopsis

`image.lowsrc`

Description

The lowsrc property of the Image object is a read/write string that specifies the URL of an alternate image (usually a smaller one) to display when the user's browser is running on a low-resolution monitor. The initial value is specified by the LOWSRC attribute of the <IMG> tag.

Setting this property has no immediate effect. If the src property is set, however, a new image will be loaded, and on low-resolution systems, the current value of the lowsrc property will be used instead of the newly updated value of src.

See Also

Image

Image.name Property — the name of an image

Availability

Navigator 3.0

Synopsis

```
image.name
```

Description

name is a read-only string property of the Image object. Its value is specified by the NAME attribute of the HTML <IMG> tag that creates the Image object. Image objects created with the Image( ) constructor function do not have names, and cannot have names assigned.

Usage

Images created in an HTML document with the <IMG> tag are listed in the document.images[ ] array in JavaScript. If an image is given a name, then the image is also stored in a property with that name in the document object. For example, an image with the attribute:

```
NAME="toggle_button"
```

could be referred to as:

```
document.toggle_button
```

See Also

Image

Image.onabort( ) Handler — invoked when user aborts image loading

Availability

Navigator 3.0

Synopsis

```
<IMG SRC="url"
     onAbort="handler"   a definition of the handler
     . . .>
image.onabort           a reference to the handler
image.onabort( );        an explicit invocation of the handler
```

Description

onabort( ) is an event handler invoked when the user aborts the loading of an image (for example, by clicking the **Stop** button). This event handler is defined by the onAbort attribute of an <IMG> tag. The value of this attribute may be any number of JavaScript statements, separated by semicolons; these statements will be executed only when the user aborts loading for the specified image.

See Also

Image, Image.onerror( ), Image.onload( )

Image.onerror() Handler — invoked on error during image loading

Availability

Navigator 3.0

Synopsis

```
<IMG SRC="url"
     onError="handler"    a definition of the handler
     . . .>
image.onerror            a reference to the handler
image.onerror();         an explicit invocation of the handler
```

Description

`onerror()` is an event handler invoked when an error occurs while the specified image is loading (for example, the network goes down, or the specified URL does not contain image data). This event handler is defined by the `onError` attribute of an `<IMG>` tag. The value of this attribute may be any number of JavaScript statements, separated by semicolons; these statements will be executed only when an error occurs while loading the specified image.

See Also

Image, Image.onabort( ), Image.onload( )

Image.onload() Handler — invoked when image finishes loading

Availability

Navigator 3.0

Synopsis

```
<IMG SRC="url"
     onLoad="handler"    a definition of the handler
     . . .>
image.onload            a reference to the handler
image.onload();         an explicit invocation of the handler
```

Description

`onload()` is an event handler invoked when the browser successfully finishes loading the image specified by an `<IMG>` tag. This event handler is defined by the `onLoad` attribute of an `<IMG>` tag. The value of this attribute may be any number of JavaScript statements, separated by semicolons; these statements will be executed when the image is completely loaded.

See Also

Image, Image.onabort( ), Image.onerror( )

Image.src Property — URL of the embedded image

Availability

Navigator 3.0

Synopsis

```
image.src
```

Description

The `src` property of the Image object is a read/write string that specifies the URL of the image to be displayed by the browser. The initial value of this property is specified by the `SRC` attribute of the `<IMG>` tag.

When you set this property to the URL of a new image, the browser will load and display that new image (or, on low-resolution systems, the image specified by the `lowsrc` property). This is very useful for updating the graphical appearance of your web pages in response to user actions, and can also be used to perform crude animation.

See Also

Image

Image.vspace Property — vertical padding for an image

Availability

Navigator 3.0

Synopsis

```
image.vspace
```

Description

The `vspace` property of the Image object is a read-only integer that specifies the number of extra blank pixels that will appear above and below the image in the browser window. The value of this property is specified by the `VSPACE` attribute of the `<IMG>` tag.

See Also

Image

Image.width Property — the width of an image

Availability

Navigator 3.0

Synopsis

```
image.width
```

Description

The width property of the Image object is a read-only integer that specifies the width of *image*. It is set by the WIDTH attribute of the <IMG> HTML tag.

The WIDTH attribute is optional in HTML, but including it greatly improves the layout time of your pages. Also, because of a bug, in Navigator 2.0 all images in a page that contains JavaScript must have WIDTH and HEIGHT attributes specified (even though the Image object is not available in 2.0).

See Also

Image

---

isNaN() Function — check for Not-a-Number

Availability

Navigator 3.0; Unix platforms in Navigator 2.0; implemented but nonfunctional in Internet Explorer 3.0

Synopsis

    isNaN(x)

Arguments

x   The value to be tested.

Returns

true if *x* is the reserved value NaN (not-a-number); false if *x* is a legal number, string, or any other type.

Description

isNaN() tests its argument to determine whether it is the reserved value NaN, which represents an illegal number (such as the result of division by zero). This function is required, because comparing a NaN with any value, including itself, always returns false, so it is not possible to test for NaN with the == operator.

The NaN value is not implmemented in Internet Explorer 3.0, so isNaN() always returns false on that platform.

A common use of isNaN() is to test the result of parseFloat() and parseInt() to determine if they represent legal numbers. You can also use it to check for arithmetic errors, such as division by zero.

See Also

Number.NaN, parseFloat(), parseInt()

java Property — the java.* package

Availability

Navigator 3.0

Synopsis

```
java
```

Description

`java` is a global property of the Window object, and is usually used without reference to any particular window. It is a synonym for `Packages.java`, and contains a read-only reference to a JavaPackage object that represents the top node of the *java.** package name hierarchy. The `java` Package contains, for example, a `lang` property which is a reference to the JavaPackage object for the *java.lang* package.

See Also

JavaPackage, Packages.java

JavaArray Object — JavaScript representation of a Java array

Availability

Navigator 3.0

Synopsis

```
javaarray.length          the length of the array
javaarray[index]          read or write an array element
```

Properties

length   A read-only integer that specifies the number of elements in the Java array represented by the JavaArray object.

Description

The JavaArray object is a JavaScript representation of a Java array, and it allows JavaScript code to read and write the elements of the array using familiar JavaScript array syntax. In addition, the JavaArray object has a `length` field which specifies the number of elements in the Java array.

When reading and writing values from array elements, data conversion between JavaScript and Java representations is automatically handled by the system. See Chapter 19 for full details.

Usage

Note that Java arrays differ from JavaScript arrays in a couple of important aspects. First, Java arrays have a fixed length that is specified when they are created. For this reason, the JavaArray `length` field is read-only. The second difference is that Java arrays are *typed*—i.e., their elements must all be of the same type of data. Attempting to set an array element to a value of the wrong type will result in a JavaScript error.

Example

java.awt.Polygon is a JavaClass object. We can create a JavaObject representing an instance of the class like this:

```
p = new java.awt.Polygon();
```

This object p has properties xpoints and ypoints which are JavaArray objects representing Java arrays of integers. We could initialize the contents of these arrays with JavaScript code like the following:

```
for(int i = 0; i < p.xpoints.length; i++)
    p.xpoints[i] = Math.round(Math.random()*100);
for(int i = 0; i < p.ypoints.length; i++)
    p.ypoints[i] = Math.round(Math.random()*100);
```

See Also

getClass(), java, JavaClass, JavaObject, JavaPackage, Packages, Chapter 19

JavaArray.length Property — the number of elements in a Java array

Availability

Navigator 3.0

Synopsis

```
javaarray.length
```

Description

The length property of the JavaArray object is a read-only integer that specifies the number of elements in the Java array represented by the JavaArray object. This property is read-only because arrays in Java have a fixed length.

See Also

getClass(), java, JavaArray, JavaClass, JavaObject, JavaPackage, Packages, Chapter 19

JavaClass Object — JavaScript representation of a Java class

Availability

Navigator 3.0

Synopsis

```
javaclass.static_field          read or write a static Java field
new javaclass( . . . )          create a new Java object
```

Properties

Each JavaClass object contains properties that have the same names as the public static fields and methods of the Java class it represents. These properties allow you to read and write the static fields of the class. Each JavaClass object has different properties; you can use a for/in loop to enumerate them for any given JavaClass object.

Description

The JavaClass object is a JavaScript representation of a Java class. The properties of a Java-Class object represent the public static fields and methods (sometimes called class fields and class methods) of the represented class. Note that the JavaClass object does not have properties representing the *instance* fields of a Java class—individual instances of a Java class are represented by the JavaObject object.

The JavaClass object implements the LiveConnect functionality that allows JavaScript programs to read and write the static variables of Java classes using normal JavaScript syntax. The JavaClass object also provides the functionality that allows JavaScript to read the static methods of a Java class, although it is the JavaMethod object that allows JavaScript to actually invoke those methods.

Besides allowing JavaScript to read and write Java variable and method values, the Java-Class object also allows JavaScript programs to create Java objects (represented by a JavaObject object) by using the `new` keyword and invoking the constructor method of a JavaClass.

The data conversion required for communication between JavaScript and Java through the JavaClass object is handled automatically by LiveConnect. See Chapter 19 for full details.

Usage

Bear in mind that Java is a *typed* language. This means that each of the fields of an object have a specific data type, and you can only set them to values of that type. Attempting to set a field to a value that is not of the correct type will result in a JavaScript error. Attempting to invoke a method with arguments of the wrong type will also cause an error.

Example

`java.lang.System` is a JavaClass object that represents the *java.lang.System* class in Java. You can read a static field of this class with code like the following:

```
var java_console = java.lang.System.out;
```

You can invoke a static method of this class with a line like this one:

```
var version = java.lang.System.getProperty("java.version");
```

Finally, the JavaClass object also allows you to create new Java objects like this:

```
var java_date = new java.lang.Date();
```

See Also

getClass( ), java, JavaArray, JavaMethod, JavaObject, JavaPackage, Packages, Chapter 19

JavaMethod Object — JavaScript representation of a Java method

Availability

Navigator 3.0

Synopsis

`javamethod( . . . )`   *invoke an instance method*

Description

The JavaMethod object is a JavaScript representation of a Java method. It is the part of Live-Connect that implements the functionality that allows JavaScript to invoke class and instance methods accessed through the JavaClass and JavaObject objects. See Chapter 19 for full details.

Usage

Bear in mind that Java is a *typed* language. This means that the arguments passed to a JavaMethod must be compatible with the type of the expected arguments. If arguments of the wrong type are passed, a JavaScript error will occur.

Example

`java.lang` is the name of a JavaPackage. It contains the JavaClass `java.lang.System` This class has a property `out` which is an JavaObject. This JavaObject has a property `println`, which is a JavaMethod. LiveConnect allows us to invoke this Java method using JavaScript syntax with code like the following:

```
java.lang.System.out.println("Hello from Java!");
```

The line of code above will write a message on the Java console. (See the **Options** menu to pop up the Java console in Navigator 3.0.)

See Also

getClass( ), java, JavaArray, JavaClass, JavaObject, JavaPackage, Packages, Chapter 19

JavaObject Object — JavaScript representation of a Java object

Availability

Navigator 3.0

Synopsis

`javaobject.field`   *read or write an instance field*

Properties

Each JavaObject object contains properties that have the same names as the public instance fields and methods (but not the static or class fields and methods) of the Java object it represents. These properties allow you to read and write the value of public fields. The properties of a given JavaObject object obviously depend on the type of Java object it represents. You can use the `for/in` loop to enumerate the properties of any given JavaObject.

Description

The JavaObject object is a JavaScript representation of a Java object. The properties of a JavaObject object represent the public instance fields and public instance methods defined for the Java object. (The class or static fields and methods of the object are represented by the JavaClass object.)

The JavaObject object implements the LiveConnect functionality that allows JavaScript programs to read and write the public instance fields of a Java object, using normal JavaScript syntax. The JavaObject also provides the functionality that allows JavaScript to read the methods of a Java object, although it is the JavaMethod object that allows JavaScript to actually invoke those methods. Data conversion between JavaScript and Java representations is handled automatically by LiveConnect. See Chapter 19 for full details.

Usage

Bear in mind that Java is a *typed* language. This means that each of the fields of an object have a specific data type, and you can only set them to values of that type. For example, the `width` field of a `java.awt.Rectangle` object is an integer field, and attempting to set it to a string will cause a JavaScript error to occur.

Example

`java.awt.Rectangle` is a JavaClass that represents the *java.awt.Rectangle* class. We can create a JavaObject that represents an instance of this class like this:

```
var r = new java.awt.Rectangle(0,0,4,5);
```

And then we can read the public instance variables of this JavaObject r with code like this:

```
var perimeter = 2*r.width + 2*r.height;
```

We can also set the value of public instance variables of r using JavaScript syntax:

```
r.width = perimeter/4;
r.height = perimeter/4;
```

See Also

getClass( ), java, JavaArray, JavaClass, JavaMethod, JavaPackage, Packages, Chapter 19

JavaPackage Object — JavaScript representation of a Java package

Availability

Navigator 3.0

Synopsis

```
package.package_name    refers to another JavaPackage
package.class_name      refers to a JavaClass object
```

Properties

The properties of a JavaPackage object are the names of the JavaPackage objects and JavaClass objects that it contains. These properties will be different for each individual JavaPackage. Note that it is not possible to use the JavaScript `for/in` loop to iterate over the list of property names of a Package object. Consult a Java reference manual to determine the packages and classes contained within any given package.

Description

The JavaPackage object is a JavaScript representation of a Java package. A package in Java is a collection of related classes. In JavaScript, a JavaPackage can contain classes (represented by the JavaClass object) and it can also contain other JavaPackage objects.

For example, the JavaPackage object named `java` has properties named `lang` and `net`, among others, that are references to other JavaPackage objects, which represent the *java.lang* and *java.awt* packages. The `java.awt` JavaPackage contains properties named `Frame` and `Button`, which are both references to JavaClass objects, and represent the classes *java.awt.Frame* and *java.awt.Button*. The `java.awt` JavaPackage object also contains a property named `image`, which is a reference to yet another JavaPackage object, this one representing the *java.awt.image* package.

As you can see, the property naming scheme for the JavaPackage hierarchy mirrors the naming scheme for Java packages. Note that there is one big difference between the Java-Package object and actual Java packages. Packages in Java are collections of classes, not collections of other packages. So the JavaPackage object named `java` does not actually represent a package in Java, but is simply a convenient placeholder for other JavaPackages that do represent *java.lang, java.net, java.io,* and other core Java packages.

On many systems, Java classes are installed in files in a directory hierarchy that corresponds to the package name. (For example, the *java.lang.String* class is stored in the file *java/lang/String.class* in my Java implementation from Sun. In other implementations, notably that from Netscape, the class files are actually stored in a large, uncompressed zip file. The directory hierarchy is still there; it is just less visible.) Therefore, instead of thinking of the JavaPackage object as representing a Java package, you may find it clearer to consider it as representing a directory in the Java class hierarchy.

In the above discussion, we've been referring to a JavaPackage object named `java`, but we haven't said where this `java` object comes from—i.e., what `java` is a property of. The `java` JavaPackage object is actually a property of every Window object, which makes it a "global" variable in client-side JavaScript. Since every JavaScript expression is evaluated in the context of one window or another, you can always just use `java`, and know that you will be referring to the JavaPackage object you want.

There are other global JavaPackage objects as well. The `sun` JavaPackage refers to Java packages from Sun Microsystems, which have names beginning with "sun." Similarly, the `netscape` JavaPackage refers to Java packages from Netscape. Finally, the `Packages` property is a JavaPackage object that contains references to each of these `java`, `sun`, and `netscape` JavaPackages. Thus, you can use `Packages.java` as a synonym for `java`, when you want to be more explicit about just what it is that you are referring to (or when you already have a local variable named `java`).

As we've said above, a JavaPackage object contains properties for each of the packages and classes it contains. If you think of a JavaPackage as representing a directory in the Java class directory hierarchy, then the properties of the JavaPackage are the contents of the directory. Each subdirectory of the directory becomes a JavaPackage property, with the package name matching the subdirectory name. Each file in the directory (these "class files" contain the Java byte code that implements the class) becomes a JavaClass property, with the property name matching the file name, after the *.class* extension is stripped off.

In Navigator 3.0 it is not possible to use the `for/in` loop to determine the names of the packages and classes contained within a JavaPackage. You must have this information in advance. You can find it in any Java reference manual, or by examining the Java class hierarchy yourself.

See Chapter 19 for further details on working with Java packages, classes, and objects.

Usage

With all this explanation behind us, it is now possible to see how we can use JavaPackage objects to refer to any Java class. The *java.lang.System* class, for example is:

```
java.lang.System
```

Or:

```
Packages.java.lang.System
```

Similarly, the *netscape.javascript.JSObject* class is:

```
Packages.netscape.javascript.JSObject
```

See Also

java, JavaArray, JavaClass, JavaObject, netscape, Packages, sun, Chapter 19

JSObject Java Class — Java representation of a JavaScript object

Availability

In the *netscape.javascript* package included with Navigator 3.0

Synopsis

```
public final class netscape.javascript.JSObject extends Object
```

Methods

call()   Invoke a method of the JavaScript object.

eval()   Evaluate a string of JavaScript code in the context of the JavaScript object.

getMember()   Get the value of a property of the JavaScript object.

getSlot()   Get the value of an array element of the JavaScript object.

getWindow()   Get a "root" JSObject that represents the JavaScript Window object of the web browser.

removeMember()
              Delete a property from the JavaScript object.

setMember()   Set the value of a property of the JavaScript object.

setSlot()   Set the value of an array element of the JavaScript object.

toString()   Invoke the JavaScript toString() method of the JavaScript object, and return its result.

Description

The JSObject is a Java class, not a JavaScript object; it cannot be used in your JavaScript programs, Instead, the JSObject is used by Java applets that wish to communicate with JavaScript by reading and writing JavaScript properties and array elements, by invoking JavaScript methods, and by evaluating and executing arbitrary strings of JavaScript code.

Obviously, since JSObject is a Java class, you must understand Java programming in order to use it.

A Java applet that wishes to use the JSObject class must obtain an initial JSObject instance that represents the web browser window that the applet is running in. The JSObject class does not define a constructor method, so the only way to obtain this initial instance is by invoking the static `getWindow()` method, and passing it the *java.applet.Applet* instance that represents the applet. This static method returns a "root" JSObject instance, and you can use the `getMember()` and `getSlot()` methods to obtain any other JSObjects that the applet requires.

Note that if an applet uses the JSObject class, it must have the `MAYSCRIPT` attribute set in its `<APPLET>` tag, or it will not be allowed to manipulate JavaScript from Java. Also, an applet that uses the JSObject class should import the class with a line like the following:

```
import netscape.javascript.JSObject;
```

To compile an applet that uses JSObject, the compiler must be able to locate that class. Depending on the vendor of your compiler, this is usually done by setting your `CLASSPATH` environment variable. The actual class file for the JSObject class is found in the `java_30` file that is part of the Navigator 3.0 distribution.

Full details on programming with the JSObject can be found in Chapter 19.

See Also

Chapter 19

JSObject.call() Java Method — invoke a method of a JavaScript object

Availability

Part of the *netscape.javascript* package included with Navigator 3.0

Synopsis

```
public Object call(String methodName, Object args[])
```

Arguments

methodName   The name of the JavaScript method to be invoked.

args[]   An array of Java object to be passed as arguments to the method.

Returns

A Java Object that represents the return value of the JavaScript method.

Description

The `call()` method of the Java JSObject class invokes a named method of the JavaScript object represented by the JSObject. Arguments are passed to the method as an array of Java objects, and the return value of the JavaScript method is returned as a Java object. Chapter 19 describes the data conversion performed to convert the method arguments from Java objects to JavaScript values and to convert the method return value from a JavaScript value to a Java object.

See Also

JSObject, Chapter 19

JSObject.eval( ) Java Method — evaluate a string of JavaScript code

Availability

Part of the *netscape.javascript* package included with Navigator 3.0

Synopsis

```
public Object eval(String s)
```

Arguments

s   A string that contains arbitrary JavaScript statements, separated by semi-colons.

Returns

The JavaScript value of the last expression evaluated in s, converted to a Java object.

Description

The eval() method of the Java JSObject class evaluates the JavaScript code contained in the String s in the context of the JavaScript object specified by the JSObject. The eval() method of the Java JSObject class behaves just like the eval() method of the JavaScript Object "class."

The argument s may contain any number of JavaScript statements, separated by semicolons; these statements will be executed in the order in which they appear. The return value of eval() is the value of the last statement or expression evaluated in s.

See Also

JSObject, Chapter 19

JSObject.getMember( ) Java Method — read a property of a JavaScript object

Availability

Part of the *netscape.javascript* package included with Navigator 3.0

Synopsis

```
public Object getMember(String name)
```

Arguments

name   The name of the property to be read.

Returns

A Java Object that contains the value of the named property of the specified JSObject.

Description

The `getMember()` method of the Java JSObject class reads and returns to Java the value of a named property of a JavaScript object. The return value may be another JSObject object, or a Double, Boolean, or String object, but is returned as a generic Object, which you must cast as necessary.

See Also

JSObject, Chapter 19

JSObject.getSlot() Java Method — read an array element of a JavaScript object

Availability

Part of the *netscape.javascript* package included with Navigator 3.0

Synopsis

```
public Object getSlot(int index)
```

Arguments

`index`   The index of the array element to be read.

Returns

The value of the array element at the specified `index` of a JavaScript object.

Description

The `getSlot()` method of the Java JSObject class reads and returns to Java the value of an array element at the specified `index` of a JavaScript object. The return value may be another JSObject object, or a Double, Boolean, or String object, but is returned as a generic Object, which you must cast as necessary.

See Also

JSObject, Chapter 19

JSObject.getWindow() Java Method — return initial JSObject for browser window

Availability

Part of the *netscape.javascript* package included with Navigator 3.0

Synopsis

```
public static JSObject getWindow(java.applet.Applet applet);
```

Arguments

applet   An Applet object running in the web browser window for which a JSObject is to be obtained.

Returns

A JSObject that represents the JavaScript Window object for the web browser window that contains the specified *applet*.

Description

The getWindow() method is the first JSObject method that any Java applet will call. JSObject does not define a constructor, and the static getWindow() method provides the only way to obtain an initial "root" JSObject from which other JSObjects may be obtained.

See Also

JSObject, Chapter 19

JSObject.removeMember() Java Method — delete a property of a JavaScript object

Availability

Part of the *netscape.javascript* package included with Navigator 3.0

Synopsis

```
public void removeMember(String name)
```

Arguments

name   The name of the property to be deleted from the JSObject.

Returns

Nothing.

Description

The removeMember() method of the Java JSObject class deletes a named property from the JavaScript object represented by the JSObject.

See Also

JSObject, Chapter 19

JSObject.setMember() Java Method — set a property of a JavaScript object

Availability

Part of the *netscape.javascript* package included with Navigator 3.0

Synopsis

```
public void setMember(String name, Object value)
```

Arguments

name   The name of the property to be set in the JSObject.

value   The value that the named property should be set to.

Returns

Nothing.

Description

The setMember( ) method of the Java JSObject class sets the value of a named property of a JavaScript object from Java. The specified *value* may be any Java Object. Primitive Java values may not be passed to this method. In JavaScript, the specified *value* will be accessible as a JavaObject object.

See Also

JSObject, Chapter 19

JSObject.setSlot( ) Java Method — set an array element of a JavaScript object

Availability

Part of the *netscape.javascript* package included with Navigator 3.0

Synopsis

```
public void setSlot(int index, Object value)
```

Arguments

index   The index of the array element to be set in the JSObject.

value   The value that the specified array element should be set to.

Returns

Nothing.

Description

The setSlot( ) method of the Java JSObject class sets the value of a numbered array element of a JavaScript object from Java. The specified *value* may be any Java Object. Primitive Java values may not be passed to this method. In JavaScript, the specified *value* will be accessible as a JavaObject object.

See Also

JSObject, Chapter 19

JSObject.toString() Java Method — return the string value of a JavaScript object

Availability

Part of the *netscape.javascript* package included with Navigator 3.0

Synopsis

```
public String toString()
```

Arguments

None.

Returns

The string returned by invoking the toString() method of the JavaScript object represented by the specified Java JSObject.

Description

The toString() method of the Java JSObject class invokes the JavaScript toString() method of the JavaScript object represented by a JSObject and returns the result of that method.

Because the Java toString() method of a JSObject simply invokes the JavaScript toString() method of the JavaScript object represented by that JSObject, Java is guaranteed to convert any JSObject to a string in the same way that JavaScript does.

See Also

JSObject, Chapter 19

Link Object — a hypertext link

Availability

Navigator 2.0, Internet Explorer 3.0; enhanced in Navigator 3.0

Synopsis

```
document.links[]
document.links.length
```

Properties

hash
: A read/write string that specifies the hash portion of the HREF URL, including the leading hash (#) mark. This portion specifies the name of an anchor within the object referred to by the URL.

host
: A read/write string that specifies the combination of the hostname and port portions of the HREF URL.

hostname
: A read/write string that specifies the hostname portion of the HREF URL.

href
: A read/write string that specifies the complete URL specified by the HREF property.

pathname   A read/write string that specifies the path portion of the HREF URL.

port   A read/write string that specifies the port portion of the HREF URL.

protocol   A read/write string that specifies the protocol portion of the HREF URL, including the trailing colon.

search   A read/write string that specifies the search or query portion of the HREF URL, including the leading question mark.

target   A read/write string property that specifies the name of a Window object (i.e., a frame or a top-level browser window) in which the HREF URL should be displayed.

Event Handlers

onclick   Statements invoked when the user clicks on the link. In Navigator 3.0, this event handler may prevent the link from being followed (e.g., after asking the user to confirm) by returning false. On Windows platforms in Navigator 3.0, this event handler does not work for links created with the <AREA> tag.

onmouseout   Statements invoked when the user moves the mouse off of the link. Available in Navigator 3.0 and later.

onmouseover   Statements invoked when the user moves the mouse over the link. The status property of the current window may be set here.

HTML Syntax

A Link object is created with standard <A> and </A> tags, with the addition of the onClick, onMouseOver and onMouseOut event-handler attributes. The HREF attribute is required for all Link objects. If the NAME attribute is also specified, then an Anchor object is also created:

```
<A HREF="url"                        the destination of the link
    [ NAME="anchor_tag" ]            creates an Anchor object
    [ TARGET="window_name" ]         where the new document should be displayed
    [ onClick="handler" ]            invoked when link is clicked
    [ onMouseOver="handler" ]        invoked when mouse is over link
    [ onMouseOut="handler" ]         invoked when mouse leaves link
>
link text or image                   the visible part of the link
</A>
```

In Navigator 3.0 and later, a Link object is also created by each <AREA> tag within a client-side image map. This is also standard HTML with the addition of event-handler tags:

```
<MAP NAME="map_name">
    <AREA SHAPE="area_shape"
        COORDS=coordinates
        HREF="url"                   the destination of the link
        [ TARGET="window_name" ]     where the new document should be displayed
        [ onClick="handler" ]        invoked when area is clicked
```

```
      [ onMouseOver="handler" ]        invoked when mouse is over area
      [ onMouseOut="handler" ]         invoked when mouse leaves area
  >
      . . .
  </MAP>
```

Description

The Link object represents a hypertext link or a clickable area of a client-side image map in an HTML document. All links created with the <A> (and in Navigator 3.0 the <AREA>) tag are represented by Link objects and stored in the links[] array of the Document object. Note that links created by both the <A> and <AREA> tags are stored in the same array—there is no real distinction between them, and there is no special Area object that represents hypertext links in an image map.

The Link object can be thought of as a specialized form of the URL object. The destination of a hypertext link is a URL, of course, and the Link object has all of the properties of the URL object which describe that destination. These protocol, hostname, pathname and other URL properties are all documented under the URL object. The Link object is also related to the Location object, which also has a full set of URL properties that describe the URL of the currently displayed document.

The Link object has an additional target property and three event handlers that are not shared by the URL object or Location objects, however. The target property specifies a window name into which the document referred to by the hypertext link should be loaded. And the onmouseover(), onclick(), and onmouseout() event handlers specify code to be executed when the mouse passes over the hypertext link, clicks on it, and moves off or out of the link's region of the screen.

Usage

In HTML parlance, hypertext links are sometimes called "anchors" because they are created with the <A> tag, which is used both for links to other URLs and for creating named link destinations within a document. This is a confusing usage that should be avoided; in JavaScript, a hypertext link is a Link object, and a named destination for a link is an Anchor object.

See Also

Anchor, Area, Location, URL

Link.hash Property — see URL.hash

Link.host Property — see URL.host

Link.hostname Property — see URL.hostname

Link.href Property — see URL.href

Link.onclick() Handler — invoked when a Link is clicked

Availability

Navigator 2.0, Internet Explorer 3.0; enhanced in Navigator 3.0

Synopsis

```
<A onClick="handler-statements">        a definition of the handler
<AREA onClick="handler-statements">     another definition; Navigator 3.0 only
link.onclick                            a reference to the handler
link.onclick();                         an explicit invocation of the handler
```

Description

onclick() is an event-handler function invoked when the user clicks on a hypertext link. This event handler is defined by the onClick attribute of the HTML <A> or <AREA> tag that defines the hypertext link. The value of this attribute may be any number of JavaScript statements, separated by semicolons. These statements will be executed when the user clicks on the link.

The onclick() event handler is invoked before the browser follows the clicked hypertext link. This allows you to set the href, target, and other properties of the link dynamically (using the this keyword to refer to the clicked link). You may also use Window.alert(), Window.confirm(), and Window.prompt() from this event handler.

In Navigator 3.0, you may prevent the browser from following the link by returning false. If you return true, or any other value, or nothing, then the browser will follow the link as soon as onclick() returns. You might stop the browser from following a link if you used the Window.confirm() method to ask the user if they really want to follow the link and they choose the **Cancel** button, for example. In general, if you want a link that performs some action but does not cause a new URL to be displayed, it is better to use a the onclick() event handler of a Button object instead of the onclick() handler of a Link object.

Note that while this event handler returns false to tell the browser not to perform its default action (following a link), the onmouseover() event handler must return true to tell the browser not to take its default action (displaying the URL of the link). This incompatibility exists for historical reasons. The standard for Form and form element event handlers is to return false to prevent the browser from performing a default action.

Bugs

In Navigator 3.0, the onclick() event handler of the <AREA> does not work on Windows platforms. Because this is a very common platform, you should avoid using this event handler in client-side image maps. Instead, you can often specify a javascript: URL as the value of the HREF attribute of the <AREA> tag.

See Also

Link

Link.onmouseout() Handler — invoked when the mouse leaves a link

Availability

Navigator 3.0

Synopsis

`<A onMouseOut="handler-statements">`	*a definition of the handler*
`<AREA onMouseOut="handler-statements">`	*another definition; Navigator 3.0 only*
`link.onmouseout`	*a reference to the handler*
`link.onmouseout();`	*an explicit invocation of the handler*

Description

`onmouseout()` is an event-handler function invoked when the user moves the mouse off of a hypertext link. This event handler is defined by the `onMouseOut` attribute of the HTML `<A>` or `<AREA>` tag that defines the hypertext link. The value of this attribute may be any number of JavaScript statements, separated by semicolons. These statements will be executed when the user moves the mouse off of the link.

See Also

Link, Link.onmouseover()

Link.onmouseover() Handler — invoked when the mouse goes over a link

Availability

Navigator 2.0, Internet Explorer 3.0

Synopsis

`<A onMouseOver="handler-statements">`	*a definition of the handler*
`<AREA onMouseOver="handler-statements">`	*another definition; Navigator 3.0 only*
`link.onmouseover`	*a reference to the handler*
`link.onmouseover();`	*an explicit invocation of the handler*

Description

`onmouseover()` is an event-handler function invoked when the user moves the mouse over a hypertext link. This event handler is defined by the `onMouseOver` attribute of the HTML `<A>` or `<AREA>` tag that defines the hypertext link. The value of this attribute may be any number of JavaScript statements, separated by semicolons. These statements will be executed when the user moves the mouse over the link.

By default, the browser displays the URL that a hypertext link refers to in the status line whenever the mouse goes over the link. The `onmouseover()` event handler is invoked before the URL is displayed. If the handler returns `true`, then the browser will not display the URL. Thus, an event-handler function that returns `true` can display a custom message in the status line by setting the `Window.status` property to any desired value itself.

Note that while this event handler returns `true` to tell the browser not to perform its default action (displaying the URL of a link), the `onclick()` event handler of the Link object must return `false` to tell the browser not to take its default action (following the link). This incompatibility exists for historical reasons. The standard for Form and form element event handlers is to return `false` to prevent the browser from performing a default action.

See Also

Link, Link.onmouseout()

Link.pathname Property — see URL.pathname

Link.port Property — see URL.port

Link.protocol Property — see URL.protocol

Link.search Property — see URL.search

Link.target Property — target window of a hypertext link

Availability

Navigator 2.0, Internet Explorer 3.0

Synopsis

```
link.target
```

Description

`target` is a read/write string property of the Link object. It specifies the name of the frame or window in which the URL referred to by the Link object should be displayed. The initial value of this property is specified by the `TARGET` attribute of the `<A>` tag that creates the Link object. If this attribute is unset, then the default is for the window containing the Link to be used, so that following a hypertext link overwrites the document that contains the link.

Note that the value of `target` is the *name* of a frame or window, not an actual JavaScript reference to the frame or window itself. The name of a frame is specified by the `NAME` attribute of the `<FRAME>` tag. The name of a window is specified when the window is created with a call to the `Window.open()` method. If `target` specifies the name of a window that does not exist, then Navigator will automatically open a new window to display the URL, and any future links with the same `target` name will use that freshly created window.

Four special target names are supported. The target named `"_blank"` specifies that a new, empty browser window should be created and used to display the new URL. The target `"_self"` is the default; it specifies that the new URL should be displayed in the same frame or window as the link. The target `"_parent"` specifies that the results should be displayed in the parent frame of the frame that contains the link. Finally, the `"_top"` target specifies that the new URL should be displayed in the topmost frame—i.e., that all frames should be removed, and the new URL should occupy the entire browser window.

See Also

Form.target, Link

location Property — see Window.location

Location Object — represents and controls browser location

Availability

Navigator 2.0, Internet Explorer 3.0; enhanced in Navigator 3.0

Synopsis

```
location
window.location
```

Properties

The properties of a Location object refer the various portions of a URL, which has the following general format:

```
protocol://hostname:port/pathname?search#hash
```

See the URL object for further details on these URL properties.

hash
: The hash portion of the URL, including the leading hash (#) mark. This portion specifies the name of an anchor within a single HTML file.

host
: A combination of the hostname and port portions of the URL.

hostname
: The hostname portion of the URL.

href
: The complete URL.

pathname
: The path portion of the URL.

port
: The port portion of the URL.

protocol
: The protocol portion of the URL, including the trailing colon.

search
: The search or query portion of the URL, including the leading question mark.

Methods

reload()
: Reload the current document from the cache or the server. This method was added in Navigator 3.0.

replace()
: Replace the current document with a new one, without generating a new entry in the browser's session history. This method was added in Navigator 3.0.

Description

The Location object is stored in the location property of the Window object, and represents the web address (the "location") of the document currently displayed in that window. The href property contains the complete URL of that document, and the other properties of the Location object each describe a portion of that URL. The Location object is, in fact, a specialized form of the URL object—it has the same properties as that object does.

There is an important difference between the Location object and the URL object, however. The Location object represents the current "location" of the browser, but it also *controls* that location. If you assign a string containing a URL to the Location object, or to its href property, the web browser responds by loading the newly specified URL and displaying the document it refers to.

When you set the location or location.href properties to a URL that you have already visited, the browser will either load that URL from the cache, or will check with the server to see if the document has changed and reload it if necessary. In Navigator 2.0, it will always check with the web server. In Navigator 3.0, the action it takes depends on the **Verify Document** setting in Navigator's **Network Preferences**.

Instead of setting location or location.href to replace the current URL with a completely new one, you can also modify just a portion of the current URL by assigning strings to the other properties of the Location object. Doing this creates a new URL, with one new portion, which the browser loads and displays. For example, if you set the hash property of the Location object you can cause the browser to move to a named location within the current document (although in Navigator 2.0, the browser reloads the entire document to accomplish this; this bug is fixed in Navigator 3.0). Similarly, if you set the search property, you can cause the browser to reload the current URL with a new query string appended. If the URL refers to a CGI script, then the document resulting from the new query string may be quite different from the original document.

It is generally not so useful to set the other properties of the Location object. For example, if you loaded a document via the HTTP protocol, you would rarely be able to actually load another document simply by using the protocol property to change the URL protocol from http: to ftp:. See the URL object for a complete description of the hash, search, protocol and other properties that represent portions of a URL.

While the properties of the Location object are identical to those of the URL object, we've seen that they have quite different behavior. In Navigator 3.0, the Location object also defines methods that the URL object does not. The reload() method of the Location object reloads the current document, and the replace() method loads a new document without creating a new history entry for it—the new document "replaces" the current one in the browser's history list.

Note that the Location object bears some resemblance to the Link object which is another specialized version of the URL object. While the Location object represents and controls the current location of the browser, Link objects represent the destinations of hypertext links within a document.

See Also

Link, URL, Window.location

Location.hash Property — see URL.hash

Location.host Property — see URL.host

Location.hostname Property — see URL.hostname

Location.href Property — see URL.href

Location.pathname Property — see URL.pathname

Location.port Property — see URL.port

Location.protocol Property — see URL.protocol

Location.reload() Method — reload the current document

Availability

Navigator 3.0

Synopsis

```
location.reload()
location.reload(force)
```

Arguments

force   A Boolean argument that specifies whether the document should be reloaded, even if the server reports that it has not been modified since it was last loaded. If this argument is omitted, or if it is false, then the method will only reload the full page if it has changed since last loaded.

Returns

Nothing.

Description

The reload() method of the Location object reloads the document that is currently displayed in the window of the Location object. When called with no arguments, or with the argument false, it uses the If-Modified-Since HTTP header to determine whether the document has changed on the web server. If it has, it reloads the document from the server, and if not, it reloads the document from the cache. This is is the same action that occurs when the user clicks on Navigator's **Reload** button.

When reload() is called with the argument true, then it will always bypass the cache and reload the document from the server, regardless of the last-modified time of the document. This is the same action that occurs when the user shift-clicks on Navigator's **Reload** button.

See Also

Location, Location.replace()

Location.replace() Method — replace one displayed document with another

Availability

Navigator 3.0

Synopsis

```
location.replace(url)
```

Arguments

url   A string that specifies the URL of the new document that is to replace the current one.

Returns

Nothing.

Description

The `replace()` method of the Location object loads and displays a new document. Loading a document in this way is different than simply setting `location` or `location.href` in one important respect: the `replace()` method does not generate a new entry in the History object. When you use `replace()`, the new URL overwrites the current entry in the History object. After calling `replace()`, that is, the browser's **Back** button will not return you to the previous URL; it will return you to the URL before that one.

Usage

When you are working with multiple frames and/or JavaScript generated documents, you sometimes end up with quite a few temporary or transient documents. If there are more than just a few of these documents, it becomes annoying to the user to back out of your web site with the **Back** button. If you use the `replace()` method to load these documents, however, you can prevent this problem.

See Also

History, Location, Location.reload()

Location.search Property — see URL.search

Math Object — placeholder for mathematical functions and constants

Availability

Navigator 2.0, Internet Explorer 3.0

Synopsis

```
Math.constant
Math.function()
```

Constants

E	the constant *e*, the base of the natural logarithm.
LN10	the natural logarithm of 10
LN2	the natural logarithm of 2
LOG10E	the base-10 logarithm of *e*
LOG2E	the base-2 logarithm of *e*
PI	the constant π
SQRT1_2	1 divided by the square root of 2
SQRT2	the square root of 2

Functions

abs()	compute an absolute value
acos()	compute an arc cosine
asin()	compute an arc sine
atan()	compute an arc tangent
atan2()	compute the angle from the X axis to a point
ceil()	round a number up
cos()	compute a cosine
exp()	compute an exponent of *e*
floor()	round a number down
log()	compute a natural logarithm
max()	return the larger of two numbers
min()	return the smaller of two numbers
pow()	compute x^y
random()	compute a random number; not available on all platforms
round()	round to the nearest integer
sin()	compute a sine
sqrt()	compute a square root
tan()	compute a tangent

Description

Math is a read-only reference to a placeholder object that contains mathematical functions and constants. These functions and constants are conveniently grouped by this Math object, and are invoked with syntax like this:

```
y = Math.sin(x);
area = radius * radius * Math.PI;
```

Math is actually a "global" property of the Window object, and as such, is usually referred to as Math, rather than as *window*.Math.

Math is not a class of objects like Date and String are. The Date class, for example, defines methods that operate on Date objects; on instances of the class. Math, on the other hand is simply an object that contains references to functions. These functions happen to be invoked through the Math object, but they do not operate on that object, as methods would.

See Also

Number

Math.abs() Function — compute an absolute value

Availability

Navigator 2.0, Internet Explorer 3.0

Synopsis

```
Math.abs(x)
```

Arguments

x   Any number or numeric expression.

Returns

The absolute value of x.

Description

Math.abs() returns the absolute value of its single argument.

See Also

Math

Math.acos() Function — compute an arc cosine

Availability

Navigator 2.0, Internet Explorer 3.0

Synopsis

```
Math.acos(x)
```

Arguments

x   A number or numeric expression between -1.0 and 1.0.

Returns

The arc cosine, in radians, of the specified value x.

Description

`Math.acos()` computes and returns the arc cosine, or inverse cosine of the specified argument. The argument must be a value between -1.0 and 1.0. The return value is between 0 and π radians.

See Also

Math, Math.asin( ), Math.tan( ), Math.cos( )

Math.asin() Function — compute an arc sine

Availability

Navigator 2.0, Internet Explorer 3.0

Synopsis

```
Math.asin(x)
```

Arguments

x   A number or numeric expression between -1.0 and 1.0.

Returns

The arc sine, in radians, of the specified value x.

Description

`Math.asin()` computes and returns the arc sine, or inverse sine of its argument. The argument must be a value between -1.0 and 1.0. The return value is between $-\pi/2$ and $\pi/2$ radians.

See Also

Math, Math.acos( ), Math.atan( ), Math.sin( )

Math.atan() Function — compute an arc tangent

Availability

Navigator 2.0, Internet Explorer 3.0

Synopsis

```
Math.atan(x)
```

Arguments

x   Any number or numeric expression.

Returns

The arc tangent, in radians, of the specified value *x*.

Description

`Math.atan()` computes and returns the arc tangent, or inverse tangent, of its argument. The return value is between -$\pi/2$ and $\pi/2$ radians.

See Also

Math, Math.acos( ), Math.asin( ), Math.tan( )

Math.atan2( ) Function — compute the angle from the X axis to a point

Availability

Navigator 2.0, Internet Explorer 3.0

Synopsis

```
Math.atan2(x, y)
```

Arguments

x   The X-coordinate of the point.

y   The Y-coordinate of the point.

Returns

The counter-clockwise angle, measured in radians, between the positive X axis, and the point (*x*, *y*).

Description

The `Math.atan2()` function performs half of the conversion between Cartesian coordinates and polar coordinates. It computes and returns the angle theta of an (*x*, *y*) point.

This function is named `Math.atan2()` because it performs a similar computation to `Math.atan()`. `Math.atan2()` is passed separate *x* and *y* arguments, and `Math.atan()` is passed the ratio of those two arguments.

See Also

Math, Math.atan( ), Math.tan( )

Math.ceil() Function — round a number up

Availability

Navigator 2.0, Internet Explorer 3.0

Synopsis

```
Math.ceil(x)
```

Arguments

x   Any numeric value or expression.

Returns

The closest integer greater than or equal to *x*.

Description

Math.ceil() computes the ceiling function—i.e., it returns the closest integer value that is greater than or equal to the function argument. Math.ceil() differs from Math.round() in that it always rounds up, rather than rounding up or down to the closest integer. Also note that Math.ceil() does not round negative numbers to larger negative numbers; it rounds them up towards zero.

Example

```
a = Math.ceil(1.99);   // result is 2.0
b = Math.ceil(1.01);   // result is 2.0
c = Math.ceil(1.0);    // result is 1.0
d = Math.ceil(-1.99);  // result is -1.0
```

See Also

Math, Math.floor( ), Math.round( )

Math.cos() Function — compute a cosine

Availability

Navigator 2.0, Internet Explorer 3.0

Synopsis

```
Math.cos(x)
```

Arguments

x   A numeric value or expression, in radians.

Returns

The cosine of the specified value *x*.

Description

Math.cos() computes and returns the cosine of the specified argument. The argument should be an angle be specified in radians, and the return value will be between -1.0 and 1.0.

See Also

Math

Math.E Constant — mathematical constant *e*

Availability

Navigator 2.0, Internet Explorer 3.0

Synopsis

```
Math.E
```

Description

Math.E is the mathematical constant *e*, the base of the natural logarithms, with a value of approximately 2.71828.

See Also

Math, Math.exp( ), Math.log( ), Math.PI

Math.exp() Function — compute e^x

Availability

Navigator 2.0, Internet Explorer 3.0

Synopsis

```
Math.exp(x)
```

Arguments

x   A numeric value or expression to be used as the exponent.

Returns

e^x, *e* raised to the power of the specified exponent, x.

Description

Math.exp() computes e^x, where *e* is the base of the natural logarithms, approximately 2.71828.

Usage

You can compute x^y using Math.exp() with the following formula:

$$x^y = e^{y \ln x}$$

This formula can be expressed in JavaScript as follows:

```
Math.exp(y * Math.log(x))
```

See Also

Math, Math.log( ), Math.LN10

Math.floor( ) Function — round a number down

Availability

Navigator 2.0, Internet Explorer 3.0

Synopsis

```
Math.floor(x)
```

Arguments

x   Any numeric value or expression.

Returns

The closest integer less than or equal to x.

Description

`Math.floor()` computes the floor function—i.e., it returns the nearest integer value that is less than or equal to the function argument. `Math.floor()` rounds a floating-point value down to the closest integer. This differs from `Math.round()` which rounds up or down to the nearest integer. Also note that `Math.floor()` rounds negative numbers to be more negative, not closer to zero.

Example

```
a = Math.floor(1.99);   // result is 1.0
b = Math.floor(1.01);   // result is 1.0
c = Math.floor(1.0);    // result is 1.0
d = Math.floor(-1.01);  // result is -2.0
```

See Also

Math, Math.ceil( ), Math.round( )

Math.LN10 Constant — mathematical constant $\log_e 10$

Availability

Navigator 2.0, Internet Explorer 3.0

Synopsis

```
Math.LN10
```

Description

Math.LN10 is $\log_e 10$, the natural logarithm of 10, which has a value of approximately 2.3025850929940459011.

See Also

Math, Math.exp(), Math.LN2, Math.log(), Math.LOG2E, Math.LOG10E

Math.LN2 Constant — mathematical constant $\log_e 2$

Availability

Navigator 2.0, Internet Explorer 3.0

Synopsis

```
Math.LN2
```

Description

Math.LN2 is $\log_e 2$, the natural logarithm of 2, which has a value of approximately 0.693147180559945282623.

See Also

Math, Math.exp(), Math.LN10, Math.log(), Math.LOG2E, Math.LOG10E

Math.log() Function — compute a natural logarithm

Availability

Navigator 2.0, Internet Explorer 3.0

Synopsis

```
Math.log(x)
```

Arguments

x Any numeric value or expression greater than zero.

Returns

The natural logarithm of x.

Description

Math.log() computes $\log_e x$, the natural logarithm of its argument. The argument must be greater than zero.

Usage

You can compute the base-10 and base-2 logarithms of a number with these formulas:

$$\log_{10} x = \log_{10} e \cdot \log_e x$$
$$\log_2 x = \log_2 e \cdot \log_e x$$

These formulas translate into the following JavaScript functions:

```
function log10(x) { return Math.LOG10E * Math.log(x); }
function log2(x) { return  Math.LOG2E * Math.log(x); }
```

See Also

Math, Math.exp( ), Math.LOG2E, Math.LOG10E

Math.LOG10E Constant — mathematical constant $\log_{10} e$

Availability

Navigator 2.0, Internet Explorer 3.0

Synopsis

```
Math.LOG10E
```

Description

`Math.LOG10E` is $\log_{10} e$, the base 10 logarithm of the constant *e*. It has a value of approximately 0.43429448190325181667.

See Also

Math, Math.exp( ), Math.LN2, Math.LN10, Math.log( ), Math.LOG2E

Math.LOG2E Constant — mathematical constant $\log_2 e$

Availability

Navigator 2.0, Internet Explorer 3.0

Synopsis

```
Math.LOG2E
```

Description

`Math.LOG2E` is $\log_2 e$, the base 2 logarithm of the constant *e*. It has a value of approximately 1.442695040888963387.

See Also

Math, Math.exp( ), Math.LN2, Math.LN10, Math.log( ), Math.LOG10E

Math.max() Function — return the larger of two values

Availability

Navigator 2.0, Internet Explorer 3.0

Synopsis

```
Math.max(a, b)
```

Arguments

a, b   Any two numeric values or expressions.

Returns

The larger of the two values a and b.

Description

Math.max() returns whichever of its two arguments is larger.

See Also

Math, Math.min()

Math.min() Function — return the smaller of two values

Availability

Navigator 2.0, Internet Explorer 3.0

Synopsis

```
Math.min(a, b)
```

Arguments

a, b   Any two numeric values or expressions.

Returns

The smaller of the two values a and b.

Description

Math.min() returns whichever of its two arguments is smaller.

See Also

Math, Math.max()

Math.PI Constant — mathematical constant π

Availability

Navigator 2.0, Internet Explorer 3.0

Synopsis

```
Math.PI
```

Description

Math.PI is the constant π or pi, the ratio of the circumference of a circle to its diameter. Pi has a value of approximately 3.141592653589793116.

See Also

Math, Math.E

Math.pow() Function — compute x^y

Availability

Navigator 2.0, Internet Explorer 3.0

Synopsis

```
Math.pow(x, y)
```

Arguments

x   The number or numeric expression to be raised to a power.

y   The power that x is to be raised to.

Returns

x to the power of y, x^y

Description

`Math.pow()` raises its first argument to the power of its second argument and returns the result.

Usage

Any values of x and y may be passed to `Math.pow()`. However, if the result is an imaginary or complex number, then `Math.pow()` returns zero. In practice, this means that if x is negative, then y should be a positive or negative integer. Also, bear in mind that large exponents can easily cause floating-point overflow and return a value of infinity.

See Also

Math, Math.exp()

Math.random() Function — return a pseudo-random number

Availability

Navigator 3.0; buggy in Internet Explorer 3.0; Unix platforms only for Navigator 2.0

Synopsis

```
Math.random( )
```

Arguments

None.

Returns

A pseudo-random number between 0.0 and 1.0.

Description

`Math.random()` returns a psuedo-random number between 0.0 and 1.0. Note that in Navigator 2.0, this function only works for Unix platforms. In Internet Explorer 3.0, `Math.random()` generates pseudo-random numbers, but is not randomly seeded, so it generates the same sequence of numbers each time the browser is started.

Usage

Since `Math.random()` does not work on all platforms, you should not rely on it if you want your scripts to be really portable. If you need only a single pseudo-random number, you can often use a portion of the current time, such as (`new Date()).getSeconds()`).

If you need need a sequence of more reliably pseudo-random numbers (for a game, perhaps), you'll have to write your own pseudo-random number generator. The following code is based on a linear congruential algorithm in the book *Numerical Recipes*, and produces simple, non-cryptographic, pseudo-random numbers:

```
function random() {
  random.seed = (random.seed*random.a + random.c) % random.m;
  return random.seed / random.m;
}
random.m=714025; random.a=4096; random.c=150889;
random.seed = (new Date()).getTime()%random.m;
```

Bugs

Internet Explorer 3.0 does not randomly seed its random-number generator, so it generates the same sequence of random numbers each time the browser starts up. This bug will be fixed in a future release.

See Also

Math

Math.round() Function — round to the nearest integer

Availability

Navigator 2.0, Internet Explorer 3.0

Synopsis

```
Math.round(x)
```

Arguments

x   Any number or numeric expression

Returns

The integer closest to *x*.

Description

Math.round() rounds its argument up or down to the nearest integer.

Bugs

In Navigator 2.0, Math.round() did not correctly round very large numbers. The following workaround can be used:

```
function my_round(num)
{
    var fl = Math.floor(num);
    var ce = Math.ceil(num);
    return (fl == ce) ? num :
        ((num - fl) < (num - ce)) ? fl :
        ce;
}
```

See Also

Math, Math.ceil( ), Math.floor( )

Math.sin( ) Function — compute a sine

Availability

Navigator 2.0, Internet Explorer 3.0

Synopsis

Math.sin(*x*)

Arguments

x   An angle, in radians.

Returns

The sine of *x*.

Description

Math.tan() computes and returns the sine of its numeric argument, which must be an angle specified in radians.

Usage

To convert degrees to radians, multiply by 0.017453293 ($2\pi/360$).

See Also

Math, Math.asin( ), Math.cos( ), Math.tan( )

Math.sqrt() Function — compute a square root

Availability

Navigator 2.0, Internet Explorer 3.0

Synopsis

```
Math.sqrt(x)
```

Arguments

x   Any numeric value or expression greater than or equal to zero.

Returns

The square root of *x*.

Description

`Math.sqrt()` returns the square root of its argument, which must be greater than or equal to zero.

Usage

You can compute roots other than the square root of a number with `Math.pow()`. For example:

```
function sq_rt(x)   { return Math.pow(x,1/2); }
function cube_rt(x) { return Math.pow(x,1/3); }
```

See Also

Math, Math.pow()

Math.SQRT1_2 Constant — mathematical constant $1/\sqrt{2}$

Availability

Navigator 2.0, Internet Explorer 3.0

Synopsis

```
Math.SQRT1_2
```

Description

`Math.SQRT1_2` is $1/\sqrt{2}$, the reciprocal of the square root of 2. It has a value of approximately 0.70710678118654757274.

See Also

Math, Math.sqrt(), Math.SQRT2

Math.SQRT2 Constant — mathematical constant √2

Availability

Navigator 2.0, Internet Explorer 3.0

Synopsis

```
Math.SQRT2
```

Description

Math.SQRT2 is the constant $\sqrt{2}$, the square root of 2. It has a value of approximately 1.4142135623730951455.

See Also

Math, Math.sqrt( ), Math.SQRT1_2

Math.tan( ) Function — compute a tangent

Availability

Navigator 2.0, Internet Explorer 3.0

Synopsis

```
Math.tan(x)
```

Arguments

x An angle, measured in radians.

Returns

The tangent of the specified angle x.

Description

Math.tan( ) computes and returns the tangent of its numeric argument, which must be an angle specified in radians.

Usage

To convert degrees to radians, multiply by 0.017453293 ($2\pi/360$).

See Also

Math, Math.atan( ), Math.cos( ), Math.sin( )

MimeType Object — represents a MIME datatype

Availability

Navigator 3.0

Synopsis

```
navigator.mimeTypes[i]
navigator.mimeTypes["name"]
navigator.mimeTypes.length
```

Properties

description   A read-only string that provides an English description of the content and encoding of the type.

enabledPlugin

A reference to the Plugin object that supports this MIME type, or null, if no installed and enabled plug-in supports it.

suffixes   A read-only string that specifies a comma-separated list of the common file-name extensions associated with this MIME type.

type   A read-only string that indicates the name of the MIME datatype, such as "text/html" or "video/mpeg".

Description

The MimeType object represents a MIME type (i.e., a data format) supported by the browser. The format may be supported directly by the browser, or may be supported through an external "helper application," or a plug-in for embedded data.

Usage

The navigator.mimeTypes[] array may be indexed numerically, or with the name of the desired MIME type (which is the value of the type property). In order to check which MIME types are supported by the browser, you can loop through each element in the array numerically. Or, if you just want to check whether a specific type is supported, you can write code like the following:

```
var show_movie = (navigator.mimeTypes["video/mpeg"] != null);
```

See Also

Navigator, Plugin

MimeType.description Property — a description of a MIME type

Availability

Navigator 3.0

Synopsis

```
mimetype.description
```

Description

The description property of a MimeType object is a human-readable description (in English) of the data type described by the MimeType. This description is more verbose and understandable than the name property.

See Also

MimeType, MimeType.type, Navigator, Plugin

MimeType.enabledPlugin Property — the plug-in that handles the MIME type

Availability

Navigator 3.0

Synopsis

```
mimetype.enabledPlugin
```

Description

The `enabledPlugin` property is a reference to a Plugin object that represents the installed and enabled plug-in that handles the specified MIME type. If the MIME type is not handled by any plug-ins, then the value of this property will be `null`.

Usage

The `navigator.mimeType[ ]` array will tell you whether a given MIME type is supported by the browser in some fashion. The `enabledPlugin` property of the MimeType object, however tells you whether a particular supported type is supported with a plug-in or not (MIME types can also be supported with helper applications, or directly by the browser.) If a MIME type is supported by a plug-in, it can be embedded in a web page with the `<EMBED>` tag; otherwise it must be output in some other way.

See Also

MimeType, Plugin

MimeType.suffixes Property — common file suffixes for a MIME type

Availability

Navigator 3.0

Synopsis

```
mimetype.suffixes
```

Description

The `suffixes` property of a MimeType object is a read-only string that contains a comma separated list of filename suffixes (not including the '.' character) that are commonly used with files of the specified MIME type. For example, the the suffixes for the `text/html` MIME type are "html, htm".

See Also

MimeType, Navigator, Plugin

MimeType.type Property — the name of a MIME type

Availability

Navigator 3.0

Synopsis

```
mimetype.type
```

Description

The `type` property of a MimeType object is a read-only string that specifies the name of the MIME type. This is a unique string such as "text/html" or "image/jpeg" that distinguishes this MIME type from all others. It describes the general type of data and the data format used.

The value of the `type` property can also be used as an index to access the elements of the `navigator.mimeTypes[]` array.

See Also

MimeType, MimeType.description, Navigator, Plugin

---

name Property — see Window.name

---

navigate() Method — see Window.navigate()

---

navigator Property — reference to the Navigator object

Availability

Navigator 2.0, Internet Explorer 3.0

Synopsis

```
navigator
```

Description

The `navigator` property contains a read-only reference to a Navigator object, which provides version and configuration information about the web browser. See the Navigator object for details.

All windows have a `navigator` property that refers to a Navigator object, and all Navigator objects contain the same values. Therefore, the Navigator object is usually referred to simply as `navigator` without an explicit window reference.

See Also

Navigator, Window

Navigator Object — information about the browser in use

Availability

Navigator 2.0, Internet Explorer 3.0; enhanced in Navigator 3.0

Synopsis

```
navigator
```

Properties

appCodeName The code name of the browser.

appName The name of the browser.

appVersion Version information for the browser.

mimeTypes[ ] An array of MimeType objects describing the MIME types recognized and supported by the browser. Added in Navigator 3.0.

mimeTypes.length
 The number of elements in the mimeTypes[ ] array.

plugins[ ] An array of Plugin objects describing the installed plug-ins. Added in Navigator 3.0.

plugins.length
 The number of elements in the plugins[ ] array.

userAgent The string passed by the browser as the user-agent header in HTTP requests.

Methods

javaEnabled( )
 Test whether Java is supported and enabled in the current browser. Added in Navigator 3.0.

plugins.refresh( )
 Check for newly installed plug-ins, enter them in the plugins[ ] array, and optionally reload documents using those plug-ins. Added in Navigator 3.0.

taintEnabled( )
 Test whether the data-tainting security model is supported and enabled in the current browser. Added in Navigator 3.0.

Description

The Navigator object contains properties that describe the web browser in use. You can use its properties to perform platform-specific customization. The name of this object obviously refers to the Netscape Navigator browser, but other browsers that implement JavaScript will support this object as well.

There is only a single instance of the Navigator object, which you can reference through the navigator property of any Window object. Because of the implicit window reference, you can always refer to the Navigator object simply as navigator.

See Also

MimeType, Plugin

Navigator.appCodeName Property — the code name of the browser

Availability

Navigator 2.0, Internet Explorer 3.0

Synopsis

```
navigator.appCodeName
```

Description

`navigator.appCodeName` is a read-only string property which specifies the code name of the browser. For Navigator 2.0 and 3.0, the value of this property is "Mozilla". For compatibility, Internet Explorer 3.0 also uses "Mozilla" as the value of this property.

See Also

Navigator, Navigator.appName, Navigator.appVersion, Navigator.userAgent

Navigator.appName Property — the application name of the browser

Availability

Navigator 2.0, Internet Explorer 3.0

Synopsis

```
navigator.appName
```

Description

`navigator.appName` is a read-only string property that specifies the name of the browser. For Navigator 2.0 and 3.0, the value of this property is "Netscape". In Internet Explorer 3.0, the value of this property is "Microsoft Internet Explorer".

See Also

Navigator, Navigator.appCodeName, Navigator.appVersion, Navigator.userAgent

Navigator.appVersion Property — the platform and version of the browser

Availability

Navigator 2.0, Internet Explorer 3.0

Synopsis

```
navigator.appVersion
```

Description

`navigator.appVersion` is a read-only string property that specifies platform and version information for the browser. For Navigator 2.0 and 3.0, this property has the following format:

```
version (platform; encryption[; detail])
```

version is the version number; "2.01", for example. *platform* is a general indication of the platform. For example, "Win16" indicates a 16-bit version of Windows, "Win95" indicates Windows 95, and "X11" indicates a Unix platform running the X Window System. *encryption* is either "U" indicating a domestic U.S. release of Navigator, with strong encryption, or "I" indicating an international release with weakened encryption capabilities (to comply with U.S. government export control laws on cryptographic technologies.) Finally, the optional *detail* may provide additional information about the platform. On my platform, for example, it is the string "Linux 1.2.13 i486".

In Internet Explorer 3.0 running on Windows 95, this property has the value "2.0 (compatible; MSIE 3.0A; Windows 95)". Note that IE 3.0 reports a version number of "2.0". This is to be compatible with Navigator 2.0, which it most closely resembles. The remainder of the string does contain complete IE version information, however.

See Also

Navigator, Navigator.appCodeName, Navigator.appName,
Navigator.userAgent

Navigator.javaEnabled( ) Method — test whether Java is available

Availability

Navigator 3.0

Synopsis

```
navigator.javaEnabled()
```

Arguments

None.

Returns

`true` if, and only if, Java is supported by and enabled on the current browser.

Description

You can use `navigator.javaEnabled()` to check whether the current browser will be able to display applets, and also whether JavaScript will be able to work with Java objects through the Properties object. If Java is not available, you can use JavaScript to perform some alternative action.

See Also

Document.applets[], Navigator, Properties

Navigator.mimeTypes[ ] Property — array of supported MIME types

Availability

Navigator 3.0

Synopsis

```
navigator.mimeTypes[]
navigator.mimeTypes.length
```

Description

`navigator.mimeTypes` is an array of MimeType objects, each of which represents one of the MIME types (e.g., "text/html" and "image/gif") supported by the browser. There are `navigator.mimeTypes.length` elements in the array.

See Also

Navigator, Navigator.plugins[], MimeType, Plugin

Navigator.plugins[ ] Property — array of installed plug-ins

Availability

Navigator 3.0

Synopsis

```
navigator.plugins[]
navigator.plugins.length
```

Description

`navigator.plugins` is an array of Plugin objects, each of which represents one plug-in that has been installed along with the browser. There are `navigator.plugins.length` elements in the array. The Plugin object provides information about the plug-in, including a list of MIME types it supports.

A *plug-in* is the Netscape name for a software package that can be invoked by Navigator to display specific data types within the browser window.

See Also

Navigator, Navigator.mimeTypes[], MimeType, Plugin

Navigator.plugins.refresh() Property — make newly installed plug-ins available

Availability

Navigator 3.0

Synopsis

```
navigator.plugins.refresh([reload])
```

Arguments

reload   An optional Boolean argument that, if `true` specifies that `refresh()` should reload any pages that contain <EMBED> tags and use plug-ins. If this argument is omitted, it defaults to `false`.

Description

The `refresh()` method causes Navigator to check whether any new plug-ins have been installed. If so, the `plugins[]` array is updated ("refreshed") to include the newly installed plug-ins. If the *reload* argument is specified and is `true`, then Navigator will also reload any currently displayed documents that contain <EMBED> tags and use plug-ins.

Note the unusual synopsis for this method. `refresh()` is a method of the `plugins[]` array, not of the Navigator object. For almost all purposes, however, it is simpler to consider it a method of the Navigator object, which is why it is grouped with the methods and properties of that object here.

See Also

Navigator, Navigator.plugins[], Plugin

Navigator.taintEnabled() Method — test whether data tainting is enabled

Availability

Navigator 3.0

Synopsis

```
navigator.taintEnabled()
```

Arguments

None.

Returns

`true` if, and only if, the data-tainting security model is supported by and enabled on the current browser, `false` if the data-tainting security model is not in effect.

Description

You can use `navigator.taintEnabled()` to test whether the browser that your JavaScript code is running on uses the data-tainting security model or not. Without data tainting in effect, there are a number of restrictions on what properties your code can read. With data tainting on, there are restrictions on what kinds of data your script can send to a server in a form submission.

See Chapter 20 for a full discussion of JavaScript security, and JavaScript capabilities both with and without data tainting.

See Also

Navigator, Chapter 20

Navigator.userAgent Property — the HTTP user-agent value

Availability

Navigator 2.0, Internet Explorer 3.0

Synopsis

```
navigator.userAgent
```

Description

`navigator.userAgent` is a read-only string property that specifies the value the browser uses for the user-agent header in HTTP requests. In Navigator 2.0 and 3.0, this property is the value of `navigator.appCodeName` followed by a slash and the value of `navigator.appVersion`. For example:

```
Mozilla/2.01 (Win16; I)
```

In Internet Explorer 3.0, this property has the value "Mozilla/2.0 (compatible; MSIE 3.0A; Windows 95)". Once again, this is the value of `appCodeName` followed by a slash and the value of `appVersion`.

See Also

Navigator, Navigator.appCodeName, Navigator.appName, Navigator.appVersion

---

netscape Property — the netscape.* package

Availability

Navigator 3.0

Synopsis

```
netscape
```

Description

`netscape` is a global property of the Window object, and is usually used without reference to any particular window. It is a synonym for `Packages.netscape`, and contains a read-only reference to a JavaPackage object that represents the top node of the *netscape.** package name hierarchy. The `netscape` Package contains, for example, a `javascript` property which is a reference to the Package object for the *netscape.javascript* package.

See Also

JavaPackage, Packages.netscape

Number Object — place-holder for numeric constants

Availability

Navigator 3.0

Synopsis

```
Number.constant
```

Constructor

```
new Number(value)
```

Arguments

value   The numeric value of the Number object being created. This argument will be converted to a number, if necessary.

Returns

The newly constructed Number object

Constants

MAX_VALUE   The largest representable number.

MIN_VALUE   The smallest representable number.

NaN   Special Not-a-Number value.

NEGATIVE_INFINITY
             Special negative infinite value; returned on overflow.

POSITIVE_INFINITY
             Special infinite value; returned on overflow.

Methods

toString()   Convert a number to a string, using a specified radix (base).

valueOf()   Return the primitive numeric value contained by the Number object.

Description

Numbers are a basic, primitive data type in JavaScript. In Navigator 3.0, however, JavaScript also supports the Number object, an object type that represents a primitive numeric value. JavaScript automatically converts between the primitive and object forms as necessary. In Navigator 3.0, you can explicitly create a Number object with the Number() constructor, although there is rarely any need to do so.

The Number() constructor is actually more commonly used as a place-holder for five useful numeric constants: the largest and smallest representable numbers, positive and negative infinity, and the special Not-a-Number value. Note that these values are properties of the

Number() constructor function itself, not of individual number objects. For example, you use the MAX_VALUE property as follows:

```
biggest = Number.MAX_VALUE
```

not like this:

```
n = new Number(2);
biggest = n.MAX_VALUE
```

By contrast, the toString() method of the Number object is a method of each Number object, not of the Number() constructor function. As noted above, JavaScript automatically converts from primitive numeric values to Number objects whenever necessary. This means that we can use the toString() method with a variable that holds a number, even though that value is not actually an object:

```
value = 1234;
binary_value = n.toString(2);
```

What happens in this code is that JavaScript implicitly invokes the Number() constructor to convert the number n to a temporary Number object for which the toString() method can be invoked. It is this toString() method that is the main reason for the existence of the Number object in the first place.

See Also

Math, Object

Number.MAX_VALUE Constant — the maximum numeric value

Availability

Navigator 3.0

Synopsis

```
Number.MAX_VALUE
```

Description

Number.MAX_VALUE is the largest number representable in JavaScript. Its value is approximately 1.79E+308.

See Also

Number, Number.MIN_VALUE

Number.MIN_VALUE Constant — the minimum numeric value

Availability

Navigator 3.0

Synopsis

```
Number.MIN_VALUE
```

Description

`Number.MIN_VALUE` is the smallest (closest to zero, not most negative) number representable in JavaScript. Its value is approximately 2.22E-308.

See Also

Number, Number.MAX_VALUE

Number.NaN Constant — the special Not-a-Number value

Availability

Navigator 3.0

Synopsis

```
Number.NaN
```

Description

`Number.NaN` is a special value that indicates that the result of some arithmetic operation (such as division by zero) or mathematical function is "Not-a-Number." `parseInt()` and `parseFloat()` return this value when they cannot parse the specified string, and you might use `Number.NaN` in a similar way to indicate an error condition for some function that normally returns a valid number.

JavaScript prints the `Number.NaN` value as NaN. Note that the NaN value always compares unequal to any other number, including NaN itself. Thus, you cannot check for the Not-a-Number value by comparing to `Number.NaN`. Use the `isNaN()` function instead.

See Also

isNaN( ), Number

Number.NEGATIVE_INFINITY Constant — negative infinity

Availability

Navigator 3.0

Synopsis

```
Number.NEGATIVE_INFINITY
```

Description

`Number.NEGATIVE_INFINITY` is a special numeric value that is returned when an arithmetic operation or mathematical function generates a negative value greater than the largest representable number in JavaScript (i.e., more negative than `-Number.MAX_VALUE`).

JavaScript displays the `NEGATIVE_INFINITY` value as `-Infinity`. This value behaves mathematically like an infinity—for example, anything multiplied by infinity is infinity, and anything divided by infinity is zero.

See Also

Number, Number.POSITIVE_INFINITY

Number.POSITIVE_INFINITY Constant — infinity

Availability

Navigator 3.0

Synopsis

```
Number.POSITIVE_INFINITY
```

Description

`Number.POSITIVE_INFINITY` is a special numeric value that is returned when an arithmetic operation or mathematical function generates a value greater than the largest representable number in JavaScript (i.e., greater than `Number.MAX_VALUE`).

JavaScript displays the `POSITIVE_INFINITY` value as `Infinity`. This value behaves mathematically like an infinity—for example, anything multiplied by infinity is infinity, and anything divided by infinity is zero.

Note that when numbers "underflow," i.e., when they become less than `Number.MIN_VALUE`, JavaScript converts them to zero.

See Also

Number, Number.NEGATIVE_INFINITY

Number.prototype Property — see Function.prototype

Number.toString() Method — convert a number to a string

Availability

Navigator 3.0

Synopsis

```
number.toString([radix])
```

Arguments

radix   This optional argument specifies the base that should be used to convert the number. It should be an integer between 2 and 16. If no value is specified, then base 10 is used.

Returns

The string representation of the number in the specified *radix*.

Description

The `toString()` method of the Number object converts a Number to a string, using the specified *radix* or base. If no *radix* is specified, base 10 is used.

Usage

Because JavaScript automatically converts numeric values to temporary Number objects when needed, you can use the toString() method on numbers, even though they are primitive types rather than true JavaScript objects:

```
n = 123;
s = n.toString(16);
```

Note, however, that because of syntactic restrictions in the language, you cannot use the toString() method on numeric literals. You must assign them to variables first; i.e., you *cannot* rewrite the two lines of code above as:

```
s = 123.toString(16);
```

See Also

Number, Object.toString()

Number.valueOf() Method — see Object.valueOf()

Object Object — features of all JavaScript objects

Availability

Navigator 2.0, Internet Explorer 3.0; enhanced in Navigator 3.0

Constructor

```
new Object();
new Object(value);        Navigator 3.0
```

Arguments

value   In Navigator 3.0, this optional argument specifies a primitive JavaScript value—a number, a Boolean, a string, or a function—that is to be converted to an object.

Returns

If no *value* argument is passed, this constructor returns a newly created object, which has no properties defined. If a primitive *value* argument is specified, then the constructor creates and returns a Number, Boolean, String, or Function object wrapper around the primitive value.

Properties

constructor   A read-only reference to the JavaScript function that was the constructor for the object. This property is not defined in Navigator 2.0 or Internet Explorer 3.0.

Methods

assign()   A method, which, if defined, is used to implement the JavaScript assignment operator (=).

eval()   Evaluate a string of JavaScript code in the context of the given object. In Navigator 2.0 and Internet Explorer 3.0, eval() is a standalone function, rather than a method of Object.

toString()   A method, which, if defined, is used to convert an object to a string.

valueOf()   Return the primitive value of the object, if any. For objects of type Object, this method simply returns the object itself. For other object types, such as Number and Boolean, this method returns the primitive value associated with the object. This method was added in Navigator 3.0.

Description

The Object object is a built-in data type of the JavaScript language. It serves as the "super-class" for all other JavaScript objects, and therefore methods of the Object object are methods of all other object types. Similarly, the behavior of the Object object is shared by all other object types. The basic behavior of objects in JavaScript is explained in Chapter 7.

A number of the Object methods listed above are unusual in that they are not predefined, and are not intended to be invoked by the JavaScript code that you write. Instead these are methods that you can define for any object, and that will be invoked by the JavaScript system at appropriate times, to perform some sort of operation on the object. The toString() method is an example: once you have defined this method for an object, the system will invoke it whenever it needs to convert that object to a string.

JavaScript allows object syntax to be used to refer to properties and methods of primitive datatypes, such as JavaScript strings. When you do this with JavaScript expressions such as "hello".toUpperCase(), what actually happens is that JavaScript creates a temporary object "wrapper" for the primitive value (a string in this case) so that the method can be invoked or the property accessed. This primitive value to object conversion is performed automatically by JavaScript whenever necessary, but if you ever need to perform it yourself, you can do so by passing the primitive value to the Object() constructor.

Usage

When an Object object is newly created, it has no properties defined. As described in Chapter 7, you can add a property definition to an object simply by assigning a value to the property. Furthermore, objects can be used as associative arrays. In some cases you will want to create an "empty" object of this sort for use in your programs. You do this with:

```
blank_obj = new Object();
```

In other cases, however, you will want to use a number of objects that are all of a certain type, such as objects that represent complex numbers, for example. To do this, you should write a constructor function for your object "class" and initialize the properties of the object as desired. You may also want to define a prototype object for your constructor function that will provide methods for all objects of your new object type.

Example

Defining the `toString()` method, and also the less frequently used `assign()` and `valueOf()` methods of an object, is most efficiently done in a constructor method for your object type, or with the prototype object of your object.

```
// define a constructor for the Complex object type
function Complex(x,y) { this.x = x; this.y = y; }

// Create a dummy object to force the prototype object to be created
new Complex(0,0);

// give all Complex objects a toString() method
Complex.prototype.toString =
    new Function("return '{' + this.x + ',' + this.y + '}';");

// Create an object of this new Complex type
c = new Complex(2, 2);

// Convert the object to a string, implicitly invoking the
// toString() method, and display the string.
alert("c = " + c);    // displays string "{2,2}"
```

See Also

Array, Boolean, Function, Function.prototype, Number, String, Window, Chapter 7

Object.assign() Method — overload the assignment operator

Availability

Navigator 3.0

Synopsis

```
object.assign(value)
```

Arguments

value   The value to be assigned. The `assign()` method should, in some fashion, assign *value* to the object.

Returns

Nothing.

Description

The `assign()` method is not one you usually call explicitly in your JavaScript code. Instead you define this method for certain objects, and the system invokes the method automatically when a value is assigned to that object.

If an object o has an `assign()` method defined, then the assignment:

```
o = value;
```

is translated to the following function call:

```
o.assign(value);
```

The `assign()` method should be written to expect a single argument, which will always be the value of the right-hand side of an assignment operator. When invoked, the object will refer to the left-hand side of the assignment. The body of the method should "assign," in some appropriate fashion, the *value* to the object.

Usage

You might define the `assign()` method when you want assignment to an object to perform some sort of side effect. For example, in client-side JavaScript, assigning a URL value to the `location` field of a window object causes the browser to load that URL into the window.

Sometimes, you may want to define an `assign()` method for only one single special object. In other cases, however, you will want all instances of a class of objects to have a special assignment behavior. In this case, you should set the `assign()` method in a constructor function or a prototype object.

Example

The following code shows how you could define an `assign()` method for a class of objects so that when one object of this class is assigned to another, the object's fields will be assigned "by value," rather than assigning "by reference."

```
// Define a function suitable for use as our assign() method.
function copy_fields(value)
{
    for (field in value) this[field] = value[field];
}

// Define it as the assign() method in a prototype object, so that
// all instances of the object type have this assign() method.
MyObject.prototype.assign = copy_fields;
```

See Also

Object

Object.constructor Property — an object's constructor function

Availability

Navigator 3.0

Synopsis

```
object.constructor
```

Description

The constructor property of any object is a read-only reference to the function that was used as the constructor for that object. For example, if you create an array a with the Array() constructor, then a.constructor will be Array:

```
a = new Array(1,2,3);    // create an object
a.constructor == Array   // evaluates to true
```

One common use of the constructor property is to determine the type of unknown objects. Given an unknown value, you can use the typeof operator to determine whether it is a primitive value or an object. If it is an object, you can use the constructor property to determine what type of object it is. For example, the following function determines whether a given value is a Document object:

```
function isDocument(x) {
    return ((typeof x == "object") && (x.constructor == "Document"));
}
```

Note, however, that this technique is not possible with all object types. In Navigator 3.0 there is no Window() constructor, for example, and Window objects have their constructor property set to Object.

See Also

Object, Chapter 7

Object.eval() Method — evaluate JavaScript code in a string

Availability

Navigator 2.0, Internet Explorer 3.0; modified in Navigator 3.0

Synopsis

```
eval(code)              Navigator 2.0, Internet Explorer 3.0
object.eval(code)       Navigator 3.0
```

Arguments

code   A string that contains the JavaScript expression to be evaluated or the statements to be executed.

Returns

The value of the evaluated *code*, if any.

Description

In Navigator 2.0 and Internet Explorer 3.0, eval() is a built-in function (i.e., not a method of any object), but it behaves as if it is a method of the Window object. In Navigator 3.0, eval() has become a method of Object, so it can be invoked through a JavaScript object of any type.

eval() executes the JavaScript code in its string argument *code*. *code* may contain one or more JavaScript statements. If there is more than one statement, they must be separated from each other by semicolons. Recall that JavaScript expressions are themselves a simple type of statement, so you can also use eval() to evaluate a JavaScript expression rather than execute a statement. eval() returns the value of the last expression in *code* that it evaluates. If *code* contains only statements that have no value, eval() returns nothing.

In Navigator 2.0 and Internet Explorer 3.0, eval() evaluates the specified code in the context of the current Window object. In Navigator 3.0, it evaluates the code in the context of the object through which it is invoked. Thus, in Navigator 3.0, when you use eval() without an object specified to its left, it is implicitly invoked through the current window object, and its behavior is the same as in Navigator 2.0.

But in Navigator 3.0, eval() can also be invoked through other objects:

```
var x = 1;
o = new Object();
o.x = 2;
o.eval('x');  // evaluated in o's context; returns 2
eval('x');    // evaluated in Window context; returns 1
```

Usage

eval() provides the capability for a JavaScript program to dynamically modify the code that it executes. It gives you the ability to write a JavaScript program that acts as a JavaScript interpreter. In practice, eval() is not frequently used. In most cases, you can do anything you want with a statically defined function.

Bugs

eval() crashes Navigator 2.0 on 16-bit Windows (Windows 3.1) platforms. A workaround that is possible in some cases is to use Window.setTimeout() with a zero-millisecond delay as a replacement for eval().

See Also

Object, Window.setTimeout()

Object.prototype Property — see Function.prototype

Object.toString() Method — define an object's string representation

Availability

Navigator 2.0, Internet Explorer 3.0

Synopsis

```
object.toString()
```

Arguments

None.

Returns

A string representing the object.

Description

The `toString()` method is not one you usually call directly in your JavaScript programs. Instead, you define this method in your objects, and the system calls it whenever it needs to convert your object to a string.

The JavaScript system invokes the `toString()` method to convert an object to a string whenever the object is used in a "string context." For example, if an object is converted to a string when it is passed to a function that expects a string argument:

```
alert(my_object);
```

Similarly, objects are converted to strings when they are concatenated to strings with the + operator:

```
alert('My object is: ' + my_object);
```

The `toString()` method will be invoked without arguments, and should return a string. To be useful, the string you return should be based, in some way, on the value of the object for which the method was invoked.

Usage

The `toString()` method can be quite useful when you are debugging JavaScript programs—it allows you to print objects and see their value. For this reason alone, it is a good idea to define a `toString()` method for every object class you create.

The string returned by `toString()` can be as complex as you like, and this method need not be restricted to use in debugging, of course. For example, a `toString()` method could be defined to return HTML formatted text. If the wording and formatting are chosen appropriately, then you could use `document.write()` to output a string representation of an object directly into an HTML document!

Although the `toString()` method is usually invoked automatically by the system, there are times when you may invoke it yourself. For example, you might want to do an explicit conversion of an object to a string in a situation where JavaScript will not do it automatically for you:

```
y = Math.sqrt(x);
ystr = y.toString();
```

Note in this example that numbers have a built-in `toString()` method that you can use to force a conversion.

In other circumstances, you might choose to use a `toString()` call even in a context where JavaScript would do the conversion automatically. Using `toString()` explicitly can help to make your code clearer:

```
alert(my_obj.toString());
```

It does not generally make sense to define a `toString()` method for only a single object, so you will usually assign this method to a prototype object so that it is available to all objects in a class of objects.

Example

You might define a simple class of Circle objects and specify a toString() method for it as follows. (In Navigator 3.0, you could use a prototype object to define the method rather that setting it each time the constructor function is called.)

```
function Circle_toString() {
    return "[A circle of radius " + this.r + "]";
}

function Circle(r) {
    this.r = r;
    this.toString = Circle_toString();
}
```

See Also

Object

Object.valueOf() Method — the primitive value of the specified object

Availability

Navigator 3.0

Synopsis

```
object.valueOf();
```

Arguments

None.

Returns

The primitive value associated with the *object*, if any. Otherwise, returns the object itself.

Description

The valueOf() method of an object returns the primitive value associated with that object, if there is one. For objects of type Object, and for the client-side JavaScript objects, there is no primitive value, and this method simply returns the object itself.

For objects of type Number, however, valueOf() returns the primitive numeric value represented by the object. Similarly, it returns the primitive Boolean value associated with a Boolean object, the string associated with a String object, and the function associated with a Function object.

It is rarely, if ever, necessary to invoke the valueOf() method yourself. JavaScript does this automatically whenever an object is used where a primitive value is expected. In fact, because of this automatic invocation of the valueOf() method, it is difficult to even distinguish between primitive values and their corresponding objects. The typeof operator will show you the difference between strings and String objects and functions and Function objects, for example, but in practical terms, you can use them equivalently in your JavaScript code.

The `valueOf()` methods of the Number, Boolean, String, and Function objects convert these "wrapper" objects to the primitive values they represent. The `Object()` constructor performs the opposite operation when invoked with a number, Boolean, string, or function argument: it wraps the primitive value in an appropriate object wrapper. JavaScript performs this primitive to object conversion for you in almost all circumstances, so it is rarely, if ever, necessary to invoke the `Object()` constructor in this way.

Usage

In some circumstances, you may want to define a custom `valueOf()` method for your own objects. For example, you might define a JavaScript object type to represent complex numbers (a real number plus an imaginary number). As part of this object type, you'd probably define methods for performing complex addition, multiplication, and so on. But you might also want the ability to treat your complex numbers like ordinary real numbers by discarding the imaginary part. You might do something like the following:

```
Complex.prototype.valueOf = new Function("return this.real");
```

With this `valueOf()` method defined for your Complex object type, you could then do things like pass one of your complex number objects to `Math.sqrt()`, which would compute the square root of the real portion of the complex number.

See Also

Object, Object.toString()

---

open() Method — see Window.open()

---

opener Property — see Window.opener

Option Object — an option in a Select box

Availability

Navigator 2.0, Internet Explorer 3.0; enhanced in Navigator 3.0

Synopsis

```
select.options[i]
```

Properties

`defaultSelected`

> A read-only Boolean that specifies whether this option is selected by default. Set by the `SELECTED` attribute.

`index`   A read-only integer that specifies the index of this option within the array of options.

`selected`   A read/write Boolean that specifies whether this option is currently selected. Its initial value is specified by the `SELECTED` attribute.

text   The text that describes the option. It is the plain text (not formatted HTML text) that follows the <OPTION> tag. In Navigator 2.0 and Internet Explorer 3.0, this property is read-only. In Navigator 3.0 it is read/write.

value   A read/write string that specifies the value to be passed to the server if this option is selected when the form is submitted. The initial value is specified by the VALUE attribute.

Constructor

```
new Option([text, [value, [defaultSelected, [selected]]]])
```

Arguments

text   An optional string argument that specifies the text property of the Option object.

value   An optional string argument that specifies the value property of the Option object.

defaultSelected
                  An optional Boolean argument that specifies the defaultSelected property of the Option object.

selected   An optional Boolean argument that specifies the selected property of the Option object.

Returns

The newly created Option object.

HTML Syntax

An Option object is created by an <OPTION> tag within a <SELECT> which is itself within a <FORM>. Multiple <OPTION> tags typically appear within the <SELECT>.

```
<FORM ...>
  <SELECT  ...>
   <OPTION
       [ VALUE="value" ]          the value returned when the form is submitted
       [ SELECTED ] >             specifies whether this option is initially selected
     plain_text_label             the text to display for this option

         ...
  </SELECT>
         ...
  </FORM>
```

Description

The Option object describes a single option displayed within a Select object. The properties of this object specify whether it is selected by default, whether is is currently selected, what position it has in the options[ ] array of its containing Select object, what text it displays, and what value it passes to the server if it is selected when the containing form is submitted.

Note that although the text displayed by this option is specified outside of the <OPTION> tag, that text must be plain, unformatted text, without any HTML tags. This is so that the text can be properly displayed in list boxes and drop-down menus that do not support HTML formatting.

You can dynamically create new Option objects for display in a Select object with the Option() constructor. Once a new Option object is created, it can be appended to the list of options in a Select object by assigning it to the variable `options[options.length]`. See `Select.options[ ]` for details.

See Also

Select, Select.options[ ]

Option.defaultSelected Property — specifies whether an object is selected by default

Availability

Navigator 2.0, Internet Explorer 3.0

Synopsis

```
option.defaultSelected
```

Description

The `defaultSelected` property is a read-only Boolean that specifies whether the Option *option* is initially selected when the Select object that contains it is created. The Reset object uses this property to reset a Select object to its initial state, and you can use it to achieve the same effect in your code.

See Also

Option, Select

Option.index Property — the position of the option

Availability

Navigator 2.0, Internet Explorer 3.0

Synopsis

```
option.index
```

Description

The `index` property specifies the position or index of the Option object *option* within the `options[ ]` array of the Select object that contains it. The first Option object in the array is at index 0, and has its `index` property set to 0. The second Option has an `index` of 1, and so on.

See Also

Option, Select

Option.selected Property — whether the option is selected

Availability

Navigator 2.0, Internet Explorer 3.0

Synopsis

```
option.selected
```

Description

The `selected` property is a read/write Boolean value that specifies whether a Option object within a Select object is currently selected. You can use this property to test whether a given option is selected. You can also use it to select (by setting it to `true`) or deselect (by setting it to `false`) a given option. Note that when you select or deselect an option in this way the `Select.onchange()` event handler is not invoked.

Usage

To determine the selected options in a Select object, you can loop through the `Select.options[]` array testing the `selected` property of each item. When multiple selections are not allowed (i.e., when the `MULTIPLE` attribute does not appear in the `<SELECT>` tag), however, it is much easier to simply check use the `selectedIndex` property of the Select object.

See Also

Option, Select, Select.selectedIndex

Option.text Property — the label for an option

Availability

Navigator 2.0, Internet Explorer 3.0; enhanced in Navigator 3.0

Synopsis

```
option.text
```

Description

The `text` property is a string that specifies the text that appears to the user for the Option object *option*. The initial value of this property is whatever plain (without HTML tags) text appears after the `</OPTION>` tag and before the next `<OPTION>` tag or before the closing `</SELECT>` tag.

In Navigator 2.0, the `text` property is read-only. In Navigator 3.0, it is read/write. By setting a new value for this property, you can change the text that appears for the option within its Select object. Note that if you plan to use this technique, you should ensure that changing the option label does not make the Select object wider, or if the object must become wider, that there is no information to the right of the Select object that will become obscured when it grows.

See Also

Option, Select

Option.value Property — value returned when form is submitted

Availability

Navigator 2.0, Internet Explorer 3.0

Synopsis

```
option.value
```

Description

value is a read/write string property of the Option object. It specifies the text that is passed to the web server if the *option* is selected when the form is submitted. The initial value of value is specified by the VALUE attribute of the <OPTION> tag. If the form will be submitted to a server (as opposed to simply used by JavaScript on the client side) then each Option object within a Select object should have a distinct value.

See Also

Option, Select

Packages Object — packages of Java classes

Availability

Navigator 3.0

Synopsis

```
Packages
```

Properties

java   A reference to a JavaPackage object that represents the top node of the *java.** package hierarchy.

netscape   A reference to a JavaPackage object that represents the top node of the *netscape.** package hierarchy.

sun   A reference to a JavaPackage object that represents the top node of the *sun.** package hierarchy.

Description

The Packages property is a "global" variable in JavaScript. It is a read-only reference to a JavaPackage object, and is defined as a property of all Window objects. Because the Packages property is the same for all Window objects, you can always refer to it simply as Packages, rather than explicitly accessing it through a particular Window object.

A JavaPackage object in JavaScript is an object that contains references to other JavaPackage objects and to JavaClass objects. Each JavaPackage object represents a node in the tree of package names. The Packages property refers to a JavaPackage object that is the root of this package name hierarchy.

The `Packages` JavaPackage object contains three properties—`java`, `sun`, and `netscape`—all of which refer to other JavaPackage objects representing the *java.**, *sun.**, and *netscape.** Java packages.

Usage

The Window object also contains "global" properties named `java`, `netscape`, and `sun`, all of which are synonyms for the properties of the `Packages` object. So instead of writing `Packages.java.lang.Math`, for example, you can just write `java.lang.Math`.

See Also

JavaClass, JavaObject, JavaPackage

Packages.java Property — root of the core Java language packages

Availability

Navigator 3.0

Synopsis

```
Packages.java
```

Description

The `java` property of the `Packages` object is a JavaPackage that contains each of the packages that comprise the core Java class library. These are packages such as *java.lang*, *java.io*, and *java.applet*.

Usage

You can use the "global" `java` property anywhere you would use `Packages.java`.

See Also

JavaPackage, Packages JavaPackage, Packages

Packages.netscape Property — root of the Java packages from Netscape

Availability

Navigator 3.0

Synopsis

```
Packages.netscape
```

Description

The `netscape` property of the `Packages` object is a JavaPackage that contains each of the packages that comprise the *netscape.** class library from Netscape. The packages in this class library include *netscape.javascript*, for example.

Usage

You can use the "global" `netscape` property anywhere you would use `Pack-ages.netscape`.

See Also

JavaPackage Packages

Packages.sun Property — root of the Java packages from Sun Microsystems

Availability

Navigator 3.0

Synopsis

```
Packages.sun
```

Description

The `sun` property of the `Packages` object is a JavaPackage that contains each of the packages that comprise the *sun.** class library from Sun Microsystems. These packages are shipped with Sun's Java implementation, but are not an official part of the Java language, and so using these packages may make your programs less portable.

Usage

You can use the "global" `sun` property anywhere you would use `Packages.sun`.

See Also

JavaPackage, Packages

---

parent Property — see Window.parent

---

parseFloat( ) Function — convert a string to a number

Availability

Navigator 3.0, partial support in Navigator 2.0 and Internet Explorer 3.0

Synopsis

```
parseFloat(s)
```

Arguments

s   The string to be parsed and converted to a number.

Returns

The parsed number, or `NaN`, if *s* does not begin with a valid number. Because Navigator 2.0 and Internet Explorer 3.0 do not support `NaN`, those browsers return 0 when *s* cannot be parsed.

Description

parseFloat() is a built-in function in JavaScript; it is a core part of the language, and is not a method of any object.

parseFloat() parses and returns the first number that occurs in s. Parsing stops, and the value returned, when parseFloat() encounters a character in s that is not a valid part of the number (i.e., a sign, a digit, decimal point, exponent, etc.) If s does not begin with a number that parseFloat() can parse, then the function returns NaN, a reserved value that represents "not-a-number". You can test for the NaN value with the isNaN() function. If NaN is used with arithmetic operations, the result will always be NaN. In Navigator 2.0 (except Unix platforms) and Internet Explorer 3.0, parseFloat() returns 0 instead of NaN when the input cannot be parsed.

Bugs

In Navigator 2.0 (except Unix platforms) and Internet Explorer 3.0, the NaN return value is not implemented, and so parseFloat() returns 0 when it cannot parse a number. When you receive this return value on those platforms, you must perform additional tests to determine whether the string contains illegal input or actually contains the value 0.

See Also

isNaN(), parseInt()

---

parseInt() Function — convert a string to an integer

Availability

Navigator 3.0; partial support in Navigator 2.0 and Internet Explorer 3.0

Synopsis

```
parseInt(s)
parseInt(s, radix)
```

Arguments

s   The string to be parsed.

radix   An optional integer argument that represents the radix (i.e., base) of the
                number to be parsed.

Returns

The parsed number, or NaN, if s does not begin with a valid integer. Because Navigator 2.0 and Internet Explorer 3.0 do not support NaN, those browsers returns 0 when s cannot be parsed.

Description

parseInt() is a built-in function in JavaScript; it is a core part of the language, and is not a method of any object.

parseInt() parses and returns the first number that occurs in s. Parsing stops, and the value is returned, when parseInt() encounters a character in s that is not a valid numeral for the specified radix. If s does not begin with a number that parseInt() can parse, then the function returns NaN, a reserved value that represents "not-a-number." You can test for the NaN value with the isNaN() function. If NaN is used with arithmetic operations, the result will always be NaN.

In Navigator 2.0 (except on Unix platforms) and in Internet Explorer 3.0, NaN is not implemented, and parseInt() returns 0 instead of NaN. For these browsers parseInt() that does not distinguish between a malformed string value and a legal value 0.

radix specifies the base of the number to be parsed. Specifying 10 makes the parseInt() parse a decimal number. The value 8 specifies that an octal number (using digits 0 through 7) is to be parsed. The value 16 specifies a hexadecimal value, using digits 0 through 9 and letters A through F. *radix* can be any value between 2 and 36.

If *radix* is 0, or if it is not specified, parseInt() tries to determine the radix of the number from *s*. If *s* begins with 0x, then parseInt() parses the remainder of *s* as a hexadecimal number. If *s* begins with a 0, then parseInt() parses the number in octal. Otherwise, if *s* begins with a digit 1 through 9, then parseInt() parses it as a decimal number.

Bugs

In Navigator 2.0 (except Unix platforms) and Internet Explorer 3.0, the NaN return value is not implemented, and so parseInt() returns 0 when it cannot parse a number. When you receive this return value on those platforms, you must perform additional tests to determine whether the string contains illegal input or actually contains the value 0.

See Also

isNaN(), parseFloat()

Password Element — input field for sensitive data

Availability

Navigator 2.0, Internet Explorer 3.0; enhanced in Navigator 3.0

Synopsis

```
form.name
form.elements[i]
```

Properties

defaultValue

> A read-only string that specifies the initial value to appear in the password input field. This property is specified by the VALUE attribute of the HTML tag that created the Password element.

form

> A read-only reference to the Form object that contains the Password element.

name

> A read-only string, set by the HTML NAME attribute, that specifies the name of the Password element. This is also the *name* that can be used to reference the Password element as a property of its form.

type

> A read-only string that specifies the type of this form element. For Password elements, it has the value "password". Available in Navigator 3.0 and later.

value   In Navigator 3.0, with the data-tainting security model enabled, this property
               is a read-only string that specifies the password value entered by the user. In
               Navigator 2.0, and in 3.0 without data tainting enabled, this property exists,
               but always contains the empty string.

Methods

blur( )   Remove the keyboard focus from the Password element.

focus( )   Set the keyboard focus to the Password element. When focus is set, all
               keystrokes are automatically entered into this element.

select( )   Highlight all the text in the Password element, and enter a special mode so
               that future input replaces the highlighted text.

Event Handlers

onblur( )   Invoked when a user action causes the Password element to lose the key-
               board focus.

onchange( )   Invoked when the user changes the value in the Password element and
               moves the keyboard focus elsewhere. This event handler is not invoked for
               every keystroke in the Password element, but only when the user completes
               an edit.

onfocus( )   Invoked when a user action causes the Password element to gain the key-
               board focus.

HTML Syntax

A Password element is created with a standard HTML <INPUT> tag:

```
<FORM>
   . . .
   <INPUT
     TYPE="password"          specifies that this is a Password element
     [ NAME="name" ]          a name that can later be used to refer to this element
                              specifies the name property
     [ VALUE="default" ]      the default value transmitted when the form is submitted
     [ SIZE=integer ]         how many characters wide the element is
   >
   . . .
</FORM>
```

Description

The Password element is a text input field intended for input of sensitive data, such as passwords. As the user types characters, only asterisks appear, so that the input value cannot be
read by a bystander looking over the user's shoulder.

As an additional security precaution, JavaScript cannot read the value typed by the user
either. The value property is a read-only string that initially contains the value specified by
the VALUE attribute. The user's input is transmitted to the server when the form is submitted, but that input does not appear in this property. Setting this property has no effect on
the value transmitted. The VALUE attribute specifies the data to be transmitted if the user

does not type anything, and this default value is the only thing to which JavaScript has access.

See Also

Element, Form, Text

Password.blur() Method — see Element.blur()

Password.defaultValue Property — see Element.defaultValue

Password.focus() Method — see Element.focus()

Password.form Property — see Element.form

Password.name Property — see Element.name

Password.onblur() Handler — see Element.onblur()

Password.onchange() Handler — invoked when input value changes

Availability

Navigator 2.0, Internet Explorer 3.0

Synopsis

```
<INPUT TYPE=file
    onChange="handler-statements" . . .>     a definition of the handler
Password.onchange                            a reference to the handler
Password.onchange();                         an explicit invocation of the handler
```

Description

The `Password.onchange()` event handler is defined by the `onChange` attribute of the `<INPUT>` HTML tag that defines the Password object. The value of this attribute may be any number of JavaScript statements, separated by semicolons; these statements will be executed whenever the user changes the value in the password input field and then "commits" those changes by moving keyboard focus elsewhere (i.e., by clicking the mouse elsewhere or by typing the **Tab** or **Return** keys). This handler is intended to process a complete change to the input value, and therefore is not invoked on a keystroke-by-keystroke basis.

For security reasons, the `value` field of the Password element is not readable except in Navigator 3.0 with the data-tainting security model enabled. Since the `value` can't be read, it doesn't do much good to be notified when that value has changed.

See Also

Element.onchange(), Password.

Password.onfocus() Handler — see Element.onfocus()

Password.select() Method — see Element.select()

Password.type Property — see Element.type

Password.value Property — user input to the Password object

Availability

Navigator 2.0, Internet Explorer 3.0; enhanced in Navigator 3.0 when data tainting is enabled

Synopsis

```
password.value
```

Description

The `value` property of the Password object is a string that specifies the password entered by the user, and is the value sent over the Net when the form is submitted.

For security reasons this property may not be read or written in Navigator 2.0, or in Navigator 3.0 when the data tainting security model is not enabled. In Navigator 3.0 and later versions, when data tainting is enabled, this property may be read, but may not be set.

See Also

Password

Plugin Object — describes an installed plug-in

Availability

Navigator 3.0

Synopsis

```
navigator.plugins[i]
navigator.plugins['name']
```

Properties

description   A read-only string that contains a human-readable description of the plug-in, specified by the plug-in itself. This property may specify a full product name, information about the vendor and version, and so on.

filename   A read-only string that specifies the name of the disk file that contains the plug-in code.

length   The number of MIME types supported by the plug-in. MimeType objects describing these types are array elements of the Plugin object.

name   A read-only string that specifies the name of the plug-in. This is generally a much shorter string than `description`. The value of this property may be used as an index into the `navigator.plugins[ ]` array.

Elements

The array elements of the Plugin object are MimeType objects that specify the data formats supported by the plug-in.

Description

A *plug-in* is a software module that can be invoked by Navigator to display specialized types of embedded data within the browser window. In Navigator 3.0, plug-ins are represented by the Plugin object. This object is somewhat unusual in that it has both regular object properties and array elements. The properties of the Plugin object provide various pieces of information about the plug-in, and the array elements of it are MimeType objects that specify the embedded data formats that the plug-in supports.

Plugin objects are obtained from the plugins[] array of the Navigator object. navigator.plugins[] may be indexed numerically when you want to loop through the complete list of installed plug-ins, looking for one that meets your needs (for example, one that supports the MIME type of the data you want to embed in your web page). This array can also be indexed by plug-in name, however. That is, if you want to check whether a specific plug-in is installed in the user's browser, you might use code like this:

```
document.write( navigator.plugins("Shockwave") ?
                "<EMBED SRC="movie.dir' HEIGHT=100 WIDTH=100>" :
                "You don't have the Shockwave plug-in!" );
```

The name used as an array index with this technique is the same name that appears as the value of the name property of the Plugin.

Don't confuse the fact that Plugin objects are stored in an array of the Navigator object with the fact that each Plugin object is itself an array of MimeType objects. Because there are two arrays involved, you may end up with code that looks like these lines:

```
navigator.plugins[i][j] the jth MIME type of the ith plug-in
navigator.plugins["LiveAudio"][0] the 1st MIME type of the LiveAudio plug-in
```

Finally, note that while the array elements of a Plugin object specify the MIME types supported by that plug-in, you can also determine which plug-in supports a given MIME type with the enabledPlugin property of the MimeType object.

See Also

Navigator, MimeType, MimeType.enabledPlugin

Plugin.description Property — English description of a plug-in

Availability

Navigator 3.0

Synopsis

```
plugin.description
```

Description

The description property of a Plugin object is a read-only string that contains a human-readable English description of the specified plug-in. The text of this description is provided by the creators of the plug-in, and may contain vendor and version information, as well as a brief description of the function of the plug-in.

See Also

MimeType, Navigator, Plugin

Plugin.filename Property — the filename of the plug-in program

Availability

Navigator 3.0

Synopsis

```
plugin.filename
```

Description

The filename property of the Plugin object is a read-only string that specifies the name of the file on disk that contains the plug-in program itself. This name may vary from platform to platform. The name property is usually more useful than filename for identifying a plug-in.

See Also

MimeType, Navigator, Plugin, Plugin.name

Plugin.name Property — the name of a plug-in

Availability

Navigator 3.0

Synopsis

```
plugin.name
```

Description

The name property of a Plugin object is a read-only string that specifies the name of the plug-in. Each plug-in should have a name that uniquely identifies it.

The value of the name property can also be used as an index into the navigator.plugins[ ] array. You can use this fact to easily determine whether a particular named plug-in is installed in the current browser:

```
var sw_installed = (navigator.plugins["Shockwave"] != null);
```

Note that some plug-ins may support a configurable list of MIME types. Once you have determined that a desired plug-in is installed, you may also need to consult the Plugin.mimeTypes[ ] array to be sure that the plug-in can display the type of data you want it to.

See Also

MimeType, Navigator, Plugin, MimeType.enabledPlugin

---

prompt( ) Method — see Window.prompt( )

Radio Element — a graphical radio button

Availability

Navigator 2.0, Internet Explorer 3.0; enhanced in Navigator 3.0

Synopsis

The Radio button element is always used in groups of mutually exclusive options that have the same name. To reference one Radio element within a group, use this syntax:

```
form.radio_name[j]
form.radio_name.length
form.elements[i][j]
form.elements[i].length
```

Properties

checked
: A read/write Boolean value that specifies whether the button is checked or not.

defaultChecked
: A read-only Boolean that specifies the initial state of the radio button. May be specified with the HTML CHECKED attribute.

form
: A read-only reference to the Form object that contains the Radio element.

name
: A read-only string, set by the HTML NAME attribute, that specifies the name of the Radio button.

type
: A read-only string that specifies the type of this form element. For Radio elements, it has the value "radio". Available in Navigator 3.0 and later.

value
: A read/write string, initially set by the HTML VALUE attribute, that specifies the value returned by the Radio button if it is selected when the form is submitted.

Methods

blur()
: Removes keyboard focus from the radio button.

click()
: Simulates a click on the radio button.

focus()
: Gives keyboard focus to the radio button.

Event Handlers

onblur()
: Invoked when the radio button loses keyboard focus.

`onclick()`   Invoked when the radio button is clicked.

`onfocus()`   Invoked when the radio button is given keyboard focus.

HTML Syntax

A Radio element is created with a standard HTML <INPUT> tag, with the addition of the new `onClick` attribute. Radio elements are created in groups by specifying multiple <INPUT> tags that have the same `NAME` attribute.

```
<FORM>
  . . .
  <INPUT
    TYPE="radio"            specifies that this is a radio button
    [ NAME="name" ]         a name that can later be used to refer to this button...
                            ...or to the group of buttons with this name
                            specifies the name property
    [ VALUE="value" ]       the value returned when this button is selected
                            specifies the value property
    [ CHECKED ]             specifies that the button is initially checked
                            specifies the defaultChecked property
    [ onClick="handler" ] · JavaScript statements to be executed when the button
                            is clicked
  >
  label                     the HTML text that should appear next to the button
  . . .
</FORM>
```

Description

The Radio element represents a single graphical radio button in an HTML form. A radio button is one button in a group of buttons that represent mutually exclusive choices. When one button is selected, the previously selected button becomes deselected.

The `onClick` event handler allows you to specify JavaScript code to be executed when the button is checked or unchecked.

You can examine the `checked` property to determine the state of the button, and you can also set this property to select or deselect the button. Note that setting `checked` changes the graphical appearance of the button, but does not invoke the `onClick` event handler. The initial value of the `checked` property, and the value of the `defaultChecked` property are determined by the `CHECKED` attribute. Only one Radio element in a group may contain this attribute—it sets the `checked` and `defaultChecked` properties `true` for that element and `false` for all other Radio buttons in the group. If none of the elements have the `CHECKED` attribute, then the first one in the group will be `checked` (and `defaultChecked`) by default.

Note that the text that appears next to a Radio button is not part of the Radio element itself, and must be specified externally to the Radio's HTML <INPUT> tag.

It is good programming style to specify the `NAME` attribute for a button, and is mandatory if the radio button is part of a form that will submit data to a CGI script running on a web server. Specifying a `NAME` attribute sets the *name* property, and also allows you to refer to the button by name (instead of as a member of the form `elements` array) in your JavaScript code, which makes the code more modular and portable.

Radio elements are used in groups of mutually exclusive options, and each member of the group is given the same `NAME` attribute (the shared name defines the members of the group). So if the shared name of a group of Radio elements in form f is "opts", then `f.opts` is an array of Radio elements, and `f.opts.length` is the number of elements in the array.

Unfortunately, in Navigator 2.0, there is a bug in how Radio elements in a group are assigned to an array. See the "Bugs" section for details.

You can set the `VALUE` attribute or the `value` property of a Radio element to specify the string that will be passed to the server if the Radio element is checked when the form is submitted. Each Radio element in a group should specify a distinct `value` so that a script on the server can determine which one was checked when the form was submitted.

Usage

Radio elements can be used to present the user with a list of multiple, mutually exclusive, options. Use the Checkbox element to present a single option or to present a list of options that are not mutually exclusive.

Bugs

As described above, when a group of Radio elements share the same `NAME` attribute, JavaScript assigns them to an array that bears that name. Unfortunately, there is a bug in this process in Navigator 2.0: if the radio elements do not have event handlers specified with the `onClick` attribute, then they are assigned to the array in reverse order. This is counter-intuitive, and is an incompatibility with Navigator 3.0 in which the bug is fixed.

The workaround is to always assign an event handler, if only a dummy one, to all of your Radio elements that will be manipulated with JavaScript. You can do this by including `onClick="0"` in the <INPUT> tag for each Radio element you define. With this workaround, you can ensure that the elements will be assigned to the array in the same order in Navigator 2.0 and Navigator 3.0.

At least some versions of Navigator do not correctly select the first radio button in a group when no buttons in the group have the `CHECKED` attribute specified. Therefore you should always explicitly specify the `CHECKED` attribute for one default selection in every radio button group.

See Also

Checkbox, Element, Form

Radio.blur() Method — see Element.blur()

Radio.checked Property — whether a Radio button is selected

Availability

Navigator 2.0, Internet Explorer 3.0

Synopsis

```
radio.checked
```

Description

checked is a read/write Boolean property of the Radio object. If the Radio button is checked, then the checked property is true. If the Radio is not checked, then checked is false.

If you set checked to true, then the Radio button will become selected, and whichever button was previously selected will become deselected. Note, however, that setting the checked property of a radio button to false will have no effect, because at least one button must always be selected, and you cannot deselect a radio button except by selecting some other button.

Note that setting the checked property does not cause the Radio's onClick event handler to be invoked. If you want to invoke that event handler, you must do so explicitly.

See Also

Radio

Radio.click() Method — see Element.click()

Radio.defaultChecked Property — initial state of a Radio button

Availability

Navigator 2.0, Internet Explorer 3.0

Synopsis

```
radio.defaultChecked
```

Description

defaultChecked is a read-only Boolean property of the Radio object. It is true if the Radio button is initially selected—i.e., if the CHECKED attribute appears in the Radio's HTML <INPUT> tag. If this tag does not appear, then the Radio button is initially deselected, and defaultChecked is false.

Usage

You can use the defaultChecked property to reset a group of radio buttons back to its default state. You might do this when the user selects a **Reset** button in a form, for example. You can reset a group of radio buttons with the following function:

```
function resetRadio(radio_group) {
    var i;
    for(i = 0; i < radio_group.length; i++) {
        if (radio_group[i].defaultChecked) {
            radio_group[i].checked = true;
            break;
        }
    }
}
```

See Also

Radio

Radio.focus() Method — see Element.focus()

Radio.form Property — see Element.form

Radio.name Property — see Element.name

Radio.onblur() Handler — see Element.onblur()

Radio.onclick() Handler — invoked when a Radio button is selected

Availability

Navigator 2.0, Internet Explorer 3.0

Synopsis

```
<INPUT TYPE="radio"                    a definition of the handler
       onClick="handler-statements">
radio.onclick                          a reference to the handler
radio.onclick();                       an explicit invocation of the handler
```

Description

onclick() is an event handler invoked when the user clicks on a Radio button. This event handler is defined by the onClick attribute of the HTML <INPUT> tag that defines the Radio button. The value of this attribute may be any number of JavaScript statements, separated by semicolons; these statements will be executed when the user clicks on (i.e., checks or unchecks) the button.

See Also

Radio

Radio.onfocus() Handler — see Element.onfocus()

Radio.type Property — see Element.type

Radio.value Property — value returned when form is submitted

Availability

Navigator 2.0, Internet Explorer 3.0

Synopsis

```
radio.value
```

Description

`value` is a read/write string property of the Radio object. It specifies the text that is passed to the web server if the radio button is checked when the form is submitted. The initial value of `value` is specified by the `VALUE` attribute of the Radio's HTML `<INPUT>` tag. If the form will be submitted to a server (as opposed to simply used by JavaScript on the client side) then each radio button in a group must have a distinct `value`.

Usage

Note that the `value` field does not specify whether or not the radio button is currently selected; the `checked` property specifies the current state of the Radio object.

See Also

Radio

Reset Element — a button to reset a form's values

Availability

Navigator 2.0, Internet Explorer 3.0; enhanced in Navigator 3.0

Synopsis

```
form.name
form.elements[i]
```

Properties

form   A read-only reference to the Form object that contains the Reset element.

name   A read-only string, set by the HTML `NAME` attribute, that specifies the name of the Reset element. This is also the *name* that can be used to reference the Reset element as a property of its form.

type   A read-only string that specifies the type of this form element. For Reset elements, it has the value "reset". Available in Navigator 3.0 and later.

value   A read-only string, set by the HTML `VALUE` attribute, that specifies the text to appear in the button. If no `VALUE` is specified, then (in Navigator) the button will be labelled "Reset" by default.

Methods

blur()   Removes keyboard focus from the Reset button.

click()   Simulates a click on the Reset button.

focus()   Gives keyboard focus to the Reset button.

Event Handlers

`onblur()`   Invoked when the Reset button loses keyboard focus.

`onclick()`   Invoked when the Reset button is clicked.

`onfocus()`   Invoked when the Reset button is given keyboard focus.

HTML Syntax

A Reset element is created with a standard HTML `<INPUT>` tag, with the addition of the `onClick` attribute:

```
<FORM>
    ...
  <INPUT
    TYPE="reset"              specifies that this is a Reset button
    [ VALUE="label" ]         the text that is to appear within the button
                              specifies the value property
    [ NAME="name" ]           a name that can later be used to refer to the button
                              specifies the name property
    [ onClick="handler" ]     JavaScript statements to be executed when the button
                              is clicked
  >
    ...
</FORM>
```

Description

The Reset element has the same properties and methods as the Button element, but has a more specialized purpose. When a Reset element is clicked on, all input elements in the form that contains it will have their values reset back to their initial default values. (For most elements this means to the value specified by the HTML `VALUE` attribute.) If no initial value was specified, then a click on the Reset button will "clear" any user input from those elements.

Usage

If no `VALUE` attribute is specified for a Reset element, it will be labelled **Reset**. In some forms, it may be better to label the button **Clear Form** or **Defaults**.

In Navigator 3.0, you can simulate the action of a Reset button with the `reset()` method of the Form object. Also in Navigator 3.0, the `onreset()` event handler of the Form object will be invoked before the form is reset. This event handler can cancel the reset by returning `false`.

See Also

Button, Element, Form

Reset.blur() Method — see Element.blur()

Reset.click() Method — see Element.click()

Reset.focus() Method — see Element.focus()

Reset.form Property — see Element.form

Reset.name Property — see Element.name

Reset.onblur() Handler — see Element.onblur()

Reset.onclick() Handler — invoked when a Reset button is clicked

Availability

Navigator 2.0, Internet Explorer 3.0; enhanced in Navigator 3.0

Synopsis

```
<INPUT TYPE="reset"                        a definition of the handler
        onClick="handler-statements">
reset.onclick                              a reference to the handler
reset.onclick();                           an explicit invocation of the handler
```

Description

The `Reset.onclick()` event handler is defined by the `onClick` attribute of the HTML `<INPUT>` tag that defines the Reset button. The value of this attribute may be any number of JavaScript statements, separated by semicolons; these statements will be executed when the user clicks on the Reset button.

The Reset button has the special function of resetting all form elements to their default value. This event handler may add any additional functionality to the Reset button. In Navigator 2.0, there is no way for the `onclick()` event handler to cancel the reset action or to prevent the fields from being reset. In Navigator 3.0, however, the `onclick()` handler may return `false` to prevent the Reset object from resetting the form.

See Also

Button, Button.onclick(), Form.onreset(), Form.reset(), Reset

Reset.onfocus() Handler — see Element.onfocus()

Reset.type Property — see Element.type

Reset.value Property — the label of a Reset button

Availability

Navigator 2.0, Internet Explorer 3.0

Synopsis

```
reset.value
```

Description

The value property is a read-only string that specified the text that appears within the Reset button. It is specified by the VALUE attribute of the <INPUT> tag that created the button. If no VALUE attribute is specified, the default value is "Reset".

See Also

Element.value, Reset

scroll() Method — see Window.scroll()

Select Element — a graphical selection list

Availability

Navigator 2.0, Internet Explorer 3.0; enhanced in Navigator 3.0

Synopsis

```
form.element_name
form.elements[i]
```

Properties

form
: A read-only reference to the Form object that contains the Select element.

length
: A read-only integer that specifies the number of elements in the options[] array (i.e., the number of options that appear in the Select element).

name
: A read-only string, set by the HTML NAME attribute, that specifies the name of the Select element. This is also the *name* that can be used to reference the Select element as a property of its form.

options
: An array of Option objects, each of which describes one of the options displayed within the Select element.

selectedIndex
: A read-only (read/write in Navigator 3.0) integer that specifies the index of the selected option within the Select element. If the Select element has its MULTIPLE attribute set and allows multiple selections, then this property only specifies the index of the first selected item or −1 if none are selected.

type   A read-only string that specifies the type of this form element. For Select ele-
              ments, it has the value "select-one" or "select-multiple". Available in
              Navigator 3.0 and later.

Methods

blur()   Removes keyboard focus from the Select element.

click()   Simulates a click on Select element.

focus()   Gives keyboard focus to the Select element.

Event Handlers

onblur()   Invoked when the Select element loses keyboard focus.

onchange()   Invoked when the user selects or deselects an item.

onfocus()   Invoked when the Select element is given keyboard focus.

HTML Syntax

A Select element is created with a standard HTML <SELECT> tag, with the addition of the
new onChange event-handler attribute. Options to appear within the Select element are created with the <OPTION> tag:

```
<FORM>
    . . .
<SELECT
    NAME="name"                      a name that identifies this element; specifies name property
    [ SIZE=integer ]                 number of visible options in Select element
    [ MULTIPLE ]                     multiple options may be selected, if present
    [ onChange="handler" ]           invoked when the selection changes
    [ onBlur="handler" ]             invoked when element loses focus
    [ onFocus="handler" ]            invoked when element gains focus
>
<OPTION VALUE="value1" [SELECTED]> option_label1
<OPTION VALUE="value2" [SELECTED]> option_label2
    .
    .                                other options here
    .
</SELECT>
    . . .
</FORM>
```

Description

The Select element represents a graphical list of choices from which the user may select. If
the MULTIPLE attribute is present in the HTML definition of the element, the user may select
any number of options from the list. If that attribute is not present, the user may select only
one option, and options have a "radio button" behavior—selecting one deselects whichever
was previously selected.

The options in a Select element may be displayed in two distinct ways. If the SIZE attribute
has a value greater than 1, or if the MULTIPLE attribute is present, they are displayed in a
list box which is SIZE lines high in the browser window. If SIZE is smaller than the

number of options, the list box will include a scrollbar so that all the options are accessible. On the other hand, if SIZE is specified as 1, and MULTIPLE is not specified, the currently selected option is displayed on a single line and the list of other options is made available through a drop-down menu. The first presentation style displays the options clearly but requires more space in the browser window. The second style requires minimal space, but does not display alternative options as explicitly.

The options[] property of the Select element is the most interesting. This is the array of Option objects that describe the choices presented by the Select element. The length property specifies the length of this array (as does options.length). See the documentation of the Option object for details.

In Navigator 3.0, the options displayed by the Select element may be dynamically modified. You can change the text displayed by an Option object simply by setting its text property. You can change the number of options displayed by the Select element by setting the options.length property. And you can create new options for display with the Option() constructor function. See Select.options[] and Option for details.

See Also

Element, Form, Option

Select.blur() Method — see Element.blur()

Select.click() Method — see Element.click()

Select.focus() Method — see Element.focus()

Select.form Property — see Element.form

Select.length Property — number of options in a Select object

Availability

Navigator 2.0, Internet Explorer 3.0

Synopsis

```
select.length
```

Description

The length property of a select object is a read-only integer that specifies the number of elements in the select.options[] array. select.length refers to the same value as select.options.length.

See Also

Option, Select

Select.name Property — see Element.name

Select.onblur( ) Handler — see Element.onblur( )

Select.onchange( ) Handler — invoked when the selection changes

Availability

Navigator 2.0, Internet Explorer 3.0

Synopsis

```
<SELECT onChange="handler-statements" ...>    a definition of the handler
select.onchange                                a reference to the handler
select.onchange();                             an explicit invocation of the handler
```

Description

The `Select.onchange()` event handler is defined by the `onChange` attribute of the
`<SELECT>` HTML tag that defines the Select object. The value of this attribute may be any
number of JavaScript statements, separated by semicolons; these statements will be executed whenever the user selects or deselects an option.

Bugs

In the Windows versions of Navigator 2.0, when the Select object is displayed in its drop-
down menu form, the `onchange()` event handler is not invoked immediately after a choice
is made; it is not invoked until the user clicks somewhere else on the page. This bug has
been fixed in Navigator 3.0.

This is a severe enough bug (on a very common platform) that `onchange()` should be considered nonfunctional in Navigator 2.0. If you require immediate notification of changes,
consider replacing your Select object with Checkbox or Radio objects, and using their
`onclick()` event handlers.

See Also

Option, Select

Select.onfocus( ) Handler — see Element.onfocus( )

Select.options[ ] Property — the choices in a Select object

Availability

Navigator 2.0, Internet Explorer 3.0; enhanced in Navigator 3.0

Synopsis

```
select.options[i]
select.options.length
```

Description

The options[ ] property contains an array of Option objects, each of which describe one of the selection options presented within the Select object *select*. The options.length property specifies the number of elements in the array, as does the *select*.length property. See the Option object for further details.

In Navigator 3.0, you can modify the options displayed in a Select object in any of the following ways:

- If you set options.length to 0, all options in the Select object will be cleared.

- If you set options.length to a value less than the current value, then the number of options in the Select object will be decreased, and those and the end of the array will disappear.

- If you set an element in the options[ ] array to null, then that option will be removed from the Select object, and the elements above it in the array will be moved down, changing their indices, to occupy the new space in the array.

- If you create a new Option object with the Option( ) constructor (see the Option reference entry), you can add that option to the end of list of options in the Select object by assigning the newly created option to a position at the end of the options[ ] array. To do this, set options[options.length].

See Also

Option, Select

Select.selectedIndex Property — the selected option

Availability

Navigator 2.0, Internet Explorer 3.0; extended to be writable in Navigator 3.0

Synopsis

select.selectedIndex

Description

The selectedIndex property of the Select object is an integer that specifies the index of the selected option within the Select object. If no option is selected, selectedIndex is -1. If more than one option is selected, selectedIndex specifies the index of the first one only.

In Navigator 2.0, selectedIndex is a read-only property. In Navigator 3.0, it is read/write: by setting the value of this property, you cause the specified option to become selected. You also cause all other options to become deselected, even if the Select object has the MULTIPLE attribute specified. When doing list-box style selection (instead of drop-down menu selection) you can deselect all options by setting selectedIndex to -1. Note that changing the selection in this way does not trigger the onchange( ) event handler.

Usage

When the MULTIPLE attribute is specified and selection of multiple options is allowed, the selectedIndex property is not very useful. In this case, to determine which options are selected, you should loop through the options[ ] array of the Select object, and check the selected property of each Option object.

See Also

Option, Select

Select.type Property — type of form element

Availability

Navigator 3.0

Synopsis

```
select.type
```

Description

`type` is a read-only string property shared by all form elements; it specifies the type of the element. The Select object is unusual in that there are two possible values for the `type` property. If the Select object allows only a single selection (i.e., if the `MULTIPLE` attribute does not appear in the object's HTML definition), the value of the `type` property is "select-one". If the `MULTIPLE` attribute does appear, the value of the `type` attribute is "select-multiple".

See Element.type for more information.

See Also

Element.type, Select

self Property — see Window.self

setTimeout() Method — see Window.setTimeout()

status Property — see Window.status

String Object — support for strings

Availability

Navigator 2.0, Internet Explorer 3.0; enhanced in Navigator 3.0

Constructor

```
new String(value)        Navigator 3.0 only
```

Arguments

value   The initial value of the String object being created. This argument will be converted to a string, if necessary.

Returns

A newly created String object that holds the string *value*, or the string representation of *value*.

Properties

length	The number of characters in the string.

Methods

anchor()	Return a copy of the string, in an <A NAME=> environment.
big()	Return a copy of the string, in a <BIG> environment.
blink()	Return a copy of the string, in a <BLINK> environment.
bold()	Return a copy of the string, in a <B> environment.
charAt()	Extract the character at a given position from a string.
fixed()	Return a copy of the string, in a <TT> environment.
fontcolor()	Return a copy of the string, in a <FONT COLOR=> environment.
fontsize()	Return a copy of the string, in a <FONT SIZE=> environment.
indexOf()	Search the string for a character or substring.
italics()	Return a copy of the string, in a <I> environment.
lastIndexOf()	Search the string backwards for a character or substring.
link()	Return a copy of the string, in a <A HREF=> environment.
small()	Return a copy of the string, in a <SMALL> environment.
split()	Convert a string to an array of strings, using a specified delimiter character.
strike()	Return a copy of the string, in a <STRIKE> environment.
sub()	Return a copy of the string, in a <SUB> environment.
substring()	Extract a substring of a string.
sup()	Return a copy of the string, in a <SUP> environment.
toLowerCase()	Return a copy of the string, with all characters converted to lower case.
toUpperCase()	Return a copy of the string, with all characters converted to upper case.

Description

Strings are a basic data type in JavaScript. The String object type exists to provide methods for operating on string values. The length property of a String object specifies the number of characters in the string. The String class defines a number of methods, most of which simply make a copy of the string with HTML tags added before and after. Other methods, however, perform more interesting functions: extracting a character or a substring from the string, or searching for a character or a substring, for example.

Background Details

The string datatype and the String object are not the same. In Navigator 2.0, however, they are indistinguishable. In Navigator 3.0, you can use the `typeof` operator to distinguish them (a string has type "string" and a String object has type "object") but you can also use them interchangeably. The reason that string values and String objects can be used interchangeably is that JavaScript converts between these two types whenever necessary. When you invoke a String object method on a string value (which is not an object and cannot have methods), JavaScript converts that value to a temporary String object, allowing the method to be invoked. This temporary String object is not available to the program.

In Navigator 3.0, you can use the String object constructor method to create String objects that are not temporary, and that can actually be used by your programs. It is rarely, if ever, necessary to do this, but if you do, the String object you create can be used interchangeably with a string value. When an object is used where a string value is required, the object's `toString()` method is automatically invoked by JavaScript to convert the object to a string. If the object is a String object, the resulting value will be the string value that is required.

Example

A number of the String methods are used for creating HTML:

```
link_text = "My Home Page".bold();
document.write(link_text.link("http://www.djf.com/~david"));
```

The code above embeds the following string into the HTML document that is currently being parsed:

```
<A HREF="http://www.djf.com/~david"><B>My Home Page</B></A>
```

Other methods of the String object perform more interesting functions. The following code, for example, extracts the 3rd through 5th characters of a string and converts them to upper-case letters:

```
s.substring(2,5).toUpperCase();
```

See Also

Chapter 3

String.anchor() Method — add an HTML anchor to a string

Availability

Navigator 2.0, Internet Explorer 3.0

Synopsis

```
string.anchor(name)
```

Arguments

name   The value of the NAME attribute of the HTML <A> tag, i.e., the name of the anchor to be created.

Returns

A copy of *string*, enclosed within `<A NAME="`*name*`">` and `</A>` `HTML tags.`

Description

`String.anchor()` returns a copy of the string for which it is called, surrounded by `<A>` and `</A>` HTML tags. The `NAME` attribute of the `<A>` tag is set to the *name* argument. If the resulting string is appended to an HTML document (with `Document.write()` for example), it defines an anchor, with a name of *name*, which can be the target of a hypertext link.

Example

The following two JavaScript fragments evaluate to identical strings:

```
'Chapter 1: Introduction'.anchor('ch01');'
'<A NAME="ch01">Chapter 1: Introduction</A>'
```

See Also

String, String.link()

String.big() Method — make a string <BIG>

Availability

Navigator 2.0, Internet Explorer 3.0

Synopsis

```
string.big()
```

Arguments

None.

Returns

A copy of *string*, enclosed within `<BIG>` and `</BIG>` HTML tags.

See Also

String, String.small()

String.blink() Method — make a string <BLINK>

Availability

Navigator 2.0, Internet Explorer 3.0

Synopsis

```
string.blink()
```

Arguments

None.

Returns

A copy of *string*, enclosed within `<BLINK>` and `</BLINK>` HTML tags.

See Also

String

String.bold() Method — make a string bold with `<B>`

Availability

Navigator 2.0, Internet Explorer 3.0

Synopsis

```
string.bold()
```

Arguments

None.

Returns

A copy of *string*, enclosed within `<B>` and `</B>` HTML tags.

See Also

String, String.italics()

String.charAt() Method — get the *n*th character from a string

Availability

Navigator 2.0, Internet Explorer 3.0

Synopsis

```
string.charAt(n)
```

Arguments

n   The index of the character that should be returned from *string*.

Returns

The *n*th character of *string*.

Description

`String.charAt()` returns the *n*th character of the string *string*. The first character of the string is numbered 0. If *n* is not between 0 and *string.length* - 1, then this method returns an empty string. Note that JavaScript does not have a character datatype that is distinct from the string type, so the returned character is a string of length 1.

See Also

String, String.indexOf( ), String.lastIndexOf( )

String.fixed() Method — make a string fixed-width with <TT>

Availability

Navigator 2.0, Internet Explorer 3.0

Synopsis

```
string.fixed()
```

Arguments

None.

Returns

A copy of *string*, enclosed within <TT> and </TT> HTML tags.

See Also

String

String.fontcolor() Method — set a string's color with <FONT>

Availability

Navigator 2.0, Internet Explorer 3.0

Synopsis

```
string.fontcolor(color)
```

Arguments

color   A string that specifies the color name or value to be used as the value of the COLOR attribute in the <FONT> HTML tag.

Returns

A copy of *string*, contained within <FONT COLOR="*color*"> and </FONT> HTML tags.

Usage

Colors are specified either as one of the standard color names recognized by JavaScript, or as red, green, and blue color values, expressed as six hexadecimal digits in the form RRGGBB.

Example

The first two lines of the following code fragment have the same effect as the second two:

```
var s1 = 'Red'.fontcolor('red');
var s2 = 'Gray'.fontcolor('A0A0A0');     red, green, & blue are all 0xA0
var s1 = '<FONT COLOR="red">Red</FONT>'
var s2 = '<FONT COLOR="A0A0A0">Gray</FONT>'
```

See Also

String, String.fontsize( ), Appendix G

String.fontsize( ) Method — set a string's font size with <FONT>

Availability

Navigator 2.0, Internet Explorer 3.0

Synopsis

```
string.fontsize(size)
```

Arguments

size   An integer between 1 and 7 or a string that starts with a + or - sign fol-
                 lowed by a digit between 1 and 7. If an integer is specified, it is an
                 absolute font size specification. If a string beginning with + or - is speci-
                 fied, it is a font size specification relative to the <BASEFONT> font size.

Returns

A copy of *string*, contained within <FONT SIZE="*size*"> and </FONT> HTML tags.

Example

The first two lines of the following code fragment have the same effect as the second two:

```
s1 = 'Chapter 1'.fontsize(6);
s2 = 'SMALLCAPS'.fontsize('-1');
s1 = '<FONT SIZE="6">Chapter 1</FONT>'
s2 = '<FONT SIZE="-1">SMALLCAPS</FONT>'
```

See Also

String, String.big( ), String.small( )

String.indexOf( ) Method — search a string

Availability

Navigator 2.0, Internet Explorer 3.0

Synopsis

```
string.indexOf(substring)
string.indexOf(substring, start)
```

Arguments

substring   The substring that is to be searched for within *string*.

start   An optional integer argument that specifies the position within *string*
               at which the search is to start. Legal values are 0 (the position of the
               first character in the string) to *string*.length-1 (the position of the
               last character in the string). If this argument is omitted, then the search
               begins at the first character of the string.

Returns

The position of the first occurrence of *substring* within *string* that appears after the *start* position, if any, or –1 if no such occurrence is found.

Description

`String.indexOf()` searches the string *string* from beginning to end to see if it contains an occurrence of *substring*. The search begins at position *start* within *string,* or at the beginning of *string,* if *start* is not specified. If an occurrence of *substring* is found, then `String.indexOf()` returns the position of the first character of the first occurrence of *substring* within *string*. Character positions within *string* are numbered starting with zero.

If no occurrence of *substring* is found within *string,* then `String.indexOf()` returns –1.

Bugs

In Navigator 2.0 and 3.0, if *start* is greater than the length of *string,* then `indexOf()` returns the empty string rather than -1.

See Also

String, String.charAt( ), String.lastIndexOf( ), String.substring( )

String.italics( ) Method — make a string italic with <I>

Availability

Navigator 2.0, Internet Explorer 3.0

Synopsis

```
string.italics()
```

Arguments

None.

Returns

A copy of *string,* enclosed within <I> and </I> HTML tags.

See Also

String, String.bold( )

String.lastIndexOf( ) Method — search a string backwards

Availability

Navigator 2.0, Internet Explorer 3.0

Synopsis

```
string.lastIndexOf(substring)
string.lastIndexOf(substring, start)
```

Arguments

substring   The substring that is to be searched for within *string*.

start   An optional integer argument that specifies the position within *string* at which the search is to start. Legal values are 0 (the position of the first character in the string) to *string*.length-1 (the position of the last character in the string). If this argument is omitted, then the search begins at the last character of the string.

Returns

The position of the last occurrence of *substring* within *string* that appears before the *start* position, if any, or −1 if no such occurrence is found within *string*.

Description

String.lastIndexOf() searches the string from end to beginning to see if it contains an occurrence of *substring*. The search begins at position *start* within *string*, or at the end of *string* if *start* is not specified. If an occurrence of *substring* is found, then String.lastIndexOf() returns the position of the first character of that occurrence. Since this method searches from end to beginning of the string, the first occurrence found will be the last one in the string that occurs before the *start* position.

If no occurrence of *substring* is found, then String.lastIndexOf() returns −1.

Note that although String.lastIndexOf() searches *string* from end to beginning, it still numbers character positions within *string* from the beginning. The first character of the string has position 0, and the last has position *string*.length-1.

See Also

String, String.charAt(), String.indexOf(), String.substring()

String.length Property — the length of a string

Availability

Navigator 2.0, Internet Explorer 3.0

Synopsis

```
string.length
```

Description

The String.length property is an integer that indicates the number of characters in the specified *string*. For any string *s*, the index of the last character is s.length-1.

See Also

String

String.link() Method — add a hypertext link to a string

Availability

Navigator 2.0, Internet Explorer 3.0

Synopsis

```
string.link(href)
```

Arguments

href   The URL target of the hypertext link that is to be added to the string. This string argument specifies the value of the HREF attribute of the <A> HTML tag.

Returns

A copy of *string*, enclosed within <A HREF="*href*"> and </A> HTML tags.

Example

The following two JavaScript fragments evaluate to identical strings:

```
'Section 1-1'.link('ch01#sect1')
'<A HREF="ch01#sect1">Section 1-1</A>'
```

See Also

String, String.anchor()

String.prototype Property — see Function.prototype

String.small() Method — make a string <SMALL>

Availability

Navigator 2.0, Internet Explorer 3.0

Synopsis

```
string.small()
```

Arguments

None.

Returns

A copy of *string*, enclosed within <SMALL> and </SMALL> HTML tags.

See Also

String

String.split() Method — break a string into an array of strings

Availability

Navigator 3.0

Synopsis

```
string.split();
string.split(delimiter);
```

Arguments

delimiter   The character or string at which the *string* will be split. If no delimiter is specified, then the returned array has only one element, the string itself.

Returns

An array of strings, created by splitting *string* into substrings, at *delimiter* boundaries.

Description

The split() method creates and returns an array of substrings of the specified string. These substrings are created by splitting the string at every occurrence of the specified *delimiter*. The delimiter character or characters are not part of the returned substrings.

If no *delimiter* is specified, then the string is not split at all, and the returned array contains only a single, unbroken string element.

Unfortunately, there is no way to specify more than one delimiter string or character to use. For example, there is no way to tell it to treat any of the space, newline and tab characters as delimiters.

Note that the String.split() method is the inverse of the Array.join() method.

Example

The split() method is most useful when you are working with highly structured strings. For example:

```
s = "1,2,3,4,5"
a = s.split(",");
```

Another common use of the split() method is to parse commands and similar strings by breaking them down into words delimited by spaces:

```
words = sentence.split(' ');
```

See Also

Array.join( ), String

String.strike() Method — strike-out a string with <STRIKE>

Availability

Navigator 2.0, Internet Explorer 3.0

Synopsis

```
string.strike()
```

Arguments

None.

Returns

A copy of *string*, enclosed within <STRIKE> and </STRIKE> HTML tags.

See Also

String

String.sub() Method — make a string a subscript with <SUB>

Availability

Navigator 2.0, Internet Explorer 3.0

Synopsis

```
string.sub()
```

Arguments

None.

Returns

A copy of *string*, enclosed within _{and} HTML tags.

See Also

String, String.sup( )

String.substring() Method — return a substring of a string

Availability

Navigator 2.0, Internet Explorer 3.0

Synopsis

```
string.substring(from, to)
```

Arguments

from   An integer that specifies the position within `string` of the first character of the desired substring. `from` must be between 0 and `string.length-1`.

to   An optional integer that is one greater than the position within `string` of the last character of the desired substring. `to` must be between 1 and `string.length`.

Returns

A new string, of length `to-from`, which contains a substring of `string`. The new string contains characters copied from positions `from` to `to-1` of `string`.

Description

`String.substring()` returns the specified substring of `string`. If `from` equals `to`, `String.substring()` returns an empty (length 0) string. If `from` is greater than `to`, this method first swaps the two arguments before proceeding.

Usage

`String.substring()` can be a confusing function to use. It is important to remember that the character at position `from` is included in the substring, but that the character at position `to` is not included in the substring. One notable feature of assigning the arguments this way is that the length of the returned substring is always equal to `to-from`.

Often it is more convenient to extract a substring of a string by specifying the start character and the desired length of the substring. You can do this with a function like the following:

```
function substring2(string, start, length) {
    return string.substring(start, start+length);
}
```

See Also

String, String.charAt(), String.indexOf(), String.lastIndexOf()

String.sup() Method — make a string a superscript with <SUP>

Availability

Navigator 2.0, Internet Explorer 3.0

Synopsis

```
string.sup()
```

Arguments
None.

Returns
A copy of *string*, enclosed within `<SUP>` and `</SUP>` HTML tags.

See Also
String, String.sub()

String.toLowerCase() Method — convert a string to lowercase

Availability
Navigator 2.0, Internet Explorer 3.0

Synopsis
```
string.toLowerCase()
```

Arguments
None.

Returns
A copy of *string*, with all uppercase letters converted to lowercase.

See Also
String, String.toUpperCase()

String.toUpperCase() Method — convert a string to uppercase

Availability
Navigator 2.0, Internet Explorer 3.0

Synopsis
```
string.toUpperCase()
```

Arguments
None.

Returns
A copy of *string*, with all lowercase letters converted to uppercase.

See Also
String

Submit Element — a button to submit a form

Availability

Navigator 2.0, Internet Explorer 3.0; enhanced in Navigator 3.0

Synopsis

```
form.name
form.elements[i]
form.elements['name']
```

Properties

form   A read-only reference to the Form object that contains the Submit element.

name   A read-only string, set by the HTML NAME attribute, that specifies the name of the Submit element. This is also the *name* that can be used to reference the Submit element as a property of its form.

type   A read-only string that specifies the type of this form element. For Submit elements, it has the value "submit". Available in Navigator 3.0 and later.

value   A read-only string, set by the HTML VALUE attribute, that specifies the text to appear in the button. If no VALUE is specified, then (in Navigator) the button will be labelled "Submit Query" by default.

Methods

blur()   Removes keyboard focus from the Submit button.

click()   Simulates a click on the Submit button.

focus()   Gives keyboard focus to the Submit button.

Event Handlers

onblur()   Invoked when the Submit button loses keyboard focus.

onclick()   Invoked when the Submit button is clicked.

onfocus()   Invoked when the Submit button is given keyboard focus.

HTML Syntax

An Reset object is created with a standard HTML <INPUT> tag, with the addition of the onClick attribute:

```
<FORM>
   . . .
   <INPUT
     TYPE="submit"              specifies that this is a Submit button
     [ VALUE="label" ]          the text that is to appear within the button
                                specifies the value property
     [ NAME="name" ]            a name that can later be used to refer to the button
                                specifies the name property
     [ onClick="handler" ]      JavaScript statements to be executed when the button
                                is clicked
   >
```

```
   . . .
</FORM>
```

Description

The Submit element has the same properties and methods as the Button object, but has a more specialized purpose. When a Submit button is clicked, it submits the data in the form that contains the button to the server specified by the form's ACTION attribute, and loads the resulting HTML page sent back by that server.

Usage

Form data may also be submitted by invoking the Form.submit() method. The Submit.onclick() event handler can define additional JavaScript statements to be executed when a Submit button is clicked, but this event handler cannot prevent the form from being submitted (if it fails input verification tests, for example).[*] To cancel a form submission, you must use the Form.onsubmit() event handler.

If no VALUE attribute is specified for a Submit object, it will be labelled **Submit Query**. In some forms, it may make more sense to label the button **Submit** or **Done** or **Send**.

See Also

Button, Element, Form, Form.onsubmit(), Form.submit()

Submit.blur() Method — see Element.blur()

Submit.click() Method — see Element.click()

Submit.focus() Method — see Element.focus()

Submit.form Property — see Element.form

Submit.name Property — see Element.name

Submit.onblur() Handler — see Element.onblur()

Submit.onclick() Handler — invoked when a Submit button is clicked

Availability

Navigator 2.0, Internet Explorer 3.0; enhanced in Navigator 3.0

Synopsis

```
<INPUT TYPE="submit"                    a definition of the handler
       onClick="handler-statements">
```

---

[*] This event handler *can* abort a submission in Navigator 3.0; see the reference entry for details.

        `submit.onclick`   *a reference to the handler*
        `submit.onclick();`   *an explicit invocation of the handler*

Description

The `Submit.onclick()` event handler is defined by the `onClick` attribute of the HTML `<INPUT>` tag that defines the Submit button. The value of this attribute may be any number of JavaScript statements, separated by semicolons; these statements will be executed when the user clicks on the Submit button.

The Submit button has the special function of submitting a form to the server. This event handler may add any additional functionality to the Submit button. In Navigator 2.0, there is no way for this `onclick()` event handler to cancel the submit action or to prevent the form from being submitted; use the `Form.onsubmit()` event handler to perform input validation and to cancel form submission if necessary.

In Navigator 3.0, the `onclick()` event handler may return `false` to prevent the Submit object from submitting the form.

See Also

Button, Button.onclick(), Form, Form.onsubmit(), Form.submit(), Submit

---

Submit.onfocus() Handler — see Element.onfocus()

Submit.type Property — see Element.type

Submit.value Property — the label of a Submit button

Availability

Navigator 2.0, Internet Explorer 3.0

Synopsis

        `submit.value`

Description

The `value` property is a read-only string that specifies the text that appears within the Submit button. It is specified by the `VALUE` attribute of the `<INPUT>` tag that created the button. If no `VALUE` attribute is specified, the default `value` is "Submit Query".

See Also

Element.value, Submit

---

sun Property — the sun.* Java package

Availability

Navigator 3.0

Synopsis

```
sun
```

Description

sun is a global property of the Window object, and is usually used without reference to any particular window. It is a synonym for Packages.sun, and contains a read-only reference to a JavaPackage object that represents the top node of the *sun.** Java package name hierarchy.

See Also

JavaPackage, Packages.sun

---

taint() Function — taint a value or window

Availability

Navigator 3.0 with data tainting enabled

Synopsis

```
taint()
taint(value)
```

Arguments

value   The value for which a tainted copy is to be made. If this argument is not specified, then taint() adds taint to the current window instead.

Returns

A tainted copy of *value*, if it is a primitive data type, or a tainted reference to *value*, if it is an object type.

Description

The taint() function is used when the data-tainting security model is in effect. See Chapter 20 for details on this security model. JavaScript automatically associates taint with data values that are potentially private, and which should not be "stolen" by scripts. If you have additional sensitive data that is not automatically tainted by JavaScript, you can add taint to it with the taint() function.

taint() does not taint the value it is passed; instead, it returns a tainted copy of that value, or a tainted reference to that value for object types. (Note that taint is associated with primitive values and with references to objects, not with the objects themselves.)

Sometimes taint is carried not by data values, but by the control flow of a program. In this case, you may want to add taint to the entire window in which JavaScript code runs. You can do this by calling taint() with no arguments.

See Also

untaint(), Chapter 20

Text Element — a graphical text input field

Availability

Navigator 2.0, Internet Explorer 3.0; enhanced in Navigator 3.0

Synopsis

```
form.name
form.elements[i]
```

Properties

defaultValue
: A read-only string that specifies the initial value to appear in the input field. Specified by the VALUE attribute of the <INPUT> tag.

form
: A read-only reference to the Form object that contains the Text element.

name
: A read-only string, set by the HTML NAME attribute, that specifies the name of the Text element. This is also the *name* that can be used to reference the Text element as a property of its form.

type
: A read-only string that specifies the type of this form element. For Text elements, it has the value "text". Available in Navigator 3.0 and later.

value
: A read/write string that specifies the value contained in the input field (which is also the value sent to the server when the form is submitted). The initial value of this property is specified by the VALUE attribute.

Methods

blur( )
: Remove the keyboard focus from the Text element.

focus( )
: Set the keyboard focus to the Text element. When focus is set, all keystrokes are automatically entered into this element.

select( )
: Highlight all the text in the Text element, and enter a special mode so that future input replaces the highlighted text.

Event Handlers

onblur( )
: Invoked when a user action causes the Text element to lose the keyboard focus.

onchange( )
: Invoked when the user changes the value in the Text element and moves the keyboard focus elsewhere. This event handler is not invoked for every keystroke in the Text element, but only when the user completes an edit.

onfocus( )
: Invoked when a user action causes the Text element to gain the keyboard focus.

HTML Syntax

A Text element is created with a standard HTML <INPUT> tag, with the addition of optional attributes for event handlers:

```
<FORM>
    . . .
    <INPUT
      TYPE="text"              specifies that this is a Text element
    [ NAME="name" ]            a name that can later be used to refer to this element
                               specifies the name property
    [ VALUE="default" ]        the default value transmitted when the form is submitted
                               specifies the defaultValue property
    [ SIZE=integer ]           how many characters wide the element is
    [ MAXLENGTH=integer ]      max allowed number of input characters
    [ onBlur="handler" ]       the onblur() event handler
    [ onChange="handler" ]     the onchange() event handler
    [ onFocus="handler" ]      the onfocus() event handler
    >
    . . .
</FORM>
```

Description

The Text element represents a text input field in a form. The SIZE attribute specifies the width, in characters, of the input field as it appears on the screen, and the MAXLENGTH attribute specifies the maximum number of characters the user will be allowed to enter.

Besides these HTML attributes, value is the main property of interest for the Text element. You can read this property to obtain the user's input, or you can set it to display arbitrary (unformatted) text in the input field.

Usage

Use the Password element instead of the Text element when the value you are asking the user to enter is sensitive information, such as a password that should not be displayed openly on the screen. Use a Textarea element to allow the user to enter multiple lines of text.

When a form contains only one Text or Password element, the form will automatically be submitted if the user strikes the **Return** key in that Text or Password element. In many forms, this is a useful shortcut. In some, however, it can be confusing if the user strikes **Return** and submits the form before entering input into other form elements such as Checkboxes and Radio buttons. You can sometimes minimize this confusion by placing Text elements with their default submission action at the bottom of the form.

See Also

Element, Form, Password, Textarea

Text.blur() Method — see Element.blur()

Text.defaultValue Property — see Element.defaultValue

Text.focus() Method — see Element.focus()

Text.form Property — see Element.form

Text.name Property — see Element.name

Text.onblur() Handler — see Element.onblur()

Text.onchange() Handler — invoked when input value changes

Availability

Navigator 2.0, Internet Explorer 3.0

Synopsis

```
<INPUT TYPE=text
       onchange="handler-statements" ...>     a definition of the handler
text.onchange                                  a reference to the handler
text.onchange();                               an explicit invocation of the handler
```

Description

The `Text.onchange()` event handler is defined by the `onChange` attribute of the `<INPUT>` HTML tag that defines the Text object. The value of this attribute may be any number of JavaScript statements, separated by semicolons; these statements will be executed whenever the user changes the value in the input field and then "commits" those changes by moving keyboard focus elsewhere (i.e., by clicking the mouse elsewhere or by typing the **Tab** or **Return** keys). This handler is intended to process a complete change to the input value, and therefore is not invoked on a keystroke-by-keystroke basis. Also, note that the `onchange()` event hander is *not* invoked when the `value` property of a Text object is set by JavaScript.

See Also

Text, Text.blur(), Text.focus(), Text.onblur()

Text.onfocus() Handler — see Element.onfocus()

Text.select() Method — see Element.select()

Text.type Property — see Element.type

Text.value Property — user input to the Text object

Availability

Navigator 2.0, Internet Explorer 3.0

Synopsis

```
text.value
```

Description

value is a read/write string property of the Text object. The initial value of value is specified by the VALUE attribute of the <INPUT> tag that defines the Text object. When the user types characters into the Text object, the value property is updated to match the user's input. If you set the value property explicitly, the string you specify will be displayed in the Text object. This value property contains the string that is sent to the server when the form is submitted.

See Also

Text

Textarea Element — a multiline text input area

Availability

Navigator 2.0, Internet Explorer 3.0; enhanced in Navigator 3.0

Synopsis

```
form.name
form.elements[i]
```

Properties

defaultValue

> A read-only string that specifies the initial value to appear in the input field. This default value is whatever plain text appears between the <TEXTAREA> and </TEXTAREA> tags.

form

> A read-only reference to the Form object that contains the Textarea element.

name

> A read-only string, set by the HTML NAME attribute, that specifies the name of the Textarea element. This is also the *name* that can be used to reference the Textarea element as a property of its form.

type

> A read-only string that specifies the type of this form element. For Textarea elements, it has the value "textarea." Available in Navigator 3.0 and later.

value

> A read/write string that specifies the value contained in the Textarea (which is also the value sent to the server when the form is submitted). The initial value of this property is the same as the defaultValue property.

Methods

blur( )   Remove the keyboard focus from the Textarea element.

focus( )   Set the keyboard focus to the Textarea element. When focus is set, all keystrokes are automatically entered into this element.

select( )   Highlight all the text in the Textarea element, and enter a special mode so that future input replaces the highlighted text.

Event Handlers

onblur( )   Invoked when a user action causes the Textarea element to lose the keyboard focus.

onchange( )   Invoked when the user changes the value in the Textarea element and moves the keyboard focus elsewhere. This event handler is not invoked for every keystroke in the Textarea element, but only when the user completes an edit.

onfocus( )   Invoked when a user action causes the Textarea element to gain the keyboard focus.

HTML Syntax

A Textarea element is created with standard HTML <TEXTAREA> and </TEXTAREA> tags, with the addition of optional attributes for event-handlers:

```
<FORM>
  ...
  <TEXTAREA
    [ NAME="name" ]                      a name that can later be used to refer to this element
    [ ROWS=integer ]                     how many lines tall the element is
    [ COLS=integer ]                     how many characters wide the element is
    [ WRAP=off|virtual|physical ]        how word wrapping is handled
    [ onBlur="handler" ]                 the onblur() event handler
    [ onChange="handler" ]               the onchange() event handler
    [ onFocus="handler" ]                the onfocus() event handler
  >
    plain_text                           the initial text; specifies defaultValue
  </TEXTAREA>
  ...
</FORM>
```

Description

The Textarea element represents a text input field in a form. The NAME attribute specifies a name for the element. This is mandatory if the form is to be submitted, and also provides a convenient way to refer to the Textarea element from JavaScript code. The COLS attribute specifies the width, in characters, of the element as it appears on the screen, and the ROWS attribute specifies the height, in lines of text, of the element. The WRAP attribute specifies how long lines should be handled: the value off specifies that they should be left as is; the value virtual specifies that they should be displayed with line breaks but transmitted without; and the value physical specifies that they should be displayed and transmitted with line breaks inserted.

Besides these HTML attributes, value is the main property of interest for the Textarea element. You can read this property to obtain the user's input, or you can set it to display arbitrary (unformatted) text in the Textarea. The initial value of the value property (and the permanent value of the defaultValue property) is the text that appears between the <TEXTAREA> and </TEXTAREA> tags.

Usage

If you need only a single line of input text, use the Text element. If the text to be input is sensitive information, such as a password, use the Password element.

See Also

Element, Form, Password, Text

Textarea.blur() Method — see Element.blur()

Textarea.defaultValue Property — see Element.defaultValue

Textarea.focus() Method — see Element.focus()

Textarea.form Property — see Element.form

Textarea.name Property — see Element.name

Textarea.onblur() Handler — see Element.onblur()

Textarea.onchange() Handler — invoked when input value changes

Availability

Navigator 2.0, Internet Explorer 3.0

Synopsis

```
<TEXTAREA
    onchange="handler-statements" ...>    a definition of the handler
</TEXTAREA>
textarea.onchange                         a reference to the handler
textarea.onchange();                      an explicit invocation of the handler
```

Description

The Textarea.onchange() event handler is defined by the onChange attribute of the <TEXTAREA> HTML tag that defines the Textarea object. The value of this attribute may be any number of JavaScript statements, separated by semicolons; these statements will be executed whenever the user changes the value in the Textarea and then "commits" those changes by moving keyboard focus elsewhere (i.e., by clicking the mouse elsewhere or by typing the **Tab** or **Return** keys). This handler is intended to process a complete change to the input value, and therefore is not invoked on a keystroke-by-keystroke basis. Also, note that the `onchange()` event hander is *not* invoked when the `value` property of a Textarea object is set by JavaScript.

See Also

Textarea, Textarea.blur(), Textarea.focus(), Textarea.onblur()

Textarea.onfocus() Handler — see Element.onfocus()

Textarea.select() Method — see Element.select()

Textarea.type Property — see Element.type

Textarea.value Property — user input to the Textarea object

Availability

Navigator 2.0, Internet Explorer 3.0

Synopsis

```
textarea.value
```

Description

`value` is a read/write string property of the Textarea object. The initial value of `value` is the same as the `defaultValue` property—the plain text (i.e., without any HTML tags) that appears between the `<TEXTAREA>` and `</TEXTAREA>` tags. When the user types characters into the Textarea object, the `value` property is updated to match the user's input. If you set the `value` property explicitly, the string you specify will be displayed in the Textarea object. This `value` property contains the string that is sent to the server when the form is submitted.

Bugs

In Navigator 2.0, the Textarea object required the use of platform-specific newline characters or newline sequences. Thus, appending the "\n" character (newline character for Unix) to the `value` property of a Textarea object would not actually start a new line on Windows platforms (which use a sequence of "\r\n" to delimit lines), for example. In Navigator 3.0, this problem has been resolved—any newline character or sequence is automatically mapped to the correct platform-specific sequence.

To workaround the bug on Navigator 2.0 platforms, you'll need a variable that contains the platform-specific newline sequence. One easy way to obtain such a "newline" variable is to create your Textarea element with a default value which consists of a single blank line. Then you can copy the `value` property of this element; it will contain the newline sequence required on the current platform.

See Also

Textarea

top Property — see Window.top

toString() Method — see Object.toString()

unescape() Function — decode an escaped string

Availability

Navigator 2.0, Internet Explorer 3.0

Synopsis

```
unescape(s)
```

Arguments

s   The string that is to be decoded or "unescaped."

Returns

A decoded copy of s.

Description

The unescape() function is a built-in part of JavaScript; it is not a method of any object.

unescape() decodes a string encoded with escape(). It creates and returns a decoded copy of s. It decodes s by finding and replacing character sequences of the form %xx, where xx is two hexadecimal digits. Each such sequence is replaced by the single character represented by the hexadecimal digits in the Latin-1 encoding.

Thus, unescape() decodes the string:

```
Hello%20World%21
```

to:

```
Hello World!
```

See escape() for more information on this encoding and decoding technique.

See Also

escape( ), String

untaint() Function — untaint a value or window

Availability

Navigator 3.0 when data tainting is enabled

Synopsis

```
untaint()
untaint(value)
```

Arguments

value   The value for which a non-tainted copy is to be made. If this argument is not specified, then untaint( ) removes taint from the current window instead.

Returns

An untainted copy of *value*, if it is a primitive data type, or an untainted reference to *value*, if it is an object type.

Description

The untaint( ) function is used when the data-tainting security model is in effect. See Chapter 20 for details on this security model. JavaScript automatically associates taint with data values that are potentially private, and which should not be "stolen" by scripts. If you need to allow these values to be exported by scripts, you must use untaint( ) to make untainted copies.

untaint( ) does not remove from the taint the value it is passed; instead, it returns an untainted copy of that value, or an untainted reference to that value for object types. (Note that taint is associated with primitive values and with references to objects, not with the objects themselves.)

Sometimes taint is carried not by data values, but by the control flow of a program. In this case, you may need to remove taint from an entire window in which JavaScript code runs. You can do this by calling untaint( ) with no arguments. Note, however, that you can only do this if the window carries only the taint of the script that calls untaint( ). If the window has been tainted by other scripts, it cannot be untainted.

See Also

taint( ), Chapter 20

URL Object — a Universal Resource Locator

Availability

Navigator 2.0, Internet Explorer 3.0

Synopsis

```
window.location
document.links[i]
```

Properties

hash   A read/write string that specifies the hash portion of the URL, including the leading hash (#) mark. This portion specifies the name of an anchor within the object referred to by the URL.

host   A read/write string that specifies the combination of the hostname and port portions of the URL.

hostname   A read/write string that specifies the hostname portion of the URL.

href	A read/write string that specifies the complete URL.
pathname	A read/write string that specifies the path portion of the URL.
port	A read/write string that specifies the port portion of the URL.
protocol	A read/write string that specifies the protocol portion of the URL, including the trailing colon.
search	A read/write string that specifies the search or query portion of the URL, including the leading question mark.

Description

The URL object represents a URL—the location of an object on the Web. The various properties of the URL object are strings that contain various portions of the URL, such as the protocol, the hostname, and the query string.

The Area, Link, and Location objects are kinds of URL objects—they contain all of the properties of the URL object, plus additional properties of their own. URL objects cannot be used on their own, but may be used through the Link and Area objects in the Document.links[] array and the Location object referred to by the Window.location property.

See Also

Area, Link, Location

URL.hash Property — the anchor specification of a URL

Availability

Navigator 2.0, Internet Explorer 3.0

Synopsis

    URL.hash

Description

hash is a read/write string property of the URL object. It specifies the anchor portion of a URL, including the leading hash (#) mark. For example, the hash property of the following (fictitious) URL is "#result".

    http://www.ora.com:1234/catalog/search.html?JavaScript#result

This anchor portion of a URL refers to a named position within the data referenced by the URL. In HTML files positions are named with anchors created with the <A NAME="*anchor_name*"> tag.

See Also

Area, Document.links[], Link, URL, Window.location

URL.host Property — the hostname and port portions of a URL

Availability

Navigator 2.0, Internet Explorer 3.0

Synopsis

```
URL.host
```

Description

host is a read/write string property of the URL object. It specifies the hostname and port portions of a URL. For example, the host of the following (fictitious) location is "www.ora.com:1234".

```
http://www.ora.com:1234/catalog/search.html?JavaScript#result
```

See Also

Area, Document.links[ ], Link, URL, Window.location

URL.hostname Property — the hostname portion of a URL

Availability

Navigator 2.0, Internet Explorer 3.0

Synopsis

```
URL.hostname
```

Description

hostname is a read/write string property of the URL object. It specifies the hostname portion of a URL. For example, the hostname of the following (fictitious) location is "www.ora.com".

```
http://www.ora.com:1234/catalog/search.html?JavaScript#result
```

See Also

Area, Document.links[ ], Link, URL, Window.location

URL.href Property — the complete URL specification

Availability

Navigator 2.0, Internet Explorer 3.0

Synopsis

```
URL.href
```

Description

href is a read/write string property of the URL object. It specifies the complete text of the URL, unlike other URL properties which specify only portions of the URL.

See Also

Area, Document.links[ ], Link, URL, Window.location

URL.pathname Property — the path portion of a URL

Availability

Navigator 2.0, Internet Explorer 3.0

Synopsis

```
URL.pathname
```

Description

pathname is a read/write string property of the URL object. It specifies the pathname portion of a URL. For example, the pathname of the following (fictitious) location is "/catalog/search.html".

```
http://www.ora.com:1234/catalog/search.html?JavaScript#result
```

See Also

Area, Document.links[ ], Link, URL, Window.location

URL.port Property — the port portion of a URL

Availability

Navigator 2.0, Internet Explorer 3.0

Synopsis

```
URL.port
```

Description

port is a read/write string property of the URL object. It specifies the port portion of a URL. For example, the port of the following (fictitious) location is "1234".

```
http://www.ora.com:1234/catalog/search.html?JavaScript#result
```

See Also

Area, Document.links[ ], Link, URL, Window.location

URL.protocol Property — the protocol portion of a URL

Availability

Navigator 2.0, Internet Explorer 3.0

Synopsis

    URL.protocol

Description

protocol is a read/write string property of the Location and the Link objects. It specifies the protocol portion of a URL, including the trailing colon. For example, the protocol of the following (fictitious) location is "http:"

    http://www.ora.com:1234/catalog/search.html?JavaScript#result

See Also

Area, Document.links[], Link, URL, Window.location

URL.search Property — the query portion of a URL

Availability

Navigator 2.0, Internet Explorer 3.0

Synopsis

    URL.search

Description

The search is a read/write string property of the URL object. It specifies the query portion of a URL, including the leading question mark. For example, the search of the following (fictitious) location is "?query=JavaScript&matches=666".

    http://www.ora.com:1234/search.html?query=JavaScript&matches=666#result

Note that the search string (also known as a query string) is not parsed: it still contains the "?" prefix—which you can remove with String.substring(1)—and, more important, it is not split along the "&" delimiter into individual variables. See the split method of the String object for an easy way to break it up in Navigator 3.0.

See Also

Area, Document.links[], Link, String.split( ), URL, Window.location

window Property — see Window.window

Window Object — a web browser window or frame

Availability

Navigator 2.0, Internet Explorer 3.0; enhanced in Navigator 3.0

Synopsis

self	*the current window*
window	*the current window*

Properties

closed
: A read-only Boolean that specifies whether a window has been closed. Available in Navigator 3.0 and later.

defaultStatus
: A read/write string that specifies the default message to appear in the status line.

document
: A reference to the Document object contained in the window.

frames[]
: An array of frames contained by this window.

history
: A reference to the History object for this window.

java
: A reference to the JavaPackage object that is the top of the package name hierarchy for the core *java.** packages that comprise the Java language.

length
: The number of elements in the frames[] array. Same as frames.length. Read-only.

location
: A reference to the Location object for this window.

Math
: A reference to an object holding various mathematical functions and constants.

name
: A string that contains the name of the window. The name is optionally specified when the window is created with the open() method. In Navigator 2.0 and Internet Explorer 3.0, this property is read-only. In Navigator 3.0 and later it is read/write.

navigator
: A reference to the Navigator object that applies to this and all other windows.

netscape
: A reference to the JavaPackage object which is the top of the Java package name hierarchy for the *netscape.** Java packages from Netscape.

opener
: A read/write property that refers to the Window object that called open() to create this window. Available in Navigator 3.0 and later.

Packages
: A reference to a JavaPackage object that represents the top of the Java package name hierarchy.

parent
: A reference to the parent window or frame of the current window. Only useful when the current window is a frame rather than a top-level window.

self   A reference to the window itself. A synonym of `window`.

status   A read/write string that specifies the current contents of the status line.

sun   A reference to the JavaPackage object which is the top of the Java package name hierarchy for the *sun.** Java packages from Sun Microsystems.

top   A reference to the top-level window that contains the current window. Only useful when the current window is a frame rather than a top-level window.

window   A reference to the window itself. A synonym of `self`.

Methods

alert( )   Display a simple message in a dialog box.

blur( )   Take keyboard focus from the top-level browser window; this sends the window to the background on most platforms.

clearTimeout( )
                Cancel a pending timeout operation.

close( )   Close a window.

confirm( )   Ask a yes-or-no question with a dialog box.

focus( )   Give the top-level browser window keyboard focus; this brings the window to the front on most platforms.

open( )   Create and open a new window.

prompt( )   Ask for simple string input with a dialog box.

scroll( )   Scroll the document displayed in the window.

setTimeout( )
                Execute code after a specified amount of time elapses.

Event Handlers

onblur( )   An event handler invoked when the window loses focus.

onerror( )   An event handler invoked when a JavaScript error occurs.

onfocus( )   An event handler invoked when the window gains focus.

onLoad( )   An event handler invoked when the document (or frameset) is fully loaded.

onUnload( )   An event handler invoked when the browser leaves the current document or frameset.

Description

The Window object represents a browser window or frame. It is documented in detail in Chapter 11*[/XRF].

In client-side JavaScript, all expressions are evaluated in the context of the current Window object. This means that no special syntax is required to refer to the current window, and you can use the properties of that window object as if they were variables. For example, you can write document rather than *window*.document. Similarly, you can use the methods of the current window object as if they were functions: alert() instead of *window*.alert().

The Window object does have window and self properties that refer to the window object itself. You can use these when you want to make the current window reference explicit rather than implicit. In addition to these two properties, the parent, and top properties and the frames[ ] array refer to other Window objects related to the current one.

To refer to a frame within a window, use:

```
frames[i] or self.frames[i] // frames of current window
window.frames[i] // frames of specified window
```

To refer to the parent window (or frame) of a frame, use:

```
parent or self.parent // parent of current window
window.parent // parent of specified window
```

To refer to the top-level browser window from any frame contained within it, use:

```
top or self.top // top window of current frame
window.top // top window of specified frame
```

New top-level browser windows are created with the Window.open() method. When you call this method, save the return value of the open() call in a variable, and use that variable to reference the new window. In Navigator 3.0, the opener property of the new window is a reference back to the window that opened it.

In general, the methods of the Window object manipulate the browser window or frame in some way. The alert(), confirm() and prompt() methods are notable: they interact with the user through simple dialog boxes.

Since JavaScript code is evaluated in the context of the Window object in which it is running, the Window object must contain references (or references to references) to all the other JavaScript objects of interest. That is, it is the root of a JavaScript "object hierarchy." Many of the properties of the Window object are references to other important JavaScript objects. Most of these properties refer to an object particular to the window. The location property of a Window, for example, refers to the Location object of the window.

A number of Window properties, however, refer instead to "global" objects. The navigator property is one of these: it contains a reference to the Navigator object, which contains version information about the browser. Every Window object contains a navigator property which is a reference to this same Navigator object. Because all JavaScript expressions are evaluated in the context of a Window object, there is no way to define global variables such as navigator except by making them properties of every Window object. Other "global" properties of this sort are Math, Packages, java, sun, and netscape.

See Chapter 11 for an in-depth overview of the Window object, and see the individual reference pages for complete details on all the Window properties, methods, and event handlers.

See Also

Document, Chapter 11

Window.alert() Method — display a message in a dialog box

Availability

Navigator 2.0, Internet Explorer 3.0

Synopsis

```
window.alert(message)
```

Arguments

message   The plain text (not HTML) string to display in a dialog box popped up over *window*.

Returns

nothing.

Description

The alert() method displays the specified *message* to the user in a dialog box. The dialog box contains an **OK** button that the user can click to dismiss the dialog box.

The dialog box that is displayed is non-modal. That is, the user can continue to interact with the browser window while the dialog is displayed. JavaScript execution continues while the dialog is displayed; it does *not* pause until the user dismisses the dialog.

Usage

Perhaps the most common use of the alert() method is to display error messages when the user's input to some form element is invalid in some way. The alert dialog can inform the user of the problem and explain what needs to be corrected to avoid the problem in the future. The appearance of the alert() dialog box is platform-dependent, but generally it contains graphics that indicate that the message indicates an error, a warning, or an alert of some kind. While alert() can display any desired message, the "alert" graphics of the dialog mean that this method is not appropriate for simple informational messages like "Welcome to my home page" or "You are the 177th visitor this week!"

Note that the *message* displayed in the dialog is a string of plain text, not formatted HTML. You can use the newline character, \n, in your strings to break your message across multiple lines. You can also do some very rudimentary formatting using spaces and can approximate horizontal rules with underscore characters, but the results you achieve will depend greatly on the font used in the dialog, and will thus be system dependent.

In Netscape Navigator, the message displayed is prefaced with "JavaScript Alert:". The alert box in Microsoft Internet Explorer does not display any similar indication that the message comes from a JavaScript program; this has been raised as a possible security concern.

See Also

Window, Window.confirm(), Window.prompt()

Window.blur() Method — remove keyboard focus from a top-level window

Availability

Navigator 3.0

Synopsis

```
window.blur()
```

Arguments

None.

Returns

Nothing.

Description

The `blur()` method removes keyboard focus from the top-level browser window specified by the Window object. If the Window object is a frame, then keyboard focus is given to the top-level window that contains that frame. On most platforms, a top-level window will be sent to the background, to the bottom of the window stack, when it has focus taken from it.

See Also

Window, Window.focus()

Window.clearTimeout() Method — cancel deferred execution

Availability

Navigator 2.0, Internet Explorer 3.0

Synopsis

```
window.clearTimeout(timeoutId)
```

Arguments

timeoutId   A value returned by `setTimeout()` that identifies the timeout to be cancelled.

Returns

Nothing.

Description

The `clearTimeout()` method cancels the execution of code that has been deferred with the `setTimeout()` method. The *timeoutId* argument is a value returned by the call to `setTimeout()` and identifies which (of possibly more than one) block of deferred code to cancel.

See Also
Window, Window.setTimeout()

Window.close() Method — close a browser window

Availability
Navigator 2.0, Internet Explorer 3.0

Synopsis
```
window.close()
```

Arguments
None.

Returns
Nothing.

Description
The close() method closes the top-level browser window specified by *window*. A window can close itself by calling self.close() or simply close(). In Navigator, if *window* is the only open window, then close() closes it and Navigator exits.

In Navigator 3.0, only windows that are opened by JavaScript can be closed by JavaScript. This prevents malicious scripts from causing the user's browser to exit.

In Navigator 2.0 and 3.0, there is no meaningful way to close a frame within a window. Thus, the close() method should only be invoked for Window objects that represent top-level browser windows, not those that represent frames.

See Also
Window, Window.open()

Window.closed Property — specifies whether a window has been closed

Availability
Navigator 3.0

Synopsis
```
window.closed
```

Description
The closed property of the Window object is a read-only Boolean value that specifies whether the window has been closed. When a browser window closes, the Window object that represents it does not simply disappear. The Window object continues to exist, but its closed property is set to true.

Usage

Once a window has been closed, you should not attempt to use or manipulate it in any way. If your code needs to use a window that may be closed without your program's knowledge, then you should be sure to always test the `closed` property before using the Window object.

See Also

Window, Window.close()

Window.confirm() Method — ask a yes-or-no question

Availability

Navigator 2.0, Internet Explorer 3.0

Synopsis

```
window.confirm(question)
```

Arguments

question   The plain text (not HTML) string to be displayed in the dialog. It should generally express a question you want the user to answer.

Returns

`true` if the user clicks the **OK** button, or `false` if the user clicks the **Cancel** button.

Description

The `confirm()` method displays the specified `question` in a dialog box that pops up over `window`. The appearance of the dialog is platform-dependent, but it generally contains graphics that indicate that the user is being asked a question. The dialog contains **OK** and **Cancel** buttons that the user can use to answer the question. If the user clicks the **OK** button, then `confirm()` returns `true`. If the user clicks **Cancel**, then `confirm()` returns `false`.

The dialog box that is displayed by the `confirm()` method is *modal*—that is, it blocks all user input to the main browser window until the user dismisses the dialog by clicking on the **OK** or **Cancel** buttons. Since this method returns a value depending on the user's response to the dialog, JavaScript execution pauses in the call to `confirm()` and subsequent statements are not executed until the user responds to the dialog.

Usage

Note that the `question` displayed in the dialog is a string of plain text, not formatted HTML. You can use the newline character, \n, in your strings to break your question across multiple lines. You can also do some very rudimentary formatting using spaces and can approximate horizontal rules with underscore characters, but the results you achieve will depend greatly on the font used in the dialog, and will thus be system dependent.

Also, there is no way to change the labels that appear in the buttons of the dialog box (to make them read "Yes" and "No", for example). Therefore, you should take care to phrase your question or message in such a way that "OK" and "Cancel" are suitable responses.

See Also

Window, Window.alert( ), Window.prompt( )

Window.defaultStatus Property — the default status line text

Availability

Navigator 2.0, Internet Explorer 3.0

Synopsis

```
window.defaultStatus
```

Description

`defaultStatus` is a read/write string property that specifies default text to appear in the window's status line. In Navigator, the status line is used to display the browser's progress while loading a file, and to display the destination of hypertext links that the mouse is over. While it is not displaying any of these transient messages, the status line is, by default, blank. However, you can set the `defaultStatus` property to specify a default message to be displayed when the status line is not otherwise in use, and you can read the `default-Status` property to determine what the default message is. The text you specify may be temporarily overwritten with other messages, such as those that are displayed when the user moves the mouse over a hypertext link, but the `defaultStatus` message will always be redisplayed when the transient message is erased.

If you set `defaultStatus` for a Window object that is a frame, the message you specify will be visible whenever the mouse is within that frame (whether or not that frame has focus). When you specify `defaultStatus` for a top-level window that contains no frames, your message is always visible when the window is visible. If you specify `defaultStatus` for a top-level window that contains frames, your message is only visible when the mouse is over the borders that separate the frames. Thus, in order to guarantee visibility of a message in a framed document, you should set `defaultStatus` for all frames in the document.

Usage

`defaultStatus` is used to display semi-permanent messages in the status line. To display transient messages, use the `status` property.

The `defaultStatus` property remains set when the browser moves from one page to another. If you set this property, you should be sure to reset it to the empty string (`""`) to restore the status line to its default blank state when the message is no longer applicable. A good way to do this is with the `onUnload()` event handler. Note that not all sites will be this considerate, so it is also a good idea to protect your web pages from other sites' default status messages by setting or resetting the `defaultStatus` property when your page is first loaded.

See Also

Window, Window.status

Window.document Property — the Document of the Window

Availability

Navigator 2.0, Internet Explorer 3.0

Synopsis

```
window.document
```

Description

The `document` property contains a read-only reference to the Document object that describes the document contained in *window*, which can be any top-level window or frame. See the Document object for further details.

See Also

Document, Frame, Window

Window.focus( ) Method — give keyboard focus to a top-level window

Availability

Navigator 3.0

Synopsis

```
window.focus()
```

Arguments

None.

Returns

Nothing.

Description

The `focus()` method gives keyboard focus to the top-level browser window specified by the Window object. If the Window object is a frame, then keyboard focus is given to the top-level window that contains that frame. On most platforms, a top-level window will be brought forward, to the top of the window stack, when it is given focus.

See Also

Window, Window.blur( )

Window.frames[] Property — list of frames within a window

Availability

Navigator 2.0, Internet Explorer 3.0

Synopsis

```
window.frames[i]
window.frames.length
```

Description

The `frames` property is an array of references to Window objects, one for each frame contained within the specified `window`. The `frames.length` property contains the number of elements in the `frames[]` array, as does the `window.length` property. Note that frames referenced by the `frames[]` array may themselves contain frames and may have a `frames[]` array of their own.

See Also

Frame, Window

Window.history Property — the History of the Window

Availability

Navigator 2.0, Internet Explorer 3.0

Synopsis

```
window.history
```

Description

The `history` property contains a read-only reference to the History object of `window`, which may be any top-level window or frame. See the History object for further details.

See Also

History, Window

Window.java Property — see java

Window.length Property — number of frames in the window

Availability

Navigator 2.0, Internet Explorer 3.0

Synopsis

```
window.length
```

Description

The `length` property specifies the number of frames contained in `window`, which may be any top-level window or frame. `length` also specifies the number of elements in the `window.frames[]` array.

See Also

Frame, Window, Window.frames[]

Window.location Property — the URL of the window

Availability

Navigator 2.0, Internet Explorer 3.0

Synopsis

```
window.location
```

Description

The location property contains a read-only reference to the Location object of *window*, which may be any top-level window or frame. See the Location object for further details. Note that while the location property itself is read-only, the properties of the Location object to which it refers are read/write, and can be used to make the browser go to any specified web address.

See Also

Location, Window

Window.Math Property — see Math

Window.name Property — the name of a window

Availability

Navigator 2.0, Internet Explorer 3.0; enhanced in Navigator 3.0.

Synopsis

```
window.name
```

Description

The name property is a string that specifies the name of *window*, which may be any top-level window or frame. This property is read-only in Navigator 2.0 and Internet Explorer 3.0, and is read/write in Navigator 3.0. The name of a top-level window is initially specified by the *name* argument of the Window.open() method. The name of a frame is initially specified by the NAME attribute of the <FRAME> HTML tag.

The name of a top-level window or frame may be used as the value of a TARGET attribute of an <A> or <FORM> tag. Using the TARGET attribute in this way specifies that the hyperlinked document or the results of form submission should be displayed in the named window.

The initial window opened by Navigator, and any windows opened with the **New Web Browser** menu item initially have no name (i.e., name == ""), and so these windows cannot be addressed with a TARGET attribute from a separate top-level window. In Navigator 3.0, you can set the name attribute to remedy this situation.

See Also

Form, Frame, Link, Window

Window.navigate() Method — load a new URL

Availability

Internet Explorer 3.0

Synopsis

```
window.navigate(url)
```

Arguments

url   A string that specifies the URL to be loaded and displayed.

Returns

Nothing.

Description

The Window.navigate() method of Internet Explorer loads ("navigates to") the specified url into the specified window.

This method is an incompatible extension to JavaScript—it is not supported by Navigator 2.0 or 3.0—and is therefore best avoided. The same purpose can be accomplished both in Navigator and Internet Explorer by simply assigning the desired url to the location property of the desired window.

See Also

Location, Window.location

Window.navigator Property — see navigator and Navigator

Window.netscape Property — see netscape

Window.onblur() Handler — invoked when window loses focus

Availability

Navigator 3.0

Synopsis

```
<BODY                                 a definition of the handler
    [ onBlur="JavaScript statements" ]
        . . .
>
<FRAMESET                             another way to define the handler
    [ onBlur="JavaScript statements" ]
        . . .
>
```

```
window.onblur=handler-func          defining the handler directly
window.onblur();                    an explicit invocation of the handler
```

Description

onblur() is an event handler invoked by the browser when a top-level browser window loses the input focus, either because the user has switched to some other window, or because focus was explicitly transferred to another browser window with the Window blur() or focus() methods.

The onblur() event handler can be defined in HTML by specifying the onBlur attribute of the <BODY> or <FRAMESET> tag of the document or frameset that occupies the top-level window. The value of this attribute may be any number of JavaScript statements, separated by semicolons. This event handler may also be defined by assigning a function to the onblur property of the Window object.

Usage

If your web page does some sort of animation, you might use the onblur() event handler to stop the animation when the window doesn't have the input focus, on the theory that if the window doesn't have the focus, then the user probably can't see it or isn't paying attention to it.

See Also

Window, Window.blur(), Window.focus(), Window.onfocus()

Window.onerror() Handler — invoked when a JavaScript error occurs

Availability

Navigator 3.0

Synopsis

You register an onerror() event handler like this:

```
window.onerror=handler-func
```

Navigator invokes the handler like this:

```
window.onerror(message, url, line)
```

Arguments

message   A string that specifies the error message for the error that occurred.

url   A string that specifies the URL of the document in which the error occurred.

line   A number that specifies the line number at which the error occurred.

Returns

true if the handler has handled the error and JavaScript should take no further action. false if JavaScript should post the default error message dialog box for this error.

Description

The onerror() event handler of the Window object is invoked when a JavaScript error occurs in code executing in that window. The default error handler installed by JavaScript displays an error dialog box. You can customize error handling by providing your own onerror() event handler.

You define an onerror() event handler for a window by setting the onerror property of a Window object to an appropriate function. Note that unlike other event handlers in JavaScript, the onerror() handler cannot be defined in an HTML tag.

When the onerror() handler is invoked, it is passed three arguments. The first is a string specifying the error message. The second is a string specifying the URL of the document in which the error occurred. And the third is a number that specifies the line number at which the error occurred. An error handling function may do anything it wants with these arguments: it may display its own error dialog, or may log the error in some way, for example. When the error handling function is done, it should return true if it has completely handled the error and wants JavaScript to take no further action. Or, it should return false if it has merely noted or logged the error in some fashion and still wants JavaScript to display the error message in its default dialog box.

Note that while this event handler returns true to tell the browser to take no further action, most Form and form element event handlers return false to prevent the browser from performing some action, such as submitting a form. This inconsistency can be confusing.

You can turn off error handling entirely for a window by setting the onerror property of the window to null. If you will later want to turn error handling back on, you should first save the default error handler in a temporary variable, so you can restore the onerror property to its default value.

Example

The following code shows how you might write and register an error handler for a window. Instead of reporting the error in a dialog box, this handler reports the details in a form that it creates directly in the document itself. The form contains a button that will send the details of the error off to the author of the web page.

```
<script>
function p(s) { document.writeln(s) }  // shorthand

// define the error handler. It generates an HTML form so
// the user can report the error to the author.
function report_error(msg, url, line)
{
    // Output a form that reports the error
    p('<P><HR SIZE=5><DIV align=center>');
    p('<H1>SORRY!  A JavaScript Error Has Occurred</H1>');
    p('<FORM ACTION="mailto:bugs@wahoo.com" METHOD=post
    p('      ENCTYPE="text/plain">');
    p('You can help the author debug this program by clicking here: ');
```

```
        p('<INPUT TYPE="submit" VALUE="Report Error">');
        p('</DIV><DIV align=right>');
        p('<BR>Your name (optional): <INPUT SIZE=60 NAME="name" VALUE="">');
        p('<BR>Message: <INPUT SIZE=60 NAME="message" VALUE="'
                + msg + '">');
        p('<BR>URL: <INPUT SIZE=60 NAME="url" VALUE="' + url + '">');
        p('<BR>Line Number: <INPUT SIZE=60 NAME="line" VALUE="'
                + line + '">');
        p('<BR>Browser Version: <INPUT SIZE=60 NAME="version"'
                + 'VALUE="' + navigator.userAgent + '">');
        p('</DIV>');
        p('</FORM>');
        p('<HR SIZE=5><P>');

        return true;     // tell the browser not to report the error itself
    }


    // now register the error handler
    window.onerror = report_error;
    </script>
```

See Also

Window

Window.onfocus() Handler — invoked when window is given focus

Availability

Navigator 3.0

Synopsis

```
<BODY                                  a definition of the handler
    [ onFocus="JavaScript statements" ]
        . . .
>


<FRAMESET                              another way to define the handler
    [ onFocus="JavaScript statements" ]
        . . .
>

window.onfocus=handler-func            defining the handler directly
window.onfocus();                      an explicit invocation of the handler
```

Description

onfocus() is an event handler invoked by the browser when a top-level browser window is given the input focus, because either the user has switched to the browser window, or focus was transferred to the window with the Window focus() or blur() methods.

The onfocus() event handler can be defined in HTML by specifying the onFocus attribute of the <BODY> or <FRAMESET> tag of the document or frameset that occupies the top-level window. The value of this attribute may be any number of JavaScript statements, separated by semicolons. This event handler may also be defined by assigning a function to the `onfocus` property of the Window object.

Usage

If your web page does some sort of animation, you might use the `onfocus()` event handler to start the animation and the `onblur()` handler to stop it, so that it only runs while the user is paying attention to the window.

See Also

Window, Window.blur(), Window.focus(), Window.onblur()

Window.onload() Handler — executed when a document finishes loading

Availability

Navigator 2.0, Internet Explorer 3.0

Synopsis

```
<BODY                                    a definition of the handler
    [ onLoad="JavaScript statements" ]
        . . .
>


<FRAMESET                                another way to define the handler
    [ onLoad="JavaScript statements" ]
        . . .
>


window.onload=handler-func               defining the handler directly
window.onload();                         an explicit invocation of the handler
```

Description

`onload()` is an event handler invoked by the browser when a document or frameset is completely loaded into the browser. The `onload()` handler is defined by the `onLoad` attribute of the `<BODY>` or `<FRAMESET>` HTML tags. The value of this attribute may be any number of JavaScript statements, separated by semicolons.

When the `onload()` event handler is invoked, you can be certain that the document has fully loaded, and therefore that all scripts within the document have executed, all functions within scripts are defined, and all forms and other document elements have been parsed and are available through the Document object.

Usage

If any of your document's event handlers depend on the document being fully loaded, you should be sure to check that it is loaded before executing those handlers. If the network connection were to stall out after a button appeared in the document, but before the parts of the document that the button relied on were loaded, then when the user clicks the button they will get unintended behavior or an error message. One good way to verify that the document is loaded is to use the `onload()` handler to set a variable, `loaded`, for example, to `true`, and to check the value of this variable before doing anything that depends on the complete document being loaded.

Bugs

JavaScript is supposed to guarantee that the `onload()` handler for each frame in a window will be invoked before the `onload()` handler for the window itself. Unfortunately, Navigator 2.0 does not always do this. Thus in a framed document, you may need to check that each of your individual frames has fully loaded.

See Also

Window, Window.onunload()

Window.onunload() Handler — executed when the browser leaves a page

Availability

Navigator 2.0, Internet Explorer 3.0

Synopsis

```
<BODY                                      a definition of the handler
    [ onUnload="JavaScript statements" ]
        . . .
>


<FRAMESET                                  another way to define the handler
    [ onUnload="JavaScript statements" ]
        . . .
>


window.onunload=handler-func               defining the handler directly
window.onunload();                         an explicit invocation of the handler
```

Description

`onunload()` is an event handler invoked by the browser when it unloads (i.e., leaves) a document or a frameset. The `onunload()` handler is defined by the `onUnload` attribute of the `<BODY>` or `<FRAMESET>` HTML tags. The value of this attribute may be any number of JavaScript statements, separated by semicolons.

The `onunload()` event handler provides the opportunity to perform any necessary "clean-up" of the browser state before a new document is loaded. For example, an `onunload()` handler might restore the `Window.defaultStatus` property (the default message in the status line) to the empty string.

When the browser leaves a site using frames, the `onunload()` handlers for each frame will be invoked before the `onunload()` handler of the browser itself.

Usage

The onunload() handler is invoked when the user has instructed the browser to leave the current page and move somewhere else. Therefore, it is almost never appropriate to delay the loading of the desired new page by popping up dialog boxes (with Window.confirm() or Window.prompt() for example) from an onunload() event handler.

See Also

Window, Window.onunload()

Window.open() Method — open a new browser window or locate a named window

Availability

Navigator 2.0, Internet Explorer 3.0; enhanced in Navigator 3.0

Synopsis

```
window.open(url, name, [features, [replace]])
```

Arguments

url

A string that specifies the URL to be displayed in the new window, or the empty string for a blank window. This argument is optional in Navigator 2.0 and 3.0, but is required in Internet Explorer 3.0.

name

A string of alphanumeric and underscore characters that specifies a name for the new window. This name can be used as the value of the TARGET attribute of <A> and <FORM> HTML tags. If this argument names a window that already exists, then the open() method will not create a new window, but will simply return a reference to the named window. In this case, the features argument is ignored. This argument is optional in Navigator 2.0 and 3.0, but is required in Internet Explorer 3.0.

features

A string that specifies which features of a standard browser window are to appear in the new window. The format of this string is specified below. This argument is optional; if it is not specified, then the new window will have all standard features.

replace

An optional Boolean argument that specifies whether the url that is loaded into the new page should create a new entry in the window's browsing history or replace the current entry in the browsing history. If this argument is true then no new history entry will be created. This argument is not supported by Navigator 2.0 or Internet Explorer 3.0, although those browsers will ignore it if it is specified. Also, notice that it doesn't make much sense to use this argument for newly created windows; it is intended for use when changing the contents of an existing window.

Returns

A reference to a Window object, which may be newly created, or to an already existing one.

Description

The open() method looks up an already existing window or opens a new browser window. If the *name* argument specifies the name of an existing window, then a reference to that window is returned. The returned window will display the URL specified by *url*, but the *features* argument will be ignored. This is the only way in JavaScript to obtain a reference to a window which is known only by name.

If the *name* argument is not specified, or if no window with that name already exists, the the open() method creates a new browser window. The created window displays the URL specified by *url*, has the name specified by *name*, and has the size and controls specified by *features* (the format of this argument is described later in this entry). If *url* is the empty string, then open() opens a blank window.

The *name* argument specifies a name for the new window. This name may only contain alphanumeric characters and the underscore character. It may be used as the value of the TARGET attribute of an <A> or <FORM> tag in HTML, to force documents to be displayed in the window.

With Navigator 3.0, when you use Window.open() to load a new document into a named window, you can also use the *replace* argument to specify whether the new document will have its own entry in the window's browsing history, or whether it will replace the history entry of the current document. If *replace* is true, the new document will replace the old. If this argument is false is or not specified, then the new document will have its own entry in the Window's browsing history. This argument provides functionality much like that of the Location.replace() method.

The *features* argument is a comma-separated list of features to appear in the window. If this optional argument is empty or not specified at all, then all features will be present in the window. On the other hand, if *features* specifies any one feature, then any features that do not appear in the list will not appear in the window. The string should not contain any spaces or other whitespace. Each element in the list has the format:

> *feature[=value]*

For most features, the *value* is yes or no. For these features, the equals sign and the *value* may be omitted—if the feature appears, yes is assumed, and if it doesn't no is assumed. For the width and height features, the *value* is required and must specify a size in pixels.

The available features and their meanings are listed here. Note, however, that on X11 platforms in Navigator 2.0, only the width and height features work, and new browser windows are not created with any of the standard controls, even when the *features* argument is omitted entirely.

toolbar	The browser toolbar, with **Back** and **Forward** buttons, etc.
location	The input field for entering URLs directly into the browser.
directories	Directory buttons, such as "What's New" and "What's Cool" in Netscape.

status   The status line.

menubar   The menu bar.

scrollbars   This feature enables horizontal and vertical scrollbars when they are necessary.

resizable   If this feature is not present or is set to no, then the window will not have resize handles around its border. (Depending on the platform, the user may still have ways to resize the window.) Note that a common bug is to misspell this feature as "resizeable", with an extra "e".

width   This feature must be followed by a value that specifies the width of the window in pixels.

height   This feature must be followed by a value that specifies the height of the window in pixels.

Don't confuse this Window.open() method with the document.open() method; the two perform very different functions. For clarity in your code, you may want to use window.open() instead of open(). (Recall that the window property is simply a way to explicitly refer to the current window.)

Bugs

In Navigator 2.0, on X11 and Macintosh platforms, the *url* argument is ineffective. The solution is to call open() once to create the window, and then call it again to set the URL, or better, to use location property of the new (blank) window to load the desired URL.

On X11 platforms in Navigator 2.0, only the width and height features work, and new browser windows are not created with any of the standard controls, even when the *features* argument is omitted entirely.

See Also

Location.replace(), Window, Window.close()

Window.opener Property — the window that opened this one

Availability

Navigator 3.0; read-only in Internet Explorer 3.0

Synopsis

     window.opener

Description

The opener property is a read/write (read-only in Internet Explorer 3.0) reference to the Window object that contained the document that called open() to open this top-level browser window. This property is only valid for Window objects that represent top-level windows; not those that represent frames.

The opener property is useful so that a newly created window can refer to variables and functions defined in the window that created it.

Usage

The `opener` property does not exist in Navigator 2.0. You can use the following code for backward compatibility:

```
var newwin = open();
if (newwin != null && newwin.opener == null)
    newwin.opener = self;
```

p. 266-7

See Also

Window, Window.open()

Window.Packages Property — see Packages

Window.parent Property — the parent of a frame

Availability

Navigator 2.0, Internet Explorer 3.0

Synopsis

```
window.parent
```

Description

The `parent` property is a read-only reference to the Window object that contains *window*. If *window* specifies a top-level window, then `parent` refers to the window itself. If *window* is a frame, then the `parent` property refers to the top-level window or frame that contains *window*.

Usage

The `parent` property is generally only useful for frames rather than for top-level windows. With a function like the following, you can use the property to determine whether a given Window object is a top-level window or a frame:

```
function is_toplevel(w) { return (w.parent == w); }
```

See Also

Window, Window.top

Window.prompt() Method — get string input in a dialog

Availability

Navigator 2.0, Internet Explorer 3.0

Synopsis

```
window.prompt(message)
window.prompt(message, default)
```

Arguments

message   The plain text (not HTML) string to be displayed in the dialog. It should ask the user to enter the information you want. On Windows platforms, only one line messages are allowed.

default   An optionally specified string or integer which will be displayed as the default input in the dialog. If `null` is specified, or if this argument is not passed at all, then `prompt()` displays the string "<undefined>" as the default value. Pass the empty string ("") to make `prompt()` display an empty input box.

Returns

The string entered by the user, or the empty string if the user did not enter a string, or `null` if the user clicked **Cancel**.

Description

The `prompt()` method displays the specified *message* in a dialog box that also contains a textual input field and **OK**, **Clear**, and **Cancel** buttons. Platform-dependent graphics in the dialog help to indicate to the user that her input is desired.

The *default* argument specifies the text that initially appears in the input field. If *default* is `null`, or if this optional argument is not passed at all, then the initial text is "<undefined>". If *default* is the empty string ("") then the input field is initially empty. Otherwise, the input field displays the string or number that is passed as the *default*.

If the user clicks the **Cancel** button, `prompt()` returns `null`. If the user clicks the **Clear** button, `prompt()` erases any current text in the input field. If the user clicks the **OK** button, `prompt()` returns the value current value displayed in the input field. Note, however, that if the input field is displaying "<undefined>" because the *default* argument was `null` or unspecified, then `prompt()` returns the empty string and not the string "<undefined>". Also note that `prompt()` always returns the user's input as a string value, even if *default* was specified as a numeric value. If necessary, you can use `parseInt()` or `parseFloat()` to convert the returned string to a number.

The dialog box that is displayed by the `prompt()` method is *modal*—that is, it blocks all user input to the main browser window until the user dismisses the dialog by clicking on the **OK** or **Cancel** buttons. Since this method returns a value depending on the user's response to the dialog, JavaScript execution pauses in the call to `prompt()`, and subsequent statements are not executed until the user responds to the dialog.

Usage

Note that the *question* displayed in the dialog is a string of plain text, not of formatted HTML. Unlike the message displayed by the `alert()` and `confirm()` methods, the message displayed by `prompt()` may only be a single line long on Windows platforms.

See Also

Window, Window.alert(), Window.confirm()

Window.scroll( ) Method — scroll a document in a window

Availability

Navigator 3.0

Synopsis

```
window.scroll(x, y)
```

Arguments

x   The X-coordinate to scroll to.

y   The Y-coordinate to scroll to.

Returns

Nothing.

Description

The `scroll()` method moves the window's document within the window, so that the specified *x* and *y* coordinates of the document appear in the upper-left corner of the window.

The X coordinate increases to the right, and the Y coordinate increases down the page. Thus, `scroll(0,0)` always places the top-left corner of the document in the top-left corner of the window.

See Also

Window

Window.self Property — the window itself

Availability

Navigator 2.0, Internet Explorer 3.0

Synopsis

```
window.self
```

Description

The `self` property contains a reference to the Window object specified by *window*, i.e., *window*.`self` is identical to *window*. Because a reference to the current top-level window or frame is implicit in all JavaScript expressions, the *window* in the above expressions can be omitted and you can simply use `self` to refer to the current window.

Usage

The `self` property provides a way to explicitly refer to the current window or frame when necessary (for example, when passing a the current window to a function). The `self` property is also sometimes useful for code clarity. Using `self.name` to refer to the name of the current window or frame is less ambiguous than simply using `name`, for example.

The `window` property is a synonym for the `self` property.

See Also

Window, Window.window

Window.setTimeout( ) Method — defer execution of code

Availability

Navigator 2.0, Internet Explorer 3.0

Synopsis

```
window.setTimeout(code, delay)
```

Arguments

code   A string that contains the JavaScript code to be executed after the *delay* has elapsed.

delay   The amount of time, in milliseconds, before the JavaScript statements in the string code should be executed.

Returns

An opaque value (a "timeout id") that can be passed to the clearTimeout() method to cancel the execution of *code*.

Description

The setTimeout() method defers the execution of the JavaScript statements in the string *code* for *delay* milliseconds. Once the specified number of milliseconds have elapsed, the statements in *code* are executed normally. Note that they are executed only once. To execute code repeatedly, *code* must itself contain a call to setTimeout() to register itself to be executed again.

The statement in the string *code* are executed in the context of *window*—i.e., *window* will be the current window for those statements. If more than one statement appears in *code*, the statements must be separated from each other with semicolons.

Bugs

In Navigator 2.0 memory allocated by JavaScript is not freed until the browser leaves a web page. Each call to setTimeout() consumes some memory, and the deferred code generally consumes memory as well. Thus, if a page performs some sort of infinite loop (for example, a status-bar animation using Window.setTimeout() and Window.status), then memory will slowly be consumed, and Navigator may crash if the user remains on the page for a long time.

See Also

Window, Window.clearTimeout()

Window.status Property — specify a transient message

Availability

Navigator 2.0, Internet Explorer 3.0

Synopsis

```
window.status
```

Description

status is a read/write string property that specifies a transient message to appear in the window's status line. The message generally appears only for a limited amount of time— until it is overwritten by another message, or until the user moves the mouse to some other area of the window, for example. When a message specified with status is erased, the status line returns to its default blank state, or to the default message specified by the defaultStatus property.

Although only top-level windows have a status line, the status property of frames may also be set. Doing so displays the specified message in the top-level window's status line. Transient messages set by frames will be visible regardless of which frame currently has focus or which frame the mouse is in. This differs from the behavior of the defaultStatus property.

Usage

status is used to display transient messages in the status line. To display semi-permanent messages, use the defaultStatus property.

In general, setting the status property is only useful from event handlers and in code fragments deferred with the Window.setTimeout() method. If you set status directly from a script, the message will not be visible to the user. It will not be displayed right away, and when it is displayed, it will likely be immediately overwritten by a browser message such as "Document: done".

If you want to set the status property in the onMouseOver() event handler of a hypertext link, you must return true from that event handler. This is because the default action when the mouse goes over a link is to display the URL of that link, thereby overwriting any status message set by the event handler. By returning true from the event handler, you cancel this default action and leave your own status message displayed (until the mouse moves off of the link).

See Also

Window, Window.defaultStatus

Window.sun Property — see sun

Window.top Property — the window of a frame

Availability

Navigator 2.0, Internet Explorer 3.0

Synopsis

```
window.top
```

Description

The `top` property is a read-only reference to the Window object that is the top-level window that contains *window*. If *window* is a top-level window itself, then the `top` property simply contains a reference to *window*. If *window* is a frame, then the `top` property contains a reference to the top-level window that contains the frame. Note that the `top` property refers to a top-level window even if *window* refers to a frame contained within another frame (which may itself be contained within a frame, and so on). Compare this with the `Window.parent` property.

Usage

Certain operations, such as setting the `status` and `defaultStatus` properties only are useful when performed on a top-level window. When JavaScript code running in a frame needs to operate on its top-level window, it can use the `top` property. For example, it could display a message in the message line as follows:

```
top.defaultStatus = 'Welcome to my Home Page!';
```

See Also

Window, Window.parent

Window.window Property — the window itself

Availability

Navigator 2.0, Internet Explorer 3.0

Synopsis

```
window.window
```

Description

The `window` property is identical to the `self` property; it contains a reference to the Window object specified by *window*. That is, *window*.`window` is identical to *window* itself. Because a reference to the current top-level window or frame is implicit in all JavaScript expressions, the *window* in the above expressions can be omitted and you can simply use `window` to refer to the current window.

Usage

The `window` property (and its synonym, `self`) provides a way to explicitly refer to the current window or frame when necessary, or when convenient for code clarity. To open a new window in an event handler, for example, it is necessary to use `window.open()`, because `open()` by itself would be confused with the `Document.open()` method.

See Also

Window, Window.self

IV

Appendices

- Appendix A, *JavaScript Resources on the Internet*
- Appendix B, *Known Bugs*
- Appendix C, *Differences between Navigator 2.0 and 3.0*
- Appendix D, *JavaScript Incompatibilities in Internet Explorer 3.0*
- Appendix E, *A Preview of Navigator 4.0*
- Appendix F, *Persistent Client State: HTTP Cookies*
- Appendix G, *JavaScript and HTML Color Names and Values*
- Appendix H, *LiveConnected Navigator Plug-Ins*

This part summarizes the differences between JavaScript in versions of Netscape Navigator, as well as the differences in the version of JavaScript implemented in Microsoft Internet Explorer. It also contains a list of known JavaScript bugs, the Netscape specification for Internet "cookies," and other important details useful to the serious JavaScript programmer.

JavaScript Resources on the Internet

There are quite a few web sites that are useful to JavaScript programmers. This appendix lists some of the highlights.

A.1 Official Netscape Documentation

The official JavaScript documentation from Netscape can be found in the online *Netscape Navigator Handbook*. You can get there by selecting the **Handbook** entry in the **Help** menu of Netscape Navigator and following the links to the JavaScript documentation.

The official JavaScript documentation is titled *The JavaScript Guide*, and in Navigator 3.0, you can link to it directly at:

http://home.netscape.com/eng/mozilla/3.0/handbook/javascript/index.html

This URL is likely to change for future versions of Navigator, however.

You are unlikely to find anything in the Navigator 3.0 version of this JavaScript documentation that you cannot also find in this book. As the JavaScript documentation is updated during the Navigator 4.0 beta cycle, you may find it quite useful, however.

A.2 Discussion of JavaScript

The primary worldwide forum for discussion (in English) of JavaScript is the Usenet newsgroup *comp.lang.javascript*. As with many Usenet newsgroups, this one can have a lot of traffic, and can sometimes be difficult to keep up with.

If you don't care for the quality or quantity of discussion that occurs in such a large, widely distributed forum, you may prefer to try to find (or start!) a smaller mailing list or chat room dedicated to the discussion of JavaScript. One of the main JavaScript mailing lists (with a moderately large volume of traffic) is hosted by *inquiry.com*. See the list homepage for directions on how to subscribe to this list:

> *http://www.inquiry.com/techtips/js_pro/maillist.html*

Note that this mailing list is also available in digest form, which can be very convenient.

If you are a member of Netscape's DevEdge developer's program, you might also try the JavaScript newsgroup hosted by Netscape:

> *snews://secnews.netscape.com/netscape.devs-javascript*

Note that this newsgroup uses the "secure news" `snews:` protocol rather than the traditional `news:`.

A.3 Examples and Links for Further Exploration

There are several good sites that include collections of JavaScript examples and/or contain links to various JavaScript resources. The largest site is probably Gamelan, the official Java directory site for JavaSoft. This site contains JavaScript information under the heading of "Related Technologies". You can get to the main Gamelan page at:

> *http://www.gamelan.com/*

And you can find the JavaScript specific listings at:

> *http://www.gamelan.com/pages/Gamelan.related.javascript.html*

Another useful site is "The JavaScript Index"; it contains links to useful JavaScript examples, as well as pointers to JavaScript tutorials and other resources. "JSI", as it is known, is maintained by Andrew Wooldridge, and is at:

> *http://www.c2.org/~andreww/javascript/*

Finally, Yahoo! has a collection of JavaScript resources. You can find it at:

> *http://www.yahoo.com/text/Computers_and_Internet/Programming_Languages/*
> *JavaScript/*

A.4 FAQ Lists

As this appendix is written, there is no particularly good FAQ (Frequently Asked Questions) list for JavaScript. The most often cited FAQ list is found at the "JavaScript 411" site:

http://www.freqgrafx.com/411/

This site, and the FAQ were developed by Andy Augustine of Frequency Graphics. They were quite useful for Navigator 2.0 and during the Navigator 3.0 beta period. Currently, however, neither the site nor the FAQ appears to be actively maintained, and as this appendix is written, the material they contain is unfortunately fairly dated.

There is no FAQ list for the *comp.lang.javascript* newsgroup, at least not one that is regularly posted to *news.answers*. (Perhaps some enterprising reader of this book will take it upon themselves to start one!)

B

Known Bugs

In order to program effectively in JavaScript, or any language, it is important to have an idea of what features don't work as advertised. This appendix discusses the known bugs in various versions of JavaScript.

B.1 Known JavaScript Bugs in Navigator 3.0

The bugs detailed in the sections below comprise the complete list of JavaScript bugs that were known to the developers of JavaScript at Netscape when this book went to press. Unfortunately, not all of these bugs have been fully researched, and some of the descriptions are vague. They've been arranged by topic, and in approximate order of severity and the frequency with which they are encountered.

B.1.1 History.go() Doesn't Work with Frames

The `History.go()` method may not work correctly when a window contains multiple frames. Use `History.back()` and `History.forward()` instead.

B.1.2 Table Bugs

There are a couple of JavaScript bugs in Navigator 3.0 that relate to HTML tables.

B.1.2.1 Images in tables

When an `<IMG>` tag appears in a table cell, two JavaScript Image objects will be created to represent it. If the `<IMG>` tag appears in a table nested within a table, four Image objects may be created. Only the last Image object created for a given <IMG> tag has a working src property. Because an unexpected number of Image objects are created, it is difficult to correctly use the Document.images[] array to refer to them.

As a workaround, give all of your images names with the NAME attribute, and refer to them by name as properties of the Document object. When JavaScript creates multiple objects with the same name, it stores them in an array by that name. If an image named "outside" is specified outside of any HTML tables, you can refer to it as document.outside. However, if an image named "inside" is created within a table, two Image objects with this name will be created, and they can be referred to as document.inside[0] and document.inside[1]. It is the latter image that has the correctly working src property.

The following function demonstrates a workaround to this bug. Given an image name, it returns the working Image object with that name. It works correctly for images that are not part of tables, and will continue to work correctly even after this bug has been patched.

```
function getImage(image_name)
{
    var i = document[image_name];
    if (i.length)                    // If the image is actually an array...
        return i[i.length-1];        // then return the last image in it.
    else return i;                   // Otherwise return the single Image.
}
```

B.1.2.2 Document.write() in nested tables

Calling document.write() from within a nested table can sometimes result in incorrectly formatted text, which may include portions of JavaScript code that appears within <SCRIPT> and </SCRIPT> tags.

Using document.write() within tables is not nearly so buggy as it could be in Navigator 2.0, but nevertheless, it is still a good idea to sidestep these problems by using document.write() to dynamically generate the entire table, including all relevant HTML tags, rather than just generating the contents of a static HTML table.

B.1.3 Bugs with Dynamically Generated Documents

Navigator 3.0 contained a lot of changes that allow it to print and save the dynamically generated content of documents, which is something that was *not* possible in Navigator 2.0. Unfortunately, these changes seem to have left (or created) some residual bugs, and the exact circumstances under which these bugs can occur are not always clear.

B.1.3.1 Event handlers in regenerated documents

For very complex implementation-specific reasons, if your JavaScript program generates a document into a separate window or frame, you may find that the event handlers in the generated document stop working if your program ever regenerates that document. There are two steps you can take to avoid this problem. The first is to not call document.open() for the window or frame into which you are generating your document. While it is good style to call this function, it is not actually necessary, because calling document.write() on a closed document implicitly re-opens the document. The only time document.open() is actually necessary is when you want to open a document for some MIME type other than "text/html".

The other way to avoid this problem, if you really do want to call document.open(), is to store the return value of document.open() into a global variable. The return value of this method is typically ignored but it is actually the new Document object. Because of the particular genesis of this bug, simply storing this return value is sufficient to prevent the event handlers from breaking.

B.1.3.2 Content disappears upon resize

In some generated documents, at least those containing Applets, resizing the browser may cause document content to disappear. As a workaround to this problem, you can try calling document.write() with the empty string before each <APPLET> tag in the document. That is, insert do-nothing lines like the following before your <APPLET> tags:

```
<!-- Bug workaround for NN 3.0 -->
<SCRIPT LANGUAGE="JavaScript">document.write("");</SCRIPT>
```

B.1.3.3 onClick() event handlers ignored

Under certain conditions, which are not yet understood, an onClick() event handler in a generated document may fail to work. Since it is not yet understood what triggers this problem, no standard workaround has been found yet.

B.1.4 LiveConnect Bugs

LiveConnect, described in Chapter 19, *LiveConnect: JavaScript and Java*, is a new and powerful addition to Navigator 3.0. As such, it is not surprising that some bugs remain. Actually, most LiveConnect bugs are really missing features, rather than actual buggy implementation.

B.1.4.1 Can't call Java method with nonsystem object arguments

JavaScript cannot call any Java method that takes an object as an argument if the type of that object is not one of the standard system classes. For example, if an applet defines a helper class called *Helper*, JavaScript could not invoke a method that expected an argument of type *Helper*. The workaround is to define any affected methods so that they take arguments of type *java.lang.Object*, and then, within the method, to cast those arguments to the actual desired type.

B.1.4.2 Java network activity can cause exception

If JavaScript invokes Java code that performs networking, it may cause an exception to be thrown. If you encounter this problem, a workaround you can try is to perform the networking in a separate thread, and have JavaScript call the method that starts the networking thread.

B.1.4.3 Accessing applets before they are loaded

If you attempt to use LiveConnect to interact with a Java applet before the applet is fully loaded, you will see an error dialog, and the applet will be inaccessible to JavaScript even after it has finished loading. To avoid this situation, use the `onLoad()` event handler of the Window object to be sure that everything has finished loading before attempting to interact with applets.

B.1.4.4 Problems with overloaded methods

If a class contains overloaded methods (i.e., methods with the same name but different arguments), JavaScript may not be able to correctly figure out which one to call. In beta releases of Navigator 3.0, JavaScript could only invoke the first overloaded method that it found in the class. That problem has been resolved, however, and overloaded methods usually work now.

If you encounter trouble with overloaded methods, a workaround is to give them different names, or to add a new method that simply calls the correct overloaded method for you.

B.1.5 Form Bugs on Windows Platforms

There are a few bugs related to event handlers and form elements that occur on Windows platforms only.

B.1.5.1 onBlur() and onFocus()

`onBlur()` and `onFocus()` event handlers of Form elements are never invoked on Windows platforms.

B.1.5.2 onClick() in reset button

On Windows platforms, you can't prevent a Form from being reset by returning false from the `onClick()` event handler of the Reset button object.

B.1.5.3 FileUpload bug

For important security reasons, the `value` field of the FileUpload object cannot be set by JavaScript programs. This is not a bug. Unfortunately, on Windows platforms, you cannot correctly read the the `value` property after the user has clicked the **Browse** button of the form element to select a file. The `value` property is only correct if the user actually types in the filename. As a workaround, you can try calling the `focus()` and `blur()` methods of the FileUpload object before attempting to read the `value` property.

B.1.6 Window Size on Unix Platforms

On Unix platforms, when you open a new window with the `Window.open()` method, the width and height specifications may be overridden and ignored if X resources specify window width and height, or if Navigator was started with the standard `X -geometry` command line argument. The only workaround to this bug is to be satisfied with the default window size and not try to override it with X resources or command-line arguments.

B.2 Known JavaScript Bugs in Internet Explorer 3.0

Although there are undoubtedly at least some bugs in the implementation of client-side JavaScript in Internet Explorer 3.0, Microsoft has not made a list of bugs available to the public. Or rather, it made such a list briefly available on its web site and then withdrew it.

Despite this questionable tactic of Microsoft's, the truth is that the issue of bugs in Internet Explorer 3.0 is usually overshadowed by the issue of compatibilitiy with Navigator 3.0. Any bugs can simply be considered yet another incompatibility to watch out for. See Appendix D, *JavaScript Incompatibilities in Internet Explorer 3.0*, for details.

B.3 Commonly Encountered JavaScript Bugs in Navigator 2.0

Navigator 2.0 has a lot of bugs. This is a fact of life and a source of frequent frustration. By being aware of the most important and most frequently encountered bugs, you can begin to reduce the amount of frustration you'll have to endure when programming with the Navigator 2.0 version of client-side JavaScript—and, more important, the amount of frustration your customers endure when they run your JavaScript code with Navigator 2.0.

If you're wondering why this relatively long section has been devoted to Navigator 2.0 bugs, when presumably these have all been fixed in Navigator 3.0, remember that it doesn't matter what version of Navigator you run; it is the user's version that counts. Even with Navigator 3.0 released in final form, your scripts may still be run on many Navigator 2.0 platforms.

Navigator 2.0 is sufficiently buggy that apparently no one has attempted to make a complete list of all known bugs (if Netscape has one, they are not releasing it). The reason is simple: trying to produce a definitive list of bugs, for versions 2.0, 2.0.1, and 2.0.2, running on Windows 3.1, Windows 95, Windows NT, the Macintosh, and each of the many flavors of Unix that are supported would be a huge undertaking. Documenting all the bugs in all the versions on all the platforms in detail would probably require a book longer than this one.

For that reason, this section does not attempt to be a definitive list of bugs in Navigator 2.0. Instead, the aim is to inform you of the most serious and most commonly encountered bugs so that you will know how to avoid them and how to work around them when you can't avoid them. In a heterogeneous environment like the Internet, users of your scripts will be running a variety of Navigator versions on a variety of platforms. In effect, *a bug on any one popular platform is a bug on all platforms*, since the affected code or object cannot be safely used. For that reason, the bugs listed here are not categorized by platform or version.

Note that with release 2.0.2, development stopped on version 2.0 of Navigator. Thus, the bugs listed here will remain in the installed base of Navigator 2.0 browsers.

After describing the commonly encountered bugs, this chapter ends with a short section on debugging techniques that you may find useful for your scripts.

B.3.1 Security Hobbles

The first possibility you should consider when you encounter a strange bug in a script is to check whether you are violating Navigator's security restrictions. Remember that in versions 2.0.1 and 2.0.2, a script cannot read any properties of a window if the contents of that window came from a different server (i.e., a different host or a different protocol running on the same host) than the script did. The implications of this one restriction are far-reaching and have many implications for referencing properties across windows or frames. In particular, if you see the "Window has no properties" or "access disallowed from scripts at *url* to documents at *url*" error messages, you've probably run up against this security hobble.

See Chapter 20, *JavaScript Security*, for a list of a few more security restrictions. These restrictions are inconvenient and annoying, but they aren't really bugs; just limitations in the capabilities of JavaScript. Many of these restrictions may be lifted when data tainting becomes the default security model in Navigator 4.0.

B.3.2 General Bugs

This section covers general bugs that don't apply to any one particular JavaScript object.

B.3.2.1 Printing and saving generated text

When you output text to a document using the Document.write() method, Navigator can display this text. Unfortunately, because of the way HTML parsing works in Navigator, text generated by JavaScript cannot be printed or saved to a file. There is no workaround, except to replace your client-side JavaScript with a server-side CGI script.

A bug related to the previous one is that when the web browser is resized, all JavaScript in the web page is re-interpreted. This bug is fixed in 3.0 along with the printing bug.

Another related Navigator (non-JavaScript) bug is that when Navigator prints forms, it does not print the contents of the form elements.

B.3.2.2 JavaScript and tables

In general, JavaScript and tables do not mix well in Navigator 2.0. If you can, simply avoid putting JavaScript code in web pages that contain tables. If you cannot avoid it, then don't put form elements within tables—the table algorithm parses table contents twice, causing contained form elements to be created twice, and what are supposed to be single form elements end up in arrays of elements. Also, do not try to use JavaScript to output a portion (one or a few cells) of a table. If you need to generate some of the table with JavaScript code, use JavaScript to generate the entire table. These table problems have been fixed (mostly) in 3.0.

B.3.2.3 Line length limit

JavaScript was designed not to impose arbitrary length restrictions on lines of code. Unfortunately, because of a bug in the HTML parser, JavaScript complains if any lines in your program are over 254 characters long. Usually, the only time this occurs is when you have a very long string, in which case the end of the string gets truncated, and JavaScript complains of an "Unterminated string literal." The workaround is to break up your long lines and to avoid long strings. If you must use long strings, break them up into chunks that are shorter than 254 characters and use + to concatenate them.

B.3.2.4 Script size limit

Because of the nature of the 16-bit architecture of Windows 3.1, there is a limit on the length of scripts that can be handled on this platform. Programmers have reported having problems on this platform when their scripts reach 20Kb to 40Kb in length. A solution is to break the script up into separate modules and load each module into a separate frame or window, and then (carefully!) make function calls between frames or windows. When a script gets this long, another solution you should seriously consider is converting it to a CGI script run on the server, instead of forcing the user to download all the code.

B.3.2.5 Conversion of floating-point values to strings

The code used by JavaScript to convert floating-point values to strings is buggy and you will often see floating-point values displayed with a lot of trailing 9s. For example, the following code:

```
i = .15
alert(i);
```

will usually display a dialog box containing a string like ".14999999999995" instead of the ".15" that you would expect. This is a particular problem when dealing with numeric values that represent money. A workaround is to multiply your value by 100, and use the Math.round() method to round the result to the nearest integer. If you divide by 100 at this point, you'll have the same problem of trailing 9s, so the only solution is to convert your value times 100 to a string, use the String.substring() method to extract the dollars digits and cents digits, and then print these strings out, adding your own decimal point.

B.3.2.6 Date and time bugs

In Navigator 2.0, the Date object has quite a few bugs and is almost unusable. On Macintosh platforms, the time returned is off by an hour, and on all platforms, time zones are not handled well. Also, prior to version 2.0.2, there was a Navigator bug (not directly a JavaScript bug) in the handling daylight savings time. A side effect of this is that Navigator 2.0 and 2.0.1 cannot correctly determine whether a document on a server is newer than the cached version and so the **Reload** button does not always work correctly.

You can usually use the Date object to print out the current date, and you can use it to compute the interval (in milliseconds) between two dates or times in the same time zone, but you should probably not attempt more sophisticated uses of it than that.

B.3.2.7 lastIndexOf()

The String method `lastIndexOf()` should search a string backward starting from the specified character position within the string (0 for the first character, and `string.length` - 1 for the last character). In 2.0, however, it begins the search one character before the specified character. The workaround in 2.0 is to add 1 to the desired index.

B.3.2.8 eval()

Using the `eval()` function crashes Navigator 2.0 and 2.01 when running on Windows 3.1 platforms. This bug is fixed in 2.02, however. The workaround is to avoid `eval()`, or to use the `Navigator` object to check what platform the script is running on, and refuse to run on a Windows 3.1/Navigator 2.0 or 2.01 platform.

B.3.3 Window and Frame Bugs

The bugs described below affect the Window object and related areas of JavaScript. Some of them are suprisingly subtle, and because the Window object is so important in client-side JavaScript, these bugs may have wide reaching impact.

B.3.3.1 Window.open() method

The `Window.open()` method takes three arguments, a URL to display in the window, a window name, and a list of browser features that should be present or absent in the new window. Unfortunately, there are bugs with the first and third arguments.

On the Macintosh and some Unix platforms, the URL specified as the first argument to `Window.open()` is ignored. A commonly proposed workaround is to call `open()` a second time with the same URL specified. Another workaround is to set the `location.href` property of the window after it is created. For example, the second block of JavaScript code should be used instead of the first block:

```
// problems on Mac and Unix
var w = open("http://www.ora.com");

// following works on all platforms
var w = open("");
w.location.href = "http://www.ora.com";
```

In addition, the list of window features specified by the third argument to `Window.open()` does not work on Unix platforms running the X Window System. Width and height may be specified with this third argument, but no other features may be specified—all windows will be created without a menubar, toolbar, status line, and so on.

B.3.3.2 Dangling references

As discussed in Chapter 11, *Windows and the JavaScript Name Space*, the JavaScript memory management model is inadequate in Navigator 2.0. Because all objects allocated by a window are freed when the window unloads, references to those objects from other windows can be left dangling if the user closes the window or unexpectedly points the browser to a new page. If you attempt to use one of these references to a no-longer-existing object, you may get a corrupt value, or you may actually crash the browser.

It is debatable whether this is a bug or just an unfortunate misfeature of the JavaScript architecture in Navigator 2.0. In any case, the solution is to be very careful with your cross-window references.

B.3.3.3 Frame properties overwrite others

This is a bug that occurs only in a very specific situation, but it is bizarre and puzzling when you encounter it for the first time. When a window contains named frames, the references to those frames are stored in properties of the window. JavaScript apparently allocates the first few property "slots" of the window object for these frames. If you create other properties of the Window object before the frames are created, and if the window is a newly created one, then these properties may take up those first property "slots." Later, when the frame references are stored in those slots, the value of your properties will be overwritten.

This situation occurs only in a couple of specific cases. The first is when you have a `<SCRIPT>` tag that sets properties before a `<FRAMESET>` tag that defines frames.

(Doing this is probably a poor programming practice, by the way.) The second is when you have a script that sets properties in a window and then generates the frames itself by explicitly outputting the necessary <FRAMESET> and <FRAME> tags.

A related bug that serves to make this bug even more mysterious is that frame properties of a Window object are not detected by a for/in loop until they have actually been used once by a script!

B.3.3.4 onLoad() event handler called early

When a document that does not contain frames but does contain images is loaded into a window, the Window object's onLoad() event handler may be called before the document is actually completely loaded. In this case, you cannot rely on onLoad() to tell you when the document is fully loaded and all document objects are defined. Therefore, you should be sure to check that the elements you want to access really exist before attempting to use them. For example, you might check that the last element of the last form is created before doing any manipulation of forms. If the element is not created when you check it, you can use setTimeout() to defer the code to be executed and to check again later.

B.3.3.5 Dialogs in onUnload()

Invoking the alert(), confirm(), or prompt() dialogs from an onUnload() event handler may crash Navigator. The only workaround is to avoid the temptation to do this—don't try to pop up a dialog to say good-bye to the user when they leave your page!

B.3.3.6 Scripts in framesets

Scripts that appear after a <FRAMESET> tag in a document will not be executed. This is not actually a bug, but a fact of the JavaScript architecture. Scripts may appear in the <HEAD> or <BODY> of a document. An HTML file that defines a frameset has a head—that portion that appears before the frameset—but does not have a body; the frameset is a substitute for the document body, and JavaScript rules do not allow scripts within frameset definitions.

JavaScript does allow scripts before the beginning of a frameset, but unless you have a good reason to do this, it probably isn't a good idea.

B.3.3.7 Status and defaultStatus

When you query the value of the status property of a Window, you get the value of the defaultStatus property of that Window, even if there is a status message currently displayed by the browser.

Also, on some platforms the defaultStatus message is not properly restored after a status message is displayed. For example, if you set the status property to a special message from the onMouseOver() event handler of a hypertext link, then this message may not be erased when the user moves the mouse off the link. You can address this problem by using setTimeout() to register a function to be executed after a couple of seconds which will explicitly set the status property to be the same as the defaultStatus.

B.3.3.8 setTimeout() memory leak

As discussed in Chapter 12, *Programming with Windows*, Navigator 2.0 does not reclaim any memory used by a page until that page unloads. The setTimeout() method allocates memory each time it is called, even when called repeatedly with the same string argument. Therefore, pages that perform repetitive actions (such as animation) with setTimeout() will allocate more and more memory, and may eventually crash the browser.

B.3.4 Document Object Bugs

These bugs affect the Document object.

B.3.4.1 Document background color

You can set the Document.bgColor property at any time to change the background color of a document. Unfortunately, on Unix/X11 platforms, and possibly some others, doing this also erases any text displayed in the window. If you really want to change the document color, you will have to reload or rewrite the document contents, which will cause a noticeable flicker after the color changes.

B.3.4.2 Closing the current document

Calling Document.close() on a document that contains the currently running script may crash the browser. The solution is to not do this. Obviously, any time Navigator crashes, it is a bug. But just as obviously, closing a document that contains the code that is currently being executed is not a useful thing to do, and it is not clear what such an attempt should actually do.

B.3.4.3 Overwriting the current script

If you call Document.write() on the current document from an event handler or timeout, or call a function that calls Document.write() from an event handler or timeout, you will implicitly close the current document and open a new one to perform the write into. What this does is erase the contents of the document, *including the currently executing function or event handler.* At best you will get undefined results if you attempt to do this. Often, though, you will crash the browser.

The solution, of course, is to not do this. Note that you can safely overwrite the document of a separate frame or window.

B.3.5 Form Bugs

This section describes bugs that affect HTML forms and the elements they contain.

B.3.5.1 Images and form event handlers

A strange but very commonly encountered bug is the following: If a document contains images *and* forms, then all the <IMG> tags must have WIDTH and HEIGHT attributes, or the event handlers of the form may be ignored. Usually, adding these tags speeds document loading times, so it is a good idea to get in the habit of using them with all images.

An alternative workaround is to follow your forms with an empty pair of <SCRIPT> and </SCRIPT> tags.

B.3.5.2 Backward radio and checkbox arrays

When an HTML form contains more than one element with the same name, then those elements will be stored in an array by that name. This is commonly done for radio buttons and checkboxes. The elements are supposed to appear in the array in the same order that they appear in the HTML source. For obscure reasons, however, if the elements do not have event handlers defined, then they will be placed in these arrays backward. If some of the elements have event handlers and some do not, then they will be placed in the array in some chaotic order. The solution is to provide an event handler for each element, even if it is only a dummy handler like the following:

```
<INPUT TYPE="checkbox" NAME="opt" VALUE="case-sensitive" onClick="0">
```

Of course, the order the elements are placed in the array is only an issue if you want to read or write the properties of those elements from your JavaScript code. If the form will simply be submitted to a server, then you don't have to worry about this bug.

B.3.5.3 Form method property

The `method` property of a Form object specifies the technique used to submit the contents of a form to a server. This property should be a read/write property, but in Navigator 2.0, it is read-only and may be set only when the form is defined in HTML.

B.3.5.4 Mutable string values

In JavaScript, strings are immutable objects, which means that the characters within them may not be changed and that any operations on strings actually create *new* strings. Strings are assigned by reference, not by value. In general, when an object is assigned by reference, a change made to the object through one reference will be visible through all other references to the object. Because strings cannot be changed, however, you can have multiple references to a string object and not worry that the string value will change without your knowing it.

Unfortunately, however, the `value` property of the Text and Textarea objects is a *mutable* string in Navigator 2.0. Thus, if you assign the `value` property to a variable, and then you set (or the user types) new text into the Text or Textarea object, the string your variable refers to will change.

The way to prevent this behavior is to force the `value` property to be copied by value rather than by reference. You can do this by creating a new string object with the + operator. Add the empty string to the `value` property to create a new string that contains the same text as the `value` property:

```
var address = document.form1.address.value + "";
```

Differences between Navigator 2.0 and 3.0

There have been quite a few changes between Navigator 2.0 and Navigator 3.0. Some of these are differences in the core JavaScript language—differences between JavaScript 1.0 and JavaScript 1.1. Others are the addition of new objects, the implementation of LiveConnect, and changed functionality in existing objects. The changes are listed below. Details can be found on the various reference entries, and in the main chapters of the book.

C.1 Core Language Changes

There have been quite a few additions and improvements to the core JavaScript language, and to the way that it is embedded in HTML files:

- The `typeof` and `void` operators have been added. See Chapter 4, *Expressions and Operators.*

- The `constructor` property of all objects completements the `typeof` operator as a way to determine the type of objects. (The `type` property the Element object serves a similar purpose for HTML form elements). See Chapter 7, *Objects* and the Object.constructor reference entry.

- Constructor functions may now have a prototype object that defines methods, constants, and default properties shared by all objects created by the constructor. See Chapter 7, and the Object.constructor reference entry.

- The String object is now a true JavaScript object, with a constructor, and a new `split()` method.

- The Boolean and Number objects have been added. The Number object defines several useful constants.

- The Function object now supports a constructor for the creation of "anonymous" functions. See Chapter 6, *Functions.*

- The Array object provides a useful constructor for the creation of arrays, and also new sort(), reverse(), and join() methods. Array handling in JavaScript 1.1 is much improved over JavaScript 1.0. See Chapter 8, *Arrays.*

- The Math.random() method works on all platforms in JavaScript 1.1, and the Not-a-Number value, NaN, and the isNaN() function are implemented on all palatforms. This means that parseInt() and parseFloat() can now correctly return NaN to signal invalid input.

- The eval() function of JavaScript 1.0 has become a method of all objects in JavaScript 1.1. This allows JavaScript code to be evaluated in the context of any desired object. When used as a function in JavaScript 1.1, eval() will evaluate the code in the context of the current window, just as it did in JavaScript 1.0.

- All objects can now be given an assign() method, which essentially overloads the assignment operator for that particular object. See Chapter 7.

- Files of pure JavaScript code, given the *.js* file extension, may now be included within HTML files with the SRC attribute of the <SCRIPT> tag. See Chapter 10, *Client-Side Program Structure.*

- You can specify code that requires JavaScript 1.1 and should not be run on JavaScript 1.0 platforms with the LANGUAGE="JavaScript1.1" attribute of the <SCRIPT> tag. See Chapter 10.

- JavaScript code can also be embedded within HTML tags between &{ and }; using the new JavaScript entity. See Chapter 10.

C.2 LiveConnect

In Navigator 3.0, LiveConnect is the "glue" that connects JavaScript with Java and with Navigator plug-ins. It has the following new features:

- The JavaPackage object represents a Java package.

- The JavaClass object represents a Java class.

- The JavaObject object represents a Java object.

- The `JavaArray` object represents an array in Java.

- The `JavaMethod` object represents a Java method.

- The `getClass()` method returns the JavaClass object for any given JavaObject object.

- The Java class *netscape.javascript.JSObject* represents a JavaScript object from within Java applets.

- The `applets[]` array of the Document object is an array of JavaObject objects that represent the applets embedded in the document.

- The `embeds[]` array of the Document object is an array of JavaObject objects that represent the embedded objects in the document, and allow JavaScript to control the Navigator plug-ins that display those objects.

See Chapter 19, *LiveConnect: JavaScript and Java* for details on all of these new objects, functions, and arrays.

C.3 JavaScript Security

There have been several important changes to JavaScript security in Navigator 3.0. See Chapter 20, *JavaScript Security* for complete details.

- The `Document.domain()` property allows large web sites that use multiple web servers to circumvent the restriction that scripts from one host can't read the properties of windows or documents that come from another host.

- A new security model, based on data tainting, is experimental in Navigator 3.0. When enabled, this new model makes significant changes to the security restrictions placed on JavaScript programs. It also makes new properties and array elements of the History object available, and allows the `value` property of the Password object to be read.

- The `taint()` and `untaint()` functions were added in Navigator 3.0 as part of the new data-tainting security model. The `taintEnabled()` method of the Navigator object was also added.

C.4 Image Manipulation

Navigator 3.0 supports image manipulation with the following powerful new features. Chapter 16, *Special Effects with Images*, has complete details.

- The Image object represents an image, either on-screen or off. Setting the `src` property of an Image object will cause it to load (and display if it is an on-screen image) the image stored at the specfied URL.

- The `Document.images[]` array contains a complete list of the images displayed within a document.

- The `Image()` constructor allows the creation of off-screen images, which can be used to preload images that will be required for animations or other image manipulation techniques.

- The `onload()`, `onerror()`, and `onabort()` event handlers of the Image object help determine the status of images that are loading.

- The `complete` property of the Image object specified whether it is still being loaded or not.

C.5 *The Window Object*

The Window object is one of the most important in JavaScript. It has a number of new features in Navigator 3.0:

- The `Window.scroll()` method scrolls the contents of a window to specified *x* and *y* coordinates.

- The `Window.focus()` and `Window.blur()` methods give and remove keyboard focus from a window. Calling `focus()` will raise the window to the top of the desktop stacking order on most platforms.

- The `onfocus()` and `onblur()` event handlers are invoked when a window gains or loses the input focus.

- The `onerror()` event handler of the Window object is invoked when a JavaScript error occurs; it gives a JavaScript program the opportunity to handle errors in its own way.

- The `Window.opener` property refers to the Window object that most recently called the `open()` method on it.

- The `Window.closed` property specifies whether a window has been closed.

- The `name` property of the Window object is now read/write, so that windows (including the unnamed initial window) can change their names for use with the `TARGET` attribute of various HTML tags.

- A fourth, optional argument has been added to the `Window.open()` method; it allows JavaScript programs to specify whether the URL loaded into the specified window should create a new entry in the History array or whether it should replace the current entry.

C.6 The Location Object

The Location object supports two important new methods in Navigator 3.0:

- The `replace()` method of the Location object causes the specified URL to be loaded and displayed, but instead of creating a new entry in the hisory array for that URL, it overwrites the URL of the current entry in the array.

- The `reload()` method of the Location object reloads the current document.

C.7 Forms and Form Elements

There are several new features of the Form object and of the form elements that it contains in Navigator 3.0:

- The Form object now supports a `reset()` method that resets the value of all elements within the form.

- The Form object also supports a corresponding `onreset()` method, invoked when the form is reset by the user.

- All form elements now have a `type` property that specifies what type of element they are.

- The `onclick()` event handler of all form elements that support it is now cancelable—the event handler may return `false` to indicate that the Browser should not execute the default action for that button. This affects the Reset and Submit elements.

- The options displayed within a Select element can now be dynamically updated by JavaScript programs. The `options[]` array of the Select element and its `length` property have special behavior that manipulates the displayed options, and the new `Option()` constructor allows the creation of new Option object for display within the Select element.

C.8 Miscellaneous Changes

There have also been a few miscellaneous changes in Navigator 3.0:

- Hypertext links created by <AREA> tags within client-side image maps create Link objects just like <A> tags do. These objects become part of the `links[]` array of the Document object.

- Link objects support a new `onMouseOut()` event handler, triggered when the mouse passes out of the link's "hot spot" or trigger area.

- The Document object has a new URL property which is the preferred name for what was the Document.location property. The location property is deprecated because it is too easily confused with the location property of the Window object.

- New Plugin and MimeType objects represent installed Navigator plug-ins and MIME type data formats that are supported by the browser. These objects appear in the plugins[] and mimeTypes[] arrays of the Navigator object, and allow JavaScript programs to determine whether a particular client supports required plug-ins or data formats. Furtherore, the plugins.refresh() method of the Navigator object causes the browser to check for newly installed plug-ins and optionally reload affected web pages.

- The javaEnabled() method of the Navigator object specifies whether Java is supported and enabled on the current platform.

D

JavaScript Incompatibilities in Internet Explorer 3.0

There are quite a few differences between the version of JavaScript supported by Internet Explorer 3.0 and those "definitive" versions supported by Navigator 2.0 and 3.0. This is understandable, because although Netscape calls JavaScript an "open" standard, they weren't ready to release the implementation of their incomplete Navigator 2.0 version of it. Therefore Microsoft was left in the position of reverse-engineering the language on a tight release schedule.

Because of the incompatibilities between the Microsoft and Netscape versions of JavaScript, it can be frustrating to write JavaScript code that works correctly on both platforms, and some programmers may simply choose to avoid the issue by writing code for JavaScript 1.1 only, and requiring users to use Navigator 3.0 or a later version. Compatibility with Internet Explorer 3.0 can be acheived, however, and the partial list of differences in this appendix should help. Note that you'll also find these differences detailed througout the chapters and reference pages of this book.

D.1 Language Version

JavaScript in Internet Explorer was developed during the Navigator 3.0 beta cycle, so the Microsoft engineers modeled it mostly after the stable Navigator 2.0 platform. As a result, IE 3.0 supports a version of JavaScript that is essentially JavaScript 1.0. This means that IE does not support many of the interesting new features of JavaScript 1.1: the Image object, the Plugin and MimeType objects, the Number and Boolean objects, and so forth. It does not define `applets[]` or `embeds[]` arrays in the Document object. Because it does not support the Number object, it does not define the `MAX_VALUE`, `MIN_VALUE`, and other constants that exist as properties of that object. Like Navigator 2.0 on most platforms, IE 3.0 does not support the Not-a-Number (`NaN`) value.

On the other hand, the Microsoft engineers did get a few important 1.1 features into their implementation. For example, IE 3.0 does support the `Window.opener` property, the `typeof` operator, and even object prototypes (although it doesn't work for strings.) IE 3.0 also supports the Array object of Navigator 3.0, although it does not support the `join()`, `sort()` and `reverse()` methods of that object.

D.2 Case Sensitivity

One major difference between Navigator and Internet Explorer is that the "object model" (as Microsoft calls it) in Internet Explorer is not case-sensitive. Because IE can also be scripted with the non–case-sensitive VBScript language, all the HTML and browser objects such as Window, Document and Form are not case sensitive. Thus, in IE, you could write code that invoked `DOCUMENT.WRITE()` instead of `document.write()`. Don't expect code like this to work in Navigator, however! See Chapter 2, *Lexical Structure*, for details.

D.3 Form Values and String Conversion

The JavaScript interpreter in Internet Explorer 3.0 does not always convert objects to strings when they are used in a "string context". This happens most notably when objects are assigned to the `value` field of form elements. To make this work correctly, you have to explicitly convert the object to a string, either by invoking its `toString()` method or by adding the empty string to it. To display the date and time in a form, for example, you'd have to use code like this:

```
today = new Date();
document.forms[0].dateandtime.value = today.toString()
```

or like this:

```
today = new Date();
document.forms[0].dateandtime.value = today + "";
```

If you encounter this conversion problem in other contexts, the workaround is the same.

D.4 Object Model Differences

There are a few other differences in support for HTML and browser objects in Navigator and Internet Explorer 3.0:

- The Window.open() method does not correctly load the argument specified in the first argument in IE 3.0. This same bug exists for some platforms in Navigator 2.0. The workaround is to first open a new window and then load the desired document by setting the location property. Also, the Window.name property is read-only in IE 3.0.

- The Document.open() method in IE 3.0 ignores the MIME type argument, if any is passed. It assumes that all documents are of type "text/html".

- IE 3.0 records cookies only when the document is loaded via the http: protocol. Documents loaded from the local disk (as they commonly are when being developed or tested) cannot use cookies.

- The blur() method of form elements behaves differently (and probably more sensibly) in IE 3.0 that it does in Navigator. The difference is detailed in the Element.blur() reference entry.

- The History.go() method can only move backward or forward a single step at a time in IE 3.0, and the History.length property always returns 0.

D.5 Garbage Collection

Internet Explorer 3.0 uses a "true" garbage collection scheme. This means that it never has problems with object cycles as Navigator 3.0, with its reference counting scheme, does. It also means that it avoids all the problems that plague Navigator 2.0's garbage collection scheme. For a full discussion of garbage collection, see Chapter 11, *Windows and the JavaScript Name Space.*

D.6 Security

Navigator 2.0.2 and Navigator 3.0 implement a very restrictive "hobble" in the interests of security: a script running in one window cannot read the properties of another window unless the contents of that window were loaded from the same server as the script. Internet Explorer 3.0 implements security measures, but this is not one of them. This means that users of IE 3.0 may be vulnerable to malicious scripts that steal information. See Chapter 20, *JavaScript Security* for a full discussion of JavaScript security issues.

D.7 Communication with Java

In Navigator 3.0, JavaScript can communicate with Java in a very full-featured way through LiveConnect. Internet Explorer 3.0 does not support LiveConnect, and future versions of this browser probably won't either. Instead, IE 3.0 allows JavaScript programs to treat applets as ActiveX objects, and read and write fields and invoke methods of those applets. Note however that IE 3.0 does not suport the `applets[]` array of the Document object—applets must be referred to by name. Also, note that IE 3.0 mechanism for communication with Java is not nearly so full-featured as LiveConnect. See Chapter 19, *LiveConnect: JavaScript and Java* for details.

D.8 Supported but Nonfunctional Properties

In Internet Explorer 3.0, a number of the properties supported by Navigator 2.0 and 3.0 are "supported" only in the sense that they can be used without causing errors. These properties may not return meaningful values when read and/or do not cause any changes when set. Some properties, like `Document.alinkColor` are non-functional simply because the browser as a whole does not support the feature (special colors for activated links, in this case). Others are simply not supported presumably because the engineers at Microsoft did not have the time to implement them. These include the `action`, `encoding`, `method` and `target` properties of the Form object and the `length` property of the History object.

The `isNaN()` function also falls into the category of "supported but nonfunctional." Because IE 3.0 does not support `NaN` values, the `isNaN()` function always returns `false`.

D.9 Miscellaneous Differences

Other differences between Navigator and Internet Explorer 3.0 are small details about the way values are computed and printed:

- The `for/in` statement in IE 3.0 does not always enumerate the same object properties that Navigator does. It does enumerate all user-defined properties, which is its primary function. But predefined properties of built-in objects are not always listed.

- The && and || operators behave somewhat differently in Navigator and Internet Explorer, although, since JavaScript is an untyped langauge, the difference is usually irrelevant. When the first operand of the && operator evaluates to true, then the operator returns the value of the second operand in Navigator. In Internet Explorer, this second operand is first converted to a Boolean value, and that value is returned. Thus the expression

  ```
  true && 10
  ```

  evaluates to 10 in Navigator but to true in Internet Explorer. This may seem like a major difference, but because JavaScript is an untyped langauge, it rarely matters. The && operator is almost always used in a Boolean context, such as the expression of an if statement, so even when Navigator returns a value like 10, that value will be immediately converted to the Boolean value true within that context. The same evaluation difference occurs when the first operand of the || operator evaluates to false.

- In Internet Explorer 3.0, Boolean values implicitly are converted to strings differently than they are in Navigator. The value true is converted to the string −1, and the value false is converted to the string 0. If you actually want them to be converted to the strings "true" and "false", you must convert them explicitly by adding them to the empty string.

- User-defined function values are also converted to strings differently in IE 3.0. In Navigator, functions are converted to a string that includes the complete body of the function. In fact, you can even use eval() function to define the function in some other window. This does not work in Internet Explorer, which omits the function body from its string representation of functions.

A Preview
of Navigator 4.0

This appendix offers a glimpse at the new JavaScript functionality coming in Navigator 4.0, which will be part of the Netscape Communicator suite. This book was printed before the first beta release of Navigator 4.0 was available, however, so the details here are somewhat speculative and based on rumor. By the time you read this, beta versions of 4.0 may well be available. If so, perhaps this appendix will serve to pique your interest in downloading it.

E.1 New Language Features

Navigator 4.0 will feature JavaScript version 1.2. This new version of the language is slated to support several important new features:

- JavaScript 1.2 may support a `switch` statement, like that in C and Java.

- The `delete` operator, which is depricated in JavaScript 1.1, will rise from the grave. In JavaScript 1.2, this operator will actually delete or remove properties of object or top-level variables.

- JavaScript 1.2 will feature true garbage collection rather than the reference counting used by Navigator 3.0.

- JavaScript 1.2 will support regular expressions. This support will presumably be built into the String class.

E.2 Dynamic HTML

Navigator 4.0 will support some very powerful new JavaScript features that allow it to create dynamic documents. These exciting new features are the subject of much speculation, but unfortunately, the details are still not known outside of Netscape, and the following descriptions must be somewhat vague.

* Navigator 4.0 should support a number of new JavaScript event handlers, which will enable JavaScript programs to respond to individual keystrokes, and to mouse-button press and release events, rather than to a simple "on click" event.

* Navigator 4.0 will support a new <LAYER> tag, will will allow HTML text and objects to be positioned at absolute cordinates within a window, and to be stacked on top of each other (hence the name "Layer"). It is expected that this will mean that many HTML objects in JavaScript will have x and y coordinate properties, and that JavaScript programs may even be able to set layer coordinates to dynamically move "layers" within the document.

* Navigator 4.0 will support style sheets and will also include a feature known as "JavaScript Style Sheets." This is expected to give JavaScript programs control over the style in which documents are displayed. It is worth noting that Microsoft is working on a competing technology for dynamic HTML documents code-named "Trident."

E.3 Other New Features

Navigator 4.0 will also support several other new features:

* In Navigator 4.0, the data-tainting security model may be enabled by default. If so, this will substantially relax many of the security hobbles described in Chapter 20, *JavaScript Security*. These hobbles will be replaced, to some extent, with a suite of new user confirmation dialogs that will appear when JavaScript detects a possible security violation. Some existing scripts may have to be rewritten to avoid posting these dialogs when they are not strictly necessary.

* Navigator 4.0 will provide methods that allow JavaScript programs to query the current browser window size, the screen resolution, and screen color depth. These new methods will presumably be implemented as part of the Navigator object.

- Navigator 4.0 will include a working Anchor object, and the anchors in a document will finally be available through the anchors[] array of the Document object. Because of the absolute positioning changes described above, properties of the anchor object will include their x and y coordinates within the document.

- Navigator 4.0 will provide support for embedded objects with the <OBJECT> tag. It is not clear what the overlap between this tag and the <EMBED> tag will be nor in what way the <OBJECT> tag will be accessible to JavaScript programs.

Persistent Client State: HTTP Cookies

Author's note: This appendix contains the complete text of the HTTP Cookie specification from Netscape. This document can also be found at:

http://home.netscape.com/newsref/std/cookie_spec.html

It is a "preliminary specification", and, as such, is subject to change. Because it is "preliminary" Netscape warns that it should be used "with caution". Since the specification was originally written, however, the use of cookies has become commonplace, and the details described here are much more stable than they were when this specification was first written. While this specification constitutes the "final word" on cookies, it is aimed at CGI programmers and at the implementors of web servers and browsers. The JavaScript interface to cookies is described in Chapter 15, Saving State with Cookies.

F.1 Copyright

NOTE   This is a preliminary specification—use with caution.

F.2 Introduction

Cookies are a general mechanism which server-side connections (such as CGI scripts) can use to both store and retrieve information on the client side of the connection. The addition of a simple, persistent, client-side state significantly extends the capabilities of web-based client/server applications.

F.3 Overview

A server, when returning an HTTP object to a client, may also send a piece of state information which the client will store. Included in that state object is a description of the range of URLs for which that state is valid. Any future HTTP requests made by the client which fall in that range will include a transmittal of the current value of the state object from the client back to the server. The state object is called a *cookie*, for no compelling reason.

This simple mechanism provides a powerful new tool which enables a host of new types of applications to be written for web-based environments. Shopping applications can now store information about the currently selected items, for-fee services can send back registration information and free the client from retyping a user-id on next connection, sites can store per-user preferences on the client, and have the client supply those preferences every time that site is connected to.

F.4 Specification

A cookie is introduced to the client by including a `Set-Cookie` header as part of an HTTP response; typically this will be generated by a CGI script.

F.4.1 Syntax of the Set-Cookie HTTP Response Header

This is the format a CGI script would use to add to the HTTP headers a new piece of data which is to be stored by the client for later retrieval.

```
Set-Cookie: name=value; expires=date;
path=path; domain=domain_name; secure
```

`name=value`

This string is a sequence of characters excluding semicolons, commas, and white space. If there is a need to place such data in the name or value, some encoding method such as URL style %XX encoding is recommended, though no encoding is defined or required.

This is the only required attribute on the Set-Cookie header.

expires=*date*

The expires attribute specifies a date string that defines the valid lifetime of that cookie. Once the expiration date has been reached, the cookie will no longer be stored or given out.

The date string is formatted as:

    Wdy, DD-Mon-YYYY HH:MM:SS GMT

This is based on RFC 822, RFC 850, RFC 1036, and RFC 1123, with the variations that the only legal time zone is GMT and the separators between the elements of the date must be dashes.

expires is an optional attribute. If not specified, the cookie will expire when the user's session ends.

NOTE   There is a bug in Netscape Navigator version 1.1 and earlier. Only cookies whose path attribute is set explicitly to "/" will be properly saved between sessions if they have an expires attribute.

---

domain=*domain_name*

When searching the cookie list for valid cookies, a comparison of the domain attributes of the cookie is made with the Internet domain name of the host from which the URL will be fetched. If there is a tail match, then the cookie will go through path matching to see if it should be sent. "Tail matching" means that domain attribute is matched against the tail of the fully qualified domain name of the host. A domain attribute of *acme.com* would match host names *anvil.acme.com* as well as *shipping.crate.acme.com.*

Only hosts within the specified domain can set a cookie for a domain and domains must have at least two (2) or three (3) periods in them to prevent domains of the form: *.com, .edu,* and *va.us.* Any domain that falls within one of the seven special top level domains listed below only require two periods. Any other domain requires at least three. The seven special top level domains are: *com, edu, net, org, gov, mil,* and *int.*

The default value of domain is the host name of the server which generated the cookie response.

path=*path*

> The path attribute is used to specify the subset of URLs in a domain for which the cookie is valid. If a cookie has already passed domain matching, then the pathname component of the URL is compared with the path attribute, and if there is a match, the cookie is considered valid and is sent along with the URL request. The path */foo* would match */foobar* and */foo/bar.html*. The path / is the most general path.
>
> If the path is not specified, it as assumed to be the same path as the document being described by the header which contains the cookie.

secure

> If a cookie is marked secure, it will only be transmitted if the communications channel with the host is a secure one. Currently this means that secure cookies will only be sent to HTTPS (HTTP over SSL) servers.
>
> If secure is not specified, a cookie is considered safe to be sent in the clear over unsecured channels.

F.4.2 Syntax of the Cookie HTTP Request Header

When requesting a URL from an HTTP server, the browser will match the URL against all cookies and if any of them match, a line containing the name/value pairs of all matching cookies will be included in the HTTP request. Here is the format of that line:

```
Cookie: NAME1=OPAQUE_STRING1; NAME2=OPAQUE_STRING2 ...
```

F.4.3 Additional Notes

- Multiple Set-Cookie headers can be issued in a single server response.

- Instances of the same path and name will overwrite each other, with the latest instance taking precedence. Instances of the same path but different names will add additional mappings.

- Setting the path to a higher-level value does not override other more specific path mappings. If there are multiple matches for a given cookie name, but with separate paths, all the matching cookies will be sent. (See examples below.)

- The expires header lets the client know when it is safe to purge the mapping but the client is not required to do so. A client may also delete a cookie before its expiration date arrives if the number of cookies exceeds its internal limits.

- When sending cookies to a server, all cookies with a more specific path mapping should be sent before cookies with less specific path mappings. For example, a cookie "name1=foo" with a path mapping of / should be sent after a cookie "name1=foo2" with a path mapping of */bar* if they are both to be sent.

- There are limitations on the number of cookies that a client can store at any one time. This is a specification of the minimum number of cookies that a client should be prepared to receive and store:

  - 300 total cookies;

  - 4 kilobytes per cookie, where the name and the OPAQUE_STRING combine to form the 4 kilobyte limit;

  - 20 cookies per server or domain (note that completely specified hosts and domains are treated as separate entities and have a 20-cookie limitation for each, not combined).

  Servers should not expect clients to be able to exceed these limits. When the 300-cookie limit or the 20-cookie-per-server limit is exceeded, clients should delete the least recently used cookie. When a cookie larger than 4 kilobytes is encountered the cookie should be trimmed to fit, but the name should remain intact as long as it is less than 4 kilobytes.

- If a CGI script wishes to delete a cookie, it can do so by returning a cookie with the same name, and an expires time which is in the past. The path and name must match exactly in order for the expiring cookie to replace the valid cookie. This requirement makes it difficult for anyone but the originator of a cookie to delete a cookie.

- When caching HTTP, as a proxy server might do, the Set-cookie response header should never be cached.

- If a proxy server receives a response which contains a Set-cookie header, it should propagate the Set-cookie header to the client, regardless of whether the response was 304 (Not Modified) or 200 (OK).

  Similarly, if a client request contains a Cookie: header, it should be forwarded through a proxy, even if the conditional If-modified-since request is being made.

F.5 Examples

Here are some sample exchanges which are designed to illustrate the use of cookies.

F.5.1 First Example Transaction Sequence

Client requests a document, and receives in the response:

```
Set-Cookie: CUSTOMER=WILE_E_COYOTE; path=/;
            expires=Wednesday, 09-Nov-99 23:12:40 GMT
```

When client requests a URL in path / on this server, it sends:

```
Cookie: CUSTOMER=WILE_E_COYOTE
```

Client requests a document, and receives in the response:

```
Set-Cookie: PART_NUMBER=ROCKET_LAUNCHER_0001; path=/
```

When client requests a URL in path / on this server, it sends:

```
Cookie: CUSTOMER=WILE_E_COYOTE; PART_NUMBER=ROCKET_LAUNCHER_0001
```

Client receives:

```
Set-Cookie: SHIPPING=FEDEX; path=/foo
```

When client requests a URL in path / on this server, it sends:

```
Cookie: CUSTOMER=WILE_E_COYOTE; PART_NUMBER=ROCKET_LAUNCHER_0001
```

When client requests a URL in path */foo* on this server, it sends:

```
Cookie: CUSTOMER=WILE_E_COYOTE; PART_NUMBER=ROCKET_LAUNCHER_0001; SHIPPING=FEDEX
```

F.5.2 Second Example Transaction Sequence

Assume all mappings from above have been cleared.

Client receives:

```
Set-Cookie: PART_NUMBER=ROCKET_LAUNCHER_0001; path=/
```

When client requests a URL in path / on this server, it sends:

```
Cookie: PART_NUMBER=ROCKET_LAUNCHER_0001
```

Client receives:

```
Set-Cookie: PART_NUMBER=RIDING_ROCKET_0023; path=/ammo
```

When client requests a URL in path */ammo* on this server, it sends:

```
Cookie: PART_NUMBER=RIDING_ROCKET_0023; PART_NUMBER=ROCKET_LAUNCHER_0001
```

NOTE   There are two name/value pairs named PART_NUMBER due to the inheritance of the / mapping in addition to the */ammo* mapping.

G

JavaScript and HTML Color Names and Values

HTML and JavaScript allow colors to be specified for such things as text color, link color, document background, and even the background of table cells. Colors can be specified in a fully general *#RRGGBB* format, in which *RR*, *GG*, and *BB* are each two hexadecimal digits which represent the intensity of red, green, and blue primaries in the color. Two hexadecimal digits provide 8 color values, or 256 possible levels for each of the red, green, and blue primaries. Using the color specification scheme, you would use "#000000" for black and "#FFFFFF" for white. "#00FF00" would produce a very intense green, and "#A0A0A0" would produce a gray color.

Because it can be difficult to determine the hexadecimal values for the colors you desire, HTML and JavaScript also allow certain colors to be specified by name. The HTML 3.2 standard defines sixteen standard color names that should be supported by all conforming browsers. These colors are listed in Table G-1. This list of sixteen colors was chosen to match the 16 colors supported on old VGA display hardware. Note that the HTML 3.2 standard does not specify the actual color values for each of these named colors, so they may be displayed somewhat differently by different browsers.

Table G-1: Standard Color Names in HTML 3.2

aqua	gray	navy	silver
black	green	olive	teal
blue	lime	purple	white
fuchsia	maroon	red	yellow

Navigator 2.0 and 3.0 and Internet Explorer 3.0 each support all of the standard colors listed in Table G-1. In addition to these standard colors, Navigator also recognizes quite a few other color names, which are listed in Table G-2. Because these color names are not standardized in any way,[*] it is not really a good idea to rely on them in production web pages that may be viewed on web browsers that do not support these color names. For that reason, Table G-2 also lists the hexadecimal color string equivalents for each of these colors. If you use the color name while developing a JavaScript program, you can replace it with the corresponding color value for the release version of that program.

Table G–2: Colors

Color Name	Color Value	Color Name	Color Value
aliceblue	#F0F8FF	lightsalmon	#FFA07A
antiquewhite	#FAEBD7	lightseagreen	#20B2AA
aqua	#00FFFF	lightskyblue	#87CEFA
aquamarine	#7FFFD4	lightslategray	#778899
azure	#F0FFFF	lightsteelblue	#B0C4DE
beige	#F5F5DC	lightyellow	#FFFFE0
bisque	#FFE4C4	lime	#00FF00
black	#000000	limegreen	#32CD32
blanchedalmond	#FFEBCD	linen	#FAF0E6
blue	#0000FF	magenta	#FF00FF
blueviolet	#8A2BE2	maroon	#800000
brown	#A52A2A	mediumaquamarine	#66CDAA
burlywood	#DEB887	mediumblue	#0000CD
cadetblue	#5F9EA0	mediumorchid	#BA55D3
chartreuse	#7FFF00	mediumpurple	#9370DB
chocolate	#D2691E	mediumseagreen	#3CB371
coral	#FF7F50	mediumslateblue	#7B68EE
cornflowerblue	#6495ED	mediumspringgreen	#00FA9A
cornsilk	#FFF8DC	mediumturquoise	#48D1CC
crimson	#DC143C	mediumvioletred	#C71585
cyan	#00FFFF	midnightblue	#191970
darkblue	#00008B	mintcream	#F5FFFA

---

[*] Programmers familiar with the X Window System may recognize the color names in this table, at least the bizarre ones such as "papayawhip"; the color names and values are derived from the "color database" shipped with the X11 distribution.

Table G–2: Colors (continued)

Color Name	Color Value	Color Name	Color Value
darkcyan	#008B8B	mistyrose	#FFE4E1
darkgoldenrod	#B8860B	moccasin	#FFE4B5
darkgray	#A9A9A9	navajowhite	#FFDEAD
darkgreen	#006400	navy	#000080
darkkhaki	#BDB76B	oldlace	#FDF5E6
darkmagenta	#8B008B	olive	#808000
darkolivegreen	#556B2F	olivedrab	#6B8E23
darkorange	#FF8C00	orange	#FFA500
darkorchid	#9932CC	orangered	#FF4500
darkred	#8B0000	orchid	#DA70D6
darksalmon	#E9967A	palegoldenrod	#EEE8AA
darkseagreen	#8FBC8F	palegreen	#98FB98
darkslateblue	#483D8B	paleturquoise	#AFEEEE
darkslategray	#2F4F4F	palevioletred	#DB7093
darkturquoise	#00CED1	papayawhip	#FFEFD5
darkviolet	#9400D3	peachpuff	#FFDAB9
deeppink	#FF1493	peru	#CD853F
deepskyblue	#00BFFF	pink	#FFC0CB
dimgray	#696969	plum	#DDA0DD
dodgerblue	#1E90FF	powderblue	#B0E0E6
firebrick	#B22222	purple	#800080
floralwhite	#FFFAF0	red	#FF0000
forestgreen	#228B22	rosybrown	#BC8F8F
fuchsia	#FF00FF	royalblue	#4169E1
gainsboro	#DCDCDC	saddlebrown	#8B4513
ghostwhite	#F8F8FF	salmon	#FA8072
gold	#FFD700	sandybrown	#F4A460
goldenrod	#DAA520	seagreen	#2E8B57
gray	#808080	seashell	#FFF5EE
green	#008000	sienna	#A0522D
greenyellow	#ADFF2F	silver	#C0C0C0
honeydew	#F0FFF0	skyblue	#87CEEB
hotpink	#FF69B4	slateblue	#6A5ACD

Table G-2: Colors (continued)

Color Name	Color Value	Color Name	Color Value
indianred	#CD5C5C	slategray	#708090
indigo	#4B0082	snow	#FFFAFA
ivory	#FFFFF0	springgreen	#00FF7F
khaki	#F0E68C	steelblue	#4682B4
lavender	#E6E6FA	tan	#D2B48C
lavenderblush	#FFF0F5	teal	#008080
lawngreen	#7CFC00	thistle	#D8BFD8
lemonchiffon	#FFFACD	tomato	#FF6347
lightblue	#ADD8E6	turquoise	#40E0D0
lightcoral	#F08080	violet	#EE82EE
lightcyan	#E0FFFF	wheat	#F5DEB3
lightgoldenrodyellow	#FAFAD2	white	#FFFFFF
lightgreen	#90EE90	whitesmoke	#F5F5F5
lightgrey	#D3D3D3	yellow	#FFFF00
lightpink	#FFB6C1	yellowgreen	#9ACD32

LiveConnected Navigator Plug-Ins

Netscape Navigator 3.0 ships (on some platforms, at least) with three built-in plug-ins that have support for LiveConnect. These plug-ins are LiveAudio, LiveVideo, and Live3D. Recall from Chapter 19, *LiveConnect: JavaScript and Java* that you can interact with plug-ins from JavaScript in the same way that you interact with Java applets. The sections below briefly describe the LiveConnect API provided by each of these plug-ins.

Note that this appendix does *not* provide full documentation for these plug-ins. In particular, it does not explain how to use the <EMBED> tag to embed data for these plug-ins into an HTML document. Some of these plug-ins define quite a few attributes for use with <EMBED> and have fairly complex HTML syntax. You can find details at:

> *http://home.netscape.com/comprod/products/navigator/version_3.0/*
> *development/*

Once you understand how these various plug-ins work, this appendix should serve as a convenient reference to their LiveConnect APIs. It won't teach you about the plug-ins themselves, however.

H.1 LiveAudio

The LiveAudio plug-in plays audio files in most common formats, including AIFF, AU, MIDI, and WAV. It is bundled with Navigator 3.0 on Windows and Macintosh platforms. Its LiveConnect API consists of the following 14 methods:

end_time(*seconds*)

Specify the time at which the audio clip should stop playing. Calling this method overrides the STARTTIME attribute.

`fade_from_to(`*`from, to`*`)`

    Fade the sound from the volume *from* to the volume *to*. Both volumes should be volume percentages expressed as integers between 0 and 100.

`fade_to(`*`volume`*`)`

    Fade the sound to the specified *volume*. This argument specifies volume as a percentage of maximum volume and should be expressed as an integer between 0 and 100.

`GetVolume()`

    Returns the current volume of the sound, as an integer between 0 and 100. This number represents a percentage of maximum volume.

`IsPaused()`

    Returns `true` if the sound is paused; `false` otherwise.

`IsPlaying()`

    Returns `true` if the sound is playing; `false` otherwise.

`IsReady()`

    Returns `true` if the sound has completed loading and the plug-in is ready to play it.

`pause()`

    Pause sound playing, without restarting at the beginning.

`play(`*`loop, url`*`)`

    Play the sound specified by *url*. If *loop* is `true`, then the sound should be played over and over again continuously. If *loop* is `false`, then it should be played only once. Otherwise, if *loop* is an integer, it specifies the number of times that the sound should be played. This *loop* argument corresponds closely to the HTML `LOOP` attribute.

`setvol(`*`volume`*`)`

    Sets the volume of the sound to *volume*. This argument represents the volume as a percentage of the maximum volume and should be expressed as an integer between 0 and 100.

`start_at_beginning()`

    This method overrides the `start_time()` method or the `STARTTIME` HTML attribute and forces the sound to be played from the beginning.

`stop()`

    Stop playing the sound.

StopAll()

> Stop playing the sound and all other sounds controlled by the LiveAudio plug-in.

stop_at_end()

> Calling this method overrides the end_time() method and the ENDTIME HTML attribute and forces the sound to be played all the way to the end.

H.2 LiveVideo

The LiveVideo plug-in displays AVI format movies, and is bundled with Navigator on Windows 95 and Windows NT platforms. It has a fairly simple LiveConnect API, consisting of just four methods:

play()

> Play the movie, starting at the current location.

stop()

> Stop playing the movie.

rewind()

> Return to the beginning of the movie.

seek(*frame*)

> Skip to the specified frame number within the movie.

H.3 Live3D

The Live3D plug-in displays VRML worlds. In order to use it, you will have to understand VRML technology. The API consists of the following ten methods and two callbacks:

AnimateObject(*obj*, *url*)

> Animate the object *obj* using the animation file specified by *url*. Supported animation formats include VUEformat from Autodesk.

DeleteObject(*obj*)

> Delete the specfied object *obj* from the scene graph.

GotoViewPoint(*viewpoint*, *frames*)

> Move the virtual camera to the named *viewpoint*. Animate the move using the number of frames specified by *frames*.

HideObject(*obj*)

Hide the specified object *obj*.

LoadScene(*url*, *frame*)

Load a new scene from the specified *url* into the specified *frame*. If *frame* is null, then the scene is loaded into the current frame.

MorphObject(*obj*, *num_vertices*, *coordinates*, *frames*, *morphtype*)

This method morphs the object *obj* by interpolating its vertices onto those specified by *coordinates*. The interpolation is animated over the number of frames specified by *frames*. The *morphtype* argument specifies what type of morph should be performed. It should be one of "ONCE", "BACKFORTH", or "LOOP".

onAnchorClick()

This is not a method but an event handler. It is invoked when an anchor within the 3D scene is clicked.

onMouseMove()

This event handler is invoked whenver the mouse moves within the Live3D plug-in window.

SetBackgroundImage(*url*)

This method load the specified *url* as the background image for the current scene. Various image formats are supported, including PNG, RGB, GIF, JPEG, BMP and RAS.

SetAnchorObject(*obj*, *url*)

Sets the "anchor" or hypertext link of the specified object *obj* to the specified *url*.

ShowObject(*obj*)

Makes the specified object *obj* visible.

SpinObject(*obj*, *pitch*, *yaw*, *roll*, *local*)

This method spins the specified object *obj*. The *pitch*, *yaw*, and *roll* arguments are Boolean values that specify which axes the object should be rotated around. If *local* is false, then the rotation occurs in world coordinate space; otherwise it occurs around the geometric center of the object.

Index

Symbols

& (bitwise and) operator, 60
&& (logical and) operator, 59, 609
&{} for entities, 166, 600
' (apostrophe), 32
* (multiplication) operator, 54
\ (backslash), 32
!= (inequality) operator, 56
! (logical not) operator, 59
{} (braces), 70, 80
[] (brackets), 45, 67, 75, 114, 121, 137
^ (bitwise exclusive or) operator, 60
, (comma) operator, 66, 75
$ (dollar sign), 34
. (dot) operator, 67, 101, 130, 137
" (double quote), 31
= (assignment) operator, 56, 61, 118
    combined with operations, 62
== (equality) operator, 55
> (greater than) operator, 57–58
>= (greater than or equal) operator, 57–58
>> (shift right with sign) operator, 61
>>> (shift right zero fill) operator, 61
– (minus) operator, 54
– (negation) operator, 54
–– (decrement) operator, 55
< (less than) operator, 57–58
<!-- --> (comment tags), 29, 270–272
<= (less than or equal) operator, 57–58
<< (shift left) operator, 60
() (parentheses), 43–44, 53, 68, 86

% (modulo) operator, 54
| (bitwise or) operator, 60
|| (logical or) operator, 59, 609
+ (plus/concatenate) operator, 41, 54,
    57–58, 134, 191
++ (increment) operator, 55
?: (conditional) operator, 63
; (semicolon), 29, 69
' (single quote), 31
/ (division) operator, 54
// (comment marker), 29
/**/ (comment markers), 29
~ (bitwise not) operator, 60

Numbers

√2/2 constant, 470
√2 constant, 471

A

<A> tags, 229, 337, 522
about:cache URL, 313
abs( ), 458
access operators, 66
accessing object properties (see objects)
accumulator, 319
acos( ), 458
ACTION attribute, 406
action property, 406
ActiveX, 308
adding (see defining)

About the Author

David Flanagan is a consulting computer programmer, user interface designer, and trainer. His previous books with O'Reilly & Associates include the best-selling *Java in a Nutshell*, *X Toolkit Intrinsics Reference Manual*, and *X Volume 6C, Motif Tools: Streamlined GUI Design and Programming with the Xmt Library*. David has a degree in computer science and engineering from the Massachusetts Institute of Technology.

Colophon

Our look is the result of reader comments, our own experimentation, and feedback from distribution channels. Distinctive covers complement our distinctive approach to technical topics, breathing personality and life into potentially dry subjects.

The animal on the cover of *JavaScript: The Definitive Guide* is a Javan rhinoceros. All five species of rhinoceros are distinguished by their large size, thick, armor-like skin, three-toed feet, and single or double snout horn. The Javan rhinoceros, along with the Sumatran rhinoceros, is one of two forest-dwelling species. The Javan rhinoceros is similar in appearance to the Indian rhinoceros, but smaller and with certain distinguishing characteristics, primarily skin texture.

Rhinoceroses are often depicted standing up to their snouts in water or mud. In fact, they can frequently be found just like that. When not resting in a river, rhinos will dig deep pits in which to wallow. Both of these resting places provide a couple of advantages. First, they give the animal relief from the tropical heat and protection from blood-sucking flies. (The mud that the wallow leaves on the skin of the rhinoceros provides some protection from flies, also.) Second, mud wallows and river water help support the considerable weight of these huge animals, thereby relieving the strain on their legs and back.

Folklore has long held that the horn of the rhinoceros possesses magical and aphrodisiacal powers, and that humans who gain possession of the horns will gain those powers, also. This is one of the reasons why rhinoceroses are a prime target of poachers. All species of rhinoceros are in danger, and the Javan rhino is the most precarious. There are fewer than 100 of these animals still living. At one time Javan rhinoceroses could be found throughout southeastern Asia, but they are now believed to exist only in Indonesia and Vietnam.

Edie Freedman designed the cover of this book, using a 19th-century engraving from the Dover Pictorial Archive. The cover layout was produced with Quark XPress 3.3 using the ITC Garamond font.

The inside layout was designed by Nancy Priest and Mary Jane Walsh. Text was prepared in SGML using the DocBook 2.1 DTD. The print version of this book was created by translating the SGML source into a set of gtroff macros using a filter developed at ORA by Norman Walsh. Steve Talbott designed and wrote the underlying macro set on the basis of the GNU troff -gs macros; Lenny Muellner adapted them to SGML and implemented the book design. The GNU groff text formatter version 1.09 was used to generate PostScript output. The text and heading fonts are ITC Garamond Light and Garamond Book; the constant-width font used in this book is Letter Gothic. The illustrations that appear in the book were created in Macromedia Freehand 5.0 by Chris Reilley.

 # More Titles from O'Reilly

Developing Web content

Building Your Own WebSite

By Susan B. Peck & Stephen Arrants
1st Edition July 1996
514 pages, ISBN 1-56592-232-8

 This is a hands-on reference for Windows® 95 and Windows NT™ users who want to host a site on the Web or on a corporate intranet. This step-by-step guide will have you creating live Web pages in minutes. You'll also learn how to connect your web to information in other Windows applications, such as word processing documents and databases. The book is packed with examples and tutorials on every aspect of Web management, and it includes the highly acclaimed WebSite™ server software 1.1 on CD-ROM.

Web Client Programming with Perl

By Clinton Wong
1st Edition Winter 1997
250 pages (est.), ISBN 1-56592-214-X

 Web Client Programming with Perl teaches you how to extend scripting skills to the Web. This book teaches you the basics of how browsers communicate with servers and how to write your own customized Web clients to automate common tasks. It is intended for those who are motivated to develop software that offers a more flexible and dynamic response than a standard Web browser.

JavaScript: The Definitive Guide

By David Flanagan
2nd Edition February 1997
672 pages, ISBN 1-56592-234-4

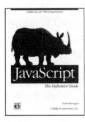 This definitive reference guide to JavaScript, the HTML extension that gives Web pages programming language capabilities, covers JavaScript as it is used in Netscape 3.0 and 2.0 and in Microsoft Internet Explorer 3.0. Learn how JavaScript really works (and when it doesn't). Use JavaScript to control Web browser behavior, add dynamically created text to Web pages, interact with users through HTML forms, and even control and interact with Java applets and Navigator plug-ins.

HTML: The Definitive Guide

By Chuck Musciano & Bill Kennedy
1st Edition April 1996
410 pages, ISBN 1-56592-175-5

 A complete guide to creating documents on the World Wide Web, this book describes basic syntax and semantics and goes on to show you how to create beautiful, informative Web documents you'll be proud to display. The HTML 2.0 standard and Netscape extensions are fully explained.

Designing for the Web: Getting Started in a New Medium

By Jennifer Niederst with Edie Freedman
1st Edition April 1996
180 pages, ISBN 1-56592-165-8

 Designing for the Web gives you the basics you need to hit the ground running. Although geared toward graphic designers, it covers information and techniques useful to anyone who wants to put graphics online. It explains how to work with HTML documents from a designer's point of view, outlines special problems with presenting information online, and walks through incorporating images into Web pages, with emphasis on resolution and improving efficiency.

WebMaster in a Nutshell

By Stephen Spainhour & Valerie Quercia
1st Edition Fall 1996
374 pages, ISBN 1-56592-229-8

 Web content providers and administrators have many sources of information, both in print and online. WebMaster in a Nutshell pulls it all together into one slim volume—for easy desktop access. This quick-reference covers HTML, CGI, Perl, HTTP, server configuration, and tools for Web administration.

For information: **800-998-9938**, 707-829-0515; **info@ora.com; http://www.ora.com/**
To order: **800-889-8969** (credit card orders only); **order@ora.com**

Java Programming

Exploring Java

By Patrick Niemeyer & Joshua Peck
1st Edition May 1996
426 pages, ISBN 1-56592-184-4

Exploring Java introduces the basics of Java, the hot new object-oriented programming language for networked applications. The ability to create animated World Wide Web pages has sparked the rush to Java. But what has also made this new language so important is that it's truly portable. The code runs on any machine that provides a Java interpreter, be it Windows 95, Windows NT, the Macintosh, or any flavor of UNIX.

Java in a Nutshell

By David Flanagan
1st Edition February 1996
460 pages, ISBN 1-56592-183-6

Java in a Nutshell is a complete quick-reference guide to Java, the hot new programming language from Sun Microsystems. This comprehensive volume contains descriptions of all of the classes in the Java 1.0 API, with a definitive listing of all methods and variables. It also contains an accelerated introduction to Java for C and C++ programmers who want to learn the language *fast*.

Java Virtual Machine

By Troy Downing & Jon Meyer
1st Edition Winter 1997
380 pages (est.), ISBN 1-56592-194-1

This book is a comprehensive programming guide for the Java Virtual Machine (JVM). It gives readers a strong overview and reference of the JVM so that they may create their own implementations of the JVM or write their own compilers that create Java object code.

Java Language Reference

By Mark Grand
1st Edition January 1997
450 pages (est.), ISBN 1-56592-204-2

The *Java Language Reference* will be an indispensable tool for every Java programmer. Part of O'Reilly's new series on the Java language, this edition describes Java Version 1.0.2. It covers the syntax (presented in easy-to-understand railroad diagrams), object-oriented programming, exception handling, multithreaded programming, and differences between Java and C/C++.

Java Fundamental Classes Reference

By Mark Grand
1st Edition Winter 1997
330 pages (est.), ISBN 1-56592-241-7

The *Java Fundamental Classes Reference* provides complete reference documentation for the Java fundamental classes. These classes contain architecture-independent methods that serve as Java's gateway to the real world and provide access to resources such as the network, the windowing system, and the host filesystem.

Java AWT Reference

By John Zukowski
1st Edition Winter 1997
700 pages (est.), ISBN 1-56592-240-9

The *Java AWT Reference* provides complete reference documentation on the Abstract Windowing Toolkit (AWT), a large collection of classes for building graphical user interfaces in Java. Part of O'Reilly's new Java documentation series, this edition describes Version 1.0.2 of the Java Developer's Kit. The *Java AWT Reference* includes easy-to-use reference material on every AWT class and provides lots of sample code to help you learn by example.

For information: **800-998-9938**, 707-829-0515; **info@ora.com; http://www.ora.com/**
To order: **800-889-8969** (credit card orders only); **order@ora.com**

World Wide Web Journal

Fourth International World Wide Web Conference Proceedings

A publication of O'Reilly & Associates
and the World Wide Web Consortium (W3C)
Winter 1995/96
748 pages, ISBN 1-56592-169-0

The *World Wide Web Journal* provides timely, in-depth coverage of the W3C's technological developments, such as protocols for security, replication and caching, HTML and SGML, and content labeling. It also explores the broader issues of the Web with Web luminaries and articles on controversial legal issues such as censorship and intellectual property rights. Whether you follow Web developments for strategic planning, application programming, or Web page authoring and designing, you'll find the in-depth information you need here.

The *World Wide Web Journal* is published quarterly. This issue contains 57 refereed technical papers presented at the Fourth International World Wide Web Conference, held December 1995 in Boston, Massachusetts. It also includes the two best papers from regional conferences.

Key Specifications of the World Wide Web

A publication of O'Reilly & Associates
and the World Wide Web Consortium (W3C)
Spring 1996
356 pages, ISBN 1-56592-190-9

The key specifications that describe the architecture of the World Wide Web and how it works are maintained online at the World Wide Web Consortium. This issue of the *World Wide Web Journal* collects these key papers in a single volume as an important reference for the Webmaster, application programmer, or technical manager.

In this valuable reference, you'll find the definitive specifications for the core technologies in the Web: Hypertext Markup Language (HTML), Hypertext Transfer Protocol (HTTP), and Uniform Resource Locators (URLs), plus the emerging standards for portable graphics (PNG), content selection (PICS), and style sheets (CSS).

The Web After Five Years

A publication of O'Reilly & Associates
and the World Wide Web Consortium (W3C)
Summer 1996
226 pages, ISBN 1-56592-210-7

As the Web explodes across the technology scene, it's increasingly difficult to keep track of myriad new protocols, standards, and applications. The *World Wide Web Journal* is your direct connection to the work of the World Wide Web Consortium (W3C) as it helps members understand the forces behind current developments and leads the way to further innovation.

This issue is a reflection on the web after five years. In an interview with Tim Berners-Lee, the inventor of the Web and Director of the W3C, we learn that the Web was built to be an interactive, intercreative, two-way medium from the beginning. At the opposite scale, as a mass medium, are urgent questions about the Web's size, character, and users. These issues are addressed in selections from the MIT/W3C Workshop on Web Demographics and Internet Survey Methodology, along with commerce-related papers selected from the Fifth International World Wide Web Conference, which took place from May 6–10 in Paris.

Building an Industrial Strength Web

A publication of O'Reilly & Associates
and the World Wide Web Consortium (W3C)
Fall 1996
244 pages, ISBN 1-56592-211-5

Issue 4 focuses on the infrastructure needed to create and maintain an "Industrial Strength Web," from network protocols to application design. Included are the first standard versions of core Web protocols: HTTP/1.1, Digest Authentication, State Management (Cookies), and PICS. This issue also provides guides to the specs, highlighting new features, papers explaining modifications to 1.1 (sticky and compressed headers), extensibility, support for collaborative authoring, and using distributed objects.

Perl

Programming Perl, 2nd Edition

By Larry Wall, Tom Christiansen, & Randal L. Schwartz
2nd Edition September 1996
676 pags, ISBN 1-56592-149-6

 *Programming Perl*, second edition, is the authoritative guide to Perl version 5, the scripting utility that has established itself as the programming tool of choice for the World Wide Web, UNIX system administration, and a vast range of other applications. Version 5 of Perl includes object-oriented programming facilities. The book is co-authored by Larry Wall, the creator of Perl.

Perl is a language for easily manipulating text, files, and processes. It provides a more concise and readable way to do many jobs that were formerly accomplished (with difficulty) by programming with C or one of the shells. Perl is likely to be available wherever you choose to work. And if it isn't, you can get it and install it easily and free of charge.

This heavily revised second edition of *Programming Perl* contains a full explanation of the features in Perl version 5.003. It covers version 5.003 syntax, functions, library modules, references, debugging, and object-oriented programming.

Learning Perl

By Randal L. Schwartz, Foreword by Larry Wall
1st Edition November 1993
274 pages, ISBN 1-56592-042-2

 *Learning Perl* is ideal for system administrators, programmers, and anyone else wanting a down-to-earth introduction to this useful language. Written by a Perl trainer, its aim is to make a competent, hands-on Perl programmer out of the reader as quickly as possible. The book takes a tutorial approach and includes hundreds of short code examples, along with some lengthy ones. The relatively inexperienced programmer will find *Learning Perl* easily accessible. Each chapter of the book includes practical programming exercises. Solutions are provided for all exercises.

CGI Programming on the World Wide Web

By Shishir Gundavaram
1st Edition March 1996
450 pages, ISBN 1-56592-168-2

 This book offers a comprehensive explanation of CGI and related techniques for people who hold on to the dream of providing their own information servers on the Web. It starts at the beginning, explaining the value of CGI and how it works, then moves swiftly into the subtle details of programming.

Perl 5 Desktop Reference

By Johan Vromans
1st Edition February 1996
44 pages, ISBN 1-56592-187-9

 This is the standard quick-reference guide for the Perl programming language. It provides a complete overview of the language, from variables to input and output, from flow control to regular expressions, from functions to document formats—all packed into a convenient, carry-around booklet. Updated to cover Perl version 5.003.

Mastering Regular Expressions

By Jeffrey E. F. Friedl
1st Edition January 1997
368 pages, ISBN 1-56592-257-3

 Regular expressions, a powerful tool for manipulating text and data, are found in scripting languages, editors, programming environments, and specialized tools. In this book, author Jeffrey Friedl leads you through the steps of crafting a regular expression that gets the job done. He examines a variety of tools and uses them in an extensive array of examples, dedicating an entire chapter to Perl.

For information: **800-998-9938**, 707-829-0515; **info@ora.com; http://www.ora.com/**
To order: **800-889-8969** (credit card orders only); **order@ora.com**

Stay in touch with O'Reilly

Visit Our Award-Winning World Wide Web Site

http://www.ora.com/

VOTED

"Top 100 Sites on the Web" —*PC Magazine*

"Top 5% Websites" —*Point Communications*

"3-Star site" —*The McKinley Group*

Our Web site contains a library of comprehensive product information (including book excerpts and tables of contents), downloadable software, background articles, interviews with technology leaders, links to relevant sites, book cover art, and more. File us in your Bookmarks or Hotlist!

Join Our Two Email Mailing Lists

LIST #1 NEW PRODUCT RELEASES: To receive automatic email with brief descriptions of all new O'Reilly products as they are released, send email to: listproc@online.ora.com and put the following information in the first line of your message (NOT in the Subject: field, which is ignored): **subscribe ora-news "Your Name" of "Your Organization"** (for example: **subscribe ora-news Kris Webber of Fine Enterprises)**

LIST #2 O'REILLY EVENTS: If you'd also like us to send information about trade show events, special promotions, and other O'Reilly events, send email to: **listproc@online.ora.com** and put the following information in the first line of your message (NOT in the Subject: field, which is ignored): **subscribe ora-events "Your Name" of "Your Organization"**

Visit Our Gopher Site

- Connect your Gopher to **gopher.ora.com**, or
- Point your Web browser to **gopher://gopher.ora.com/**, or
- telnet to **gopher.ora.com** (login: **gopher**)

Get Example Files from Our Books Via FTP

There are two ways to access an archive of example files from our books:

REGULAR FTP — ftp to: **ftp.ora.com** (login: **anonymous**—use your email address as the password) or point your Web browser to: **ftp://ftp.ora.com/**

FTPMAIL — Send an email message to: **ftpmail@online.ora.com** (write "help" in the message body)

Contact Us Via Email

order@ora.com — To place a book or software order online. Good for North American and international customers.

subscriptions@ora.com — To place an order for any of our newsletters or periodicals.

software@ora.com — For general questions and product information about our software.
- Check out O'Reilly Software Online at **http://software.ora.com/** for software and technical support information.
- Registered O'Reilly software users send your questions to **website-support@ora.com**

books@ora.com — General questions about any of our books.

cs@ora.com — For answers to problems regarding your order or our products.

booktech@ora.com — For book content technical questions or corrections.

proposals@ora.com — To submit new book or software proposals to our editors and product managers.

international@ora.com — For information about our international distributors or translation queries.
- For a list of our distributors outside of North America check out: **http://www.ora.com/www/order/country.html**

O'REILLY™

101 Morris Street, Sebastopol, CA 95472 USA

TEL 707-829-0515 or 800-998-9938 (6 A.M. to 5 P.M. PST)

FAX 707-829-0104

TO ORDER: **800-889-8969** (CREDIT CARD ORDERS ONLY); **order@ora.com; http://www.ora.com/**

OUR PRODUCTS ARE AVAILABLE AT A BOOKSTORE OR SOFTWARE STORE NEAR YOU.

Titles from O'Reilly

INTERNET PROGRAMMING

CGI Programming on the
    World Wide Web
Designing for the Web
HTML: The Definitive Guide
JavaScript: The Definitive Guide
Learning Perl
Programming Perl, 2nd Edition
Regular Expressions
WebMaster in a Nutshell
Web Client Programming with Perl
    (Winter '97)
The World Wide Web Journal

USING THE INTERNET

Smileys
The Whole Internet User's Guide
    and Catalog
The Whole Internet for Windows 95
What You Need to Know:
    Using Email Effectively
What You Need to Know: Bandits on the
    Information Superhighway

JAVA SERIES

Exploring Java
Java AWT Reference (Winter '97 est.)
Java Fundamental Classes Reference
    (Winter '97 est.)
Java in a Nutshell
Java Language Reference (Winter '97 est.)
Java Threads
Java Virtual Machine (Winter '97)

SOFTWARE

WebSite™ 1.1
WebSite Professional™
WebBoard™
PolyForm™
Statisphere™

SONGLINE GUIDES

Gif Animation Studio
NetActivism
NetLaw (Winter '97)
NetLearning
NetResearch (Winter '97)
NetSuccess for Realtors
Shockwave Studio (Winter '97 est.)

SYSTEM ADMINISTRATION

Building Internet Firewalls
Computer Crime:
    A Crimefighter's Handbook
Computer Security Basics
DNS and BIND, 2nd Edition
Essential System Administration,
    2nd Edition
Getting Connected:
    The Internet at 56K and Up
Linux Network Administrator's Guide
Managing Internet Information Services
Managing Usenet (Spring '97)
Managing NFS and NIS
Networking Personal Computers
    with TCP/IP
Practical UNIX & Internet Security
PGP: Pretty Good Privacy
sendmail, 2nd Edition (Winter '97)
System Performance Tuning
TCP/IP Network Administration
termcap & terminfo
Using & Managing UUCP
Volume 8: X Window System
    Administrator's Guide

UNIX

Exploring Expect
Learning GNU Emacs, 2nd Edition
Learning the bash Shell
Learning the Korn Shell
Learning the UNIX Operating System
Learning the vi Editor
Linux in a Nutshell (Winter '97 est.)
Making TeX Work
Linux Multimedia Guide
Running Linux, 2nd Edition
Running Linux Companion
    CD-ROM, 2nd Edition
SCO UNIX in a Nutshell
sed & awk, 2nd Edition (Winter '97)
UNIX in a Nutshell: System V Edition
UNIX Power Tools
UNIX Systems Programming
Using csh and tsch
What You Need to Know:
    When You Can't Find Your
    UNIX System Administrator

WINDOWS

Inside the Windows 95 Registry

PROGRAMMING

Advanced PL/SQL
Applying RCS and SCCS
C++: The Core Language
Checking C Programs with lint
DCE Security Programming
Distributing Applications Across
    DCE and Windows NT
Encyclopedia of Graphics File
    Formats, 2nd Edition
Guide to Writing DCE Applications
lex & yacc
Managing Projects with make
Oracle Performance Tuning
Oracle Power Objects
Oracle PL/SQL Programming
Porting UNIX Software
POSIX Programmer's Guide
POSIX.4: Programming for
    the Real World
Power Programming with RPC
Practical C Programming
Practical C++ Programming
Programming Python
Programming with curses
Programming with GNU Software
Pthreads Programming
Software Portability with imake,
    2nd Edition
Understanding DCE
Understanding Japanese Information
    Processing
UNIX Systems Programming for SVR4

BERKELEY 4.4 SOFTWARE DISTRIBUTION

4.4BSD System Manager's Manual
4.4BSD User's Reference Manual
4.4BSD User's Supplementary
    Documents
4.4BSD Programmer's Reference
    Manual
4.4BSD Programmer's Supplementary
    Documents

X PROGRAMMING
THE X WINDOW SYSTEM

Volume 0: X Protocol Reference Manual
Volume 1: Xlib Programming Manual
Volume 2: Xlib Reference Manual
Volume. 3M: X Window System
    User's Guide, Motif Edition
Volume. 4: X Toolkit Intrinsics
    Programming Manual
Volume 4M: X Toolkit Intrinsics
    Programming Manual,
    Motif Edition
Volume 5: X Toolkit Intrinsics
    Reference Manual
Volume 6A: Motif Programming
    Manual
Volume 6B: Motif Reference Manual
Volume 6C: Motif Tools
Volume 8 : X Window System
    Administrator's Guide
Programmer's Supplement for Release 6
X User Tools (with CD-ROM)
The X Window System in a Nutshell

HEALTH, CAREER, & BUSINESS

Building a Successful Software Business
The Computer User's Survival Guide
Dictionary of Computer Terms
The Future Does Not Compute
Love Your Job!
Publishing with CD-ROM

TRAVEL

Travelers' Tales: Brazil (Winter '96)
Travelers' Tales: Food (Fall '96)
Travelers' Tales: France
Travelers' Tales: Gutsy Women
    (Fall '96)
Travelers' Tales: Hong Kong
Travelers' Tales: India
Travelers' Tales: Mexico
Travelers' Tales: San Francisco
Travelers' Tales: Spain
Travelers' Tales: Thailand
Travelers' Tales: A Woman's World

International Distributors

Customers outside North America can now order O'Reilly & Associates books through the following distributors. They offer our international customers faster order processing, more bookstores, increased representation at tradeshows worldwide, and the high-quality, responsive service our customers have come to expect.

EUROPE, MIDDLE EAST AND NORTHERN AFRICA (except Germany, Switzerland, and Austria)

INQUIRIES
International Thomson Publishing Europe
Berkshire House
168-173 High Holborn
London WC1V 7AA, United Kingdom
Telephone: 44-171-497-1422
Fax: 44-171-497-1426
Email: **itpint@itps.co.uk**

ORDERS
International Thomson Publishing Services, Ltd.
Cheriton House, North Way
Andover, Hampshire SP10 5BE,
United Kingdom
Telephone: 44-264-342-832 (UK orders)
Telephone: 44-264-342-806 (outside UK)
Fax: 44-264-364418 (UK orders)
Fax: 44-264-342761 (outside UK)
UK & Eire orders: **itpuk@itps.co.uk**
International orders: **itpint@itps.co.uk**

GERMANY, SWITZERLAND, AND AUSTRIA

International Thomson Publishing
Königswinterer Straße 418
53227 Bonn, Germany
Telephone: 49-228-97024 0
Fax: 49-228-441342
Email: **anfragen@oreilly.de**

AUSTRALIA

WoodsLane Pty. Ltd.
7/5 Vuko Place, Warriewood NSW 2102
P.O. Box 935, Mona Vale NSW 2103
Australia
Telephone: 61-2-9970-5111
Fax: 61-2-9970-5002
Email: **info@woodslane.com.au**

NEW ZEALAND

WoodsLane New Zealand Ltd.
21 Cooks Street (P.O. Box 575)
Wanganui, New Zealand
Telephone: 64-6-347-6543
Fax: 64-6-345-4840
Email: **info@woodslane.com.au**

ASIA (except Japan & India)

INQUIRIES
International Thomson Publishing Asia
60 Albert Street #15-01
Albert Complex
Singapore 189969
Telephone: 65-336-6411
Fax: 65-336-7411

ORDERS
Telephone: 65-336-6411
Fax: 65-334-1617

JAPAN

O'Reilly Japan, Inc.
Kiyoshige Building 2F
12-Banchi, Sanei-cho
Shinjuku-ku
Tokyo 160 Japan
Telephone: 81-3-3356-5227
Fax: 81-3-3356-5261
Email: **kenji@ora.com**

INDIA

Computer Bookshop (India) PVT. LTD.
190 Dr. D.N. Road, Fort
Bombay 400 001
India
Telephone: 91-22-207-0989
Fax: 91-22-262-3551
Email: **cbsbom@giasbm01.vsnl.net.in**

THE AMERICAS

O'Reilly & Associates, Inc.
101 Morris Street
Sebastopol, CA 95472 U.S.A.
Telephone: 707-829-0515
Telephone: 800-998-9938 (U.S. & Canada)
Fax: 707-829-0104
Email: **order@ora.com**

SOUTHERN AFRICA

International Thomson Publishing Southern Africa
Building 18, Constantia Park
240 Old Pretoria Road
P.O. Box 2459
Halfway House, 1685 South Africa
Telephone: 27-11-805-4819
Fax: 27-11-805-3648

O'REILLY™

TO ORDER: **800-889-8969** (CREDIT CARD ORDERS ONLY); **order@ora.com**; **http://www.ora.com**
OUR PRODUCTS ARE AVAILABLE AT A BOOKSTORE OR SOFTWARE STORE NEAR YOU.

O'REILLY™

O'Reilly & Associates, Inc.
101 Morris Street
Sebastopol, CA 95472-9902
1-800-998-9938

Visit us online at:
**http://www.ora.com/
orders@ora.com**

O'REILLY WOULD LIKE TO HEAR FROM YOU

Nineteenth century wood engraving
of a bear from the O'Reilly &
Associates Nutshell Handbook®
Using & Managing UUCP.

POST CARD

BUSINESS REPLY MAIL
FIRST CLASS MAIL   PERMIT NO. 80   SEBASTOPOL, CA

Postage will be paid by addressee

O'Reilly & Associates, Inc.
101 Morris Street
Sebastopol, CA 95472-9902